PENGUIN BOOKS
THE AGE OF WRATH

Abraham Eraly is the author of four acclaimed books on premodern Indian history—*Gem in the Lotus: The Seeding of Indian Civilisation*, *The First Spring: The Golden Age of India*, *The Age of Wrath: A History of the Delhi Sultanate* and *The Last Spring: The Lives and Times of the Great Mughals* (also published in two volumes, as *Emperors of the Peacock Throne* and *The Mughal World*). He was born in Kerala and was educated there and in Chennai. He has taught Indian history in colleges in India and the United States, and was the editor of a current affairs magazine for several years.

PRAISE FOR THE BOOK

'[The] definitive biography of the great Mughals'—*Financial Express*

'*The Age of Wrath* is simple in its focus and stunning in its research. Savour it in bits and keep a few Post-its handy to bookmark the facts scattered throughout the book. Deceptively simple yet daunting and swathed in endless layers. For any lover of history, there are nuggets peppered throughout the book'—*Sunday Standard*

'A fascinating and comprehensive account'—*Deccan Herald*

'Offers an insightful perspective on a part of Indian history of which extremely little is written or researched about'—*Time Out*

'This is history written in a manner of good fiction, mixing anecdote with analysis, without sacrificing erudition'—*Business Standard*

ABRAHAM ERALY

THE AGE
of
WRATH

A History of the Delhi Sultanate

PENGUIN BOOKS

An imprint of Penguin Random House

PENGUIN BOOKS

USA | Canada | UK | Ireland | Australia
New Zealand | India | South Africa | China | Singapore

Penguin Books is part of the Penguin Random House group of companies
whose addresses can be found at global.penguinrandomhouse.com

Published by Penguin Random House India Pvt. Ltd
4th Floor, Capital Tower 1, MG Road,
Gurugram 122 002, Haryana, India

First published in Viking by Penguin Books India 2014
Published in Penguin Books 2015

Copyright © Abraham Eraly 2014

ISBN 9780143422266

Typeset in Sabon by Eleven Arts, New Delhi
Printed at Repro India Limited

In the history which I am writing I will allow no partiality or prejudice to mingle.

—Baihaqi,
11th-century Ghaznavid chronicler

In most parts of my work I simply relate without commenting, unless there be a special reason for doing so.

—Al-Biruni
11th-century Ghaznavid chronicler

It is the duty of a historian . . . to have no hope of profit, no fear of injury, to show no partiality . . . or animosity . . ., to make no difference between friend and stranger, and to write nothing but with sincerity.

—Khafi Khan
17th-century Mughal chronicler

Contents

Acknowledgements

While working on the penultimate draft of this book, I had the good fortune to have two perceptive readers, Jayashree Nambiar and Priya Vijayaraghavan, to look through the draft and make suggestions. I had this help from Jayashree for my last book also, but Priya is someone whom I had never met or even spoken to on the phone. She had sent me an email a couple of years back commenting on my previous books, and we have been in touch with each other on and off by email since then. When I finished the draft of this book I requested her to read through it, and she readily agreed.

It is important for a writer to have his text checked by a discerning reader, for quite often what is crystal clear to the writer is confusing to the reader. In this I was blessed with having the comments of Jayashree and Priya.

On the publisher's side, I am grateful to Chiki Sarkar and Paromita Mohanchandra of Penguin for their help and advice. I am also greatly indebted to Meena Bhende, whose meticulous copy editing of my text has been invaluable to me.

A COUPLE OF years ago, when I was working on an early draft of this book, I had a surprise visitor, a close friend of mine of my student days, now a phenomenally successful businesswoman in a faraway country, whom I had not seen for well over forty years. That evening, when we were strolling on the boulevard along the beach in Pondicherry, she asked me to tell her the most moving incident I had come across while researching for this book.

So I told her about Ibn Battuta, a Moroccan traveller who had spent several years in Delhi in the mid-fourteenth century as a courtier of Sultan Muhammad Tughluq, and was then sent to China by the sultan as his ambassador.

On his way to China, Battuta spent a few months in Maldives, and there, on a tiny island which had just one little mud hut, he came across the only man living there. 'He had,' recounts Battuta in his memoirs, 'a wife and children, a few coco-palms, and a small boat which he used for fishing . . . The island also had a few banana trees . . . I swear I envied that man, and wished that the island had been mine, that I might have made it my retreat until the inevitable hour should befall me.'

Battuta had over the years moved among some of the richest and most powerful men of the age, but the one person he envied most was this poor, solitary islander.

When I told this story to my friend, her eyes glazed over with tears, and we walked in silence for a while. She was, she then told me, saddened by the many personal sacrifices she had to make in her pursuit of success.

'Well, every achievement has its price,' I told her consolingly. 'No pain, no gain.'

'And no cliché, no wisdom,' she rejoined, laughing.

This book is dedicated to that witty and wise long-lost friend of mine.

Preface

This book completes my four-volume study of the history of pre-modern India.

The four volumes in the set, all published by Penguin in India, are: *Gem in the Lotus: The Seeding of Indian Civilisation*; *The First Spring: The Golden Age of India*; *The Age of Wrath: A History of the Delhi Sultanate*; and *The Last Spring: The Lives and Times of the Great Mughals*. *The Last Spring* was later published as two paperback books: *Emperors of the Peacock Throne* and *The Mughal World*.

I hope to follow up this set with a summation book, to link India's past with its present, and to examine the historical processes by which India became the kind of nation it is today.

As in my previous books, I have in this book tried to portray the life of the people in the past, rather than merely chronicle events.

Historians, according to Mughal chronicler Muhammad Hadi, are like 'thirsty explorers in the desert.' Often there is not enough water to quench their thirst. There is, for instance, very little data in primary sources on the socio-cultural history of early medieval India, or on the life of the common people. But the source books have a good amount of material on the life of kings, and that enlivens the history of the age with human drama.

Another major problem that we have with early medieval Indian history is that our main sources of information about it are the accounts given by Arab, Persian and Turkish chroniclers. These are inevitably one-sided, though they seldom deliberately falsify facts. We have virtually no Indian sources for the history of this age.

PART I

OVERVIEW

What matters it to us whether
Rama reigns or Ravana reigns?

—A MEDIEVAL INDIAN SAYING

Challenge and Response

The inception of the second millennium CE marked the beginning of a radically new and transformative phase in the history of India, which would last nearly as long as the millennium itself. During virtually this entire period a good part of India was under the political and socio-cultural dominance of invaders, first under Turks, then under Mughals, and finally under Britishers.

These invaders were entirely unlike all the previous invaders of India. Although several other races had entered India over the millennia as invaders or migrants, in time they all had merged indistinguishably into the Indian socio-cultural milieu. This did not happen with Turks, Mughals or Britishers. Nor was there any significant general change in the life and culture of Indians under the influence of these invaders, except during the latter period of the British rule. Indians and these invaders coexisted, but they did not blend. They were like oil and water in the same pot.

The first phase of this millennial history of foreign rule in India began with the invasion of India by Turks and the establishment of the Delhi Sultanate. This development had a radically transmutative effect on the political make-up of India, the displacement of virtually the entire traditional ruling class of India by the invaders. More importantly, the Turkish invasion resulted in the superimposition of a wholly contradistinctive foreign civilisation over Indian civilisation.

Curiously, there was no awareness at all among medieval Indians, even among the ruling class, about the historic nature of the Turkish invasion. The lack of this awareness meant that there was no general, united opposition by the rulers or the people of India against Turks. Turks were not seen by Indians as

3

aliens, but as just another component in the ever roiling regional, racial, tribal, linguistic, socio-cultural, religious, sectarian and political diversity of India. So even while Turks were mopping up Hindu kingdoms one after the other, the rajas and their chieftains went on with their usual endless petty squabbles and battles among themselves, as if nothing whatever in their world had changed.

But everything in their world had in fact changed radically. Turks were entirely different from all the previous invaders of India, and Indians of this age were entirely different from what their forefathers had been in the previous age. India had absorbed all the pre-Turkish invaders and migrants into its society and culture because India was then, for a thousand years from around the middle of the first millennium BCE to around the middle of the first millennium CE, a marvellously vital and creative civilisation, which was far more advanced than the civilisations of most of the invaders and migrants. In dismal contrast to this, Indian civilisation at the time of the Turkish invasion was in an awfully decadent and comatose state, while Turks had a youthful, vibrant and advanced civilisation.

Besides, the socio-religious systems and culture of Indians and Turks were far too divergent from each other to have any transformative influence on each other. Basically, the problem was that Islam was too adamantine to be influenced by Hinduism, and Hinduism was too effete to respond creatively to Islam. There was no consonance at all between the two religions in any respect: while Islam was monotheistic, Hinduism was polytheistic; while Hinduism was a malleable, multilayered religion which was forever in flux, Islam was a monolayered and relatively immutable religion. And while Islam was an aggressive, proselytising religion, which was intolerant of other religions, Hinduism was a passive, non-proselytising religion, which could companionably coexist with any other religion, or any number of other religions. Similarly, while Hinduism was an inclusive religion, which could accommodate within it any number of diverse deities, beliefs and practices, and could be anything to anybody, Islam was an exclusive religion, which had only one god and one basic set of beliefs and practices.

Furthermore, while Islamic society was egalitarian and had no hereditary social divisions, Hindu society was rigidly hierarchic and was divided into many hereditary castes occupying different rungs in society and performing their allotted exclusive socio-economic functions. Likewise, while Hindu society was a closed society, and its caste divisions were hereditary, into which one could enter only by being born into it, Islamic society was an open society, into which anyone from any background could enter as an equal member on becoming a Muslim. And while Muslims feasted on beef, Hindus venerated the cow and regarded cow slaughter and beef eating as most heinous sins.

Basically, while Hindu society could have possibly accommodated Islamic religious beliefs and social practices within it by assigning to them particular religious and socio-cultural spaces, as it had done over the centuries with numerous Indian tribal cults and the cults of migrants and invaders, Muslim society could not possibly have accommodated Hindu religious beliefs and social practices within it without totally compromising its socio-religious identity—without ceasing to be Islam, in fact.

Because of this polarity between Hinduism and Islam in all matters, they exerted no significant influence on each other, except in the case of a few peripheral mystic sects in both religions. Yet, despite their total contrariety in every facet of life, Hindus and Muslims coexisted without any major conflict or communal violence for very many centuries.

The orthodox Muslim policy towards the people of other religions was to induce them to become Muslims, and to extirpate those who resisted conversion, sparing only Jews, Christians and Zoroastrians, who were treated as zimmis, protected non-Muslims. But as Islam spread outside the Middle East, the concept of zimmis was, for various practical reasons, liberally interpreted to include in it people of other religions also. In the case of Hindus, Muslim rulers necessarily had to be accommodative towards them, for Hindus provided several indispensable services in the economy, government and army of the Muslim state. In any case it would have been physically impossible for Turks to exterminate Hindus, because of the vastness and diversity of the Hindu population.

INDIA IN PREMODERN times was often regarded by foreigners as a paradise on earth. Typically, Abdullah Wassaf, an early fourteenth century Persian writer, states:

> It is asserted that paradise is in India,
> Be not surprised because paradise itself
>   is not comparable to it.

This was a highly chimerical image of India, but not too different from the common premodern perception of India by foreigners. There was however another view of India by medieval foreigners, which, although it also saw India as a land of fabulous natural resources, regarded it as an uncongenial place to live in, because of its torrid climate. India, according to Khondamir, an early sixteenth century chronicler, 'consumed the body as easily as flame melts a candle.'

That apprehension presumably was the reason why Mahmud Ghazni decided not to annex India and rule over it, even though he had the proven military capability to do that. Similarly, Timur also decided against occupying India—although he swept through a good part of North India, plundering its wealth and slaughtering its people, he remained in India only for about six months, and quickly sped back to his home in Central Asia, heeding the advice of one his top nobles, who warned him: 'If we establish ourselves permanently therein, our race will degenerate and our children will become like the natives of those regions, and in a few generations their strength and valour will diminish.'

These views about the debilitating effect of Indian climate were highly exaggerated, just as the contrary views about India as a paradise were highly exaggerated. But Indian climate did certainly have an enervating effect on its people, as is evident from the fact that all the invaders who settled in India were in turn, after a couple of centuries, defeated and displaced by fresh invaders—Arabs by Ghaznavids, Ghaznavids by Ghuris, Ghuris by Mughals, and Mughals by Persians and Britishers.

But why did some invaders choose to settle down in India, while others disdained to do so? The crucial factor in this seems to have been that the invaders who chose India as home were mostly those who had been driven out of their homeland—or were in imminent danger of being driven out—by their more aggressive neighbours. They were taking refuge in India as much as invading it.

These migrant invaders chose India presumably because they saw it as a soft target, and also because of its reputation for fabulous riches. But why did the medieval Indian kingdoms, many of them ruled by Rajputs renowned for their martial valour, succumb so abjectly to Turks, even though the armies of the rajas were invariably much larger than those of Turks? And then again why were Turks so easily routed by Mughals, and Mughals in turn by Persians and Britishers? Why did each new invader rout the previous invader? India had never in its several millenniums long history prevailed over invaders, except in a couple of minor cases. Why?

A reason that is commonly given for this is that there was no united stand by Indian kings against invaders. There could in fact be no such united stand by them, because, from the Indian point of view, there was no we/they divide between Indians and invaders. The Indian ruling class viewed Turks not as foreigners but as a component in the ever-shifting population conglomeration of India. And the establishment of the Turkish rule in India was seen by them as just an aspect of the normal political turmoil in India. As for the common people, it made virtually no difference in their lives whether rajas or sultans ruled over them.

There was no concept of India as a nation at this time. Indians did not look like one people or speak like one people—the language of the people of one region of India was entirely unintelligible to the people of the other regions of India. And each of these regional groups was itself divided into several discrete socio-cultural groups based on caste and sect. India in medieval times was just a geographical region, like Europe, not a nation. At best India could be considered as a distinct civilisation, but in this too India was not much different from Europe. India was in fact even more fragmented than Europe, because of the innumerable sectarian and caste divisions among each of its regional people.

In any case, the lack of political unity is hardly a convincing reason for the dismal military performance of Indian kings against invaders, for many of the Indian kings had under their command greater resources in men and materials than the invaders. But what mattered in battles was not the numerical strength of the army, but its martial spirit and energy, and in this the Indian armies were inferior to the invading armies, perhaps because of the sweltering, debilitating climate of India.

The awareness of this adverse effect of Indian climate on people made some of the invaders conduct their campaigns into India only during the relatively cool months of the year. Mahmud Ghazni, for instance, conducted his raids into India mostly during the cool, rainless months between October and February; similarly, Timur took care to restrict his Indian campaign to the six months between September and March.

THE ONE APPARENT advantage that Indian kings had over invaders was that their armies were invariably much larger than those of the invaders. But this numerical advantage of the Indian armies was more than negated by the decisive superiority of the invaders in martial spirit, weaponry, regimental discipline, and innovative tactics. Indeed, the vast size of Indian armies often proved to be a disadvantage, as their size was mostly made up of ill-trained and ill-disciplined hordes who could not act effectively in concert.

In contrast, Turks had certain crucial military advantages over Indians. Their cavalry, which constituted their main military division, was far superior to the Indian cavalry in every respect, in men as well as in mounts. The Indian armies mainly depended on their elephant corps, but elephants, though forbidding in appearance and terrifying as they charged into the enemy ranks, were no match to the storming, whirling charge of the Turkish cavalry. Elephants were in fact quite often a menace to their own side, for when wounded in battle or otherwise frightened they ran pell-mell, causing great havoc in their own army.

More than all this, Turks as aggressors swooping down from the cool Afghan mountains had irresistible kinetic energy, while the Indian armies were mostly made up of plainsmen normally leading a sedentary life in an enervating climate, and their posture, as defenders, was generally static. Psychologically too Indians were at a disadvantage, as they suffered from the victim syndrome, and were often sluggish in battle, unlike the spirited Turks. Moreover, the fatalistic value system of Indians inculcated in them a generally defeatist attitude. In contrast, Turks were energised by their religious fervour; they believed that they had the favour of god with them and were therefore invincible. And indeed they did prove to be invincible. Equally, they were energised by the irresistible lure of plunder.

A peculiarity of Indian history is that though India was repeatedly invaded by foreigners over the millennia, Indians themselves had never ventured out of the subcontinent for conquests, except for some transient, trade related naval campaigns into south-east Asia by Cholas during the classical age. Indians were always the conquered, never the conquerors. One reason for this could be that Indians had no compelling survival need to venture into other lands, as the subcontinent was mostly quite fertile, and it provided the people with all their basic requirements. Foreign conquest was therefore not a survival requirement for Indians.

Another reason why Indians never ventured out of the subcontinent was that geographically India is like a mammoth canyon, separated from the Eurasian landmass by the high mountains bordering it on the north, and from the rest of the world by the seas bordering its peninsula. This topography made it easy for invaders from the northern highlands to sweep down the mountains into India, but made it virtually impossible for Indians to clamber up the mountains and invade foreign lands. Nor could Indians in premodern times cross the seas to seek any major conquest, as the necessary seafaring facilities were not then available. An equally important reason— perhaps the most important reason—why Indians never ventured outside the subcontinent is that they were generally a rather torpid people, and did not have the energy or the spirit to go adventuring over the mountains or across the seas.

TURKS, ACCORDING TO medieval Muslim chroniclers, suffered no notable military reverses in India, except once, in the first battle of Tarain in 1191. But was the conquest of India really all that easy for Turks? Our only sources of information on it are Muslim chroniclers, several of whom were the courtiers of the sultans about whom they wrote. Do their accounts present the true picture of what happened? The career prospects and the personal fortunes of these chroniclers depended on the sultans about whom they wrote, whom they could offend only at great personal risk. Says Barani, courtier-chronicler of Muhammad Tughluq: 'We were traitors who were prepared to call black white . . . Avarice and the desire

for worldly wealth led us into hypocrisy, and as we stood before the king
. . . fear of our fleeting lives and equally fleeting wealth deterred us from
speaking the truth before him.'

Modern historians therefore have to approach the medieval chronicles
with some scepticism, especially as the data in them are often confusing and
sometimes contradictory. Besides, even where these reports seem absolutely
factual, we have to note that their factuality is one-sided and partisan.
From another perspective, the story they tell would probably have had a
different nuance.

We have no Indian accounts at all about what happened during the Turkish
invasion of India, or about the history of the Delhi Sultanate. For instance,
incredible though it might seem, there is no reference at all in any medieval
Indian text about Mahmud Ghazni's many devastating raids deep into India.
In fact, there is virtually no mention at all in medieval Indian texts about any
of the momentous political and cultural developments then taking place in
India. Apparently Indian chroniclers considered those events as not worth
recording. Instead they went on writing their inane romances. And that in itself
is significant, as a reflection of the general Indian disconnect with mundane
reality. Indians were great mythmakers, but not good chroniclers of history. As
Al-Biruni, an eleventh century Ghaznavid intellectual notes, 'Indians attach
little importance to the sequence of events.'

WITH THE ESTABLISHMENT of the Delhi Sultanate the political history
of India once again acquired a dominant theme, seven centuries after the
collapse of the Gupta Empire. Though there had been a few large and
important kingdoms in India in the intervening period, none of them had the
all-India prominence that the Gupta Empire had, or that the Delhi Sultanate
came to have.

The establishment of the Muslim empire in India had three distinct phases,
each widely separated in time. It began with the Arab conquest of Sind in
the early eighth century, followed nearly three centuries later by Mahmud
Ghazni's pillaging raids deep into India, and finally, yet two centuries later,
by the invasion of India by Muhammad Ghuri and the establishment of the
Delhi Sultanate.

The first of these invasions, the Arab conquest of Sind, came, for some
inexplicable reason, only at the very end of the Arab imperial expansion,
even though Arabs, as seafaring traders, had been in close contact with India
for many centuries even before the founding of Islam, and the prospect of
pillaging India's fabled riches, and of battling with India's heathens, would
have been irresistible lures for them. In fact, even when Arabs finally sent an
army into India, it was not a wanton act by them, but was provoked by the

collusion of the raja of Sind with the pirates who were harassing Arab ships in the Arabian Sea.

The Arab army invading Sind was commanded by Muhammad Qasim, who was only seventeen years old then, but proved to be an exceptionally able general and a most sagacious administrator. He won most of the battles he fought, and, what is more important, won the hearts of the conquered people by his fair and generous treatment of them—by his 'honesty, prudence, justice, equity, and generosity', as *Chach-nama*, a contemporary Arab chronicle, states. And it was Qasim who introduced in India the practice of Muslim rulers treating the local people as zimmis, and allowing them, on the payment of jizya, the poll tax, to lead their traditional way of life without any interference.

The Arab rule in Sind lasted three centuries, but all through its history it remained a minor, peripheral realm of little significance in the history of India or of Arabia. And the kingdom was finally wiped out, ironically, not by any Indian king, but by another Muslim invader, Mahmud Ghazni, a Turk.

AFTER THE ARAB conquest of Sind, India had a respite from foreign invasions for nearly three centuries, till Mahmud Ghazni's raids into India in the early eleventh century. Mahmud had, during the solemn ceremony of receiving the Caliphate honours on his accession to the throne of Ghazni, taken a vow to wage jihad, holy war, every year against the idolaters of India. He could not keep that vow to the letter, but he did lead more than a dozen campaigns into India during his thirty-two-year reign. The sultan had two motives in his Indian raids: to slaughter heathens and to gather plunder. He fought for god and mammon, but quite probably more for mammon than for god. These were however interconnected motives, each reinforcing and energising action in the other.

Curiously, Mahmud, unlike most other invaders, had no hunger for land. Had he desired it, he could have easily annexed a good part of North India to his kingdom, but he did not have the patience for empire building. Except Punjab and Sind—the gateways to India, which he needed to keep open for his raids—Mahmud did not annex any territory in India.

The final and decisive phase of the Muslim invasion of India was launched by Muhammad Ghuri, a late twelfth and early thirteenth century sultan of Ghazni, who was presumably inspired by what he had heard about the legendary exploits of Mahmud Ghazni in India. Muhammad's raids into India were nowhere near as spectacular as those of Mahmud, but they had a far greater transformative effect on Indian history, as they led to the founding of the Delhi Sultanate, with which began an entirely new epoch in Indian history.

The Delhi Sultanate was established in 1206, nearly six centuries after the founding of Islam, and it endured for 320 years, till 1526, when Babur invaded

India and established the Mughal Empire. The history of the Sultanate is divided into five dynastic periods, and within each of these dynasties too there were several internal upheavals, assassinations of kings, and violent usurpations. It is on the whole quite a sordid story. Though there were a few kings of exceptional ability and achievements in the Sultanate, many of the sultans were worthless scamps. Some were barely sane. And some were blatant sexual perverts. The worst of these abhorrent sultans was Mubarak, Ala-ud-din Khalji's successor, who, according to Barani, 'cast aside all regard for decency, and presented himself [at the durbar] decked out in female trinkets and apparel,' and he made his cronies scamper stark naked in the durbar hall, insult the assembled great nobles in foul language, and 'defile and befoul their garments.'

For all its flaws, the Delhi Sultanate had a few rare distinctions, such as having the only woman ever to sit on the throne of Delhi: Raziya. And she, despite the purdah restrictions that normally cloistered upper class Muslim women, ruled the empire with distinction for three years, but was then overthrown and killed by a band of hyper-orthodox nobles. 'Sultan Raziya was a great monarch,' comments medieval chronicler Siraj. 'She was endowed with all the qualities befitting a king. But she was not of the right sex, and so in the estimation of men all her virtues were worthless.'

The Sultanate also had the rare distinction of having a king who voluntarily relinquished his throne while still in his youth and went into retirement. This was Alam Shah of the Sayyid dynasty, who then moved from Delhi to Budaun, a charming little town on the banks of Ganga, where he lived in blissful obscurity for thirty years, till his death, free of all the cares and tribulations that harry a crowned head.

THE FIRST OF the five dynasties of the Delhi Sultanate was the Slave Dynasty. It was founded by Qutb-ud-din Aibak, Muhammad Ghuri's viceroy in India, who set up the Indian territories of the Ghuri empire as an independent kingdom on the death of Muhammad. The dynasty he founded came to be known as the Slave Dynasty because its sultans were all manumitted slaves or their descendants. They were not however ordinary slaves, but royal slaves, like Mamluks of medieval Egypt, and they, far from being an underclass, constituted a politico-military aristocracy, who could aspire for the highest offices in the government, and even rise to be sultans, as indeed three of them did. It was not a disgrace but a distinction to be a royal slave.

The Slave Dynasty ruled the Sultanate for 84 years, from 1206 to 1290, and it had ten sultans belonging to three different but related families. The second dynasty, that of Khaljis, was the shortest reigning dynasty of the Sultanate; it was in power for only 30 years, till 1320, and had six sultans. The third dynasty, that of Tughluqs, had the longest history of all the Delhi dynasties; it ruled for 94 years, till 1414, and had 11 sultans. The next dynasty, that of Sayyids, ruled for 37 years, till 1451, and had four sultans. The last dynasty, that of Lodis, had three sultans, and it endured for 75 years, till the Mughal invasion of 1526.

The expansionist phase of the Sultanate history was the one and a quarter century period from its founding in the first decade of the thirteenth century to the second quarter of the fourteenth century. The empire was at its greatest territorial extent during the reign of Muhammad Tughluq, when it stretched over virtually the entire subcontinent, except over Kerala in the deep south, Kashmir in the far north, and a few pockets here and there. Curiously, the reign of Muhammad Tughluq, which marked the culmination of the territorial expansion of the Sultanate, also marked the beginning of its fragmentation.

The greatest of the Delhi sultans was Ala-ud-din Khalji, the second ruler of the second dynasty of the Sultanate. He was illiterate—like Akbar, the great Mughal emperor—but was a brilliant, radical reformer. In that age of minimal governments, Ala-ud-din ran a maximal government. A totalitarian and exceptionally able ruler, he firmly controlled nearly every facet of life in his empire. Although he did all that no doubt primarily to quench his thirst for power, his rule was also most beneficial to his subjects, who lived in greater security and material comfort under him than under any other Delhi sultan. Ala-ud-din was an autocrat, but a benevolent autocrat.

Ala-ud-din had to his credit the introduction of several daringly innovative and brilliantly successful administrative and economic reforms, some of which were many centuries ahead of his time, and were rather like those of a modern welfare state. The most remarkable aspect of his reign was his futuristic economic reforms, through which he firmly regulated every segment of the economy, particularly its market operations, by balancing the demand and supply of goods, and fixing their prices. Ala-ud-din backed up these market reforms by setting up an elaborate intelligence network, which enabled him to maintain total control over everything that happened in the empire. States Barani: 'No one could stir without the sultan's knowledge.'

Another radical reformer of the Delhi Sultanate was Muhammad Tughluq, but while Ala-ud-din was successful in everything he did, Muhammad was a dismal failure in everything he did. Soon after his accession Muhammad conceived several fascinating political and socio-economic reforms, which—particularly the introduction of token currency—were, as ideas, quite sound, and would have been beneficial to the sultanate if they had been implemented efficiently. But they all failed miserably in execution, and produced results that were the opposite of what the sultan had intended. This was because Muhammad lacked the pragmatism, patience and perseverance needed to execute his schemes successfully. He was an obsessive daydreamer. And it was only in his daydreams that he was able to fulfil himself.

The picture of Muhammad that emerges from medieval chronicles is of a psychotic Jekyll-and-Hyde personality, a bizarre blend of antithetical qualities, of good and evil, overweening arrogance and abject humility, murderous savagery and touching compassion. There was an element of revolting fiendishness in some of the punishments that he meted out. Thus when Gurshasp, his nephew, rose in revolt against him, not only was he flayed alive, but his flesh was cooked with rice and served to his wife and children. In another instance, when a pious and venerable Muslim described the sultan as a tyrant, he was forcibly fed human excrement, on the sultan's orders.

MUHAMMAD HAD NO sons, and so was succeeded by his cousin Firuz, and that marked an amazing transition in the history of the Sultanate, from hellish chaos to heavenly tranquillity. Muhammad and Firuz were entirely unlike each other in character, temperament and policies—Muhammad was an egomaniac, flighty and unpredictable, ever pursuing some chimerical goal or other, and given to savage violence; in contrast, Firuz was a stable, dependable ruler, with a good sense of what was viable and necessary, and was essentially a man of peace. While Muhammad wanted the world to adjust to him, Firuz adjusted himself to the world. And, more than anything else, Firuz was concerned with the stability of his empire and the welfare of its people, rather than with self-fulfilment. He was the right person in the right place at the right time.

Firuz was the most humane of the Delhi sultans. He reversed the prevailing royal view that people should serve the king, and held that the king should serve the people. Public welfare, not personal fulfilment, was his objective. He was especially caring towards the lowly. The Delhi Sultanate under Firuz was the closest that any government in medieval India came to being a welfare state.

The death of Firuz was followed by a period of political chaos, during which the Sultanate fragmented into a number of independent kingdoms, some of which had larger territory and greater power than the Sultanate. But the Sultanate, though considerably attenuated, endured for 114 years more, till the Mughal invasion. During this period the Sultanate was ruled by two successor dynasties, Sayyids and Lodis. The disintegration of the Sultanate continued under Sayyids, and by the end of their rule the kingdom was confined to just the city of Delhi and its neighbouring villages. As a common satirical jingle of the time had it,

> From Delhi to Palam
> Is the realm of Shah Alam.

There was some revival of the fortunes of the kingdom under Lodis, but their history ended abruptly in 1526, when Babur invaded India and established the Mughal Empire. But its last ruler, Ibrahim, had the distinction of being the only sultan of Delhi to die in battle, despite the innumerable battles they fought all through their over-three-century-long history.

One Land, Two Worlds

The political history of the Delhi Sultanate was quite a roller-coaster ride. There were spectacular highs and lows in it, but hardly any progress. It is on the whole a sordid tale of treachery, rebellions, usurpations and fiendish reprisals. The sultans were particularly savage in dealing with their refractory or rebellious subjects, having them disembowelled or flayed alive, thrown alive into blazing fire, fed to wild animals, and thrown under elephants' feet to be trampled to death. Such bestial punishments were meted out even to the rebellious members of the royal family.

'Amputation of hands and feet, ears and noses, tearing out the eyes, pouring molten led into the throat, crushing the bones of the hand and feet with mallets, burning the body with fire, driving iron nails into the hands, feet, and bosom, cutting the sinews, sawing men asunder—these and many similar tortures were practised' by sultans against criminals and rebels, notes Sultan Firuz Tughluq in his memoirs. Suspects were invariably tortured to extract confession from them, and tortured so savagely that they often confessed even to crimes they had not committed, preferring death to torture. 'People consider death a lighter affliction than torture,' notes Battuta, a fourteenth century Moorish traveller in India.

The punitive action of kings against rebels often involved mass slaughter, with no distinction made between the innocent and the guilty, for the objective of kings was more to terrorise people and keep them submissive, than merely to punish the guilty. Thus Balban once, in retaliation for the contumacy of some villagers, ordered his soldiers to burn down their villages and 'slay every man there . . . The blood of the rioters ran in streams, heaps of the slain were

15

to be seen near every village and jungle, and the stench of the dead reached as far as Ganga,' reports Barani.

Predictably, the conduct of the Sultanate army was most savage in enemy territory, and entailed the slaughter of thousands and thousands of people, both soldiers and common people. Thus, according to Mughal chronicler Ferishta, Bahmani sultan Ahmad Shah during his invasion of Vijayanagar 'overran the open country, and wherever he went, he put to death men, women and children, without mercy . . . Wherever the number of the slain amounted to 20,000, he halted for three days, and made a festival in celebration of the bloody event.'

The ruthless suppression of adversaries and criminals was an essential survival requirement for rulers nearly everywhere in the medieval world. In India this was so with rajas as well as sultans, though Hindu kings, ruling over their own people, were not normally as virulent as Muslim rulers, conquerors ruling over an alien people.

THE TENDENCY OF Muslim rulers in India to be oppressive towards their Hindu subjects was heightened by the fact that most of their values and practices were diametrically opposite to those of Hindus. Muslim society, unlike the caste segmented Hindu society, was fundamentally egalitarian, and had no birth determined status divisions in it, so anyone could rise to any position, depending solely on his ability. Even a slave could rise to be a king, as indeed some of them did in the Delhi Sultanate.

This egalitarianism of Muslim society was particularly evident in the early history of the Delhi Sultanate, during which there was, till the reign of Balban, no great status difference even between the sultan and his nobles. The sultan was then more a leader than a ruler, a *primus inter pares*. Later however sultans generally claimed that the occupation of the throne endowed them with *farr*, divine effulgence, which distinguished them from all others. But whatever be their pretence, the real basis of royal authority, of sultans as well as of rajas, was their military might, their ability to coerce others to submit to their will. In principle the primary duty of kings was to protect their subjects and to provide for their welfare, but in practice their primary concern, often their sole concern, was to preserve and expand their power.

The throne however was no bed of roses. The sultan, for all his great power, led a perilous life, for the sword of an enemy or a rebel always hung over his head. But these perils were more than compensated by the incredible powers and privileges that he enjoyed, particularly his godlike power over the lives and fortunes of his subjects.

The primary concern of most medieval rulers, sultans as well as rajas, was to retain their seat on the throne. But some of them were also, commendably, keen and knowledgeable patrons of art, literature and learning, and some were distinguished scholars and writers themselves. These cultural accomplishments however made virtually no difference in their performance as rulers; in that it was only their administrative and military capabilities that really mattered. Muhammad Tughluq was probably the most erudite of the Delhi sultans, but he was a pathetic failure as a ruler; on the other hand, Ala-ud-din Khalji was illiterate, but was the most successful of the Delhi sultans.

But even under capable rulers, the story of most medieval Indian kingdoms was marred by internal upheavals. The politics of the Delhi Sultanate during most of its history was, typically, a dizzying whirl of Byzantine conspiracies and counter-conspiracies, in which life was nightmarish for those in the inner circle of power. No one, including the sultan, was ever secure in his office, or even safe in his life. For instance, among the five descendants of Iltutmish who sat on the throne of Delhi, all except one were overthrown and killed.

The main reason for this ever-swirling political chaos was that there were no well-defined and generally accepted rules of royal succession. The throne belonged to whoever could seize it. Imprisoning or killing one's rivals—even one's father or brother—to gain or to secure the throne was not considered a crime, but as legitimate and normal political conduct. Kings were often murderers. In India, as Mughal emperor Babur would later remark in his memoirs, 'there is . . . this peculiarity . . . that any person who kills the ruler and occupies the throne becomes the ruler himself. The amirs, viziers, soldiers and peasants submit to him at once and obey him.'

MEDIEVAL INDIAN STATES were all essentially military dictatorships, established and preserved through military action. The primary occupation of most of their kings was waging wars, to suppress rebellions, to defend or expand their kingdom, and to gather plunder. They were all warlords. They ruled over the kingdom, but rarely governed it. Civil administration, except revenue collection, had only a low priority for most kings. With very rare exceptions, providing good government and caring for the welfare of the people hardly ever concerned them.

Even the maintenance of law and order had only a low priority for most medieval Indian kings. Lawlessness was therefore widely prevalent in medieval India. There were countless robber bands in jungles all over India at this time, and whenever the political authority weakened they rampaged through the countryside, at times even through towns, pillaging and killing people. Protection against them was primarily the concern of the local people, seldom that of the king. And when the king acted against brigands, it was mainly to safeguard his revenue, hardly ever to protect the people. Indeed, kings themselves at times acted like brigands, pillaging their own subjects, to collect the overdue taxes from them.

One of the most disturbing aspects of the medieval Indian kingdoms was the universality of corruption in them, from the highest to the lowest level. Taking bribes was not a secret, devious act in India at this time, but was done openly, and was widely accepted as the normal and natural state of affairs by everyone. Provincial governors and other high government officials, even the sultan himself, were not above seeking recompense for doing favours, the only difference being that in their case the offerings they received were treated as presents, not bribes. And just as subordinates gave bribes to their superiors to win favours from them, superiors often gave bribes to their subordinates to secure their loyalty, except that these offerings were also called presents, not bribes. Loyalty was invariably on sale in medieval India. Nearly everyone, at all levels of government and society, was perfidious.

Curiously, despite all the socio-political turbulences in medieval India, normal life seems to have been fairly comfortable for most people there, though only at the very basic level. India was blessed with rich natural resources, so the one essential survival requirement of the common people, food, was easily available for all at affordable prices in normal times. What is shocking about the medieval Indian society is the appalling disparity between the incredible opulence and wanton lifestyle of the ruling class and the dreary subsistence level existence of the common people. 'Those in the country are very miserable, whilst the nobles are extremely opulent and delight in luxury,' observes Athanasius Nikitin, a Russian traveller in India in the fifteenth century.

The worst horror that the common people in medieval India had to face in their normal life was the visitation of famine which ravaged the land periodically. Agricultural production at this time was almost wholly dependent on the monsoon, so when the rains failed, famine felled thousands and thousands of people in one sweep. And those who survived did so by eating whatever they could find, however filthy or rotten, even putrefied carrion, and by taking to cannibalism. 'One day I went out of the city, and I saw three women . . . cutting into pieces and eating the skin of a horse which had been dead some months,' reports Battuta. 'Skins were cooked and sold in the markets. When bullocks were slaughtered, crowds rushed forward to catch the blood, and consumed it for their sustenance.' Adds Barani: 'Famine was very severe, and man was devouring man.'

THE SOCIO-CULTURAL AND political profile of India changed radically with the establishment of the Delhi Sultanate. Never before in its millenniums-long history had India faced a challenge as potent and irreconcilable as that of

Turco-Afghans, and never before had it failed to absorb invaders and migrants smoothly into its society and culture.

India at the time of the Turkish invasion had been in a dormant state for several centuries, remaining hermetically sealed within the subcontinent, with virtually no contact with the outside world. One would have expected that the Turkish invasion would awaken India from its slumber and stimulate it to transform itself to meet the Turkish challenge. But what happened was the opposite of this: instead of responding to the challenge of Islam, Hindu society curled up tighter into itself.

The aggressive presence of Turks in India made virtually no difference in the life and culture of most Indians. Nor did the contact with Hindus make any notable difference in the life and culture of most Muslims. Their civilisations were totally unlike each other in every respect to have any major influence on each other.

Hindus were treated as second class citizens in Muslim states, but as citizens nevertheless. They had their own rights. In any case, the discriminatory treatment that Hindus received at the hands of Muslim rulers would not have troubled them much, for most Indian communities were subject to worse discrimination in their own sharply stratified caste society. True, Hindus and Muslims did live separately and did not mix socially; but then so did the different Hindu castes live separately and did not mix socially. Even in the matter of jizya, not many Hindus would have felt it as a particularly discriminative tax, for Muslims too had to pay a community tax, zakat. Besides, jizya was usually imposed on individuals only in towns, while in villages, where most Hindus lived, it was assessed as a collective tax. Muslim rulers did slaughter a large number of Hindus, and demolish many of their temples and shrines, but Hindus seem to have taken all that fatalistically, as they normally did with nearly everything else in their lives.

There was hardly any display of resentment by Hindus against Turks. Nor were there any notable communal clashes during the many-centuries-long Muslim rule in India. This was largely because the establishment of Muslim rule in India made no notable difference in the lives of most Hindus, as most of them lived in villages, where there were scarcely any Muslims, and the lives of the people there were largely unaffected by the establishment of Muslim rule.

The only Hindu class that suffered any great material or social deprivation under Muslim rule was the ruling class, particularly the rajas, most of whom lost of their wealth and power. But several of the rajas saved some of their status and wealth by serving the sultans in subordinate positions. Similarly, most Hindu zamindars and chieftains served the sultans in various administrative capacities. And so did Brahmins, presumably in large numbers, and they were therefore rewarded by the sultans (except Firuz Tughluq) by exempting them, as a community, from the payment of jizya. As for Hindu commoners, very many of them served in the army and the administration of the sultans. Hindus quite probably constituted the majority of government employees in Muslim states. In a sense it was Hindus who ran the government for the sultans.

HINDUISM, BEING A non-proselytizing religion, posed no threat to Islam. Rather, being a polymorphic religion, it was tolerant and accommodative towards Islam, as it was towards its own diverse castes and sects. But the tolerance of Hindu society was tolerance by segregation; it was in fact a form of intolerance. Every community was free to live in whichever way it liked, but none was allowed to intrude into the cultural or social space of other communities. This meant that Hindu society, despite its appearance of tolerance, was in fact a highly discriminatory, inequitable and intolerant society, which sharply and unalterably segregated people by religion, sect and caste, and treated each group differently.

However, Hindu caste segregation involved no overt oppression, as it was birth determined, and was not the result of any social action by any group. Nor did caste segregation lead to any notable social tension. Even though segregation was an oppressive practice, lower caste Hindus did not generally feel oppressed by it, but accepted the circumstances of their life fatalistically, as a natural and inevitable outcome of the transmigratory process, the conditions of their life being predestined by their acts in their previous lives. Besides, the pervasive fatalistic attitude of the Indians of the age made them passively accept the conditions of their life, whatever those conditions were, and not struggle against them, as they believed that those conditions were inexorably fated by their karma.

And, paradoxical though it might seem, India's social diversity was the basis of its social cohesion and efficiency, for the different castes, though they were rigidly segregated from each other socially, were tightly integrated with each other in their functions, with each caste, from the highest to the lowest, including the outcastes, occupying a specific social niche and providing an exclusive and indispensible service in society. The different castes were like the different organs and limbs of a living being.

The caste society was a cooperative society. The diverse castes in it were not adversaries, but co-operators. And together they all constituted one cohesive society. The caste system thus enabled Hindu society, despite its diversity and appalling inequity, to function efficiently and peacefully for very many centuries.

Unfortunately, the caste system had a negative side to it, which nullified most of its benefits—it was a singularly unjust system, and was awfully wasteful of human resources, for its division of labour was based not on the merit of individuals, but on their birth. And it kept society sedated, in a state of coma, precluding mutation and progress.

In contrast to this birth-determined social segregation in Hindu society, Muslim society was basically egalitarian. Similarly, though both Hindu and Muslim societies had slaves, their treatment of slaves was entirely different from each other. Being a slave in Muslim society, unlike in Hindu society, was not an insurmountable handicap or degradation, for all professional and political avenues were open to slaves, depending on their ability.

As in the case of slaves, Hindu and Muslim societies differed greatly in their treatment of women. In upper-class Muslim society, women had to observe purdah, and were secluded in the zenana, the female quarters of their home. They were not allowed to have any contact with any men other than the members of their immediate family. And when they appeared in public, they had to wear the burqa, a shapeless, sack-like outer garment that covered their entire body from head to foot, leaving only a narrow veiled opening over the eyes. There were no such restrictions on Hindu women. However, Hindu women were not normally allowed to own property or to divorce their husband, but these rights were enjoyed by Muslim women.

Another difference in the social practices of Hindus and Muslims was that while some Hindu communities, such as Rajputs, considered the birth of a girl child as a misfortune, and female infanticide was widespread among them, that practice was strictly prohibited in Muslim society. Similarly, while polyandry and matrilineal families were common in some Hindu communities—particularly among Nairs in Kerala—these were virtually unknown in Muslim society. On the other hand, deviant sexual practices, like homosexuality and pederasty, were very rare among Hindus, but were fairly common among Muslims. Even some of the sultans were bisexual or homosexual, and some held court dressed as women.

A SOCIAL PRACTICE that was widely prevalent in medieval India, among Hindus as well Muslims, was polygamy. Muslims were however permitted to have only four wives, but in Hindu society there was no restriction at all about the number of wives a man could have. As for concubines, both societies permitted men to have as many of them as they desired or could afford, with some kings and nobles maintaining incredibly large harems. For instance, the sultan Begarha of Gujarat, according to contemporary chroniclers, had as many as 4000 women in his harem.

As for prostitution, Hindus and Muslims held totally opposite views on it. Islam considered prostitution as a major sin, but Hindus viewed it as a normal and legitimate aspect of social life. In ancient India, in the Mauryan Empire for instance, there were even state run brothels. Similarly, in medieval India brothels were run as a government sanctioned service in Vijayanagar.

Another oddity in medieval Hindu society was the practice of ritual suicide, in which people in woe or debility, because of illness or old age, drowned themselves in a holy river, such as Ganga, to escape from the miseries of life and to attain salvation. Jauhar, mass ritual suicide, was yet another Hindu practice, but this was restricted to the ruling class and the military aristocracy. Another form of ritual suicide—again practised mainly, though not exclusively, by the Hindu aristocracy—was sati, self-immolation by the widow or widows of a dead king or chieftain on his funeral pyre.

Islam considered all these as abominable practices, but it was only very rarely that sultans intervened in them, for Hindus as zimmis were normally free to practice their traditional customs without any interference. It was in any case impossible to lay down uniform rules in dealing with Hindu social and religious practices, for there were countless variations in them, depending on sect and caste and region.

As in social practices, so also there were great variations in the cuisine and dining practices of Indians, and these had become quite rigid in early medieval times. Society in ancient and early classical India was quite permissive in the matter of food, and allowed all, irrespective of their class and sex, including the priestly class, the freedom to eat whatever they liked, even beef, drink alcohol, and take psychotropic drugs. The scene changed altogether in the middle of the first millennium CE, when the caste system tightened its iron grip on Hindu society. Caste regulations then defined and enforced the rules about food and drink applicable to each caste, and these rules played a crucial role in segregating castes. The old adage that you are what you eat thus acquired a new meaning in India.

Some of the nobles of early medieval India were incredible gluttons. Battuta, for instance, speaks of an Ethiopian officer in India who 'was tall and corpulent, and used to eat a whole sheep at a meal, and . . . [drink] about a pound and a half of ghee.' Even more fantastic were the dietary practices attributed to Sultan Begarha of Gujarat, a man of gigantic size and gargantuan appetite, who, according to legend, ate about fourteen kilos of food every day, and, most curious of all, his daily diet included a swig of poison!

HINDU CIVILISATION WAS in an awful state of degeneration in early medieval times, especially when compared with its marvellous effulgence in the preceding age. This decline affected all facets of Indian civilisation. Culture putrefied. The caste system straitjacketed society, thereby hampering human enterprise and thwarting social progress. Commercial economy collapsed, and India gradually subsided into a stagnant, barely self-sustaining agrarian economy. Towns decayed; many of them were deserted, and they turned into crumbling relics. Instead of the urban sophistication that had characterised the classical Indian civilisation, now, in the early medieval period, crude rusticity characterised it. There was no more any creative energy in Indian civilisation. 'I can only compare their mathematical and astronomical literature, as far as I know it, to a mixture . . . of pearls and dung, or of costly crystals and common pebbles,' comments Al-Biruni.

This dismal state of Indian culture worsened further during the Delhi Sultanate period, because the main sustenance of cultural activity in pre-modern times was royal patronage, and Indian culture lost that patronage at this time, as most of the Hindu kingdoms had been conquered by Turks. Indian culture at this time also suffered from the vandalization and destruction of some of India's ancient cultural institutions and religious structures by Turks, most notably the demolition of the renowned Buddhist university of Nalanda in Bihar. Fortunately such destruction was mostly confined to the early period of the Delhi Sultanate. Some later sultans even took special care to preserve India's cultural heritage. The contribution of Firuz Tughluq in this was particularly commendable, such as he arranging for the translation of several ancient Sanskrit texts into Persian, and the meticulous care with which he had two Asoka pillars—they were over one and a half millenniums old—transported from the provinces to Delhi and erecting them there. Another commendable trans-cultural activity of the age was the contribution of some Muslim scholars, Al-Biruni in particular, in deferentially studying Indian culture and writing books on them.

Another fascinating cultural development in India during the early middle ages was the shift of creative activity from mainstream culture to regional culture, particularly in literature. Though a good number of new works continued to be written in Sanskrit at this time, these were all of little merit. But the decline of Sanskrit literature opened up literary space for regional languages to grow and flourish. Sanskrit, or rather Prakrit, had spawned a number of regional offshoots in North India in the late classical period, and from around the eighth century on some of these languages began to produce literatures of their own, and this gathered considerable momentum in the succeeding years.

One of the most interesting cultural developments of the middle ages was that, in contrast to the moribund state of Sanskrit literature, Tamil, the only other ancient Indian language which had a literature of its own, remained vibrantly alive at this time. But the ethos of Tamil literature in medieval times changed totally from what it had been in the classical period. While Tamil in the classical period produced sensitive secular literature, depicting the chiaroscuro of everyday life, its miseries and pleasures, mainly under Buddhist and Jain influence, its emphasis now shifted to religious literature, both devotional and expository, under the influence of resurgent Hinduism and its devotional cults. Religious fervour now replaced the calm reflective tone that had earlier characterised Tamil literature. There was also a good amount of fascinating literary activity in the regional offshoots of Tamil at this time—in Kannada, Telugu and Malayalam. Also, there was some high-quality creative activity in Persian literature in India during the Sultanate period, and some of these writers, particularly Amir Khusrav, were admirers of the Indian literary tradition and were influenced by it.

SUCH CREATIVE INTERACTIONS between Hindu and Muslim cultures were, however, rare, because of their totally contrary nature. This was particularly evident in the architecture of temples and mosques. While the structure of the Hindu temple was complex, dark and mysterious, the structure of the mosque was bright and open, its lines smooth, simple and elegant. Their very construction methods were different—while arch and dome were the defining characteristics of Muslim architecture, India had no tradition of dome building, and arches were built in India by the method of corbelled horizontal courses, unlike the superior Muslim practice of building them with voussoirs.

Similarly, while Muslims abhorred the depiction of living beings in art as sinful imitations of god's work, Hindu art was primarily figurative, in painting as well as in sculpture. Mosques were entirely free of figurative art, and used only floral, calligraphic, arabesque and geometric designs for decoration, but Hindu temples generally teemed with the sculptures and paintings of people, gods, animals and mythological creatures. Furthermore, Hindu temple art often depicted men and women in erotic play, which Muslims considered as totally repugnant.

The only cultural field in which Hindu and Muslim traditions exerted any notable mutual influence was in music. In early medieval times Indian classical music split into two distinct streams, Carnatic music of South India, and Hindustani music of North India, because North Indian music at this time came under the influence of Perso-Arabic musical tradition, while South Indian music remained virtually unaffected by it. Further, Hindustani music at this time became primarily court music (because its main patrons now, consequent of the collapse of the Hindu political power in North India, were sultans and Muslim nobles) while Carnatic music (flourishing mainly in peninsular India, in regions outside Muslim rule) largely retained its old character as devotional music. Besides, Carnatic music remained primarily vocal music, as most of its compositions were written to be sung; in contrast, musical instruments came to play a much larger role in Hindustani music, and it used far more instruments than Carnatic music.

THE TURKISH INVASION of India and the establishment of Islam as the religion of the dominant ruling class in India dramatically changed the religious ethos of the subcontinent. Over the millennia Hinduism had absorbed into it the beliefs and practices of numerous Indian tribes as well as of many foreign migrants. Hinduism could possibly have accommodated Islam too into its capacious multi-sectarian fold, but Islam was not susceptible to such absorption, for its monotheism was totally incompatible with Hindu polytheism. 'They (Hindus) totally differ from us in religion, as we believe in nothing in which they believe, and vice versa,' comments Al-Biruni. Because of this total contrariness between Hinduism and Islam they did not even exert any notable influence on each other.

This however was true only of the orthodox sects of both religions. In contrast to this, there were some intensely devotional new movements in both religions at this time, and there was a fair amount of interaction between these various movements. In Hinduism, the most notable of the devotional movements were the Bhakti cults that came to prominence in the centuries immediately preceding the Turkish invasion of India. These supercharged devotional cults originated in South India around the sixth century, and, gradually, over the next few centuries, spread all over the subcontinent.

The Bhakti sages held that only total and unswerving *bhakti* (devotion to god) could save man from the pitfalls of life and earn him salvation. And for this one did not have to go to temples or perform rituals, for god is latent in every man, and this god within can be roused through loving devotion. This was also the view of Sufis in Islam. They held that god realisation cannot be achieved through conventional religious practices, but only though obsessive, passionate devotion to god, and by awakening one's intuitive faculties through intense meditation. Such meditation, Sufis believed, would enable the devotee to gain insights into the true nature of god, and that this knowledge would liberate him from all worldly bonds, so that he becomes one with god.

Another fascinating religious development in the middle ages was the rise to prominence of several mystical religious movements in India, in both Hinduism and Islam. The mystics disregarded conventional religious barriers and drew their followers from both Hinduism and Islam, and they had no hesitation to freely incorporate elements of different faiths in their teachings. 'There is only one god, though Hindus and Muslims call him by different names,' stated Haridasa. And Kabir asserted:

> *All that lives and dies,*
> *They are all one.*
> *The this and that haggling*
> *is done.*

PART II

PRELUDE

The Hindu Shahi dynasty is now extinct, and of the whole house there is no longer the slightest remnant in existence. We must say that, in all their grandeur, they never slackened in their ardent desire for doing that which is good and right, that they were men of noble sentiment and noble bearing.

—AL-BIRUNI

1

Triumph and Tragedy

The Arab imperial expansion is one of the most dazzling military sagas in world history, a tornado of awesome kinetic energy and speed that swept through a vast stretch of land from the frontiers of China to the shores of the Atlantic Ocean, covering Central Asia, Afghanistan, the Middle East, North Africa, as well as Spain and southern France, an area more extensive than the Roman empire at its height. And all this was achieved within the span of just a century after the death of Prophet Muhammad, the founder of Islam, in CE 632. Arabs believed that they had the power of god with them and were therefore invincible. And indeed they did prove to be invincible.

Inexplicably it was only in the last phase of this imperial expansion, in the second decade of the eighth century, that Arabs made their first major military move into India, although India was at this time famed for its riches, and Arab chieftains had been for over half a century right at the border of India, in Afghanistan, and India was a familiar country for them, for they, as seafaring traders, had a many-centuries-long commercial relationship with Indians.

The history of the commercial relationship between India and Arabia goes back to ancient times, and this amicable relationship continued even after Arabs, galvanised by Islam, turned their primary interest from trade to empire-building. Arab traders had many settlements in India in early medieval times, at port cities and royal capitals, where Indian kings in their characteristic tolerant religious spirit had allowed them to build their homes and mosques, practice their religion without any restriction, and maintain their distinctive lifestyle. Some Indian kings even employed Arabs in top administrative and military positions, and some had Arab contingents in their armies.

There was however an irritant in the Indo-Arab relationship, the menace of pirates operating out of Indian harbours, which hampered Arab shipping and trade. This prompted Arab rulers to send a couple of naval expeditions into Indian coastal waters, to chastise the pirates. But these were minor incidents. And their purpose was to secure the sea trade, not to conquer territory. It was in any case impossible to conquer land from the sea in that age.

There is only one recorded instance of a caliph even considering sending an exploratory contingent into India. This was by Caliph Usman of the mid-seventh century, who at one time thought of sending an army into Sind. But he was, according to the ninth-century Persian historian Al-Biladuri, advised against it by an explorer. 'Water is scarce there, the fruits are poor, and the robbers are bold,' the explorer warned. 'If few troops are sent there, they will be slain; if many, they will starve.'

What finally made Arabs send an army into Sind was a piracy related incident. There are three different versions of what provoked this action, but the generally accepted account is that what led to it was the capture of an Arab ship by pirates off the port city of Debal in the Indus delta. The pirates not only plundered the ship but also seized the Arab girls who were on it, the orphan daughters of the Muslim traders who had died in Sri Lanka. The incident, particularly the capture of the girls, roused the wrath of Hajjaj, the pugnacious Arab governor of Iraq, and he then sent an imperative letter to Dahar, the king of Sind, demanding that he should immediately free the girls, punish the pirates, and make reparation for the damage caused. But Dahar claimed that he was helpless to do anything in the matter. 'They are pirates who have captured these women, and over them I have no authority,' he wrote to Hajjaj. The reply was probably disingenuous, for several of the coastal rulers of India at this time were known to connive with pirates and share their booty. In any case, Hajjaj considered the reply evasive or deceitful, and he sent two punitive forces against Dahar, one by land and the other by sea. But both these forces were routed in Sind, and their commanders slain.

HAJJAJ THEN SENT, with the Caliph's permission, a full-fledged army to invade Sind, and gave the command of this campaign to Muhammad Qasim, his nephew and son-in-law, who was then the governor of Shiraz in Persia. Muhammad was only seventeen years old at this time, but he conducted the Sind campaign with a sagacity way beyond his age, and proved to be resourceful and ingenious in military strategies as well as in diplomacy and administration.

The Caliph took care to provide Muhammad with a strong army for this campaign: 6000 picked Syrian cavalry, the flower of the Arab armies, backed by a large camel corps and a baggage train of some 3000 camels. Several more troops and adventurers joined the army on its way to India, motivated by religious zeal and the prospect of plunder. Heavy siege weapons were sent to Sind by sea, and this included a monstrously huge ballista ironically named 'Bride', which required some 500 men to operate it. Muhammad, states Al-Biladuri, 'was provided with all he could require, without omitting even thread and needles.'

Setting out on the campaign, Muhammad adventurously took the hazardous but short Makran seacoast route—the 'waterless inferno' through which Alexander had retreated from India in the fourth century BCE—to advance into Sind. The army seems to have endured the perils of the journey well, and it reached Sind in good shape. And, although it suffered some initial reverses in Sind, it had little difficulty in storming into Debal by scaling its ramparts.

Muhammad was usually humane and fair in his treatment of the defeated enemy, but at Debal, where he had his first major military engagement in India, he was utterly ruthless in the carnage he inflicted on the people there, presumably to terrify the chieftains of Sind into submission by a demonstration of the doom that awaited them if they resisted him, and no doubt also to rouse the ferocity of his own soldiers with bloodlust and the prospect of plunder. Arabs ravaged Debal for three whole days, slaughtering all the adult men who refused to become Muslims, enslaving their wives and children, and plundering the town of all its wealth. Muhammad then sent the customary one-fifth of the plunder to the Caliph, and divided the rest among his soldiers.

Muhammad stationed a garrison in Debal to secure his line of communication and supply, and then proceeded northward along the Indus, to confront his main adversary, the king Dahar. He met very little resistance as he advanced, and a couple of towns along his route surrendered to him peacefully, though there were also a few places where he had to fight his way through. Muhammad, notes Al-Biruni in his eleventh-century chronicle, advanced 'sometimes fighting with sword in hand, sometimes gaining his ends by treaties, leaving to the people their ancient beliefs, except in the case of those who wanted to become Muslims.'

MUHAMMAD WAS OFTEN brilliantly innovative in his military tactics. One such tactic he used was to divide his army into two divisions while attacking forts, one to fight during daytime, and the other to fight at night, thus giving no rest to the defenders, while his own soldiers always remained well-rested and fresh. Because of such tactics, and the sheer ferocity of his soldiers, Muhammad was usually victorious in his battles.

As in military tactics, so also in diplomacy Muhammad was quite ingenious, winning over the local chieftains to his side. According to Al-Biladuri, Muhammad counselled the people of Sind to surrender to him peacefully, promising them that if they did so they would not be molested in any way, but would be given full protection, and that their 'temples shall be unto us, like the churches of Christians, the synagogues of Jews, and the fire temple of the Magians.' But he also warned them that if they resisted him, he would be absolutely ruthless in suppressing them. And this warning was demonstrated by him in several places, where he faced resistance, by indiscriminately slaughtering the enemy soldiers as well as the common people, and by enslaving their women and children. He also desecrated a number of temples, or demolished them to build mosques in their place. In one temple he defiled the idol by attaching a piece of beef to its neck.

This dual policy of Muhammad was quite successful. His military ferocity scared off many of his potential adversaries—sometimes they fled by the back gate of their fort when Arabs entered it by its front gate—or induced them to submit to him prudently, without resistance. Some chieftains even sided with Muhammad and assisted him in his campaign. As for the general public, according to *Chach-nama*, a near-contemporary chronicle of the Arab conquest of Sind, Muhammad won them over by his 'honesty, prudence, justice, equity, and generosity.' He took particular care to give 'protection to artificers, merchants and the common people,' and at times even compensated those whose properties were plundered by his soldiers. Because of all this, in some places people even greeted Muhammad as a saviour, by 'ringing bells, beating drums and dancing.'

Muhammad's magnanimous treatment of the local people—mostly Hindus and Buddhists—involved a liberal interpretation of the injunctions of Koran, which allow Muslim armies to spare only the 'people of the book' (Jews, Christians and Zoroastrians) and their religious places, but require all other infidels to be put to death if they did not become Muslims. Hajjaj in fact cautioned Muhammad on this. 'The great god says in Koran, "O true believers, when you encounter unbelievers, strike off their heads." The above command of the great god is a great command and must be respected and followed,' he warned. 'You should not be so fond of showing mercy, as to nullify the virtue of the act. Henceforth grant pardon to none of the enemy and spare none of them, or else all will consider you a weak-minded man.'

Koran, however, is not entirely consistent in its injunctions on this, and in one place it says, 'Make war upon such of those . . . who believe not in god . . . until they pay tribute out of hand, and are humbled.' This command was often liberally interpreted to mean that non-Muslims should not be harried in any way if they paid jizya and conducted themselves humbly. It was this policy that Muhammad adopted. And Hajjaj himself later approved it. As 'the chief inhabitants [of Sind] . . . have made submission, and have agreed to pay taxes to the Caliph, nothing more can be properly required from them,' he wrote to Muhammad. 'They have been taken under our protection, and we cannot in any way stretch out our hands upon their lives or property. Permission is given to them to worship their gods. Nobody must be forbidden or prevented from following his own religion. They may live in their houses in whatever manner they like . . . [They should be allowed to] live without any fear, and strive to better themselves . . . You deserve praise and commendation for your military conduct, and for the pains you have taken in protecting the people, ameliorating their condition, and managing the affairs of the government.'

MUHAMMAD'S FAR-SIGHTED AND conciliatory policy towards Sindhis paid good dividends, for many local chieftains, as well as the gentry and the common people, responded to it by peacefully submitting to him. And several of them, including some chieftains, even a son of Dahar, became Muslims, and took Arab names—mainly, we may assume, to retain their power or to gain other temporal advantages, though some probably had a genuine change of faith. There does not seem to have been any large number of forced conversions by Muhammad. According to *Chach-nama*, the good conduct of Muhammad 'dispelled the fear of the Arab army from the minds of those who offered allegiance, and brought those to submission who were inimically disposed.'

Another major reason for the easy submission of Sindhis to Arabs was their general belief, based on an ancient astrological prediction, that it would be futile for them to resist Arabs, for they (Arabs) were destined to be victorious. 'In the books of the Buddhists it is predicted, upon astrological calculations, that Hindustan shall be captured by Muhammadans . . . It is the will of god,' stated a local chieftain to his clansmen as he prepared to surrender to Muhammad.

Yet another factor that facilitated the easy advance of Muhammad in Sind was that a good number of the people there at this time were Buddhists, and they, notes *Chach-nama*, peacefully surrendered to Muhammad, telling him, 'Our religion is one of peace and quiet; fighting and slaying, as well as all blood-shedding are prohibited to us.' This pacific attitude of Buddhists was motivated, apart from their anxiety to prevent carnage, by their desire to protect their business interests, for they were the dominant commercial community in Sind, and antagonising Arabs would have seriously harmed their business.

It was on the whole a smooth passage for Muhammad in Sind. But during his northward thrust to confront Dahar he was delayed for some months on the western bank of the Indus, as a number of his soldiers were there afflicted with scurvy, and many of his horses died of some disease. Hajjaj then sent him medicines and reinforcements, and eventually, in June 712, Muhammad crossed the river and advanced on the fortress of Brahmanabad, where Dahar was stationed.

As Muhammad approached the fortress, he was confronted (according to an evidently exaggerated account) by Dahar with a huge army consisting of 50,000 cavalry. He even had 500 Arabs in his army, according to *Chach-nama*. 'A dreadful conflict ensued, such as had never been heard of,' comments Al-Biladuri. Dahar, as was usual among Indian kings, led his army mounted on a huge elephant. His high visibility was meant to inspire his army, but it also made him an easy target for enemy sharpshooters. And, as it happened, an Arab soldier 'shot his naphtha arrow into Dahar's howdah and set it on fire,' reports *Chach-nama*. Dahar then, according to Al-Biladuri, 'dismounted and fought valiantly, but was killed towards the evening. The idolaters then fled, and Musulmans glutted themselves with massacre.' Dahar's head was severed and sent to the Caliph as a trophy, along with his share of the booty taken in the campaign.

As the Arabs charged into the fortress, one of Dahar's queens committed sati, but another, Rani Ladi, surrendered and eventually married Muhammad. Two of Dahar's maiden daughters, Suryadevi and Parmaldevi, who were found in the fort, were sent by Muhammad to the Caliph, as a part of the homage due to him.

After capturing Brahmanabad, Muhammad spent some time there, organising the administration of the conquered territories. He then continued his northward advance, fighting several battles along the way, and captured the city of Multan.

It had been a brilliant campaign by Muhammad all along. But presently he was overtaken by a dreadful misfortune, which ended his career while it was still in full bloom.

THE CAUSE OF Muhammad's tragic end is given variously in contemporary chronicles. According to *Chach-nama*, this was a vengeance wreaked on him by the two Sind princesses he had sent to the Caliph's harem. The story, as told in *Chach-nama*, is that one night some days after the princesses arrived, the Caliph had the older princess, Suryadevi, brought to him. When he made her sit down, 'and she uncovered her face . . . [he] was enamoured of her surpassing beauty and charms. Her powerful glances robbed his heart of patience, and he laid his hand upon her and drew her towards him.' But she shrank away from his touch and stood up, and said that she was not worthy of him, for Muhammad had violated her before sending her to him. This so enraged the Caliph that he right away, without any enquiry whatever, despatched an imperative order to Muhammad that he should, directly on receipt of the order, 'suffer himself to be sewed up in a hide and sent to the capital.'

Muhammad obeyed immediately, as expected of a loyal Arab officer. He was then tightly sewed up in a hide and sent to Baghdad in a locked chest.

Predictably he died of suffocation on the way. When the chest arrived at the Caliph's palace, he showed the corpse to Suryadevi, to impress her with his power. 'The virtuous . . . [princess then] put off the veil from her face, placed her head on the ground,' and told the Caliph that he had made a dreadful mistake in punishing Muhammad. 'It is proper that a king should test with the touchstone of reason and weigh in his mind whatever he hears from friend or foe,' she told him. 'And when it is found to be true and indubitable, then orders compatible with justice should be given . . . Your gracious mind is wanting in reason and judgement. Muhammad Qasim respected our honour, and behaved like a brother or son to us, and he never touched us . . . with a licentious hand. But he had killed the king of Hind and Sind, he had destroyed the dominion of our forefathers, and he had degraded us from the dignity of royalty to a state of slavery. Therefore, to retaliate and to revenge these injuries, we uttered a falsehood before the Caliph . . . Through this fabrication and deceit we have taken our revenge.' The Caliph then, overcome with remorse and wrath, 'bit the back of his hand' and immediately ordered the princesses to be entombed alive, thus inflicting on them a fate similar to that suffered by Muhammad.

This tragic tale is usually discounted by historians as mere romance, but the story is no more incredible than many other similar historical accounts of royal vengeance, though some of the detail in it—the words spoken by the princess, for instance—are obviously frills added to it by its raconteur. The plausibility of the *Chach-nama* story is also indicated by the fact that this work was written not long after the Arab invasion of Sind, so the writer could not have deviated too far from the actual events without exposing himself to ridicule. The other account of Muhammad's end—that he was tortured and put to death by the Caliph due to family enmity—is of a later period, though it is possible that family enmity was also a factor in the Caliph's ill-treatment of Muhammad. Whatever it was that actually happened, it is certain that Muhammad's life ended tragically. He had been in Sind for only about three years, but during that short period he had won the affection of the people there by his prudence and benevolence so that, according to Al-Biladuri, 'the people of Hind wept for him' on hearing his tragic end.

The history of Arabs in Sind after the departure of Muhammad is obscure. Presently the Arab power declined everywhere in Eurasia, and Turks seized from them the political and military leadership in the Muslim world. Although the Arab state in Sind endured for some three centuries, it made no major gains in territory or power during this period. The successors of Muhammad did at one time, in the second quarter of the eighth century, overrun a good part of Rajasthan and Gujarat, and advanced as far as Ujjain, but these gains were transitory, for Arabs were presently pushed back into Sind by Chalukyas of northern Deccan and Pratiharas of Malwa. The Arab expansion northward towards Kashmir and Kanauj was also repulsed, by Lalitaditya of Kashmir and Yasovarman of Kanauj.

The Arab power in India was thus mostly confined to Sind, but there it endured till the early eleventh century. And it was finally extinguished, ironically, not by any Indian king, but by another Muslim invader, Mahmud Ghazni. On the whole, the occupation of Sind by Arabs, though it is a fascinating story, was an event of little consequence in Indian history. It was an isolated, peripheral event, which had no connection at all with either the Indian raids of Mahmud Ghazni three centuries later, in the early eleventh century, or the establishment of the Delhi Sultanate yet another two centuries later, in the early thirteenth century, events which would radically transform the very texture and pattern of Indian history.

2

For God and Mammon

After the Arab conquest of Sind, India had a respite from invasions for nearly three centuries, till the Ghaznavid invasion in the early eleventh century. In the meantime, by the second decade of the ninth century, the far-flung Arab empire had begun to crack up like a clay field in high summer, and several of its provinces became virtually independent kingdoms, even though Muslim rulers everywhere generally acknowledged the nominal overlordship of the Caliph.

One of the major kingdoms that emerged out of the splintered Arab empire was the Samanid kingdom of Central Asia, spread over Khurasan and Transoxiana, and had Bukhara as its capital. In time the Samanid kingdom too splintered into several independent states. In 963 Alptigin, a Turkic slave who had risen to high office under the Samanids and served them as their governor in Khurasan, rebelled against his king, seized the city of Ghazni in eastern Afghanistan, and established an independent kingdom there. Ghazni, states Mughal emperor Babur in his autobiography, was at that time 'a very humble place'. But it had a grand historical destiny. And it would play a decisive role in the history of medieval India.

Alptigin died soon after founding the kingdom, and was succeeded by three rulers in quick succession: a son, a son-in-law, and a royal slave. The slave, Pirai—whom medieval chronicler Siraj describes as 'a very depraved man'— was overthrown by the nobles of Ghazni in 977, and they raised Sabuktigin, a favourite slave and son-in-law of Alptigin, to the throne.

The nobles favoured Sabuktigin because he was a man of proven ability, and had also taken care to win their support. According to Khondamir, an early-sixteenth-century chronicler, 'the chief men of Ghazni saw the signs of greatness and nobility, and the fires of felicity and prosperity on the forehead of Sabuktigin, who widely spread out the carpet of justice, and rooted out injury and oppression, and who, by conferring different favours on them, had made friends of the nobles, the soldiers, and the leading men of the state.'

Apart from having these laudable personal qualities, Sabuktigin also claimed royal pedigree—he traced his lineage to the last Persian monarch, whose descendants had, during the Arab invasion of Persia, fled to Turkistan, where they, having intermarried with the local people, eventually came to be considered as Turks. When Sabuktigin was around twelve years old, he was captured by a rival tribe, and was later taken to Bukhara by a slave trader. There he was bought by Alptigin, under whose favour he rapidly rose in rank, and in time achieved renown as a general.

Ghazni was a tiny kingdom at the time of Alptigin's death, and was confined to just the city and its environs. Sabuktigin greatly expanded the kingdom, extending its frontiers up to the Amu Darya in the north, the Caspian Sea in the west, and eastward across the mountains up to the upper Indus Valley. According to Al-Biruni, Sabuktigin had chosen 'the holy war as his calling,' and this led him to launch several campaigns against King Jayapala of the Hindu Shahi dynasty of Punjab. There is however no evidence of any great religious zeal in the campaigns of the sultan. His invasion of Punjab was in any case inevitable, given his expansionist ambitions, and the normal hostile posture of kings against their immediate neighbours.

Jayapala ruled over an extensive kingdom stretching from western Punjab to eastern Afghanistan, but he, according to medieval Arab historian Al-Utbi, found 'his land grow narrow under his feet' because of Sabuktigin's aggressions. Jayapala then, following the classic dictum that offence is the best form of defence, advanced against Sabuktigin with his army—'he rose with his relations, generals and vassals, and hastened with his huge elephants to wreak his revenge upon Sabuktigin,' states Al-Utbi.

THE ENSUING BATTLE went on for several days, but still remained inconclusive, and was not going too well for the Ghaznavids. What saved them was a miracle. There was, according to Al-Utbi, a ravine close to the Hindu camp, and in it a lake of absolute purity and miraculous properties. 'If any filth was thrown into it, black clouds collected, whirlwinds arose, the summits of mountains became black, rain fell, and the neighbourhood was filled with cold blasts until red death supervened.' Sabuktigin, baffled in the battlefield, decided to invoke the supernatural, and had some filth thrown into the lake. Suddenly, 'the horrors of the day of resurrection rose up before wicked infidels, and fire fell from heaven on them.' A fierce hailstorm accompanied by loud claps of thunder then swept through the valley, and 'thick black vapours' enveloped the Indian army, so they could not even 'see the road by which they could flee.'[1]

Jayapala, faced with this strange adversity, then pleaded for peace. Sabuktigin was inclined to grant it, but his belligerent son Mahmud wanted total victory. Hearing of this, Jayapala warned Sabuktigin: 'You have seen the impetuosity of Hindus and their indifference to death . . . If, therefore, you refuse to grant peace in the hope of obtaining plunder, tribute, elephants and prisoners, then there is no alternative for us but to mount the horse of stern determination, destroy our property, take out the eyes of our elephants, cast our children into fire, and rush on each other with sword and spear, so that all that will be left to you are stones and dirt, and dead bodies and scattered bones.' Sabuktigin knew that this was not a hollow threat, so he granted peace to the raja on his promise of paying tribute and ceding some territories.

Jayapala reneged on that promise, and, according to Mughal chronicler Ferishta, organised a confederacy of several North Indian rajas against Sabuktigin. It was a matter of survival for him, as the very existence of his kingdom was being threatened by the rapidly expanding Ghaznavid sultanate. But the ensuing battle was once again won by Sabuktigin, despite the vast army that Jayapala deployed. This time his victory was due to the innovative battle tactic he adopted, after carefully reconnoitring the enemy deployment. Sabuktigin, according Al-Utbi, 'ascended a lofty hill from which he could see the whole army of the infidels, which resembled scattered ants and locusts, and he felt like a wolf about to attack a flock of sheep.' Returning to his camp, Sabuktigin divided his army into several contingents of 500 soldiers each and sent them in relays against the Indian army, to attack and retreat, attack and retreat, so that the Indian soldiers became utterly exhausted as the battle progressed while the bulk of the Turkish army remained fresh. At that stage Sabuktigin sent his entire army charging into battle in a fierce onslaught, and routed the Indian army, which 'fled, leaving behind them their property, utensils, arms, provisions, elephants, and horses.' Following the victory, Sabuktigin annexed the western part of the Hindu Shahi kingdom, up to Peshawar.

The crucial factor that led to Sabuktigin's victory—apart from the ingenious battle tactic he used—was that the Indian cavalry, according to Ferishta, was far inferior to the Turkish cavalry using Central Asian bloodstock. Moreover, the Central Asian soldiers of the sultan were very much hardier than Indian soldiers. The 'greatest pleasure [of the Ghaznavid cavalrymen] was to be in saddle, which they regarded as if it were a throne,' claims Al-Utbi. The Ghaznavids also had a psychological advantage over the Indian soldiers,

---

[1] Nine centuries later, an invading British Indian army was confounded by a similar snowstorm in Afghanistan.

in that they were valorous unto death, in the absolute certainty that if they died fighting infidels they would straightaway go to heaven and enjoy eternal bliss there. Their weapons too were superior to those of Indians, in that they used the composite bow—made of two pieces of wood joined together with a metal band—which, as Sarkar describes it, was 'the most dreaded weapon of antiquity'.

Sabuktigin was an exceptionally successful monarch, and in every field of government his achievements were substantial. 'Amir Sabuktigin,' states Siraj, 'was a wise, just, brave and religious man, faithful to his agreements, truthful in his words and not avaricious for wealth. He was kind and just to his subjects.' He was also a prudent and cautious monarch, and he, despite all his military successes, took care to acknowledge the overlordship of the Samanid rulers of Bukhara, and he aided them in their battles against rebels. For those services he was rewarded by the Samanid sultan with the governorship of the province of Khurasan. And Sabuktigin in turn conferred that governorship on Mahmud, his eldest son.

SABUKTIGIN DIED IN 997, after an eventful reign of twenty years, and was succeeded by his son Mahmud, after a brief war of succession. Mahmud was not Sabuktigin's chosen successor—his preference was for Ismail, his younger son. But that choice was an expression of his sentiment, not of his judgement, for Ismail was a weakling compared to Mahmud. Mahmud seems to have been the son of a concubine of the sultan, and that also probably weighed against him in the eyes of Sabuktigin, even though in Islamic law all one's children, whether born of a wedded wife or a mistress, are equally legitimate. In any case, the sword was the final arbiter of princely destinies, so a dead king's will was no barrier to an ambitious prince in his pursuit of power.

Sabuktigin seems to have had a presentiment about Mahmud's future greatness even at the very time of his birth. 'A moment before his birth, Amir Sabuktigin saw in a dream that a tree had sprung from the fireplace in his house, and grew so high that it covered the whole world with its shadow,' writes Siraj. 'Waking up startled from his dream, he began to reflect upon the import of it. At that very moment a messenger came, bringing the tidings that the Almighty had given him a son. Sabuktigin was greatly delighted by the news, and he said, "I name the child Mahmud". On the same night he was born, an idol temple in India, in the vicinity of Peshawar, on the banks of the Sind, collapsed,' portending the iconoclastic zeal that Mahmud would come to have as sultan.

Mahmud was in Khurasan at the time of his father's death, and from there he wrote a conciliatory letter to Ismail suggesting that he should leave the crown to him (Mahmud) and accept the governorship of Balk and Khurasan, a substantial portion of the kingdom. Ismail rejected the offer. Mahmud then advanced on Ghazni with his army, routed Ismail in a battle, and imprisoned him for life, but generously provided him with all material comforts. Mahmud, aged twenty-seven, then ascended the throne.

Mahmud's accession to the throne was then legitimised by the Caliph by sending to him a robe of investiture and by conferring on him the title Yamin-ud-Daulah (Right-hand-of-the-empire), so his dynasty thereafter came to be known as the Yamini dynasty. Mahmud responded to the Caliphate honour by taking a solemn vow, at the formal ceremony of receiving the laurels, to undertake jihad, holy war, every year against the idolaters of India.

MAHMUD COULD NOT keep his vow to the letter, because of his several military engagements in Central Asia, but he did lead more than twelve campaigns into India, perhaps as many as seventeen campaigns, during his thirty-two-year reign. The avowed objective of Mahmud's Indian campaigns, according to Al-Utbi, was 'to exalt the standard of religion, to widen the plain of right, to illuminate the words of truth, and to strengthen the power of justice.' Mahmud, adds Ferishta, wanted to 'root out the worship of idols from the face of all India.'

Mahmud did indeed 'convert as many as a thousand idol temples into mosques,' according to Siraj. But the passion for plunder was an equally strong motive, or perhaps an even stronger motive, in Mahmud—he fought for god as well as for mammon, but quite probably more for mammon than for god. These were however interconnected motives, each reinforcing and energising the other.

India was the ideal land for Mahmud to glut both his passions simultaneously, for Hindu temples were depositories of immense treasures, so sacking them earned him great religious merit as well as vast treasures. There was also an important morale boosting military advantage in demolishing temples and smashing their idols, for these were, in the eyes of Ghaznavid soldiers, convincing demonstrations of the invincible power of their god, and the utter powerlessness of Hindu gods. Sometimes the fragments of the smashed idols were sent to Ghazni for embedding them in thoroughfares there, for people to tread on and desecrate them.

Muslim rulers were by convention required to offer three options to their infidel adversaries: become Muslims and be privileged citizens, or live as zimmis (protected non-Muslims: second class citizens), or be killed. But the invaders in the frenzy of battle almost never paused to offer their foes those choices. The religious fervour of Mahmud's army expressed itself primarily in slaughter, plunder and destruction, but hardly ever in active pursuit of proselytisation. Even the small number of conversions that Mahmud made were done at the point of the sword—it was Islam or death for the vanquished. There was no serious attempt by him to propagandise Islam. Consequently, many of those who became Muslims to save their lives and properties, apostatised when the tide of Ghaznavid invasion receded. Mahmud's campaigns had hardly any enduring religious effect in India.

There was clearly a strong element of self-serving opportunism in Mahmud's posture of religious fervour, for he had no hesitation in inducting a large number of Hindus into his army under their own commanders, or even in deploying them in battles against rival Muslim kingdoms in Central Asia. According to Al-Utbi an army he once deployed in Central Asia consisted of 'Turks, Indians, Khaljis, Afghans and Ghaznavids.' It is significant that Mahmud was as ruthless in his fight against Muslims of the 'heretic' Ismaili sect as he was in his fight against Hindus, and he had no qualms whatever about destroying the centuries-old Muslim kingdom of Multan, massacring a large number of Ismailis there, desecrating their mosques, and, as Al-Utbi reports, in levying from them '20,000,000 dirhams with which to alleviate their sins.'

Religious fervour evidently subserved Mahmud's temporal goals of amassing booty and expanding his power. As for his soldiers, the prospect of booty was undoubtedly their primary motive, though it was religious frenzy and bloodlust that galvanized them. Often, in a single raid into India, they obtained several times more wealth than they could have ever dreamed of acquiring in a whole lifetime of mundane toil. Apart from material treasures, the Turks also seized a large number of people in India—men, women and children—for serving them as slaves, or for selling them to slave traders back home.

WARS EVERYWHERE IN the medieval world were savage. Mahmud's Indian campaigns were particularly so. This savagery was often deliberately inflamed by Mahmud, as it served the dual purpose of rousing the ferocity of his soldiers, and of terrifying the enemy. These were the major factors that enabled Mahmud to be invariably victorious in his battles—and those victories in turn endowed him with an aura of invincibility, so that his adversaries often fled on his very approach, as before a tornado of fire. And this craven flight of adversaries in turn boosted the self-confidence of Mahmud and his soldiers, and they came to regard themselves as invincible. And indeed, they became invincible.

Sometimes, when confronted with an overwhelming enemy force, Mahmud prostrated on the ground ardently praying for god's help—and that, whether god intervened or not, did ignite the valour of his soldiers, so they won the ensuing battle. Mahmud however was not a reckless adventurer. His raids, for all their seeming impetuosity, were not random, impulsive acts, but were all very carefully planned, after meticulously gathering information about his adversaries by sending spies to scout them out. And he avoided needless risks.

On one occasion, during his 1008 campaign against Shahi king Anandapala, son of Jayapala, he lay entrenched before the enemy for as many as forty days, unwilling to risk launching an attack against the vast enemy horde, but sought to provoke Anandapala to attack, which he unwisely did in the end, and was routed. It was this potent combination of caution, meticulous planning, and faith-driven battlefield ferocity that made Mahmud invincible.

There is a good amount of information on Mahmud and his campaigns in medieval Arabic and Persian chronicles, which are generally reliable in recording the broad sweep of events in his life. But some of the details in the chronicles are suspect. The accounts of the havoc caused by Mahmud in India, and of the amount of booty he seized there, often seem exaggerated in the chronicles, evidently to glorify the heroism and religious fervour of the sultan. For instance, in one campaign he is said to have taken, apart from a vast amount of treasure, 380 elephants and 53,000 captives. And in another campaign he is reported to have captured 500 elephants! Similarly, the slaughter attributed to Mahmud is often preposterous—15,000 in one battle, 20,000 in another battle, and, most incredible of all, 50,000 in the temple town of Somnath—all that with sword and spear and arrows, in battles that usually lasted just a few hours!

But even if we discount the exaggeration in these accounts, it cannot be denied that Mahmud's raids were horrendous orgies of animal ferocity. Ghaznavids killed not only the enemy soldiers, but also common folks in countless numbers. Only women and children were usually—but not always—spared, but they, as well as numerous men, were seized as slaves, and were afterwards taken to Ghazni. There, reports Al-Utbi, 'merchants from distant cities came to purchase the slaves, so that . . . [many lands in Central Asia] were filled with them, and the fair and the dark, the rich and the poor, were commingled in common slavery.' There was a good demand for Indian slaves in Central Asia at this time, and they normally fetched a good price, though at one time the Afghan slave market was so overstocked with Indian slaves that their price plummeted, and a slave could be bought for as little as a couple of dirhams.

Curiously, Mahmud, unlike most other invaders, had no hunger for land. Had he desired it, he could have easily annexed a good part of North India to his kingdom, but he did not have the patience for empire building. Except Punjab and Sind—the gateways to India, which he needed to keep open for his raids—Mahmud did not annex any territory in India. His Indian campaigns were like bandit raids—he swept through the land rapidly, fought several quick battles, slaughtered enemy soldiers and people in multitudes, destroyed temples and smashed idols, enslaved thousands of people, seized immeasurable booty, and then sped back to Ghazni. He had no desire to settle in India, perhaps because of its torrid climate, which, as Khondamir puts it, 'consumed the body as easily as flame melts a candle.'

Mahmud was proud of the incredible amount of booty he seized in India, and once, on returning from a raid, he piled up the treasures he had collected on carpets in the courtyard of his palace, for people to admire it and extol him. And Ghazni, enriched by the vast treasures that Mahmud and his soldiers brought from India, became a fabulously rich city, where, as Wolseley Haig puts it, 'mosques, colleges, caravanserais and hospices sprang up on every side.'

MAHMUD'S IDEAL CAMPAIGN schedule was to arrive in India soon after the monsoon ended, and to return to Ghazni before the monsoon set in again and the rivers became unfordable. When the season of rain ended, the season of plunder began.

Mahmud had five rainless and cool months, October to February, for his Indian campaigns. But the exigencies of war and the waywardness of weather often wrecked his plans. Nature itself was a vicious adversary that Mahmud had to contend with in India—torrential rivers, waterless deserts, deep ravines, jungles infested with ferocious animals and venomous reptiles. Once, his passage into India was blocked for a couple of months by a snowstorm that covered his route with heavy snowdrifts; another time he lost all his booty while crossing a flooded river. Sometimes vengeful native guides led him into forbidding marshes, as they did once, when he was returning from Kashmir; or led him into desert infernos, as they did once, when he was returning from Gujarat. Still he persisted relentlessly with his campaigns. And fortune invariably favoured him.

The response of Indian kings to the Ghaznavid invasion was usually craven, if we are to believe the partisan testimony of Muslim chroniclers. According to these chroniclers, the rajas often fled from Mahmud's path, even when they had under their command armies that were much larger than that of Mahmud. Often, on Mahmud's approach, they sneaked out from their forts in the middle of the night, and hid in thick forests till Mahmud left the area. Such craven responses were at least in part due to the widely prevalent fatalistic attitude of Indians, which made them believe that victory and defeat were not in their hands, but as fate decreed. They were therefore defeated in their minds even as they entered the battlefield, and were more ready to flee than to fight. There are only very few recorded instances of Indian kings offering heroic resistance to Mahmud.

Sometimes Indian kings purchased peace from Mahmud by surrendering to him their treasures as he approached their capital—and sometimes they passed on this burden to their helpless subjects, by levying on them a special tax called Turushka-danda. And sometimes, to prevent annihilation, the rajas embraced Islam, though they often apostatised later—thus Sukhapala, a grandson of King Jayapala of Punjab, became a Muslim and changed his name to Nawasa Shah, but he later reverted to Hinduism. To change religion was an act of no great import for Indians; in polytheistic India, Islam was often seen as just a constituent in the heterogeneous political, social, religious and sectarian make-up of India.

THERE WAS AT this time no concept of India as a nation, and therefore no recognition of the invader as an alien. India was just a geographical region. For Indian kings, Ghazni was just another kingdom which, though militarily more dangerous and culturally more divergent than the kingdoms in the subcontinent, was nevertheless merely another element in their normal political milieu. Not surprisingly Indian kings continued to fight with each other even as Mahmud was storming through the land. And Hindu soldiers had no scruple at all to serve under the virulently anti-Hindu Mahmud, or, presumably, to be deployed by him even against Hindu rajas.

Because of all this, it was only very rarely that Indian kings formed alliances to fight an invader. There are in fact only two recorded instances of rajas rallying together against the Ghaznavids, and both these were in support of the Hindu Shahi rajas of Punjab, Jayapala and his son Anandapala. According to Ferishta, in 1008, when Mahmud invaded Punjab, several Hindu rajas sent contingents in support of Anandapala. There was indeed something akin to a national response against this invasion. 'The Hindu females on this occasion sold their jewels, and sent the proceeds from distant parts to their husbands, so that they, being supplied with all the necessaries of the march, might be earnest in the war,' records Ferishta. 'Those who were poor contributed from their earnings by spinning cotton, and other labour.' But this concerted action, it should be noted, was not because Mahmud was an alien and a Muslim, but because he posed a threat to the power of all the local rajas and to the life and property of the common people.

But even these allied forces, despite their vast numbers, were not able to defeat the Ghaznavids. None of the Indian kings ever, not even once, prevailed over Mahmud in the innumerable battles he fought in India. This universal rout of Indian kings by Mahmud was primarily because of the lack of regimental discipline in Indian armies, and by their inability to make tactical innovations. Indian military strategies and political attitudes were shackled to moribund traditions, not dynamically related to evolving historical realities. There was thus no way that Indian armies could succeed against the well-trained and well-disciplined Ghaznavid army, which was capable of rapid, coordinated manoeuvres and decisive tactical innovations.

A much vaunted heroic act of Indian kings was to perform, when faced
with certain defeat in battle, the fearsome rite of jauhar, ritual mass suicide,
in which they killed their women and children, or consigned them into a mass
funeral pyre, and then rushed out of their fort into the enemy lines to kill and
be killed. The objective of Indian kings in executing jauhar was not to defeat
the enemy but to get themselves killed—it was an entirely defeatist and futile
act, even if viewed as an act of honour, to avoid the ignominy of defeat. There
was nothing heroic or honourable about slaughtering helpless women and
children, or in committing mass suicide.

On all this, however, we have only the accounts of Muslim chroniclers,
and these have to be taken with some scepticism, especially as their stories
are often confusing and contradictory. We cannot be therefore certain that
Mahmud was always victorious in his battles as the chroniclers claim. There
are no references at all in Indian texts to Mahmud's raids.

MAHMUD'S FIRST INCURSION into India, probably in 1000 CE, seems to
have been just a border raid, perhaps to test the field. His first major campaign
was against his immediate eastern neighbour, the king Jayapala of Punjab, with
whom Sabuktigin had earlier clashed. In September 1001 Mahmud, heading
a 15,000-strong cavalry force, swooped down from the mountains and swept
towards Peshawar. There he was confronted by Jayapala with an army of 12,000
cavalry, 30,000 infantry and 300 elephants. In the ensuing battle, which lasted
just a few hours, Mahmud overwhelmed Jayapala by the sheer ferocity of his
cavalry charge. Some 15,000 Indian soldiers were killed in the battle, and the
raja, along with some princes, were captured by Mahmud. The raja and the
princes were later released by Mahmud on payment of substantial ransoms.
And on their release they were, according to Al-Utbi, sped on their way with
contemptuous 'smacks on their buttocks' by the Turks.

Returning to his kingdom, Jayapala, out of the humiliation of the repeated
defeats he had suffered at the hands of the Ghaznavids, committed ritual suicide
by mounting a funeral pyre. He was then succeeded by his son Anandapala, and
under him also the conflict between the two kingdoms continued. Mahmud, we
are told by Al-Utbi, 'stretched upon him (Anandapala) the hand of slaughter,
imprisonment, pillage, depopulation, and fire, and hunted him from ambush
to ambush, over hill and dale, over soft and hard ground of his territory, and
his followers either became a feast to rapacious wild beasts of the passes and
plains, or fled away in distraction.'

The conflict between the Ghaznavids and the Hindu Shahis went on
intermittently for another two decades—altogether for some four decades,
from the time of Sabuktigin—till around 1020, when Punjab was annexed by
Mahmud. 'The Hindu Shahi dynasty is now extinct, and of the whole house

there is no longer the slightest remnant in existence,' reports Al-Biruni. 'We must say that, in all their grandeur, they never slackened in their ardent desire for doing that which is good and right, that they were men of noble sentiment and noble bearing.'

Beyond Punjab, the campaigns of Mahmud took him deep into the Indo-Gangetic Plain, as far as Kanauj on the Ganga. On the way to Kanauj, Mahmud raided Mathura, an ancient sacred city of Hindus and the reputed birthplace of Krishna, a divine incarnation. The city had many splendid temples, and Mahmud, we are told by Al-Utbi, was awed by their grandeur, particularly by the main temple there. 'If anyone should wish to construct a building equal to this, he would not be able to do it without expending a hundred thousand red dinars, and it would occupy two hundred years, even though the most experienced and able workmen were employed,' he is reported to have remarked. But this admiration did not prevent Mahmud from ordering the demolition of the temple. 'All the temples [in Mathura] should be burnt with naphtha and fire, and levelled to the ground,' he ordered. The city was pillaged for twenty days by the Turks, till they glutted themselves with plunder.

THE MOST CELEBRATED campaign of Mahmud was against the temple city of Somnath on the seashore in Gujarat, and it was also his last important Indian campaign. Mahmud set out from Ghazni on this campaign in October 1024, leading a huge army of 30,000 cavalry, and accompanied by a multitude of volunteers who joined him on the way, drawn by the lure of booty. He reached Multan in November and headed for Gujarat through the desert of Rajasthan, characteristically making meticulous preparations for the journey through the desert, loading several hundreds of camels with water and provisions, and requiring each soldier to carry with him fodder, water and food sufficient for several days.

Mahmud reached Somnath in January 1025. In medieval chronicles there are several different descriptions of Somnath, and of Mahmud's exploits there. Of these, the most colourful account is in the thirteenth century Arabic chronicle by Kazwini. 'Among the wonders of that place was the temple in which was placed the idol called Somnath,' he writes. 'This idol was in the middle of the temple without anything to support it from below, or to suspend it from above. It was held in the highest honour among Hindus, and whoever beheld it floating in the air was struck with amazement, whether he was a Muslim or an infidel. Hindus used to go on pilgrimage to it whenever there was an eclipse of the moon, and would then assemble there to the number of more than a hundred thousand . . . Everything that was most precious was brought there as offerings, and the temple was endowed with more than 10,000 villages.' It was a fabulously rich temple, bursting with the treasures it had accumulated over many centuries. Water from the holy river Ganga, some 1200 kilometres away, was brought every day to Somnath to wash the temple. 'A thousand Brahmins were employed there for worshipping the idol and for attending on pilgrims, and 500 damsels sang and danced at its door.' There were 300 barbers there, for tonsuring pilgrims.

The people of Somnath were initially unperturbed by Mahmud's invasion, for they firmly believed that it was their deity that had drawn Mahmud there so as to annihilate him for his sins of desecrating and destroying numerous temples elsewhere in India. So they assembled on the ramparts of the town to taunt and jeer at the Muslim army deployed just outside the town, even though their chieftain had prudently fled by sea to the safety of a nearby island. As it happened, the faith of the people was entirely misplaced. Somnatha, their god, let them down dismally.

The Turks responded to the jeers of the crowd with showers of arrows, and drove off the hecklers from the ramparts. They then climbed on to the ramparts by leaning ladders against them, and then, entering the town, engaged its defenders in fierce street-fights, slaughtering very many of them. This went on till dusk, when the Turks, having not yet fully eliminated the defenders, prudently withdrew from the town. But the next morning they resumed the attack. 'Indians,' writes Kazwini, 'made a desperate resistance. They would go weeping and crying into the temple to seek [god's] help, and then issue forth to battle and fight till all were killed. The number of the slain exceeded 50,000.'

Mahmud then exultantly entered the temple. According to Kazwini, 'The edifice was built upon fifty-six pillars of teak. The shrine of the idol was dark, but was lighted by jewelled chandeliers of great value. In front of the entrance to the cella was a chain of gold weighing 200 mans.' But the greatest marvel of it all was that the idol remained suspended in midair without any visible support. 'The king looked upon the idol with wonder,' and asked his officers about what the explanation of it could be, and one of them said that 'the canopy was made of loadstone, and the idol of iron, and that the ingenious builder had skilfully contrived that the magnet would not exert a greater force on any one side. Hence the idol was suspended in the middle.' That explanation indeed proved correct, for 'when two stones were removed from the canopy, the idol swerved to one side, when more were taken away it inclined still further, until at last it rested on the ground.'

Other sources offer different descriptions of the temple and of what Mahmud did there. According to them, the main deity of the temple was Shiva, symbolised by a huge phallic idol made of hewn stone, which, embedded deep in the floor, stood over two metres high from the floor. And alongside it were several small gold and silver idols. The sight of the phallic idol enraged Mahmud, and he raised his mace to smash it. At that point some of his officers tried to dissuade him, saying that the temple priests were offering a fabulous ransom to save the idol. Mahmud scornfully rejected their plea, saying, 'I desire that on the day of resurrection I should be summoned with the words, "Where is that Mahmud who broke the greatest of the heathen idols?" rather than by these: "Where is that Mahmud who sold the greatest of the heathen idols?"'

As it happened, smashing the idol proved to be of religious as well as material benefit to Mahmud, for when the idol was shattered it was found to have, in a cavity within it, gems worth over a hundred times the ransom offered for it. The temple was then razed to the ground. According to Siraj, Mahmud carried the Somnatha idol with him to Ghazni, where it was split 'into four parts. One part he placed in the Friday Mosque in Ghazni, one he placed at the entrance of the royal palace, the third he sent to Mecca, and the fourth to Medina,' for people to tread on them. As Kazwini states, the booty that fell to Mahmud at Somnath 'exceeded twenty-thousand-thousand [gold] dinars'—twenty million dinars—probably amounting to over six tons of gold.

Mahmud spent a fortnight at Somnath, then set out to return to Ghazni with his incalculable loot, cautiously taking a route different from the one by which he had arrived, which his enemies would have expected him to take. But his journey through Kutch and Sind, the route that he now took, proved to be perilous, as his guide, a devotee of the Somnath deity, led him into a waterless desert in Sind. Mahmud had the guide put to death, and marched on praying to god for relief. He finally managed to extricate himself from that desert trap, though many of his soldiers perished there. But that was not the end of his trials. Further along the route he was greatly harried by Jat tribesmen. Finally, after a great many ordeals, Mahmud reached Ghazni in the spring of 1026, and there received fresh laudatory titles from the Caliph, who confirmed him as the ruler of Khurasan, Hindustan, Sistan and Khvarazm. The following year Mahmud led another expedition into India, his last, to punish the Jats who had harassed him on his return from Somnath. The last three years of Mahmud's life were spent in military engagements in Central Asia.

MAHMUD WAS QUITE ill in the last couple of years of his life. As in the accounts of many other facets of his life, medieval chroniclers differ about the nature of the illness that felled the indomitable sultan. 'Opinions differ as to his disease: some say it was consumption, others a disease of the rectum, and others dysentery,' notes Mir Khvand, a fifteenth-century Persian historian. According to Khondamir, the sultan 'died of consumption or of disease of the liver . . .'

'During the time of his illness he used to ride and walk about just as he did when in health, although physicians forbade him doing so,' states Mir

Khvand. 'It is said that two days before his death he ordered all the bags of gold and silver coins which were in his treasury, and all the jewels, and all the valuables which he had collected . . . to be brought to his presence. They were accordingly all laid out in the courtyard of his palace, which, in the eyes of spectators, appeared like a garden full of flowers of red, yellow, violet, and other colours. He looked at them with sorrow, and wept very bitterly . . . [Afterwards] he reviewed all his personal slaves, his cattle, Arab horses, camels, etc., and after casting his eye upon them, and crying with great sorrow and regret, returned to his palace.'

The sight of all his treasures and acquisitions no doubt evoked in Mahmud memories of the great perils and triumphs of his life, of the power he once had over men and circumstances, and also the realization of the futility of it all, the tragedy of his life, the tragedy of all life, that every man dies alone, leaving behind everything he had cherished in life. Mahmud died weeping. And that redeems him. Partly.

Mahmud died in Ghazni in April 1030, aged 59, after a reign of 33 years. He died on a stormy, dark night of pelting rain, a night that perfectly matched the turbulence of his life. He was buried in the blue palace in Ghazni.

MAHMUD WAS A man of demoniac energy, and he was engaged in ceaseless wars during his entire reign, in which he slaughtered many thousands of people and ravaged vast tracts of land. His military campaigns extended over a vast area stretching east-west from the banks of the Ganga to the shores of the Caspian Sea, and north-south from the shores of the Aral Sea to Gujarat. Of this, his Indian campaigns constituted the dominant part, in which he, as Al-Biruni states, 'utterly ruined the prosperity of the country, and performed there wonderful exploits, by which the Hindus became like atoms and dust scattered in all directions.'

Mahmud's nature, writes Al-Utbi, 'was contrary to the disposition of men, which induce [them] to prefer a soft to a hard couch, and the splendour of the cheeks of pomegranate-bosomed girls to well-tempered sword blades.' His was a singularly sanguinary career. But then, it was a sanguinary age, and the career of Mahmud differs from that of most other kings of the age only in the incessancy of his campaigns, not in the nature of his campaigns. And it has to be noted that while he was an absolute terror to his adversaries, he was, as modern historian K. M. Panikkar notes, 'a just and wise monarch to his own subjects.'

The character of Mahmud was a complex mixture of several contradictory elements. 'He was very bigoted in religion . . . [and] was exceedingly covetous in seizing the riches of wealthy people,' states Mir Khvand. Confirms Khondamir: Mahmud was 'excessively greedy in accumulating wealth . . . [and he had an insatiable] thirst for worldly glory.' Adds Ferishta: Mahmud had 'the sordid vice of avarice.'

Yet, despite such vices, and the despotic power that he exercised, Mahmud had no hesitation to bow before the lowliest of his subjects when they charged him of misdeeds or incompetence. According to *Zinatu-l Majalis*, a late sixteenth century compilation of historical anecdotes, once when an old woman—whose son was killed along a caravan route in Ghazni—publicly rebuked Mahmud for the poor security conditions in his kingdom, and warned him to 'keep no more territory than . . . [he could] manage,' he bowed to her in humility and humbly accepted her rebuke.

There was a poignant trace of melancholy in Mahmud. Once, while drinking wine, his thoughts turned to his father, and with tears welling up in his eyes he said to a courtier: 'My father had established very good rules for the management of the country, and took great pains in enforcing them. I thought that . . . [after my father's demise] I would enjoy the exercise of my power in peace and security . . . I also considered that . . . I should become a great king. But the truth was revealed to me when he died . . . for since his departure I have not had one day's happiness. You think I drink this wine for pleasure, but this is a great mistake. I take it merely as a device to gain . . . [some] peace.'

For all his savagery, there are aspects of the character and life of Mahmud that draw our sympathy. Part of the making of his complex persona was his self-consciousness about his unprepossessing looks. According to Ferishta, Mahmud's face was heavily pock-marked. 'His features were very ugly,' states Hamdullah Mustaufi, a fourteenth century chronicler. 'One day, regarding his own face in a mirror, he became thoughtful and depressed. His vizier inquired as to the cause of his depression, to which he replied, "It is generally understood that the sight of kings adds vigour to the eye, but the form with which I am endowed is enough to strike the beholder blind." The vizier then consoled him, saying, "Scarcely one man in a million looks on your face, but the qualities of your mind cast their influence on every one. Study, therefore, to maintain an unimpeachable character, so that you may be the beloved of all hearts."'

Mahmud was particularly diffident in matters of love. According to Muhammad Ufi, an early-thirteenth-century Persian chronicler, Mahmud 'had been long enamoured . . . [of a slave-girl]. He was sincerely attached to her, and was anxious to espouse her. But it occurred to him that he might by this act incur the reproaches of the neighbouring kings and princes and forfeit the respect and esteem of his servants. He entertained this apprehension for a long time.' But one day he told a courtier about his predicament. 'Will not the neighbouring kings call me a fool?' he asked the courtier. 'And will not you also, my servants and slaves, speak ill of me in respectable society? I ask your advice in this matter. Have you ever heard or read in any history of kings wedding the children of their slaves?' The courtier then reassured Mahmud, saying, 'Many cases similar to this have occurred. Several kings . . . [have] married their own slave girls.' It was only then that Mahmud had the courage to marry the girl.

ONE OF THE most redeeming qualities of Mahmud was that he was a man of wide cultural interests. A good part of the enormous treasure that he plundered from India was used to turn Ghazni into an elegant city of great architecture and high culture, one of the grandest cities of the age. The sultan set up there a great library—with books in many languages—and a museum, and he built there a magnificent Jami Masjid, which became renowned as the Bride of Heaven, one of the finest expressions of Islamic architecture.

Mahmud was an ardent patron of learning, literature and the arts. He had 'a great propensity to poetry,' observes Ferishta. 'No king ever had more learned men at his court, kept a finer army, or displayed more magnificence.' According to Mustaufi, the sultan 'was a friend to learned men and poets, on whom he bestowed munificent presents, insomuch that every year he expended upon them more than 400,000 dinars.' He is said to have maintained some 400 poets at his court, to one of whom he once gifted 14,000 silver coins as a reward for composing a single ode that pleased him. Similarly, on three occasions he is said to have poured pearls into the mouth of another poet, for composing elegant extempore verses. And once, when the Chandella king Vidyadhara sent to him an adulatory poem, he conferred on the king the command of 15 fortresses in India. There is probably some exaggeration in these accounts of Mahmud's bounty, but there is no doubt he was a man of keen cultural interests.

Among the many litterateurs in Mahmud's court the most renowned were Firdausi (the author of the great Persian epic *Shah-nama*) and Al-Biruni (mathematician, philosopher, astronomer, historian and Sanskrit scholar). Firdausi would later fulminate against the sultan, and deride him as the niggardly son of a concubine, but that was an expression of the poet's grudge against Mahmud, for having rewarded him, for *Shah-nama*, with silver coins instead of the gold coins he had expected. When Firdausi wrote the first 1000 verses of the epic, Mahmud had given him 1000 dinars (gold coins) as reward. His finished work had 60,000 verses, so he expected to be rewarded with 60,000 dinars, but got only 60,000 dirhams (silver coins). This greatly vexed Firdausi—perhaps not so much for not getting the reward he expected, as for not getting the recognition he desired—and he, according to Khondamir, peevishly gave away all the reward money in random gifts: 20,000 dirhams to a bath-keeper, 20,000 to a sherbet seller, and 20,000 to the officer who had brought him the money. He then composed about forty verses as a satire on the sultan, introduced them into *Shah-nama*, and then fled from Ghazni to

Tus in Khurasan for safety. Some years later Mahmud is said to have regretted his niggardliness, and sent to Firdausi 60,000 dinars. But as the bearers of this reward entered Firdausi's residence by one gate, his coffin was carried out by the other gate. 'An only daughter was his heiress, to whom the emissaries of the sultan then offered . . . [the reward], but she, from the pride inherent in her disposition, refused the reward and said, "I have enough wealth to last me to the end of my days; I have no need for this money,"' reports Khondamir.

MAHMUD'S DEATH WAS followed by a battle between two of his sons over the throne. The sultan had nominated his younger son Muhammad as his successor, preferring him over his eldest and ablest son Masud. But this choice—as in the case of Sabuktigin's choice of Ismail over Mahmud to succeed him—was an expression of his sentiment, not of his judgement. Mahmud was well aware of this, and once told a noble who favoured Masud: 'I know that Masud excels Muhammad in every respect, and after my death the kingdom will devolve upon him, but I take this trouble now on behalf of Muhammad, so that the poor fellow may enjoy some honour and gratification during my lifetime, for after my death it will not be so safe for him. May god have mercy on him.' Mahmud seems to have disliked Masud, for 'Masud, from his excessive haughtiness' often spoke presumptuously and harshly to his father, notes Khondamir. According to Nizam-ul Mulk, an eleventh-century chronicler, 'Sultan Mahmud was always on bad terms with his eldest son Masud.'

Mahmud had a poor opinion about his sons, and a bleak view of the future of his empire. 'Masud is a proud fellow and thinks there is nobody better than himself,' he once observed. 'Muhammad is stout of heart, generous, and fearless, but if Masud indulges in pleasure, wine, and the like, Muhammad outdoes him. He has no control over himself, has no apprehension of Masud and is heedless of the important concerns of life . . . Masud . . . will devour him.'

That prognostication of Mahmud proved true. Masud was not at all perturbed by his father choosing Muhammad for the throne, for he knew that it was the sword, not parental choice, that would finally determine royal succession. So when a khan expressed to Masud his dismay over Mahmud's choice of successor, the prince said, 'Don't grieve about it. The sword is a truer prophet than the pen.' And indeed, in the battle between the two princes following the death of the sultan, Masud easily routed Muhammad, blinded and imprisoned him, and ascended the throne.

But Masud himself, for all his conceit, proved to be a disaster as sultan, who sometimes even cravenly chose flight over fight when confronted by enemies. The history of the Ghaznavid dynasty after the death of Mahmud is a sordid tale of endless internecine clashes between brothers, cousins, uncles and nephews, as well as recurrent rebellions by nobles and provincial governors, brutal assassinations, mass murders, mutinies and invasions. There was hardly ever any peaceful royal succession in Ghazni. Only six of the fifteen sultans of the post-Mahmud history of the kingdom died natural deaths while still on the throne; the rest were deposed or murdered. Many of the reigns were very short, a couple of the sultans occupying the throne for just a few weeks. Once a boy of three was raised to the throne in a palace intrigue; his reign lasted just one week.

Even more bizarre than these succession strifes were the rebellions by royal officers. In one such incident, an officer overthrew and put to death his king (along with eleven princes) and ascended the throne, but was himself overthrown and killed by the royal guards in about a month. On another occasion the guards of the royal treasury themselves plundered the treasures. And so it went on. Astonishingly, despite all this chaos, some of the Ghazni sultans had long and relatively peaceful reigns. Such was the case of Sultan Ibrahim of the second half of the eleventh century, who ruled for forty-two years, which was the longest reign in the entire history of the Ghaznavid kingdom; even his son and successor Masud had a fairly long reign, of seventeen years. But these were exceptional cases, just interludes of tranquillity in the swirling chaos in the sultanate following the death of Mahmud.

And as the kingdom slid into terminal and irreversible decline, its very existence was threatened by Seljuq Turks from the west, and by Ghuris from the north. The relationship between the rulers of Ghazni and Ghur was particularly vicious. Matters came to a head when two Ghuri princes were treacherously put to death by the sultan Bahram of Ghazni. That provoked Ala-ud-din Husain, the ruler of Ghur, to seek vengeance. In 1151 he stormed into Ghazni, and for a whole week his soldiers raged though the city, pillaging, slaughtering people, and burning buildings. 'For seven nights and days he gave it (the city) to the flames,' reports Siraj. 'During these seven days the clouds of smoke so darkened the sky that day seemed to be night, and the flames so lighted the sky at night that night looked like day. Plunder, devastation, and slaughter were continuous on these seven days. Every man that was found was slain, and all the women and children were made prisoners. Under the orders of the conqueror, [the remains] of all the Mahmudi kings, with the exception of Mahmud, Masud and Ibrahim, were dragged out from their graves and burnt. All this time, Ala-ud-din sat in the palace of Ghazni occupied with drinking and debauchery.'

Later, when Ala-ud-din returned to Ghur, Bahram, who had, on being defeated by Ala-ud-din, fled to Punjab for refuge, returned to Ghazni. Then it was the turn of Saljuq Turks to menace the kingdom, and in 1157 they drove out Bahram's successor Khusrav Shah from Afghanistan into Punjab. Lahore then became the last sanctuary of the Yamini dynasty. But even in Lahore their reign lasted only for about three decades, for in 1186 Ghuri prince Muizz-ud-din Muhammad invaded Punjab, seized Lahore, and imprisoned Khusrav Malik, the son and successor of Khusrav Shah. Six years later, in 1192, Khusrav Malik—who, according to Siraj, was 'exceedingly gentle, liberal, and modest, but fond of pleasure'—was murdered in prison by the Ghuris, as he was a security risk.

'The house of Mahmud had now come to its end; the sun of its glory had set, and the registrar of fate had written the mandate of its destruction,' observes Siraj. The Ghazni kingdom had in all 22 sultans, including usurpers, in its 223 years long history from its founding in 963 to its final extinction in 1186. The average reign of the Ghaznavid kings was only about ten years, and some of them occupied the throne for only just a few days.

PART III

SLAVE SULTANS

Sultan Raziya was a great monarch. She was wise, just, and generous, a benefactor to her kingdom, a dispenser of justice, the protector of her subjects, and the leader of her armies. She was endowed with all the qualities befitting a king. But she was not of the right sex, and so in the estimation of men all her virtues were worthless.

—MINHAJ SIRAJ

1

Last Rajas, First Sultans

The kingdom of Ghazni, founded in 963, endured in Afghanistan for nearly two centuries, till 1157, when Saljuq Turks invaded the kingdom and drove its sultan, Khusrav Shah, out of Ghazni into Punjab. But in a few years, in 1173, the Saljuqs themselves were driven out of Ghazni by another invader, Sultan Ghiyas-ud-din Muhammad of Ghur, a mountain kingdom in northern Afghanistan. Ghiyas-ud-din then installed his brother, Shihab-ud-din Muhammad, generally known as Muhammad Ghuri, as the ruler of Ghazni.

Muhammad's occupation of the throne of Ghazni evidently electrified him with memories of the epic exploits of Mahmud Ghazni, and inspired him to invade India. And, although his campaigns were nowhere near as spectacular as those of Mahmud, their results were far more enduring, for they led to the establishment of the Delhi Sultanate, which marked the decisive stage in the nearly one millennium-long history of the dominance of the subcontinent by foreign people that began with the Ghaznavid incursions into India in the last quarter of the tenth century and ended with the withdrawal of the British from India in the mid-twentieth century.

Muhammad's first incursion into India, in 1175, was directed against Gujarat, which was the target of Mahmud Ghazni's most celebrated campaign a century and half earlier. But this proved to be a perilous adventure for Muhammad, though the initial stages of the campaign went off smoothly for him. The sultan entered India through the Gomal Pass in the Sulaiman Range southeast of Ghazni and headed for the city of Multan, which he seized from its Ismaili ruler. He then advanced to the fortress of Uch, which he was able to occupy without a fight, as it was surrendered to him by its malcontent and treacherous queen after putting its ruler, her husband, to death, on Muhammad

59

promising to marry her daughter. Muhammad then proceeded to Gujarat, trudging through the forbidding Great Indian Desert. Taking that route was a grave mistake, for the perils of the desert utterly exhausted his army by the time it reached Gujarat, so it was there easily routed with great slaughter by Mularaja, the Chalukya king of Gujarat, in a battle fought at the foot of Mt. Abu. Muhammad then prudently retreated to Ghazni with the ragged remnants of his army.

For his next Indian campaign, in 1179, Muhammad astutely took the northern route, through the Khyber Pass, and advanced into Punjab. This was essentially a pillaging raid, like Mahmud's raids, and was followed by a few similar raids in the succeeding years. But gradually the nature and objective of his campaigns changed, from depredation to conquest. This change was particularly evident after his 1186 annexation of western Punjab from Khusrav Malik, the last Ghaznavid sultan there.

The occupation of western Punjab opened for Muhammad the gateway into the Indo-Gangetic Plane, the heartland of India. The region was politically fragmented at this time, and consisted of a number of kingdoms of varying sizes. Many of these kingdoms were ruled by Rajput rajas, the most prominent of whom were Prithviraja of Ajmer in Rajasthan and Jayachandra of Kanauj in Uttar Pradesh. Prithviraja's kingdom extended from Rajasthan northward into eastern Punjab, and that made him the immediate neighbour and inevitable adversary of Muhammad, especially as the sultan's raids extended deep into the northern districts of Prithviraja's kingdom.

A military conflict between Prithviraja and Muhammad then became inevitable. And as Prithviraja prepared for war he was joined by a number of local Rajput chieftains, whose lands had been ravaged, and their women violated, by Turks.

Prithviraja then, accompanied by allied rajas, set out to confront Muhammad. He commanded, according to an evidently hyperbolic account, an incredibly large army of 200,000 cavalry, 3000 elephants, and a vast horde of infantry. The opposing forces met at Tarain, a hundred-odd kilometres north-west of Delhi, and in the ensuing battle Rajputs completely routed Turks. Muhammad himself was severely wounded in the battle by a javelin thrown at him by a Hindu chieftain, and he very nearly collapsed on the battlefield, but was saved by an alert and agile soldier, who sprang up behind the sultan on his horse, steadied him, and galloped away to safety with him.

THIS WAS IN 1191. Muhammad was honour-bound to avenge his defeat. So, after recuperating in Ghazni and replenishing his army, he once again, in the very next year, advanced into India to confront Prithviraja. And once again the opposing forces met at Tarain. The accounts of the composition of the rival armies and what happened in the battle are given variously in different sources. According to one account, Prithviraja led into this battle an even larger army than the one he had deployed in the first battle of Tarain—300,000 cavalry, 3000 elephants and countless foot soldiers! Further, he is said to have had with him 150 Hindu chieftains, who swore to defeat Turks or die in the battle.

More credible is the account of the deployment given in *Hammira-mahakavya*, an epic poem by the fourteenth century Jain writer Nayachandra Suri. According to Suri, Prithviraja, overconfident because of his previous easy victory over Muhammad, advanced against the sultan with a small body of soldiers, as his top generals and several divisions of his army were then engaged in campaigns elsewhere. His minister Somesvara saw the folly of the raja's move and tried to dissuade him from advancing, but Prithviraja, apparently viewing the advice as impudent and inauspicious, cut off the ears of the minister in a rage and dismissed him. Somesvara then, clearly seeing the writing on the wall, defected to Turks.

Muhammad is said to have led into this battle a cavalry force of 52,000, which is quite probably an exaggerated figure. Some sources even give the strength of his cavalry as 120,000! But whatever the actual size of the two armies, the Rajput army certainly would have been very much larger than the Turkish army. So the only way Muhammad could win the battle against Prithviraja was by adopting some daringly ingenious tactics.

Muhammad was equal to the challenge. He divided his army into five divisions, and at dawn on the day of the battle sent four of the divisions, all mounted archers, to attack the Rajputs from all four sides. They were told to attack the enemy in waves and shower them with arrows, and then, every time the enemy advanced, quickly retreat by pretending flight. Muhammad's objective was to harry, bewilder and disarray the Rajput army. And it worked. By late afternoon, when the Rajput army had become totally disordered, Muhammad charged into it with the fifth division of his cavalry that he had held in reserve, and routed it. Prithviraja then got down from his elephant, mounted a horse and attempted to flee from the battlefield, but was overtaken and captured.

There are two different versions of what subsequently happened to the raja. According to one account, Muhammad, along with the captive raja, proceeded from the battlefield to Ajmer, the Rajput capital. There he initially restored Prithviraja to his throne, as a tributary ruler, but later executed him, suspecting him of being treasonous, and enthroned his son. Other sources state that Prithviraja was caught and beheaded while attempting to flee from Tarain after the battle.

Muhammad's next target was Delhi. But there was hardly any opposition to him there, and the city was surrendered to him by its governor after a token resistance. The sultan then appointed Qutb-ud-din Aibak, his trusted general, as his deputy in India, and retired to Ghazni. But he was back in India the very next year, to confront Jayachandra, who ruled over an extensive kingdom in the Gangetic Valley, with Kanauj as his capital. Jayachandra had stood morosely aloof when several other Rajput chiefs rallied to the support of Prithviraja in his battles against Muhammad, for there was intense political rivalry between Prithviraja and Jayachandra, as was natural and inevitable between neighbouring kings. And this antipathy was aggravated by bitter personal animosity between the two kings, because of Prithviraja's 'abduction' of Jayachandra's daughter Samyogita.

THE PRITHVIRAJA-SAMYOGITA romance is celebrated in *Prithviraja-raso*, an epic Sanskrit poem. This work as it exists now is of uncertain date and authorship, and has several different versions, but its core section is traditionally attributed to Chand Bardai, who is said to have been a court poet of Prithviraja. According to the epic, Samyogita was enamoured of the raja's heroic persona, and had been in secret romantic correspondence with him for quite a while. Meanwhile Jayachandra arranged, as was required by royal custom, the *swayamvara* ceremony of the princess, for her to choose a groom from among the princes who had assembled in a hall in the palace on the invitation of the raja. Prithviraja was deliberately not invited to the ceremony, and Jayachandra compounded that slight by placing at the door of the *swayamvara* hall a mock statue of Prithviraja, depicting him as a doorkeeper.

As was customary, Samyogita then walked down the line of the seated princes with a flower garland in her hand, to choose a groom by garlanding him. But she passed them all one by one and went to the door of the hall and, as the astounded princes watched, garlanded Prithviraja's statue. And in an instant she was seized by the raja, who was hiding nearby with a few cohorts—evidently by secret arrangement with the princess—and they sped off on horses to Ajmer, repulsing the pursuing soldiers of Jayachandra.

In general terms there is nothing improbable about the story, though many of its details are no doubt dreamed up by the poet. This incident is said to have happened between the first and second battle of Tarain. The rout of Prithviraja in the second battle of Tarain therefore delighted Jayachandra; according to folklore, he even celebrated the event by organising a festive illumination in his capital. But he was not fated to savour that euphoria for long, because Turks presently descended on Kanauj, and in a battle fought on the banks of Yamuna, the raja, an easy target on his grand elephant, was shot dead by a Ghuri archer, upon which the Rajput army predictably scattered. This was followed, as usual, by an orgy of carnage and rapine by Turks. Jayachandra was the last great Hindu monarch of North India, and the extinction of his dynasty was a major event in the history of medieval India.

Soon after defeating Jayachandra, Muhammad returned to Ghazni with the vast booty he had gathered. He would lead a few more campaigns into India, and collect more booty, but he does not seem to have had any intention to shift his capital to India and live there. His last Indian campaign was in 1206, to reinforce Aibak in his battle against Khokars, a fierce martial tribe of the upper Indus Valley. On the conclusion of that campaign, the sultan set out, as usual, to return to Ghazni, and on the way he camped on the banks of Indus to rest for a while. And there, in mid-March that year, he was assassinated.

It is not clear who the assassins were, or what their motive was. Possibly they were vengeful Ismailis of Sind—whose kingdom Muhammad had overrun in his very first Indian campaign—or, more likely, they were Khokars, a large number of whom Muhammad's army had just recently slaughtered. Whoever the assassins were, they came in a small band of three or four daredevils, who swam across Indus and entered the royal camp through its unguarded riverfront. 'On the king's return from Lahore towards Ghazni . . . [he pitched his camp] on the bank of a pure stream in a garden filled with lilies, jasmines and other flowers,' writes Hasan Nizami, an early thirteenth century chronicler. 'There, while he was engaged in the evening prayer, some impious men . . . came running like the wind towards His Majesty . . . and on the spot killed [the guards, and then] . . . ran up towards the king and inflicted five or six desperate wounds upon the lord of the seven climes, and his spirit flew above the eight paradises and the battlements of the nine heavens, and joined those of the ten evangelists.'

MUHAMMAD HAD NO sons. That left the field wide open for his three chief nobles—Aibak in Delhi, Yildiz in Ghazni, and Qabacha in Multan—to grapple with each other for power, even though they were closely related to each other. On Muhammad's death Aibak in Delhi promptly assumed sovereign power, but this was challenged by Yildiz, Aibak's father-in-law, who, in possession of Ghazni, declared himself as the successor of Muhammad Ghuri and claimed suzerainty over all the late sultan's territories. The third contestant for the throne was Qabacha, Aibak's son-in-law, who declared himself to be an independent ruler in Multan, and sought to widen his territory by advancing on Lahore.

Of the two challengers whom Aibak confronted, Yildiz was the more serious one, so he decided to deal with him first, and promptly swept into Afghanistan with an army, and expelled him from Ghazni. But his triumph was short-lived, for Yildiz soon regained his power in Ghazni, and forced Aibak to retreat to

India. And Yildiz, hovering at the frontier of India, would remain a threat to Aibak and his successors in Delhi for about a decade.

Aibak was originally a native of Turkistan, but was enslaved as a boy, and, after being sold and resold a couple of times, he was in his teenage taken to Ghazni by a slave trader, and there he was bought by Muhammad Ghuri. Aibak rose rapidly in the service of the sultan, because of his energy, efficiency, dedication, and nobility of character. The name Aibak means moon-face, indicating beauty, but physically Aibak was hardly personable. 'He was not comely in appearance,' states Siraj. But the richness of his talents more than compensated for his poor looks. Aibak, comments Siraj, 'was a brave and liberal king. The almighty had bestowed on him such courage and generosity that in his time there was no king like him from the east to the west . . . He was possessed of every quality and virtue.'

In 1195 Aibak was appointed the viceroy of India by Muhammad, as a reward for his successful campaign against Gujarat, which he had undertaken to avenge the defeat that Muhammad had suffered there early in his career. Muhammad, writes medieval chronicler Sirhindi, 'sent a canopy of state to Malik-Khutb-ud-din [Aibak] and conferred on him the title sultan.' That honour presaged Aibak's eventual accession to the throne of Delhi.

In every sense Aibak was the real founder of the Delhi Sultanate. Muhammad's campaigns, rather like those of Mahmud, were primarily plundering raids, and he left it to Aibak to consolidate and extend the Ghuri conquests in India. And Aibak achieved that objective with consummate skill. Then, on the death of Muhammad, the Turkish territories in India under the governorship of Aibak became an independent kingdom, not just a province of the Ghuri empire. And presently, as Afghanistan was conquered by the Mongols, the connection of the Delhi Sultanate with Ghuri entirely ceased.

Aibak was tirelessly active all through his rule in Delhi, as governor and as sultan, conquering new territories and suppressing rebellions. These campaigns were essential for stabilising the Turkish rule in India, but they also served to keep the Turkish army active and in fine fettle, and to boost the morale of the soldiers with a constant feed of rich plunder.

It is difficult to see Aibak as a ruthless fanatic or as a savage invader, but these are the qualities that Muslim chroniclers laudatorily attribute to him, no doubt with considerable exaggeration. 'His bounty was continuous and his slaughter was continuous,' states Siraj. In Varanasi, according to Nizami, Aibak 'destroyed nearly one thousand temples, and raised mosques on their foundations.' And in his campaign against the Khokars, he was, according to Nizami, so ruthless in exterminating them that 'there remained not one inhabitant [there] to light a fire.'

THE MILITARY CAMPAIGNS that Aibak personally led were confined to the central and western Indo-Gangetic Plain; he left the conquest of the eastern Gangetic Plain to the initiative and enterprise of his lieutenant, Bakhtiyar Khalji. Bakhtiyar, according to Siraj, 'was a very smart, enterprising, bold, courageous, wise, and experienced man.' But he, like Aibak, was not physically personable. His appearance, according to Siraj, was rather gorilla-like, his arms reaching down to his calves. But his lack of handsomeness was more than offset by his enormous physical power and energy. Taunted by envious nobles, he is said to have once even subdued an elephant in a single combat.

Aibak recognised Bakhtiyar's potential and assigned to him the conquest of Bihar and Bengal, and in this he was phenomenally successful. But he was also phenomenally destructive—he was responsible for the destruction of the great Buddhist University of Nalanda in Bihar, though it has to be noted, as an extenuating circumstance, that he mistook the walled university to be a fort, and Buddhist monks to be Brahmins. As Siraj describes the scene, 'Great plunder fell into the hands of the victors. Most of the inhabitants of the place were Brahmins with shaven heads. They were put to death. Large numbers of books were found there, and when Muhammadans saw them, they called for some persons to explain their contents, but all the men had been killed. It was then discovered that the whole fort and city was a university.'

After subduing Bihar the general advanced into Bengal, which had been under the rule of the Sena dynasty for several centuries. Bakhtiyar with characteristic impetuosity rode into Nadia, the then capital of Bengal, with an escort of just eighteen cavalrymen, leaving his army behind. Nobody challenged him and his men, for they were taken to be horse traders. They 'did not molest any man, but went on peaceably and without ostentation . . . In this manner he (Bakhtiyar) reached the gate . . . [of the royal palace, and there] he drew his sword and commenced the attack,' writes Siraj. 'At this time the raja (Lakshmana-sena) was at his dinner, and gold and silver dishes filled with food were placed before him according to the usual custom. All of a sudden a cry was raised at the gate of his palace.' Hearing the commotion and learning about the attack, 'the raja fled barefooted by the rear door of the palace, and his whole treasure, and all his wives, maid servants, attendants, and women fell into the hands of the invader. Numerous elephants were taken, and such booty was obtained by the Muhammadans as is beyond all compute.'

Meanwhile Lakshmana-sena fled to east Bengal, a heavily forested region, and set up his rule there, but was not pursued there by Bakhtiyar. Lakshmana-sena was an aged, scholarly king, a patron of poets, and a poet himself. Jayadeva, the renowned author of *Gita-Govinda*, is said to have adorned his court. Quite probably the raja was not martially inclined. Besides, there was an ancient and widely believed prophecy that Muslim rule would be established in Bengal at this time. Bakhtiyar therefore had little difficulty in subjugating most of Bengal.

Bakhtiyar's sword now rested on the slopes of the Himalayas. Beyond the mountains lay the mysterious land of Tibet, which set Bakhtiyar dreaming. His thirst for adventure was insatiable, and it now led him to launch an invasion of Tibet. He set out on this campaign with a large force of 10,000 cavalry, but the operation turned out to be a total disaster, because of the extreme weather of Tibet as well as the virulence of the local tribesmen. Bakhtiyar gained nothing whatever from the campaign, but lost a good number of his soldiers in it, and himself barely managed to escape with his life.

This was a humiliation that Bakhtiyar could not bear. 'He would thereafter never go out, because he felt ashamed to look on the wives and children of those who had perished [in that campaign],' writes Siraj. 'If ever he did ride out, all people, women and children, from their housetops and the streets, cried out cursing and abusing him.' According to Siraj, Bakhtiyar's mental distress led to the collapse of his health, and presently he 'took to bed, and died.' Other sources however state that he was put out of his misery by his fellow officer, Ali Mardan, who subsequently assumed the leadership of the Khalji clan of Bakhtiyar.

Bakhtiyar died in 1206. Four years later, in 1210, Aibak died in Lahore, in an accident while playing polo. 'The sultan,' writes Siraj, 'fell from his horse in the field while he was playing *chaugan*, and the horse came down upon him, so that the pommel of the saddle entered his chest, and killed him.'

Aibak had ruled North India in all for fifteen years, eleven years as the deputy of Muhammad Ghuri, and the last four years as a sovereign, 'during which he wore the crown, and had the *khutba* read and coin struck in his name,' records Siraj. The Delhi Sultanate that he founded would endure for 320 years, from 1206 to 1526, till Babur conquered Delhi and established the Mughal Empire.

WHY DID THE Indian kingdoms, many of them ruled by Rajputs renowned for their martial valour, collapse so rapidly and abjectly? The reason that is commonly given for this is that Indian kings made no united stand against Turks. There could in fact be no such united stand by them, because, from the Indian point of view, there was no we/they divide between Indians and Turks. Turks were seen by Indians as just one element—though a new element—in the racial, linguistic, socio-cultural and political agglomeration of India. There was no sense of any unique Indianess among the people or the rulers anywhere in India at this time. Indians did not look like one people or speak like one people—the language of one regional group was entirely unintelligible to the other regional groups. And each of these regional groups was itself divided into several distinct socio-cultural groups based on caste and sect. India was a landmass, at best a civilisation, like Europe, but not a nation.

Because of all this, Turks were hardly ever seen by Indians as aliens. Several other races from outside the subcontinent had entered India over the centuries, and they were all absorbed into the local society over time, and Indians presumably did not see Turks as any different from these earlier invaders and migrants.

But of course Turks were different. Unlike the previous invaders and migrants, they could not be absorbed into Indian society, for there was an insurmountable barrier between them and the people of India. The problem was primarily religious. Polytheistic and poly-religious Indians had no problem in accommodating Turks and Islam in their society without in any way compromising their society and religion, but monotheistic Turks could not possibly accommodate Indians in their society without fundamentally altering the composition and ethos of their society and religion. The divide between the two civilisations was insurmountable.

The Turkish invader was of course seen by the threatened Indian rajas as an enemy. But not as an alien—for the rajas, Turks were not much different from their enemies within India. The local rajas in fact persisted in their self-destructive internecine wars even when the Turks were invading India. Indeed, in several instances Indian chieftains and royal commanders defected to Turks, or connived with them against their own rajas. And very many Hindu soldiers served in the Turkish army. There was no sense among Indian kingdoms that they were facing a common danger from Turks. Though there were a few instances of rajas banding together to oppose Turks, these were evidently the banding together of subordinate chieftains under their overlord, as indicated by the very large number of the confederate chieftains—fifty of them!—joining Jayapala in his first battle of Tarain against Muhammad Ghuri.

The absence of concerted military action by the rajas cannot however be considered as the decisive factor that led to their rout by Turks, for many of the Indian kingdoms were much larger in size, population and resources than Ghazni, and the rajas often fielded armies which were very much larger than the Turkish army.

But this numerical advantage of the Indian armies was more than negated by the decisive superiority of the Turkish army in weaponry, regimental discipline, innovative tactic, and group martial spirit. Indeed, the vast size of the Indian armies often proved to be a disadvantage, as their size was mostly made up of ill-trained and ill-disciplined hordes who could not act efficiently in concert. As individual soldiers, Rajputs, who constituted a large section of North Indian armies, were a match, or more than a match, to Turks in valour.

But the lack of regimental training and discipline nullified that advantage. On the whole Indians had very little chance of prevailing over Turks.

The main dependence of Turks was on their cavalry, which was far superior to the Indian cavalry in every respect, in men as well as in mounts. In contrast, the main dependence of Indian armies was on their elephant corps, but elephants, though forbidding in appearance, were no match for the storming, whirling charge of the Turkish cavalry. Elephants were in fact quite often a menace to their own side, for when wounded in battle or otherwise frightened they ran pell-mell, causing havoc in their own army.

Equally decisive was the Turkish ability to rapidly innovate their tactics to suit any emergent military situation, and execute lightning manoeuvres, while Indians were slaves of tradition, and they generally fought in the same manner regardless of the actual military situation.

Besides all this, Turks, as aggressors swooping down from the cool Afghan mountains, had irresistible kinetic energy, while Indians were mostly plains people leading a sedentary life in an enervating climate, and their posture, as defenders, was generally static. Psychologically too Indians were at a disadvantage, as they suffered from the victim syndrome, and were often sluggish in battle, unlike the spirited Turks. Moreover, the fatalistic value system of Indians inculcated in them a generally defeatist attitude. In some cases Indians were also demoralised by astrological predictions that the Turkish conquest of India was inevitable. In contrast, Turks were energised by religious fervour, confident in their faith that they were invincible as the soldiers of their god. Equally, they were motivated by the irresistible lure of plunder.

But is the story of the facile victory of Turks over Indians entirely true? Virtually the only sources of information of the Turkish conquest of India are Arabic and Persian chronicles. But these present only one side of the story. We do not have the Indian version of what happened and why. There is hardly any mention in the early medieval Indian texts about the momentous events that were then taking place. Apparently Indian chroniclers considered those events as not worth recording. And that in itself is significant, as a reflection of the general Indian disconnect with mundane reality.

2

Heroes and Zeroes

With the establishment of the Delhi Sultanate the political history of India once again acquired a dominant theme, seven centuries after the collapse of the Gupta Empire. Though there were a few large and important kingdoms in India in the intervening period, none of them had the all-India prominence that the Gupta Empire had, or the Delhi Sultanate came to have. And the Sultanate would endure far longer than most Indian kingdoms, for well over three centuries, till the Mughal invasion in the early sixteenth century.

The history of the Delhi Sultanate is divided into five dynastic periods— Slave, Khalji, Tughluq, Sayyid, and Lodi. The first of these dynasties is known as the Slave Dynasty because its sultans were all manumitted slaves or their descendants. They were not however ordinary slaves, but royal slaves, like the Mamluks of medieval Egypt, and they, far from being an underclass, constituted a privileged politico-military aristocracy, who could aspire for the highest offices in the government, and even rise to be sultans, as indeed three of them did. It was not a disgrace but a distinction to be such a slave.

The Slave Dynasty ruled Delhi for 84 years, from 1206 to 1290, and there were in all ten sultans in the dynasty, belonging to three different but related families, those of Aibak, Iltutmish and Balban. The founders of these ruling families were men of great ability and achievement, but many of their successors were profligate, worthless men of little or no ability to govern, or even any serious interest in governance. Some were barely sane. And a few of the sultans were overthrown and killed in family strife or court intrigue, and the reigns of some of them were very short, lasting just a few months.

The Sultanate during its early period was bedevilled by internecine rivalries and conflicts. The stature of the sultan in his relationship with his top nobles at this time was that of a first among equals than that of a sovereign over his servitors; he was more like a leader than a ruler. And there was a good amount of push and pull between the sultan and the nobles for sharing power. This was particularly so during times of royal succession, when the nobles invariably tried to test the mettle of the new sultan, to see whether they could be the masters of their master. Another perennial problem of the Sultanate was that its provincial governors were ever on the verge of rebellion, and were often in actual rebellion, aspiring to be independent rulers. The Rajput rajas—subdued by Turks but left as subordinate rulers—were also a source of constant menace to the Sultanate, as they were always waiting in the wings for an opportunity to regain their lost sovereign power. The sultans also had to deal with the depredations of hill tribes; they were present in large numbers all over India, and they boldly rampaged through the countryside whenever the iron hand of the government slackened.

ALL THESE PROBLEMS manifested in an acute form on the sudden death of Aibak. Predictably, the nobles differed in their choice of a successor to Aibak. While the nobles in Lahore, where Aibak died, hastily raised to the throne Aram Shah, a son (or adopted son) of Aibak, perhaps to avoid any hiatus in government, the nobles in Delhi rejected the choice, as they considered Aram to be a callow youth unsuited to rule in those turbulent times. Instead, they chose Iltutmish, a son-in-law of Aibak and an officer of proven ability, to be the sultan. This inevitably led to a military clash between the two factions, and in it Iltutmish easily routed Aram—about whom nothing is heard thereafter—and ascended the throne in Delhi.

This was in 1211. Iltutmish was a manumitted slave of Aibak. He was originally from Turkistan, and belonged to the Ilbari tribe there, but was, as a boy, sold into slavery by his envious brothers. 'The future monarch,' writes Siraj, 'was from his childhood remarkable for beauty, intelligence, and grace, such as excited jealousy in the hearts of his brothers.' So one day they enticed him away from home, on the pretext of taking him to a horse-show, and sold him to a slave trader. Eventually, after having been resold a few times, the boy was taken to Ghazni by a slave trader, and there he was offered for sale to Muhammad Ghuri. The sultan however rejected the offer as he considered the price asked for the boy—well over 'a thousand dinars in refined gold'—too high. Aibak however took a fancy for him, and bought him (along with another slave) for 'one lakh chital coins' when the trader brought them to Delhi. Aibak, according to Siraj, 'called him his son and kept him near his person. His rank and honour increased day by day . . . [and he was in time] elevated to the rank of Amir-shikar,' Chief Huntsman, a high office, and was also put in charge of some important fiefs. These high offices that Iltutmish held facilitated his choice as sultan by the nobles.

The immediate concern of Iltutmish on his accession was to secure his vulnerable western frontier, across which there was an ever present danger of fresh invasions. There was at this time a political storm brewing in Afghanistan, which was threatening to surge over the mountains into India, and this was a matter of particular anxiety for Iltutmish. In part this development was a continuation of the problems faced by Aibak on his accession. Yildiz, who had tussled with Aibak, was in possession of Ghazni at the time of Iltutmish's accession. But in 1215 he was driven out of Afghanistan into Punjab by the sultan of Khvarazm. Yildiz then set himself up as the ruler of Lahore by seizing the city from Qabacha who was then in possession of it. The presence of Yildiz in Lahore was a menace to Iltutmish, so he marched out against him, defeated and captured him in a battle fought at Tarain. He was then taken to Delhi, paraded through the city streets, and later executed, as a warning to the other potential rivals of the sultan.

But that was not the end of the troubles for Iltutmish in his western provinces, for Qabacha reoccupied Lahore soon after the Sultan left Punjab and returned to Delhi. Iltutmish however ignored him for the time being, as he was not a major threat to him. But a couple of years later he again led his army into Punjab and drove Qabacha out of Lahore. Qabacha then fled southward and took refuge in the city of Uch. But Iltutmish did not directly pursue him there, for he was at this time faced with a great menace that loomed over the north-western mountains of India. This was the Mongol tornado which, having swept through Central Asia, was now threatening India.

In 1221 Mongols under Chingiz Khan occupied Khvarazm. The sultan of Khvarazm then fled to India for refuge, and, in pursuit of him, Mongols themselves stormed into India and headed towards Indus. But there, on the banks of the river, for some mysterious reason, perhaps deterred by the sweltering climate of India, or by some ill omen, Chingiz Khan turned back and returned to Afghanistan. This was a lucky break for Iltutmish—if Chingiz Khan had advanced further east he would have caused dreadful havoc in the Delhi Sultanate. Freed from that anxiety, Iltutmish then returned to Punjab to deal with Qabacha. Qabacha then fled from Uch on the sultan's approach and took refuge in an island fortress on Indus, but was pursued there too by the royal forces. He then tried to escape from there in boat, but drowned in the river while fleeing.

Iltutmish then turned to Bengal, where Ali Mardan, a barely sane megalomaniac, had assumed sovereign power on Aibak's death, and preened himself as the monarch of the whole world. Once, according to Siraj, when an impoverished merchant requested for a donation from him, 'the king enquired what his native place was. He replied, Isfahan [in Persia]. The king then ordered a *firman* (decree) to be written, granting to him Isfahan as his *jagir*.' Besides being grotesquely delusional, Ali Mardan was also 'a cruel and sanguinary man,' notes Siraj. All this was too much even for his own nobles, so they eventually murdered him and placed one of their colleagues on the throne. At that point Iltutmish, freed from anxiety about his western frontier, marched into Bengal and brought it under his control. But the relief was only temporary. Trouble continued to brew in Bengal, and it was only after some five years that Iltutmish was finally able to establish his authority there with reasonable firmness.

Rebellion would however erupt again and again in Bengal during the reigns of the latter sultans, and the region would remain in a state of turbulence throughout the entire history of the Sultanate. And so would several other provinces of the empire. The realms of Hindu rajas in the Indo-Gangetic Plain were also always in turmoil. Soon after Aibak's death, several of the rajas broke free from the control of the Sultanate and assumed belligerent postures, so they had to be subjugated all over again. In all this, the problems that Iltutmish faced were typical of the problems that the sultans would face all through the history of the Delhi Sultanate. The character of Delhi Sultanate during its entire history was more like that of a military occupation than that of an established state, so its authority had to be periodically reasserted through military action.

ILTUTMISH WAS ABLE to overcome most of the problems he faced and re-establish the royal authority over all the lands over which Aibak had ruled. There was even some territorial expansion under him, into Madhya Pradesh, so that his empire extended right across North India, from Indus in the west to Brahmaputra in the east. Iltutmish also managed to keep his turbulent Turkish nobles under reasonable subordination, and he introduced a fair amount of decorum in the royal court, along the lines of the Persian court etiquette, in the place of the casualness that had been the norm there before him.

These reforms of Iltutmish raised the stature of the sultan well above that of the nobles. But what was gain for the sultan was loss for the nobles. They had traditionally enjoyed a near equal status with the sultan, but now they were his servitors. Their loss was not so much of power as of status, but status was as important to them as power. The top nobles of the empire then formed an informal league called The Forty, to countervail the supremacy of the sultan. All the great fiefs of the empire, as well as all the highest offices in the government and the army, were held by these nobles, and they would play, from behind the throne, a crucial role in the affairs of the Delhi Sultanate for many years.

The quarter century long reign of Iltutmish was one of substantial achievements, in recognition of which he was honoured by the Caliph by sending to him a robe of honour, and by issuing an edict designating him as Sultan of India. The Qutb Minar, the colossal victory tower in Delhi, today stands as a fitting monument to the great sultan—though the construction of the tower was begun by Aibak, he had built only its bottom storey; it was Iltutmish who completed the edifice.

Iltutmish enjoyed as high a reputation for benevolence, as for administrative efficiency and martial prowess. 'It is firmly believed that no king so benevolent, so sympathising, and so respectful to the learned and to elders as he was' had ever ruled the empire, states Siraj. And Ibn Battuta, the Moroccan scholar-traveller who was in India in the fourteenth century, adds: 'He was just, pious and virtuous. Among his noteworthy characteristics was the zeal with which he endeavoured to redress wrongs, and to render justice to the oppressed.' Symbolic of this was the great bell that Iltutmish set up at the entrance of the royal palace, which people could ring to draw the sultan's attention and seek justice. 'When the sultan heard the bell, he immediately inquired into the case and gave satisfaction to the complainant,' records Battuta.

Unfortunately, the sultan was beset with several personal misfortunes in the last phase of his life. His eldest and favourite son, crown prince Nasir-ud-din Mahmud, died in Bengal at this time under mysterious circumstances. There was even an assassination attempt on the sultan at this time, when a band of Ismailis stormed into the Great Mosque in Delhi during the Friday prayers, and cut through the congregation towards the sultan, who barely managed to escape before the would-be assassins reached him. A few months later, while he was conducting a campaign against the turbulent Khokars of Punjab, he was stricken with a serious illness, and had to be carried back to Delhi on a litter.

As his life was ebbing away, the courtiers urged him to nominate a successor, so as to avert the horrors of a disputed succession. Iltutmish then named his eldest daughter Raziya as his successor. 'The sultan,' writes Siraj, 'discerned in her countenance the signs of power and bravery, and, although she was a girl and lived in seclusion, . . . [the sultan] put her name in writing as the heir of the kingdom, and successor to the throne.' And when the courtiers demurred about this on the ground that Raziya was a woman, Iltutmish told them: 'My sons are devoted to the pleasures of youth, and not one of them is qualified to be the king . . . After my death you will find that there is no one more competent to guide the state than my daughter.'

THE SULTAN'S CHOICE of Raziya for the throne was not merely an expression of sentiment, but of sound judgement as well, for the princess was a very capable woman, and had a good amount of administrative experience, as Iltutmish had often left her in charge of the government when he was away on military campaigns, and she had, according to Siraj, exercised royal authority with great dignity. Still, Iltutmish's choice of her for the throne was unconventional. Even though there were a few instances in Arab history of women playing an open role in politics, and even leading armies into battle, the normal practice in Islamic societies was for royal women, however ambitious and able they were, to play politics only from behind the harem screen, and not openly. Not surprisingly, the Delhi nobles abhorred the idea of being subservient to a woman, and on the death of Iltutmish they disregarded his choice and placed his eldest surviving son, Rukn-ud-din Firuz, on the throne.

Ironically, even in choosing Firuz, what the nobles in effect got was a woman's rule, and that too of a petty, vindictive and vicious woman, for Firuz had no interest in ruling, and he left all the power to his mother, Shah Turkan, a low-born former handmaid of Iltutmish. Firuz was entirely feckless. His only virtue was generosity, but even that he turned into a vice by his excesses. He was 'a very generous and handsome king, full of kindness and humanity . . . No king in any reign had ever scattered gifts, robes of honour, and grants in the way he did,' writes Siraj. 'But all his lavishness sprang from his inordinate addiction to sensuality, pleasure and conviviality. He was so entirely addicted to revelry and debauchery that he often bestowed his honours and rewards on bands of singers, buffoons and catamites. He scattered his riches to such a heedless extent that he would ride out drunk upon an elephant through the streets and bazaars, throwing tankas of red gold around him for the people to pick up and rejoice over.'

Meanwhile Shah Turkan, 'in blind fury and vindictiveness', set about avenging the indignities that she had suffered in the royal harem at the hands of the high-born wives of Iltutmish, by putting some of them to death in an ignominious manner, and by subjecting others to various gross humiliations. She even blinded a young son of Iltutmish and had him later put to death, fearing that he might grow up to be a threat to Firuz. She also hatched a plot to kill Raziya. In that environment of gross misrule several provincial governors broke out in rebellion, and when Firuz marched out against them, Raziya cleverly manipulated public sentiment in Delhi and incited a popular uprising against Shah Turkan. The people of Delhi, writes Siraj, 'rose and . . . seized the royal palace and made the mother of the sultan a prisoner.' And when Firuz, deserted by many of his officers, returned to Delhi, he too was imprisoned, and presently put to death. The reign of Firuz, according to Siraj, lasted just six months and twenty-eight days.

RAZIYA WAS THEN proclaimed the sultan by public acclaim. According to Isami, a mid-fourteenth century chronicler, when Firuz was overthrown, and the nobles were discussing to whom they should give the crown, Raziya, 'waved her scarf from a window and said to them, *'Here I am, the daughter of his majesty; the crown befits my head. It was I whom the king had chosen as his heir-apparent . . . Since you set the crown on the head of another person against the king's orders, you have came to grief . . . [Give the crown to me for a few years to test my ability.] Should I acquit myself as a ruler better than a man, you might keep me on the throne. Should you see things otherwise, you may remove the crown from my head and give it to whomsoever you please . . . [On hearing Raziya, the nobles concluded that] a daughter is better than an ill-bred son. Many a woman has been the vanquisher of men in battle; many a man has owed his position to a woman. If this daughter of the king is raised to the throne . . . she would prove to be better than the sons of the king.' So they offered the throne to Raziya. And in November 1236 she ascended the throne, assumed the title Raziya-ud-din, and issued coins bearing that title.

But Raziya's accession was resented by some of the provincial governors, who then threateningly converged on Delhi with their armies. But Raziya managed to sow dissension among the governors, so the confederacy collapsed before it could do any harm, and the confederate nobles scattered. Several of the fleeing nobles were then captured and executed by royal officers. Raziya's energy and decisiveness in dealing with the crisis earned the admiration of several of the vacillating nobles, and won them over to her side.

Raziya then broke free from the conventional constraints of harem ladies, and one day three years after her accession, 'threw off the dress and veil of women, put on a tunic and cap, and thus appeared in public. When she rode on elephant all men clearly saw her,' records Siraj. And 'she rode on horseback as men ride, armed with a bow and quiver, and surrounded by courtiers. She did not veil her face,' adds Battuta.

These practices of Raziya were most offensive to the orthodox Muslim nobles of the Sultanate, who were under the sway of ancient prejudices, and they decided to oust her. But they bided their time, waiting for an opportunity or excuse to overthrow her. A good part of Raziya's persona as sultan involved her posturing as a man. But her biology betrayed her. She could pretend to others to be a man, but not to herself. And it was her yearning for intimate male companionship that eventually brought about her downfall—that, and her attempts to reduce the power of The Forty by selecting several of her principal officers from outside that elite group.

One of Raziya's favourite officers was Jalal-ud-din Yaqut, an Abyssinian, whose elevation to the post of *Amir-i-Akhur*, Master of the Stables, a very high office, was deeply resented by Turkish nobles, especially as she was suspected of having an amorous relationship with him. A conspiracy was then hatched by a group of nobles headed by Aitigin, the Lord Chamberlain, to depose her. They did not however dare to move against her in Delhi, as she enjoyed decisive popular support there. But in the summer of 1240, when she was on a campaign against a provincial rebel in southern Punjab, the conspirators swung into action, killed Yaqut and the other close associates of Raziya who had accompanied her on the campaign, and threw her into prison in the Bhatinda fort. And in Delhi they raised Muiz-ud-din Bahram, Iltutmish's third son, as sultan.

But Raziya was only down, not out. Not yet. She now used the lure of high office to entice Altuniya, the governor of Bhatinda, who was her captor, to ally with her. She married him, and together they advanced on Delhi with an army. But fortune no longer favoured her. In the ensuing battle her army was utterly routed by the Delhi forces. 'Not even one horseman remained with her,' states Isami. She and Altuniya then fled from the battlefield, but they both fell into the hands of the local people. There are three different versions of what happened then: according to Siraj, both of them were forthwith killed by their captors, but Sirhindi states that their captors 'despatched them in fetters to the sultan, who put them both to death,' and Battuta claims that it was a peasant who killed Raziya, to steal her ornaments.

Raziya had reigned for three years and six days. She was buried on the banks of Yamuna, and a small tomb was erected there to mark her grave. In time the tomb became a place of pilgrimage, as it was 'considered a place of sanctity,' states Battuta. 'Sultan Raziya was a great monarch,' comments Siraj. 'She was wise, just, and generous, a benefactor to her kingdom, a dispenser of justice, the protector of her subjects, and the leader of her armies. She was endowed with all the qualities befitting a king. But she was not of the right sex, and so in the estimation of men all her virtues were worthless.'

BAHRAM ON HIS accession assigned, presumably as previously agreed with the nobles, the highest executive power in the Sultanate to Aitigin and designated him as Naib-i-Mamlikat, regent of the kingdom. But if the nobles expected Bahram to be a mere figurehead, a puppet in their hands, they were soon disabused of that fancy. Bahram was a bizarrely schizophrenic person, gentle and shy as well as savage and bloodthirsty. He was, according to Siraj, 'a fearless, intrepid and sanguinary man . . . [but was also] shy and unceremonious, and had no taste for gorgeous attire which kings love to wear, nor for the belts, accoutrements, banners and other insignia of royalty.'

As sultan, it was Bahram's vicious side that was most evident—he was brutally repressive towards nobles, even towards his benefactors. Thus when Aitigin, who was primarily instrumental in placing him on the throne, offended him by marrying one of his sisters, and took to the practice of keeping an elephant and a band at the entrance of his mansion, as at the entrance of the royal palace, Bahram had him promptly executed. These tyrannical acts of Bahram sent a shiver of anxiety through the nobles—an 'uneasy feeling spread like an epidemic' among the nobles, states Siraj. The politics of the Delhi Sultanate at this time was a dizzying whirl of Byzantine conspiracies and counter-conspiracies, in which life was nightmarish for those in the inner circle of power. The only solution to their awful predicament was to depose the sultan, the nobles decided, and one day in the summer of 1242, they, according to Isami, 'bound him hand and foot in fetters and threw him into prison,' and later had him murdered. Bahram had reigned for just over two years.

The nobles then assembled at the tomb of Iltutmish and chose Ala-ud-din Masud, a grandson of Iltutmish, to ascend the throne. Masud at the time of his accession was, according to Siraj, 'a generous and good-natured prince, possessed of many estimable qualities.' However, after a year or so of his reign he fell under evil influences, and turned into a bloodthirsty tyrant. He 'acquired the habit of seizing and killing his nobles,' reports Siraj. 'He became confirmed in his cruelty; all his excellent qualities were perverted, and he gave himself up to unbounded licentiousness, pleasure, and hunting . . . [Moreover] he was given to depravity.' So in June 1246 the nobles once again seized control of the situation, deposed Masud and threw him into prison, where he soon died, or was murdered. Masud had reigned for four years.

The nobles then enthroned Iltutmish's youngest son, Nasir-ud-din Mahmud, an affable and devout prince, who, according to Isami, 'ruled the country righteously, not like the other foolish princes.'

3

The Divine Right Sultan

With the accession of Nasir-ud-din Mahmud began the slow process of restoring the political stability of the Delhi Sultanate, which had been in an awful state of turmoil for a decade after the death of Iltutmish. But Mahmud, a mild and unassertive prince, himself had virtually nothing to do with this transformation. The crucial role in it was played by Ghiyas-ud-din Balban, an eminent Turkish noble, who assumed supreme power in the Sultanate on Mahmud's accession, and wielded that power for forty years, from 1246 to 1287, first as the regent of Mahmud for two decades, and then, on Mahmud's death, as sultan, for another two decades. During this entire period there was only one brief interruption in his career, during his regency, when he was out of power for about two years, due to the manoeuvres of his political rivals.

Mahmud, who was about seventeen years old at the time of his accession, had no aptitude for governing, no interest in it either, and was content to leave that responsibility entirely to Balban. Mahmud 'was a mild, kind, and devout king, and he passed much of his time making copies of the Holy Book,' notes Barani, a mid-fourteenth century historian of the Sultanate. Mahmud lived very frugally. It is said that once when his wife asked him to take some money from the treasury and buy a slave girl to do the domestic work in the royal quarters, he rejected the request saying that the treasury belonged to the people, and was not for the personal use of the sultan.

These retiring, saintly qualities, though commendable in themselves, were unsuited in a sultan in the turbulent environment then existing in the Sultanate. Though Iltutmish had made a serious effort to systematise the administration of the Sultanate, what he achieved was altogether lost in the chaos that followed his death. 'During the reigns of his sons, the affairs of the country had fallen into confusion,' observes Barani. 'The treasury was empty, and the royal court had but little in the way of wealth and horses. The Shamsi slaves had become khans, and they divided among themselves all the wealth and power of the kingdom, so that the country came under their control.'

But these nobles themselves were divided into various cabals and were forever at each other's throat. 'None [of the nobles] would give precedence . . . to another,' continues Barani. 'In possessions and display, in grandeur and dignity, they vied with each other, and in their proud vaunts and boasts every one exclaimed to the other, "What art thou that I am not, and what will thou be that I shall not be?" The incompetence of the sons of Iltutmish, and the arrogance of the Shamsi slaves, thus brought into contempt that throne which had been among the most dignified and exalted in the world.'

The worst period in all this was the decade long interregnum between the death of Iltutmish and the accession of Mahmud, when royal authority was often impudently flouted by provincial governors and top nobles, some of whom nurtured the ambition of becoming sultans themselves. Besides that, there was at this time the persistent problem of resurgent Rajput rajas challenging the authority of the sultan to regain their independence. There was also the problem of turbulent hill tribes and bandits freely roaming around in the countryside, menacing traders and travellers as well as the common people. And above all, there was the ominous presence of Mongols in the northwest, threatening to engulf the Sultanate. The future of the Sultanate looked most uncertain.

The Delhi Sultanate at the time of Mahmud's accession covered a broad swath of land in North India, but the territory had not yet been consolidated into a viable, stable state. Indeed, before Balban took charge of the situation soon after Mahmud's accession, the Sultanate was in grave danger of disintegrating into total chaos. Balban stabilised the situation substantially, despite the jealousies and intrigues of rival nobles.

DURING ALMOST ALL the twenty years of Mahmud's reign Balban served as the regent of the Sultan, and bore the grand title Ulugh Khan (Great Khan). 'He, keeping Nasir-ud-din as a puppet, carried on the government, and used many of the insignia of royalty even while he was only a Khan,' reports Barani. The rule of Mahmud was in fact the rule of Balban.

Balban began his career in India as a slave of Iltutmish, who purchased him in Delhi in 1233. He was of the lineage of a clan of chieftains in Turkistan, but was enslaved as a child and brought to Gujarat by a slave trader. There he was bought by a Turk who, according to Siraj, 'brought him up carefully like a son. Intelligence and ability shone out clearly in his countenance . . . [so he was] treated with special consideration' by his master, who eventually brought him to Delhi and sold him to Iltutmish. Balban, according to Battuta, 'was short in stature and of mean appearance.' But his high mental stature and talents more than compensated for his poor physical appearance. Iltutmish, Siraj notes, regarded Balban to be 'a youth of great promise, so he made him his personal attendant, placing, as one might say, the hawk of fortune on his hand.'

Balban rose rapidly in the service of the Sultanate, and in time became a member of The Forty, the elite band of Turks serving the sultan. And even in that elite group Balban stood out, surpassing the other nobles by his 'vigour, courage and activity.' Raziya appointed him as her Chief Huntsman, an important and confidential post. 'Fate proclaimed that the earth was to be the prey of his fortune, and world the game of his sovereignty,' comments Siraj. Later, when Bahram became the sultan, he raised Balban to the post of Master of the Horse. 'The steed of sovereignty and empire thus came under his bridle and control,' remarks Siraj. 'His success was so great that other nobles began to look upon him with jealousy, and the thorn of envy began to rankle in their hearts. But it was the will of god that he should excel them all, so that the more the fire of their envy burnt, the stronger did the incense of his fortune rise from the censer of the times.' In 1243 Balban was appointed Amir-i-Hajib, Lord Chamberlain, by Sultan Masud.

Balban's star rose even more rapidly when Masud was succeeded by Mahmud, especially after the sultan married his daughter. Balban was then appointed to the premier post of Naib-i-Mamlikat, and he in turn filled most of the key positions in the government with his nominees, and appointed his brother Kashli Khan as Lord Chamberlain. These posts were not, however, sinecures, for Balban demanded credible performance from all his officers, just as he himself worked untiringly.

But the very success of Balban created its own problems, for it roused the envy of rival nobles, who then worked in secret to oust him from his high office. The prime mover in the plot against Balban was Raihan, the Wakil-i-dar, superintendent of the sultan's household establishment, a position that gave him easy access to the royal family. A wily conspirator, he won the support of the sultan's mother and several disgruntled nobles, and, craftily working behind the scenes, he gradually roused resentment in Mahmud himself against Balban's dominance. And eventually, in the winter of 1252–53, he persuaded the sultan to shift Balban out of Delhi and send him to his fief, and also to remove his brother, Kashli Khan, from his office. It was the hope of the conspirators that Balban would resist these slights, and thus give them the opportunity to destroy his power altogether. But to their disappointment, Balban obeyed the royal order without a murmur. Discomfited, Raihan then struck a second blow, and got the sultan to transfer Balban abruptly from his fief to another fief. But once again Balban obeyed without protest.

But Balban was not withdrawing from power politics, only biding his time. Presently, the envy of the nobles about Balban came to be overshadowed by their growing resentment over Raihan, a Hindu convert to Islam, lording over them, the Turkish nobles. A group of these nobles then appealed to Balban to return to Delhi. In the ensuing manoeuvres and counter-manoeuvres, and in the face of the threat of a military conflict between rival factions, the sultan was persuaded by his advisers to dismiss Raihan from the court and reappoint Balban and his brother to their previous posts.

The sultan acted on that advice, and Balban returned to his old office in January 1255, after having been out of it for about two years. He then held that post till Mahmud's death in February 1266.

MAHMUD WAS THE only one of Iltutmish's descendants to have a long reign—of twenty years—while all the others ruled only for short periods, the shortest reign, of just seven months, being that of Rukn-ud-din Firuz, the first successor of Iltutmish. In fact, among the five descendants of Iltutmish who sat on the throne of Delhi—three sons, one daughter, and one grandson—all except Mahmud were overthrown and killed by the nobles.

Mahmud however was sultan only in name, for during virtually his entire reign it was Balban who actually ruled the kingdom. So Balban's accession to the throne on the death of Mahmud was a natural and inevitable transition, from being the de facto ruler to being the de jure ruler. Mahmud is said to have designated Balban to succeed him; the choice was in any case inevitable, for no prince of Iltutmish's lineage was then alive, and a ruler of the calibre and experience of Balban was essential at this time to prevent anarchy from engulfing the kingdom.

Balban reinforced his entitlement to the throne by claiming to be a descendant of Afrasiyab, the legendary Turkish royal hero, and thus placing himself well above all the other nobles of the Sultanate (his potential rivals) in social status. And this claim of royal lineage by Balban was a crucial determinant of the nature of his rule, for it enabled him to assume an exalted posture as sultan, and to adopt a demeanour and conduct to match the high pedigree that he claimed and the high office that he occupied.

The primary characteristics of Balban as sultan were his high sense of responsibility and unremitting hard work. He would not allow carelessness or sloth to erode his power in any way. As sultan, he gave up all the convivial pleasures that he had previously enjoyed, maintained his distance from nobles, and showed no intimacy with anyone. 'Sultan Balban, while he was a khan, was addicted to wine drinking, and was fond of giving entertainments;

two or three times in a week he would give banquets and gamble with his guests . . . But after he came to the throne he allowed himself no prohibited indulgences,' observes Barani. His only remaining addiction was hunting, but that too he used to subserve his political purpose, as a means of exercising his army preparatory to launching military campaigns. In all matters he now strictly followed Islamic regulations. And at meals he preferred the company of Muslim clerics, with whom he discussed theological matters.

Balban now took care to present a forbiddingly stern, impassive façade to the public. Though behind this façade he still remained subject to common human dispositions and emotions, he kept them all under the strict control of his iron will. But if self-control and implacability are indispensable qualities required in a sultan, so was magnanimity. So Balban did sometimes, though rarely, condone the incompetence of his officers, and once even pardoned army deserters. And we are told that he often wept at sermons in the mosque. Balban's general outward appearance of cold-blooded efficiency was a triumph of will over nature.

BALBAN, UNLIKE MOST of his predecessors on the throne, had a very lofty concept of kingship. Most of the sultans of Delhi who preceded Balban, except Iltutmish, were little more than first among equals. This, Balban felt, was a major weakness of the Sultanate, which led to laxity in administration and disarray in the empire, with courtiers and provincial governors constantly trying to tussle with the sultan and erode his power. From his long experience as regent—and perhaps under the influence of the ancient Persian concept of monarchy—Balban felt that the throne had to be raised well above the level of the nobles. And to do that, he enunciated the concept of the sultan as the vicegerent of god. This claim was not just an expression of royal vanity—the high status that Balban claimed was not for himself as a person, but for the office of the sultan, and it constituted a political concept of broad practical significance, which found expression in Balban's own impeccable conduct, and in the strict manner in which he ran the government.

An essential expression of Balban's exalted concept of kingship was his insistence that courtiers on approaching the sultan should prostrate before him and kiss the throne or the sultan's feet. Court etiquette now became rigidly formal, and it was required to be strictly observed by all. In court, and in public, Balban was always escorted by a praetorian guard with drawn swords, which helped to create the needed physical and psychological distance between the sultan and all others. 'No sovereign,' concludes Barani, 'had ever before exhibited such pomp and grandeur in Delhi . . . [Through all the] years that Balban reigned he maintained the dignity, honour, and majesty of the throne in a manner that could not be surpassed. Certain of his attendants who waited on him in private assured me they never saw him otherwise than fully-dressed. During the whole time that he was khan and sultan . . . he never conversed with persons of low origin or occupation, and never indulged in any familiarity, either with friends or strangers, by which the dignity of the sovereign might be lowered. He never joked with anyone, nor did he allow anyone to joke in his presence; he never laughed aloud, nor did he permit anyone in his court to laugh.' In Balban's court, frivolity was a serious misdemeanour, if not a crime.

BALBAN'S LONG YEARS as the de facto ruler of the Sultanate had given him ample time to reflect on the changes that were needed in government to consolidate royal power and to ensure efficient administration. He therefore introduced a number of administrative reforms soon after his accession. One of his key measures was to set up an elaborate network of carefully selected confidential spies and news reporters at all the sensitive spots in the empire and among all potential rebels, including his sons, for he believed that the crucial requirement for maintaining effective control over the empire was to have accurate and detailed information about all the significant developments everywhere in the empire.

Balban also took a number of decisive measures to systematise administrative procedures and to reform the army—he abolished many of the sinecures that had proliferated in the Sultanate over the decades, confiscated the lands of the fief-holders who were no longer rendering the services for which grants had been given to them, and cashiered a number of worthless or superannuated military officers. 'Many of the grantees were old and infirm, many more had died, and their sons had taken possession of the grants as an inheritance from their fathers,' notes Barani. 'All these holders of service lands called themselves proprietors, and professed to have received the lands as free gift form Sultan Iltutmish . . . Some of them went leisurely to perform their military duties, but the greater part stayed at home making excuses, the acceptance of which they secured by presents and bribes of all sorts to the deputy muster-master and his officials.' Balban initially ordered all these grants to be taken back by the state and the grantees to be given subsistence allowances, but later, rather uncharacteristically, he rescinded the order on compassionate grounds.

Such shows of clemency were rare in Balban. He normally insisted on unremitting efficiency from his officers, and treated inefficiency and failure to perform assigned duties as unpardonable offences. And he was utterly ruthless in enforcing discipline and hard work among his officers, and in punishing the tardy, for that, he believed, was the only way to ensure dependable service from them. Thus, when Amin Khan, the governor of Oudh, who was sent to suppress a rebellion in Bengal, was defeated by the rebel and he tamely retreated, Balban ordered him 'to be hanged over the gate of Oudh,' reports Barani.

Balban was equally stern and uncompromising in the administration of justice, and would, according to Barani, show 'no favour to his brethren or children, to his associates or attendants.' Thus when Malik Baqbaq, a top noble and governor of Budaun, flogged to death one of his servants, Balban, on receiving the complaint about it from the servant's wife, had the noble himself flogged to death, and had the news-writer, who had failed to report the noble's crime to Balban, hanged over the city gate. Similarly, when another top noble, Haibat Khan, slew a man in a drunken rage, Balban had 500 lashes given to the noble, and then handed him over to the widow of the slain man, saying, 'This murderer was my salve, he is now yours. Do you stab him as he stabbed your husband.' Though the khan then managed to purchase his life from the widow for 20,000 tankas, he thereafter never again appeared in public, out of shame.

BALBAN DID NOT have the common vanity of kings to gain glory through conquests. This was not because he was averse to military campaigns, but because he considered that it would be imprudent for him to seek fresh conquests when the territories that were already in the empire were not properly consolidated, and the empire itself was periodically menaced by Mongol raids. Balban's primary focus during his entire rule, as regent and as sultan, was on the consolidation of the empire, its proper administration, and its protection against Mongol raids, and not on seeking fresh conquests. Once when some of his courtiers suggested that he should seek renown through conquests, he outright rejected the proposal. 'I have devoted all the revenues of my kingdom to the equipment of my army, and I hold all my forces ever ready and prepared to . . . [meet the threat of Mongol invasion]. I will never leave my kingdom, nor will I go to any distance from it. In the reigns of my patrons and predecessors there was none of this problem with the Mongols, so they could lead their armies wherever they pleased, subdue the dominions of Hindus, and carry off gold and treasures, staying away from their capital a year or two. If this anxiety [about the Mongols] . . . were removed, then I would not stay one day in my capital, but lead forth my army to capture treasures and valuables, elephants and horses, and would never allow the Rais and Ranas to repose in security at a distance.'

Mongols had first forayed into India during the reign of Iltutmish, and had since then raided India several times, and were a constant menacing presence in western Punjab. 'No year passed without the Mongols forcing their way into Hindustan and . . . [raiding] different towns,' notes Barani. The Mongol threat to the Sultanate was not so much of the conquest of territory as of plunder, destruction and carnage. As the early medieval chronicler Juwaini puts it, 'Mongols came, razed, burnt, slaughtered, plundered, and departed.'

In India the Mongol depredations were largely confined to the Indus Plain west of the Sutlaj. When they advanced further east, they, despite their fearsome reputation for savagery, were invariably routed by the Sultanate forces, for the Mongol army was not a professional army but a horde, and was no match to the trained and disciplined army of the Sultanate. Often, on the approach of the Sultanate army, Mongols fled without fighting, not wanting to risk losing the plunder that they had already gathered.

Turks detested Mongols as uncouth savages. 'Their eyes were so narrow and piercing that they might have bored a hole into a brass vessel, and their stench was more horrible than their colour,' writes medieval poet Amir Khusrav, colouring his description with bardic fancy. 'Their heads were set on their bodies as if they had no necks, and their cheeks resembled leathern bottles, full of wrinkles and knots. Their noses extended from cheek to cheek, and their mouths from cheekbone to cheekbone; their nostrils resembled rotten graves, and from them the hair descended as far as the lips. Their moustaches were of extravagant length, but the beards about their chins were very scanty. Their chests, in colour half black, half white, were covered with lice which looked like sesame growing on a bad soil. Their whole bodies, indeed, were covered with these insects, and their skins were as rough-grained as shagreen leather, fit only to be converted into shoes. They devoured dogs and pigs with their nasty teeth . . . The king marvelled at their beastly countenances and said that god had created them out of hellfire.'

By the mid-thirteenth century, Lahore had become a Mongol dependency, with its Turkish governor acknowledging the suzerainty of Mongols and paying tribute to them. Around this time the governor of Sind also transferred his allegiance from the Sultanate to Mongols. It was feared that Mongols might even advance on Delhi. Balban, who was the regent of the Sultanate at this time, met the challenge of Mongols with a combination of astute diplomacy, unwinking vigilance, and display of military might, and he was able to avert any serious damage to the empire to be caused by them. With Mongols dominant in Afghanistan and Central Asia, Turks in India had at this time nowhere to retreat to—India was now their homeland, and they had to protect it at all cost in order to survive. Balban therefore took care to maintain good relationship with Hulagu Khan, the Mongol viceroy in Iran and a grandson of Chingiz Khan, and obtained from him the assurance that Mongols would not advance beyond Satluj. This rapport prompted Hulagu to send, in 1259, a goodwill mission to Delhi, which was accorded a grand reception by Balban, which included also a cautionary demonstration of the military might of the Sultanate.

The peace with the Mongols did not however last long. Occasional Mongol forays into the Sultanate continued, and by around 1279 major Mongol incursions resumed. But Balban had by then, during the period of relative peace with the Mongols, reorganised his western frontier defences under the command of his eldest son Muhammad, who was appointed as the supreme commander of the frontier forces. Mongols were not therefore allowed to operate beyond Satluj, and their raids were mostly confined to the region west of Indus.

BALBAN WAS AS much concerned with internal security as with external security. The countryside, even the neighbourhood of Delhi, was at this time periodically marauded by predatory tribes and bands of brigands. Of particular menace were Meos of Mewat, the heavily forested region on the southern and western flanks of Delhi. 'At night they used to come prowling into the city, giving all kinds of trouble, depriving the people of their rest; and they plundered the country houses in the neighbourhood of the city,' states Barani. 'In the neighbourhood of Delhi there were large and dense jungles, through which many roads passed. The disaffected . . . and the outlaws . . . [of this region] grew bold and took to robbery on the highway, and they so beset the roads that caravans and merchants were unable to pass through them . . . [Because of their ravages] the western gates of the city were shut at afternoon prayer, and no one dared to go out of the city in that direction after that hour . . . [The Mewatis would assault] the water-carriers and the girls who were fetching water, and would strip them and carry off their clothes. These daring acts . . . caused a great ferment in Delhi.'

This was an affront that Balban could not tolerate, and he personally set out on a campaign to exterminate the Mewatis. For twenty days he had his soldiers ravage the Mewati habitats with deliberate and ruthless savagery, slaughtering the people there wholesale, the frenzy of the soldiers being roused by Balban's offer of a tanka for every severed head, and two tankas for every living prisoner. Several Mewati leaders were captured and taken to Delhi, and were executed there in various gruesome ways—some were thrown under elephants to be trampled to death, while others were cut to pieces or flayed alive. Despite all this, the Mewatis became active again a few months later, so Balban once again marched out against them, and this time massacred some 12,000 people there. Then, to prevent the recurrence of the problem, he cleared the forests around Delhi, set up military outposts there, and settled Afghan soldier-farmers in vulnerable areas, giving them tax-free lands.

Elsewhere in the Sultanate too Balban was ruthless in dealing with any kind of turmoil. Thus when lawlessness broke out in Katehr in north-western Uttar Pradesh, Balban, according to Barani, personally led a contingent of soldiers into the region, and ordered them to 'burn down Katehr and destroy it, to slay every man, and to spare none but women and children . . . He remained for some days in Katehr and directed the slaughter. The blood of the rioters ran in streams, heaps of the slain were to be seen near every village and jungle, and the stench of the dead reached as far as Ganga.' And, as in Mewat, in Katehr too, to secure the region, Balban cleared the jungles, laid new roads, and constructed several forts in vulnerable areas. These measures led to a general improvement of law and order in the Sultanate, which in turn led to greater material prosperity, as commercial transport became secure, and farmers were freed from the harassment of brigands.

EVEN MORE SERIOUS than the problems of brigandage was the problem of the insubordination of provincial governors that perennially bedevilled the Sultanate. Bengal was particularly vulnerable to this hazard, so that its capital, Lakhnawati, earned the sobriquet Bulghakpur, City of Rebellion. 'The people of this country had for many long years evinced a disposition to revolt,' observes Barani. 'And the disaffected and evil disposed among them generally succeeded in alienating the loyalty of the governors.' Balban therefore appointed Tughril, one of his most 'cherished slaves,' as the governor of Bengal. Tughril was, according to Barani, 'a very active, bold, courageous and generous man,' and Balban believed that Bengal would be safe under his governorship. But soon after Tughril settled in Bengal, 'ambition laid its egg in his head,' and he broke out in rebellion. Balban then directed Amin Khan, the governor of Oudh, to suppress the rebellion, but he was easily routed by Tughril. Balban probably suspected treachery in Amin Khan's tame retreat from Bengal, and it so roused his wrath that he had him executed forthwith. But the two other contingents that he thereafter sent against Tughril also suffered defeat. These reverses were humiliating to Balban, and a threat to his authority, so he himself then proceeded to Bengal, with the awful resolve never to return except with the rebel's head.

That unnerved Tughril, and on Balban's approach he fled eastward from Lakhnawati, hoping that the sultan would not pursue him there. But Balban was relentless in his pursuit. So, as the royal army closed in on him, Tughril retreated further eastward, towards Tripura. But he was pursued there too, and was soon overtaken and captured by a small band of royal soldiers, who immediately beheaded him. Balban then returned to Lakhnawati with a large number of captured rebel soldiers. There, to serve as a warning to other potential rebels, Balban 'ordered gibbets to be erected along both sides of the great bazaar, which was more than a *kos* (two miles) in length,' reports Barani. 'He ordered all the sons and sons-in-law of Tughril, and all the men who had served him or borne arms for him, to be slain and placed upon the gibbets . . . This so horrified the beholders that they themselves nearly died of fear.'

Balban then appointed his son Bughra Khan as the governor of Bengal, after taking from him an oath 'that he would recover and secure the country of Bengal and that he would not hold convivial parties, nor indulge in wine and dissipation.' The sultan also warned him about the awful fate that awaited anyone rebelling against royal authority.

Balban then set out for Delhi, herding a large number of captured deserters from the royal army who had joined Tughril. He intended to gibbet them all in Delhi, but was dissuaded from that dreadful reprisal by the qazi, who, according to Barani, threw himself at the feet of the sultan and interceded for the prisoners. The appeal moved the sultan, and he pardoned most of the deserters, and even the others he banished or imprisoned only for short periods. Balban's Bengal campaign altogether took three years.

'FROM BEING A MALIK he became a khan, and from being a khan he became a king,' writes Barani, describing the career of Balban. 'When he attained the throne he imparted to it new lustre; he brought the administration into order, and restored to efficiency institutions whose power had been shaken or destroyed. The dignity and authority of government was restored, and his stringent rules and resolute determination caused all men, high and low, throughout his dominions, to submit to his authority . . . [He ruled the empire] with dignity, honour and vigour.'

On the whole Balban had very substantial achievements to his credit. And, though he was utterly ruthless in enforcing his will, he was never rash or capricious, but deliberate in all that he said and did, and always in perfect self-control. By the end of his reign security and order by and large prevailed in the sultanate, in so far as they could prevail anywhere in India in the thirteenth century.

Then tragedy struck.

In 1285, Balban's eldest and favourite son, Muhammad, the heir apparent—whom 'his father loved . . . dearer than his own life,' according to Barani—was killed in Multan in a battle against Mongols. Balban was devastated by the tragedy, although he maintained a façade of imperturbable composure in public. 'The sultan was now more than eighty years old, and though he struggled hard against the effects of his bereavement, day by day they became more apparent,' notes Barani. 'By day he held his court, and entered into public business as if to show that his loss had not affected him; but at night he poured forth his cries of grief, tore his garments, and threw dust upon his head . . . The reign of Balban now drew to a close, and he gradually sank under his sorrow.'

The death of Muhammad was not just a personal loss for the sultan, but an irreparable loss for the dynasty, for Muhammad was a highly cultured, earnest and able prince. 'The court of the young prince,' reports Barani, 'was frequented by the most learned, excellent and accomplished men of the time . . . [Poets] Amir Khusrav and Amir Hasan served at his court . . . [They were richly rewarded by the prince, and they used to say that] they had very rarely seen a prince so excellent and virtuous . . . [as Muhammad]. At his entertainments they never heard him indulge in foolish or dirty talk, whether wine was drunk or not; if he drank wine, he did so in moderation, so as not to become intoxicated and senseless.'

In 1287, two years after Muhammad's death, Balban himself died. The major concern of Balban in his last days was to decide on who should succeed him. His initial choice was Bughra Khan, his second son. Balban summoned him from Lakhnawati, and said to him: 'Grief for your bother has brought me to my deathbed, and who knows how soon my end may come? This is no time for you be absent, for I have no other son to take my place. [My grandsons] Kaikhusrav (son of Muhammad) and Kaiqubad (son of Bughra Khan) . . . are young, and have not experienced the heat and cold of fortune. Youthful passions and indulgence would make them unfit to govern my kingdom, if it should descend to them. The realm of Delhi would again become a child's toy, as it was under the successors of Iltutmish . . . Think over this. Do not leave my side. Cast away all desire of going to Lakhnawati.'

Bughra Khan did not heed the advice. He was, comments Barani, 'a heedless prince,' who did not care for the throne of Delhi with all its onerous responsibilities and endless problems, and yearned for a life of ease in Lakhnawati. So after a couple of months in Delhi, when Balban's health improved a little, he returned to Lakhnawati 'without leave from his father.' Balban then summoned some of his intimate nobles and told them to raise Kaikhusrav to the throne. 'He is young and incapable of ruling as yet, but what can I do?' Balban lamented. Three days later the sultan died.

On his death the nobles wilfully set aside Balban's choice and raised Kaiqubad to the throne, and there followed several years of chaos in the Sultanate. 'From the day that Balban, the father of his people, died, all security of life and property was lost, and no one had any confidence in the stability of the kingdom,' comments Barani.

Kaiqubad was seventeen or eighteen years old at this time. According to Barani, the prince 'was a young man of many excellent qualities. He was of an equable temper, kind in disposition and very handsome. But he was fond of pleasure and sensual gratifications. From his childhood till the day he came to the throne, he had been brought up under the eye of the sultan, his grandfather. Such strict tutors had been placed over him that he never had the idea of indulging in any pleasure, or the opportunity for gratifying any lust. His tutors . . . watched him so carefully that he never cast his eyes on any fair damsel, and never tasted a cup of wine. Night and day his austere guardians watched over him. Teachers instructed him in the polite arts and manly exercises, and he was never allowed to do any unseemly act, or to utter any improper speech. When, all at once, and without previous expectation, he was elevated to such a mighty throne . . . all that he had read, heard and learned, he immediately forgot; his lessons of wisdom and self-restraint were thrown aside, and he plunged at once into pleasure and dissipation of every kind . . . His ministers likewise, and the young nobles of his court, his companions and friends, all gave themselves up to pleasure. The example spread, and all ranks, high and low, learned and unlearned, acquired a taste for wine drinking and amusements . . . Night and day the sultan gave himself entirely to dissipation and enjoyment.' Vice and immorality became widespread. Mosques were empty of worshippers, but wine shops flourished. Adds Ferishta: 'There were ladies of pleasure everywhere, and every street rang with music and mirth.'

IN THAT CHAOTIC environment, Nizam-ud-din, the able, crafty and ambitious nephew and son-in-law of the kotwal of Delhi, assumed the supreme power in the empire as Naib-i-mulk, deputy ruler of the sultanate. 'The government of the country was in his hands,' observes Barani. Nizam-ud-din filled all the key positions in the government with his own men, eliminated many of the rival nobles, executing or imprisoning them, and even had the prince Kaikhusrav murdered. And he encouraged Kaiqubad to sink ever deeper into debauchery, presumably hoping that this would eventually enable him to seize the throne.

These developments in Delhi troubled even the easygoing Bughra Khan, who now ruled as the sultan of Bengal. He wrote to Kaiqubad to mend his ways, and, getting no satisfactory response, set out with his army to confront his son. And Kaiqubad too set out with his army to meet his father. In a while both armies, advancing from opposite directions, came face to face with each other, and camped on the opposite banks of Gogra (Sarayu), a tributary of Ganga at the frontier of the two kingdoms. Fortunately there was no clash between the two armies, quite probably because of the indulgent nature of Bughra Khan, whose objective in any case was not to subjugate or overthrow his son, but to induce him to be assertive and strong as a ruler. It was then decided that father and son should meet to resolve matters. There was however some squabble between the two camps about protocol, whether the sultan of Delhi should go to meet the sultan of Bengal, or whether the sultan of Bengal should go to meet the sultan of Delhi. But eventually Bughra Khan, affable as ever, crossed the river (at a time fixed by astrologers as auspicious) and went to Kaiqubad's camp

Kaiqubad received his father with regal pomp, in court, sitting on the throne and attended by arrayed nobles. Approaching the throne, Bughra Khan, as Barani describes the scene, 'bowed his head to the earth, and three times kissed the ground, as required by the ceremonial of the Delhi court.' But the sight of his father prostrating before him so overwhelmed Kaiqubad with emotion that he flung aside all formalities, and, 'descending from the throne, cast himself at his father's feet . . . Father and son then burst into tears and embraced each other . . . and the sultan rubbed his eyes upon his father's feet. This sight drew tears also from the eyes of the beholders too. The father then took his son's hand and led him to the throne, intending himself to stand before it for a while; but the sultan got down, and conducting his father to the throne, seated him there on his right side. Then, getting down, he bent his knees, and sat respectfully before him . . . Afterwards they had some conversation together in private. And then Bughra Khan retired across the river to his own camp.'

Would the father's advice be heeded by the son? Bughra Khan was sceptical. Returning to his camp he commented: 'I have said farewell to my son and to the kingdom of Delhi, for I know full well that neither my son nor the throne of Delhi will long exist.'

That presentiment came true. The gist of Bughra Khan's advice to his son was to mend his easy-going ways, get rid of Nizam-ud-din, and take charge of the government. Returning to Delhi, Kaiqubad did indeed for a while heed his father's advice; he transferred Nizam-ud-din to Multan, and, when he hesitated to leave, had him poisoned. But the change of his ways did not last long. In an engaging story told by Barani, one day 'a lovely girl met him on the road, and addressed some lines of poetry to him . . . The sultan was overpowered by her charms . . . [He] called for wine, and, drinking it in her presence, himself recited some verses, to which she in turn replied in verse.'

The incident signalled Kaiqubad's reversion to his old self-indulgent ways; indeed, he now immersed himself deeper in debauchery, to make up for the lost days of pleasure. He thereafter paid no attention at all to the affairs of the state. That created a power vacuum in Delhi, and presently the empire swirled into total chaos. 'What little order had been maintained in the government was now entirely lost,' comments Barani. 'The affairs of the court now fell into the greatest confusion.'

Kaiqubad himself came to a wretched end. He was now struck by paralysis, and was confined to bed, barely alive. The nobles then placed his three-year-old son, Kayumars, on the throne, and set up a regency council to administer the empire. But there were divisions and deadly rivalries among the nobles, and the contending cabals plotted against each other, and drew up black lists, planning to eliminate their opponents.

Out of this churning chaos, a new leader rose to the top, Malik Jalal-ud-din Khalji, the commander of the army. As the political chaos in Delhi became worse confounded, Khalji, who was stationed in a suburb of Delhi, sent his sons in a daring foray into the city, and had the infant sultan seized and brought to his camp. 'The sons of Jalal-ud-din, who were all audacious fellows, went publicly at the head of 500 horse to the royal palace, seized the infant sultan, and carried him off to their father,' writes Barani. 'This created great excitement in the city; the high and low, small and great, poured out of the twelve gates of the city, and took the road . . . to rescue the young prince.' But the kotwal (whose sons were held as hostages by Jalal-ud-din) appeased them and persuaded them to return to the city.

Jalal-ud-din then assumed the office of Naib, and ruled the kingdom in the name of Kaiqubad. This charade went on for three months. Then one day Jalal-ud-din sent one of his officers and had Kaiqubad murdered. 'This man . . . found the sultan lying at his last gasp in the room of mirrors,' records Barani. 'He despatched him with two or three kicks, and threw his body into Yamuna.'

It was a sordid end to a sordid life. Nothing is known about what happened to the infant sultan. Jalal-ud-din then formally ascended the throne. And with that began a new epoch in the history of the Delhi Sultanate.

PART IV

KHALJIS

I issue such orders as I consider to be for the good of the state, and the benefit of the people . . . I do not know whether this is lawful or unlawful. Whatever I think to be for the good of the state, or suitable for the emergency, that I decree.

—SULTAN ALA-UD-DIN KHALJI

1

The Reluctant Sultan

Jalal-ud-din Khalji ascended the throne in mid-June 1290. His coronation was held in Kilughari, a suburb of Delhi, not in the city, for he thought it would be imprudent for him to enter the city then, as the dominant Turkish population of Delhi was hostile to him, considering him to be an Afghan usurper, not a Turk. The people of Delhi, observes Barani, 'hated Khalji maliks . . . [They] had been for eighty years governed by sovereigns of Turkish extraction and were averse to the succession of Khaljis . . . They said that no Khalji had ever been a king, and that the race had no right or title to [the throne of] Delhi.' Though Islam does not discriminate against people on the basis of their race, Muslim communities often did show such prejudices.

The prejudice of Turks was however misplaced in this case, for Khaljis were actually ethnic Turks. But they had settled in Afghanistan long before the Turkish rule was established there, and had over the centuries adopted Afghan customs and practices, intermarried with the local people, and were therefore looked down on as non-Turks by pure-bred Turks.

This snobbish aversion of the old Turkish nobility in Delhi for Khaljis did not however last long. Presently, as was to be expected, the nobles generally acquiesced to Jalal-ud-din's accession and flocked to him, their material interests overriding their tribal prejudice. Besides, as Barani comments, 'the excellence of Jalal-ud-din's character, his justice, generosity, and devotion, gradually removed the aversion of the people.'

Jalal-ud-din nevertheless decided not to take up his residence in Delhi, presumably to avoid rousing the antagonism of the people there, and also because he felt that it would be presumptuous for him to sit on the throne of Balban, his former lord. So he completed the palace complex and gardens left unfinished by Kaiqubad at Kilughari, and took up his residence there. The princes and the nobles too then built their bungalows there, and soon several bazaars also came up there. 'In three or four years houses sprang up on every side, and the markets became fully supplied,' reports Barani. The suburb then came to be known as Shahr-i-Nau, the New City.

Jalal-ud-din was in his seventies when he ascended the throne. His old age and long subservient service under the Delhi sultans made him rather unassertive as a monarch, and this was disappointing to his pugnacious clansmen and relatives, who wanted to flaunt their newly acquired power and status, and advance the interests of their clan. Typically, when Jalal-ud-din first entered Delhi as sultan and went to the Red Palace of Balban, he, instead of riding into the courtyard of the palace, as sultans did, respectfully dismounted at the gate. And on entering the palace he wept bitterly, thinking of the inconstancy of temporal fortunes, and remembering how he had on so many occasions stood before the great sultan in humility and awe, but how now a dreadful misfortune had fallen on the sultan's family.

JALAL-UD-DIN'S ACCESSION TO the throne, instead of inflating his ego, instilled in him great humility. Though he, as the warden of the western marches, was reputed for his fierce martial spirit, now, as sultan in his old age, he turned out to be, in the eyes of his clansmen, disgustingly mild, more concerned with his afterlife than with his temporal life. Although Jalal-ud-din on his accession did favour his sons and several of his relatives and clansmen with appointments to important positions in the kingdom, that only fuelled their personal ambitions for even higher positions, and made them still more disgruntled with the sultan.

Jalal-ud-din's ostentatious displays of humility were particularly embarrassing to Khalji nobles. He would not punish even those who sought to overthrow him. Thus when Malik Chhajju, a nephew of Balban and the governor of Kara in Uttar Pradesh, rebelled and advanced on Delhi with an army to claim the throne as his inheritance, but was defeated and brought in chains before the sultan, Jalal-ud-din was moved to tears on seeing the prince in bonds, and he not only released him but also entertained him with wine in his private chambers, even spoke appreciatively of the rebel's loyalty to his uncle. And when one of the sultan's nobles upbraided him saying that his conduct was 'unseemly and injudicious,' he said that he would rather relinquish the throne than ruin his afterlife by shedding the blood of fellow Muslims.

Similarly, when it was reported to Jalal-ud-din that a group of Turkish nobles in their cups were prattling about overthrowing and killing him—one of the nobles, notes Barani, 'said that he would finish off the sultan with a hunting knife, and another drew his sword and said he would make mince-meat of him'—his initial response was to dismiss the report, saying, 'Men often drink too much and say foolish things; do not report drunken stories to me.' But when these reports persisted, he one day summoned the tipplers to the court, flung down his sword before them and challenged, 'Is there one among you who is man enough to take this sword and fight it out fairly with me?' The abashed nobles then pleaded that their 'drunken ravings' should not be taken seriously. And the sultan, his eyes 'filled with tears at these words,' merely banished them from the court for a year. According to Barani, 'Jalal-ud-din always treated his nobles, officers, and subjects with the greatest kindness and tenderness. He never visited their offences with blows, confinement, or other severity, but treated them as a parent treats his children.'

This leniency of the sultan extended even to thieves, whom he often released after taking from them an oath that they would never again steal. Similarly, when a large number of Thugs, a murderous robber band, were captured near Delhi, the sultan's punishment for them was merely to transport them to Bengal and release them there!

ALL THIS DISGUSTED the Khalji nobles, and they, according to Barani, 'whispered to each other that the sultan did not know how to rule, for instead of slaying the rebels he had made them his companions . . . He had none of the awesomeness and majesty of kings, . . . [nor the qualities of] princely expenditure and boundless liberality, [nor] the . . . severity, by which enemies are repulsed and rebels put down.' In fact, one of his top nobles, Malik Ahmad Chap, the deputy lord chamberlain—whom Barani describes as 'one of the wisest men of the day'—one day boldly told Jalal-ud-din all this to his face, and warned him that his indulgent conduct would kindle rebellions, for 'punishments awarded by kings are warnings to men.' The sultan listened patiently to the harangue, but in the end he said, 'If I cannot reign without shedding the blood of Muslims, I would renounce the throne, for I cannot endure the wrath of god.'

This reluctance to shed the blood of fellow Muslims inhibited Jalal-ud-din even in his military campaigns. Thus when he invaded Ranthambhor in Rajasthan, and found that it would be difficult to capture the fort without a lot of bloodshed, he abandoned the campaign. And when Ahmad Chap chided him about it, he said: 'I am an old man. I have reached the age of eighty years, and ought to prepare for my death. My only concern should be with matters that may be beneficial [to me] after my death.'

But whatever be Jalal-ud-din's failings, no one could accuse him of cowardice or timidity, for he was a veteran of very many battles, particularly against fierce Mongols, and had won renown for his valour. Even his detractors, as Barani notes, conceded that Jalal-ud-din 'was not wanting in courage and warlike accomplishments.' His disengagement from military pursuits as sultan was not because of cowardice, but because of his assessment of the state of the Sultanate, and of the values and conduct that were appropriate for him in his old age. According to Amir Khusrav, Jalal-ud-din believed that the Sultanate was not strong enough to assert itself decisively, and that therefore the best policy for the sultan would be to rule with tolerance and mildness.

There is only one recorded instance of Jalal-ud-din behaving tyrannically. This was in the case of Sidi Maula, a bizarre dervish who had, according to Barani, 'peculiar notions about religion . . . He kept no servant or handmaid, and indulged in no passion. He took nothing from anyone, yet expended so much that people were amazed, and used to say that he dealt in magic.' He built a grand hospice in Delhi where a large number of people were served, twice every day, 'bounteous and various meals . . . as no khan or malik could furnish.'

The dervish was patronised by many of Delhi's elite, including Khan Khanan, the sultan's eldest son. But he had many enemies too, and they accused him of planning to assume the role of the Caliph. Jalal-ud-din, a hyper-orthodox Muslim, considered the dervish's beliefs and practices as abominable, so one day he ordered him to be manacled and brought to him at the royal palace. The sultan then expostulated with him for a while, presumably hoping to induce him to change his ways. But that was of no avail. Jalal-ud-din then, out of sheer exasperation, cried out: 'Oh . . . avenge me of this maula!' Immediately the dervish was set on with a dagger by a bystander, and was then trampled to death by an elephant on the orders of Arkali Khan, a son of the sultan. This sacrilegious act, according to the chroniclers of the age, brought divine wrath on the city in the form of a devastating dust storm—'a black storm arose which made the world dark,' states Barani—which was in a while followed by a severe famine.

DESPITE HIS OLD age, and his generally pacifist attitude, the embers of his fiery old spirit still smouldered in Jalal-ud-din, and they did sometimes flare up. This it did especially when he had to deal with Mongols, his old adversaries. Thus when a vast horde of well over 100,000 Mongols entered India in 1292, he promptly marched out against them, defeated their advance force in a fierce encounter, imposed peace on them on his own terms, and forced their main army to retreat from India. The sultan also gained a religious objective in this encounter, by inducing a few thousand Mongols to become Muslims and settle in a suburb of Delhi, where they came to be known as New Muslims. The sultan even gave one of his daughters in marriage to a Mongol prince, Ulghu, a descendant of Chingiz Khan, who had become a Muslim.

There were a couple of other major military campaigns during the reign of Jalal-ud-din, but the sultan himself had little to do with them, for they were organised and led by his nephew, Ala-ud-din, the governor of Kara. In the first of these campaigns, towards the close of 1292, Ala-ud-din invaded Malwa and raided Bhilsa town. The campaign yielded a vast booty, which Ala-ud-din then dutifully presented to the sultan, and was in turn rewarded by the sultan by adding Oudh to his fief.

The success of his Malwa campaign whetted Ala-ud-din's ambition. Soon he set out on a fresh campaign, to raid Devagiri, the capital city of the Yadava kingdom in Deccan, to which he was lured by the city's reputation for fabulous wealth. Devagiri, according to Barani, 'was exceedingly rich in gold and silver, jewels and pearls, and other valuables.' Ala-ud-din had only a relatively small contingent with him on this campaign, a cavalry force of just three or four thousand and a couple of thousand infantrymen, but the sheer speed and energy of his attack offset that limitation—he stormed into Devagiri in a lightening swift move, overpowered its king, Ramachandra, and seized from him a vast booty, and then sped back to Kara.

This was the first incursion into peninsular India by a Sultanate army, but its purpose was not to conquer territory, but to gather plunder. And the campaign had, for Ala-ud-din, a secret personal motive also—to obtain funds to finance his plan to usurp the throne of Delhi. In this he was instigated by his officers in Kara, who were formerly, a few years earlier, associated with the rebellion of Malik Chhajju. These officers told Ala-ud-din that the indispensable prerequisite for the success of his usurpation plan was to acquire adequate funds, to recruit a strong army, and to induce desertions from the enemy camp. 'Get plenty of money, and then it would be easy to conquer Delhi,' they advised. Ala-ud-din therefore did not seek, as was conventionally required, the sultan's permission for his Devagiri campaign, nor did he forward to the sultan the booty that he got there. The Devagiri campaign was the prelude to Ala-ud-din's rebellion.

THESE ACTIONS OF Ala-ud-din roused the suspicion of the nobles in Delhi about his intentions, and they warned Jalal-ud-din about it. But the sultan gave no credence to those warnings, for Ala-ud-din was his nephew (brother's son) and son-in-law, whom he had brought up from his childhood and had always treated as his own son. The sultan not only disregarded the warning of the nobles, but even upbraided them for their distrustful attitude. 'The guileless heart of the sultan relied upon the fidelity of Ala-ud-din,' notes Barani.

Meanwhile Ala-ud-din wrote to the sultan apologising for conducting the unauthorised campaign and promising to send all the booty to Delhi. And in Delhi, Ala-ud-din's brother Almas Beg worked on the sentiments of the sultan by telling him that Ala-ud-din was distraught with anxiety about the possible anger of the sultan, and was thinking of fleeing to Bengal, or even committing suicide. To reassure Ala-ud-din, the sultan then, on Almas Beg's entreaty, set out to Kara by boat on the Ganga, escorted by a small cavalry force travelling along the river bank on the right side. When the party reached Kara, they found Ala-ud-din's forces drawn up in battle array on the opposite bank, but this was explained by Almas Beg as the preparation to offer a formal, ceremonial reception to the sultan, and he persuaded him to go over to the riverbank where Ala-ud-din was waiting. The gullible sultan, now in his dotage, then crossed over to where Ala-ud-din stood, escorted by just a few royal attendants.

'The sultan,' writes Barani, 'was so blinded by his destiny that although his own eyes saw the treachery, he would not return . . . [When the sultan disembarked, Ala-ud-din] advanced to receive him . . . When he reached the sultan he fell at his feet, and the sultan, treating him as a son, kissed his eyes and cheeks, stroked his beard, gave him two loving taps upon the cheek, and said, "I had brought thee up from infancy, why art thou afraid of me?" . . . The sultan then took Ala-ud-din's hand, and at that moment the stony-hearted traitor gave the fatal signal . . . [and his officer assigned for the task] struck at the sultan with a sword. But the blow fell short and cut his own hand. He again struck and wounded the sultan, who then ran towards the river, crying, "Ah thou villain, Ala-ud din! What hast thou done!" . . . [Then another officer] ran after . . . [the sultan], threw him down, cut off his head, and bore it dripping with blood to Ala-ud-din.' All the royal officers who had accompanied the sultan across the river were also then slain. 'The venerable head of the sultan was then placed on a spear and paraded about . . . And while the head of the murdered sovereign was yet dripping with blood, the ferocious conspirators brought the royal canopy and elevated it over the head of Ala-ud din.'

The royal military escort on the opposite bank of the river watched this horrid scene with dismay, but there was nothing that they could do about it, as it would have been suicidal to cross the river and confront Ala-ud-din, as the sultan was already dead, and Ala-ud-din's army was very much larger than the sultan's military escort. So the royal contingent quickly retreated to Delhi. Meanwhile the spear-mounted severed head of Jalal-ud-din was sent around for display in the nearby areas, as the proof of Ala-ud-din's triumph and succession.

This was in July 1296. Jalal-ud-din had reigned for just six years when he was assassinated.

2

Sikandar Sani

When the news of the assassination of Jalal-ud-din reached Delhi, his widow, Malika-i-Jahan, immediately placed her youngest son, Qadr Khan, 'a mere lad', on the throne, presumably because her eldest surviving son, Arkali Khan, was away in Multan at that time, and the throne could not be left vacant. But this hasty act of the queen—whom Barani describes as 'one of the silliest of the silly'—created divisions among the Delhi courtiers. And it so upset Arkali Khan that he made no move to aid his mother and defend the family throne.

Ala-ud-din was at this time hesitating about his next move, but the news of Arkali Khan's discontent emboldened him to proceed to Delhi right away. As Ala-ud-din set out for Delhi he, in his characteristic spirit of caution and daring, took care to win over the local people to his side by literally showering on them, at every stage along his way to Delhi, gold and silver coins, by using a portable catapult. People in droves therefore flocked to him. A large number of soldiers also joined him along the way, so that in a couple of weeks, by the time he reached the environs of Delhi, his army burgeoned into a formidable legion of 50,000 horse and 60,000 infantry. In public perception the future now clearly belonged to Ala-ud-din, so there was a general scramble, particularly among the nobles and the top officers of the Sultanate, to join him. 'He then won over the maliks and amirs by a large outlay of money, and those unworthy men, greedy for gold . . . and caring nothing for loyalty . . . joined Ala-ud-din,' observes Barani. 'He scattered so much gold that the faithless people easily forgot the murder of the late sultan, and rejoiced over his succession.'

Meanwhile Malika-i-Jahan sent an army from Delhi under royal officers to block Ala-ud-din's advance, but they, instead of opposing him, promptly defected to him, and were, according to Barani, rewarded by Ala-ud-din with 'twenty, thirty, and even fifty mans of gold. And all the soldiers who were under these noblemen received each three hundred tankas.' In that predicament Malika-i-Jahan wrote to Arkali Khan in Multan requesting him to forgive her folly of raising her young son to the throne ('I am a woman, and women are foolish,' she wrote) and asking him to rush to Delhi and mount the throne. But Arkali—whom Barani describes as 'one of the most renowned warriors of the time', and would have probably made a great sultan—declined the offer, as most of the nobles had by then joined Ala-ud-din, and it was too late to stop him. She then sent Qadr Khan, the boy sultan, with an army to oppose Ala-ud-din, 'but in the middle of the night the entire left wing of his army deserted to the enemy with great uproar,' records Barani. Qadr Khan then hastily retreated to Delhi, and he and his mother collected whatever treasure they could immediately gather and fled from the city for Multan in the dead of the night.

Ala-ud-din then advanced on Delhi, even though it was, as Barani notes, 'the very height of the rainy season' and roads had turned into marshes. But his progress was slow, and it was only towards the end of 1296, some five months after he murdered his uncle, that he reached Delhi.

ALA-UD-DIN ENTERED DELHI with great pomp, and was formally enthroned there, and he took up his residence in the Red Palace of Balban. His immediate concern was to win over to his side the prominent people of the city, and this he successfully did by liberally scattering gold and honours among them. 'He had committed a deed unworthy of his religion and position, so he deemed it . . . [prudent] to cover up his crime by scattering honours and gifts upon all classes of people,' states Barani, whose own father and uncle were among the principal beneficiaries of Ala-ud-din's bounty. 'People were so deluded by the gold which they received that no one ever mentioned the horrible crime that the sultan had committed.'

After securing his position in Delhi, Ala-ud-din sent an army to Multan, where it captured Arkali Khan and Qadr Khan along with their principal followers. The princes were, on the orders of Ala-ud-din, immediately blinded, and were later put to death, and their mother was taken to Delhi and locked up in a prison. 'The throne was now secure. The revenue officers, the elephant keepers with their elephants, the kotwals with the keys of the fort, the magistrates, and the chief men of Delhi went over to Ala-ud-din, and a new order of things was established,' records Barani. 'His wealth and power were great, so whether individuals gave their allegiance or whether they did not, mattered little, for the khutba was read and coins were struck in his name.'

In the second year of his reign Ala-ud-din turned to the task of firming up his authority over the nobles. He had, during the early stages of his usurpation, distributed vast wealth among the nobles to win them over to his side, but he was sagacious enough to know that, though this was crucially beneficial to him initially, it entailed a major risk, as it inflated the ego of the nobles with the feeling that the sultan had come to power because of their support, and that he was now indispensably dependent on them for remaining in power. Ala-ud-din therefore, now that he was secure on the throne, wanted to make it clear to the nobles that instead of he being dependent on their support, they were dependent on his favour.

To prove this point he dismissed from service or otherwise disgraced several of his top officers. He was particularly severe with the nobles who had switched sides and had opportunistically joined him as he usurped the throne, deeming them to be untrustworthy men—those who had betrayed their former master could very well betray their present master as well, he felt. 'The maliks of the late king, who deserted their benefactor and joined Ala-ud-din, and received gold by *mans* and obtained employments and territories, were all seized in the city and in the army, and thrown into forts as prisoners,' records Barani. 'Some were blinded and some were killed. Their houses were confiscated . . . and their villages were brought under the public exchequer. Nothing was left for their children . . . Of all the amirs of Jalal-ud-din, only three were spared by Ala-ud-din . . . These three persons had never taken money from Sultan Ala-ud-din. They alone remained safe, but all the other Jalali nobles were exterminated root and branch.' Ala-ud-din spared the three high-principled loyalists of Jalal-ud-din, because he felt that such people could be trusted, and that their unfailing loyalty to their master merited respect.

ALA-UD-DIN WAS IN many respects a most unusual person—and a most unusual monarch. And he was amazingly successful in all that he did, even in the many revolutionary reforms that he introduced, some of which were far, far ahead of his times. 'The character and manners of Sultan Ala-ud-din were strange,' states Barani. 'He was bad-tempered, obstinate, and hard-hearted, but the world smiled upon him, fortune befriended him, and his schemes were generally successful. So he became . . . more reckless and arrogant . . . He was by nature cruel and implacable, and his only concern was for the welfare of his kingdom. No consideration of religion, no regard for the ties of brotherhood or filial relationships, no care for the rights of others, ever troubled him.' He was entirely unsentimental and ruthlessly efficient. Success was all that mattered to him.

And, most unusual of all in that age of minimal governments, Ala-ud-din ran a maximal government. There was hardly anything in the empire that he did not seek to control and manipulate. And he had to his credit the introduction of several daringly innovative and brilliantly successful administrative and economic reforms. Curiously, he was illiterate—as was the great Mughal emperor Akbar—but that proved to be an advantage for him, as he could innovate freely, without being burdened by conventional wisdom.

'He was a man of no learning and he never associated with men of learning. He could not read or write a letter,' scorns Barani. 'But when he became king, he came to the conclusion that polity and government are one thing, and the rules and decrees of religion are another. Royal commands belong to the king, legal decrees rest upon the judgment of kazis and muftis. In accordance with this opinion, whatever affair of the state came before him, he only looked to the public good, without considering whether his mode of dealing with it was lawful or unlawful. He never asked for legal opinions on political matters, and very few learned men visited him.'

Barani's comment that Ala-ud-din 'only looked to the public good' was meant as a criticism, but to the modern reader it would seem to be a high compliment. The sultan ruled his vast empire with firmness and energy, even with wisdom, and on the whole his rule was beneficial to the people, and under him they lived in greater security and comfort than under any other king of the Delhi Sultanate.

Ala-ud-din was undeniably one of the greatest rulers in Indian history. Unfortunately, in contrast to his splendid public achievements, he had to endure much misery in his private life. He had married his cousin, Jalal-ud-din's daughter, but she turned out to be a veritable shrew, as was her mother, and the two of them together made his domestic life utterly wretched. 'The wife of Ala-ud-din tormented him,' states Ibn Battuta, a fourteenth century Moorish traveller in India. The sultan was a maniac for control, but he could not control his wife. Though he had other wives, domestic disharmony would have been galling to him, especially as he was obsessed with being in control of everything.

The sultan compensated the miseries of his private life with outstanding achievements in his public life. 'One success followed another,' reports Barani. 'Despatches of victory came in from all sides; every year he had two or three sons born; affairs of the state went on according to his wish and to his satisfaction; his treasury was overflowing, boxes and caskets of jewels and pearls were daily displayed before his eyes; he had numerous elephants in his stables and 70,000 horses in the city and environs; two or three regions were subject to his sway; and he had no apprehension of enemies to his kingdom or of any rival to his throne.'

Ala-ud-din had several major military achievements to his credit. But he was not rapacious in his conquests, and was usually generous and honourable in his treatment of the rajas he subjugated, and he often reinstated them on their thrones as subordinate rulers. He was no doubt a despot, as the rulers of the age invariably were, but he was not a whimsical despot. All his policies were formulated, and actions taken, only after very careful consideration, not on impulse. He, as even Barani admits, usually 'consulted and debated with wise men by night and by day as to the best means' for achieving his goals. He was even amenable to criticism, and often rewarded those who boldly gave him sensible though unpalatable advice. And, most unusual and laudable of all, he had a genuine concern for the welfare of the common people. Also, contrary to what Barani says, Ala-ud-din enjoyed the company of scholars and creative people, and was a patron of Amir Khusrav and Amir Hasan, renowned poets.

ALA-UD-DIN WAS INVARIABLY successful in all his ventures, and his successes, if we are to believe Barani, fantastically inflated his ambition. 'His prosperity intoxicated him,' states Barani. 'Vast desires and great aims beyond him, or a hundred thousand like him, laid their seeds in his brain, and he entertained fancies which had never occurred to any king before him. In his exaltation, ignorance, and folly, he quite lost his head, forming the most impossible schemes and nourishing the most extravagant desires.'

Some of Ala-ud-din's schemes, as reported by Barani, were certainly megalomaniacal. 'If I am inclined, I can . . . establish a new religion and creed; and my sword, and the swords of my friends, will bring all men to adopt it,' he once told his nobles. He also dreamed of world conquest. 'I have wealth and elephants and forces beyond calculation. My wish is to place Delhi in charge of a vicegerent, and then I myself will go out into the world, like Alexander, in pursuit of conquest, and subdue the whole habitable world,' he vaunted. 'Every region that I subdue I will entrust to one of my trusty nobles, and then proceed in quest of another. Who is there that will stand against me?' He even assumed the title Sikandar Sani (Second Alexander), and had the title stamped on his coins and inserted in the *khutba* read at Friday prayers. 'His companions, although they saw his . . . folly and arrogance, were afraid of his violent temper, and applauded him,' comments Barani.

It was Barani's uncle Ala-ul Mulk, the kotwal of Delhi and one of the close associates of Ala-ud-din from the time before his accession, who finally opened the sultan's eyes to the absurdity of his chimeric schemes. This noble used to attend the royal court only on the new moon days because of his 'extreme corpulence,' but one day when he attended the court, the sultan asked his opinion about his grand projects. And the kotwal made bold to submit: 'Religion and law and creeds should never be made the subjects of discussion by Your Majesty, for these are the concerns of prophets, not the business of kings. Religion and law spring from heavenly revelation; they are never established by the plans and designs of man . . . The prophetic office has never appertained to kings, and never will . . . though some prophets have discharged the function of royalty. My advice is that Your Majesty should never talk about these matters.' The sultan, according to Barani, 'listened, and hung down his head in thought . . . After a while he said, "Henceforth no one shall ever hear me speak such words."'

But what about his plan for world conquest, Ala-ud-din then asked. 'The second design is that of a great monarch, for it is a rule among kings to seek to bring the whole world under their sway,' the kotwal admitted, but cautioned that what was possible for Alexander might not be possible for any king anymore. 'These are not the days of Alexander,' the kotwal cautioned. 'But what is the use of my wealth, and elephants and horses, if I remain content with Delhi, and undertake no new conquests?' the sultan persisted. 'What will then be said of my reign?' The kotwal then advised the sultan that before planning world conquest he should first effectively defend his kingdom against persistent Mongol incursions, and then conquer the vast unconquered regions of the Indian subcontinent. But even these practicable goals, the kotwal warned, would be difficult to achieve 'unless Your Majesty gives up drinking excessively, and keeps aloof from convivial parties and feasts.' Ala-ud-din was pleased with this frank and sensible counsel, and he honoured the kotwal with a robe of honour and various other valuable gifts.

ALA-UD-DIN HEEDED THE Kotwal's advice, and thereafter focussed his attention on realisable goals, such as expanding his empire and tightening its administration. And in both these he was exceptionally successful. There was a substantial expansion of the territory of the Delhi Sultanate during his reign, so the kingdom became the absolutely dominant political and military power in the subcontinent. But the sultan was not a rash adventurer. His military policy, as in everything else he did, was a potent combination of daring and caution. He took particular care to treat the conquered rajas honourably, and he cautioned his officers setting out on conquests that they should 'avoid unnecessary strictness' towards the rajas, and should treat them respectfully, so as to turn enemies into allies. And to ensure that his orders on all these matters were strictly carried out by his officers, Ala-ud-din kept himself fully informed about the movements and activities of his army, by setting up outposts all along its route, to carry news about the army to him, and to carry his instructions back to the army. As a result of these wise and benevolent and yet strict policies of the sultan, 'subjugated countries and enemies became his ardent supporters,' states Barani.

A major military concern of Ala-ud-din, as of most Delhi sultans, was to defend his kingdom against recurrent Mongol depredations across the north-western frontier of India. In the early part of his reign—in the eight years from 1298 to 1306—there were as many five major Mongol incursions into India, in some of which they plundered the very environs of Delhi, and in one instance even entered the city itself for looting.

The Mongol threat was primarily of plunder and carnage, not of territorial conquest. Their campaigns were rather like the raids of Mahmud Ghazni; and, like Mahmud, the only major Indian territory they seized was western Punjab, the gateway to India, which they had to keep open and under their control to facilitate their raids. Mongols were a mountain people, and they abhorred the hot, humid climate of the Indian plains. Nor did the prospect of a peaceful settled life in India suit their restless, turbulent nature. On the couple of occasions when bands of captured Mongols were induced by the sultan to settle down in the environs of Delhi, they could not bear to live there for long, and in time many of them fled back to Afghanistan and Central Asia. Even some two centuries later, when Babur invaded India and established the Mughal Empire, several of his chieftains disdained to settle down in India but returned to their homeland.

India was for the Mongols a fabulously rich land to plunder periodically, but not a desirable place to occupy and live. They raided India whenever they needed fresh loot, which was often, for plunder was essential for their sustenance, as preys were for predatory animals. There were presumably numerous Mongol raids into India during the Sultanate period, of which only the major ones are recorded in history. During most of these incursions they, when confronted by the Sultanate army, quickly fled back to Afghanistan, so as not to risk losing their loot by engaging in battles. It was only on very rare occasions that they stood their ground and fought. The many decisive Indian victories against Mongols that the Turkish chroniclers have recorded were in most cases quite probably hollow victories, merely chasing the fleeing Mongols.

The first recorded Mongol incursion into India during the reign of Ala-ud-din was in its second year, in early 1298, but they were as usual driven back by an army sent by the sultan. But they came again the very next year, a vast horde of some 200,000 men, who crossed the Indus and stormed towards Delhi, where they camped on the banks of the Yamuna, and besieged the city. On the approach of Mongols, the people in the suburbs of Delhi fled into the city for refuge, and that led to an acute shortage of provisions in the city and the near collapse of the civic order there. 'Great anxiety prevailed in Delhi,' reports Barani. 'All men, great and small, were in dismay. Such a concourse had crowded into the city that the streets and markets and mosques could not contain them.'

The Mongol problem had to be met head-on, Ala-ud-din then decided, and he set out from Delhi with his army to confront the raiders, though he was advised by the ever cautious kotwal to temporise with them rather than risk all in a battle. 'If I were to follow your advice, to whom can I then show my face?' the sultan asked the kotwal. 'How can I then go into my harem? Of what account will the people then hold me? And what would then happen to the daring and courage which is necessary to keep my turbulent people in submission? Come what may, I will tomorrow march into the plain of Kili.'

Fortunately, Mongols were routed in the ensuing battle. But they swept into India again a couple of years later, again with a very large cavalry force, and they once again headed straight for Delhi and camped on the banks of the Yamuna, plundering the suburbs of the city and even foraying into the city itself, forcing Ala-ud-din to take refuge in the fort of Siri. 'Such fear of Mongols and anxiety as now prevailed in Delhi had never been known before,' notes Barani. Fortunately, Mongols suddenly retreated on their own accord after two months, apparently sated with plunder. 'This . . . preservation of Delhi seemed, to wise men, one of the wonders of the age,' concludes Barani.

THE MONGOL RAIDS were a direct challenge to the authority of the sultan. They could not be allowed to go on, Ala-ud-din decided. It was not enough to drive back Mongols whenever they raided India, he held; what was needed was to take strong deterrent measures to avert their raids altogether. He therefore had the old forts along the route of Mongols repaired, and also had some new forts built, and he provided them all with stockpiles of weapons, provisions and fodder. Frontier forts 'were garrisoned with strong, select forces, and were ever kept in a state of defence preparedness; and the fiefs on the route of Mongols were placed under amirs of experience, and the whole route was secured by the appointment of tried and vigilant generals,' reports Barani.

But none of that deterred the Mongols, and they raided India again in 1305. This time however they avoided the strongly defended Delhi, but rampaged through the Doab—the tongue of land between Ganga and Yamuna—pillaging, burning and butchering. But once again they were routed by the Sultanate army. A large number of Mongols were taken as prisoners in this battle, some 8000 of them, and they were all then ruthlessly slaughtered, and their severed heads cemented into the walls of Ala-ud-din's fortress at Siri.

Despite that awful carnage, Mongols raided India again the very next year, but were once again routed. The slaughter in this battle, according to the early fourteenth century chronicler Wassaf, was several times greater than that in the previous battle, but the figure he gives seems exaggerated. 'After the battle an order was issued by Ala-ud-din to gather together the heads of all those who had been slain,' he writes. 'On counting them . . . they were found to amount to 60,000, and . . . a tower was built of these heads before the Badaun Gate [of Delhi], in order that it might serve as a warning . . . to future generations.'

This tower, according to Ferishta, could be seen there even two and a half centuries later, during the reign of Akbar. The Mongols who were captured were thrown under elephants to be trampled to death, and their women and children were sold into slavery. 'So many thousands [of Mongols] were slain in battle and in the city that horrid stenches arose' from the rotting bodies, reports Barani. 'Streams of blood flowed.'

This was the last major Mongol incursion into India during Ala-ud-din's reign; India was free of their menace during the last ten years of his reign, except for a minor incursion in 1307–08. Mongols were evidently deterred by the severity of the Ala-ud-din's reprisals against them; besides, they were at this time having internal troubles in Central Asia, which also hindered their activities. 'The Mongols conceived such a fear and dread of the army of Islam that all fancy for coming to Hindustan was washed clean out of their breasts,' comments Barani. 'All fear of the Mongols entirely departed from Delhi and the neighbouring provinces. Perfect peace and security prevailed everywhere.'

ALA-UD-DIN, LIKE MOST kings of the age, considered it his indispensable royal duty to conquer new territories, to demonstrate his spirit and might. Besides that, waging wars served three essential requirements of the medieval state: that of gathering booty to replenish the royal treasury, inspiriting its soldiers with the prospect of plunder, and keeping the army in fighting trim. Ala-ud-din therefore sent out his army for conquests nearly every other year of his reign, except in his last few years, when illness incapacitated him. But because of his anxiety about Mongol raids, these campaigns were initially, in the first decade of his reign, confined to Rajasthan, Madhya Pradesh and Gujarat, the regions close to Delhi. But later, after his apprehension about the Mongol raids waned, he sent his forces storming far afield, almost to the southern tip of India.

The first of the major expansionist military campaigns of Ala-ud-din was against Gujarat, in 1298, the second year of his reign. Though Gujarat had been raided and plundered by Turks several times previously, it had not yet been annexed by the Sultanate. The primary objective of Ala-ud-din too was to gather plunder, but he also intended to annex this commercially important region to his empire. The invading army 'plundered . . . all Gujarat,' reports Barani. 'The wives and daughters, the treasure and elephants of Raja Karna (of the Vaghela dynasty that ruled Gujarat at this time) fell into the hands of Muslims,' though the raja himself, along with a young daughter, managed to escape and take refuge with the king of Devagiri in Deccan.

After routing the raja, the Sultanate army advanced to the temple city of Somnath, plundered its renowned Shiva temple—which had been rebuilt after it was sacked by Mahmud Ghazni in the early eleventh century—and sent its idol to Delhi, where its fragments were laid on the ground at the entrance of the Friday Mosque for the faithful to tread on.

From Somnath the Sultanate army proceeded to the flourishing port city of Khambhat (Cambay), plundered its merchants and obtained a vast booty—and, what turned to be far more valuable to the sultan, the army there seized a young, handsome and exceptionally talented slave eunuch named Kafur, who bore the nickname Hazardinari (Thousand Dinars), as his original price was one thousand dinars. Taken to Delhi, Kafur became an intimate of the sultan—his 'beauty captivated Ala-ud-din,' says Barani—and he would in time play a central role in the history of the times.

The invasion of Gujarat, like everything else that Ala-ud-din did, was remarkably successful, and the kingdom was annexed by the Sultanate. But the success of the campaign was somewhat marred by a mutiny in the Sultanate army when it was on its way back to Delhi. The trouble erupted, according to Barani, when the generals demanded that all soldiers should hand over to them one-fifth of the spoils they got in Gujarat, and 'instituted inquisitorial inquiries about it' to ensure that this was done. Though the mutiny was easily suppressed, its ringleaders managed to escape. So when the army returned to Delhi, the families of the rebel leaders were, in reprisal, subjected to dreadful punishments. 'The crafty cruelty which had taken possession of Ala-ud-din induced him to order that the wives and children of the mutineers, high and low, should be cast into prison,' states Barani. 'This was the beginning of the practice of seizing women and children for the faults of men.' Further, Nusrat Khan, one of the army generals, whose brother had been murdered by the mutineers, in revenge 'ordered the wives of the assassins to be dishonoured and exposed to most disgraceful treatment; he then handed them over to vile persons to make common strumpets of them. Their children he caused to be cut to pieces on the heads of their mothers. Outrages like this are practised in no religion or creed. These and similar acts . . . filled the people of Delhi with amazement and dismay, and every bosom trembled.'

ALA-UD-DIN'S NEXT MILITARY target was the fort of Ranthambhor in Rajasthan. Though Rajasthan was not, in terms of spoils, a particularly inviting region for Turks to conquer, its control was of crucial strategic importance to the Sultanate, as the route from Delhi to central and peninsular India passed through the region. Rajasthan therefore had to be secured before the Sultanate could expand southward. Besides, it was dangerous for the Sultanate to let the turbulent Rajput rajas remain in power in the very backyard of Delhi. Moreover, Ranthambhor was an impregnable fort, which could serve as an excellent outpost of Delhi. All this made its conquest essential for the Sultanate.

Aibak had captured this fort during the early history of the Sultanate, but it had subsequently changed hands several times, and was at this time in the possession of a Rajput raja. Recognising the strategic importance of Ranthambhor, Ala-ud-din himself led the army against it, and he succeeded in capturing it after a protracted siege and much bloodshed. A factor in Ala-ud-din's success at Ranthambhor was the defection of the raja's minister, Ranmal, to him. Characteristically, after capturing the fort, Ala-ud-din executed Ranmal—the sultan had no tolerance for those who betray their masters, even in the instances in which he benefited from their defections. The raja of Ranthambhor, Hamir Deva, was also executed. The kingdom of Ranthambhor was then annexed by the Sultanate, and its fort was placed under the command of a Turkish general.

During the Ranthambhor campaign Ala-ud-din very nearly lost his life in a coup attempt by his brother's son, Akat Khan. This happened on the sultan's way to Ranthambhor, when he was diverting himself by hunting in a forest near his camp. It was early morning and he was sitting on a stool in a clearing in the woods, accompanied by just a few guards, waiting for the game to be driven towards him by his soldiers. As Barani describes the scene, seeing Ala-ud-din to be virtually defenceless, Akat Khan with a contingent of New Muslim cavalry soldiers galloped up to him, 'shouting "Tiger! Tiger!" and began to discharge arrows at him. It was winter, and the sultan was wearing a large overcoat. He jumped up . . . and seizing the stool on which he had been sitting, made a shield of it. He warded off several arrows, but two pierced his arm, though none reached his body.' Apparently he fainted then, because of the loss of blood. Meanwhile the sultan's guards covered him with their bucklers, and, as the attackers galloped up, they shouted that the sultan was dead. 'Akat Khan was young, rash and foolish. He had made a violent attack on his sovereign, but he lacked the decision and resolution to carry it through, and cut off the sultan's head. In his folly and rashness he took another course.'

Confronted by the royal guards who stood firm with their swords drawn around the fallen sultan, Akat Khan dared not dismount and lay his hands on the sultan. Instead he galloped back to the royal camp and 'seated himself on the throne of Ala-ud-din, and proclaimed to the people of the court in a loud voice that he had slain the sultan.' The courtiers believed him, as they felt that he would not have dared to sit on the throne if Ala-ud-din was not actually dead. So 'the chief men of the army came to pay their respects to the new sovereign. They kissed the hand of that evil doer and did homage. Akat Khan in his egregious folly then attempted to go into the harem,' but there his entry was barred by the guards who warned him that he had to first produce the sultan's severed head before he could enter the harem.

Meanwhile Ala-ud-din regained consciousness, and his attendants dressed his wounds. He then reflected on what had happened, and concluded that Akat Khan would not have dared to do what he did, if he did not have the support of many royal officers and courtiers. He therefore felt that it would not be safe for him to return to his camp, and that the best course of action for him would be to retreat somewhere and regroup his forces. But one of his officers strongly argued against that course of action, and urged him to return immediately to the camp, and assured him that as soon as the people in the camp realised that he was safe, they would flock to him.

Ala-ud-din heeded that advice. He then proceeded to the camp, and was on the way joined by many of his men, so that by the time he reached the camp he had an escort of five or six hundred solders. 'He immediately showed himself on a high ground, and being recognized, the assembly at the royal tent broke up, and his attendants came forth with elephants to receive him,' records Barani. 'Akat khan then rushed out of the tents and fled on horseback.' But he was pursued, captured and immediately beheaded. And those who had connived with Akat Khan's plot were 'scourged to death with thongs of wire.'

This was a testing time for Ala-ud-din. Around the time of the Ranthambhor incident, two other nephews of his, provincial governors, also rose in rebellion against him. But they were soon captured by royal forces and sent to the sultan in Ranthambhor, where he had them punished in his presence—'they were blinded by having their eyes cut out with knives like slices of a melon,' reports Barani. 'The sultan's cruel, implacable temper had no compassion for his sister's children.'

At this time there was also an insurrection in Delhi, in which a group of discontented officers under one Haji Maula—an officer of 'violent, fearless and malignant character,' as Barani describes him—broke into the royal treasury, took out bags of gold coins from there, and distributed the money among themselves and their followers, and raised a distant descendant of Iltutmish (pretentiously named Shahinshah—King of Kings) to the throne. Fortunately for Ala-ud-din, the rebellion fizzled out quickly—it was suppressed within a week by loyal officers, and the pretender and his sponsor, along with many of their followers, were put to death.

ALA-UD-DIN RETURNED TO Delhi from Rajasthan in mid-1301, but in early 1303 he once again set out for Rajasthan, this time to capture the fort of Chitor, the possession of which, like that of Ranthambhor, was strategically important to him, to secure the route of his planned campaigns into central and peninsular India. In addition to these compelling strategic considerations, Ala-ud-din, according to a colourful romantic legend, was drawn to Chitor by what he had heard about the enchanting beauty of Padmini, the queen of

Rana Ratan Singh of the kingdom. This legend has a few variations, but in broad terms the story is that Padmini spurned the sultan outright, and would not even agree to let him see her just once. The most she conceded was to allow him to fleetingly see her reflection in a mirror. But that momentary glimpse further inflamed Ala-ud-din's passion, and he decided to capture her somehow.

This inevitably led to a battle between the armies of the raja and the sultan, in which the vastly superior Turkish army vanquished the Rajput army, even though Rajputs fought with great valour. Rajputs then retreated into the fort, where they barricaded themselves and performed the awesome rite of *jauhar*, in which Padmini and all the women in the fort flung themselves into an immense blazing pyre built there, preferring death to dishonour. When that rite was over, the gates of the fort were flung open, and the raja and his men hurtled out into the plain and tore into the arrayed enemy army, to kill and be killed, till all the Rajputs perished.

This story is told with many colourful frills in the bardic lore of Rajasthan, but there is no record of it at all in any contemporary chronicle. All that Barani says about Ala-ud-din's Chitor campaign is that 'the sultan then led forth an army and laid siege to Chitor, which he took in a short time and returned home.' In fact, Amir Khusrav's statement that after taking Chitor, the sultan ordered the 'massacre of 30,000 Hindus,' specifically excludes the possibility of *jauhar* having been performed there on this occasion.

The story also does not quite match what we know of Ala-ud-din's character. He was a down-to-earth, hard-headed monarch, and it is unlikely that he had any serious romantic vulnerability. He did indeed seize and take into his harem the queens of some of the rajas he defeated, but that was for him like appropriating any other valuable asset of the enemy.

The earliest textual reference to the Padmini episode is in Malik Muhammad Jaisi's epic Hindi poem *Padmavat*. This was written in the mid-sixteenth century, nearly two and a half centuries after Ala-ud-din's conquest of Chitor, and is therefore of doubtful credibility. Moreover, *Padmavat* is a romance and not a historical work. The story is also mentioned by a few later chroniclers, such as Abul Fazl and Ferishta, but they were obviously just repeating popular legends. Still, despite all these negative factors, it is possible that there is some tiny kernel of truth in the story, though most of its details are clearly bardic embellishments.

IN 1305, TWO years after the capture of Chitor, Ala-ud-din sent his army into the kingdom of Malwa, which he had previously invaded, during his governorship of Kara, but whose rulers had since then, 'rubbed their eyes with the antimony of pride, and . . . had forsaken the path of obedience,' states Amir Khusrav. 'A select body of royal troops . . . suddenly fell on those blind and bewildered men . . . The blows of the sword then descended upon them, their heads were cut off, and the earth was moistened with . . . [their] blood.'

The capture of Malwa cleared the path for the expansion of the Sultanate into peninsular India. Other circumstances also favoured the southward expansion of the Sultanate. The Mongol incursions, which had troubled the Sultanate for several decades, ceased around this time, and that enabled Ala-ud-din to withdraw several divisions of his army from his western frontier, and send them sweeping deep into peninsular India. The Sultanate was also relatively free of provincial rebellions at this time. 'Wherever Ala-ud-din looked around upon his territories, peace and order prevailed,' writes Barani. 'His mind was free from all anxiety.' He could therefore launch into his expansionist ambitions with ease of mind.

Ala-ud-din was the first ruler of the Sultanate to extend his kingdom into peninsular India, and also the first to carry out raids deep into South India, bringing virtually the entire Indian subcontinent within the ambit of his army. But his objective in these campaigns was not to annex the entire region to his empire, but to gather plunder and to claim tribute from the local rulers.

His first target in the peninsula was Devagiri in western Deccan. This town had a special appeal for Ala-ud-din, for he had raided it when he was the governor of Kara, and it was the plunder that he got from there that provided him the resources he needed to successfully execute his plan to usurp the Delhi throne. Ala-ud-din had imposed a tribute on the raja of Devagiri during that campaign, but no tribute had been received from him for three years. So in 1307 he sent a large army into Devagiri to enforce its compliance. This army was commanded by Malik Kafur, who had entered the service of Ala-ud-din just a decade earlier but had since risen rapidly in official hierarchy, and was now designated as Malik Naib, Lieutenant of the Kingdom. The Devagiri campaign was Kafur's first major military assignment, and he executed it with expedition and efficiency, which would mark all his subsequent campaigns also. On capturing the Devagiri fort, he stripped it of all its treasures, seized its war elephants, and took them all to Delhi along with Ramadeva, the captured raja, his wives and children.

In Delhi the raja was received with courtesy and honour by Ala-ud-din. 'The sultan showed great favour to the raja, gave him a canopy, and the title Rai-i-rayan (King of Kings),' reports Barani. 'He also gave him a lakh of tankas, and [after a few months] sent him back in great honour, with his wives, children, and dependents, to Devagiri, which place he confirmed in his possession. The raja was ever afterwards obedient, and sent his tribute regularly as long as he lived.' Ramadeva would also provide invaluable assistance to the sultanate army in its subsequent campaigns in the peninsula; Devagiri in fact served as the base for Ala-ud-din's peninsular military operations.

There is an engaging romantic tale associated with the Sultanate's conquest of Devagiri, as with its conquest of Chitor, but this story has greater credibility, for it is told by the contemporary poet Amir Khusrav. The story, as told in *Ashiqa*, a long poem of Amir Khusrav, is that when Malik Kafur set out for Devagiri he was instructed by Ala-ud-din's Rajput wife Kamala Devi (formerly the queen of Gujarat) to look for her young daughter Deval Devi, whom her father Karna had taken with him when he fled from Gujarat and took refuge in Devagiri during Ala-ud-din's conquest of Gujarat some nine years earlier. The princess was now around 13 years old, and was betrothed to a son of the king of Devagiri. But while she was being escorted from her provincial residence to Devagiri for the marriage with the prince, a group of Sultanate soldiers, who were picnicking at the Ellora cave shrines, chanced upon her and seized her. She was then sent to her mother in Delhi, and there, according to the legend, Khizr Khan, Ala-ud-din's eldest son, fell desperately in love with her. She was, according to Isami, a mid-fourteenth century chronicler, 'a soul-enticing and heart-ravishing beauty . . . The beautiful girl captivated his heart and he became a slave of her coquetry and guiles.' The lovers were eventually, after many twists and turns of events, happily united in marriage.

IN 1309, THE very year after Malik Kafur returned to Delhi from Devagiri, Ala-ud-din sent him again into the peninsula, this time against Warangal, ruled by Prataparudra Deva of the Kakatiya dynasty. This was the second expedition that Ala-ud-din sent against Warangal. Six years earlier he had sent an army into the kingdom under the command of Fakhr-ud-din Jauna, the future Muhammad Tughluq. For some inexplicable reason Muhammad took the difficult and unfamiliar eastern route, through Orissa, to invade Warangal. Predictably, as in nearly everything that Muhammad would later do as sultan, the campaign failed disastrously—it was beset by the difficulties of the route and by incessant rains, and the army suffered a humiliating defeat in Warangal, and had to retreat in disarray.

Ala-ud-din's objective in his new campaign against Warangal was to gather booty and obtain tribute, so he instructed Malik Kafur that if the raja surrendered his treasure, elephants and horses, and agreed to send a yearly tribute, he 'should accept these terms and not press the raja too hard.' The Sultanate army this time sensibly took the traditional western route, and was on the way able to secure assistance and reinforcements from Ramadeva of Devagiri. The raja, notes Barani, 'sent men forward to all villages on the route, as far as the border of Warangal, with orders for the collection of fodder and provisions for the army, and warning that if even a bit of rope was lost [by the army] they would have to answer for it. He sent on all stragglers to rejoin the army, and he added to it a force of Marathas, both horse and foot. He himself accompanied the march several stages, and then took leave and returned.'

The raja of Warangal was reputed to have a huge army, and his fort had, apart from its stone walls, a strong earthen wall around it, which was so well-compacted that stones from catapults rebounded from it like nuts, according to medieval sources. The fort was also girded by two deep moats, one around the earthen wall, and the other around the fort itself. Predictably, the Sultanate army faced stubborn resistance there, but they eventually managed to fill up the outer moat, then breach the earthen wall, and storm the main fort. The raja then surrendered, and, according to Barani, presented to Kafur '100 elephants, 7000 horses, and large quantities of jewels and valuables. He (Kafur) also took from him a written engagement to annually send treasure and elephants [to Delhi].'

Among the treasures that Kafur got in Warangal was a fabulous diamond, which Amir Khusrav describes as 'unparalleled in the whole world.' It probably was the famed Koh-i-Nur (Mountain of Light) diamond, which the Mughal emperor Babur got in Agra when he captured the city in 1526, and which eventually, after it changed hands several times, became part of the British crown jewels in 1877, when Queen Victoria was proclaimed the empress of India. Babur estimated the value of the diamond to be so high as to be sufficient to feed the whole world for two days.

KAFUR RETURNED TO Delhi in June 1310, bearing very many camel loads of treasure, and was accorded a grand reception by the sultan. But he was too restless by nature to remain inactive in Delhi. So in November 1310, five months after he returned to Delhi, he again set out with his army, this time for South India. Advancing through Devagiri he headed for Dvarasamudra in Karnataka, the capital of Hoysala king Vira Ballala. The raja did not have the strength to oppose the invasion, so he prudently sued for peace, agreed to surrender his treasures, and send an annual tribute to Delhi. 'Thirty-six elephants, and all the treasures of the place fell into the hands of the victors,' reports Barani.

Kafur then set out for the Tamil country. He met with virtually no resistance there, as the local rajas and chieftains, realising, from the experience of the other peninsular kingdoms, the futility of resistance, fled on Kafur's approach, leaving their towns and temples to be freely plundered by the invading army. Though Kafur's progress this time was hampered by torrential rains and heavy floods, he nevertheless resolutely continued his southward thrust, plundering and ravaging the temple cities of Chidambaram and Srirangam, as well as the Pandyan capital Madurai. He then swerved eastward and headed for the temple town of Rameswaram on the shore of the Bay of Bengal, there to sack the town and pillage the temple. The Khalji army, writes Amir Khusrav, advanced to 'the shore of the sea as far as Lanka, and spread the odour of the amber-scented faith.'

This was the farthest point that any army from North India had ever penetrated into South India, and Kafur is said to have built a mosque in Rameswaram to mark that historic feat. Kafur's passage through South India was quick and easy, and he had to fight no major battles there, so he could return to Delhi in late October 1311, after having been away for less than one year. And he was once again received by Ala-ud-din with great honour, in a special durbar. Kafur had brought with him an immense booty—'612 elephants, 96,000 mans of gold, several boxes of jewels and pearls, and 20,000 horses,' according to Barani. The quantity of the booty brought by Kafur astonished the people of Delhi. 'No one,' comments Barani, 'could remember anything like it, nor was there anything like it recorded in history.'

The last major military campaign of Ala-ud-din's reign was against Devagiri, where Ramadeva's successor Singhana had turned refractory, and had defaulted the payment of tribute. So in 1313 the sultan sent Malik Kafur into Devagiri, and in the ensuing battle he defeated and killed the raja, and annexed the kingdom to the Sultanate. From Devagiri, Kafur then made forays into Telingana, Karnataka and Tamil Nadu, to reassert the supremacy of Delhi over the South Indian kingdoms. Kafur spent about three years in the peninsula, but was recalled to Delhi in 1315 due to Ala-ud-din's rapidly failing health.

These were the major military campaigns of Ala-ud-din's reign. Apart from these, there were several minor campaigns also during his reign. But the objective of Ala-ud-din in most of these campaigns was to gain political dominance, to gather plunder and to secure tribute, not to annex territory. His campaigns made Ala-ud-din absolutely the dominant ruler of India, but apart from Gujarat, Rajasthan, Malwa and Devagiri, very little new territory was brought under the rule of the Sultanate during his reign. In most cases, the defeated rulers were reinstated on their throne with honour, on their promise of paying regular tribute to the sultan. In this, as in everything else he did, Ala-ud-din was entirely pragmatic, as he found no merit in annexing faraway lands that he could not effectively govern.

3

Radical Reformer

Ala-ud-din 'shed more innocent blood than ever any Pharaoh was guilty of,' states Barani. But this comment is more an expression of Barani's hyper-orthodox prejudice against the unorthodox sultan than an objective assessment. Though Ala-ud-din was indeed a sanguinary despot, that was not a unique trait in him, but a common characteristic of most Delhi Sultans. What distinguished Ala-ud-din was not his despotism or brutality, but his radical and futuristic political and economic reforms, which greatly enhanced the power and efficiency of the government, and even promoted the welfare of the people.

Ala-ud-din was a daringly original and in many respects a startlingly modern reformer. Though he was illiterate, many of his reforms showed excellent grasp of economic planning and administrative control. And on the whole his reforms and regulations, particularly his market regulations, were greatly beneficial to people. A Sufi sage would later ascribe philanthropic motives to Ala-ud-din's market regulations, but that is a hyperbole. It is not that Ala-ud-din was indifferent to the welfare of the people—indeed, some of his statements specifically and strongly express his concern for the public weal—but the basic objective of all his policies and actions was to make the government more efficient and strong, and thus to consolidate and enhance royal power.

The sultan in the early years of his reign was beset by a number of political and socio-economic problems, and that convinced him that there was something very wrong with the polity of the Sultanate, and that sweeping reforms were imperative. He therefore decided to investigate, together with his advisors, the causes of the problems he faced, and to find efficient solutions for them—not just to solve the problems as they arose, but to prevent such

118

problems from ever again arising. And then, having determined the causes of the problems faced by the state, he took a number of sagacious policy decisions, and executed them with relentless resolve, so that not only did peace and security as never before prevail in the empire, but also his subjects by and large lived a more prosperous, contended and secure life than at any other time in the history of the Delhi Sultanate. 'During the whole period of Sultan Ala-ud-din's reign, the situation of the county was very good and prosperous,' concedes Barani. 'Administration was carried on efficiently and successfully.'

In all his policies and actions Ala-ud-din was entirely open-minded and pragmatic, unrestrained by political conventions and precedents, as well as by religious prescripts. 'Oh, doctor, thou art a learned man, but thou has had no experience,' he once told a kazi who presumed to advise him on politics. 'I am an unlettered man, but I have seen a great deal.' Practicality was the sole guide of Ala-ud-din. And he was entirely unsentimental in this, and would not allow even his tribal or blood relationships sway his judgements in any way.

ALA-UD-DIN WAS UTTERLY ruthless in the pursuit of his goals, and had no qualms whatever in slaughtering thousands of people in cold blood if that was necessary to consolidate his power and achieve his goals. Thus when a conspiracy of New Muslims against him was discovered, he unhesitatingly ordered the total extermination of the tribe. 'Twenty or thirty thousand New Muslims were killed, of whom probably only a few had any knowledge [of the intended revolt],' reports Barani. 'Their houses were plundered, and their wives and children turned out.'

Riots were fairly common in Delhi at this time, but Ala-ud-din put an end to them by dealing with the rioters with deliberate ferocity. 'By the sultan's command every rioter was most tenaciously pursued, and put to death,' reports Barani. 'Their heads were sawn in two and their bodies divided.' From Ala-ud-din's point of view, this was the right and proper thing to do, for it produced the desired result. 'After these punishments, breaches of peace were never heard of in the city,' concedes Barani.

Muslim religious leaders generally condemned many of the policies and actions of Ala-ud-din as irreligious and fiendish. But the sultan was unmoved by such excoriations. He, according to Barani, 'held that matters of administration have nothing to do with religious laws.' Even in his personal life Ala-ud-din was hardly religious. 'The sultan,' censures Barani, 'said no prayers, did not attend the Friday prayer in the mosque . . . He was not careful at all about prayers and religious fasting.'

Once when a kazi expounded to him what was lawful and unlawful according to Islamic conventions, Ala-ud-din told him, 'When troopers do not appear at the muster, I order three years pay to be taken from them. I place wine-drinkers and wine-sellers in pits of incarceration. If a man debauches another man's wife, I cut off his organ, and the woman I cause to be killed. Rebels . . . I slay; their wives and children I reduce to beggary and ruin. Extortion I punish with torture . . . and I keep the extortionist in prison, in chains and fetters, until every *jital* is restored. Political criminals I confine and chastise. Wilt thou say that all this is unlawful?'

The kazi then rose from his seat, and moved to the place reserved for suppliants in the durbar hall, and there placed his forehead on the ground in submission and said, 'My liege! Whether you send me, your wretched servant, to prison, or whether you order me to be cut in two, all these are unlawful, and finds no support in the sayings of the Prophet, or in the exposition of the learned.'

'The sultan,' records Barani, 'heard all this and said nothing, but put on his slippers and went into his harem.' The kazi too then went home. 'The next day he took the last farewell of all his people, made a propitiatory offering, and performed his ablutions. Thus prepared for death, he proceeded to the court.' But contrary to general expectation, Ala-ud-din called the kazi forward and honoured him with a ceremonial robe, and presented to him a large sum of money. Strong himself, Ala-ud-din appreciated strength and candour in others. And he said to the kazi: 'Although I have not studied the Science or the Book, I am a Mussulman of a Mussulman stock. To prevent rebellion, in which thousands perish, I issue such orders as I consider to be for the good of the state and the benefit of the people . . . I do not know whether this is lawful or unlawful. Whatever I think to be for the good of the state, or suitable for the emergency, that I decree.'

Self-willed, Ala-ud-din always made up his own mind on all matters, but he also took care to hold detailed consultations with his top officers on all important issues, and to ponder over their views before deciding on what he should do. And he encouraged his courtiers to speak to him frankly. 'Rest assured that I will not harm you,' he once told a kazi. 'Only reply with truth and sincerity to whatever question I may put to you.'

Ala-ud-din was ruthless, but not thoughtless. And he applied himself unswervingly to the implementation of his policies—he was as meticulous in the execution of his plans, as he was in their conception. Because of all this, most of his reforms were successful, even though many of them were daringly innovative and way ahead of the times.

ONE OF THE immediate concerns of Ala-ud-din on his accession was to secure the integrity of the empire by effectively dealing with the perennial problem of insurgency plaguing the Sultanate, caused by his ambitious close relatives and top nobles aspiring to usurp the throne, and by provincial governors seeking to establish independent kingdoms. There was also the recurrent problem of subordinate Hindu rajas and chieftains seeking to regain their independence.

There were four successive insurrections in the early part of Ala-ud-din's reign, one of which very nearly led to his overthrow and assassination. These crises prompted Ala-ud-din to ponder over what he needed to do to prevent the recurrence of rebellions and to ensure that his government ran smoothly.

Ala-ud-din then, as usual, held extensive discussions with his councillors—'for several nights and days,' according to Barani—to decide on how to deal with the problem of insurgency. He then concluded that there were four basic causes for insurrections: 1/ The sultan's neglect of public affairs, and his inattention to the activities of his subjects. 2/ Convivial wine parties held by nobles, which were occasions for loose talk and the hatching of conspiracies. 3/ 'The intimacy, affection, alliances, and intercourse of maliks (military commanders) and amirs (noblemen) with each other, so that if anything happens to one of them a hundred others get mixed up in it.' 4/ 'Money, which engenders evil and strife, and brings forth pride and disloyalty. If men had no money, they would attend to their own business, and would never think of riots and revolts, [and would not be able to win the support] of low and turbulent people.'

After thus deciding on the nature of the problems that the state faced, Ala-ud-din set about devising solutions to them. And these solutions, like much else that he did, were audaciously original and yet eminently practical, though also quite harsh. His first measure was to deprive the people of the material means and the leisure to hatch rebellions, by yoking them to the drudgery of earning their livelihood and preventing them from accumulating wealth. The sultan, reports Barani, 'ordered that wherever there was a village held by proprietary right, in free gift, or as a religious endowment, it should . . . be brought back under the exchequer. People were pressed and amerced, money was exacted from them on every kind of pretence. Many were left without any money, till at length it came to pass that excepting maliks and amirs, officials, Multanis (moneylender-traders) and bankers, no one possessed even a trifle of cash. So vigorous was the confiscation that, beyond a few thousand tankas, all the pensions, grants of land and endowments in the country were appropriated [by the state]. The people were all then so absorbed in obtaining the means of living that the name of rebellion was never mentioned.'

Ala-ud-din's second measure was to set up an elaborate intelligence network, to gather information on all that was going on in the empire, which he considered to be the absolute prerequisite for running an efficient government. This intelligence gathering was done with such thoroughness that, according to Barani, 'no one could stir without the sultan's knowledge, and whatever happened in the houses of nobles, great men, and officials was communicated to the sultan by his reporters. Nor were the reports neglected, for explanations . . . [on the matter reported] were demanded [from the nobles]. The system of reporting went to such a length that nobles dared not speak aloud even in the largest palaces, and if they had anything to say, they communicated it by signs. In their own houses, night and day, dread of the reports of spies made them tremble. No word or action which could provoke censure or punishment was allowed to transpire. The transactions in the bazaars, the buying and selling, and the bargains made, were all reported to the sultan by spies.'

'THIRDLY, HE PROHIBITED wine-drinking and wine-selling, as also the use of intoxicating drugs. Dicing also was forbidden . . . Vintners and gamblers and beer-sellers were turned out of the city,' reports Barani. The sultan, according to his courtier poet Amir Khusrav, considered wine as 'the mother of all wickedness,' and he himself now entirely gave up drinking wine and holding wine parties. All the china and glass vessels in the royal banqueting room were smashed, and jars and casks of wine in the royal cellars were emptied on the road—so much wine was poured into the streets that pools and puddles formed there as in the rainy season, reports Barani.

To enforce prohibition, Ala-ud-din ordered that 'taverns should be set on fire, and that drummers should go around proclaiming vigorously that whoever drinks will be punished severely,' reports Isami. All prohibition violators who were caught were imprisoned. And when jails became filled up with prisoners, which they soon did, a number of them were, according to Barani, confined in 'pits for the incarceration of offenders dug outside the Badaun gate [of Delhi], which is a great thoroughfare.' Many died in these pits, and many 'were taken out half-dead.'

But nothing could prevent the habitual imbibers from finding some way to circumvent the prohibition rules and gratify their craving. Clandestine distilling and consumption of liquor now became common, and many travelled to the suburbs of Delhi to enjoy their drinks in peace and at leisure. A good amount of liquor was also smuggled into Delhi 'by hundreds of tricks and devices, and by all sorts of collusion.' These widespread violations of prohibition rules eventually constrained Ala-ud-din to modify the rules and permit private distillation and drinking of liquor, provided that liquor was not sold or consumed publicly, and that 'drinking parties were not held.' Prohibition was the only measure of Ala-ud-din that did not quite succeed.

Ala-ud-din also banned prostitution, as a companion measure to prohibition. The prostitutes then had to 'sit in their houses, patching up their skirts with the greatest repentance and rubbing their hands together,' states the Khusrav. 'All the roots of sin and avarice have been cut off.'

The last of Ala-ud-din's socio-political regulations was to virtually forbid the holding of convivial parties by nobles, by ordering that 'noblemen and great men should not visit each other's houses, or give feasts, or hold meetings,' reports Barani. Marriage alliances between noble families were now required to be formed only with the consent of the sultan. Inevitably, 'feasting and hospitality fell quite into disuse' in Delhi.

ALONG WITH THESE socio-political regulations, Ala-ud-din also introduced certain administrative reforms, which were essential for the effective implementation of his policies and for the smooth functioning of the government. He paid special attention to the lower rungs of bureaucracy, particularly to those working in the districts, for these officers, Ala-ud-din knew, were the foundation stones of the state's administrative superstructure, and any weakness in them would adversely affect the efficiency of the entire government. All through the history of the Delhi Sultanate, nearly all subordinate government officers were Hindus, and among them the conduct of the hereditary revenue collectors was a major concern for Ala-ud-din, for many of them were notoriously corrupt, lording over the peasants and gorging on the produce of their hard labour, and also cheating the government of its dues.

Ala-ud-din therefore sought to curb the powers of the traditional village officers by depriving them of their privileges and withdrawing the perquisites and concessions that they had traditionally enjoyed, thus in effect reducing them to the level of common peasants. 'I have discovered that the khuts and muqaddams (village headmen) ride upon fine horses, wear fine clothes, shoot with Persian bows, make war upon each other, and go out hunting; but of the tribute, poll tax, house tax and pasture tax, they do not pay even one jital (coin),' Ala-ud-din observed. 'They levy separately the khut's share from the villages, give parties and drink wine, and many of them pay no tax at all . . . Nor do they show any respect for my officers . . . I have therefore taken measures . . . so that at my command they are ready to creep into holes like mice.' The suppression of the arbitrary powers of village chieftains and revenue collectors not only facilitated the efficient functioning of the government at the local level, but also benefited peasants, as it freed them from the oppressions and extortions of by chieftains.

Another important administrative measure of Ala-ud-din was to deal with the corruption of royal officials, which was endemic in the Delhi Sultanate. Government servants, the sultan noted, 'were in the habit of taking bribes and committing embezzlements . . . They falsify accounts and defraud the state of revenue.' Ala-ud-din dealt with this problem with a two-pronged measure. On the one hand, he kept strict surveillance over the work of government servants, and inflicted severe punishments on the corrupt, so that 'it was no longer possible for anyone to take one tanka (coin) or any single thing from either a Hindu or Mussulman by way of bribe.' At the same time the sultan increased the salaries of officials so that they would not have any survival compulsion to resort to corruption—'I have directed that the salary of superintendents and other officials shall be fixed at such a rate as to allow them to live respectably,' he announced.

ONE OF THE topmost concerns of Ala-ud-din throughout his reign was to maintain the strength and discipline of his army. That was essential for preserving the integrity of the empire against the persistent problems of provincial rebellions and Mongol raids. Besides, the booty that military campaigns brought was a major source of revenue for the Sultanate. In view of all this Ala-ud-din quite early in his reign decided, according to Barani, that the one indispensable requirement for the maintenance of the stability and security of the empire was to have a large standing army—'and not only a large, but a choice army, well-armed, well-mounted, with archers, and all ready for immediate service.'

But the maintenance of such an army would involve enormous expenditure, which would empty the royal treasury in just a few years, Ala-ud-din realised. The only way that this could be managed was to substantially lower the salaries of officers and soldiers. And for this to be feasible, it was necessary to bring down the prices of provisions and other essential supplies, so that soldiers could maintain a good standard of living on a low salary. But how could the prices of provisions be brought down? 'The sultan then consulted with his most experienced ministers as to the means of reducing the prices of provisions without resorting to severe and tyrannical punishments,' reports Barani. 'His councillors replied that the necessaries of life would never become cheap until the price of grain was fixed by regulations and tariffs.'

Heeding that advice, Ala-ud-din then issued a series of seven market regulations. First of all, he issued an order regulating the prices of grains, and this was so rigorously enforced that 'this scale of prices was maintained as long as Ala-ud-din lived . . . whether the rains were abundant or scanty,' states Barani in his detailed report about the price control measures of Ala-ud-din. Secondly, to ensure that traders complied with the regulated prices, the sultan appointed a senior officer, 'a wise and practical man,' as the controller of markets.

But prices could not be controlled through administrative measures alone, Ala-ud-din knew. He was well aware that the key means to control prices was to control supplies, and that the royal order fixing prices could be maintained only if it was backed by balancing supply and demand. Therefore, to regulate the supply of grain, he ordered, as his third measure of market control, that 'all the *khalisa* villages (whose revenues were reserved for the royal treasury) in the Doab should pay their tribute in kind,' and that those in some of the other nearby areas should pay half their tribute in grain. As a result of this order, grains from the districts arrived in Delhi in caravans, so 'there never was a time when there were not two or three royal granaries full of grain in the city. When there was a deficiency of rain, or when for any reason the caravans [bringing grain] did not arrive, and grain became scarce in the markets, then the royal stores were opened and the corn was sold at the tariff price.'

To further regulate the supply of essential goods, Ala-ud-din 'ordered that the names of all the merchants of the empire, whether Mussulmans or Hindus, should be registered in the book of the Diwan . . . Merchants were required to sign engagements whereby they were compelled to bring a certain quantity of wares to town and to sell them at the rates fixed by the sultan.'

Fourthly, Ala-ud-din placed grain dealers and transporters under the authority of the controller of markets. And to control them effectively, they, along with their families, were forced to settle in villages along the Yamuna near Delhi, and a supervisor was placed over them to ensure their proper conduct.

The fifth market control measure of Ala-ud-din was to prohibit regrating. 'This was so rigidly enforced that no merchant, farmer or retailer, or anyone else could hold back secretly . . . [even a small amount of grain, or sell even a small amount of it] above the regulated price.' Sixthly, 'engagements were taken from provincial revenue officers and their assistants that they would ensure that the corn-carriers were supplied with corn by peasants on the field at a fixed [farm] price.' The order also thoughtfully granted that, 'to give the villagers a chance of profit, they were [to be] permitted to carry their corn into the market and sell it at the regulation [market] price.'

Lastly, the sultan maintained a hands-on control over the market by requiring three different sources—market superintendent, reporters and spies—to send to him daily reports on market rates and transactions. He also took care to ensure that the three sources served as checks on each other, in order to prevent any of them from falsifying their reports in any way.

'ALL THE WISE men of the age were astonished at the evenness of the price [of grains] in the markets,' comments Barani. Whether the season was favourable or unfavourable for cultivation, there was no scarcity of provisions in Delhi, and their prices remained unvarying. 'This was indeed the wonder of the age, which no other monarch was able to achieve.' Even luck favoured Ala-ud-din, for the monsoon was regular during most of his reign, and harvests were abundant.

Controlling the prices of food-grains was only the first step in Ala-ud-din's market control measures, which in their final formulation were very comprehensive, and covered virtually the entire gamut of market operations.

The prices of 'piece goods, garments, sugar, vegetables, fruits, animal oil, and lamp oil' were all regulated by Ala-ud-din, notes Barani. The prices of maid servants and concubines, as well as of male slaves, were also fixed. 'The price of a serving girl was fixed from five to twelve tankas, of a concubine at 20, 30, or 40 tankas. The price of a male slave was 100 or 200 tankas or less . . . Handsome lads fetched from 20 to 30 tankas; the price of slave labourers was 10 to 15 tankas, and of young domestic slaves 17 or 18 tankas . . . Great pains were taken to secure low prices for all things sold in the stalls in the markets, from caps to shoes, from combs to needles . . . Even in the case of articles of the most trifling value, the sultan took the greatest trouble to fix their prices and settle the profit of the vendors.' In the case of luxury items, their purchase was permitted only with the written permission of the Diwan.

These price control measures were enforced with great rigour, with Ala-ud-din personally inquiring regularly into all aspects of market operations in every bazaar in Delhi. Violators of the price regulations were severely punished. Merchants then sought to circumvent the price regulations by using short weights—'They sold their goods according to the stipulated rate, but they cheated the purchasers in the weight, especially ignorant people and children,' reports Barani. Ala-ud-din investigated this matter by sending children to buy various things and take them to him, and he then had the items weighed. If any deficiency was found, 'the inspector took from . . . [the particular] shop whatever was deficient, and afterwards cut from the shopkeeper's haunches an equal weight of flesh, which was thrown down before his eyes. The certainty of this punishment kept the traders honest, and restrained them from giving short weight and resorting to other knavish tricks.'

'From fear of the police, people both high and low, whether belonging to the market or not, became careful about their behaviour, obedient, and submissive, and subdued with fear and awe,' continues Barani. 'Nor did anyone dare to swerve a needle's point from the letter of the law, to increase or diminish any of the royal standard prices, or to indulge in vain desires and excesses of any sort.'

These were all restrictive measures, which kept the market operations within the parameters prescribed by Ala-ud-din. But the sultan also initiated certain positive measures to stimulate the economy, such as advancing money from the royal treasury to traders for financing their business, and freeing cultivators from exploitation by village chieftains.

ALA-UD-DIN SUPPLEMENTED THESE market regulations with a number of revenue reforms, to augment the financial resources of the empire. He collected a variety of urban and rural taxes, and took particular care to systematise agricultural taxes, which were by far the main sources of revenue of the state. He classified farmlands into different categories, and assessed tax on them on the basis of the average yield per given measure of land in a given area. 'Half [the produce] was required to be paid [as tax] without any diminution,' states Barani. In addition to the tax on agricultural produce, peasants had to pay tax on milch cattle, as well as a general grazing tax.

All these revenue measures were rigorously enforced by the sultan. 'People were brought to such a state of obedience that one revenue officer could string together by the neck twenty khuts, muqaddams and chaudharys (village headmen) and enforce payment by blows,' notes Barani. 'Blows, confinement in the stocks, imprisonment and chains, were all employed to enforce payment.'

Ala-ud-din preferred to collect taxes directly from cultivators rather than through village headmen. This was done to prevent tax collectors from cheating the government, or exploiting peasants, and to ensure, as Barani notes, that 'the burden of the strong might not fall upon the weak, and there might be but one law for the payment of the revenue for both the strong and the weak.' The tax pressure of Ala-ud-din was on the rich, not on the poor. Characteristically, he abolished the various concessions and privileges that village headmen had traditionally enjoyed, and collected from them the full tax due on their lands. He also prohibited them from levying on cultivators any cess of their own. This severity of Ala-ud-din with village headmen and traditional tax collectors was beneficial to common peasants, towards whom the sultan was generally protective.

Ala-ud-din was also strict in dealing with parasitic government tax officials, as he was in dealing with village headmen and traditional rural tax collectors. Royal officers who held land grants in lieu of pay were strictly forbidden to levy any additional cesses on their own. And 'collectors, clerks, and other officers employed in revenue matters, who took bribes and acted dishonestly, were all dismissed,' notes Barani. 'There was no chance of a single tanka being taken dishonestly or as bribe from any Hindu or Mussulman. The revenue collectors and officers were so coerced and checked that for [cheating the government even] five hundred or a thousand tankas they were imprisoned and kept in chains for years . . . [Consequently] clerkship came to be considered . . . [a wretched profession], and no man would give his daughter to a clerk. Death was deemed preferable to revenue employment.'

THE MARKET AND revenue reforms of Ala-ud-din resulted in a substantial reduction in the prices of essential commodities. And this enabled the sultan, as he had planned, to regulate the salaries of soldiers, and to increase the size of his army. 'At the present time the imperial army consists of 475,000 . . . warriors, whose names are recorded by the imperial muster-master, and whose pay and rations are entered in the regulations of the deputy-victualler,' records Wassaf. There was also an increase in the number of war elephants in the Sultanate army at this time—according to Wassaf, there were as many as 400 elephants in the royal stables alone.

The army of Ala-ud-din was quite probably the largest, the best organised, and the best equipped army in the entire history of the Delhi Sultanate. The sultan took particular care to ensure that soldiers and their equipment met his quality specifications. 'All the men were inspected by the muster-master. Those who were skilled in archery and the use of arms passed, and were paid the price of their horses. The horses were then branded,' notes Barani. These soldiers were paid in cash, instead of with land assignments, as was usually done by the Delhi sultans. Ala-ud-din met the cash requirement for this by appropriating all the land near Delhi in the Doab as khalisa, royal estate, the revenue from which went directly into the royal treasury, rather than into provincial coffers.

And just as Ala-ud-din carefully monitored the recruitment of his soldiers, so also he kept a close watch on the operations of the army when it was in the field. 'It was the practice of the sultan, when he sent an army on an expedition, to establish posts on the road,' states Barani. 'Relays of horses were stationed at every post, and at every half or quarter kos runners were posted, and officers and report writers were posted in every town or place where horses were stationed. Every day, or every two or three days, news used to come to the sultan reporting the progress of the army, and news about the health of the sovereign was carried back to the army. False news was thus prevented from being circulated in the city or in the army. This exchange of accurate information between the court and the army was of great public benefit.'

Another major concern of Ala-ud-din was the maintenance of law and order in the empire, for that was essential for the success of all his reforms. India was at this time infested with numerous wild bandit tribes, who disdained the authority of the state, and threatened to hamper the success of the socio-economic reforms of the sultan. As in everything else, Ala-ud-din dealt with this problem decisively, so that, according to Barani, 'dacoits and lawless men themselves turned into the guards of the roads. Not a single thread of travellers was ever reported to be lost. Peace and safety like this and to this extent were not found in any other period.'

ALA-UD-DIN IS SOMETIMES accused of unfair persecution of Hindus. Indeed, he was very severe in his treatment of them. But it was political expediency, not religious bigotry, that was the prime determinant of his policies and actions towards Hindus. He treated Hindus harshly not because of their religion, but because they, as a disaffected subject people, were a major source of disquiet in the kingdom.

Ala-ud-din believed that it was wealth that fomented disaffection and rebellion among Hindus, and he therefore decided that it was an imperative political necessity that they should be reduced to poverty. 'I know that Hindus will never become submissive and obedient till they are reduced to poverty,' he maintained. 'I have therefore given orders that just sufficient shall be left to them from year to year, of corn, milk and curds, but that they shall not be allowed to accumulate wealth and property.'

Ala-ud-din's measures to keep Hindus subservient were, according to Barani, so effective 'that contumacy and rebellion, and riding on horses, carrying of weapons, wearing of fine clothes, and eating betel, entirely ceased among chaudharys (land owners) and other opulent men . . . It was in fact not possible for a Hindu to hold up his head, and in the houses of Hindus there was not a sign of gold and silver and articles of luxury . . . In consequence of their impoverished state, the wives of the landed proprietors and chief men even used to come to the houses of the Mussulmans and do [domestic] work there, and receive wages for it.'

There is no doubt considerable exaggeration in these reports of Barani; they quite probably reflect what the orthodox cleric would have liked to see, not the reality. This is equally true of an approbatory comment on the prevailing conditions of Hindus that Barani attributes to a kazi: 'As soon as the revenue collector demands the sum due from him, [the Hindu] pays the same with meekness and humility, coupled with utmost respect, and free from reluctance, and he, should the collector chooses to spit into his mouth, opens the same without hesitation, so that the official may spit into it . . .'

ALA-UD-DIN WAS ONE of the most extraordinary rulers in Indian history, indeed in world history. He was a radical reformer, and was exceptionally successful in all that he did, though many of his reforms were several centuries ahead of his time.

This success of Ala-ud-din elicited admiration from even so adverse a critic as Barani—the sultan, he writes, was 'brilliant . . . [in his] political and administrative measures . . . During his reign, either through his agency or the beneficent ruling of providence, there were several remarkable events and matters which had never been witnessed or heard of in any age or time, and probably will never again be seen.' Barani then goes on to list ten major achievements of Ala-ud-din's reign: 1/ Cheapness of all the necessities of life; 2/ invariable success in military campaigns; 3/ rout of the Mongols; 4/ maintenance of a large army at a small cost; 5/ political stability resulting from the suppression and prevention of rebellions; 6/ safety on roads in all directions; 7/ honest dealings of the bazaar people; 8/ erection and repair of mosques, minarets, and forts, and the excavation of tanks; 9/ the prevalence of 'rectitude, truth, honesty, justice, and temperance in the hearts of Muslims in general during the last ten years of his reign'; and 10/ the flourishing of many learned and great men 'without the patronage of the sultan.' Ala-ud-din, observes Ibn Battuta, 'was one of the best of sultans, and people of India eulogise him highly.'

People by and large enjoyed peace and security, even prosperity, during the reign of Ala-ud-din. As a kazi once remarked, Ala-ud-din had driven criminals into 'mice holes, and has taken cheating, lying and falsifying out of them . . . [And he] has managed the bazaar people as no king ever has done since the days of Adam.' 'None dared make any babble or noise,' states Afif, a fourteenth century chronicler. 'None dared to pick up [even] a fallen jewel from the street,' claims Amir Khusrav.

Ala-ud-din was a compulsive workaholic, and he drove his officers as hard as he drove himself. Indeed, royal officers played a crucial role in the achievements of the sultan. As Barani states, 'During the whole period of Sultan Ala-ud-din's reign, the situation of the county was very good and prosperous due to the bravery, mutual cooperation and farsightedness of officials and soldiers. Administration was carried on efficiently and successfully.' A part of the credit for the success of Ala-ud-din's reign should therefore go to his officers—but all the credit for laying down impeccable government regulations, finding talented officers, earning their loyalty, and getting the best out of them, should go to the sultan.

Another remarkable aspect of Ala-ud-din's reign was that he, despite his authoritarianism and ruthlessness, also showed a genuine concern for the welfare of the common people, and sought to free them from exploitation by tax collectors and village headmen. And in his tax policy he sought to ensure that, as Barani states, 'heavy burdens were not placed upon the poor.' Further, in times of poor harvest, and when there was a general scarcity of provisions, Ala-ud-din made sure that 'if in such a season any poor . . . person went to the market, and did not get assistance, the overseer [of the market] received punishment whenever the information reached the king's ears.'

People on the whole led a better life under Ala-ud-din than under any other king of the Delhi Sultanate. 'No more prosperous times than his had ever fallen to the lot of any Muhammadan sovereign,' states Afif. Ala-ud-din was on the whole a beneficent ruler to his subjects.

But he was not a benign ruler. Rather, he was singularly brutal in extirpating all who stood in his path. Even in that sanguinary age, Ala-ud-din's reign stood out for its excesses. All that can be said in extenuation of the sultan in this is that he could not have achieved much of what he did without such ruthlessness.

4

The Reign of Eunuchs

The last years of Ala-u-din's life were dismal. 'The prosperity of Ala-ud-din at length declined,' writes Barani. 'Success no longer attended him. Fortune proved, as usual, fickle, and destiny drew her poniard to destroy him.' The sultan was also plagued by debilitating health problems at this time. He suffered from acute oedema, and 'day by day his malady grew worse . . . Under his mortal disorder the violence of his temper increased tenfold.' Instead of the carefully calculated and decisive actions that had characterised his reign till then, he now became petulant and impulsive. 'Cares assailed him on many sides . . . He drove away his wise and experienced ministers from his presence, and sent his councillors into retirement . . . The reins of government fell into the hands of slaves and worthless people. No wise man remained to guide him.'

Presently the grand political edifice that Ala-ud-din had built up with sagacity and perseverance over many years began to crumble. And succession manoeuvres now turned the royal court into a snake-pit, with rivals rearing up, hissing and spitting venom on each other. In 1312 Ala-ud-din nominated his oldest surviving son, Khizr Khan, as his successor, and that led to the prince's mother (Malika-i-Jahan) and her brother (Alp Khan, the governor of Gujarat, who was also the father-in-law of the prince) becoming the prime manipulators in the court. Khizr Khan played virtually no role in all this—he was, according to Barani, a weakling, an indolent voluptuary addicted 'to pleasure and debauchery . . . [over whom] buffoons and strumpets had gained mastery'

Ala-ud-din's confidant and chief advisor at this time was Malik Kafur, but he was uncomfortable in the vicious, noxious environment then prevailing in the royal court. He evidently despised Khizr Khan, and the prince, as well as his mother and father-in-law, were no doubt wary of Kafur. There was also 'a deadly enmity' between Malik Kafur and Alp Khan. Because of all this, Kafur wanted to get away from Delhi, and he persuaded the sultan to send him on a military campaign into peninsular India, and he spent three years there, engaged in various battles, till he was called back to Delhi, because of the sultan's failing health.

Back in Delhi, Kafur gained complete ascendancy over the ailing sultan, and he planted in his mind the suspicion that Alp Khan was planning some political move in concert with Malika-i-Jahan. Kafur then, according to Barani, 'induced the sultan to have Alp Khan killed . . . [and] he caused Khizr Khan to be made a prisoner and sent to the Gwalior fort, and he had the mother of the prince turned out of the Red Palace.' The ensuing turbid political environment in Delhi led, as usual, to rebellions in the provinces, particularly in Gujarat, Chitor and Devagiri. In the midst of these unsettling developments, in early January 1316, the great sultan, who had for twenty years ruled the empire with awesome authority, passed away. 'The rule of the sultan was tottering when death seized him,' comments Barani. Ala-ud-din, according to Amir Khusrav, died 'partly through bodily infirmity and partly through mental distress.' The future looked bleak indeed for the Khalji dynasty.

'ON THE SECOND day after the death of Ala-ud-din, Malik Kafur assembled the principal nobles and officers in the palace, and produced a will of the late sultan which he had caused to be drawn up in favour of Malik Shihab-ud-din (a son of Ala-ud-din by the Devagiri raja Ramadeva's daughter), and removing Khizr Khan from being the heir apparent,' reports Barani. 'With the assent of the nobles he then placed Shihab-ud-din upon the throne. But as the new sovereign was just a child five or six years old, he was a mere puppet in the hands of . . . Malik Kafur, [who] himself [then] undertook the conduct of the government.'

Kafur had entered the royal service in 1298, the second year of Ala-ud-din's reign, and had risen rapidly in official position, mainly because of his proven ability as military commander and wise counsellor—the sultan, according to Isami, favoured Kafur because 'his counsel had always proved appropriate and fit for the occasion.' Besides, Ala-ud-din, according to Barani, 'was infatuated with Malik Kafur, and made him the commander of his army and vizier. He distinguished him above all his other helpers and friends, and this eunuch and minion held the chief place in his regards.' And in the closing days of the sultan's reign, he became the virtual ruler of the empire. Kafur 'did not allow anyone to see the emperor, and he himself began to . . . administer the realm,' states Isami.

Barani is severely critical of Kafur, but his excoriations are not quite credible, for he was deeply prejudiced against Malik Kafur, whom he invariably described as a 'wicked fellow,' presumably because he was not a Turk but an Islamised Hindu and a eunuch. The resentment against Kafur among the Turkish nobles intensified when he blinded Khizr Khan and his brother Shadi Khan—Kafur, writes Barani, 'sent his barber to blind Shadi Khan . . . by cutting his eyes from their sockets with a razor'—and imprisoned the other sons of Ala-ud-din, except the boy sultan who was his protégé. 'His great object was to remove all the children and wives of the late sultan, all the nobles and slaves who had claims for the throne, and to fill their places with creatures of his own.'

But court politics was an unfamiliar, perilous arena for Kafur. He was a brilliant military commander, but quite unskilled in manipulative politics, and was vulnerable to the manoeuvres of his rivals. His fall was therefore inevitable. The final scene in this drama was enacted one night when Kafur sought to blind Mubarak Khan, the imprisoned third son of Ala-ud-din. The soldiers whom he sent to do this were bribed by the prince with the jewelled necklace he was wearing, and he, reminding them of their long service under Ala-ud-din and of their duty to his dynasty, induced them to go back and assassinate Kafur. So they 'went with drawn swords to his sleeping room and severed his wicked head from his foul body,' reports Barani. 'They also killed his confederates.'

KAFUR'S DE FACTO RULE lasted only thirty-five days. On his assassination, the nobles in Delhi released Mubarak from prison and installed him as the regent of Shihab-ud-din, the child sultan, though he himself was only seventeen or eighteen years old then. After a few months, Mubarak imprisoned and blinded Shihab-ud-din, and himself ascended the throne, no doubt with the connivance of the ever opportunistic and scheming nobles.

In some ways Mubarak was like his father, and he, following Ala-ud-din's policy of never to trust defectors, had the assassins of Kafur, who were then strutting about as king-makers, dispersed and their leaders executed, even though the throne he occupied was their gift. And, again like Ala-ud-din, he had no compunction whatever to ruthlessly exterminate his political rivals, including his brothers and close relatives. However, he lacked his father's unwinking attention to governance; besides, he was addicted to sensual pleasures, and spent most of his time and energy in debauchery.

'Still he was a man of some excellent qualities,' notes Barani. And in the early part of his reign, he was a popular ruler. A major reason for his popularity was that he reversed many of the exacting policies of Ala-ud-din. 'On the very day of his accession he issued orders that the [political] prisoners and exiles of the late reign, amounting to seventeen or eighteen thousand in number, should all be released in the city and in all parts of the country . . .,' reports Barani.

'[Further,] six months' salary was given to the army, and the allowances and grants of nobles were increased . . . The sultan from his good nature relieved the people of heavy tributes and oppressive demands; and penalties, extortions, beatings, chains, fetters, and blows were set aside in revenue matters.'

All this was partly deliberate policy, and partly an expression of Mubarak's indolent nature. 'Through his love of pleasure, extravagance and ease, all the regulations and arrangements of the late reign fell into disuse; and through his laxity in business matters all men took their ease, being saved from the harsh temper, severe treatment, and oppressive orders of the late king,' notes Barani. 'Men were no longer in . . . fear of hearing, "Do this, but don't do that;" "Say this, but don't say that;" "Hide this, but don't hide that;" "Eat this, but don't eat that;" "Sell such as this, but don't sell things like that;" "Act like this, but don't act like that" . . . All the old regulations were now disregarded . . . and an entirely new order of things was established. All fear and awe of the royal authority vanished.'

Nearly all the 'regulations of Ala-ud-din came to an end on his death, for his son . . . was not able to maintain even a thousandth part of them,' continues Barani. The only reform of Ala-ud-din that Mubarak retained was prohibition, but even that only nominally so, for he was quite negligent in enforcing it. 'Such was the general disregard of orders and contempt for restrictions that wine shops were publicly opened, and vessels of wine by hundreds came into the city from the country.' As Ala-ud-din's market regulations were discarded by Mubarak, prices of all things rose. And so did wages. Traders 'rejoiced over the death of Ala-ud-din; they now sold goods at their own price, and cheated and fleeced people as they pleased . . . The doors of bribery, extortion, and malversation were thrown open, and a good time for the revenue officers came around . . . Hindus again found pleasure and happiness, and were beside themselves with joy. . . . [They] who had been so harassed . . . that they had not even time to scratch their heads, now put on fine apparel, rode on horseback, and shot their arrows. All through the reign of Mubarak, not one of the old rules and regulations remained in force, no order was maintained.'

'DURING THE FOUR years and four months [of Mubarak's reign] the sultan attended to nothing but drinking, listening to music, debauchery and pleasure, scattering gifts, and gratifying his lusts,' states Barani. 'The sultan plunged into sensual indulgences openly and publicly, by night and by day, and the people followed his example . . . His whole life was passed in extreme dissipation and utter negligence. Debauchery, drunkenness, and shamelessness proved his ruin . . . He cast aside all regard for decency, and presented himself decked out in the trinkets and apparel of a female before his assembled company. He gave up attendance at public prayer, and publicly broke the fast of the month of Ramadan.' He made one of his cronies, a Gujarati named Tauba, supreme in his palace, and encouraged him to insult the great nobles in foul language, and to 'defile and befoul their garments . . . Sometimes he made his appearance in company stark naked, talking obscenity.'

But Mubarak was lucky, for during his reign there was 'no deficiency in the crops, no alarm from Mongols, no irreparable calamity . . . No revolt or great disturbance arose in any quarter, not a hair of anyone was injured, and the name of grief or sorrow never entered the breast, or passed from the tongue of anyone.' The many troubles that arose in the last years of Ala-ud-din and immediately after his death 'began to abate on the accession of Mubarak. People felt secure,' concludes Barani. Though there were a couple of provincial rebellions during this period, they were minor affairs, and were easily suppressed.

Mubarak was a bizarre amalgam of wild debauchery and bestial violence. He was highly eccentric, was perhaps insane. Ferishta describes him as 'a monster in the shape of man.' There was indeed a demon lurking inside him, which at the slightest provocation burst out into the open and committed the most appalling savageries. Thus when a conspiracy to murder him was discovered, he not only had the principal plotter, Asad-ud-din, a cousin of Ala-ud-din, and his brothers and co-conspirators beheaded, but had even their children of tender years 'slaughtered like sheep,' and the women and girls of the families driven out into the streets.

The sultan was at this time swirling in a state of convulsive insecurity. He saw a traitor in every shadow, and that led him to order a series of executions of his potential rivals and enemies. Thus when he heard a rumour that some amirs were conspiring to replace him with the young son of his brother Khizr Khan, he, according to Battuta, 'seized him (the boy) by the feet and dashed his head against a stone till his brains were scattered.' He then executed his three surviving brothers, who had all been already blinded and were lodged in the Gwalior prison—their heads were hacked off, and their bodies flung into a ditch. Mubarak even executed his father-in-law, Zafar Khan, the governor of Gujarat.

'Acts of violence and tyranny like this became his common practice . . . The good qualities which the sultan had possessed were now all perverted,' comments Barani. 'He gave way to wrath and obscenity, to severity, revenge and heartlessness. He dipped his hands in innocent blood, and he allowed his tongue to utter disgusting and abusive words to his companions and attendants . . . A violent, vindictive spirit . . . possessed him.' Mubarak was like a moth dancing around the candle flame, courting self-destruction, but no one dared to caution or counsel him, fearing the consequences.

MUBARAK, AS RIZVI describes him, was 'passionately homosexual', and was 'deeply in love' with a slave officer from Gujarat named Hasan, whom he designated as Khusrav Khan and made him his closest aide. Khusrav is described with great contempt by Barani as a Parwari, which is sometimes taken to be the name of the untouchable Hindu caste of scavengers in Gujarat. But Barani's disdain for Khusrav seems to be more an expression of a Turk's prejudice against Islamised Indians (many of whom were indeed of low caste origin) than of Khusrav's actual caste origin. According to Amir Khusrav, another contemporary chronicler, Khusrav belonged to Baradus, a Hindu military caste that served as the commandos of rajas. In any case, Khusrav proved himself to be a man of considerable military acumen and prowess, as he demonstrated in his successful campaigns in the peninsula, which took him, in imitation of Kafur's campaigns, deep into the Tamil country.

The sultan, notes Barani, 'granted a canopy to Khusrav Khan, and raised him to a dignity and distinction higher than that had ever been attained by Malik Kafur. In fact, his infatuation for this infamous and traitorous Parwari exceeded that of Ala-ud-din for Malik Kafur . . . Khusrav Khan was a base, designing, treacherous, low-born fellow . . . [But the sultan raised him] from one dignity to another . . . He was made the commander-in-chief, and all the affairs of the army were in his hands.'

Mubarak's 'passion and rashness carried him so far that he raised the youth to the office of wazir, and he was so doting that he could never endure his absence even for a moment,' continues Barani. Once, according to Barani, when Khusrav was returning to Delhi after a military campaign in peninsular India, the sultan suffered such acute pangs of separation that he 'sent relays of bearers with a litter to bring him with all haste from Devagiri [to Delhi],' covering a distance of over 1100 kilometres in seven days. And another time, again according to Barani, when some royal officers warned the sultan that Khusrav was plotting a rebellion, 'fate so blinded the sultan that he would not believe [the charge], but grew angry with the accusers, [some of whom were blinded or imprisoned, and some degraded or stripped of their offices]. Whoever . . . testified to the treachery of Khusrav Khan received condign punishment, and was imprisoned or banished.'

KHUSRAV'S POSITION AT the court thus became unassailable. But despite all the favours shown to him by the sultan, Khusrav seems to have despised him. According to Barani, Khusrav 'had often thought of cutting down the sultan with his sword when they were alone together.' He had, during his peninsular campaign, evidently formulated a secret plan to usurp the throne, and on his return to Delhi persuaded Mubarak to allow him to raise a personal army from men of his own tribe. Something was clearly afoot, but Mubarak, blinded by his infatuation, saw nothing amiss. Khusrav in fact further persuaded the sultan to give him the keys of a palace gate, on the pretext that he needed it to allow his friends and relatives to come into the palace to visit him at night. When one of the nobles cautioned Mubarak against allowing Khusrav's armed men to enter the palace at night, the sultan, according to Barani, 'grossly abused him, and spurned his honest counsels.' And when Mubarak told Khusrav about the suspicions of the noble, 'the infamous wretch began to weep and lament, saying that the great kindness and distinction which the sultan had bestowed upon him had made all the nobles and attendants of the court his enemies, and they were eager to take his life. The sultan [then] said that even if the all the world were turned upside down, and all his companions were of one voice in accusing Khusrav, he would sacrifice them all for one hair on his head.'

The final scenes of the unfolding drama are described in absorbing detail by Barani. One day late at night in mid-April 1320, a band of Khusrav's armed men under the leadership of Jahariya, their captain, entered the palace and assaulted the guards there. This created an uproar, which roused the sultan from his sleep, and he asked Khusrav, who was evidently sleeping with him, to go and find out what the trouble was. 'He went and looked, and told the sultan that some of his horses had broken loose, and were running about in the courtyard, where men were engaged in catching them. Just then Jahariya and some of his followers came to the upper storey [of the palace, where the sultan was sleeping,] and they despatched the officers and door-keepers there. The [ensuing] violent uproar convinced the sultan that treason was at work, so he put on his slippers and ran towards the harem. The traitor saw that if the sultan escaped into the women's apartments, it would be difficult to consummate the plot. Prompt in his villainy, he [therefore] rushed after the sultan and seized him from behind by the hair, which he twisted tightly round his hand. The sultan then flung him down and got upon his chest, but still the rascal would not release his hold. They were in this position when Jahariya entered at the head of the conspirators . . . [and he] struck the sultan in the chest with a spear and dragged him off Khusrav, dashed him to the ground and cut off his head.' The headless trunk of the sultan was then flung into the courtyard.

When the royal guards and others realised what had happened, many of them 'fled and hid themselves,' but quite a few of them were caught and killed by the Gujaratis. The rebels then entered the harem, killed Ala-ud-din's widow, and committed many atrocities there. Khusrav's men thus took full control of the palace. 'Lamps and torches were then lighted in great numbers and a court was held.' The great nobles of the sultanate were then sent for 'and were brought into the palace and made accomplices in what happened. By daybreak the palace was full inside and out with . . . [Khusrav's men]. Khusrav Khan had prevailed. The face of the world thus assumed a new complexion. A new order of things had sprung up, and the foundation of the dynasty of Ala-ud-din was utterly razed.'

'As the day broke, Khusrav, in the presence of those nobles whom he had brought into the palace, mounted the throne and assumed the title of Sultan Nadir-ud-din . . . He had no sooner begun to reign, than he ordered all the personal attendants of the late sultan, many of whom were of high rank, to be slain. Their wives, women, children and handmaids were all given to the Parwaris and Hindus.' Khusrav then won over many nobles, even several Muslim clerics, to his side by scattering gold and other opulent gifts among them. He also took care to honour and appease several of the Khalji loyalists. Prominent among those he thus sought to placate was Fakhr-ud-din Jauna, the future Muhammad bin Tughluq, who was appointed Master of the Horse and was honoured in various ways; Khusrav was particularly keen to win over Jauna, for he was the son of Ghazi Malik, the governor of Punjab, a most respected and powerful royal officer.

CONTEMPORARY MUSLIM CHRONICLERS speak of Khusrav's usurpation of the throne as a Hindu coup. 'In the course of four or five days preparations were made for idol worship in the palace,' writes Barani. 'The horrid Parwaris sported in the royal harem. Khusrav married the wife of the late sultan; and the Parwaris, having gained the upper hand, took to themselves the wives and handmaids of the nobles and great men. The flames of violence and cruelty reached to the skies. Copies of the Holy Book were used as seats, and idols were set up in the pulpits of mosques . . . Hindus rejoiced greatly . . . boasting that Delhi had once more come under Hindu rule.' Ibn Battuta, a later chronicler confirms this, and states that 'Khusrav Khan upon becoming king, showed great favour to Hindus,' and prohibited cow slaughter.

Many of Khusrav's close followers were Hindus, and it is likely that some Hindu rites were performed by them in the palace. Because of all this, but perhaps mainly because the Turkish nobles of the sultanate could not reconcile themselves to having an Indian Muslim as their sultan, opposition to Khusrav soon began to mount. The prime mover against Khusrav was Ghazi Malik who, according to Barani, 'writhed like a snake when he heard of the overthrow of the dynasty of Ala-ud-din.' He had initially acquiesced with the usurpation of Khusrav, because any hostile move by him would have endangered the life of his son Jauna, who was in Delhi. Eventually, some two months after Khusrav's accession, Jauna, escorted by just a couple of his men, managed to escape from Delhi one afternoon and join his father in Punjab, outpacing a body of cavalrymen Khusrav sent in pursuit of him.

Ghazi Malik was then free to move against Khusrav. He tried to form a confederacy of nobles and provincial governors with the rallying cry that Islam was in danger, but not many responded to his call, as they did not want to risk their official positions, and preferred to wait for the situation to clarify before deciding which side to join. Meanwhile Khusrav, hearing of the moves of Ghazi Malik, sent an army against him under the command of his brother and another young officer. Comments Barani: 'So these two foolish, ignorant lads went forth, like newly hatched chickens just beginning to fly, to fight with a veteran warrior like Ghazi Malik . . . who twenty times had routed the Mongols.' Hearing of their advance, Ghazi Malik set out from Dipalpur to confront them, and he easily routed them in a brief encounter.

Ghazi Malik remained on the battlefield for a week, to collect and distribute the spoils, and to rest and reorganise his army. He then advanced on Delhi. Meanwhile Khusrav organised another army, distributing largesse among the soldiers. Many soldiers, according Barani, 'took the money of the wretched fellow, heaped hundreds of curses upon him, and then went to their homes.' Even one of Khusrav's top generals deserted him. But despite these setbacks, Khusrav confidently advanced to meet the army of Ghazi Malik. The ensuing battle, fought at Indarpat near Delhi in early September 1320, was closely contested, but in the end Khusrav was defeated. He then fled for his life, but was caught lurking in a garden, and was promptly beheaded. 'The effeminate wretch could not bear the attack of men,' comments Barani.

'That night, while Ghazi Malik was at Indarpat, most of the nobles and chief men and officers came from the city (Delhi) to pay their respects to him, and the keys of the palace and of the city gates were brought to him,' notes Barani. On the second day after the battle Ghazi Malik rode to the Palace of Thousand Pillars at Siri. And there, in the presence of the assembled nobles, he 'wept over the unhappy fate which had befallen . . . the sons of Ala-ud-din, his patron.' He then told the nobles: 'If you know of any son of our patron's blood, bring him forth immediately, and I will seat him on the throne, and will be the first to tender him my service and devotion. If the whole stock has been clean cut off, then do you bring forward some worthy and proper person and raise him to the throne; I will pay my allegiance to him. I have drawn my sword to avenge my patrons, not to gain power and ascend the throne.'

The nobles then told him that the entire family of Ala-ud-din had been wiped out by the usurpers. And they proclaimed: 'All of us who are here present know no one besides thee who is worthy of royalty and fit to rule.' They then took him by the hand and conducted him to the throne, 'and everyone paid him due homage.'

On 8 September 1320 Ghazi Malik thus became the sultan of Delhi, and took the title Ghiyas-ud-din Tughluq Shah.

PART V

TUGHLUQS

At present I am angry with my subjects, and they are aggrieved with me . . . No treatment that I employ is of any benefit. My remedy for rebels, insurgents, opponents, and disaffected people is the sword . . . The more the people resist, the more I inflict chastisement.

—SULTAN MUHAMMAD TUGHLUQ

1

Restoration of Normalcy

The accession of Ghiyas-ud-din Tughluq calmed the dreadful paroxysm that had afflicted the Sultanate since the closing years of Ala-ud-din Khalji's reign. Ghiyas-ud-din was a sagacious ruler, wise and moderate, caring as much for the welfare of his subjects, as for the preservation of his power. And, although he had no spectacular achievements to his credit, he restored normalcy in the Sultanate, and that in itself was a major achievement. 'In the course of one week the business of the state was brought to order, and the disorders and evils caused by Khusrav and his unholy followers were remedied,' states Barani. 'The people in all parts of the country were delighted at his accession. Rebellion and disaffection ceased, peace and obedience prevailed.'

According to Battuta, Ghiyas-ud din 'belonged to a clan of Turks called Karauna inhabiting the mountains between Sind and the country of the Turks. He was in a very humble condition, and went to Sind as a servant of a certain merchant.' Later he entered the service of the Khalji governor of Sind as a footman, and distinguished himself by his skill, bravery and devotion. After a while, he joined the royal service in Delhi, and there too won the appreciation and favour of his superiors, and rose rapidly in the official hierarchy, to eventually become one of the top nobles of the Sultanate. Ala-ud-din conferred on him the title Ghazi Malik, and appointed him as the governor of Punjab, a critically important post, responsible for the defence the empire against the depredations of Mongols. That appointment, and his commendable performance in the post, considerably enhanced his already high reputation, and made his accession to the throne of Delhi natural and inevitable after the overthrow of Khusrav.

Ghiyas-ud-din, according to Sirhindi, 'was a kind and just person, chaste and pure . . . In ingenuity, thrift, knowledge and adroitness he was unequalled.' He was not at all an overweening person, and his accession to the throne made hardly any change in his character or conduct. He never flaunted his power. His relationship with the nobles was more of camaraderie than of dominance; he led the nobles, but did not drive them. 'His nobleness and generosity of character made him distinguish and reward all those whom he had known and been connected with, and those who in former days had showed him kindness or had rendered him service,' notes Barani. 'No act of kindness was ever passed over.' Characteristically, on the very day of his accession, Ghiyas-ud-din had all the surviving relatives of Ala-ud-din and Mubarak brought to him, and he treated them 'with all due respect and honour.' He also took care to marry off the daughters of Ala-ud-din suitably. A pious Muslim, he lived a life of discipline and moderation, abjured wine drinking and all excesses. All his actions were marked by propriety. Sang poet Amir Khusrav:

He never did anything that was not replete with wisdom and sense
He might be said to wear a hundred doctors' hoods under his crown.

PRUDENCE, JUSTICE AND concern for the commonweal characterised all the policies and actions of Ghiyas-ud-din. So, despite being ever loyal to the memory of Ala-ud-din, he reversed or modified many of the former sultan's exacting regulations, so as to lighten the burden on people and to ease the pressure on administration. Having risen from among the common people, he knew their problems, sympathised with them, and did what he could to mitigate their sufferings, but without compromising the interests of the state. 'In the generosity of his nature, he ordered that the land revenues of the country should be settled on just principles,' and he substantially reduced the tax demand on farmers from what it was under Ala-ud-din, reports Barani. While Ala-ud-din had collected half the farm produce as tax, Ghiyas-ud-din limited it to one-tenth or one-eleventh of the gross produce. He also took care to remit taxes during drought years.

These sharp reductions in tax rates by the sultan would have notably reduced the revenues of the state, but they did not seriously impair its financial health, because the sultan prudently balanced them by stimulating the expansion of agriculture and trade, so that the reduction of the tax rates was offset, at least partly, by the expansion of the economy and the consequent widening of the sources of revenue of the state.

Ghiyas-ud-din held that the sensible means to increase the revenue of the state was to expand farm production, so he, according to Barani, sought to motivate farmers to increase the area under their cultivation by directing his revenue officers to ensure that 'something was left [to farmers] over and above the tribute, so that the country might not be ruined by the weight of taxation, and the way to improvement be barred.' He cautioned his officers that 'countries are ruined and are kept in poverty by excessive taxation and the exorbitant demands of kings.' The sultan also took some positive measures to facilitate the expansion of cultivation, such as digging irrigation canals, and building forts in the countryside to provide people security from brigands. On the whole Ghiyas-ud-din's revenue measures benefited the people as well as the sultan.

Ghiyas-ud-din also introduced certain administrative measures to prevent, or at least minimise, the exploitation of farmers by tax collectors—thus, instead of the usual method of remunerating the tax collectors by giving them a percentage of their revenue collection, which resulted in the collectors extorting excess payments from farmers, the sultan compensated the collectors by exempting their land holdings from taxes. Further, to protect farmers, he prohibited the use of torture for collecting tax arrears, even though he allowed torture in cases of theft and embezzlement.

The sultan was equally considerate in his treatment of Hindus—while he followed the orthodox Muslim state policy of treating Hindus as subject people and second class citizens, he took care that they were not turned destitute. According to Barani, the sultan ordered that Hindus should be left with enough (but only with just enough) sustenance to lead a productive life, so that they would not become either 'blinded by wealth' and turn rebellious, 'nor, on the other hand, be so reduced to poverty and destitution as to be unable to pursue their husbandry.'

Ghiyas-ud-din's general policy in dealing with his subjects, Hindus as well as Muslims, was to be fair but firm with them—he would not exploit the people, nor would he allow the people to cheat him. Thus when he found that Khusrav had improperly given away extensive land grants and large amounts of money to various influential people, including some religious leaders, to win their support, he ordered the resumption of those lands and demanded the refund of the money from the recipients. One of the chief beneficiaries of Khusrav's largesse was the celebrated Sufi sage Nizam-ud-din Auliya, who had received about half a million tankas from him. When Ghiyas-ud-din demanded the refund of this amount from the sage, he replied that he had distributed all the money in charity as soon as he received it, and therefore could not make the restitution. This angered the sultan and intensified his dislike of the sage, whose dervish practices he, an orthodox Muslim, in any case strongly disapproved. This ill feeling between the two would later add a curious twist to the mystery about the violent death of the sultan a few years later.

Another important administrative measure of Ghiyas-ud-din was the restoration of the postal system that Ala-ud-din had set up, but had fallen into disuse after his death. Its restoration enabled Ghiyas-ud-din to keep in regular touch with all parts of his empire, and manage its affairs efficiently.

ONE OF THE major concerns of Ghiyas-ud-din as sultan was to recover the territories that the Sultanate had lost during the turmoil following the death of Ala-ud-din, and to restore the Sultanate to its former position of absolute supremacy in the Indian subcontinent. In pursuit of this policy he sent, in the second year of his reign, an army into Warangal, where the Kakatiya ruler Prataparudra-deva had thrown off the yoke of the sultanate and was expanding his territory and power through military campaigns against his neighbours. The Sultanate army, commanded by Ghiyas-ud-din's eldest son Jauna, then invaded the kingdom and forced the raja, after a prolonged siege, to plead for peace.

But at the point of the conclusion of the campaign, the Sultanate army was suddenly thrown into turmoil by certain mysterious developments. The basic cause of the trouble was that the army had not received any news from Delhi for nearly a month—because the communication link between Delhi and the army had been cut by local rebels—and that led to all sorts of wild rumours to spread in the army. One such rumour was that Ghiyas-ud-din was dead, and that Delhi was in the throes of a political turmoil. It was also rumoured that Jauna was plotting to usurp the throne, and was planning to liquidate some of the senior army commanders whose loyalty to him was suspect. All this created great disquiet among the army commanders, and they, as well as Jauna, retreated in disorder to Devagiri, from where the prince sped to his father in Delhi with a small escort.

This is the story told by Barani. But Battuta offers another explanation for the development, and states that the rumour about Ghiyas-ud-din's death was deliberately spread by Ubaid, a poet and boon companion of Jauna, on the suggestion of the prince. This, according to Battuta, was done to enable the prince to win the support of the army in his plan to usurp the throne, but the plan failed as the army commanders suspected the truth and deserted the prince, as they did not want to be associated with the planned usurpation.

The version given by Battuta is not credible, because of its inherent improbability—Jauna, as the eldest son of the sultan, had already been designated as the heir apparent, and there was no reason for him to jeopardise that position by rebelling. Besides, subsequent developments also disprove the usurpation attempt theory. On the return of the army to Delhi, the officers who deserted Jauna were put to death by the sultan—the chief deserters 'were impaled alive, and some of the others with their wives and children were thrown under the feet of elephants,' reports Barani. In direct contrast to this, Jauna was given a fresh army and sent again against Warangal, where the raja had reasserted his independence. There was evidently no suspicion at all in the sultan about the loyalty of Jauna. This was also proved by subsequent developments. Thus a year or so later, when the sultan set out on a campaign into Bengal, he had no hesitation at all to appoint Jauna as his regent in Delhi.

Jauna's stature as the heir apparent enhanced considerably after his second Warangal campaign, which was entirely successful. The raja there once again surrendered to him after a brief resistance, and the prince then sent him, along with all his treasures, to Delhi, and annexed the kingdom to the empire. From Warangal Jauna then seems to have advanced north-eastward into Orissa and then southward into the Tamil country, but the accounts about this campaign in contemporary chronicles are confusing. But on the whole the peninsular campaign of Jauna seems to have been quite successful. This is indicated by the grand reception that the sultan accorded to the prince on his return to Delhi.

Ghiyas-ud-din then put Jauna in charge of Delhi and set out for Bengal with an army, to reassert his authority over that rebellious and strife-torn province. After a successful campaign there, which brought most of Bengal once again under the rule of Delhi, the sultan hastened back home, as some disquieting news had reached him about developments in Delhi. This concerned Jauna's association with Nizam-ud-din Auliya, and the dervish's prediction in one his trances that Jauna's accession to the throne was imminent. Other astrologers are also said to have made similar predictions. Hearing all this, Ghiyas-ud-din wrote menacing letters to the astrologers, and sent a warning to Auliya that when he returned to Delhi, the city would be too small to hold them both.

AS IT HAPPENED, it was not the sultan's threat, but the dervish's prediction, that came true. When some of Auliya's devotees warned him of the sultan's imminent arrival in Delhi, and advised him to leave the city in view of the sultan's threat, he is said to have replied, '*Hanuz Dihli dur ast!*'—Delhi is still far off!

According to Barani, when Jauna learnt of the sultan's return, he along with the great nobles in Delhi went forth to receive him, and built for his reception a temporary structure at Afghanpur, a village about a dozen kilometres from Tughluqabad, the capital that Ghiyas-ud-din had built for himself south of Delhi. When the sultan arrived at Afghanpur, the prince and the nobles ceremoniously conducted him to the reception hall they had built there, and served him a grand banquet. Then suddenly, while the sultan was still in the building, 'a calamity occurred. Like a thunderbolt falling from heaven . . . the roof of the dais on which the sultan . . . was sitting fell, crushing him and five or six other persons, so that they all died.'

Battuta describes the incident quite differently. According to him it was the sultan who ordered the reception hall to be built, and it was built on wooden pillars and beams by Jauna in the course of three days. Jauna, according to Battuta, had designed it ingeniously so that 'it would crash when elephants touched it at a certain spot . . . The sultan stopped at this building and feasted the people. After they dispersed, the prince asked the sultan for permission to parade the elephants before him.' During the parade, when the elephants passed along a particular place, the building, as Jauna had planned, collapsed on the sultan, killing him. Though Jauna then ordered pickaxes and shovels 'to be brought to dig and look for his father, he made signs to them not to hurry, and the tools were not brought till after sunset. Then they began to dig . . . Some assert that Tughluq was taken out dead; others, on the contrary, maintain that he was alive, and that an end was made of him.'

The mechanical ingenuity attributed to Jauna by Battuta in constructing the collapsible building, though not impossible, seems improbable, and so does his story of the prince making signs (obviously in front of many others) to the rescuers to delay their work. The hastily built structure was probably not quite stable. Ferishta mentions that there was a suspicion of conspiracy behind the accident, but he discredits it, and adds, 'God only knows the truth.' Assassinations of kings by their close relatives were all too common in the Delhi Sultanate, so it was natural to suspect conspiracy in every accident. But lack of a compelling motive—Jauna was after all the heir-apparent, and his father was a very old man—and the complicated and chancy device used for causing the sultan's death, as also Battuta's marked prejudice against the prince, which is evident in much of what he says about him, make the conspiracy theory implausible.

2

Sultan Quixote

Ghiyas-ud-din Tughluq died in early 1325, in the fifth year of his reign. He had built for himself an elegant mausoleum at Tughluqabad, and he was buried there on the very night of his death, in conformity with the Islamic custom of burying the deceased soon after their death. Three days later Jauna ascended the throne, and took the title Muhammad Tughluq. He remained at Tughluqabad for forty days, in extended mourning. 'When the accursed prince finished his father's burial he made a display of sorrow while at heart he was happy,' comments Isami, a contemporary chronicler virulently hostile to Muhammad.

After the period of mourning, Muhammad set out for Delhi in a ceremonial procession. The city was elaborately decorated for the occasion, and Muhammad, basking in the acclamation of the crowds lining the streets, proceeded to the palace of the early sultans of Delhi, and took up his residence there. He then, according to Isami, made a hypocritical declaration: 'The late emperor's policy was to administer justice . . . I shall do the same. The old and the aged in the realm are unto me like my father; the youth are like my brothers; . . . the children in the empire are like my own children . . . I wish prosperity, peace and long life for all, high and low . . . I shall rule with justice and enforce it to such an extent that I may fittingly be called the Just Emperor.'

Thus began, with festivities and in great optimism, the most turbulent reign in the over three centuries long history of the Delhi Sultanate. There is a good amount of information on Muhammad in contemporary chronicles. There is even an account of his reign by a foreign traveller, Ibn Battuta, a Moorish explorer, who spent about a decade in India in the mid-fourteenth century, most of it in Delhi, at the court of Muhammad. But these chroniclers were often as confused as modern scholars are about what to make of the motives and actions of Muhammad. There is even some confusion about the chronology of the reign.

The chief chronicler of Muhammad's reign was Zia-ud-din Barani, who had excellent high level political contacts in the Sultanate, as he belonged to a family of prominent royal officers from the time of his grandfather, and was himself a favourite courtier of Muhammad for some fourteen years, though he never held any official post. Being a courtier had its advantages and disadvantages for Barani as a chronicler—it enabled him to witness at close range many of the events that he wrote about, but he had to be also very careful about what he wrote, for fear of rousing the sultan's wrath. 'We were traitors who were prepared to call black white,' he frankly admits. 'Avarice and the desire for worldly wealth led us into hypocrisy, and as we stood before the king and witnessed punishments forbidden by the law, fear of our fleeting lives and equally fleeting wealth deterred us from speaking the truth before him.'

But Barani was free of those fears and anxieties when he wrote his chronicle, for it was some years after Muhammad's death and towards the end of his own life—when he was no longer a courtier, and had little to hope for or to fear from the Tughluqs—that he wrote it. He was therefore brutally candid about the sultan's misdeeds, though he was also equally appreciative of his good deeds. Battuta is even more candid about Muhammad, for he had nothing at all to fear from the Tughluqs, as he wrote his book in Morocco after returning home from his travels.

The picture of Muhammad that emerges from these and other medieval chronicles is of a psychotic Jekyll-and-Hyde personality, a bizarre blend of antithetical qualities, of good and evil, overweening arrogance and abject humility, murderous savagery and touching compassion. 'This king is of all men the fondest of making gifts and of shedding blood,' comments Battuta. 'His gate is never without some poor man enriched, or some . . . man executed, and stories are current among the people about his generosity and courage, and about his cruelty and violence . . . For all that, he is of all men the most humble and the readiest to show equity and justice . . . Justice, compassion for the needy, and extraordinary generosity' characterised his conduct. In the colourful words of Sewell, an early modern historian, Muhammad was 'a saint with the heart of a devil, or a fiend with the soul of a saint.'

Muhammad was a compulsive innovator. But he—unlike Ala-ud-din, the other great reformer sultan of early medieval India—lacked the pragmatism, patience and perseverance needed to execute his schemes successfully, even though several of the schemes he dreamed up were, in themselves, quite sound. All his grand dreams therefore turned into dreadful nightmares, for himself as well as for his subjects. Muhammad however did not see the failure of his schemes as his failure in their execution, but blamed it on the intractability and lack of vision of his subjects. And this turned him vindictive towards the people, treating them not as his subjects, whom he had the duty to protect and nurture, but as his enemies whom he had to chastise. 'I punish the people because they have all at once become my enemies and opponents,' he once told Barani. 'I have dispensed great wealth among them, but they have not become friendly and loyal. Their temper is well known to me, and I see that they are disaffected and inimical to me.'

MUHAMMAD'S FRUSTRATIONS TURNED him into a sadistic, bloodthirsty tyrant. 'The sultan was far too ready to shed blood,' reports Battuta. 'He punished small faults and great, without respect of persons, whether men of learning, piety or high station. Every day hundreds of people, chained, pinioned, and fettered, are brought to his hall, and those who are for execution are executed, those for torture are tortured, and those for beating are beaten.' Confirms Barani: 'Not a day or week passed without the spilling of much . . . blood . . . Streams of gore flowed [daily] before the entrance of his palace.' The corpses of those executed were usually flung down at the gate of the royal palace, as a warning to the public to be obedient to the sultan. These executions were carried out on all days, except on Fridays, which was a day of respite for prisoners.

Such punishments, Muhammad believed, were right and proper—and essential. 'These days many wicked and turbulent men are to be found,' he one day told Barani, justifying the savage punishments he inflicted. 'I visit them with chastisement upon the suspicion or presumption of their rebellious and treacherous deigns, and I punish the most trifling act of contumacy with death. This I will do until I die, or until people act honestly, and give up rebellion and contumacy.' Muhammad was, for a medieval sultan, quite a learned man, but his learning, instead of making him humane, only calloused him. 'The dogmas of philosophers, which are productive of the indifference and hardness of heart, had a powerful influence on him,' comments Barani. 'But the declarations of the holy books, and utterances of prophets, which inculcate benevolence and humility, and hold out the prospect of future punishment, were not deemed worthy of attention.'

In medieval chronicles there are several accounts of the savagery of Muhammad against his own subjects, slaughtering them indiscriminately, plundering and devastating their land. Thus on one occasion, following a rebellion, 'the sultan led forth his army to ravage Hindustan,' reports Barani. 'He laid the country waste from Kanauj to Dalamu, and every person that fell into his hands he slew. Many of the inhabitants fled and took refuge in jungles, but the sultan had the jungles surrounded, and every individual that was captured was killed.' Comments Sewell: Muhammad 'exterminated whole tribes as if they were vermin.'

There was an element of revolting fiendishness in some of the punishments that Muhammad meted out. Thus when Baha-ud-din Gurshasp, his cousin, rose in revolt against him, not only was he flayed alive, but his flesh was cooked with rice and sent to his wife and children. In another case, when a pious and venerable Muslim described the sultan as a tyrant, and refused to retract the charge despite being chained and starved for a fortnight, the sultan, according to Battuta, ordered him to be forcibly fed human excrement. So the wardens stretched him on his back on the ground, 'opened his mouth with pincers and dropped into it human refuse dissolved in water.'

'The cruelties of this tyrant . . . surpass all belief,' comments Nurul Haq, a Mughal chronicler. However, it should be noted that in brutality the difference between Muhammad and most other Delhi sultans was only that of degree, not of kind, though the difference in degree in this case was so extreme as to seem like difference in kind. Of the thirty-two sultans of Delhi, only a couple of them were free of such savagery. Brutality and the terror it evoked were, from the point of view of the sultans, essential for their survival as rulers in that brutal age, particularly in India, where they were a small group of alien invaders ruling over a vast and hostile subject people. But in the case of Muhammad he carried the brutality to such a senseless extreme that it turned out to be counterproductive: it undermined his power, instead of securing it.

Muhammad, concedes Ferishta, was a learned, cultured and talented prince, but adds that 'despite all these admirable qualities he was wholly devoid of mercy or consideration for his people. The punishments he inflicted were not only rigid and cruel, but frequently unjust. So little did he hesitate to spill the blood of god's creatures that when anything occurred which excited him to proceed to that horrid extremity, one might have supposed his object was to exterminate the human species altogether.'

Hanafi, a mid-sixteenth century chronicler, gives a graphic account of one of the sultan's gruesome acts of tyranny. Muhammad, Hanafi writes, 'one day . . . went on foot to the court of Kazi Kamal-ud-din, the chief justice, and told him that Shaikh-zada Jam had called him unjust; he demanded that he should be summoned and required to prove the injustice of which he accused him, and that if he could not prove it, he should be punished according to the injunction of the law. Shaikh-zada Jam, when he arrived, admitted that he had made the allegation. The sultan then enquired his reason [for doing that], to which he replied, "When a criminal is brought before you, it is entirely at your royal option to punish him justly or unjustly, but you go further than that, and give his wife and children to the executioners so that they may do what they like with them. In what religion is this practice lawful? If this is not injustice, what is it?" The sultan remained silent, but after he left the court he ordered the Shaikh-zada to be imprisoned in an iron cage.' Later he had the Shaikh cut to pieces right in front of the kazi's court. 'There are many similar stories of the atrocities he committed. Tyranny took the place of justice.'

MUHAMMAD COMPENSATED HIS many frustrations by assuming a posture of extreme arrogance, of knowing and doing everything better than everyone else in the world. The more he failed, the more haughty he became. According to Barani, the sultan's pride was so overweening that he could not bear to hear of anyone anywhere in the world as being better than him in any way. And he had, as the predictable corollary of his insane pride, a ferocious temper. But characteristically, as in everything else in him, Muhammad was a weird mixture of contrary qualities in temperament too—if he was grotesque in his wrathful arrogance, he was equally grotesque in his ostentatious displays of abject self-abasement.

The classic instance of this was the reception he accorded to the Caliph's representative when he arrived in Delhi on royal invitation. As his troubles mounted, Muhammad conceived the chimerical notion that what would save him from his vicissitudes would be to secure pontifical recognition for his rule. 'It occurred to his mind that no king or prince could exercise regal power without conformation by the Caliph of the race of Abbas,' notes Barani. So he made diligent inquires, and, on learning from travellers that the true representative of the line of Abbas was the Caliph of Egypt, he sent envoys to Egypt to seek the Caliph's formal recognition.

'His flatteries of the Caliph were so fulsome that they cannot be reduced to writing,' states Barani. And when the Caliph's representative arrived in Delhi bringing Caliphal honours and a ceremonial robe for Muhammad, 'the sultan, with all his nobles . . . went forth to meet . . . [him] with great ceremony, and he walked before him barefoot for the distance of some long bow-shots.'

On getting pontifical recognition, Muhammad considered himself to be the deputy of the Caliph in India, and he removed his own name from his coins, and substituted it with the name of the Caliph. And, predictably, he then went to absurd extremes in displaying his subservience to the caliph. 'Without the Caliph's command the sultan scarcely ventured to drink even a draught of water,' wryly comments Barani.

Around this time there arrived in India one Ghiyas-ud-din Muhammad, a great-great grandson of the Abbasid Caliph al-Mustansir of Baghdad, and the sultan received him with grovelling servility. He sent the leading ecclesiastics and theologians of the court to receive the guest in western Haryana, and himself went a good distance from Delhi to meet him. After a ceremonious exchange of gifts, the sultan held Ghiyas-ud-din's stirrup while he mounted his horse, and they rode together to Delhi with the royal umbrella held over the heads of them both. The sultan even persuaded the reluctant Ghiyas-ud-din to place his foot upon his neck!

Muhammad was generally gracious and generous—almost fawning— towards the foreigners who visited him. It was as if he sought to purchase their appreciation as he could not win it from his own people, and he hoped that the visitors would spread his renown around the world. Typically, Ghiyas-ud-din was granted surpassing privileges at the royal court, given opulent presents, provided with lavish residential facilities and assigned an extensive fief for his income. Battuta too received very generous treatment from the sultan. 'When I approached the sultan, he took my hand and shook it,' reports Battuta. 'And, continuing to hold it, he addressed me most affably in Persian, saying, "Your arrival is blessed; be at ease, I shall be compassionate to you and grant you such favours that your fellow-countrymen will hear of it and come and join you." Then he asked me where I came from and I answered him, and every time he said any encouraging word to me I kissed his hand, until I had kissed it seven times.' Battuta was then given 6000 tankas in cash, and was assigned three villages as his fief, to which two more were later added, yielding him in all a substantial annual income of 12,000 tankas. Besides, he was given ten Hindu slaves to attend on him. He was even appointed as the kazi of Delhi, even though he did not know the local language—the office was, for Battuta, a sinecure, for he was given two local assistants to do his work, so he could enjoy the royal bounty with a clear conscience.

As in his treatment of foreign visitors, the sultan was equally cordial in his relationship with foreign rulers. Typical of this was his response to a diplomatic mission from China. 'The king of China had sent valuable gifts to the sultan, including a hundred slaves of both sexes, five hundred pieces of velvet and silk cloth, musk, jewelled garments and weapons, with a request that the sultan permit him to rebuild the idol-temple which is near the mountains called Qarajil,' reports Battuta. 'It is in a place known as Samhal, to which the Chinese go on pilgrimage; the Muslim army in India had captured it, laid it in ruins and sacked it.' On receiving the Chinese request for permission to rebuild the temple, Muhammad wrote to him that under Islamic law permission to build infidel temples could be given only to those who paid poll-tax. 'If thou wilt pay the jizya we shall empower thee to build it,' he wrote. But along with this negative reply, the sultan sent to the Chinese ruler, to mollify him, even richer presents than what he had received from him: 'a hundred thoroughbred horses, a hundred white slaves, a hundred Hindu dancing and singing girls, twelve hundred pieces of various kinds of cloth, gold and silver candelabra and basins, brocade robes, caps, quivers, swords, gloves embroidered with pearls, and fifteen eunuchs.'

THERE IS VERY little information in medieval chronicles about Muhammad's private life, but he seems to have been very close to his mother, whom he always treated with the highest respect and was ever obedient to her. He was continent in sexual relationships, and prohibited the presence of women in military camps. He also abstained from drinking.

Muhammad, as sultan, had many reprehensible and ludicrous qualities, but these were compensated, though only in a small part, by a few laudable qualities. Battuta records several instances of Muhammad's concern for equity and justice. 'Once a Hindu noble claimed that the sultan had put his brother to death without cause, and cited him before the qazi,' writes Battuta. 'The sultan then walked on foot and unarmed to the kazi's court, saluted him and made obeisance, and remained standing before him, having previously commanded the kazi not to rise before him . . . when he entered the court. The qazi gave judgement against the sultan, to the effect that he must give satisfaction to his adversary for the blood of his brother, and he did so. At another time a certain Muslim claimed that the sultan owed him a sum of money. This matter too was brought before the kazi, who again gave judgement against the sultan for the payment of the debt, and he paid it.'

In the same compliant, caring spirit he did at times, though rarely, take special measures to succour the people in distress. Thus 'when a famine broke out in India and Sind, and prices became so high that [the cost of] a maund of wheat rose to six *dinars*, the sultan ordered that every person in Delhi, small or great, freeman or salve, should be given six months' provisions from the granary, at the rate of a pound and a half per person per day,' records Battuta. 'The doctors and qazis then set about compiling registers of the population of each quarter and brought the people, each of whom received six months' provisions.' Even in normal times the sultan took care to provide sustenance for the indigent in Delhi, by setting up public kitchens for feeding several thousands of them every day. He also set up hospitals for the sick, and hospices for widows and orphans.

IN RELIGION, AS in everything else, Muhammad was a bundle of contradictions, rigidly orthodox in some ways, but in other ways flagrantly unorthodox. According to Battuta, 'the ceremonies of religion are strictly complied with at his court, and he is severe in the matter of attendance at prayer and in punishing those who neglect it.' Ferishta confirms this. On the other hand, Barani and Isami denounce Muhammad as an irreligious person—Barani in fact, despite being a timorous courtier, once openly told the sultan that many of his actions, particularly the harsh punishments he meted out to rebels, had no sanction in Islamic tradition. Isami went further, and he in his chronicle denounced Muhammad as a kafir, an infidel, who sided with infidels and indulged in infidel practices, and he urged people to rise up against him.

One of the 'infidel practices' of Muhammad that outraged orthodox Muslims was his patronage of yogis, of which Battuta gives a vivid account. 'The sultan sent for me once when I was in Delhi, and on entering I found him in a private apartment with some of his intimates and two . . . yogis,' records Battuta. 'One of the yogis, who squatted on the ground, then rose up in the air above our heads, still sitting. I was so astonished and frightened by this that I fell to the floor in a faint. A potion was administered to me, and I revived and sat up . . . Meantime . . . the yogi's companion took a sandal from a bag he had with him, and beat it on the ground like one infuriated. The sandal rose in the air until it came above the neck of the . . . [yogi who had risen up in the air] and then began hitting him on the neck while he descended little by little until he sat down alongside us. Then the sultan said, "If I did not fear for your reason I would have ordered them to do still stranger things than this that you have seen." I took leave, but was affected with palpitation and fell ill.'

Another paradoxical trait of Muhammad was that he, for all the violence of his rule, was an ardent patron of Jain sage Jinaprabha Suri, who was, in conformity with the precepts of his religion, a strict practitioner of nonviolence. According to Jain sources the sultan once invited the sage to the royal palace, 'treated him with respect, seated him by his side, and offered to give him wealth, land, horses, elephants etc, all of which the saint declined. The sultan praised him [for his austerity] and issued a firman . . . for the construction of a new . . . rest-house for the monks.' The sage was then carried on an elephant to his residence, escorted by several nobles and 'to the accompaniment of varied music and dances of young women.'

Whatever be the veracity of these stories, Muhammad seems to have loved to explore other faiths, at least as an intellectual exercise, for he was, despite all his wildness, a man of learning and wide cultural interests. 'In calligraphy . . . Sultan Muhammad abashed the most accomplished scribes,' writes Barani. 'The excellence of his handwriting, the ease of his composition, the sublimity of his style, and the play of his fancy, left the most accomplished teachers and professors far behind. He was an adept in the use of metaphor. He knew by heart a good deal of Persian poetry, and understood it well . . . No learned or scientific man, or scribe, or poet, or wit, or physician, could have had the presumption to argue with him about his own special pursuit, nor would he have been able to maintain his position against the throttling arguments of the sultan.' Confirms Battuta: 'He is one of those kings whose felicity is unimpaired and surpassing all ordinary experience.'

3

Daydreamer Sultan

Muhammad Tughluq was an incorrigible daydreamer. And it was only in his dreams that he was able to fulfil himself. The problem was not with his ideas, which were mostly quite sound, but with his character, which was mercurial and erratic, and lacked the tenacity and pragmatism needed to implement his schemes successfully. In this, the contrast between Muhammad and Ala-ud-din, the other great radical reformer sultan of Delhi, could not have been greater. While Ala-ud-din was a pragmatist, motivated solely by practical considerations, Muhammad was a fantasist, who was motivated more by the excitement of his whimsies than by expediency. Muhammad was impulsive, while Ala-ud-din was deliberate and calculating. So while Ala-ud-din succeeded in almost all his reforms, Muhammad failed in everything. In nearly every case the result that Muhammad got out of his projects was the exact opposite of what he hoped for.

Even the mode of decision-making by the two sultans was entirely different. While Ala-ud-din always held detailed discussions with his councillors on every major project, though in the end he made up his own mind, Muhammad 'never talked over his projects with any of his councillors and friends,' states Barani. 'Whatever he conceived, he considered to be good, but in promulgating and enforcing the schemes he lost his hold upon the territories he possessed, disgusted his people, and emptied his treasury. Embarrassment followed embarrassment, and confusion became worse confounded. The ill feeling of the people gave rise to outbreaks and revolts . . . As more and more the people became disaffected, more and more the mind of the king was set against them, and the numbers of those brought to punishment increased. The tribute of most of the distant countries and districts was lost, and many of his soldiers and servants were scattered and left in distant lands. Deficiencies appeared in the treasury. The mind of the sultan then lost its equilibrium. In the extreme weakness and harshness of his temper he gave himself to severity . . . [Thus his] schemes led to the ruin of his empire, and the decay of the people. Every one of [his schemes] . . . led to some wrong and mischief, and the minds of all men, high and low, were disgusted with their ruler . . . When the sultan found that his orders did not work as well as he desired, he became still more embittered against his people, and he cut them down like weeds . . .'

Many of Muhammad's administrative reforms related to revenue matters, for adequacy of funds was a prerequisite for the implementation of his other ambitious plans. Soon after his accession he therefore ordered the compilation of a register of the revenue and expenditure of all the provinces of his empire, on the model of the register that was already being maintained for the districts neighbouring Delhi. For this, Muhammad directed the governors of the provinces to send to him the details of their revenue and expenditure, and these reports were, over several years, compiled into a common register for the whole empire by a host of clerks under the supervision of officers. This register, if properly maintained, would have been invaluable for systematising the revenue administration of the empire, but it is not known how effectively it was maintained, or for how long, and with what results.

Equally innovative and valuable was Muhammad's decision to set up a ministry of agriculture, to expand cultivation by converting fallow lands into farmlands, and to spread the cultivation of high value commercial crops in the place of common crops—'not one span of land should remain uncultivated . . . and whatever was being cultivated should be changed [for more valuable crops],' the sultan directed. 'Wheat should be sown instead of barley; sugarcane instead of wheat; grape and date instead of sugarcane . . .' And, to encourage farmers to make this changeover, the sultan offered them liberal loans from the royal treasury.

When this scheme to expand cultivation was promulgated, several 'greedy, impecunious men . . . came forward,' reports Barani. 'Some . . . pledged to bring one lack of bighas of wasteland under cultivation, others promised to raise a thousand horsemen from [the revenues of] wastelands—all within three years! They were given horses . . ., gold-embroidered gowns, waistbands of brocade, and cash [by the sultan].'

The scheme however failed miserably, for, as Barani observes, 'the officers entrusted with the distribution of loans [to farmers] from the public treasury took care of themselves, and appropriated the money for their own wants and necessities . . . In the course of two years about seventy lakh tankas had been issued from the treasury to the superintendents of the cultivation of wastelands, but not one hundredth or one thousandth part of what was disbursed was reproduced in agriculture.'

ANOTHER SCHEME OF Muhammad to increase the revenue of the state was the introduction of revenue farming, by which all the revenues of particular areas were for a certain period assigned to their highest bidders, on their agreement to pay the government the bid amounts irrespective of whether the revenue they collected was more, or less, than the bid amount. This scheme was initially introduced in the Deccan, but was later extended to the other provinces of the empire.

This procedure had, in theory, the double advantage of reducing the administrative burden of the state and at the same time increasing and stabilising its revenue. In practice, however, the system proved to be ruinous, to the people as well as to the government, for the successful bidders were often upstart speculators with hardly any administrative experience, who could seldom meet their extravagant revenue promises, however hard they squeezed the people. Predictably several of the franchise holders turned into rebels eventually, when faced with punitive action by the sultan for the collection of the revenue dues from them. The common people too suffered greatly, due to their exploitation by the revenue collectors. So this scheme too, like most of the other schemes of Muhammad, proved to be counterproductive, resulting in civil disturbances and the near collapse of the revenue administration of the state.

Yet another counterproductive administrative reform of Muhammad was to sharply increase the tax on the cultivators in the Doab, as he, according Barani, felt that 'he ought to get five or ten per cent more tribute from the [rich agricultural] lands there . . . [And he] collected these cesses so rigorously that cultivators there were impoverished and reduced to beggary.' Further, these taxes were assessed on the standard yield, not on the actual yield, and that added to the distress of farmers during periods of poor yield. But instead of offering relief to farmers in distress, the sultan added to their financial burden by requiring them to pay, in addition to the tax on farm produce, 'a cattle-tax, a house tax, and several other imposts of an oppressive nature,' states Mughal chronicler Badauni. All this, according to Barani, led to 'the ruin of the country and the decay of the people.' But Muhammad was unconcerned. And he, despite the all too evident problems that his tax measures caused, gradually extended them to a wide area of the empire.

Inevitably people in several places rose in rebellion against these exacting, oppressive measures of the sultan. In the Doab, farmers 'burnt their corn stacks and turned their cattle out to roam at large,' reports Barani. Muhammad responded to this peasant uprising with savage reprisals. 'Under the orders of the sultan, collectors and magistrates then laid waste the country, and they killed some landholders and village chiefs and blinded others. Such of these unhappy inhabitants as escaped formed themselves into bands and took refuge in jungles.' According to Nurul Haq, 'the sultan then gave orders that every peasant who was seized should be put to death, and that the whole country should be ravaged and given up to indiscriminate plunder . . . He himself marched out . . . and put to the sword all the remaining population and ordered their heads to displayed from the battlements of the fort. In this way he utterly depopulated whole tracts of his kingdom, and inflicted such rigorous punishment, that the whole world was aghast.'

These adversities of the people were compounded by an acute and prolonged drought that afflicted North India at this time. 'For seven whole years not a drop of rain fell from the heavens,' states Badauni. And this, according to Barani, 'produced a fatal famine in Delhi and its environs, and throughout the Doab . . . It continued for some years, and thousands upon thousands of people perished . . . All cultivation [was] abandoned . . . Man was devouring man.' Battuta states that he once saw some women stripping off the skin of a long dead horse and eating it, and that cooked hides were on sale in markets. And people gathered in butcheries to drink the blood of slaughtered cattle. In one place a man was found cooking a human foot. Cannibalism became common.

Characteristically, Muhammad then swung from one extreme posture to its total opposite, from callousness and brutality to compassion and humanism. To relieve people from the horrors of famine he then ordered grain to be issued to them from the royal granary, and he set up public kitchens to feed the destitute. Also, he tried to revive cultivation by advancing loans to farmers from the treasury to buy seeds and plough-cattle, but 'want of rain prevented cultivation,' so the misery of the people continued, notes Barani.

THE MOST RADICAL of the economic reforms of Muhammad was the introduction of token currency in the fifth year of his reign, when he issued brass or copper coins on par with the value of his silver tanka coins. He did this, according to Barani, to raise funds to finance his grandiose plan to conquer the whole known world. Besides, the sultan's 'bounty and munificence had caused a great deficiency in the treasury,' and that had to be rectified. 'So he introduced the copper money, and gave orders that it should be used in buying and selling, and should . . . [be accepted as legal tender] just as the gold and silver coins [were accepted].'

It is likely that Muhammad was inspired to introduce token currency by what he had learnt about its use in China (which had been using paper currency for some centuries) and Persia (which had adopted the practice in the thirteenth century). The idea of introducing token currency in India excited the sultan, as he had a compulsive need to try something new every now and then. Besides, he considered it as the best solution to the financial problems he faced. However, unlike the Chinese who took elaborate measures to prevent forgeries of paper currency and punished counterfeiters with death, Muhammad did not have the administrative will and skill to execute the scheme effectively. So it failed utterly.

The token coins that Muhammad issued were easily counterfeited. 'Every goldsmith struck copper coins in his workshop,' states Barani. 'The promulgation of the edict [about token currency] turned the house of every Hindu into a mint, and Hindus of the various provinces coined lakhs and crores of copper coins. With these they paid their tribute, and with these they purchased horses, arms, and fine things of all kinds. The *rais*, the village headmen and landowners, grew rich and strong upon these copper coins, but the state was impoverished.'

Soon it came to be that people in their everyday transactions would accept copper coins only for the value of its metal, not for its inscribed value. But everyone paid their dues to the government in copper coins, often in forged coins. In consequence of this, the treasury, according to Barani, 'was filled with copper coins. So low did they fall [in value] that they were not valued more than pebbles or potsherds.' As Badauni wryly comments, 'After all, copper was copper, and silver was silver.'

When the sultan found that his token currency project had failed, and that it was ruining the finances of the state, he abandoned it, 'and in great wrath he proclaimed that whoever possessed copper coins should bring them to the treasury and receive gold [or silver] coins in exchange,' reports Barani. That in effect meant that the government now bought copper at the price of silver or gold. 'Thousands of men from various quarters, who possessed thousands of these copper coins . . . now brought them to the treasury, [and received in exchange gold and silver coins] . . . So many of these copper coins were brought to the treasury, that heaps of them rose up in Tughluqabad like mountains.' The abject failure of the token currency project further embittered Muhammad, and 'he more than ever turned against his subjects.'

ANOTHER GOOD INTENTIONED scheme of Muhammad that failed miserably was the shifting of his capital from Delhi to Devagiri, nearly a thousand kilometres to the south. Devagiri was in a fairly central location in the Sultanate, and in those of days of slow communication and travel it certainly was a political and military advantage to locate the capital there, especially as Muhammad had extended his direct rule deep into South India. Besides, Devagiri, unlike Delhi, was well beyond the reach of Mongols, who were a perennial menace to the Sultanate.

Apart from these locational advantages, Devagiri had the advantage of having an impregnable fort atop a high, rocky and precipitous hill which, from

the security point of view, was an excellent place for the sultan to reside in
those turbulent times. Moreover, to live in a place far above his subjects suited
Muhammad's exalted view of his personal eminence.

The plan to shift the capital to Devagiri was therefore on the whole sensible,
and it deserved to succeed. But it failed. It failed because it was an abrupt,
impulsive, personal decision of the sultan, which was made, as Barani stresses,
'without any consultation, and without carefully examining its advantages
and disadvantages on every side.' But more than that, the move failed because
Muhammad not only shifted his capital to Devagiri, but vindictively insisted
that the entire population of Delhi also should move to it.

Muhammad's decision to shift the capital to Devagiri was made in 1327,
in the second year of his reign, but there is some confusion about whether he
initially meant only to relocate there the royal court, its offices and staff, or
whether he wanted all the people of Delhi also to move there. The reports of
Barani and Battuta, both contemporary chroniclers, speak of the forced shift of
the entire population of Delhi to Devagiri, but while Barani implies (though he
does not state it explicitly) that this was essentially an administrative measure,
Battuta describes it as a punitive measure against the people of Delhi because
of their animosity to the sultan. It is probable that the shifting of the capital
was effected in two phases, as later medieval chroniclers like Badauni, Ferishta
and Sirhindi indicate—a first phase in which the royal court was shifted there
as an administrative measure, and a second phase a couple of years later in
which the entire population of Delhi was forced to move there as a punitive
measure. Asking all the people of Delhi to move to Devagiri in the first instance
was far too senseless a measure even for a weird eccentric like Muhammad to
conceive and execute, though it was not entirely beyond him.

Muhammad renamed Devagiri (Mountain of Gods) as Daulatabad (Abode
of Prosperity) and in a few of years it did indeed become, true to its new name,
a great and splendid city, as royal officers and others dependent on the court
built their residences there, and opulent bazaars and other facilities suitable for
a royal capital were set up there. Battuta, who visited Daulatabad some years
later, found it to be an 'enormous city which rivals Delhi . . . in importance
and in the spaciousness of its planning.'

MUHAMMAD'S DECISION TO shift his residence to Devagiri would have
been quite upsetting to the people of Delhi, for the royal court was the very
heart of Delhi, and its transfer from there would have rendered the city lifeless.
The people of Delhi therefore had good reason to resent the sultan's decision,
and they seem to have expressed their feelings about it by sending anonymous
abusive letters to him, and that was probably what roused his wrath and
prompted him to order the complete evacuation of Delhi.

According to Battuta, the people of Delhi 'used to write missives reviling and insulting' the sultan, seal them and throw then into the audience hall at night, with a warning written on them that they should be opened only by the sultan. 'When the sultan broke their seal [and opened the letters] he found them full of insults and abuse. He [therefore] decided to lay Delhi in ruins, and having bought from all the inhabitants their houses . . . and paid them the price of them, he commanded them to move to Daulatabad. But they refused. So a crier was sent around the city to proclaim that no one should remain in the city after three nights. The majority [of the residents there] then complied with the order, but some of them hid in the houses. The sultan then ordered a search to be made for any persons remaining in the town, and his slaves found two men in the streets, a cripple and a blind man. They were brought before him and he gave orders that the cripple should be flung from a mangonel, and that the blind man dragged from Delhi to Daulatabad, a distance of forty days' journey. He fell to pieces on the road and of him all that reached Daulatabad was his leg. When the sultan did this, every person left the town, abandoning furniture and possessions, and the city remained utterly deserted . . . [Then] one night the sultan mounted to the roof of his palace and looked out over Delhi, where there was neither fire nor smoke nor lamp, and he said, "Now my mind is tranquil and my wrath appeased." Afterwards he wrote to the inhabitants of the other cities commanding them to move to Delhi to repopulate it. The result was only to ruin their cities and leave Delhi still unpopulated, because of its immensity, for it is one of the greatest cities in the world. It was in this state that we found it on our arrival, empty and unpopulated, save for a few inhabitants.'

Barani concurs with Battuta that the shifting of the capital to Devagiri was disastrous. 'It brought ruin upon Delhi, the city which . . . had grown in prosperity, and rivalled Baghdad and Cairo,' he writes. 'So complete was its ruin that not a cat or a dog was left among the buildings of the city, in its palaces or in its suburbs. Troops of the natives, with their families and dependents, wives and children, men servants and maid servants, were forced to move [to Devagiri]. The people, who for many . . . generations had been . . . the inhabitants of . . . [Delhi], were broken-hearted. Many, from the toils of the long journey, perished on the road, and those who arrived at Devagiri could not endure the pain of exile. They pined to death in despondency.'

Though Muhammad took care to provide various facilities for the migrants on their long journey, and helped them to settle in Devagiri, none of that compensated them for their mental agony due to the loss of their traditional domicile. 'The sultan,' continues Barani, 'was bounteous in his liberality and favours to the emigrants, both on their journey and on their arrival; but they were tender, and could not endure the exile and suffering . . . Of all the multitudes of emigrants, few only survived to return to their home' when the sultan later re-shifted the capital to Delhi.

Daulatabad remained the capital of the Sultanate for eight years. When Muhammad finally gave permission to the migrants to return to Delhi, most of them joyfully went back, though some, 'with whom the Maratha country agreed, remained in Devagiri with their wives and children,' notes Barani. But even with the return of a large number of people to Delhi, 'not a thousandth part of the [original] population [of Delhi] remained.'

MUHAMMAD HAD MUCH more success in his military campaigns for expanding the territory of his empire than in his administrative reforms. This was partly because his reign was relatively free of Mongol raids. There was only one major incursion into the Sultanate by Mongols during his reign. This was in 1327, early in Muhammad's reign, when they invaded India under the command of the Chagatai chief Tarmashirin, a Buddhist turned Muslim. The Mongol objective, as usual, was to gather plunder, not to conquer territory, so they stormed eastward through the Indo-Gangetic Plain and advanced as far as Meerut close to Delhi, pillaging and ravaging the land all along the way, and slaughtering people indiscriminately. According to Ferishta, Muhammad then bought them off with a huge ransom, and they sped back home, once again pillaging and ravaging the land all along the way. According to another account, Muhammad made a show of pursuing the Mongols up to Kalanaur in Punjab, a town that now enters history for the first time, where Mughal emperor Akbar would be born 215 years later.

Another aspect of Muhammad's policy towards Mongols was to try and absorb them into Indian population. According to Barani 'the sultan supported and patronised Mongols,' and he induced many thousands of them to come with their families and settle in India, by conferring on them various favours and spending vast sums of money on them, probably in the hope that these fierce warriors would strengthen his army and help him to achieve his various ambitious plans for conquest. But rather than adding to the strength and stability of the Sultanate, Mongol migrants only added to the turmoil of Muhammad's reign.

Despite that setback there was, during Muhammad's reign, a significant expansion of the territory of the Sultanate, deep into South India. But in the end even that turned out to be counterproductive. Unlike Ala-ud-din Khalji's sensible policy of not annexing distant territories that he could not effectively rule, but only of establishing his suzerainty over them, Muhammad sought to annex all the lands he conquered, and early in his reign he extended his direct rule deep into the peninsula as far as Madurai. Virtually all of India, except

Kashmir and Kerala at the far ends of the subcontinent, and a few small tracts in between, then came under the direct rule of Delhi.

But Muhammad was not content with this. 'The sultan in his lofty ambition had conceived it to be his mission in life to subdue the whole habitable world and bring it under his rule,' notes Barani. Shortly after the Mongol invasion early in his reign, Muhammad dreamed up a plan to conquer Central Asia—if Central Asians could invade India, why not Indians invade Central Asia? For this project the sultan recruited a vast army of 370,000 cavalry, which was maintained by him for a year, but was not deployed in any campaign, so that 'when the next year came around there were not sufficient funds in the treasury . . . to support them,' so they were disbanded, records Barani.

The sultan did however launch a military campaign into the western Himalayan foothills, perhaps in preparation for an invasion of Central Asia, as Barani states, or for an invasion of China, as Ferishta states. But this turned out to be an absolute disaster, as heavy rains impeded the army's progress, and diseases ravaged soldiers and horses. Beset by these troubles, the hapless army retreated in disorder, but they were then brutally set on by the local people. 'The whole force was thus destroyed . . . and out of all this chosen body of men only ten horsemen returned to Delhi to tell the news of its discomfiture,' reports Barani. The net result of Muhammad's plans for foreign conquests was that, as Barani comments, 'the coveted countries were not acquired, but those which he possessed were lost; and his treasure, which is the true source of political power, was expended.'

MUHAMMAD WAS BEDEVILLED by endless problems in the latter part of his reign. His vast empire then began to disintegrate, and large chunks of it broke away. And he had little control even over the remaining territories, as countless rebellions raged through the empire like wild fires. The man who wanted to rule the world could hardly control his own backyard.

'Disaffection and disturbances arose on every side,' Barani reports, 'and as they gathered strength, the sultan became more exasperated and more severe with his subjects. But his severities only increased the distress of the people . . . Insurrection followed upon insurrection . . . The people were alienated. No place remained secure, all order and regularity were lost, and the throne was tottering to its fall.' Muhammad was well aware that his repressive measures were counterproductive, but still would not modify his policy. 'When I collect my forces and put them (the rebels) down in one direction, they excite disturbance in some other quarter,' he once told Barani. 'My kingdom is diseased, and no treatment cures it. The physician cures the headache, but fever follows; he strives to allay the fever, and something else supervenes.'

The empire was clearly swirling into anarchy. What could be done about it? What had former kings done in similar circumstances, the sultan once asked Barani. Barani replied in detail to that query, and concluded: 'Of all political ills, the greatest and the most dire is the general feeling of aversion ... among all ranks of people.' But Muhammad asserted that he would not change his ways, whatever be the reaction of the people. 'At present I am angry with my subjects, and they are aggrieved with me,' he told Barani. 'The people are acquainted with my feelings, and I am aware of their misery and wretchedness. No treatment that I employ is of any benefit. My remedy for rebels, insurgents, opponents, and disaffected people is the sword. I employ punishment and use the sword, so that a cure may be affected by suffering. The more the people resist, the more I inflict chastisement.'

Barani could have then told the sultan that the problem was not with the people, but with the sultan. But he dared not say that. 'I could not help feeling a desire to tell the sultan that the troubles and revolts which were breaking out on every side, and this general disaffection, all arose from the excessive severity of His Majesty, and that if punishments were suspended for a while, a better feeling might spring up, and mistrust be removed from the hearts of the people,' Barani confesses. 'But I dreaded the temper of the king and could not say what I desired.'

THE FIRST NOTED rebellion against Muhammad was in the second year of his reign, and that was by his cousin Baha-ud-din Gurshasp, who held a fief near Gulbarga in northern Karnataka. This was a minor rebellion, and Gurshasp was easily defeated by the imperial forces sent against him. He then fled southward and took refuge with the raja of Kampili, on the banks of the Tungabhadra. As the imperial forces pursued the rebel there, the raja shut himself in the fort of Hosdurg, and when attacked there, the royal women there performed the awesome suicidal rite of jauhar, and the raja himself and several of his officers fought to death against the enemy. Those who survived—some princes and officers—were captured by the Sultanate army and taken to Delhi, where they embraced Islam. Among these converts were two brothers, Harihara and Bukka, who would later revert to Hinduism, return to the peninsula, and found the powerful Hindu kingdom of Vijayanagar.

Meanwhile, on the fall of Hosdurg, Gurshasp fled to the Hoysala kingdom, but the raja there timidly handed him over to the Sultanate army. Gurshasp was then taken to Daulatabad, where the sultan had arrived, and he was there flayed alive, and his skin, stuffed with straw, was exhibited in the chief cities of the empire as a warning to other potential rebels.

But that did not prevent rebellions. Rather, as Muhammad's reign advanced, so did the number of rebellions against him multiply, particularly in the last phase of his reign. And, as rebellions spread, so did the harshness of the sultan's response to them intensify, in an ever tightening vicious circle of rebellion and suppression.

The sultan spent his last years obsessively scurrying around fighting rebels. But it was all utterly futile, for when he put down rebellion in one place, it broke out elsewhere, and when he moved to suppress the new rebellion, rebellion broke out again in the previous place. This went on and on. The sultan's efforts were all utterly futile, like cutting off the heads of a hydra, each of which, when cut off, immediately grew back as two.

Soon the Sultanate lost most of its territory in the peninsula, where three new kingdoms then came up: the Madurai Sultanate, the Bahmani Sultanate, and Vijayanagar. Warangal too became independent. There were serious rebellions in North India also at this time. Predictably Bengal now became an independent kingdom. Oudh and north-west India too were plagued by insurgencies. And in Gujarat and Maharashtra a group of foreign migrant officers, often described as the Centurions, broke out in rebellion.

Muhammad set out from Delhi in 1345 to suppress the rebellion of the Centurions. He would never return. All circumstances now turned adverse to the sultan. During this campaign his army was plagued by famine and epidemics. And in Gujarat he was confronted by a resourceful and tenacious adversary, a cobbler turned rebel leader named Taghi, who had, according to Barani, won over to his side several of the amirs of Gujarat. Muhammad defeated Taghi, but could not capture him, as he fled to Sind.

When the sultan was in Gujarat he caught fever and was prostrated for some months. On recovery, he set out for Sind in pursuit of Taghi. In late 1350 he crossed the Indus and advanced along the banks of the river towards Tattah, where Taghi had taken refuge. On the way he kept the fast of the tenth day of Muharram, 'and when it was over he ate some fish. The fish did not agree with him, so his illness returned and fever increased,' records Barani. Though Muhammad continued his advance on Tattah by travelling by boat on the Indus, his ailment soon turned critical, and on 20th March 1351 he 'departed from this life on the banks of the Indus, at 14 kos (45 kilometres) from Tattah.' He had reigned for 26 years.

WHAT WERE THE thoughts of the sultan as he lay dying? We do not know. There is no record of anything that he said or did in his last days. But certainly his dying thoughts would have been hardly pleasant, for the grand dreams with which he began his reign had all turned into most dreadful nightmares.

Muhammad was a learned man with wide cultural interests, but that was a qualification of little value in a medieval ruler; indeed, the most successful rulers of medieval India, Ala-ud-din Khalji and Akbar, were both illiterate.

Undeniably Muhammad had some good and progressive ideas, and several of them were achievable goals. But he did not have the pragmatism or the mental stamina to think through his plans in detail, nor did he have the tenacity and toughness of character to carry them through to success in the face of problems. None—not one—of his schemes was carried to success. Muhammad, for all his posture of toughness, was a weak, wavering ruler, who blamed others for the failure of his schemes, while the faults were all of his own.

Muhammad had the potential of being an agent for revolutionary change for the good in the Sultanate, but his reign turned out to be an absolute disaster. He meant to do good, but ended up doing only harm. All contemporary sources agree that his policies resulted in the ruin of the county and the people. 'The glory of the state, and the power of the government of Sultan Muhammad . . . withered and decayed,' states Barani. In fact, paradoxical though it might seem, it was the good in him that fuelled and fanned the flames of the fiend in him—he turned devilish to punish the people who failed to appreciate the good in him! His frustrations warped his character, turned him into a raging, rampaging monster.

And that brought untold misery on his subjects. In his death, comments Badauni, 'the king was freed from his people, and they from their king.'

4

People's Sultan

As Muhammad Tughluq lay terminally ill, the anxiety about what the future portended for the Delhi Sultanate and all those associated with it swept through the imperial army. 'They were a thousand kos distant from Delhi and their wives and children, and were near the enemy and in a wilderness and desert,' reports Barani. 'So they were sorely distressed and, looking upon the sultan's expected death as preliminary to their own death, they quite despaired of returning home.'

Presently, as expected, the sultan died. And that left the army without a commander—and the empire without a ruler. So the entire Sultanate camp, which included a good number of women and children, swirled into utter chaos as it set out to return to Delhi. 'Every division of the army marched in the greatest disorder, without leader, rule, or route,' states Barani. 'No one heeded or listened to what anyone said . . . When they had proceeded a kos or two, Mongols, eager for booty, assailed them in front, and the rebels of Tattah attacked them in the rear. Cries of dismay arose on every side. Mongols fell to plundering, and carried off women, maids, horses, camels, troopers, baggage, and whatever else had been sent on in advance. They very nearly captured even the royal harem and treasure . . . Then the villagers who had been pressed into the service of the army . . . took to flight. They pillaged various lots of baggage on the right and left of the army, and then joined the rebels of Tattah in attacking the baggage train. . . . [All this plunged the army into a whirl, for] if they advanced in front they were assailed by Mongols; if they lagged behind, they were plundered by the rebels of Tattah . . . Every man was in despair for his life and goods, his wife and children.'

These troubles went on for a few days. Then, according to Barani, the top officers in the Sultanate camp gathered together and, 'after a long and anxious deliberation,' decided to offer the crown to Firuz Shah, a first-cousin of Muhammad, and they went to him and 'with one voice said, "Thou art the heir apparent and legatee of the late sultan; he had no son . . . There is no one else . . . who enjoys the confidence of the people or has the ability to reign. For god's sake save these wretched people; ascend the throne and deliver us."' Firuz, apparently in a show of becoming modesty, expressed reluctance to accept the responsibility, and said that he was planning to go on a pilgrimage to Mecca at that time. But 'all ranks, young and old, Muslims and Hindus, horse and foot, women and children, assembled, and with one acclaim declared that Firuz Shah alone was worthy of the crown.'

Then, according to Afif, the chief chronicler of Firuz's reign, Tatar Khan, a top noble, 'stood up, and taking the arm of Firuz Shah, forced him to sit on the throne . . . as heralds and attendants shouted in loud acclaim, and drums were beaten in exultation . . .'

This was on 23 March 1351, three days after the death of Muhammad. Firuz, 46 years old then, was the closest surviving male relative of Muhammad—who had no sons, but only two daughters—and therefore had a very strong claim for the throne. He had always been close to Muhammad, and had been at times appointed (along with a couple of other senior officers) by the sultan as his regent in Delhi when he went on military campaigns. And there was a general belief that Muhammad had intended Firuz to succeed him; indeed, according to Ferishta, Muhammad 'proposed making him (Firuz) his successor, and accordingly recommended him as such on his deathbed to his nobles.'

Firuz's accession was however challenged by Muhammad's sister, Khudavand-zada, on the ground that her son, as Muhammad's nephew, had the greater claim to the throne. This claim was however rejected by the nobles on the ground that the prince was too young to rule in those troubled times.[1]

Another problem that Firuz faced on his accession was that when the news of Muhammad's death reached Delhi, Khvaja Jahan—a long time close associate of Muhammad, and whom he had apparently left in Delhi as his regent when he set out for Gujarat—raised to the throne a child who he claimed was Muhammad's son. According to Afif, Khvaja did this with good intentions, 'for public welfare and the safety of the country,' to prevent the empire from disintegrating into anarchy without a sultan, for he had been told

---

[1]That thwarted the princess, but only for a while. Some years later she would make yet another attempt to seize power for her son, this time by plotting to assassinate Firuz, but that conspiracy too failed. She was then imprisoned, her husband banished, and their vast wealth confiscated by the state.

that Firuz was missing or dead. Khvaja was well over eighty years old then, and was presumably not motivated by any personal ambition in his action. Besides, he had excellent rapport with Firuz, and had always treated him like a son. He therefore had no hesitation to submit to Firuz as he approached Delhi. And Firuz in turn received him graciously, and was inclined to pardon him and retain him as the vizier. But his advisers, no doubt motivated by their own ambitions, objected to this on the ground that Khvaja's offence was too serious to be pardoned. Firuz then left the matter to be decided by the nobles, and they had the old man executed.

FIRUZ'S FATHER, SIPAH-SALAR Rajab, was the younger brother of Ghiyas-ud-din Tughluq, and they together had migrated to India from Khurasan during the reign of Ala-ud-din Khalji. In India Rajab married a Jat princess, a beautiful and spirited daughter of Rana Mall Bhatti of Dipalpur in Punjab. Firuz was their only child.

Rajab died when Firuz was seven, so the boy was brought up by Ghiyas-ud-din. And when Ghiyas-ud-din ascended the throne of Delhi, Firuz, who was then fourteen, was given a role in government, as an aid to the sultan, a post that enabled him to gain wide experience in governance. Four years later, when Muhammad ascended the throne, Firuz was appointed as deputy of the Lord Chamberlain, and was given the command of a 12,000-strong cavalry force. 'The sultan was exceedingly kind and generous to him, and keeping him constantly near his person he used to explain to him, with much intelligence, all the affairs of the state that came up for consideration,' states Afif. Later Muhammad put Firuz in charge of one of the four divisions of the Sultanate, 'so that he might acquire experience in the art of government . . . [and] become an adept in all political matters . . . [The sultan] used to keep Firuz Shah continually at work in various matters . . . to train him so that he might become thoroughly versed in the duties of royalty.'

Firuz on his accession was thus well-equipped to assume royal responsibilities. As sultan, his first task was to restore order in the army, but this was accomplished without any special effort on his part, as the mere fact that there was now a sultan on the throne immediately calmed the army and restored its discipline. Mongols and the Sind rebels were then driven away, and the army resumed its journey to Delhi in fair order. On the way the sultan received the news that Taghi, the rebel who had sorely tried Muhammad in his last days, was dead. The news was considered an auspicious portent for the success of the reign of Firuz.

As Firuz proceeded to Delhi, his followers swelled in number, and when he neared the capital, most of the chiefs there came out to greet him. On 25 August 1351 Firuz entered the capital in a triumphant procession, when 'drums of joy were beaten, and the citizens decked themselves out in their jewels and best clothes,' reports Afif. 'Pavilions were erected and decorated . . . and for twenty-one days a continual festival was maintained.'

In every respect the reign of Firuz was unlike the reign of Muhammad; the contrast between them was like that of between a pitch-dark, cyclonic night and a calm and clear dawn. Though Muhammad and Firuz were close to each other, they were entirely unlike each other in character, temperament and policies—Muhammad was an egomaniac, flighty and unpredictable, ever pursuing some chimerical scheme or other; in contrast, Firuz was a stable, dependable ruler, with a good sense of what was viable and necessary. While Muhammad wanted the world to adjust to him, Firuz adjusted himself to the world. And, more than anything else, Firuz was concerned with the stability of the empire and the welfare of its people, rather than with self-fulfilment. He was the right person in the right place at the right time.

'Sultan Firuz was a very cautious man,' states Afif. He was also very pious. 'Whenever he was about to make a journey for a month or two, he used to visit the shrines of holy men and famous kings, to invoke their aid and to cast himself on their protection, not trusting his own power and greatness . . . The sultan never transacted any business without referring to the Koran for an augury.' But despite being a devout Muslim, Firuz had a weakness was for wine, in which he indulged secretly. Also, he was a sensualist, and was particularly addicted to sexual pleasures. His harem, according to Afif, was periodically restocked with the 'beautiful slaves, dressed and ornamented in the most splendid style,' presented to him by his provincial officers. He was also passionate about hunting, like most Delhi sultans.

IN MANY RESPECTS Firuz was a model ruler, esteemed alike by his officers and his subjects. The main task of Firuz on his accession was to rebuild the foundations of the empire, which had crumbled during the calamitous reign of Muhammad. This task involved, above all, restoring the mutual trust between the ruler and the ruled. Firuz therefore first of all sought the forgiveness of the people—and of god—for the misdeeds of Muhammad. The heirs of those who had been wantonly killed or mutilated on the orders of Muhammad were 'appeased with gifts, so that they executed deeds declaring their satisfaction, duly attested by witnesses,' states Firuz in his autobiography, *Futuhat-i-Firuz Shahi*. 'These deeds were put in a chest, which was placed . . . at the head of the tomb of the late sultan, in the hope that god in his great clemency would show mercy to my late friend and patron.' Similarly, Firuz ordered that the properties which former sultans had unfairly confiscated from people should be restored to their owners. 'Villages, lands, and ancient patrimonies of every kind had been wrested from the hands of their owners in former reigns, and had been brought under the exchequer. I directed that everyone who had a claim to property should bring it forward in the law court, and, upon establishing his title . . . the property . . . should be restored to him.'

He would be a humane ruler, Firuz resolved. 'In the reigns of former kings . . . many varieties of torture were employed . . . All these things were practised so that fear and dread might fall upon the hearts of man, and that the regulations of government might be duly maintained . . . Through the mercy which god has shown to me, these severities and terrors have been exchanged [by me] for tenderness, kindness, and mercy. Fear and respect have thus taken firmer hold of the hearts of men, and there has been no need for executions, scourgings, tortures, or terrors,' Firuz writes, and goes on to approvingly quote a poem:

> Thy power is great, then mercy show:
> Pardon is better than vengeance . . .
> Boast not the hundreds thou hast slain,
> To save one life is a nobler aim . . .

This was not just a pious pretence. Firuz had a genuine concern for the welfare of the people. He reversed the prevailing royal view that people should serve the king, and held that the king should serve the people. The Delhi Sultanate under him was the closest that any government in medieval India came to being a welfare state. Firuz was especially caring towards the lowly—he was, according to Afif, 'very kind and generous to the poor'—and he introduced several measures to succour the poor. One such measure was the setting up of a free hospital for the public. 'I was by god's grace enabled to build a hospital for the benefit of everyone of high or low degree,' he states. 'The cost of medicines and food is defrayed from my endowments. All sick persons, residents and travellers, highborn and commoner, bond and free, resort thither.'

In the same spirit, Firuz 'founded an establishment for the promotion of marriages,' reports Afif. 'Many needy Muslims were distressed at having marriageable daughters, for whom they could provide no marriage portion . . . Notice was given that any man having a marriageable daughter might apply at the *diwan-i-khairat* (charity bureau) and state his case . . . to the officers of that establishment . . . who, after due enquiry, might fix an allowance [for them] . . . People, small and great, flocked to the city from all parts of the country, and received grants for purchasing housekeeping requisites for their daughters.' The charity bureau also provided succour to widows and orphans.

FIRUZ WAS ESPECIALLY concerned with the welfare of his officers and soldiers and their families, motivated as much by humane considerations as by official responsibility. Thus, on learning about the distress of the families of the soldiers who perished in the Rann of Kutch during his disastrous Sind campaign of 1362, he ordered that the children of the dead soldiers should receive the allowances of their fathers, and 'should not be troubled in any way,' states Afif. The sultan even 'directed that those who had deserted him in Gujarat [because of their sufferings in the Sind campaign] . . . and had returned home were to have their livelihood and villages continued to them. He was desirous that no one should suffer on that account.' The deserters might be reproached, but not executed, banished or amerced, the sultan ordered.

The sultan also took care to substantially increase the salaries of government officers, for their loyalty was critically important for the success of his government. Whereas the highest pay given to an officer under Muhammad was only 200,000 tankas, Firuz assigned to his officers land grants yielding between 400,000 and 800,000 tankas, depending on their rank. His vizier was even assigned villages yielding 1,300,000 tankas!

Equally, Firuz showed earnest consideration for the welfare of his common soldiers, even in small matters. For instance, when he with his army finally emerged from the wilderness in which it had got trapped for six months while returning to Delhi from Orissa after one of his campaigns, and he then sent to Delhi a message about his safety, he also solicitously 'gave public notice that all who wished to write to their families and friends might take this opportunity,' states Afif. 'This gave great satisfaction, and every man of the army, from the highest to lowest, wrote [to his family] some account of his condition,' and a camel load of letters was sent to Delhi.

Firuz was equally solicitous about the welfare of his slaves, of whom he had an incredibly large number. 'Altogether, in the city and in the various fiefs there were 180,000 slaves, for whose maintenance and comfort the sultan took especial care,' notes Afif. 'None of the sultan's predecessors had ever collected so many slaves.'

But Firuz collected slaves to serve the state, not to serve his personal vanity, and he employed them in various productive works. 'Some were placed under craftsmen and were taught the mechanical arts, so that about 12,000 slaves became artisans of various kinds . . . There was no occupation in which the slaves of Firuz Shah were not employed,' continues Afif. 'A clever and qualified superintendent was appointed over every class of [slave] artisans.' The slaves were thus turned into economic assets of the state. 'In some places they were provided for in the army, and villages were granted to them.' Some 40,000 slaves were employed as royal guards.

Because of the vast number of royal slaves, and the diversity of their functions, Firuz set up a separate government department to administer their affairs. 'A separate muster-master of the slaves, a separate treasury for the payment of their allowances . . . [and a separate group of] officers for administering the affairs of the slaves' were instituted by Firuz, reports Afif. When the royal slaves became too numerous, many of them were distributed among the amirs, 'who treated them like [their own] children, providing them with food and raiment, lodging them and training them, and taking every care of their wants. Each year they took their slaves to court and reported about their merits and abilities.' Firuz was a slave owner, but not a slave driver.

Even in the treatment of defeated enemies, Firuz was humane and magnanimous, and that attitude often turned his enemies into his allies. This regard for others was also evident in the care that Firuz took to preserve and cherish the memory of the former sultans of Delhi, rather than remain egomaniacally focussed on himself. 'It had been a rule among the sultans of Delhi that the name of the reigning monarch only was mentioned in the prayers of Sabbaths and festivals, and no reference was made to the former sultans,' states Afif. 'When Sultan Firuz came to the throne . . . he disapproved of the omission of the names of former kings, and ordered that a khutba should be said first in the names of former kings, and then one in which his own name was mentioned.'

FIRUZ WAS WILLING even to allow some laxity in official appointments, to favour those who served him. He therefore reintroduced the system of hereditary appointments to offices, a system that was disfavoured by Ala-ud-din and Muhammad, for it made birth, instead of competence, as the qualification for government employment, and it created a hereditary aristocracy which could challenge the authority of the sultan. Firuz disregarded those risks, and, according to Afif, ruled that 'if an officer of the army died, he was to be succeeded by his son; if he had no son, by his son-in-law; if he had no son-in-law, by his slave; if he had no slave, by his nearest relation; and if he had no relations, by his wives.'

This policy was in a way logical—if the throne could be inherited, why not the lesser offices? The policy no doubt adversely affected the administrative and military efficiency of the Sultanate, but would have done that only marginally, as the normal mode of recruitment of officers in the Delhi Sultanate was quite haphazard and whimsical, except during the reign of Ala-ud-din Khalji. Another deliberate laxity that Firuz introduced in administration was the reversion to the old practice of assigning fiefs to royal officers in lieu of cash payment, which again was a policy disfavoured by Ala-ud-din, to prevent officers from gaining territorial power bases independent of the sultan. Firuz also discouraged the use of spies, who were extensively used by previous sulans to keep track of what was happening in the empire and what the royal officers were doing; instead, he sought to build mutual trust between him and his officers.

Firuz was very tolerant—too tolerant, perhaps—of human frailties, and he had a tendency to condone or overlook inefficiency, corruption and misdeeds among government employees. Thus when he was told that 'many of his soldiers were old and feeble, and unfit for duty,' and that they should be removed, he, according to Afif, refused to do so, saying, 'If I remove the old and inefficient men . . . the poor old men will be greatly troubled and be reduced to distress in their old age. I do not approve of dismissing them and putting their sons in their places . . . Let an order therefore be promulgated that when a soldier grows old and incapable, his son shall succeed him, [but only] as his deputy. If he has no son, his son-in-law, and failing any son-in-law, his slave shall represent him. The veteran may thus remain at home at ease . . .'

Similarly, horses of little value were often taken to the registry office by soldiers, and were there passed as serviceable by conniving officers. Reports about this often reached the ears of the sultan, but he ignored them. And when soldiers failed to produce their horses on time at the registry office, and the matter was brought before the sultan, he granted the defaulters a grace time of two months to produce their horses. Reporting these and other such stories, Afif comments that 'the kindness of the sultan for his people was such as no father or brother could show.'

ALL THIS HOWEVER did not turn Firuz into a weak ruler. Rather, they made him a sensible ruler, who had the self-confidence to leave some laxity and flexibility in administration for the play of human foibles without feeling threatened by it. There is no evidence that his liberal policies had notably weakened the Sultanate. He was doing what was necessary to rule efficiently in the prevailing circumstances of the Sultanate. Firuz was not a weak ruler, but a wise ruler.

Indeed, Firuz had to his credit the introduction—or revival—of certain measures to improve the efficiency of the administration, as in the case of the accounting procedures he enforced. 'In this reign there were audits of the accounts of the fiefs,' states Afif. 'When the feudatory came up from his fief to the court, he was brought before the exchequer, where an audit of his accounts was held, and the results were reported to the throne . . . The managers of the kar-khanas also had to present the abstracts of their accounts to the exchequer at the end of every year, showing the balance of cash and the stores of goods with them.'

While thus tightening the revenue administration, Firuz also took care to abolish or reduce several taxes, as part of his policy of liberalising the government. He lists as many as twenty-three taxes that he abolished. 'In former reigns they used to collect frivolous, unlawful and unjust cesses . . . I had all these abolished and removed from the accounts,' he states in his autobiography, and goes on to quote a couplet expressing his principle:

Better a people's weal than treasures vast,
Better an empty chest that hearts downcast.

'Sultan Firuz made the laws of the Prophet his guide, acting zealously upon the principles they laid down, and prohibiting all that was inconsistent therewith,' states Afif. 'No demand in excess of the regular government dues was to be made, and the officer who made any such exaction had to make full reparation. . . . Such rules were made that the *raiyats* grew rich . . . Wealth abounded and comforts were general.' Similarly, while former sultans used to take for themselves four-fifth of the battle spoils, and give only one-fifth to the soldiers, Firuz reversed this ratio, in conformity with Islamic law. And when fief holders during their visit to the sultan offered him various presents, Firuz had those presents appraised, and he deducted their value from the dues payable by the fief holders to the government, so that they might not suffer any deprivation.

Firuz also abolished the benevolences that the provincial governors were previously required to give to the sultan at the time of their appointment and every year thereafter, for that burden ultimately fell on the shoulders of the common people. In the same spirit, he cancelled the debts that people owed to the treasury on the advances that were given to them by Muhammad for restoring agriculture after a devastating famine in the Doab; in fact he had the records of the debts brought to him at the court, and had them publicly cancelled.

These were not impulsive acts, but carefully planned measures. Firuz was munificent, but he was not a wastrel. He made sure that state funds were not squandered or misappropriated in any way, but served the purpose for which they were allotted, and he exercised strict control over all state expenditures. Typical of this was his control over public works. Though he was a compulsive builder of forts, palaces, mosques, and so on, he looked into every detail of the execution of those projects to make sure that these structures conformed to their approved plans in all respects, and that there was no misappropriation of the funds allotted for them.

And just as he was careful about expenditure, he was also careful about revenue collection. To systematise revenue administration, he conducted, along the lines of what Muhammad had attempted, a comprehensive survey of the revenue potential of the empire and appointed a revenue assessor to supervise the project. When the group produced its report after a survey lasting six years, Firuz made certain changes in revenue administration, particularly in lowering the revenue demand and making it uniform over the years.

THESE LIBERAL AND wise policies of Firuz galvanised economic growth and led to the spread of prosperity in the Sultanate. 'In the houses of peasants so much grain, horses and goods accumulated that one cannot describe them,' states Afif. 'Everyone had large amounts of gold and silver and countless goods. None of the women-folk of the peasantry remained without ornaments; in every peasant's house, there were clean bed-sheets, excellent bed-cots, many articles and much wealth.' According to Barani, 'cattle, food-grains and goods' filled the houses of village headmen during the reign of Firuz.

The economic expansion of the Sultanate was also stimulated by Firuz's policy of undertaking various developmental works. Of these, the most important was the construction of five major irrigation canals, the longest of which was the 241 kilometre-long canal that carried the waters of the Yamuna to Hisar in western Haryana. Firuz also built a number of reservoirs, dams and wells. All these substantially increased the area under cultivation and contributed significantly to the prosperity of the people. 'Not one village remained barren . . . nor one span of land uncultivated,' states Afif with becoming exaggeration. The government also benefited directly from the public works, as it collected an additional levy of ten percent from the cultivators who used water from the irrigation facilities built by the state.

In addition to these promotional activities, the sultan directly participated in agricultural expansion by setting up a large number of state farms producing commercial crops. Firuz, according to Afif, 'had a great liking for laying out gardens,' and he set up over a thousand of them, where fruits were grown.

As in agriculture, so too in trade, the policies of Firuz, such as the abolition of several octroi duties and the introduction of small denomination coins— which broadened everyday market activities—stimulated the expansion of trade. Firuz was also a zealous builder, who founded a number of new towns and built many palaces, caravanserais, bridges, hospitals, colleges, mosques, mausoleums, public baths, wells, and so on, and these construction projects also stimulated the expansion of economy.

All these activities of Firuz served a dual purpose—while people benefited from them, the state also benefited, as the expansion of the economy led to a substantial increase in the state revenue. Equally, the prosperity and contentment of the people resulting from the progressive policies of Firuz led to peace and stability in the empire. Firuz acted on the sound principle that the prosperity of the king, if it is to endure, has to be based on the prosperity of the people, and that the best means to increase the revenue of the state was not through extortionate tax exactions but through mild taxation that would stimulate economic growth. On the whole, the economic and revenue policies of Firuz were well-suited to promote the welfare of the people as well as of the state. According to Afif, 'no king of Delhi had ever been in receipt of such an income as Sultan Firuz.'

Gods too favoured Firuz. A good part of the prosperity of the medieval Indian state depended on agricultural prosperity, and this was as much dependent on the favour of the rain gods as on government policies. Firuz, like Ala-ud-din, was very lucky in this. 'By the blessing of god favourable seasons and abundance of the necessaries of life prevailed in the reign of Firuz Shah, not only in the capital, but throughout his dominions,' comments Afif. 'During the whole forty years of his reign there was no appearance of scarcity, and the times were . . . [as] happy' as during the reign of Ala-ud-din Khalji, which was the most prosperous period in the history of the Delhi Sultanate. And all goods and provisions at this time were as cheap as they were under Ala-ud-din. But while Ala-ud-din had to make great exertions and adopt coercive measures to achieve it, Firuz achieved it 'through the favour of god . . . without any [great] effort on his part . . . The good fortune of the sultan prevailed . . . Perfect happiness did the kingdom enjoy in those days.'

FIRUZ WAS ESSENTIALLY a man of peace. He was content with the territories he inherited, and waged no wars of conquest. He was not tempted even when he was invited by rebels in other kingdoms to invade their lands. 'Keep no more territory than you can manage,' an old woman had once warned Mahmud Ghazni. This was the wise policy that Firuz followed. His religious orthodoxy was also a factor that influenced his military policy. Typically, when one of his nobles once berated him for shedding the blood of Muslims in wars, and warned him that 'drawing the sword against the people of Islam had ten evils for every advantage . . . [the sultan's] eyes were suffused with tears . . . and he resolved never again to make war upon [fellow] Muslims,' states Afif.

But Firuz was not a pacifist. Though in many respects he was a gentle, cultured person, he maintained a huge army of 80–90,000 cavalry, and he had no hesitation to wage wars to repel invaders and to suppress rebellions. In this his actions were often as horrific as those of any other medieval ruler. But on the whole his reign was relatively peaceful, compared to the reigns of most other Delhi sultans, which were marked by near continuous wars. Predictably there were no major rebellions during his reign. And there were only two Mongol incursions, both of which were firmly repulsed. 'A fierce battle ensued, and the slaughter was great, but victory inclined to the sultan, and the Mongols fled, abandoning their camp and baggage,' records Afif about the first Mongol invasion. 'This was the first victory of the reign of Sultan Firuz.' The second Mongol raid was directed against Gujarat, but that too was easily routed.

Firuz also did make a couple of attempts to recover the territories lost to the Sultanate in the latter part of Muhammad's reign, but these were half-hearted efforts, and they achieved no notable gains. The first of these campaigns was in the third year of his reign, when he led an army against Shams-ud-din Iliyas Shah, the rebel ruler of Bengal. Iliyas retreated into East Bengal on the approach of the imperial forces, but Firuz pursued and defeated him in a battle, and drove him to take refuge in the fort of Ekdala in East Bengal. Firuz then occupied the town alongside the fort, but decided not to storm the fort, deeming that it was not worth the effort required. In this decision he was also influenced by the wailing of women in the fort—as Firuz stormed into the town, 'all the ladies and respectable women went to the top of the fort, and when they saw him, they uncovered their heads, and in their distress made great lamentations,' reports Afif. Firuz then made peace with Iliyas, rejecting the advice of some of his officers to annex Bengal, and returned to Delhi before the dreaded onset of the monsoon.

Firuz's Bengal campaign was however tarnished by a rare show of savagery by him. Before leaving for Delhi, he decided to leave for the people of Bengal a ghoulish reminder of the consequences of their rebellion. According to Afif, Firuz then 'issued an order for collecting the heads of the slain Bengalis, and a silver tanka was offered for every head. The whole army then went busily to work, and brought the heads of the slain and piled them in heaps, receiving in payment silver tankas. The heads were counted, and they amounted to rather more than 180,000.' It should be however noted that Firuz did not order the slaughter of the enemy, as sultans usually did, but only to collect the heads of those already slain in battle.

Firuz and Iliyas thereafter maintained an amicable relationship. But when Iliyas was succeeded by his son Sikandar Shah, Firuz led a second expedition into Bengal, leading an army of 70,000 cavalry, 470 elephants, and a large body of irregulars. But this was a leisurely campaign. Firuz halted for long periods at several places along the way, even founded a new city—Jaunpur, on the banks of the Gomati—on the way, so it took him several months to reach Bengal. And this campaign was no more decisive than his previous Bengal campaign. But he was able to induce Sikandar to accept his nominal suzerainty, and agree to send to him an annual tribute of forty elephants. And Firuz in turn presented Sikandar with 500 Arab and Turkish horses, and honoured him with a jewelled crown.

On the way back to Delhi from Bengal, at Jaunpur, Firuz abruptly turned southward and advanced into Orissa, a sparsely populated and densely forested region of India that had never before been subjugated by the Sultanate. His main purpose of this campaign was to hunt for elephants, as he had heard that 'elephants were as numerous as sheep' in Orissa.

On Firuz's advance into Orissa, the raja there fled to an island for refuge, but from there he sent his emissaries to the sultan to plead for peace. Firuz assured them that he had entered Orissa only for hunting, and had no hostile intentions against the raja. On this assurance, the raja, according to Afif, sent to the sultan 'twenty mighty elephants as an offering, and agreed to furnish a certain [number of] elephants yearly in payment of tribute. The sultan then sent [ceremonial] robes and an insignia to the raja.' Apart from the elephant hunt, the only other major act of Firuz in Orissa was the sacking of the renowned temple town of Puri.

The Orissa campaign was quite rewarding for Firuz, but his return journey from there very nearly ended in total disaster, for on the journey back to Delhi his army lost its way, and for six months it wandered about despairingly through trackless plains, dense jungles, and along riverbanks, searching for a way to get out of the labyrinth and get back on the road to Delhi. 'The army ascended and descended mountain after mountain, and passed through jungles and hills until they were quite in despair and utterly worn out with the fatigue of the arduous march,' reports Afif. 'No road was to be found . . . Provisions became scarce, and the army was reduced to the verge of destruction . . . At the end of six months a road was discovered . . . [and the army], after enduring great privations . . . came out into the open country.'

THE ONLY OTHER major military campaign of Firuz was against Sind, in 1362, the eleventh year of his reign. Remembering all too well the military humiliation that Muhammad had suffered in Sind in his last days, Firuz set out during this campaign with a huge army of 90,000 horse and 480 elephants. But Firuz too suffered great perils in this campaign, for a pestilence decimated his horses—'only one-fourth of them, at the utmost, remained alive,' notes Afif—and the soldiers too suffered greatly due to the scarcity of provisions.

Seeing the adversities of the imperial army, the ruler of Sind marshalled his forces and advanced from the fort of Tatta to give battle. Firuz too then arrayed his army. 'He then put on his armour, and, with baton in hand, rode through the whole array, encouraging and cheering the men,' states Afif. 'This raised the spirits of his people and inflamed their devotion.' A brief encounter followed, fought in the midst of a dust storm, in which the sultan's army charged the enemy spiritedly and drove them back into their fort.

Firuz then decided to retreat to Gujarat, to rest and reequip his army. But the journey to Gujarat turned out to be calamitous. The army was harassed all along the way by the enemy, and it lost its entire fleet of boats. Then famine struck the army. 'As no corn could be procured, carrion and raw hides were devoured; some men even were driven by extreme hunger to boil old hides, and eat them,' writes Afif in his detailed account of the army's travails. 'A deadly famine reigned, and all men saw death staring them in the face. All the horses were destroyed, and the khans and maliks were compelled to pursue their weary way on foot. Not one steed remained in the army . . . All ranks were reduced to the same state of destitution.' To make matters worse, treacherous guides led the army into the Rann of Kutch, where 'all the land is impregnated with salt . . . When with great difficulty and exertion they escaped from that salt country, they came into a desert where no bird . . . flapped its wing, where no tree was to be seen, and where no blade of grass grew.'

Then suddenly the scene changed. 'On every side clouds rolled up swiftly, cloud upon cloud; rain fell, and water-courses ran. All men . . . were delivered from trouble.'

On reaching Gujarat, the sultan advanced loans to his soldiers to reequip themselves, spending the entire revenue of Gujarat on it. Then he once again set out for Tatta. Fortunately for Firuz, his position relative to that of the Sind ruler was now the reverse of what it was during their previous confrontation. Though there were a good number of desertions in the sultan's army at this time, as many of his soldiers were reluctant to once again go through the awful toils of a Sind campaign, the army was reinforced by fresh contingents sent from Delhi, and his soldiers were well-rested and well-equipped. In contrast to this, the Sind army was in a wretched state at this time, ravaged by famine and plagued with desertions. In that predicament the ruler of Sind prudently decided to surrender. He then presented himself to Firuz without the turban on his head, and with his sword hanging from his neck, 'like a repentant criminal, and, humbly approaching the sultan, kissed his stirrup and begged for forgiveness,' reports Afif. 'The sultan then graciously placed his hand on his back, and said, 'Why were you afraid of me? I did not mean to hurt anyone, especially you. Cheer up . . . and dispel your anxiety.' Firuz then took the ruler with him to Delhi, but later restored him to the throne of Sind on he agreeing to pay an annual tribute.

These were the major military campaigns of Firuz. Though he did wage a few other wars also, they were all relatively minor operations. Notable among them was his campaign against Rohilkhand, whose raja had treacherously murdered the governor of Budaun and his two brothers. On Firuz's approach the raja fled and escaped, so the sultan took his vengeance on the local people. He was uncharacteristically savage on this occasion—perhaps because he was inflamed by religious fervour, as the slain governor and his brothers were Sayyids, presumed descendants of the Prophet Muhammad—and he ordered the general massacre of the Hindus of Rohilkhand. Not only that, he ordered his new governor there, an Afghan, to devastate the region 'with fire and sword' annually for the next five years. And Firuz himself visited the region every year for the next five years to ensure that his order was carried out.

APART FROM THESE few deviant acts, the reign of Firuz was on the whole humane and civilised.

He was the most liberal of all the rulers of the Delhi Sultanate. But he was also a rigidly orthodox Muslim, who in his autobiography proudly records that he was conferred the title Saiyidu-s Sultan by the Abbasid Caliph in Egypt, who also bestowed on him 'robes, a banner, a sword, a ring, and a foot-print as badges of honour and distinction.' All through his life Firuz 'paid much attention to the elders of religion,' states Afif. 'And towards the end of his reign he himself became a shaveling . . . Many of the khans and amirs, out of love for the sultan, [also] performed tonsure.' Firuz was particularly careful to consult the Koran for an augury before taking any major decision, for he believed that his fate was not of his own making, but was as god decreed.

Firuz had a more serious interest in religion than most other Delhi sultans, and he was strict in enforcing Islamic prescriptions among his coreligionists, and in prohibiting their un-Islamic practices. He also made a series of changes in royal customs and practices. 'It had been the practice of former kings to use vessels of gold and silver at the royal table, and to ornament their sword-belts and quivers with gold and jewels,' he writes in his autobiography. 'I forbade these things, and ordered that the fittings of my arms should be made of bone, and I commanded that only such vessels should be used as are recognised by law.' Thereafter he used only stone and ceramic tableware. Similarly, it was a custom of the Delhi sultans to decorate their private apartments with portrait paintings, but Firuz considered this as 'contrary to law, and directed that garden scenes should be painted instead,' states Afif. 'Former kings used to wear ornaments of brass and copper, silver and gold, in opposition to the Law, but these he (Firuz) interdicted . . . Pictures on banners and ensigns were also forbidden.'

It was also a custom of the former sultans to have 'figures and devices . . . painted and displayed on saddles, bridles and collars, on censers, on goblets and cups, and flagons, on dishes and ewers, in tents, on curtains and on chairs, and upon all articles and utensils . . .,' Firuz notes. 'I ordered all pictures and portraits to be removed from these things, and that such articles only should be made as are approved and recognised by law. The pictures and portraits which were painted on the doors and walls of palaces I ordered to be effaced.'

Firuz required his officers too to conform to orthodox Islamic prescriptions. 'In former times it had been the custom [of nobles] to wear ornamented garments, and men received [such] robes as token of honour from kings . . .

[And] the garments of great men were generally made of silk and gold brocades, beautiful but unlawful,' states Firuz. 'I ordered that only such garments should be worn as are approved by the Law of the Prophet . . . [and that] trimmings of gold brocade, embroidery, or braiding should not exceed four inches in width,' he states.

In revenue administration also Firuz followed religious injunctions; whatever taxes religious leaders declared as unlawful, that the sultan forbade, even when it meant substantial loss of revenue to the government. At the same time he strictly enforced the special taxes that Islamic law required to be imposed on non-Muslims.

One such measure of the sultan was to impose jizya on Brahmins. In an Islamic state all non-Muslims were required to pay jizya, but in India it 'had never been levied from Brahmins,' reports Afif. 'They had been held excused in former reigns . . . [Firuz however held that] Brahmins were the very keys of the chamber of idolatry, and the infidels were dependent on them. They ought to be therefore taxed first . . . [When the news of the sultan's decision spread] Brahmins of all the four cities [of Delhi] assembled and went . . . [to the sultan] and represented that Brahmins had never before been called upon to pay jizya . . . [and they threatened] to collect wood and burn themselves under the walls of the palace rather than pay the tax.' But Firuz remained unrelenting. 'The Brahmins remained fasting for several days at the palace until they were on the point of death. They then clearly perceived that the sultan did not intend to spare them. The Hindus of the city then assembled and told the Brahmins that it was not right for them to kill themselves on account of jizya, and that they would undertake to pay it for them . . . When Brahmins found that their case was hopeless, they went to the sultan and begged him in his mercy to reduce the amount they would have to pay.' When Firuz agreed to this, Brahmins dispersed. In a related reform, Firuz made jizya a separate tax, while previously it was included in the land tax.

THE POLICIES AND actions of Firuz were usually guided by humane and liberal principles, but sometimes, impelled by religious fervour, he violated those principles. Thus when he invaded Orissa, he not only demolished the renowned Jagannatha temple at Puri, but also rooted up its idol and took it with him to Delhi, where, according to Afif, he 'had it placed in an ignominious position,' to be defiled by Muslims. *Sirat-i-Firuz Shahi*, an anonymous medieval work, further states, no doubt with considerable exaggeration, that Firuz slaughtered such a large number of Hindus in Puri that 'no vestige of the infidels was left except their blood.' Similar acts of vandalism and carnage were committed by him in a few other places also.

There is however some uncertainty about what he did at the temple of Jvalamukhi in Kangra. Ferishta states that the sultan 'broke the idols of Jvalamukhi, mixed their fragments with the flesh of cows, and hung them in nosebags round the necks of Brahmins, and he sent the principal idol as a trophy to Medina.' But, according to Afif, 'some infidels have reported that Sultan Firuz went specially to see this idol and held a golden umbrella over its head [in veneration] . . . Other infidels have said that Sultan Muhammad Tughluq [also] had held an umbrella over the same idol.' Afif denies these claims.

There is no way of knowing what really happened in Kangra. It is possible that Firuz did not vandalise the Jvalamukhi temple, for he, though a rigidly orthodox Muslim, was also a highly cultured person, and he is known to have taken special care to preserve several ancient Indian monuments. Besides, while Muslim law prohibited the construction of new idol temples, it did not require old temples to be demolished. Though very many old Hindu temples were indeed vandalised and destroyed during the Sultanate period, and Firuz himself did that on a few occasions, it is possible that he treated the Jvalamukhi temple with special regard, especially as the temple was renowned for its vast library, which would have greatly appealed to the scholarly sultan.

Firuz did however strictly forbid the construction of new Hindu temples and shrines in his empire. 'I destroyed these edifices, and I killed those leaders of infidelity . . ., and the lower order I subjected to stripes and chastisement,' Firuz reports about one such incident. But he was careful not to go beyond what was prescribed in Islamic law. 'I forbade the infliction of any severe punishments on Hindus in general,' he states.

Firuz was particularly severe in dealing with Hindu holy-men. 'A report was brought to the sultan that there was in Delhi an old Brahmin who persisted in publicly performing the worship of idols in his house, and that the people of the city, both Muslims and Hindus, used to resort to his house to worship the idol,' reports Afif. 'This Brahmin had constructed a wooden tablet which was covered within and without with paintings of demons and other objects . . . The sultan was informed that this Brahmin had perverted Muslim women, and had led them to become infidels. An order was accordingly given that the Brahmin with his tablet should be brought into the presence of the sultan.' Muslim theologians then advised the sultan that the Brahmin should either become a Muslim or be burned. As the Brahmin refused to become a Muslim, 'orders were given for raising a pile of faggots before the door of the durbar. The Brahmin was tied hand and foot and cast into it.'

IN HIS TREATMENT of Hindus, Firuz followed the dual policy of persecuting Hindu religious leaders, and of showing favours to low-caste Hindus to induce them to become Muslims. 'I encouraged my infidel subjects to embrace the religion of the Prophet, and I proclaimed that everyone who . . . became a Muslim would be exempt from jizya,' the sultan writes in his autobiography. 'Information of this came to the ears of the people at large, and a great number of Hindus presented themselves and were admitted to the honour of Islam. Thus they came forward day by day from every quarter, and. . . were favoured with presents and honours.'

Firuz also sought to suppress heterodox Muslim sects. 'I seized them all and I convicted them of their errors and perversions,' he writes about Shias. He punished the Shia leaders and castigated their followers, 'and so by the grace of god the influence of this sect was entirely suppressed.' He was particularly repressive towards the various bizarre sects that flourished in India at this time, among Hindus as well as Muslims. He was especially severe towards the Tantric sect, which practised ritual sex. 'I cut off the heads of the elders of this sect, and imprisoned and banished the rest, so that their abominable practises were put an end to,' states Firuz.

At this time 'there was in Delhi a man named Rukn-ud-din, who was called Mahdi, because he affirmed himself to be the Imam Mahdi, who is to appear in latter days, and [he claimed] to possess [divine] knowledge,' notes Firuz. 'He led people astray into mystic practices, and perverted ideas.' Firuz publicised his condemnation of the cult, and ordered the mystic and his cult to be liquidated. People then rushed to his place, 'tore him to pieces and broke his bones into fragments,' Firuz reports approvingly. Firuz also suppressed a few other similar cults.

As in religion, so also in social practices, Firuz sought to enforce orthodox Islamic prescriptions. 'A custom and practice unauthorised by the law of Islam had sprung up in Muslim cities,' he writes. 'On holy days women riding in palanquins or carts or litters, or mounted on horses or mules, or in large parties on foot, went out of the city to the tombs. Rakes and wild fellows of unbridled passion and loose habits took the opportunity which this practice afforded for improper, riotous actions. I commanded that no woman should go out to the tombs under pain of exemplary punishment.'

FIRUZ, THOUGH HE was rigidly orthodox in religion, was also a man of wide cultural interests, and was quite liberal in his patronage of culture. Thus when he found a library of 1300 old Sanskrit manuscript volumes in the temple of Jvalamukhi, he ordered several of them—particularly a volume on natural sciences, astrology and augury—to be translated into Persian. The translation of this book was noted by Ferishta, and was appreciated even by the hyper-orthodox Mughal chronicler Badauni, though he found that some of the other translated books were 'unprofitable and trivial works on prosody, music and dancing.'

An accomplished scholar himself, Firuz was a liberal patron of the learned. And he had to his credit the setting up of several educational institutions. He was passionately fond of music, despite the fact that orthodox Muslims considered addiction to music to be a vice, though only a venial vice. Firuz was also an inventor. 'Many wonderful things were invented by Sultan Firuz in the course of his reign,' states Afif, 'and among them the most wonderful was the *tas-i-ghariyal*' for marking time and indicating the hours of prayer. And he wrote his autobiography, as Mughal emperors Babur and Jahangir would later do.

One of the passions of Firuz was to build new towns and monumental structures. 'Among the gifts which god bestowed upon me, his humble servant, was a desire to erect public buildings,' he writes. 'So I built many mosques and colleges and monasteries . . . [I also] dug canals, planted trees, and endowed [religious scholars] with lands.' Confirms Afif: 'Sultan Firuz excelled all his predecessors on the throne of Delhi in the erection of buildings; indeed no monarch of any country surpassed him [in this]. He built cities, forts, palaces, bunds, mosques, and tombs in great numbers . . . He also built monasteries, and inns for the accommodation of travellers. One hundred and twenty monasteries were built . . . The sultan also repaired the tombs of former kings.'

Firuz, according to Afif, 'had a remarkable fondness for history.' This turned him into a zealous conservationist, who took care to preserve the historical and cultural heritage of India. 'I repaired and rebuilt the edifices and structures of former kings and ancient nobles, which had fallen into decay from the lapse of time, giving the restoration of these buildings priority over my own building works,' states Firuz.

This conservationist zeal of the sultan was not confined to the monuments of the Sultanate, but extended to ancient Indian monuments as well. His most valuable contribution in this was the preservation of two Asoka pillars—one from Meerut in UP, and the other from a village near Khizrabad in Punjab—which were transported with great and respectful care from their original sites to Delhi, where they were set up in prominent sites. Firuz of course did not know what the pillars were or who had built them and when—no one knew that till the ancient Brahmi inscriptions on them were deciphered by a British philologist in the mid-nineteenth century. But apparently Firuz had a sense that they were of very ancient—they were in fact over one and a half millenniums old—and were of very great historical value.

'These columns had stood in those places (their original locations) from the days of the Pandavas, but had never attracted the attention of any of the kings who sat upon the throne of Delhi, till Sultan Firuz noticed them, and, with great exertion brought them away,' notes Afif. 'When Firuz Shah first beheld these columns, he was filled with admiration, and resolved to remove them with great care as trophies to Delhi.'

Meticulous care was taken in excavating and transporting the pillars, and this is described in detail by Afif.[2] The pillars evoked the admiration of Timur when he occupied Delhi in 1398. 'During his stay of some days in Delhi, he inspected all the monuments of former kings, and among them these two obelisks,' writes Afif. 'He declared that in all the countries he had traversed he had never seen any monuments comparable to these.'

WE KNOW NOTHING about Firuz's family life, but he had a number of sons, of whom his favourite was his eldest son, Fath Khan, who was born when the sultan was marching to Delhi after his accession in Sind. He was a talented prince, and when he died in 1374 it shattered the aged sultan, who was then in his late sixties, and he rapidly slid into mental and physical decline. For a while he even withdrew from his royal duties. Later he resumed work and carried on for over a decade. Towards the end of this period, in 1387, there was a virtual civil war fought in the streets of Delhi, between the supporters of Khan Jahan, the powerful minister who had become the de facto ruler of the empire during Firuz's debility, and the supporters of Muhammad Shah, Firuz's eldest surviving son and heir-apparent. In this, the prince prevailed. Firuz, now over eighty years old and rather senile, then appointed Muhammad Shah as his co-ruler, and conferred on him the royal title.

Unfortunately, the prince was a sybarite; he had no serious interest in governance, but devoted himself almost entirely to sensual pleasures. And this once again led to a civil strife, a popular uprising in Delhi, which forced Muhammad to flee from the city. Firuz then appointed Ghiyas-ud-din, son of Fath Khan, as the co-ruler of the empire. Firuz died soon after, in September 1388, aged 83 and, according to contemporary chronicler Sirhindi, 'worn out with weakness.'

The reign of Firuz was the golden age of the Delhi Sultanate, especially in terms of the contentment of the people. 'During the reign of Firuz Shah . . . all men, high and low, bond and free, lived happily and free from care . . . Things were plentiful and cheap, and the people were well to do . . . Nothing in the least degree unpleasant or disagreeable happened during his reign . . . The sultan being beneficent, all men, high and low, were devoted to him.' states Afif. Confirms Sirhindi: 'There has been no king in Delhi so just and merciful, so kind and religious, or such a builder [as Sultan Firuz]. His justice won for

---

[2]See Part IX, Chapter 2

him the hearts of his subjects . . . It was in no way possible that during the reign of this sovereign any strong man could tyrannise the weak. God Almighty took this gentle, beneficent and just king to his everlasting rest, after a reign of thirty-seven years and nine months.'

As an orthodox Muslim ruler over an alien, pagan people, Firuz obligatorily discriminated against his Hindu subjects, and was often oppressive and sanguinary towards them. But even in these matters his policies and actions were moderate compared to those of most other Delhi sultans, and were on the whole more than compensated by his general regard for the welfare of all his subjects. If Muslims had good reason to rejoice in the reign of Firuz, so had Hindus. Concludes modern historian Wolseley Haig: 'The reign of Firuz . . . [marks] the most brilliant epoch of Muslim rule in India before the reign of Akbar.'

5

Timurid Tornado

'The city of Delhi has been turned upside down,' bemoans Afif about the conditions there following the death of Firuz. The subsequent story of the Tughluq dynasty is a dreary tale of assassinations, usurpations and rebellions; and of feckless, worthless sultans, and their overweening, faithless ministers, who treated their masters as puppets in their hands. During the twenty-four years between the death of Firuz Tughluq in 1388 and the overthrow of the Tughluq dynasty by Khizr Khan—the founder of the Sayyid dynasty—in 1412, as many as five sultans occupied the throne of Delhi. Of them, the longest reign was that of Nasir-ud-din Mahmud Shah, which lasted 18 years, while the shortest reign, that of Ala-ud-din Sikandar Shah, lasted just six weeks. The successors of Firuz are notable only for their utter insignificance.

During this period there were sometimes two rival kings in the Sultanate, ruling from different cities at the same time. And on a couple of occasions the imperial capital itself was divided between contending sultans, and civil war raged through the streets of the city. And once when a sultan returned to Delhi after a military campaign he had to suffer the humiliation of the city gates being shut against him by a rebel officer, who kept him waiting there for about three months. Sometimes the royal officers sent to suppress rebellions themselves turned rebels. And as power weakened at the centre, the empire began to disintegrate, and several of its provinces became independent kingdoms.

On the death of Firuz his grandson Ghiyas-ud-din, whom the sultan had designated as his successor, ascended the throne. But he turned out to be an utterly worthless ruler, frivolous and addicted to sensual pleasures. He 'was young and inexperienced,' comments Sirhindi. 'He knew nothing of politics, and had seen none of the wiles of fickle fortune. So he gave himself to wine and pleasure. The business of government was entirely neglected, and the officers of the late sultan asserted their power so fearlessly that all control of the state was lost.'

The only notable though not creditable political act of Ghiyas-ud-din was to imprison his brothers, fearing that they would turn out to be threats to his power. But that action, instead of securing his power, directly led to his downfall, as it sent shivers of anxiety through his cousins, and they manoeuvred to save themselves. Abu Bakr, one of his cousins, then secretly fled from Delhi and, joined by several disgruntled nobles, organised a cabal against the sultan.

The cabal enjoyed wide support among the nobles of Delhi, and this enabled the rebels to enter the city one day without much opposition and storm into the royal palace. Ghiyas-ud-din tried to save himself by fleeing through the rear gate of the palace, but was caught and immediately beheaded. Several of his close associates were also then beheaded, and all these severed heads were then suspended from the gate of the palace, to publicise the overthrow of the sultan. The reign of Ghiyas-ud-din had lasted just six months and eighteen days.

The rebel nobles then paraded Abu Bakr through the city, seated on an elephant with a canopy over his head, and proclaimed him as the sultan. But the enthronement of Abu Bakr did not end the turmoil in the empire. It merely opened another phase of it, for his accession was immediately challenged by a rival group of nobles, who invited Muhammad, Firuz's eldest surviving son—who had been briefly the co-ruler of the empire during the last days of Firuz, but had been driven out of the city in a popular uprising because of his wild debauchery—to reclaim the throne. Muhammad then engaged Abu Bakr in a long seesaw tussle, in which he even managed to briefly gain a foothold in Delhi a couple of times, but was driven out on both occasions. However, he finally succeeded in overthrowing Abu Bakr and seizing the throne. Abu Bakr was then sent to prison, where he died a few years later. His reign had lasted nineteen months.

The rule of Muhammad lasted three and a half years, but all through his reign he was beset with rebellions. 'The business of the state day by day fell into greater confusion,' states Sirhindi. 'Affairs came to such a pass that there were amirs at just twenty kos from Delhi who shook off their allegiance [to the sultan], and made pretensions of independence.'

Muhammad died in January 1394 and was succeeded by his son Ala-ud-din Sikandar Shah. 'In a very short time,' continues Sirhindi, 'it became evident that the new sultan was even more negligent and incompetent than his father in the duties of government.' Fortunately, he fell sick and died within a month and a half of his accession. He was then succeeded by his younger brother

Nasir-ud-din Mahmud Shah, whose reign of eighteen years was the longest of the successors of Firruz, though it was interrupted by a couple of brief periods when he was out of power.

Though his reign lasted long, Mahmud was as feckless a ruler as his immediate predecessors. He left the entire business of government to his nobles, particularly to Mallu Khan, a perfidious and overambitious noble who, according to Sirhindi, 'kept Sultan Mahmud in his power as a puppet, and himself directed all the affairs of government . . . The whole business of the state then fell into the greatest disorder. The sultan gave no heed to the duties of his station, and had no care for the permanency of the throne; his whole time was devoted to pleasure and debauchery.' Inevitably, the disintegration of the empire accelerated under him, both in the loss of territories to rebels and the emasculation of the power of the sultan.

The political scene in the Sultanate became further confounded at this time, as some nobles raised another grandson of Firuz, Nusrat Shah, to the throne in Firuzabad. So there were now for a time two sultans, one in Delhi and the other in nearby Firuzabad, and this led to a protracted civil war. 'The government fell into anarchy; civil war raged everywhere, and a scene was exhibited, unheard of before, of two kings in arms against each other residing in the same capital,' reports Ferishta. 'Affairs remained in this state for three years.'

THEN SUDDENLY THE scene changed dramatically. The cause of this change was the invasion of India by Timur. Timur belonged to the Barlas tribe, a Turco-Mongol people who traced their descent to the followers of Genghis Khan. The tribe had settled in Transoxiana in Central Asia, and had over the centuries become Turkish in language and identity, Persianised in culture, and Islamised in religion.

Timur was the son of a petty chieftain in Transoxiana. This region, like most of the medieval world, was at this time swirling in military conflicts, and Timur was involved in them from his early youth. In one of these battles he was injured in the hip by an arrow, which made him lame, and he thereafter bore the Persian nickname Timur-e Lang: Timur the Lame. Despite that handicap, his career as a military leader progressed dramatically, and by the time he was in his late fifties, he had transformed his small patrimony into a vast empire stretching from the border of China to the Mediterranean, with Samarkand as its capital.

These Central Asian campaigns occupied Timur most of his life, so it was only towards the end of his life, in 1398, when he was 62, that he turned to invade India. 'About this time there arose in my heart the desire to lead an expedition against the infidels, and to become a ghazi,' Timur writes in his autobiography. 'But I was undetermined in my mind whether I should direct my expedition against the infidels of China or against the infidels and polytheists of India.'

Timur then consulted his chieftains on this. But they were divided in their opinion. Some warned him against invading India, on the ground that India had four natural defences. 'The first defence,' they said, 'consists of five large rivers, which flow from the mountains of Kashmir . . . and it is not possible to cross them without boats and bridges. The second defence consists of woods and forests and trees, which, interweaving stem with stem and branch with branch, render it difficult to penetrate into that country. The third defence is the soldiery, and landholders, and princes, and rajas of the county, who inhabit the fastnesses in those forests, and live there like wild beasts. The fourth defence consists of elephants, for the rulers of that country on the day of the battle cover their elephants with mail, and put them in the van of their army . . . They have trained them to such a pitch that, lifting with their trunks a horse and its rider, and whirling them in the air, they will dash them on the ground.'

But this view was countered by other nobles, who pointed out that Mahmud Ghazni had 'conquered . . . Hindustan with 30,000 horse . . . and had carried off many thousand loads of gold and silver and jewels from that county, besides subjecting it to a regular tribute.' And that feat, they assured, could be repeated by Timur, especially as he had 100,000 valiant Tartar horsemen under his command. And the invasion of India would not only earn him heavenly blessings, but also countless material benefits, they asserted. 'The army will be contented [with booty] and the [royal] treasury will be . . . well-filled, and with the gold of Hindustan our amir will become a conqueror of the world and famous among the kings of the earth.' This view was seconded by Timur's sons. 'If we conquer India we shall become the rulers over the seven climes,' a prince said. And another prince added: 'India is full of gold and jewels, and in it there are seventeen mines of gold and silver, diamond and ruby and emerald and tin and iron and steel and copper and quicksilver etc, and there are there plants fit for making wearing apparel, and aromatic plants, and sugarcane, and it is a country which is always green and verdant, and the whole aspect of the country is pleasant and delightful. And, as the inhabitants [of India] are chiefly infidels . . . it is right for us to conquer them.' A third view of the nobles was that it would be good to raid India, but not occupy it. 'If we establish ourselves permanently therein, our race will degenerate and our children will become like the natives of those regions, and in a few generations their strength and valour will diminish.'

Timur thought over these diverse views of his nobles and princes, and finally decided to invade India. 'My object in the invasion of Hindustan,' he told the assembled nobles, 'is to lead an expedition against the infidels, so that . . . we may convert to the true faith the people of that country, and purify the land itself of the filth of infidelity and polytheism, and we may overthrow their temples and idols and become *ghazis* and *mujahids*.'

This was Timur's declared primary objective for invading India, but he also sought material rewards, the loot of the legendary riches of India, which no doubt was the primary motive of his soldiers. 'My principal object in coming to Hindustan, and in undergoing all this toil and hardship, has been to accomplish two things,' he candidly stated once in the midst of his Indian campaign. 'The first was to wage war against the infidels . . . and by this religious warfare to acquire some claim to reward in the life to come. The other was a worldly object, that the army of Islam might gain something by plundering the wealth and valuables of the infidels. Plunder in war is as lawful as their mothers' milk to Muslims who wage war for their faith.' He would, he decided, invade India, slaughter its infidels, plunder the land, and return home. He would not settle in India.

ONCE THE DECISION to invade India was made, matters moved fast. Timur then mustered a huge army by bringing together contingents from the various provinces of his empire, and in the summer of 1398, 'in the auspicious month of Rajab,' he set out from Samarkand for India. 'I placed my foot in the stirrup at a lucky moment, and quitting my capital Samarkand, directed my course towards Hindustan,' he writes.

Timur crossed the Indus on 24 September 1398, and swept towards Delhi. Most Indian rulers and their armies, as well as the common people, fled on the approach of Timur, as they would before a wildfire, though there were also a few instances of Rajputs engaging in desperate battles after performing the awesome rite of jauhar. 'Many of the Rajputs placed their wives and children in their houses and burned them, then they rushed into the battle and were killed,' writes Timur. 'Such was the terror inspired by him (Timur) that Muslims and Hindus fled before him, some to the mountains, some to the deserts, some to the waves of the rivers, and some to Delhi,' observes Sirhindi. And when Timur closed in on Delhi, the people in the surrounding areas fled pell-mell to the city for refuge—they 'set fire to their houses and fled with their children and property and effects towards Delhi, so that the whole country was deserted,' notes Timur. Even strong forts were abandoned without a fight.

Timur's passage through India was marked by incredible savagery. 'I commanded my troops . . . to kill all men, to make prisoners women and children, and to plunder and lay waste all their property,' he writes. 'I directed towers to be built of the [severed] heads of those obstinate unbelievers . . . In the course of one hour the heads of ten thousand infidels were cut off. The sword of Islam was washed with the blood of infidels.' Typically, his order to a foraying contingent he sent to the environs of Delhi was 'to plunder and destroy and kill everyone whom they met.' Among the captives only the lives of Muslims were spared. 'I gave orders that Muslim prisoners should be separated and saved, but the infidels should all be despatched to hell with the proselytising sword.'

This ferocity was an essential part of Timur's military tactic, to inspirit his soldiers with bloodlust, and to terrify the enemy and make them flee. Religious fervour was another key factor in the invincibility of Timur's army in India, and so was its lust for plunder. 'When the soldiers gave up killing the infidels, they secured great plunder in goods and valuables, prisoners and cattle . . . The plunder exceeded all calculation,' Timur records. Yet another reason for the success of Mongols was Timur's clear understanding of battle psychology, that victory and defeat depended as much on the spirit of soldiers as on the strength of arms. And he knew how to rouse the martial spirit of his soldiers, and how to dispirit the enemy. 'I ordered my warriors to shout their battle-cry aloud, and drums and other instruments to be sounded,' Timur states about the commencement of a battle. 'The noise reverberated through the hills, and filled the hearts of the infidels with dismay and trembling, so that they wavered.' And while the enemy thus turned timorous, Timur's own soldiers became charged up, and they, 'spurring their horses, shouting their war-cry, and brandishing their swords, fell upon the forces of the enemy like hungry lions upon a flock of sheep.'

But more than all these—religious fervour, animal ferocity and lust for plunder—the reason for Timur's success was that he was a brilliant military commander and an exceptionally clever tactician, who came up with an innovative solution to every military problem he faced. A potent combination of caution and daring marked Timur's campaigns, and he took care to formulate his military tactics only after carefully analysing all the information about the military potential of the enemy provided by his spies. He also used spies to spread disinformation among the enemy, to weaken their morale with exaggerated stories about the size and fierceness of the Mongol army.

TIMUR NEVER TOOK unnecessary risks. 'I gave orders that the officers and soldiers of my army should put on their armour, and that every man should remain in his proper regiment and place, in perfect readiness,' he says about the precautions he took while advancing on Delhi. And on his preparations for the battle of Delhi he states: 'I gave orders for the camp to be carefully guarded all night to prevent a nocturnal surprise by the enemy, and the night was passed with the caution and care which are necessary in war.' He also took care to rein in the impetuosity of his soldiers, to prevent them from plunging into dangerous situations.

As a good general, Timur took excellent care of his soldiers, and they in turn were fiercely loyal to him. And he treated them all equitably. Sometimes he even redistributed the plunder among them, so that all his men gained evenly from the battle, as victory was the result of their collective effort. 'As some [soldiers] had obtained much and others little, I had it all fairly divided,' he states about what he did after a battle. Similarly, after another battle he 'directed that those who had captured many [cattle] should give a few to those soldiers who had got no share. Through this order, every man, small and great, strong and weak, obtained a share of the spoil.' If any division of his army got only little booty during a battle, Timur took care to place that division in the next battle in a position where it could collect more booty.

Timur often sought the advice of astrologers in difficult situations, but relied more on his own judgement in making decisions, which were at times against the advice of astrologers. Equally, he depended on divine favour. 'In all matters, small and great, I placed my reliance on the favour and kindness of god, and I knew that victory and conquest, defeat and flight, are each ordained by him,' he states. 'So I placed no reliance on the words of astrologers and stargazers, but besought the giver of victory to favour my arms.' Rather than heed the predictions of astrologers, Timur sought divine guidance for his actions in the omens he found in the Koran by opening it at random. He considered god to be the giver of victory in battles, and always took care to get off his horse at the end of a battle and prostrate himself on the ground to render his thanks to god for giving him victory.

IN PREPARATION FOR the attack on Delhi, Timur held a council of war, in which he instructed his officers about the tactics to be used in that crucial battle. 'All my soldiers were brave veterans, and had used their swords manfully under my own eyes. But there were none that had seen so many fights and battles as I had seen, and none of the amirs and braves of the army could compare with me in the amount of fighting I had gone through, and the experience I had gained,' he writes. 'I therefore gave them instructions as to the mode of carrying on war, on making and meeting attacks, on arraying their men, on giving support to each other, and on all the precautions to be observed in warring with an enemy. . . I ordered the amirs . . . not to be too forward nor too backward, but to act with utmost prudence and caution in their operations.'

At that meeting some of Timur's officers expressed apprehensions about confronting the war elephants of the Delhi sultan. 'It had been constantly dinned into the ears of my soldiers that the chief reliance of the armies of Hindustan was on their mighty elephants; that these animals, in complete armour, marched into battle in front of their forces, and that arrows and swords were of no use against them; that in height and bulk they were like small mountains, and their strength was such that at a given signal they could tear up great trees and knock down strongly built walls; that in the battlefield they could take up a horse and its rider with their trunks and hurl them into the air,' Timur writes.

To allay these anxieties of his soldiers, Timur ordered a deep trench to be dug around the army camp, to prevent elephants from rampaging into the camp. 'I rode around to inspect it,' he writes, 'and I ordered that the trees in the vicinity should be cut down, and brought within the trench, that their branches should be formed into a strong abatis, and that in some places planks should be set up . . . [Also,] I ordered that all the buffalos which had been taken and placed with the baggage should be brought up; I then had their heads and necks fastened to their legs and placed the animals inside the abatis.' Further, according to Yazdi, Timur 'had strong iron claws (caltrops) made and given to the infantry, who were ordered to throw them on the ground in front of the elephants' to spike their feet as they charged.

Another precaution that Timur took was to execute all the Indian prisoners kept in the army camp. There were 100,000 of them in the camp, and it was feared that they constituted a danger to the army on the eve of its battle with the sultan of Delhi, for it was reported to Timur that when a Delhi contingent made a trial attack on his camp, these prisoners 'made signs of rejoicing and uttered imprecations' against Timur. So it was deemed essential, for the safety of the army, that they all should be put to death. Timur therefore ordered 'that every man who had infidel prisoners was to put them to death, and whoever neglected to do so should himself be executed and his property given to the informer.'

TIMUR'S ADVANCE THROUGH India was swift. It took him less than three months to reach Delhi after crossing the Indus, even though he fought several battles along the way. Strangely, Sultan Mahmud made no move whatever to oppose Timur during these months, presumably hoping that this incursion, like all the previous Mongol incursions, would be just a plundering raid and it involved no threat to his throne. But Timur's campaign was different from all the previous Mongol campaigns. Even though a major motive of Timur too was to gather plunder, and he had no intention to annex the territory of the Sultanate, he clearly meant to drive Mahmud out of Delhi and occupy the city for a while—for the prestige of it, and for plundering the royal treasures. This was an invasion by a king, not a raid by a pillaging horde. Moreover, there was a strong element of religious fanaticism in Timur, which was not there in the early raids of Mongols, for they were then heathens, not yet converted to Islam.

The realisation that Timur meant to occupy Delhi at last bestirred Mahmud, and he and his chief officer Mallu Khan then marched out of the city to confront Timur. His army, indicative of the withered state of the Sultanate, was small, consisting of just 10,000 cavalry and 125 elephants, though he also had with him an infantry rabble of 40,000.

'The enemy's forces now made their appearance, and for better reconnoitring their order I rode to the top of a little hill which was hard by,' writes Timur. 'There I carefully scrutinised their array, and I said to myself that with the favour of god I would defeat them and gain victory. I then alighted from my horse . . . and performed my devotions . . . bowed my head to the ground and besought the Almighty for victory.' Returning to his camp Timur then gave final instructions to his commanders, and took his position at the centre of the array.

This was on 17 December 1398. 'The two armies now confronted each other, the drums were beaten on both sides, and shouts and cries were raised,' reports Timur in his detailed description of the encounter. 'The solders of Sultan Mahmud and Mallu Khan showed no lack of courage, but bore themselves manfully in the fight, till they could not withstand the successive assaults of my soldiers . . . [At last] their courage crumbled, and they took to flight.'

Mahmud then pulled back to Delhi. But that very night, with the enemy clamouring at the city gates, Mahmud sought safety in flight—'in the middle of that night . . . [he] fled towards the mountains and jungles,' records Timur, rather fancifully. More factually, Sirhindi states that 'when night came on, Mallu Khan and Sultan Mahmud, leaving their wives and children behind came out of the city—the sultan then fled southward to Gujarat, and Mallu Khan northward to Uttar Pradesh.

Timur then triumphantly entered Delhi, took his seat on the imperial throne, and held a court there. The leading men of the city then paid their homage to Timur. 'I had them introduced [to me] one by one, and they made their obeisances, and were admitted to the honour of kissing my throne,' writes Timur. 'I received every one of them with respect and kindness, and directed them to be seated . . . [At this time] all the Sayyids, ulama, sheikhs, and other leading Muslims arose, and . . . begged that quarter might be given to the people of Delhi, and that their lives might be spared. Out of respect to the Sayyids and ulama . . . I granted quarter to the inhabitants of the city. I then ordered my ensign and royal standard to be raised, and the drums to be beaten and music played on the tops of the gates of Delhi. Rejoicings for the victory followed.' On Friday the khutba was delivered in Timur's name in all the mosques of Delhi.

TIMUR HAD GRANTED security to the people of Delhi, but his soldiers, fired by raging rapacity, nevertheless went berserk in the city, slaughtering and plundering. It was primarily for this that they had come to India. And Timur was unable, or unwilling, to restrain them. Their rampage was however resisted by the Hindus in the city; they 'set fire to their houses with their own hands, burned their wives and children in them, and rushed into the fight and were killed,' records Timur. This resistance further inflamed the raiders. 'On that day, Thursday, and all the [following] night . . . nearly 15,000 . . . [soldiers] were engaged in slaying, plundering, and destroying. When morning broke on Friday, all my army, no longer under control, went off to the city and thought of nothing but killing, plundering, and taking prisoners.' An incredible amount of booty, far beyond all imagination, was obtained by the raiders—'rubies, diamonds, garnets, pearls, and other gems; jewels of gold and silver; . . . [gold and silver coins]; vessels of gold and silver; and brocades and silks of great value. Gold and silver ornaments of the Hindu women were obtained in such quantities as to exceed all account.' A large number of prisoners were also seized by the raiders.

'Although I was desirous of sparing them (the people of Delhi), I could not succeed, for it was the will of god that this calamity should fall upon the city . . .,' states Timur. 'By the will of god, and by no wish or direction of mine, all the three cities of Delhi—Siri, Jahan-panah and Old Delhi—had been plundered.' Mughal chronicler Nizam-ud-din Ahmad in *Tabaqat-i-Akbari* records a somewhat different version of what happened. 'Timur,' he writes, 'granted quarter to the people of the city, and appointed a number of persons to collect the ransom money. Some of the citizens, incensed by the harshness of the collectors, resisted and killed several of them. This daring incited the anger of Timur, and he gave orders to kill or make prisoners the people of the city. On that day many were captured or slain, but at length Timur was moved to pity and issued an edict of mercy.'

When at last the situation in Delhi quietened down, Timur took a ride around the three cities of Delhi. 'Siri is a round city; its buildings are lofty, and are surrounded by fortifications built of stone and brick, and they are very strong,' he noted. 'Old Delhi also has a similar fort, but it is larger than Siri . . . Jahan-panah is situated in the midst of the inhabited city. The fortifications of the three cities have thirty gates.'

Timur was so greatly impressed by the magnificence of Delhi, and by the skill of its builders and artisans, that he took many of the men with him to Central Asia. 'I ordered that all the artisans and clever mechanics, who were masters of their respective crafts, should be picked out from among the prisoners and set aside, and accordingly some thousands of craftsmen were selected to await my command,' he reports. 'All these I distributed among the princes and amirs who were present, or who were engaged officially in other parts of my dominions.' But Timur kept for himself most of the architects and masons, for he was eager to develop Samarkand—'my capital, my paradise'—

into a great centre of art and architecture. 'I had decided to build a Jami Masjid in Samarkand, the seat of my empire, which should be without a rival in any country,' he writes. 'So I ordered that all builders and stonemasons should be set apart for my own service.'

Mahmud had left 120 elephants in Delhi when he fled from the city, and Timur had them paraded before him. 'As the elephants passed by me I was greatly amused to see the tricks which their drivers had taught them. Every elephant, at the sign of its driver, bowed its head to the ground, and made its obeisance, and uttered a cry . . . When I saw these mighty animals, so well-trained and so obedient to weak man, I was greatly astonished.' He then ordered some of the elephants to be sent to his provinces in Central Asia 'so that the princes and nobles throughout my dominions might see these animals.'

TIMUR WAS FASCINATED with Delhi, and he greatly enjoyed his stay there. Yet he was anxious to move on. 'I had been in Delhi fifteen days, which time I had passed in pleasure and enjoyment, holding royal courts and giving great feasts,' he writes. 'I then reflected that I had come to Hindustan to wage war against infidels . . . I had triumphed over my adversaries, I had put to death some lakhs of infidels and idolaters . . . Now that this crowning victory had been won, I felt that I ought not indulge in ease, but rather [continue] to exert myself in warring against the infidels of Hindustan.'

So he set out again on his campaign. On 1 January 1399 he crossed the Yamuna and advanced north-westward, fighting battles all along the way, often without rest, disregarding fatigue. Once when Timur was told that at a nearby place 'a large number of infidels . . . had collected with their wives and children, and with property, goods and cattle beyond estimate,' he was initially reluctant to march against them, as 'the road thither was arduous, through jungles and thickets . . . My first thought was that I had been awake since midnight, I had travelled a long distance without halt, and had surmounted many difficulties, I had won two splendid victories with a few brave soldiers, and I was very tired, so I should stop and take rest. But then I remembered that I had drawn my sword, and had come to Hind with the resolution of waging a holy war against its infidels, and so long as it was possible to fight with them, rest was unlawful for me.'

Timur therefore promptly advanced northward into the Shiwalik Range (where the local people had taken refuge) slaughtering people and pillaging the land all along the way. 'So many of them were killed that their blood ran down the mountains and the plain,' Timur writes. In mid-January he captured Kangra, then swerved westward and, fighting as many as twenty pitched battles in thirty days, reached Jammu and sacked the city.

That was Timur's last major military engagement in India. He then crossed the Chenab, and on 6 March 1399 held a court there to bid farewell to his princes and nobles, and to send them off to their respective provinces. He himself then set out homeward. 'When I was satisfied with the destruction I had dealt out to the infidels, and the land was cleansed from the pollution of their existence, I turned back, victorious and triumphant, laden with spoil.'

On 19 March 1399 Timur crossed the Indus and left India. But there would be no rest ever for this warrior sultan, for he soon got embroiled in a series of wars in the Middle East and Central Asia. His last campaign plan was to conquer China, but when he was engaged in the preparation for it, he fell critically ill, and died soon after, in February 1405.

Timur was in India for about six months only, but those were the most devastating six months in the entire history of India, as regards the number of the towns and villages sacked, and of the people butchered. Every town and village that his army passed through was littered with the putrefying copses. Typical of Timur was the order he once gave to one of his generals: 'March up the Yamuna, and take every fort and town and village you come to, and put all the infidels of the country to the sword.' Timur's army was like a vast pack of howling, predatory animals rampaging through the land. Its blood-lust was appalling.

Yet, for all his savagery, Timur, like Mahmud Ghazni, was a man of culture. A writer himself, he loved the company of the learned and was an ardent patron of creative people. His autobiography, written in Chagatai Turkic language, is quite an engaging work, in which he describes his campaigns with cool candour. Timur had a good sense of his place in history, and he wrote his autobiography to preserve the record of his achievements. In some places he also had the account of his campaigns engraved on rock. 'I ordered an engraver on stone, who was in my camp, to cut an inscription somewhere on those defiles to the effect that I had reached this country by such and such a route, in the auspicious month of Ramadan A. H. 800,' he states.

Oddly, there was also a touching element of tenderness in the character of this most ruthless, sanguinary monarch—unbelievable though it might seem, of all the vast and opulent booty and gifts that he collected in India, what he most cherished were two white parrots presented to him by a chieftain near Delhi. These birds 'could talk well and pleasantly,' writes Timur. 'The sight of these parrots and the sound of their voices gave me great satisfaction, so I gave directions that they should be brought before me in their cages every day so that I might listen to their talk . . . They brought [to me several] rare presents from Hindustan, but I looked upon the two parrots as the best of their gifts.'

Timur was also human enough to cry sometimes, though what he shed were tears of joy. 'When I recounted the favours and mercies I had received from the Almighty—my excellent sons, the brave and renowned amirs who served under me, and the great and glorious victories I had won—my heart melted, and tears burst from my eyes,' he writes.

TIMUR HAD LAID waste a broad swath of land in North India, and he left Delhi in utter ruin and virtually depopulated. 'After the departure of Timur, the neighbourhood of Delhi, and all those territories over which his armies had passed, were visited with pestilence and famine,' observes Sirhindi. 'Many died of sickness, and many perished of hunger, and for two months Delhi was desolate.'

And this material and human devastation was followed by political chaos. The Sultanate was now in shambles, and the authority of the sultan was virtually confined to the city of Delhi and its environs. And the tussle for the throne between the descendants of Firuz, which had raged before Timur's invasion, now resumed. Soon after the departure of Timur from Delhi, the city was occupied by Nusrat Shah, a grandson of Firuz. But he was almost immediately driven out of the city by Mallu Khan, who then invited Mahmud to return to Delhi and reoccupy the throne. Mahmud, who had fled to Gujarat from Delhi on being routed by Timur, and had finally taken refuge in Malwa, then returned to Delhi. But he was miserable there, for Mallu Khan was the de facto ruler, and Mahmud a mere figurehead. So, chafing under the haughty dominance of Mallu Khan, Mahmud once again fled from the city, this time to Kanauj, where he lived as a virtual refugee, with just a few attendants.

Meanwhile Mallu Khan tried to recover some of the lost provinces of the empire, but this brought him into conflict with Khizr Khan, a former noble of the Sultanate but now the deputy of Timur in Multan. In the ensuing battle Khizr Khan defeated and killed Mallu Khan. A group of nobles headed by Daulat Khan Lodi then took charge of Delhi, and they persuaded Mahmud to reoccupy the throne of Delhi. Mahmud was not entirely without spirit and enterprise, and during this phase of his rule, which lasted seven years, he made several earnest efforts to recover some of the lost territories of the empire.

The reign of Mahmud in all lasted eighteen years, but during a good part of it he was only a nominal ruler, under the thumb of some dominant noble, and on a couple of occasions he was even a fugitive living under the protection of provincial rulers. The sultan died in early 1412, and with his death ended the history of the Tughluq dynasty.

PART VI

THREE KINGDOMS

Ahmad Shah . . . overran the open country, and
wherever he went, he put to death men, women
and children, without mercy . . . Wherever the
number of the slain amounted to 20,000, he halted
for three days, and made a festival in celebration
of the bloody event.

—FERISHTA

1

The Last Hurrah

The Delhi Sultanate was in an appalling state of disintegration at the close of the reign of the Tughluqs, and had fragmented into a number of independent kingdoms, some of which had larger territory and greater power than the Sultanate. But the Sultanate, though considerably attenuated, endured for 114 years more, till the invasion of Babur and the establishment of the Mughal rule in India in 1526. During this period, after a chaotic interregnum of two years following the death of sultan Mahmud in 1412, the Sultanate was ruled by two successor dynasties, Sayyids for thirty-seven years under four sultans, and Lodis for seventy-five years under three sultans.

The first of these two dynasties was founded by Khizr Khan, who bore the appellation 'Sayyid', which identified him as a descendant of prophet Muhammad, so the dynasty he founded came to be known as the Sayyid dynasty. The veracity of Khizr Khan's claimed lineage is uncertain, but it is likely that his forebears were Arabs, who had migrated to India in the early Tughluq period and settled in Multan. The family prospered in India, gaining wealth and power. This advancement culminated in Malik Suleiman, Khizr Khan's father, becoming the governor of Multan under the Tughluqs. When Suleiman died, Khizr Khan succeeded him to the post, but lost it during the political turmoil following the death of Firuz Tughluq.

Khizr Khan was however able to regain the post by casting his lot with Timur when he invaded India, and was rewarded by Timur with the governorship of Multan. According to Mughal chronicler Ferishta, Timur in fact appointed Khizr Khan as his viceroy in Delhi, but the Khan does not seem to have assumed that office. In any case, with the retreat of Timur from India, and the return of Mahmud Tughluq to the throne of Delhi, Khizr Khan had to be contented with Multan for the time being. But his ambition now was clearly to be the ruler of Delhi, the role that Timur had assigned to him. Over the next decade and half he considerably expanded his territory and power in western India, in preparation for the campaign to seize Delhi. During this period he in fact advanced on Delhi twice, but had to retreat on both occasions, because of the lack of provisions for his army in the devastated environs of Delhi. Then his fortune turned again. On the death of Mahmud, the last sultan of the Tughluq dynasty, the nobles of Delhi raised Daulat Khan Lodi, a powerful and respected noble, to the throne of Delhi. But before Daulat Khan could consolidate his power, Khizr Khan marched against him, occupied Delhi after a siege of four months, imprisoned Daulat Khan, and ascended the throne. Daulat Khan then disappeared from history.

THIS WAS IN June 1414. With the accession of Khizr Khan began the gradual recovery of the Sultanate from the quarter century of swirling chaos into which it had slid after the death of Firuz Tughluq. Khizr Khan had all the qualities needed to play the role of a political redeemer. 'He was generous, brave, merciful, considerate, true to his word, and kind,' writes Sirhindi, a medieval Indian chronicler. Adds Badauni: 'The Sayyid was a man in whom were manifest the virtues of Muhammad . . . and the grace of Ali . . .'

Prudence and rectitude marked all the policies and actions of Khizr Khan. And he was unswerving in his loyalty to Timur (to whom he owed his rise to power) and his descendants. Though he exercised all the powers of a sovereign, he prudently refrained from assuming the royal title, but was content to be known as the viceroy of Shah Rukh, Timur's son, to whom he took care to send tribute throughout his reign. In the first few years of his reign the khutba in Delhi was read only in the name of Shah Rukh, and it was only later that Khizr Khan added his own name in the khutba, and that too only after obtaining Shah Rukh's permission to do so. Nor did Khizr Khan mint coins in his own name. He was not enamoured of the trappings of power; he had the substance of power, and that was what mattered to him. 'Although he did not take royal titles, yet he ruled and administered his territories like a king,' comments Nurul-Haqq, a sixteenth century chronicler.

In many respects Khizr Khan was like Firuz Tughluq, particularly in the caution, moderation, benevolence and sense of justice he displayed during his reign. Like Firuz, Khizr Khan also took care to win over his rivals and adversaries by treating them with fairness and generosity. Although he necessarily gave the key positions in government to his own trusted followers, he treated the top officers of the previous reign honourably. Equally, he showed a genuine concern for the welfare of his subjects, particularly for the poor.

The Delhi Sultanate was no longer an empire at the time of Khizr Khan's accession, but only one of the many kingdoms into which the subcontinent had fragmented in the closing years of the Tughluq dynasty. Khizr Khan made some cautious moves to extend its territory, but he was not particularly successful in this, though in some cases he was able to force the local rulers to pay him the tribute due to him as their overlord. He had a good sense of what was possible in the prevailing circumstances, and he trimmed his policies to suit the constraints of his situation. He therefore often overlooked the actions of refractory provincial chieftains, for he knew all too well that even if he managed to overpower them, they would turn rebellious again when his forces withdrew from their territories. He was however particular about collecting the revenues due from the provinces, for that was the absolutely essential sustenance for his very survival as sultan. Often he had to take military action to enforce revenue collection, and in some extreme cases even had to resort to plundering the fief of the defaulter to collect the dues from him, with the royal soldiers acting like brigands.

Khizr Khan died in May 1421, after a reign of seven years. His rule was on the whole marked by positive developments, and he left the Sultanate in very much better health than how he found it.

KHIZR KHAN WAS succeeded to the throne by his son Mubarak Shah, whom he had nominated as his successor just before his death. Sirhindi describes Mubarak as the 'most excellent and worthy son' of Khizr Khan, and indeed he proved to be a ruler of energy and spirit. But he too, like most other rulers of the Sultanate, had to deal with several rebellions, the hostility of nobles, as well as with the recurrence of Mongol incursions. And his life ended tragically.

Mubarak, unlike his father, assumed all the symbols and appurtenances of a sovereign ruler, took the title Shah, and also issued coins in his own name, even though he continued to pay tribute to Shah Rukh, and took care to receive, with the respect and courtesy due from a subordinate ruler to his overlord, the robes of honour sent to him by Shah Rukh. But Mubarak's posture of independence apparently irked Mongols. And this, according to Ferishta, was the reason for the recurrence of Mongol forays into India, though it is likely that this was only an excuse used by Mongols for launching their usual predatory raids.

These Mongol raids were however a relatively minor problem for Mubarak, and he was able to deal with them effectively without much difficulty. A far more serious problem for him was the recalcitrance of senior royal officers which, though a perennial problem in the Delhi Sultanate, had become particularly acute after the collapse of the Tughluq dynasty. Mubarak's solution to the problem was to periodically transfer his top officers from their posts, in order to prevent them from entrenching themselves in their offices. This

naturally created considerable resentment among the nobles. Matters came
to a head when Mubarak clipped the wings of Sarvar-ul-Mulk, his arrogant
and overweening chief minister, by bifurcating his office and assigning its
crucial revenue functions to another noble. Sarvar-ul-Mulk avenged his virtual
demotion by fomenting a conspiracy to assassinate Mubarak. The opportunity
for the plotters came when the sultan went to inspect the progress of the work
on the city of Mubarakabad that he had founded. There, while the sultan
was preparing for the Friday prayers, a bunch of conspirators 'rushed in with
loud, hellish cries and dispatched that righteous sovereign,' reports Sirhindi.
'Mubarak Shah had reigned for thirteen years, three months, and sixteen days.'

MUBARAK HAD NO son, so he was succeeded by his nephew, Muhammad
Shah, who was, according to Sirhindi, 'a clement and generous sovereign, full
of excellent qualities.' But he was an easygoing ruler, who 'took no measures
to secure his possessions, but gave himself up to indulgence.' This enabled
Sarvar-ul-Mulk to emerge as the de facto sultan. But he could not enjoy the
fruits of his regicide for long, for his rise to supreme power was resented by
other nobles, especially as he was a Hindu convert to Islam. Presently the
royal court was riven into rival cabals, and began to seethe with conspiracies
and counter-conspiracies. And, even as Sarvar-ul-Mulk initiated measures to
eliminate his rivals, he and his cohorts were slain in a palace uprising.

But that hardly improved matters in the Sultanate. With the sultan ever
dallying in the harem and paying virtually no attention to the affairs of the
state, there was now no nucleus around which the political power in the
Sultanate could cohere. A group of disaffected nobles then sought the help
of Mahmud Shah Khalji, the ruler of Malwa, to oust Muhammad, and
Muhammad in turn sought the help of Buhlul Lodi, the governor of Sirhind,
to suppress the rebels. The ensuing civil war was inconclusive, but it saved
Muhammad's crown, though the real beneficiary of the conflict was Buhlul
Lodi, who, as the saviour of the throne, now emerged as the key player in
the unfolding political drama. Although Buhlul returned to Sirhind after the
civil war, his eyes were now very much on the throne of Delhi. And in 1443,
having substantially extended his territories and acquired some strategic
allies, he advanced on Delhi and besieged it. Although he failed to capture
the city, on returning to Sirhind he declared himself a sovereign, and took
the title Sultan Buhlul.

Muhammad died in 1445, and was succeeded by his son Ala-ud-din, who,
according to Sirhindi, turned out to be even 'more negligent and incompetent
than his father in performing the duties of government.' Ala-ud-din on his
accession assumed the grand title Alam Shah, Lord of the World, which was
most ironical, for under him the Sultanate shrank to the size of a petty state,

covering just the city of Delhi and its neighbouring villages. As a common satirical jingle of the time had it,

From Delhi to Palam
Is the realm of Shah Alam.

Still Delhi was Delhi, and to rule from there was the ultimate goal of the politically ambitious everywhere in North India. But Alam Shah was not enamoured of the city because of its vicious, churning political environment. So in the third year of his reign he moved his residence from Delhi to Budaun, a charming little town on the banks of Ganga south-east of Delhi. And there he lived in blissful obscurity for thirty years, till his death in 1478, content with the modest revenue of his principality, enjoying the pleasures of life, free of all the cares and tribulations that harry a crowned head. Delhi was left to whoever could seize power there.

ON THE DEPARTURE of Alam Shah to Budaun, the Sultanate, without a king on the throne, was on the verge of terminal collapse. To prevent that fatality, the nobles of Delhi headed by Hamid Khan, the chief executive of Alam Shah, invited Buhlul Lodi to ascend the throne in Delhi. This, according to Ni'matullah, an early seventeenth century chronicler, was the turn of fortune that Buhlul had been long expecting, for a dervish had several years earlier blessed him with the words, 'May the empire of Delhi be fortunate to you!' So, on the invitation of Hamid Khan, Buhlul rushed to Delhi with an army, and there, on 19 April 1451, 'at the . . . auspicious time which astrologers . . . and experienced Brahmins had indicated,' he ascended the throne. Thus began the 75 year long reign of the Lodi dynasty.

The Lodis were Afghans, a people of uncertain racial origin, who were mostly engaged in agriculture and horse breeding, and were also highly valued as soldiers, being hardy and valiant. Afghans were divided into various tribes, among whom the Lodi tribe was one of the most prominent. Around the late tenth century a few Lodi families migrated from their homeland to north-western India, and gradually gained prominence there as horse traders and soldiers. They made their first appearance in Indian history in the mid-fourteenth century, when Malik Shahu, an ancestor of the Lodi rulers of India, raided Multan, killed its governor, and held the region under his power for a while. Though he was soon driven off from there by Muhammad Tughluq, the event marked the beginning of the involvement of the Lodis in the turbulent politics of the Delhi Sultanate.

Later, one of Shahu's grandsons, Malik Bahram, entered the service of Firuz Shah Tughluq's governor of Multan. A few years later Bahram's son Malik

Lodi was appointed the governor of Sirhind by Sultan Khizr Khan, as a reward for the crucial help that Malik had given to him during his tussle with Mallu Khan. Malik Lodi was succeeded to the governorship of Sirhind by Buhlul Lodi, his nephew and son-in-law, and he, taking advantage of the debilitation of the Sultanate under the latter Sayyids, functioned as a virtually independent ruler. He was indisputably the most powerful noble in the Sultanate at this time. So it was natural that the nobles of Delhi should invite him to occupy the throne of Delhi left vacant by Alam Shah.

Buhlul, for all his vaulting ambition, was very cautious in all that he did. Thus he on his accession took care to write to Alam Shah a dissembling, conciliatory letter, stating, according to Sirhindi, that he had acted solely in the interest of the sultan, and that he remained as ever 'his devoted servant.' Alam Shah could not possibly have been deceived by that profession, but he did not care. 'As my father addressed you as his son, I look upon you as my elder brother, and resign kingship to your hands. I shall live in contentment at Budaun.'

HAMID KHAN, UNDER whose initiative Buhlul was crowned sultan, seems to have viewed Afghans as rustic simpletons, and he expected Buhlul to leave the running of the government in his hands. And Buhlul cannily encouraged these expectations initially, by being always deferential towards him. According to Abdullah, a late medieval chronicler, Buhlul once told Hamid Khan: 'I am a mere soldier and cannot manage even my own fief. You should be the king, and I will be the commander of your troops, and obey any injunctions you may issue.' Comments Abdullah: 'So long as Hamid Khan retained any power, Sultan Buhlul thought it expedient to pay him extreme marks of deference, and he went every day to pay his respects to him.'

All that was mere pretence. And the pretence did not last long. Soon, after Buhlul became secure on the throne, he had Hamid thrown into prison, but did that with a characteristic show of courtesy. One day in the court Qutb Khan Lodi, Buhlul's cousin, respectfully placed a chain before Hamid and told him that for political reasons it was necessary to imprison him, but that his life would be spared out of consideration for the many services that he had rendered to the sultan. Nothing more was heard of Hamid Khan thereafter.

Buhlul's actions were all characterised by similar deliberation and courtesy. And he was invariably fair in his dealings with his nobles as well as with his subjects, even with his adversaries. And this nobility of his character commanded the respect of all. 'Sultan Buhlul . . . evinced courage and generosity. His mercy and benevolence were habitual,' writes Abdullah in his long paean on Buhlul. 'He observed the rules of honesty, and had exceeding respect for the law, to the injunctions of which he strictly adhered in all his undertakings. He spent most of his time in the assemblies of the wise and in the society of holy men, and made special inquiries respecting the poor and necessitous. He never turned away any suppliant . . . He devoted extreme care to the administration of justice, and himself heard the petitions of his subjects . . .'

'He was wise, experienced, considerate, kind, friendly . . . and just,' continues Abdullah. 'Whatever came into his possession, in money, goods or new *parganas*, he distributed it all among his troops, and reserved nothing whatever for himself. He accumulated no treasure, and executed his kingly functions without parade and ostentation . . . In his social meetings he never sat on a throne, and would not allow his nobles to stand. Even during public audiences he did not occupy the throne, but seated himself upon a carpet . . . If at any time . . . [his nobles] were displeased with him, he tried so hard to pacify them that he would himself go to their houses, ungird his sword from his waist, and place it before the offended party; nay, he would sometimes even take off his turban from his head, and solicit forgiveness, saying "If you think me unworthy of the station I occupy, choose someone else, and bestow on me some other office." He maintained brotherly intercourse with all his chiefs and soldiers. If anyone was ill, he would himself go and attend on him . . . [But] he was exceedingly bold [in battle] . . . From the day that he became king, no one achieved a victory over him . . .'

At the time of the accession of Buhlul 'the whole of Hind was divided into provinces governed by petty rulers,' observes Ni'matullah. Under Buhlul there was some revival the fortunes of the Sultanate, and some expansion of its territories. Soon after his accession he was engaged in a long seesaw struggle with the sultan of the powerful kingdom of Jaunpur, whom he finally overthrew and annexed his kingdom, a success that considerably enhanced his power and prestige. He also asserted his authority over the recalcitrant chieftains in the Doab and Mewat, by waging several successful campaigns against them.

The reign of Buhlul lasted nearly 39 years, its very length, truly exceptional in that turbulent age, proving the success of his reign. This success seems even more remarkable when we consider that he had very limited resources, and that the dominant Turkish community in Delhi was scornful of Afghans because of their rugged manners and rustic speech.

BUHLUL DIED IN July 1489, aged eighty. He died, according to Ni'matullah, 'on account of excessive heat'—presumably by sunstroke—while returning to Delhi after a military campaign. His third son, Sikandar, whom the sultan had designated as his successor, considering him to be the ablest of his sons, then ascended the throne. Buhlul had, while nominating Sikandar for the throne, taken care, with his characteristic caution and prudence, to assign suitable territories and offices to his other sons, close relatives, and prominent amirs, so that the succession of Sikandar would be smooth. Still, some of the nobles objected to Sikandar's nomination, on the ground that his mother was a Hindu goldsmith's daughter. Though Sikandar overcame this objection and ascended the throne, his accession was challenged by his elder brother Barbak, to whom Buhlul had assigned the important province of Jaunpur. In the ensuing battle Sikandar easily defeated his brother, but restored him to the throne of Jaunpur, following the conciliatory policy of his father. But Barbak proved to be incompetent to rule even Jaunpur, so Sikandar eventually removed him from his office and kept him in confinement.

Sikandar was only 18 when he ascended the throne, but he was endowed with a maturity and sagacity far above his age. All contemporary chroniclers have only high praise for the sultan, for the lofty qualities of his mind and heart, even for his physical charm. 'He was,' states Abdullah, 'remarkable for his beauty, which was unsurpassed, and . . . whoever looked on him yielded his heart captive to him.' According to Ni'matullah, astrologers had, on the birth of Sikandar, predicted that he would adorn 'the garden of sovereignty with verdure and brightness.' He would indeed fulfil that prediction.

'Sultan Sikandar,' states Abdullah in his effulgent praise of the monarch, 'was a most illustrious monarch and of a benevolent disposition; he was famous for his liberality, honour and politeness; he had no desire for pomp and ceremonies, and cared not for processions and magnificent dresses. No one who was profligate or of bad character had access to him. He . . . was exceedingly god-fearing and benevolent . . . just and courageous . . . and he was constantly . . . trying to render his subjects happy. He personally assisted the wretched . . . Every winter he sent clothes and shawls for the benefit of the needy, and distributed a certain amount of money to them every Friday . . . He ordained that twice a year he should be furnished with detailed accounts of the meritorious poor in his empire, whom he then supplied with means sufficient to support them for six months, each receiving according to his needs . . .' Adds Ni'matullah: 'He was . . . endowed with the quality of mildness, and was eminently benevolent, highly dignified and refined . . . He was a paragon or bravery and justice . . .'

Abdullah and Ni'matullah, early seventeenth century chroniclers, are our main sources of information on the Lodi dynasty, but the portraits they paint of Buhlul and Sikandar are so radiant that they strain credibility. Their exaggerations are however exaggerations of facts, we should assume; they are not fiction. These chroniclers had no vested interest in falsifying the portraits of the Lodi sultans, for they wrote their chronicles over eight decades after the fall of the Lodi dynasty, and had therefore nothing to gain or lose from what they wrote. The problem with their accounts is their hyperbolic narrative style, not their bias.

SIKANDAR'S REIGN WAS a period of cultural efflorescence in the Sultanate. The sultan himself, according to Badauni, was a poet, who wrote in Persian under a pen-name. He was keenly interested in all literary and scholarly activities, as well as in music. Most commendably, he paid particular attention to the preservation of old manuscripts, and arranged for the translation of several Sanskrit texts into Persian, particularly an ancient Indian text on medicine. He was also a keen sportsman—'he enjoyed himself in field sports,' states Ni'matullah. Hunting and polo, the common pastimes of the Delhi sultans, were the favourite pastimes of Sikandar too, but he was also keen on fishing, particularly in summer, when he, according to Ni'matullah, often pitched his tents on the banks of the Yamuna, 'whither he retired in order to avoid the heat, and amuse himself with fishing.'

But despite his benevolent disposition, wide-ranging cultural interests, and broad social concerns, Sikandar was a hyper-orthodox Muslim who regarded it his sacred duty to demolish temples and induce his non-Muslim subjects to become Muslims. 'His zeal for Islam surpassed all bounds,' comments Ni'matullah. He 'entirely ruined the shrines of Mathura, the mine of heathenism, and turned the principal Hindu places of worship into caravanserais and colleges,' reports Abdullah. 'Their stone images were given to butchers to serve them as meat-weights.'

Several such acts of Sikandar are recorded in medieval chronicles. Once when he was told of a Brahmin who maintained that both Islam and Hinduism were true religions, and were merely different but equally valid means for god realisation, he sought the opinion of his theologians on whether the view was valid, and whether, if it was valid, the two communities should live in peace and harmony. The theologians asserted that the Brahmin's view was most pernicious, and that he should be forced to become a Muslim, since he admitted the truth of Islam, and that he should be put to death if he refused. As the Brahmin refused to become a Muslim—he obviously saw no reason to change religion since his own religion was as true as Islam—he was put to death.

Some of the incidents of the sultan's persecution of non-Muslims given in medieval chronicles might be exaggerations, meant to laud the sultan's religious zeal, but there is little doubt that his passion for enforcing Islamic precepts was quite extreme. Indeed, some of his anti-infidel actions went beyond what was expected of even a most orthodox Muslim ruler, and were criticised even by some Muslim religious leaders. Thus, according to Abdullah, a cleric once told Sikandar 'that it would be very improper for him to destroy ancient idol temples, and that he ought not forbid [Hindus] from performing their accustomed rites . . .' Hearing this, the sultan 'placed his hand on his dagger, and exclaimed, "You side with the infidels! I will first put an end to you, and then massacre the infidels." But the cleric stood his ground, and replied:

"Everyone's life is in the hand of god . . . Whoever enters the presence of a tyrant must beforehand prepare himself for death." The sultan then rose and left in a huff. But he took no action against the cleric.

As in persecuting non-Muslims, Sikandar was equally fervid in suppressing the semi-idolatrous practices of some Muslim sects, such as taking out processions with relics. He also forbade women from going on pilgrimages to the tombs of saints, as that was an unorthodox practice. At the same time he sought to promote Islam by building many new masjids throughout his dominions, manned by state-funded staff.

All this he did in conformity with what was expected of an orthodox Muslim ruler. There were however two matters in which the sultan deviated from the orthodox Muslim prescriptions—he shaved his beard, and he drank wine secretly. 'You are a Mussulman monarch, and yet wear no beard,' a Muslim sage once upbraided him. 'This is contrary to the institutions of Islam, and particularly improper in a king.' To that the sultan replied: 'My beard is thin; if I allow it to grow it will look ill, and men will scoff at me.' As for the sultan drinking wine, he did it for health reasons, claims Abdullah. Ni'matullah also states that Sikandar drank wine 'as a medicinal tonic, in privacy, for the exhilaration of his spirit, and he did it in a decent and refined way.'

SIKANDAR CONDUCTED HIMSELF decorously at all times, and was formal even in his conversation. 'The sultan's conversation,' states Abdullah, 'was under discipline, and he was never desultory.' And just as Sikandar was reserved and ceremonial in all that he did, he required his courtiers to observe formal etiquette in his presence. While the court practices under Buhlul were informal, and the sultan was then considered as no more than a *primus inter pares*, a first among equals, the scene changed altogether under Sikandar. The sultan now elevated himself to a far higher plane than his courtiers, who were required to treat him with high respect, and conduct themselves with becoming decorum. 'Every chief had his assigned place in his presence, where he always stood,' notes Abdullah. And 'every work had its appointed time,' adds Ni'matullah.

These were not whimsical acts of the personal vanity of the sultan, but expressions of a well-considered policy to enforce discipline and efficiency in administration. A crucial aspect of this policy was that Sikandar required his provincial governors to submit their accounts regularly for auditing by central government officers. Defaulters and embezzlers were sternly punished.

Further, to keep track of all that was happening everywhere in the empire, Sikandar set up an elaborate intelligence network, so that well-informed, prompt and effective action could be taken to redress abuses and rectify faults. 'He possessed a retentive memory,' states Abdullah. 'He daily received an account of the prices of all things, and an account of what had happened in the different districts of his empire. If he perceived the slightest appearance of anything wrong, he caused instant inquiries to be made about it.' And when he sent his army on a campaign, he kept in constant touch with it twice every day, in the morning and the evening, whatever be the distance involved, sending instructions to it and receiving information from it. In all this Sikandar seems to have modelled himself on the policies and conduct of Ala-ud-din Khalji.

Sikandar, according to Ni'matullah, 'executed all his affairs with discernment, keenness and penetrating insight.' And he was untiring in his work. 'On occasions he remained so engrossed in administrative work from morning till evening and the hour for retiring, so he performed all the five daily prayers at one and the same [time and at the same] place,' states Ni'matullah. Official work often kept him awake till late at night, sometimes even till daybreak, so he had to catch up with sleep by taking a nap at midday. Sikandar, according to Abdullah, 'generally preferred the night for listening to the petitions of the needy; he also devoted a portion of it for regulating the affairs of the empire, and for writing firmans to the governors of provinces, and letters to the monarchs of the time.'

THE MAIN FOCUS of Sikandar's reign was on tightening the administration of the state rather than on expanding its territory. And, as in everything else, he was cautious and deliberate in his military policy also. He launched no major campaigns of conquest, sought no territory beyond what he could effectively govern. Rather than waging wars against his adversaries, he endeavoured to win them over through conciliatory policies. 'He put an end to wars and disputes with the other monarchs and nobles of the age, and closed the road of contention and strife,' states Abdullah. 'He contented himself with the territory bequeathed to him by his father, and passed the whole of his life in the greatest safety and enjoyment.'

However, though Sikandar avoided wars of conquest, he, following the policies of his father, launched a number of campaigns to assert his authority over the provinces of the kingdom and to consolidate the state, so that the Sultanate under him became the most powerful state in the subcontinent, though still a dwarf compared to what it had been under Khaljis and Tughluqs. One of the main military challenges that Sikandar faced was to keep under control the ever turbulent Rajput chieftains, but he was largely successful in that endeavour. In 1504 he shifted his capital from Delhi to the new township he founded in Agra, partly to keep the Rajputs under close watch, but also because Delhi had by this time become quite dilapidated.

On the whole Sikandar's reign was marked by peace and prosperity. Comments Ni'matullah: 'During the springtime of his rule, the garden of the world blossomed forth anew . . . On the cradle of his rule people lived in peace, security and contentment.' The sultan, by his wise and moderate policies, 'won the hearts of both the high and the low,' states Abdullah. 'During his reign everything was cheap, and safety and security prevailed . . . The public roads in his territory were so well secured that there was not a sign of highwaymen and robbers throughout his dominions . . . Grain, merchandise and goods of all description were so cheap during his reign that even people with small means could live comfortably . . . In his reign business was carried on in a peaceful, honest, straightforward way. A new sort of life obtained, for people high and low were polite, and self-respect, integrity, and devotion to religion prevailed, such as had never been the case in former reigns . . .

> It was a wonderful age. All enjoyed peace.
> In every house was pleasure and festivity . . .
> No one saw rebellion, even in his dreams . . .'

Sikandar died in November 1517, at the age of 46, after a reign of 28 years and some months. 'Sikandar was taken ill with a disease of the throat, which daily became worse,' writes Abdullah. '[He] became weaker every day . . . [and] by degrees his illness arrived at such a pitch that his throat would allow him neither to swallow food nor to drink water, and the passage of his breath was choked.'

SIKANDAR WAS SUCCEEDED on the throne by his eldest son Ibrahim. His coronation was one of the grandest celebrations in the history of the Delhi Sultanate. 'On that day, all those who were attached to the royal person prepared the tents, embroidered with gold and adorned with jewels, and spread carpets of various colours, worked with gold thread,' writes Ahmad Yadgar, an early seventeenth century chronicler. 'They placed the throne . . . covered with costly gems and jewels of great value, on a colourful carpet. The tributary kings and nobles wore beautiful dresses and embroidered garments . . . Horses and elephants were decked with the most magnificent trappings. So splendid a coronation had never been witnessed, and the people . . . long remembered the day on which this fortunate and youthful monarch obtained the crown.' This was the last hurrah of the Delhi Sultanate.

On the accession of Ibrahim some of the nobles in Delhi persuaded him—presumably hoping to clip his power—to partition the empire and give Jalal Khan, his uterine brother, the independent charge of Jaunpur. Ibrahim acted on this suggestion. But a few months later some other nobles in Delhi warned him that he had committed a grave error in dividing the kingdom, because

Two souls cannot occupy one body,
Nor two monarchs one kingdom.

So Ibrahim revoked the arrangement with his brother and sought to repossess Jaunpur. Jalal naturally would not agree to this. 'Sultan Ibrahim, of his own accord, gave me a portion of the inheritance which our father left, because I was his own brother, the son of the same mother,' he asserted. 'He has now broken the phial of the connection which we derived from our parent's womb with the stone of unkindness.' The issue evidently could be settled only on the battlefield. But Jalal was no match to Ibrahim, who chased him from place to place, finally captured him, and sent him to be imprisoned in the fort of Hansi, where his other four brothers were confined. But Jalal was assassinated on the way to Hansi, presumably on the order of Ibrahim.

Except for this ruthless act, the reign of Ibrahim was relatively clean, in so far as the reign of any medieval ruler could be clean. The prosperity that the Sultanate enjoyed under Buhlul continued under Ibrahim for a while. According to Abdullah, during Ibrahim's reign 'corn, clothes, and every kind of merchandise were cheaper than they had ever been known to be in any other reign, except perhaps in the time of Sultan Ala-ud-din Khalji, but even that is doubtful. Moreover, in the time of the later, the cheapness was achieved by means of every kind of disgusting interference and oppression, and by a hundred thousand enforcements and punishments; whereas the cheapness of . . . [farm produce in] this reign was occasioned by abundant harvests . . . Rain fell in the exact quantity that was needed, and the crops were consequently luxuriant, and the produce increased tenfold beyond the usual proportion.'

This state of peace and prosperity did not however last long. Presently one trouble after another began to beset the kingdom. 'Sultan Sikandar's death was followed by an internecine strife,' notes Ni'matullah. 'All his regulations were undone, low and mean persons won ascendency over the high and the noble, and caused disorder and disturbance. Administrative and financial affairs were thrown into total disorder. Although Sultan Ibrahim devised ways and adopted measures to rectify matters, these [very] steps unwittingly caused the undoing of his Sultanate.'

These problems were in part caused by the odd personality of Ibrahim. But the views of medieval chroniclers on this are rather confusing. According to Ni'matullah, the 'wrath and violence of the sultan,' his implacability and 'ill temper, kept the courtiers and nobles of the realm in perpetual dread and suspicion.' On the other hand, Yadgar states that Ibrahim was 'celebrated for his personal beauty and excellent disposition,' though a few pages later he notes that some nobles held that the sultan was 'fickle' and of 'evil disposition.' Some even held that 'the king had gone mad.'

These harsh condemnations of Ibrahim by the nobles probably have a good amount of exaggeration in them, and were tainted by their resentment of the disciplinary measures that the sultan imposed on them. Ibrahim was indeed a medieval tyrant, but he was not very much worse so than most other Delhi sultans. But he clearly did not trust his nobles, and suspected, rightly, malice in them towards him, and he sought to keep them on a tight leash.

Ibrahim wanted total subservience from his nobles, and, to achieve that goal he sought to create a suitable psychological distance between himself and them. This led to a further tightening of the formal court etiquette introduced by Sikandar. According to Ferishta, Ibrahim declared that 'kings should have no relations or clansmen, but all should be considered as subjects and servants of the state. The Afghan chiefs, who had hitherto been allowed to sit in the [king's] presence, were now constrained to stand in front of the throne, with their hands crossed on the breast.'

ALL THIS CREATED considerable resentment among the nobles, whose support was the very base on which the royal throne rested. The situation became worse after Ibrahim's conquest of Gwalior, a Rajput kingdom that had long defied his predecessors. 'When the sultan had conquered Gwalior . . . he waxed very proud, so that he began to maltreat and punish the nobles of his father,' writes Yadgar. '[He] has put 23 of them . . . to death without any cause . . . Some he suspended from walls, and caused others to be burnt alive.' Once he had a whole group of troublesome nobles exterminated by blowing up with gunpowder the building where they had assembled.

'The sultan has lost his sense; he cannot distinguish between those who serve him well and those who serve him ill,' commented a grandee. His capricious tyranny made many nobles writhe in anxiety, and it ignited several rebellions. But Ibrahim was also fortunate in having several dedicated nobles in his service, who would not under any circumstance betray him, not necessarily out of loyalty to his person, but out of loyalty to his dynasty. Thus when Azam Humayun, a top noble, was warned that Ibrahim might harm him, and that he should save himself by rebelling, he refused, even though he had then a cavalry force of 30,000 under his command. 'I cannot act thus,' he said. 'I cannot turn aside and blacken my face, let what may happen.' Predictably, he was presently imprisoned by Ibrahim, and later slain.

Ibrahim had several honourable grandees like Azam in his service, so he had no difficulty in crushing the rebel nobles. The real threat to his throne came from outside India, from Babur, the Mughal ruler of Kabul. But what directly led to the invasion of Babur was the discontent of Ibrahim's nobles, particularly of Daulat Khan Lodi, the long time governor of Punjab. His son, Dilwar Khan, who was in Delhi, had an inkling of the sultan's ill will towards his father, so he secretly fled from Delhi to Punjab to warn his father. The warning threw Daulat Khan 'into deep meditation,' writes Yadgar. 'He reflected that if he rebelled he would be accused of ingratitude, and that if he fell into the clutches of the sultan's wrath, he would not escape alive.' He also feared that he might not able to prevail over Ibrahim in a military confrontation. So he finally decided to send his son to Kabul to invite Babur to invade India and overthrow Ibrahim. Around this time Alam Khan, a disaffected uncle of Ibrahim, also made a similar appeal to Babur.

This was an opportune development for Babur, for he was at this time being menaced by Uzbegs on the west, and was thinking of India as a possible refuge. So in 1524 he invaded Punjab, and, in alliance with Daulat Khan, defeated the army sent against him by Ibrahim. But instead of handing over the province to the Khan, as the latter had expected, Babur annexed the province to his kingdom and appointed his own officers there. This resulted in the breakup of the alliance, so Babur returned to Kabul to prepare a fresh invasion. During his previous campaign his sole objective was to acquire Punjab as a safe retreat from the menace of the Uzbegs, but he had a much grander plan now, to conquer and rule over Hindustan.

In November 1525, Babur again set out from Kabul for India. He first consolidated his position in Punjab, and then sped—'like a roaring lion', as Yadgar puts it—south-eastward towards Delhi, and pitched his camp between Yamuna and the town of Panipat, some 80 kilometres north of Delhi.

Ibrahim Lodi was close by, to the south of Panipat, in a good blocking position to prevent the Mughals from advancing further into India. There was some disquiet in the Sultanate army at this time because some astrologers had predicted that Ibrahim would be defeated in the battle. This apparently induced Ibrahim to hold a grand celebration in his army camp on the day before the battle, to counter the demoralising effect of the astrological predictions and to inspirit his army.

Ibrahim, according to Yadgar, 'summoned all his nobles and soldiers and ordered them to dress themselves in the best clothes they had with them. He caused his embroidered tents and satin canopies to be erected, and made all the preparations for a fiesta. He threw amongst them all the gold, jewels, pearls and *ashrafis* which he possessed, and said, "O friends, tomorrow we shall do battle with the Mughal army. If I gain victory, I will endeavour to please you; if I do not, be at least content with these presents and my declared intentions." The whole of that day was spent in feasting and rejoicing. On the morrow they made ready for war.'

THE BATTLE BETWEEN the rival forces was fought on 20 April 1526. It was a fiercely contested battle—'so desperate a battle, indeed, had never been seen,' comments Yadgar. Still, the battle lasted only just a few hours, from sunrise to noon. And Babur, though his army was much smaller than that of Ibrahim, defeated him decisively through the use of clever and innovative tactics.

As the trend of the battle became evident, an Afghan noble appealed to Ibrahim to leave the battlefield, saying, 'If the king is saved, it will be easy to find another army, and again make war against the Mughals.' But Ibrahim rejected the plea. 'O Mahmud Khan, it is a disgrace for kings to flee from the field of battle,' he said. 'Look here, my nobles, my companions, my well-wishers and friends have partaken of the cup of martyrdom . . . My horse's legs are dyed with blood up to its chest . . . It is better that I should be like my friends, [lying] in the dust and in blood.'

And that was how it would be. Ibrahim fell in the battle, the first and only sultan of Delhi to die in battle. He had been much vilified in life, but death entirely redeemed his honour. After the battle, Babur went to see Ibrahim lying dead in the battlefield. He 'beheld that powerful sultan prostrate in the dust and weltering in blood, the royal crown fallen from his head, the state canopy also on the ground,' reports Yadgar. Ibrahim's valour in battle elicited the admiration of Babur, and he had the sultan's body shrouded richly, and buried honourably at the very spot where he had fallen.

'Sultan Ibrahim's reign lasted eight years, eight months and thirteen days,' states Ni'matullah. 'He was buried in the western suburb of Panipat and his resting place is now frequented by singers and minstrels. Pilgrims make offerings every Friday night to the departed spirit of the sultan and offer charity to the poor.'

Soon after the battle Babur sent his son Humayun to occupy and secure Agra, the Lodi capital. Babur followed him there presently, but did not immediately enter the city. He pitched his camp in the maidan outside Agra and remained there for a week, presumably waiting for an auspicious time to enter the city.

On 10 May 1526, he ceremoniously entered Agra and took up his residence in the royal palace there, as the emperor of Hindustan. And with that ended the over three centuries long history of the Delhi Sultanate.[1]

---

[1]For the details of Babur's invasion of India, see *The Last Spring*, Chapter 2.

2

The Snake Pit

The Delhi Sultanate had attained its greatest territorial extent under Muhammad Tughluq, when it stretched over virtually the entire Indian subcontinent. But it was fancy rather than earnest purpose that motivated Muhammad in his conquests, and the final consequence of the venture, as in nearly everything else he did, was the opposite of what he desired, for the mammoth expansion of its territory made the empire ungovernable, and eventually, towards the end of his reign, led to the beginning of its disintegration. Though this process was interrupted during the reign of Firuz Tughluq—who sensibly focussed his attention on governing efficiently what remained of the empire, rather than on recovering the lost provinces—the atrophying of the empire accelerated after his death, so that by the end of the Tughluq dynasty, the Sultanate had shrunk in size to a tiny state, covering just the city of Delhi and its suburbs. There was some revival of the fortunes of the Sultanate under the Sayyid and Lodi dynasties, but the fate of the kingdom was finally sealed by the invasion of Babur in 1526.

The history of India during almost the entire period of the Delhi Sultanate was one of incessant wars, rebellions and internecine conflicts. The number of these rebellions and conflicts multiplied several times during the final phase of the Delhi Sultanate, when the subcontinent fragmented into numerous kingdoms, which constantly engaged each other in war.

The story of these warring splinter kingdoms, many of them quite small and transient, is dreary. In most cases what we know of their history is a bare list of their kings, the rebellions they faced, and the battles they fought. And even the veracity of these incidents is in many cases uncertain, as their accounts vary from chronicler to chronicler, depending on their partisan affiliation. No worthwhile story can be told of them. The process of the fragmentation of the Sultanate, and the perpetual clashes between these fragments that went on during this period, are, as historical trends, very significant, but the details of the history of the numerous individual kingdoms are of little significance. The pattern of events is important, but not the details of individual events.

THE MOST NOTABLE of the numerous successor kingdoms of the Delhi Sultanate were Sind, Multan, Rajput principalities, Gujarat, Malwa, Khandesh, Jaunpur, Kashmir, Bengal, Orissa, Telingana, Bahmani, and Vijayanagar. Some of the kings of these states were legendary characters, of varied and rich talents, and they deserve to be noticed. One of these notable kings was Rana Kumbha, the mid-fifteenth century ruler of the Rajput kingdom of Mewar. He was a celebrated playwright, an eminent literary critic who wrote an acclaimed commentary on Jayadeva's *Gita Govinda*, and was a knowledgeable patron of musicians and architects. Unfortunately, he later went insane and was assassinated by his son.

Equally notable was Sultan Mahmud Begarha of Gujarat, though for entirely different reasons. A late contemporary of Rana Kumbha, Begarha's very appearance was bizarre. He was a gigantic man, with a beard that reached down to his waist, and a moustache that was so long that it had to be pulled up over both sides of his face and tied into a coiffure. Also, he had a gargantuan appetite, to match his size. And, most curious of all, he took a swig of poison with his meals, which turned his breath, sweat, spittle, semen, urine and faeces deadly poisonous. Not surprisingly, Begarha's sexual appetite matched his size, and he is said to have kept several thousand women in his harem—he needed so many of them, for every woman he slept with died soon after the coitus, poisoned by his deadly ejaculation.[1]

Among the provinces of the Delhi Sultanate, the one that occupied the most unique position was Bengal, which pulsed to a rhythm somewhat different from that of the other regions of the empire. Bengal had always enjoyed a fair amount of autonomy, because of its ethnic and cultural distinctiveness, and its great distance from Delhi. And it invariably broke free from the Sultanate at the first sign of political debility in Delhi. The region also went through some very peculiar political convulsions during the medieval period. And it has the distinction of being the only medieval Muslim state ever to be ruled by a Hindu. According to Ferishta, the de facto ruler of Bengal in the early fifteenth century was a Hindu zamindar named Ganesa.

Ganesa exercised regal powers for about seven years, but apparently without assuming the royal title. But his son, who became a Muslim, did ascend the

---

[1]More on Begarha in Part VII, Chapter 1

throne, and the dynasty remained in power for nearly a quarter century, but was eventually ousted by a member of the resurgent old dynasty. After this, in the late fifteenth century, Bengal was ruled by Ethiopians for a few years, and then by an Arab.

As in Bengal, the politics of Kashmir too did not quite conform to the Indo-Gangetic Plain pattern. Buddhism had been the dominant religion of Kashmir for many centuries, but it virtually disappeared from there in early medieval times. The state however came under a Buddhist king briefly in the early fourteenth century, when Rinchana, an invader from western Tibet, established his rule there. Rinchana was however a Buddhist only nominally, and was quite savage in his conduct—once, while suppressing a rebellion, he not only impaled the rebels but 'ripped open with sword the wombs of the wives of his enemies' and tore out the foetuses in them. But at the other end of the political spectrum, Kashmir in the fifteenth century had the distinction of having had one of the most liberal and tolerant Muslim rulers of medieval India, Zaynul Abidin, who rebuilt some of the Hindu temples demolished by his predecessor, prohibited cow slaughter, permitted sati, allowed the Hindus who had been forcibly converted to Islam to revert to their ancestral faith, and encouraged Brahmins to occupy high official positions.

OF ALL THE many independent kingdoms that emerged out of the fragmented Delhi Sultanate, the most important were two peninsular kingdoms, Bahmani and Vijayanagar, both founded at around the same time: Vijayanagar in 1336 and Bahmani a decade later, in 1347. The histories of these two kingdoms, like that of most other Indian kingdoms of this age, are marked by periodic internal turmoils, internecine conflicts, and endless wars with their neighbours. But unlike the histories of most other kingdoms of the age, which are bare lists of events, there is a good amount of detailed information about these two states and their rulers, in the accounts of Muslim chroniclers, as well as of foreign travellers who visited the region at this time, so their stories can be told in some detail.

Of these two kingdoms, the Bahmani Sultanate endured as a unified state for only about a century and a half, till 1490, and then gradually broke up into five independent kingdoms. However, titular Bahmani sultans continued to occupy their throne till 1527, so that the Sultanate may be said to have endured nominally for 180 years. Vijayanagar endured longer as a unified state, for 229 years, till 1565, when the armies of a league of Deccani sultans in a joint campaign routed the Vijayanagar army in a decisive battle and reduced the kingdom to the status of a minor state. Eventually, even this truncated kingdom fragmented into a number of independent principalities. However, the last reigning dynasty of Vijayanagar survived till the mid-seventeenth century, ruling over Chandragiri, a small realm in South India, so the history of Vijayanagar may be said to have lasted in all for 300-odd years. In the end nearly all the peninsular kingdoms, of rajas as well as of sultans, were obliterated during the tidal sweep of the Mughal empire into the peninsula in the sixteenth and seventeenth centuries.

The primary activity of the Bahmani and Vijayanagar kings, as well as of the kings of their successor states, was to wage war against each other, and this went on all through their history. These were singularly savage wars, involving the slaughter of very many thousands of people, soldiers as well as civilians. According to Ferishta, during the reign of the mid-fourteenth century Bahmani sultan Muhammad Shah 'nearly 500,000 unbelievers fell by the swords of the warriors of Islam, by which the population of the Carnatic was so reduced that it did not recover for several ages.'

Curiously, these wars were fought not to exterminate the enemy, but to gather plunder and to collect tribute—and, most importantly, to vaingloriously demonstrate the military prowess of kings. It was a game, but a savage game. Some districts of the enemy territory were sometimes annexed by the victor, but there was hardly ever any annexation of the whole enemy kingdom. For instance, the only major territory that changed hands back and forth, again and again, during the numerous wars between Vijayanagar and Bahmani kingdoms was the fertile and mineral rich Raichur Doab between Krishna and Tungabhadra rivers. And, although the warring peninsular kings usually belonged to rival religions, Hinduism and Islam, this divergence was hardly ever a decisive factor in their relationships, though a religious colouration was sometimes given to their wars, to rouse the zeal of the soldiers, and to justify the brutal reprisals that the adversaries inflicted on each other. Indeed, Hindu and Muslim rulers at times allied with each other to wage wars against the states ruled by kings of their own religion.

THE BAHMANI KINGDOM had in all eighteen sultans in its 180-year long history, though its last five sultans were mere figureheads. The kingdom was founded during the political turmoil of the closing years of the reign of Muhammad Tughluq, when several of his provincial chieftains rebelled against him and founded independent kingdoms. One such chieftain was Hasan Gangu, who seized control of Daulatabad and set himself up as an independent ruler there. On his investiture he took the title Ab'ul Muzaffar Ala-ud-din Bahman Shah, so the kingdom he founded came to be known as the Bahmani Sultanate.

There is considerable uncertainty about Hasan's background. According to a fascinating but improbable story told by Ferishta, Hasan was originally a farm labourer, who one day, while ploughing his master's field on the outskirts of Delhi, dug up a copper pot full of gold coins, and he dutifully took it to the landlord, a Brahmin named Gangu. And Gangu, awestruck by Hasan's probity, took him to the sultan, who then rewarded him by appointing him a captain in his army. The Brahmin then predicted, on the basis of the astrological calculations he made, that Hasan would one day become a king. And this destiny Hasan eventually fulfilled.

Other medieval sources tell a less romantic but more vaunting story, and trace Hasan's ancestry to the ancient Persian king Bahman. Ferishta however dismisses this story as a fabrication by the sycophantic courtiers of the sultan. 'I believe his origin was too obscure to be traced,' Ferishta states, and goes on to assert that Hasan took the appellation Bahman as a 'compliment to his former master . . . the Brahmin, a word often pronounced as Bahman. The king himself was by birth an Afghan.'

Hasan ascended the throne in August 1347 and ruled for eleven years. A short while after his accession he shifted his capital from Daulatabad to the southern city of Gulbarga, presumably to be further away from Delhi. Over the next few years he consolidated his position by launching a number of military campaigns, to subdue refractory chieftains, to expand his territory, to exact tribute, and to seize plunder and war materials. The perennial conflict between the Bahmani Sultanate and the Vijayanagar kingdom also began during the reign of Hasan, in the very second year of his reign. This was followed by another clash five years later. The results of these campaigns are given differently by the two kingdoms, each claiming victory over the other. However that may be, by the end of Hasan's reign the Bahmani Sultanate covered a fairly large area in central Deccan, from the Tungabhadra northward up to the Penganga, and from the Telingana Plateau westward up to the Arabian Sea, covering parts of Marathi, Kannada and Telugu linguistic regions. Hasan regarded his military achievements to be grand enough for him to assume the title Second Alexander and stamp it on his coins, probably in imitation of Ala-ud-din Khalji.

HASAN DIED IN 1358, aged 67, after a prolonged illness, and was succeeded by his eldest son Muhammad Shah I. Muhammad's mettle was tested right at the beginning of his reign by the Hindu kingdoms of Warangal and Vijayanagar, each impudently demanding that he should surrender certain territories to it. Muhammad met that insolence with an even greater insolence on his part, by treating the two rajas as his vassals, and accusing them of neglecting to send him, their overlord, the customary presents on his accession. He then demanded that they should therefore send to him, in reparation for their discourtesy, all their elephants loaded with treasures. Warangal's response to this was to send an army to seize the territory it demanded from the sultan. But the raja was defeated in the ensuing battle, and he had to purchase peace by sending to the sultan a large quantity of gold coins and several war elephants. The peace between them did not however last long, and hostilities between the two kingdoms broke out again and again in the following years. The raja was the loser in all those battles, and he had to surrender to the sultan the fortress of Golconda, and even his treasured turquoise throne, which thereafter became the throne of the Bahmani kings.

Bukka, the Vijayanagar king, too had no success against Muhammad. The raja invaded the Raichur Doab soon after Muhammad's accession, hoping to annex that rich region to his kingdom. But on Muhammad's impetuous advance against him, Bukka, 'not withstanding his vast army consisting of 30,000 cavalry, besides infantry,' hastily retreated, reports Ferishta. But the raja left behind a good part of his camp, presumably to entice the enemy soldiers to plunder the camp, and thus distract them from pouncing on him. The Bahmani army then, according to Ferishta, swept into the defenceless camp, and 'put to death, without distinction, men, women, children, free and slave, to the number of 70,000 souls.'

The sultan then crossed the Tungabhadra into Vijayanagar territory. Meanwhile Bukka reassembled his scattered forces and turned to confront Muhammad. The ensuing battle was hard-fought and lasted from dawn till evening, in which the Bahmani army suffered heavy losses. Its wings were routed early on and their commanders killed, but its centre held, and in the end it prevailed over the Vijayanagar army by the effective use of its artillery— manned by European and Middle Eastern gunners—and by the headlong charge of its cavalry. Bukka then retreated into the fortified city of Vijayanagar. Muhammad did not have the means to storm the city, so he turned to ravage the countryside, indulging in unconscionable, indiscriminate slaughter of thousands and thousands of people.

This carnage forced Bukka to sue for peace. During the ensuing peace negotiations, the Vijayanagar envoys expostulated with the sultan about the slaughter of civilians by his army. 'No religion requires the innocent to be punished for the crimes of the guilty, more especially helpless women and children,' they submitted. They then suggested that since Bahmani and Vijayanagar kingdoms were likely to remain neighbours for many generations, it would be desirable that 'a treaty should be made between them not to slaughter helpless and unarmed inhabitants in future battles.' Muhammad, according to Ferishta, was 'struck with the good sense of this proposal, [and he] took an oath that he would not thereafter put to death a single enemy after a victory, and would also bind his successors to observe the same line of conduct. From that time to this, it has been the general custom in the Deccan to spare the lives of prisoners of war, and not to shed the blood of an enemy's unarmed subjects.'

Unfortunately, this humane undertaking was not kept up by Muhammad's successors, or by the Vijayanagar rajas. Pillaging and slaughtering the common people wantonly was the routine rather than the exception in medieval Indian wars, and neither Bahmani nor Vijayanagar would ever altogether cease committing such excesses.

Muhammad himself however maintained peace in the latter years of his reign. His focus during this period was on improving the administration of the Sultanate and on promoting culture. He made several changes in the administrative system of the Sultanate, and gave his provincial governors a great amount of autonomy, but ensured their discipline and subordination by regularly touring through the provinces. He also took care to improve the law and order in the state, and is said to have secured its roads by executing some 20,000 brigands. In the field of culture, Muhammad's patronage turned Gulbarga into a major centre of culture and learning in India. And it was under his patronage that Deccani architecture acquired its distinctive style, as in the great mosque he built in Gulbarga.

Muhammad died in 1375, and was buried beside his father. 'He was,' comments Ferishta, 'respected in his life, and after his death remembered on account of his virtues.' And on his tomb was engraved this solacing aphorism: 'All is vanity!'

MUHAMMAD WAS SUCCEEDED by his son Ala-ud-din Mujahid, a handsome man of awesome physical prowess. But he was ill-fated, for after a brief reign of three years he was assassinated by his cousin Daud, who then ascended the throne. But Daud himself was assassinated within a few weeks by Ala-ud-din's partisans, who then raised Daud's brother, Muhammad, to the throne. The reign of Muhammad II was largely peaceful and lasted nineteen years. He was a rather unusual ruler for that age and place, for he was a learned man—lauded as an Aristotle by his courtiers—and a man of peace and culture, who showed a genuine concern for the welfare of his subjects, such as providing famine relief—though only for Muslims—and by establishing several orphanages and free schools.

Muhammad II was succeeded by his eldest son Ghiyas-ud-din, a seventeen-year-old youth, but he was blinded and overthrown within two months by Tughalchin, the chief of the Turkish slaves in the royal service, who then raised the sultan's younger brother Shams-ud-din to the throne. But the arrangement lasted only five months, as the new sultan in turn was blinded and overthrown by his cousin Firuz Shah, who then ascended the throne.

The quarter-century-long reign of Firuz was the most engaging period in the history of the Bahmani Sultanate. Firuz, like his uncle Muhammad II, was a highly cultured, talented and liberal monarch. He was a linguist and a gifted calligrapher, and a keen and knowledgeable patron of literature, art and music, who delighted in the company of writers and intellectuals. A keen student of astronomy, he had to his credit the building of a major observatory near Daulatabad.

According to medieval chronicler Tabataba, Firuz was 'a good, just, generous king, who supported himself by copying the Koran, and the ladies of whose harem used to support themselves by embroidering garments and selling them.' This is quite probably an idealized account. The reality would not have been quite so edifying. Still, there is no doubt that Firuz was a highly successful monarch, who had substantial accomplishments to his credit in nearly every sphere of government. Ferishta describes him as the greatest of the Bahmani kings.

In administration, Firuz had the wisdom and broadmindedness to appoint a good number of Hindus, particularly Brahmins, to high positions in government, and that no doubt improved the efficiency of his administration. Firuz was equally successful in his military campaigns. For three decades since Muhammad Shah's invasion of Vijayanagar in 1367, there had been no major military conflict between the two Deccani kingdoms, but the wars resumed in earnest during the reign of Firuz. The aggressor this time was king Harihara II of Vijayanagar, who in 1398 invaded the Raichur Doab with a mammoth army of about 30,000 cavalry and 900,000 infantry. Advancing north through the Doab, he deployed his forces along the southern bank of the Krishna, his army covering a vast area measuring roughly 27-by-27 kilometres, according to medieval Muslim chroniclers. The size of the Vijayanagar army, and the land area it covered, are no doubt vastly exaggerated by these writers, to glorify the victory of their hero over such immense odds. In contrast to the vast Vijayanagar horde, the Bahmani army deployed against it is said to have been a cavalry force of just 12,000.

WHATEVER THE ACTUAL strength of the rival forces, Firuz would have had only a much smaller army than that of Harihara. In the face of the massive deployment of the Vijayanagar army along the Krishna riverbank it would have been suicidal for the Sultanate army to cross the river and engage the enemy. Some means therefore had to be found to divert the attention of the Vijayanagar forces, to enable the Sultanate army to cross the river safely. In that predicament one of Firuz's officers suggested a clever stratagem to him. This officer, Siraj-ud-din, was an expert juggler, and was also proficient in music and dance, and he offered to infiltrate into the Vijayanagar camp with a small troupe of followers in the guise of wandering minstrels, and cause some turmoil there, taking advantage of which Firuz could then cross the river and surprise the enemy, it was suggested.

The plan worked out perfectly. Siraj-ud-din and a band of two dozen companions entered the periphery of the Vijayanagar camp one day, and gradually, over several days, gained such a high esteem as entertainers that they were summoned to perform before Harihara's son in the army camp. That the entertainers were Muslims roused no suspicion, for the Vijayanagar army itself had a good many Muslim soldiers and officers in it. On receiving the prince's invitation, Siraj-ud-din sent a secret message to Firuz informing him of the developments and requesting him to be ready to cross the river and attack the Vijayanagar army during the chaos he would cause in their camp.

As usual, Siraj-ud-din's performance was given at night, and it involved, among several other items, a display of startling skills with sword and dagger. As the prince and his cohorts relaxed watching the show, Siraj-ud-din and his comrades suddenly pounced on them and cut them down, then killed the royal bodyguards, and, in the ensuing confusion, escaped from the camp. Soon, as the news of the incident spread, and along with it several fantastic rumours, the Vijayanagar camp was thrown into utter turmoil. Taking advantage of this, the Bahmani army crossed the Krishna, and at dawn stormed into the Vijayanagar camp. Harihara, grieving over the death of his son, and faced with the disorder in his camp, was in no position to stand and fight, so he quickly withdrew to Vijayanagar, his capital, carrying his son's body with him. Firuz chased him in hot pursuit, plundering the countryside all along the way, and this forced Harihara to purchase peace from Firuz by paying him a very substantial indemnity.

After this, Firuz was for a while engaged in campaigns in the north of his kingdom, to consolidate his power. Then he once again turned against Vijayanagar. There is an engaging romantic legend associated with this campaign. The story centres on Parthal, the stunningly beautiful daughter of a poor goldsmith in Mudgal, a town in the Raichur Doab. On hearing about her great beauty, Devaraya I, who had succeeded Harihara to the throne of Vijayanagar, demanded her for his harem. But the girl declined the proposal. So Devaraya, enraged, swept into the Doab with a small contingent of 5000 horse, and sent a band of his soldiers to abduct the girl. But by the time the soldiers reached Mudgal, the girl and her parents had fled north across the Krishna, so the contingent vented its frustration by pillaging the region before returning to Vijayanagar. Parthal was eventually married to Firuz's son, Hasan Khan.

FIRUZ USED DEVARAYA'S intrusion into the Raichur Doab as an excuse to mount a fresh invasion into Vijayanagar. In the ensuing battle, fought beside the city of Vijayanagar, Firuz was defeated by Devaraya, and he himself was wounded. He then fell back to his fortified camp some distance away from the city, where he was able to defend himself successfully against Devaraya's repeated attacks. He in turn then sent his soldiers to ravage and despoil the countryside all around. Devaraya then, to protect his people, sent envoys to Firuz to arrange peace, and it was concluded on the terms dictated by Firuz, under which Devaraya agreed to pay a huge sum as indemnity to the sultan, and also to give him a daughter in marriage with suitable endowments.

Ferishta offers a detailed account of the marriage, which throws interesting sidelights on the social practices of the age. According to Ferishta, 'though the rajas of Carnatic had never yet married their daughters except to persons of their own caste, and giving them to strangers was highly disgraceful, yet Devaraya, out of necessity, complied [with the demand of Firuz], and preparations for celebrating the nuptials were made by both parties . . . [By then] both sides of the road between [Vijayanagar] city and the sultan's camp . . . were lined with shops and booths, in which jugglers, buffoons, dancers, and mimics of Carnatic displayed their feats and skill to amuse passengers.'

The princess was then ceremoniously taken to the sultan's camp, where presumably a Muslim marriage ceremony was performed. A few days after the marriage, the sultan along with his bride set out for Vijayanagar, to visit the raja. On the way the couple were formally received by the raja, and he escorted them to the city with great pomp. 'From the gate of the city to the palace, a distance of six miles, the road was spread with cloth of gold, velvet, satin, and other rich stuffs. The two kings rode on horseback together, between ranks of beautiful boys and girls, who waved plates of gold filled with incense and silver flowers . . . Upon their arrival at the palace gate, the sultan and the raja dismounted from their horses and moved into a splendid palanquin, set with valuable jewels, and in it they were carried together to the apartments prepared for the reception of the bride and bridegroom . . . The sultan, after being treated with royal magnificence for three days, took his leave of the raja, who pressed upon him richer presents than given previously, and accompanied him for four miles on his way, and then returned to the city.' Firuz had expected the raja to accompany him all the way to his camp, and was upset that he did not do this, so the enmity between the two persisted.

FIRUZ WAS IN many ways an admirable ruler, sagacious, spirited and enterprising. But he was also addicted to carnal indulgences. He drank heavily, perhaps for relief from his many onerous duties, and he is said to have maintained a harem of 800 women of different nationalities. This self-indulgent lifestyle eventually ruined his health and he became, as Wolseley Haig puts it, 'a jaded and feeble voluptuary.' In the end, being no longer able to function effectively as a ruler, he was forced to abdicate the throne in favour of his brother Ahmad. This was in September 1422. Firuz died the following month—or was probably strangled or poisoned, according to some sources.

Ahmad was in every respect quite unlike his suave brother, and was rather rustic in his outlook and lifestyle. But he was considered a saint—he was in fact called *vali* (saint) by the common people—and was given to ostentatious displays of his saintly powers. Thus, when the kingdom was once ravaged by a severe drought, he devoutly climbed to the top of a hill near his capital, and there, before the awed eyes of the assembled multitudes, prayed for rain—and indeed rain clouds presently appeared scudding over the horizon, and there was a heavy downpour.

Saint or not, Ahmad was as aggressive and brutal towards his neighbours as any other Bahmani sultan, and he waged several successful wars against them—against Warangal, Malwa, Gujarat, and, as usual, against Vijayanagar, which was the perennial adversary of Bahmani sultans. Ahmad's very first military campaign, right after his accession, was against Vijayanagar. For this, he led an army of 40,000 cavalry, and encamped on the northern bank of the Tungabhadra at his chosen ford, preparing to invade Vijayanagar. Devaraya II, the king of Vijayanagar, countered that move by assembling, on the southern bank of the river, an immense force of about a million soldiers, consisting of cavalry, infantry and gunners. That blocking deployment of the Vijayanagar army made it far too risky for the sultan to attempt to cross the river there. He therefore sent a contingent of his army at night some distance upstream, to cross the river secretly and suddenly fall on the rear of the Vijayanagar army. This surprise attack threw the Vijayanagar army into disarray, taking advantage of which the main body of the Bahmani army crossed the river, engaged the enemy in battle, and routed it.

What followed was unprecedented even in the history of the savage wars between these two kingdoms. 'Ahmad Shah . . . overran the open country, and wherever he went, he put to death men, women and children, without mercy,' writes Ferishta. 'Wherever the number of the slain amounted to 20,000, he halted for three days, and made a festival in celebration of the bloody event.' It was as if Ahmad meant to exterminate a whole people. He also destroyed the Hindu temples he came across along the way, and deliberately slaughtered very many cows, to outrage and mortify Hindus. Leaving thus a trail of wanton destruction and senseless carnage, Ahmad advanced on Vijayanagar city. There the raja, Devaraya II, appalled by the woes of his subjects, purchased peace by paying a substantial tribute to the sultan. And Ahmad, to heap on the raja an abject humiliation on top of his shame of military rout, insisted that he should be escorted part of the way into the Sultanate by the raja's son. The raja had no alternative but to comply. Fortunately for Vijayanagar, this was the only war that Ahmad waged against it.

There was substantial expansion in the territory of the Bahmani Sultanate during Ahmad's reign, particularly towards the east, through his annexation of Warangal. This eastward expansion prompted the sultan to shift his capital north-eastwards, from Gulbarga to Bidar. The charm of Bidar's environment and its relatively salubrious climate also attracted the sultan.

The last years of Ahmad were spent whirling around, engaged in several futile wars, mainly against Gujarat and Malwa, in none of which he was particularly successful, and in some cases he had to accept humiliating terms for peace. At last, in April 1436, when the sultan was around 64 years old, death relieved him of his miseries and frustrations. His son and successor, Ala-ud-din Ahmad, built, over the sultan's grave in the outskirts of Bidar, a magnificent tomb richly adorned with elegant calligraphic inscriptions.

THE ACCESSION OF Ala-ud-din to the throne was contested by his brother Muhammad, who demanded that he should be given an equal share in the honours and privileges of the sultan, or, alternately, that the kingdom should be divided between them. Ala-ud-din could not possibly concede those extravagant demands, so the dispute had to be settled in the battlefield. In the ensuing battle the sultan defeated his brother, but generously pardoned him, restored him to favour, and assigned to him the governorship of the critically important Raichur Doab. The brothers lived amicably thereafter.

The war between Bahmani and Vijayanagar resumed during the reign of Ala-ud-din with the usual savagery. Typical of the brutality of these conflicts was the warning that, according to Ferishta, Ala-ud-din once issued to Devaraya II, the king of Vijayanagar, that if the raja executed the two Muslim officers whom he had captured in a battle, he (the raja) would have to pay a heavy price for it, 'as it was a rule of the princes of his family to slay a 100,000 Hindus in revenge for the death of a single Muslim.'

Ala-ud-din's character was a curious mixture benevolence and tyranny, and he was cavalier and mercurial in his policies and actions. Equally, he was indifferent in observing the routine formalities expected of a sultan; he even relegated the public audience—which royal custom required him to hold every day—to just once in four or five months. And he spent a good amount of his time in the harem, where he had collected some thousand women.

Ala-ud-din preened himself as a just ruler, and he took the title *Al-adil*: The Just. Yet he allowed himself to be manipulated, perhaps while in an inebriated state, by a group of Deccani nobles to cause the murder of several foreign nobles, of whose growing prominence the Deccani nobles were envious. Characteristically the sultan then swung around in contrition and summarily executed the leaders of the Deccani party.

There were various other similar oddities in the reign of Ala-ud-din. For instance, he had to his credit the building of a large hospital in his capital where free treatment and medicines, even free food, were provided to poor patients.

At the same time he was, according to Ferishta, very harsh in his treatment of vagrants, whom he punished 'by employing them in removing filth from the streets, in dragging heavy stones, and in performing all manner of laborious work, in order that they might reform, and either earn their livelihood by industry, or quit the country altogether.' Similarly, though Ala-ud-din presented to the public a sternly orthodox Muslim persona, his private life did not quite match that image. He drank wine himself, but severely punished others for drinking. 'If any person, after admonition and moderate correction, was convicted of drinking wine, it was decreed that molten lead should be poured down his throat, whatever might be the rank of the offender,' records Ferishta.

For some mysterious reason Ala-ud-din was always reluctant to hold durbar, and he finally had an excuse for dispensing with it altogether. This was related to his execution of a number of foreigners in his service. Some of these officers were Sayyids, the presumed descendants of prophet Muhammad, and their execution greatly scandalised many. And one day an Arab trader, hearing that the sultan had taken the title *Al-adil*, shouted at him in the open court: 'No, by god! Thou art not just, generous, clement, or compassionate, O tyrant and liar! Thou hast slain the pure seed of the prophet!' The sultan is said to have wept in humiliation at the charge, and retired to his private chambers, never again to emerge from there.

ALA-UD-DIN DIED IN 1458, and was succeeded by his eldest son Humayun, who turned out to be a vicious, sadistic monster. There were several rebellions during his brief reign of three years, but they were all suppressed by him with revolting brutality. The first of these rebellions was by Hasan Khan, one of Humayun's brothers, who escaped from the prison where he was confined, and attempted to take over Bidar, the capital, when Humayun was away on a campaign. The kotwal (chief police officer of the city) repulsed the attack, but Hasan managed to escape. Meanwhile Humayun stormed back into the capital, where he vented his wrath on the kotwal, for allowing Hasan to escape. The officer was locked up in an iron cage in public view, and there bits of his flesh were cut off every day and offered to him to eat as the only food he could have during the few days he lived under the torture.

Meanwhile Hasan was captured and brought to Bidar, where he, along with his family members, dependants and followers were put to death in various barbarous ways. 'Humayun Shah, now abandoning himself to the full indulgence of his cruel propensities, and mad with rage, directed stakes to be set up on both sides of the king's *chowk* (square), and caused vicious elephants and wild beasts to be placed in different parts of the square,' writes Ferishta. 'In other places cauldrons of scalding oil and boiling water were also prepared as instruments of torture. The king, ascending a balcony in order to glut his eyes on the spectacle, first cast his brother, Hasan Khan, before a ferocious tiger, which soon tore the wretched prince to pieces and devoured him on the spot ... [Several of Hasan's] associates were then beheaded in the king's presence, and the women of their families, innocent and helpless, were dragged from their houses and were violated and ill-treated in the palace square by ruffians, in a manner too indecent to relate ... About seven thousand persons, including women and servants, none of whom had even the most remote involvement in this rebellion, besides menials, such as cooks, scullions, and others, were put to death, some being stabbed with dagger, others hewn in pieces with hatchets, and the rest flayed by [pouring on them] scalding oil or boiling water.'

'From this moment Humayun threw off all restraint, and seized at will the children of his subjects, tearing them from their parents to gratify his passions,' continues Ferishta. 'He would frequently stop nuptial processions in the street and seize the bride, and then send her to the groom's house after enjoying her. He was in the habit of putting the females of his own house to death for the most trivial offences. When any of the nobles were obliged to attend him, so great was their dread that they took leave of their families, as if preparing for death.' Fittingly, he himself was stabbed to death by one of his African maidservants when he was in a drunken stupor.

The only commendable act of Humayun was his appointment of Mahmud Gawan as his chief minister. Gawan, an Iranian migrant of exceptional ability and prudence, had arrived in Deccan during Ala-ud-din's reign, and he would serve the Sultanate most creditably in top administrative and military positions for well over three decades, through the reigns of four sultans, exerting a mature, stabilising influence on the turbulent politics of the Bahmani kingdom.

HUMAYUN WAS SUCCEEDED by his son Nizam Shah, a boy just eight years old. The accession of the boy king was seen by some of Bahmani's neighbours—Orissa, Warangal and Malwa—as an opportunity for making inroads into its territory, but they were all easily repulsed by the Bahmani army. Nizam had the advantage of being under the tutelage of his sagacious and resourceful mother, who, along with Mahmud Gawan as the chief minister of the state, efficiently managed the affairs of the state at this time.

Nizam unexpectedly died after a reign of just two years—he died on the very day of his marriage. He was then succeeded by his nine-year-old younger brother, Muhammad Shah III, who ruled the kingdom for nearly two decades. During almost his entire reign Muhammad had the benefit of having Gawan as his chief minister, who introduced several essential administrative reforms in the state, and also considerably expanded its territory through effective military action against its neighbours. Unfortunately, the very success of Gawan damned him in the eyes of his envious rivals in the government, and they instigated the sultan to execute him by levelling a false charge of treason against him.

The tragedy was the culmination of the long-festering strife between Deccani and Paradesi (foreign) officers of the kingdom, involving professional rivalry compounded by racial and sectarian hostility. This rivalry had a long history going back to the time well before the arrival of Gawan in the kingdom, and it would persist long after his death. Bahmani sultans generally tended to favour foreigners—Turks, Arabs, Mughals, and Persians—for appointment in top administrative and military positions, because they were generally more cultured and efficient than Deccanis, who were rather crude, and were often unlettered. Typically, Ala-ud-din Ahmad, the mid-fifteenth century sultan of the kingdom, had a large number of foreigners in his service, and they were assigned the place of honour in the court, on the right side of the throne, while the native officers were kept on the left side. The antagonism between the two groups was also fuelled by their sectarian differences—while most of the foreigners were Shias, Deccanis were predominantly Sunnis. The Deccani faction also had the support of Abyssinians in the royal service.

The rivalry between the two groups often led to riots. Once, during the reign of Nizam Shah, 'the Deccani troops, the Abyssinians, and the mob, entered the fort and put to death every foreigner they found within, amounting to nearly 300, among whom were several persons of high rank and eminent character,' reports Ferishta. Later, during the reign of Mahmud, Muhammad III's successor, there was a 20 day long riot in Bidar between Deccanis and Paradesis. And on a subsequent occasion, the foreigner group set about, with the Sultan's connivance, slaughtering the Deccanis for three whole days.

Gawan was a victim of this long-festering tussle for power between Paradesis and Deccanis, although he personally remained fair and neutral in this conflict, and occupied himself solely with the task of running the government efficiently. But his very success rankled Deccanis, who saw him as an obstacle to their rise to the top echelons of the government. Moreover, the administrative reforms that Gawan introduced, though they improved the efficiency of the government, curtailed the powers of the provincial chiefs, who were mostly Deccanis. They then forged a letter to implicate Gawan in a conspiracy against the sultan, and showed it to him. And the sultan—who himself was probably squirming under Gawan's dominance—immediately, without any proper enquiry, summoned Gawan to him, and peremptorily asked him what the proper punishment for a traitor was. To this Gawan replied: 'Death by the sword.' The sultan then flung the forged letter at Gawan. On reading it, Gawan said: 'This is manifest forgery. The seal is mine, but not the writing.' But the sultan, angrily disregarding this protest, peremptorily ordered him to be executed right away. Gawan then knelt down and recited a short prayer, and, as the sword fell, he exclaimed: 'Praise be to god for the blessing of martyrdom!''

This was in April 1481. Gawan was then 78 years old, and probably did not have very many more years to live, so he could die without regrets. But his execution portended ill for the Sultanate, for several of the foreign nobles, who were the strongest pillars of the state, then left for their provinces, and so did several of the conscientious Deccani nobles, and this presaged the disintegration of the Sultanate. Muhammad himself presently realised the dreadfulness of what he had done, and, overcome with grief and remorse, soon drank himself to death, screaming in his dying moment that Gawan was rending his heart.

MUHAMMAD DIED IN March 1482, aged just 28. After him, five of his descendants followed him on the throne of Bidar, but they were kings only in name, being mere puppets in the hands of domineering nobles. Besides, the Sultanate during this period gradually broke up into four independent kingdoms: Bijapur, Ahmadnagar, Berar and Golconda. The rulers of these kingdoms continued to profess allegiance to the Sultan in Bidar, but that was only a formality, and involved no real subservience. And though the sultan continued to sit on the throne, he had virtually no power at all even in Bidar, the royal capital. The last of these titular sultans was Kalimullah, and when he died in 1528, Bidar lost even its nominal overlordship, and it became just another kingdom, like the other four kingdoms into which the Bahmani state had split.

This splintering of the Sultanate multiplied by several times the points of friction and conflict in the peninsula, and the scene became quite chaotic, as endless wars now raged between these splinter kingdoms, as well as between them and the other peninsular kingdoms, all confusedly slithering over each other in ever-shifting alliances and hostilities, like a bunch of rat-snakes in a snake-pit. Religion played hardly any role in this—Muslim kingdoms often allied with Vijayanagar against fellow Muslim kingdoms; and sometimes Vijayanagar factions sought the help of Muslim kingdoms in their internal conflicts.

There was however one decisive battle in this seemingly never-ending melee, when four of the successor states of the fragmented Bahmani Sultanate—Bijapur, Ahmadnagar, Golconda and Berar—united to give a virtual deathblow to Vijayanagar in a battle fought at Talikota in January 1565.[1] But after the Talikota battle, the Muslim states once again turned snarling on each other. And so it went on for several more decades, till the seventeenth century, when

---

[1]For details of the battle, see the next chapter

the Mughals, who had been pushing into the peninsula for some years, finally obliterated most of the kingdoms in the region.

Such is the story of the Bahmani Sultanate. It is not an edifying tale. However, the Deccan sultanates did make some noteworthy contributions in the field of culture, by blending Indian and Persian streams in art and architecture, and by giving a strong local flavour to their rule. For instance, Ali Adil Shah, the late-sixteenth-century sultan of Bijapur, integrated his rule with the life of the local people by patronising Telugu culture, and by giving land grants to Brahmins and Hindu temples, and by not enforcing the collection of jizya. He was also an ardent patron of learning, who maintained a large library of books on various subjects, and was so avid about books that he carried several of them with him in boxes even when he travelled.

In administration the Deccan sultanates followed the usual pattern of Muslim states, the only notable developments being the reforms introduced by Gawan. Even these were not radical reforms, but meant only to tighten the prevailing system, so as to curb the power of provincial governors who often functioned as virtual potentates. Gawan divided the existing four provinces of the Bahmani Sultanate into eight provinces so as to reduce the area under the rule of each governor, and to make the administration of the provinces more manageable. He also placed some districts in the provinces directly under central administration, which collected for itself the revenue from them. Further, Gawan sought to curtail the military power of the governors by allowing them to occupy only one fort in their territory, the other forts being kept under the direct control of the sultan. And the royal officers who were given land assignments as pay were made accountable to the sultan for their income and expenditure.

AN EVENT OF critical historical importance of this age was the arrival of European naval fleets in the Indian seas. A Portuguese fleet under the command of Vasco-da-Gama arrived at the Kerala port city of Calicut (Kozhikode) in 1498, nearly three decades before the invasion of India by Mughals under Babur. Then gradually, over the next few decades, the Portuguese entrenched themselves in a few enclaves on the coast of peninsular India. Their main interest was in overseas trade, and this brought them into conflict with Arabs, who had till then dominated the Arabian Sea trade. In a series of naval campaigns in the early sixteenth century, the Portuguese broke the Arab sea power, and that enabled them to virtually monopolise the sea trade around India.

This development made it imperative for the peninsular kingdoms to maintain good relationship with the Portuguese, to ensure that the critically important overseas supply of horses from the Middle East and Central Asia for their armies was not disrupted. And this in turn enabled the Portuguese to play a role, though only a minor role, in local political affairs. They also did some missionary work at this time, converting a number of local Hindu families to Christianity, and even inducing some families of the ancient Syrian Christian community of Kerala to shift their affiliation from the Syrian Orthodox Church to the Roman Catholic Church, which the Portuguese claimed was the only true Christian church.

None of this particularly bothered Indian kings. But when the Portuguese intruded into the Vijayanagar kingdom and took to temple looting, it became imperative for Ramaraya, the king of Vijayanagar, to chastise them. He then launched a dual attack on their settlements, in Goa (on the west coast) and in San Thome (on the east coast), plundering the residents there and exacting punitive tribute. That apparently taught the Portuguese a lesson, for they desisted from giving any more trouble to the raja. The Portuguese in any case had no future in India. Though they dominated the Indian seas for about a century, they made no notable territorial gains in the subcontinent, and in the late sixteenth century, as the Portuguese power declined in Europe, so did their politico-economic role everywhere in the world, including India.

3

The City of Victory

The entire medieval history of India, stretching over a period of about thousand years, from the eighth to the eighteenth century, was dominated by Muslim invaders and rulers. During this period there were only two Hindu kingdoms of subcontinental prominence, that of Vijayanagar and of Marathas. No one would have foreseen this destiny for either of these kingdoms at the beginning of their history, for they were both then obscure mountain kingdoms. This was particularly so in the case of Vijayanagar, which within just a few decades of its founding rose to become one of the two dominant kingdoms of peninsular India, rivalling the Bahmani Sultanate, the other dominant peninsular kingdom.

The early history of Vijayanagar is obscure, shrouded in diverse legends. The kingdom apparently evolved out of Kampili, a chiefdom in the rocky highlands on the northern bank of Tungabhadra. Two related developments facilitated its ascendancy—the subjugation of the long established Hindu kingdoms of South India by Muhammad Tughluq in the first half of his reign, followed soon after, in the second half of his reign, by the collapse of his power in South India. It was out of the political debris left by these developments that Vijayanagar rose to prominence.

According to a plausible and widely held tradition, Vijayanagar was founded by two adventurous brothers, Harihara and Bukka, sons of Sangama, the chieftain of Kampili. But the founding of a Hindu kingdom was not the destiny that their early political career had portended, for it was as minions of the Delhi Sultanate, and not as champions of Hindu political revival, that they first appeared in history. The story is that the brothers were captured by Muhammad Tughluq during his peninsular campaign, and were taken to

Delhi, where they were converted to Islam, and then sent back to Kampili to administer it as imperial officers. But about a decade later, when the Delhi Sultanate's power in the peninsula crumbled, the brothers lost their power base. However, they then rehabilitated themselves by opportunistically reverting to Hinduism and founding a Hindu principality on the southern bank of Tungabhadra. In this venture they were crucially helped by the blessing and support of Vidyaranya, a revered Hindu sage of the region. Vidyaranya, it is said, advised Harihara, the older brother, to adopt Virupaksha, a Shaivite deity, as his patron god, and rule the kingdom as a surrogate of the god, so as to overcome the persisting public misgivings about the legitimacy of he taking on the role of a Hindu raja, because of his former conversion to Islam.

Harihara's Shaivite affiliation of was a factor in he choosing a site on the southern bank of Tungabhadra for his capital, for it was close to the temple of Virupaksha. Fortuitously—though Harihara would not have known anything about it—the region where the capital was founded had ancient historical associations going back to the period of the third century BCE Mauryan emperor Asoka, whose rock inscriptions have been found along Tungabhadra nearly fifty kilometres from the site chosen by the raja for his capital. The capital was named Vijayanagar, City of Victory, and the kingdom itself came to be known by that name. The kingdom and the city would indeed live up to the portent of that name.

Strategically the site was an excellent choice for the capital of the new kingdom, for the river border provided it a barrier against any military menace that might emanate from the north, the main direction from which it could expect invasions. Further, the site was bordered by three rocky hills, the slopes of which were covered with granite boulders, and that provided another impenetrable defence to Vijayanagar. Over a period of about a decade, Harihara linked together the three hills by building between them high and broad cyclopean walls bordered with deep ditches, so the city became virtually impregnable on all sides. In fact, only once in its long history was Vijayanagar city ever stormed.

Harihara was crowned king in Vijayanagar in April 1336. Under him and his successors the kingdom grew rapidly in territory and power, and at its height covered virtually the entire southern half of peninsular India, from river Krishna down to the tip of India, covering three distinct linguistic regions—of Telugu, Kannada and Tamil—so the kingdom is often described as an empire. The dynasty that Harihara founded was named Sangama dynasty, in memory of the raja's father, and it ruled Vijayanagar for a century and a half, till around 1486. This dynasty was succeeded by three other dynasties—Saluva, Tuluva and Aravidu—and the kingdom endured in all for over three centuries, till the mid-seventeenth century. But it became considerably attenuated after its calamitous defeat at the hands of the Deccan Sultanates in the battle of Talikota in 1565. In its final phase even this small kingdom fragmented into a number of principalities, all of which were obliterated during the expansion of the Mughals and the Marathas into South India in the late seventeenth century.

THE KINGS OF Vijayanagar were Telugus, but the expansion of their kingdom was mainly into the Kannada and Tamil regions to its south, for it was beyond their power to expand northward to any significant extent, as the territory there was mostly under the rule of powerful Muslim kingdoms, initially under the Delhi Sultanate, and subsequently under the Bahmani Sultanate and its successor kingdoms. Its southward expansion too at first seemed impossible, for right next to it on the south was the large and long-established Kannada kingdom of Hoysalas, which was just then reemerging as an independent kingdom after having been subject to the Delhi Sultanate for a couple of decades. Hoysalas paid no attention to the founding of Vijayanagar, as their king Ballala III was then preoccupied with a military campaign in the Tamil country, to expand his kingdom southward. Moreover, Vijayanagar was at this time a far too insignificant a principality for Ballala to bother about. Even when Harihara began to flex his military muscle and make incursions into the northern districts of the Hoysala kingdom, Ballala ignored him as a peripheral nuisance, and not a threat to his kingdom.

But presently the scene changed altogether. Ballala's southern campaign ended in disaster, as he was defeated and killed by the sultan of Madurai. And this soon led to the collapse of the Hoysala kingdom. But what was misfortune for Hoysalas was good fortune for Harihara. He now sent his army to invade the Hoysala lands and, overcoming the often unexpectedly stiff resistance of the feudal chieftains there, eventually, in 1346, in a campaign lasting some three years, annexed the whole kingdom.

Vijayanagar thus became the leading Hindu kingdom of the peninsula, indeed, of the whole of India. This achievement was celebrated by Harihara and his brothers by holding a grand victory festival, *vijayotsava*, in 1346. But presently, in the very year after Harihara's victory celebration, there arose, immediately to the north of Vijayanagar, a Muslim kingdom, the Bahmani Sultanate, with which, and with its successor sultanates, Vijayanagar would be embroiled in a two centuries long see-saw military conflict, which would finally end in the virtual destruction of the Vijayanagar kingdom.

Harihara died around 1356, after a reign of twenty years. He had no children, and so was succeeded by his brother Bukka I. The Vijayanagar kingdom had been built by the joint effort of Harihara and his four brothers, and its provinces were held by the raja's brothers as virtually independent rulers, as their share of the kingdom, and which their children in turn inherited and divided among themselves as their patrimony. Bukka viewed this as a pernicious arrangement which would eventually lead to the fragmentation and collapse of the kingdom. He therefore appointed his own sons as provincial governors whenever the opportunity arose, so that the kingdom could be more effectively brought under royal control.

There was considerable expansion of the territory of Vijayanagar under Bukka. He extended it southward by invading and annexing the Sultanate of Madurai, so the territory of Vijayanagar extended as far south as Rameswaram; he also extended the kingdom eastward by annexing portions of the Reddy kingdom of Kondavidu. He was not however successful in his clash with Muhammad Shah, the Bahmani sultan. According to Ferishta—whose account might be biased in favour of the sultan—Bukka was routed by the sultan and had to agree to peace on the sultan's terms. However that be, the vast expansion of the territory of Vijayanagar under Bukka, and the diversity of the ethnic groups in it, turned the kingdom almost into an empire.

An equally important aspect of Bukka's reign was that he was a liberal and progressive monarch. Though he was a staunch Hindu, who proudly bore the title Vedamarga-Pratishthapaka (Establisher of the Path of the Vedas), and sought to revitalise Hinduism by commissioning fresh commentaries to be written on ancient Hindu texts, it was not blind faith but open, earnest enquiry that marked his religious outlook. Most commendably, he considered it his duty as king to extend equal protection and patronage to the people of all religions and sects in his kingdom, such as Jains and Buddhists, and even to the followers of non-Indian religions like Jews, Christians and Muslims. Bukka also had broad cultural interests and was a keen patron of poets, such as Nachanna Soma, the renowned Telugu poet of the age.

BUKKA DIED IN 1377, and was succeeded by his son Harihara II, who assumed the grand title, Rajadhiraja, King of Kings, which was not entirely unjustified, considering the vastness of the kingdom he ruled over. But the title was more than a mere status posture; it was also an expression of the raja's aggressive military policy. He launched a number of military campaigns against his neighbouring kingdoms, in most of which he was victorious; his army is said to have invaded even Sri Lanka and exacted tribute from its king. And he, like nearly every king of Vijayanagar, battled repeatedly with the Bahmani Sultans. Under him the territory of Vijayanagar expanded eastward into Kondavidu and westward into Konkan, and this enabled him to dominate the immensely profitable overseas trade through the eastern and western peninsular ports, the revenue from which significantly added to the resources of his kingdom.

Harihara II reigned for 28 years, and died in 1404. His death was followed by a two-year-long succession struggle between his three sons, in which his youngest son, Devaraya I, emerged victorious. The sixteen years of Devaraya's reign were marked by continuous wars—with the Bahmani Sultanate, with the Velamas of Rachakonda and the Reddys of Kondavidu. He is also known to have invaded Kerala and subjugated several chieftains there. Because of these victories over tough adversaries, or because he was addicted to wildlife hunting, Devaraya bore the sobriquet Gajabetekara: Hunter of Elephants.

But there was much more to Devaraya's reign than his military campaigns. He was, like his grandfather Bukka, an ardent patron of scholars, writers and artists, whom he often honoured by literally showering them with gold coins and gems. He himself was reputed to have been a distinguished scholar, and under him Vijayanagar became the main centre of Hindu culture in peninsular India. Devaraya also undertook several major public works, such as the construction of a massive dam across Tungabhadra, and a 24-kilometre-long aqueduct from the river to his capital, to provide water for the city. He also built several waterworks to irrigate farmlands.

There is much confusion about the immediate successors of Devaraya, but it seems likely that he was succeeded by his son Ramachandra, whose reign lasted only for about six months. He was succeeded by his brother Vijaya. But Vijaya had no interest at all in governance, and he left it to his son Devaraya to run the government, and this prince eventually succeeded him to the throne. Devaraya II 'was of an olive colour, of a spare body, and rather tall,' states Abdur Razzak, the Persian envoy in peninsular India, who saw him in 1443. 'He was exceedingly young, for there was only a slight down upon his cheeks, and none upon his chin. His whole appearance was very prepossessing.' Devaraya II, like several of his predecessors, was a keen patron of literature, and his court was adorned by the celebrated Telugu poet Srinatha.

The main occupation of Devaraya II, as that of most other Vijayanagar kings, was to wage wars against his neighbours, particularly against the Bahmani Sultanate. But he had no success against the Sultanate—in fact, according to Ferishta, the raja, defeated by Sultan Ahmad Shah, had to agree not to molest the sultan's territories thereafter, and to pay him an annual tribute.

The raja then, according to Ferishta, 'called a general council of his nobles and principal Brahmins' to inquire why Vijayanagar invariably lost its wars with Bahmani, and was reduced to paying tribute to it, even though its territories, population and revenue far exceeded those of the Sultanate, 'and in like manner its army was far more numerous.' After due deliberation, the council concluded that the victory of Bahmani was due to the superiority of its cavalry and archers. Devaraya then gave orders to recruit a large number of Muslims into his army, and he 'allotted to them jagirs, erected a mosque for their use in the city of Vijayanagar, and commanded that no one should molest them in the exercise of their religion. He also ordered a copy of the

Koran to be placed before his throne, on an ornate desk, so that Muslims might perform the ceremony of obeisance before him, without violating their religious regulations. He also made all Hindu soldiers learn the discipline of the bow . . . [from Muslim soldiers, so that he at length came to have in his army] 2000 Muslims and 60,000 Hindus well skilled in archery, besides 80,000 cavalry and 200,000 infantry, armed in the usual manner with pikes and lances.' These changes considerably enhanced the military might of Vijayanagar and enabled it to become, during the reigns of Krishnadeva and Ramaraya, the dominant power of peninsular India.

Devaraya died in May 1446. 'In the evil year Kshaya, in the wretched second [month] Vaisakha, on a miserable Tuesday, in . . . [the dark fortnight], on the fourteenth day, the unequalled store of valour, Devaraya, alas, met with death,' states an inscription at Sravana Belgola.

THE DEATH OF Devaraya was followed, as on the death of several other Vijayanagar kings, by a period of chaos and succession struggles. His four successors were all effete and utterly incompetent to meet the challenges faced by the kingdom. They would be the last rulers of the Sangama dynasty, and during their rule the kingdom suffered a substantial loss of territory—it lost large tracts of its eastern districts to the king of Orissa, and on the west coast it lost Goa and its adjoining areas to the Bahmani sultan. The loss of Goa was a major blow to Vijayanagar, for it was heavily dependent on Goa for the import of horses from the Middle East, which its army critically needed.

The last two kings of the Sangama dynasty were depraved, wicked scamps. According to Fernao Nuniz, a Portuguese trader who spent some three years in Vijayanagar in the mid-sixteenth century, Virupaksha, the penultimate king of the dynasty, 'cared for nothing but women and to fuddle himself with drink.' And his life ended bizarrely, murdered by one of his sons. This prince then, disdaining to ascend the throne himself, raised one of his brothers, Praudha Devaraya, to the throne. But this raja proved to be even more wicked and dissolute than his father, and he immediately freed himself from the debt of gratitude he owed to his parricide brother by assassinating him, and then plunged into a life of wanton debauchery. But before he could do much harm, he was deposed by Saluva Narasimha, one of the leading provincial chieftains of the kingdom, who then ascended the throne. Devaraya offered no resistance to the usurper, but cravenly fled from the capital on the approach of Narasimha. Thus ended, around 1486, the rule of the Sangama dynasty.

Narasimha, who had his fief at Chandragiri in southern Andhra Pradesh, had functioned as a virtually independent ruler for quite some years, and had over the years considerably expanded the territory under his control. Because of the misrule of the last couple of kings of the Sangama dynasty, several provincial chiefs of Vijayanagar, particularly in the southern and eastern provinces of the kingdom, transferred their allegiance to Narasimha. So his position on his accession to the throne was quite strong, though he, like most other rulers of the kingdom, inevitably had to face several internal challenges.

Narasimha ruled for about five years, during which he was engaged in a number of battles, against his adversaries in the kingdom, and to protect the Vijayanagar territory from rival kingdoms. He was mostly successful in these campaigns. But the Saluva dynasty he founded barely survived him. Though Narasimha had two sons, they were too young to rule at the time of his death, so he on his deathbed he entrusted them—and the kingdom—to the care of his trusted minister, Narasa Nayaka, requesting him to rule as the regent till the boys came of age.

On Narasimha's death, his eldest son, Timma, was crowned king, but the boy was soon killed in a palace intrigue, so Narasa Nayaka placed the raja's second son, Immadi Narasimha, on the throne, but kept him under his tutelage and himself ruled as the de facto king. But Narasa Nayaka himself died in a few years, upon which his son, Vira Narasimha, took over as the regent. But Vira Narasimha had none of his father's scruples. Presently he got rid of his ward by assassination, then himself ascended the throne, and founded the Tuluva dynasty, the third dynasty of the kingdom.

This usurpation led to widespread unrest in the kingdom, and several rebellions erupted in its provinces. At this time there was also an invasion of the kingdom by Adil Shah of Bijapur. In the midst of all these troubles Vira Narasimha himself died, in 1509. The major concern of the raja at the time of his death was to secure the throne for his children, so he (according to Nuniz) instructed Saluva Timma, his trusted Brahmin minister, to blind his brothers and raise one of his sons to the throne. But Timma sensibly disregarded the royal mandate and offered the throne to Krishnadeva, the raja's youngest brother—half-brother, actually—who then ascended the throne, in August 1509.

KRISHNADEVA WAS IN his early twenties at the time of his accession, and had hardly any administrative or military experience. But he turned out to be the most celebrated ruler of Vijayanagar, who was exceptionally successful in administration as well as in military campaigns. In the initial years of his reign, he had the great advantage of having the sagacious counsel of Saluva Timma, whom the raja affectionately called *appaji*, revered father.

The kingdom that Krishnadeva inherited was, at the time of his accession, beset with several rebellions and invasions, but the raja prevailed over all his adversaries, and in time raised Vijayanagar to the stature of the most powerful kingdom in the peninsula. The first invasion he faced, soon after his accession, was by Mahmud Shah, the Bahmani sultan, who, though he was little more than a figurehead at this time, was prodded by his nobles to lead an army against Vijayanagar. But the raja was equal to the challenge; he not only routed the enemy army massed at his frontier, but pursued it into the Bahmani territory, trounced it again in a second battle, and then went on to capture Gulbarga, the old capital of the Sultanate, as well as Bidar, its new capital. The raja then restored Mahmud Shah to the throne—perhaps because he was innocuous, or perhaps because the sultan was expected to add another unsettling element in the turbulent politics of the disintegrating Sultanate. The raja then returned to Vijayanagar.

After the Bahmani campaign, Krishnadeva was for a couple of years engaged in suppressing a rebellion in southern Karnataka. This was followed by a major campaign by him to recover the eastern provinces of the kingdom lost to Gajapati, the king of Orissa, during previous regimes. This was a prolonged, five year long campaign, but it ended in total victory for Krishnadeva—he not only recovered the lost provinces but even stormed into Cuttack, Gajapati's capital. There was however no vindictiveness in Krishnadeva's treatment of Gajapati; rather, he concluded a generous peace treaty with him, by which he agreed to treat river Krishna as the boundary between their kingdoms, and returned to Gajapati all the lands that he (Krishnadeva) had conquered north of the river. And Gajapati in turn gave one of his daughters in marriage to Krishnadeva, to seal their alliance with a family bond.

The other major wars of Krishnadeva were against Golconda and Bijapur, independent kingdoms that had emerged out of the fragmented Bahmani Sultanate. In the war against Bijapur, the raja occupied Gulbarga, destroyed its fortifications, and placed a Bahmani prince, a son of Mahmud Shah, on the throne there as his ward, presumably in the hope of resuscitating the Bahmani dynasty under Vijayanagar patronage. He also took two of the sultan's brothers with him to Vijayanagar, where they were provided with all princely amenities, but were treated as the raja's dependants, symbols of his dominance over the Sultanate.

On his return to his capital from the Bijapur campaign, Krishnadeva abdicated the throne in favour of his infant son born to him in his old age, and himself carried on the administration as chief minister, presumably to ensure the eventual smooth succession of the prince. But the prince died after a few months, poisoned in a palace intrigue. Krishnadeva's only other son was a baby at this time, just eighteen months old, so it was impossible for the raja to arrange his succession. He therefore set his half-brother Achyuta free from confinement and designated him as his successor.

KRISHNADEVA WAS A peerless warrior king and a great military strategist, who was never, even once, defeated in battle. He invariably led his army in person, and often fought in the frontline of his army, thus inspiring valour in his soldiers. He also paid scrupulous attention to the welfare of his soldiers, and after every battle he usually went around the battlefield to take care of the wounded and to offer them solace. Not surprisingly, his soldiers were fiercely loyal to him, which in part explains why he was invincible.

As in military matters, Krishnadeva was thorough in administrative matters also, and was meticulously attentive to every detail. He toured around his kingdom regularly, to ensure that its provinces remained firmly under his control and functioned efficiently. Every aspect of life in his kingdom received similar attention from him. And he took particular care to stimulate the economy of the state. Agricultural prosperity was crucial for the welfare of his kingdom, so he made a major effort to improve the irrigation system in the state by repairing the existing tanks and canals and constructing some new ones, and for this he even recruited the services of a Portuguese engineer. Krishnadeva also lightened the tax burden on the people by abolishing vexatious minor taxes, like the marriage tax, reflecting his general concern for the welfare of the people.

Krishnadeva was equally renowned for his patronage of scholars, writers and artists, and his court was adorned by a group of eight Telugu literary luminaries, known as the Ashtadiggajas. The raja himself was a distinguished poet, and had to his credit the composition of *Amukta-malyada*, an epic poem in Telugu on Andal—a saint poet of the Tamil Bhakti movement—and of her intense longing for union with god Vishnu. Krishnadeva was a deeply religious person, and he regularly visited temples, often accompanied by his queens, to offer worship. And it was Krishnadeva who ordered the sculpting of the gigantic statue of Narasimha—carved out of a single granite boulder—which still stands in the ruins of Vijayanagar. According to Domingo Paes, an early sixteenth century Portuguese traveller in India, the raja also built near Vijayanagar a new palace complex in honour of his favourite wife, Nagala Devi, named it Nagalapur after her, and made it his favourite residence.

There is a good amount of information, in Indian as well as foreign sources, about the reign of Krishnadeva, much more than about any other Vijayanagar king. These sources also provide vivid descriptions of the appearance and manners of the raja. 'This king,' writes Paes, 'is of medium height, and of fair complexion and good figure, rather fat than thin; he has on his face smallpox marks. He is the most feared and perfect king that could possibly be, cheerful of disposition and very merry; he is one that seeks to honour foreigners, and receives them kindly, asking about all their affairs . . . He is a great ruler and a man of much justice . . . is gallant and perfect . . . in all things . . . The king was clothed in certain white cloths embroidered with many roses in gold, and with a *pateca* of diamonds of very great value on his neck, and on his head he had a cap of brocade in fashion like Galician helmet, covered with a piece of fine stuff all of fine silk, and he was barefooted.'

The only fault that Paes could find in Krishnadeva was that he was 'subject to sudden fits of rage,' and he sometimes, though rarely, treated fallen enemies with unbecoming contempt. Thus, after his 1520 campaign, in which he captured Raichur from Adil Shah, the sultan of Bijapur, he treated the sultan's envoy with utter disdain, and to his plea that the conquered territories might be restored to the sultan, he haughtily replied that if the sultan came and kissed his feet, he will return the lands.

Such insulting behaviour was however unusual in Krishnadeva, for he was normally mature, sober and thoughtful in all his conduct, in his private as well as public life. And there is a fair amount of data about the private life of the raja, unlike about most other kings of the age. 'This king has twelve lawful wives, of whom there are three principal ones, the sons of each of these three being heirs of the kingdom, but not those of the others,' reports Paes. These principal wives are in all respects provided everything equally by the raja 'so that there may never be any discord or ill feeling between them; all of them are great friends, and each one lives by herself.'

Paes also reports on the king's daily routine: 'This king is accustomed every day to drink a three-quarter pint of oil of gingili (sesame) before daylight, and he anoints himself all over with the said oil; he covers his loins with a small cloth and takes in his arms great weights made of earthenware [and exercises with them], and then, taking a sword, he exercises himself with it till he has sweated out all the oil, and then he wrestles with one his wrestlers. After this labour he mounts a horse and gallops about the plain in one direction and another till dawn . . . Then he goes to bathe, and a Brahmin bathes him . . .' After this morning exercise routine, the raja goes to a pavilion to attend to public business.

KRISHNADEVA DIED IN 1529 and was succeeded by Achyuta, his designated heir, but his succession set off family tensions, with Krishnadeva's son-in-law, Ramaraya, proclaiming Krishnadeva's infant son as king, and seeking to rule the kingdom in the infant's name. This could have led to a civil war, but Achyuta reconciled Ramaraya by sharing power with him. This arrangement however did not last long, and presently, when Achyuta was away from the capital on a campaign, Ramaraya took full control of the government, and he seized and imprisoned Achyuta when he returned to the capital. This was followed by a confusing period of usurpation, counter-usurpation and provincial rebellions, which was, strange though it might seem, brought to an end by Adil Shah, the sultan of Bijapur, who arrived in Vijayanagar as an invader to take advantage of the disarray in the kingdom, but stayed on to affect reconciliation between Achyuta and Ramaraya. By this agreement Ramaraya recognised Achyuta as the king of Vijayanagar, and Achyuta in turn granted Ramaraya full autonomy in his fief. The terms of this agreement were faithfully observed by both princes, and Achyuta ruled in peace till his death in 1542. Adil Shah got a large sum of money, twelve elephants and some horses as his reward for arranging the reconciliation.

Achyuta on his death was succeeded by his minor son Venkata, with his maternal uncle Tirumala ruling the kingdom on his behalf, as his regent. This was followed, as usual in similar situations in Vijayanagar history, by a prolonged and confusing tussle between various contenders for power, in which Adil Shah also got repeatedly involved, as previously. In the course of this turmoil Tirumala strangled Venkata, his ward, slaughtered many members of the royal family, and ascended the throne himself. But his reign was short-lived, for presently Ramaraya advanced against him with an army. Faced with immanent deposition, Tirumala, according to Ferishta, 'shut himself up in the palace, and, becoming mad from despair, blinded all the royal elephants and horses, also cut off their tails, so that they might be of no use to the enemy. All the diamonds, rubies, emeralds, other precious stones, and pearls, which had been collected [by the Vijayanagar rajas] in the course of many ages, he crushed to powder between heavy millstones, and scattered them on the ground. He then fixed a sword blade on a pillar in his apartment, and ran his breast upon it with such a force that it pierced through and came out at the back, thus putting an end to his existence.'

Ramaraya then raised Sadashiva, a nephew of Achyuta, to the throne, and himself ruled the state as its de facto king. He held Sadashiva under close guard, but kept up the pretence of subservience to the raja by periodically going to prostrate before him. 'Ramaraaje now became roy of Beejanuggur without a rival,' states Ferishta. And he then came to be known as Bade Ramaraya: Ramaraya the Great.

During Ramaraya's de facto rule there was a substantial increase in the number of Muslim officers in high positions in Vijayanagar, in administration as well as in the army. And just as Adil Shah had previously involved himself in the internal affairs of Vijayanagar, now Ramaraya began to intervene in the tussles between the Deccan sultanates, sending his army into their territories. He also engaged in complex diplomatic manoeuvres to prevent the sultanates from uniting and threatening Vijayanagar. In the same aggressive spirit, he sent a military contingent deep into South India, to deal with the rebels there and to extend his dominance right up to Kanniyakumari, at the very tip of India, where he had his army set up a victory tower, to symbolise his absolute dominance in the peninsula. He also conducted a successful campaign to subdue the Portuguese who had, in Goa as well as in San Thome, presumed to take law into their own hands, looting temples and converting Hindus to Christianity.

These aggressive military activities of Ramaraya however constituted only one aspect of his reign. He, like several other Vijayanagar rulers, was a highly cultured man, and a zealous patron of artists and writers, and under his patronage several writers, in Telugu as well as in Sanskrit, flourished in his court. He was also a keen builder, and some of the finest temples of the Vijayanagar period were built by him. And he, though a staunch Vaishnavite himself, was, again like several other Vijayanagar kings, quite tolerant and liberal in religious matters, and treated all people fairly, irrespective of their religious and sectarian affiliation.

THE AGGRESSIVE MILITARY campaigns of Krishnadeva and Ramaraya shifted the balance of power in the peninsula in favour of Vijayanagar. While previously the rajas were invariably the losers in their wars with the sultans, now they were invariably the winners, especially after the Sultanate splintered into five independent kingdoms. This military dominance of Vijayanagar threatened the very survival of the peninsular Muslim kingdoms, and induced them finally to unite against Vijayanagar. In the ensuing battle, the battle of Talikota, Vijayanagar was decisively defeated by the sultans, never again to rise to prominence.

The specific circumstances that led to the battle are not known. Ferishta attributes it to the arrogant and insulting conduct of Ramaraya towards the Muslim kingdoms of the Deccan, and to the atrocities his troops committed in those kingdoms, desecrating or destroying mosques, butchering Muslims and molesting their women. This was the normal mode of conduct of most medieval Indian armies in enemy territories, and in any case these excesses were no different from the excesses committed by the sultanate troops in the Vijayanagar territory. Ramaraya does not seem to have had any religious motive in his military campaigns, but was only seeking to establish the political dominance of Vijayanagar in the peninsula. Similarly, the objective of the sultanates in uniting against Vijayanagar was not religious, but political, to ensure their survival as independent kingdoms, though a religious colouration was also given to the campaign by the sultans, to rouse the valour of their soldiers. The sultans, according to Ferishta, felt that the king of Vijayanagar, 'who had bound all the rajas of the Carnatic to his yoke, required to be checked and his influence removed from the countries of Islam, in order that their people might repose in safety from the oppression of unbelievers, and their mosques and holy places no longer subject to pollution from infidels.'

In the summer of 1564 four of the five Deccan sultanates—Bijapur, Golconda, Ahmadnagar and Bidar—buried their rivalries and mutual grudges and formed a confederacy against Vijayanagar. Berar stood sullenly aloof from this league, as it was still smarting from the wounds it had received in its conflicts with its neighbouring Muslim kingdoms. The four confederates then sealed their union with marriage alliances. And in the last week of December that year the armies of the four kingdoms assembled together on the plains near Talikota, a small town in Bijapur, and then advanced to the Krishna, the river that at this time marked the northern frontier of Vijayanagar.

Ramaraya was well aware of these developments, and he too organised his forces. His army, according to one estimate of Ferishta—he gives different figures in different places in his account of the battle—consisted of 900,000 infantry, 45,000 cavalry, 2,000 elephants, and 15,000 auxiliaries. These are incredible figures, and are hard to believe, but Ramaraya certainly would have had an army that was much larger than the combined armies of the sultans. From this vast force Ramaraya detached a strong contingent and sent it to the Krishna riverbank, to prevent the enemy from crossing the river.

Confronted with this blocking deployment of the Vijayanagar army, the sultans used a ruse to cross the river. Seemingly disheartened by the impossibility of crossing the river at their chosen ford, they began to march upstream, pretending to look for another ford. Seeing this, the Vijayanagar contingent kept pace with them on the opposite bank, and this went on for three days. Then suddenly the allied army, as planned, reversed its course and quickly, within just a day, doubled back to its selected ford, and immediately sent an advance contingent across the river. This met with no resistance, as the Vijayanagar soldiers were nowhere nearby. That night the rest of the allied army also crossed the river.

The details of the ensuing battle given in various reports are partisan and contradictory. The battle, fought on 23 January 1565, a Tuesday, is usually called the battle of Talikota, though it was actually fought on a plain between two villages, Rakshasi and Tangadi, some 50 kilometres south of Talikota, and is therefore also known as the battle of Rakshasi-Tangadi. The allied forces, as Sewell describes the scene, were drawn up 'in a long line, . . . each division with the standards of the twelve Imams waving in the van . . .' The Ahmadnagar contingent was stationed at the centre of this deployment, and it had at its front 600 pieces of ordnance disposed in three lines, one behind the other, with the heavy artillery in front, behind it the lighter artillery, and the swivel guns in the rear. And in front of this artillery deployment were stationed 2,000 foreign archers, to conceal the guns from the enemy.

The particulars of the deployment of the Vijayanagar army is not known, but it was commanded by Ramaraya himself, though he was now a very old man—'he was ninety-six years old, but was as brave as a man of thirty,' according to Diogo do Couto, a sixteenth century Portuguese chronicler. The battle began with the Vijayanagar army shooting rockets at the allied army, and peppering it with fire from matchlocks and light guns. Then their cavalry charged. At that point the archers masking the Deccani artillery fell back, and the guns opened up, causing great havoc in the Vijayanagar army.

This was the decisive movement in the battle. As the Vijayanagar army staggered under the impact of the artillery salvoes, the Deccani cavalry charged into them ferociously and scattered them in a short, swift action. Ramaraya himself was captured during the melee, and was immediately beheaded on the orders of Nizam Shah. His severed head was then mounted on a long spear and displayed to the enemy, and the sight of this is said to have so demoralised the Vijayanagar soldiers that they immediately broke up and fled.

The battle lasted only just a few hours, as in the case of most medieval Indian battles, in which the worsted army usually took to flight without attempting to regroup. Though Hindu accounts speak of a more than six-months-long war, and even of single battles lasting as long as twenty-seven days, these are evidently just self-consoling myths.

The sultans won the battle mainly because of their superior artillery (under the command of Rumi Khan, a Turk) and cavalry. The desertion of two Muslim commanders and their contingents from the Vijayanagar army during the battle was also a crucial factor in the rout of the Vijayanagar army. 'When the armies were joined, the battle lasted but a [short] while, not the pace of four hours, because two traitorous captains [in the Vijayanagar army] . . . with their companies turned their faces against their king, and made such disorder in his army, that . . . [the soldiers in bewilderment] set themselves to flight,' reports Caesar Frederick, an Italian traveller who was in Vijayanagar in 1567.

THE VICTORY OF the Deccani army was decisive. According to Ferishta, so great was the slaughter in the battle—some 100,000 soldiers are said to have perished in the Vijayanagar army alone—that the waters of a stream flowing alongside the battlefield turned red with blood. The flight of the Vijayanagar army was so pell-mell that they left behind in their camp large quantities of equipments and a good amount of treasure, for the victors to pillage. 'The plunder,' notes Ferishta, 'was so great that every private man in the allied army became rich in gold, jewels, effects, tents, arms, horses, and slaves.' The sultans reserved for themselves only the captured elephants.

After the battle the allied army took a break for a few days, to rest and to reorganise themselves. Then they set out for Vijayanagar city. The people of the city had initially no sense of the peril they faced, as no Muslim army had ever entered the strongly fortified city, even when, victorious in battle, it had ravaged the environs of the city. But the gravity of the situation dawned on the people when the princes and nobles scurrying back from the battlefield gathered their treasures, loaded those on elephants, and fled from the city for safe refuges far away. They also carried with them Sadashiva, the phantom king.

'Then a panic seized the city,' writes Sewell. 'The truth became at last apparent. This was not merely a military defeat; it was a cataclysm. All hope was gone . . . Nothing could be done but to bury all treasures, to arm the younger men, and to wait. Next day the place became a prey to the robber tribes and jungle people of the neighbourhood. Hordes of . . . [them] pounced down on the hapless city and looted the stores and shops, carrying off great quantities of riches.' According to Couto, this went on day after day, for six days.

Then the allied forces entered the city. 'The enemy had come to destroy, and they carried out their object relentlessly,' continues Sewell. 'With fire and sword, with crowbars and axes, they carried on day after day their work of destruction. Never perhaps in the history of the world has such havoc been wrought, and wrought so suddenly, on so splendid a city, teeming with a wealthy and industrious population in the full plenitude of prosperity one day, and on the next, seized, pillaged and reduced to ruins, amid scenes of savage massacre and horrors beggaring description.' Caesar Frederick, who visited the city two years after the battle, noted: 'The houses still stand, but [are] empty, and there is dwelling in them nothing but tigers and other wild beasts.'

THE DESPOLIATION AND devastation of the city went on for five months without respite. Meanwhile, with Ramaraya dead, his brother Tirumala took charge of the titular raja and set up his government at Penugonda, about 190 kilometres south-east of Vijayanagar, in a defensible, rugged hilly region in the Anantapur district of the modern state of Andhra Pradesh. But Tirumala was immediately challenged by Ramaraya's son Timma, who had no hesitation even to seek the help of the sultan of Bijapur against his uncle. This move was countered by Tirumala by seeking the help of the sultan of Ahmadnagar. Soon the Vijayanagar chieftains and the Deccan sultans got once again embroiled in several shifting alliances and counter-alliances.

Around this time several chieftains of Vijayanagar threw off their allegiance to the raja and set up their own petty kingdoms. Some of these new states— Madurai under Nayaks, for instance—grew into powerful and enduring kingdoms, but most regions of Vijayanagar simply collapsed into anarchy. And many of the *palayagars*, who were responsible for maintaining law and order in the districts of the kingdom, now reversed their role and took to banditry. Vijayanagar thus began to implode. Tirumala did not have the resources—or the energy: he was an old man now—to bring the rebels to submission, but he had the wisdom to adopt a realistic policy, of acknowledging the virtual independence of the rebel chieftains in return for their symbolic recognition of the overlordship of the raja and of his own de facto authority. Vijayanagar thus became an agglomeration of semi-independent principalities with Tirumala as its head. And it survived in that loose, withered and crumbling state for nearly another century.

Tirumala did the best that anyone could possibly have done to preserve the truncated kingdom in the given circumstances. And this, he felt, entitled him to be the de jure as well as the de facto king. So in 1570, five years after the battle of Talikota, he crowned himself at Penugonda as the king of Vijayanagar, and founded the Aravidu dynasty, the last dynasty of Vijayanagar. He then divided the kingdom into three roughly linguistic provinces, and assigned these to each of his three sons: the Telugu region to his eldest son Sriranga; the Karnataka region to his second son Rama, and the Tamil country to his third son Venkatapathi. Soon after making this division Tirumala abdicated the throne in favour of his son Sriranga, and thereafter devoted himself to scholarly and religious pursuits. It is not clear what happened to Sadashiva, the phantom king, but it is likely that he was assassinated.

Vijayanagar continued to fragment under Sriranga and his four successors, though it had also a few brief periods of revival. The last phase of the history of Vijayanagar is mostly a story of pathetic, feckless rajas, and of usurpations, rebellions, civil wars, and recurrent invasions by the Deccan sultans. During the reign of the last of these kings, Sriranga III, the Deccan sultans swept into Vijayanagar in a coordinated attack and divided the kingdom among themselves. Sriranga thus became a king without a kingdom, and in 1649 he fled to Mysore to take refuge with the raja there, and died there a couple of years later. Thus ended the three century long history of Vijayanagar. All that remained of this once great kingdom were a few small principalities here and there, but even these were presently mopped up by the expanding Maratha kingdom, which had emerged as the dominant power in India after the decline of the Mughals.

VIJAYANAGAR IS OFTEN portrayed as the champion of the revival of Hindu political power, religion and culture, and as an inveterate antagonist of Muslim kingdoms. But this is not borne out by facts. Though Vijayanagar was the most powerful Hindu kingdom that existed in the entire Indian subcontinent during the nearly half a millennium period from the conquest of India by Turks at the close of the twelfth century to the establishment of the Maratha state by Shivaji in the mid-seventeenth century, and though its rajas were all devout Hindus, and several of them were keen and knowledgeable patrons of Hindu religion and culture, the primary motive of the rajas was to gain and expand their political power, and not to resuscitate Hindu religion and culture. In fact, Harihara and Bukka, the founders of the Vijayanagar kingdom, had at the outset of their political career embraced Islam, because it suited them then, but later reverted to Hinduism, because it suited them then.

Being a Hindu kingdom was incidental to the political history of Vijayanagar. It is significant that the initial territorial expansion of Vijayanagar was not into any Muslim kingdom, but into the Hindu kingdom of Hoysalas, and that too when Hoysalas were engaged in a conflict with the Muslim kingdom of Madurai. Indeed, the expansion of Vijayanagar in its entire history was mostly into Hindu kingdoms, and not into Muslim kingdoms. And throughout its history Vijayanagar was as much engaged in battles with Hindu kingdoms as with Muslim kingdoms. Nor did Vijayanagar kings have any hesitation to ally with sultans against Hindu kings. But then, nor did sultans have any hesitation to ally with Hindu kings against Muslim rulers. The wars of these kings hardly ever had anything to do with religion, but were fought primarily to defend or conquer territory. Though a religious colouration was often given to these campaigns, this was done primarily to gain military advantage by igniting the martial fervour of their soldiers.

In the case of both Bahmani and Vijayanagar, religion subserved politics. Vijayanagar was not an anti-Muslim state. It in fact had a large number of Muslim officers and soldiers in its army, that too in the critically important divisions of cavalrymen, archers, cannoneers and musketeers. Devaraya II in particular took care to show various special favours to his Muslim soldiers; he built a mosque for them, and even placed a copy of Koran on a desk in front of his throne. As for the Deccan sultanates, they all had a large number of Hindu contingents in their army, and their rulers sometimes entrusted the defence of key forts to Hindu officers, as Nizam Shah of Ahmadnagar is recorded to have done.

The Vijayanagar rajas were generally quite liberal in their religious attitudes. 'The king allows such freedom that every man may come and go and live according to his own creed without suffering any annoyance . . . whether he is a Christian, Jew, Moor or Heathen,' notes Duarte Barbosa, a Portuguese chronicler in India in the first quarter of the sixteenth century. 'Great equity and justice is shown to all, not only by the ruler but by the people to one another.' There were several instances of acts of liberalism by sultans also. Thus when Sultan Ali Adil Shah of Bijapur heard of a tragedy in the family of King Ramaraya of Vijayanagar—the death of a son of Ramaraya—he personally went to Vijayanagar to console him. And Ramaraya in turn received the sultan with utmost courtesy; Ramaraya's wife even nominally adopted the young sultan as her son. But on the whole the rajas, being polytheists, were far more tolerant in religious matters than the sultans, who were monotheists.

This liberality and religious tolerance of the rajas however generally applied only in their treatment of their own subjects. In the enemy territory they often acted as vandals, destroying mosques or using them as stables, and enslaving or slaughtering Muslims, and violating their women. This was the common practice of all invading armies during medieval times. In fact, the excesses of Hindu armies in this were not usually as excessive as those of Muslim armies.

On the whole the Vijayanagar rajas provided as good a government as was possible in that age and place. They cleared forests and brought new lands under cultivation, built dams and tanks and irrigation canals. Trade was encouraged. They also systematised revenue administration, rationalised the tax system and abolished vexatious minor taxes. All this contributed to the prosperity and contentment of the people—as well as, of course, to the power of the raja. 'In power, wealth, and extent of the country' Vijayanagar was much superior to the Bahmani Sultanate, concedes Ferishta. Exclaims Razzak: 'The city of Vijayanagar is such that the pupil of the eye has never seen a place like it, and the ear of intelligence has never been informed that there existed anything to equal it in the world.' Vijayanagar, according to Paes, was 'the best provided city in the world.'

There was however a dark side to this effulgent picture. The kingdom was ever riven by internal dissensions and conflicts, and was engaged in incessant wars with other kingdoms. Its political history, like the history of most early medieval Indian kingdoms, is a sordid story, though it also had a few periods of impressive material prosperity and cultural efflorescence.

PART VII

POLITY

If a holy man eats half his loaf,
he will give the other half to a beggar.
But if a king conquers all the world,
he will still seek another world to conquer.

—SAADI, PERSIAN POET

1

Ram-Ravan Syndrome

The history of early medieval India was like a roller-coaster ride—there were spectacular highs and lows in it, but hardly any progress. This was true of nearly all the kingdoms of the age, those of rajas as well as of sultans. It is on the whole a sordid tale of treachery, rebellions, usurpations, murders, fiendish punishments, and barbaric mass slaughter.

The dominant Indian kingdom of the age was the Delhi Sultanate. This was essentially an alien military dictatorship—it was established by conquest, and was preserved by ceaseless military campaigns throughout its over three-century-long history. Except in a few rare cases, mostly in the peninsula, the Turco-Afghans, unlike the Mughals who succeeded them as the dominant rulers of India, did not sink their roots into the Indian soil, but remained aliens throughout their history. Though theirs was not a foreign rule in the sense that their home base was outside India, theirs was essentially a rule by foreigners.

The Turco-Afghans were a miniscule community in India, ever struggling for survival in the vast and churning sea of native Indians and their subjugated but not pacified rajas. That vulnerability put the sultans in a state of perpetual insecurity, which in turn disposed them, for self-preservation, to be brutal oppressors of the natives.

The survival anxiety of the sultans was further intensified by the fact that the Turco-Afghans even among themselves lacked unity, and were riven into various factions. The Delhi Sultanate was ever seething with conspiracies and rebellions. The law that prevailed in it all through its history was the law of the jungle. Its provincial governors often assumed postures of rivalry with their sultan, and they tended to rebel and establish independent kingdoms whenever the central authority in Delhi weakened. And when one uprising

259

was suppressed by the sultan, another uprising broke out elsewhere in the empire. And the rebel governors and chieftains chastised by the sultan often turned rebels again when the royal forces withdrew. Sometimes the officer sent to suppress a rebellion himself turned rebel. This went on and on.

In Delhi itself the sultan was ever under the threat of being overthrown or assassinated, and of having his throne usurped by one of his top nobles or close relatives, particularly by his brothers, as it did indeed happen on several occasions. Even the reign of the ruthlessly efficient Ala-ud-din Khalji was beset with rebellions; there were, as the fourteenth-century chronicler Barani notes, several successive insurrections at one stage during his reign; there was even an attempted assassination of the sultan by one of his nephews seeking to usurp the throne.

This roiling state of affairs went on all through the history of the Delhi Sultanate. There was hardly a year, perhaps even hardly a month, free of internal military clashes somewhere in the empire. Scarcely anyone had any enduring loyalty to anyone. Those who plotted to betray their sultan often had betrayers against them in their own group. And those who bowed before a sultan one day unhesitatingly bowed before his assassin the next day.

All this gave the Delhi Sultanate a disquieting appearance of transience. Yet, amazingly, the Sultanate endured for over three centuries. There were, however, as many as five dynasties in the history of the Delhi Sultanate—Slave, Khalji, Tughluq, Sayyid and Lodi—and within each of these dynasties too there were several internal upheavals and usurpations. The Delhi Sultanate had, in all, 33 sultans in its 320-year-long history, their reigns averaging less than ten years. In contrast, during the entire history of the Mughal Empire, which was of about the same length as the history of the Delhi Sultanate, there was only one ruling dynasty, and during the 181-year-long high period of its history, from the invasion of Babur to the death of Aurangzeb, it had just six emperors, and the average length of their reign was over thirty years, which was more than three times the length of the average reign of the Delhi sultans. There were hardly any enduring periods of internal peace during the history of the Sultanate, except perhaps for a while during the reigns of Ala-ud-din Khalji and Firuz Tughluq. Though there were some attempts to consolidate and systematise the administration of the empire by some sultans, these had no lasting results.

A CURIOUS ASPECT OF the history of the Delhi Sultanate was the opportunistic collaboration of rajas with sultans. The rajas, if they had acted in concert, could have probably obliterated the Sultanate. Fortunately for the Sultanate, there was no prospect of any such alliance among the rajas, as there was absolutely no national spirit in that age, no awareness of India as a distinct nation, or of Indians as a distinct people. The rajas were solely concerned with preserving or augmenting their personal power and fortune. And to gain that objective they were often willing to collaborate with the sultans against their own compatriots.

The attitudes of the Muslim political class were also equally opportunistic. Just as there were many instances of rajas allying with sultans against fellow Hindu rulers, there were also many instances of sultans allying with rajas or using Hindu military contingents, against fellow Muslim rulers. Even Mahmud Ghazni, despite his reputation as a ruthless exterminator of Hindu kingdoms, had a large Hindu contingent in his army, and so had his son Masud. Masud in fact treated his Hindu officers in every way as equals to his Muslim officers, and employed them in the same high offices in which he employed his Muslim officers. Indeed, he valued their services so highly that he sternly warned his Muslim officers against offending the religious sensibilities of their fellow Hindu officers in any way.

Similarly, a Muslim governor of Gujarat under the Delhi Sultanate at one time 'encouraged the Hindu religion . . . and promoted . . . the worship of idols,' in order to gain the support of Hindus for his planned rebellion against the Delhi sultan, states Ferishta, a late sixteenth century Mughal chronicler. And, in a similar development in Hindu polity, king Devaraya of Vijayanagar took care to place a copy Koran on a desk in front of his throne, so that his Muslim officers could perform obeisance before him, without violating their religious injunctions.

It was all a power game. And in that game religion invariably subserved the political and military goals of kings. So sultans often collaborated with rajas in their battles, even in their battles against Muslim kingdoms; conversely, rajas often collaborated with sultans in their battles, even in their battles against Hindu kingdoms. For nobles and common people too religion usually subserved their temporal interests. And just as Hindu soldiers and officers freely served under sultans, so also Muslim soldiers and officers freely served under rajas.

And there is at least one instance of a Hindu being the ruler of a Muslim kingdom. This was Ganesa, a zamindar in Bengal in the early fifteenth century, who, according to Ferishta, 'attained great power and predominance during Shihab-ud-din's reign, and became the de-facto master of the treasury and kingdom.' And on the death (or assassination) of the sultan, Ganesa usurped the royal power and ruled Bengal for about seven years, though he probably did not physically occupy the throne. But on Ganesa's death, his son, who had become a Muslim, ascended the throne and ruled the state for sixteen years; and he, though outwardly a Muslim, appointed Brahmins as his ministers, and even had a Brahmin as his court priest.

Elsewhere in India too the relationship between the Hindu and Muslim ruling classes was quite fluid. Hindu chieftains and zamindars in Muslim kingdoms generally held virtually independent sway over extensive territories, and they were not usually interfered with by the sultans as long as they regularly paid to the sultans the tributes and taxes due to them. This was not, however, a relationship of mutual trust and compliance, for payments from the local chieftains often had to be exacted from them by force by the sultans, and payments were usually withheld by the chieftains whenever the power of the overlord weakened. But this was the normal conduct of local chieftains everywhere in India, irrespective of whether the king was a Hindu or a Muslim.

MEDIEVAL ISLAMIC SOCIETY was basically egalitarian. It had no caste-like divisions, so any person of any social or racial background could aspire to any position in it, including that of the sultan. In principle no one could ascend the throne by birthright, but could do so only by virtue of his merit or power, and on being acknowledged as sultan by the leaders of the Muslim community.

This political fluidity was the main reason for the many violent succession conflicts in the history of the Delhi Sultanate. Indeed, such conflicts were considered as the legitimate means for proving the capabilities of the contenders. And proving one's merit for the throne often meant exterminating one's rivals. Peaceful succession to the throne was rare in the Sultanate—or, for that matter, in Hindu kingdoms, in Vijayanagar, for instance. Though there were a few instances of the courtiers choosing the sultan by consensus from among the rival contenders, normally they had no choice but to acknowledge as sultan the man who gained the throne, by inheritance or by force. The courtiers then affirmed their allegiance to the new sultan by taking a formal oath of fealty to him.

Initially, till the reign of Balban, there was no great status difference between the sultan and his nobles; the sultan was then a *primus inter pares*, a first among equals, more a leader than a ruler. Later however the sultans generally claimed that the occupation of the throne endowed them with *farr*, divine effulgence, which distinguished them from all other people. Balban further claimed that he was ruling as the vicegerent of god on earth, thereby implying that the sultan had the divine right or sanction to be the ruler, and that to disobey him would be to disobey god. But this quasi-divine attribute of the sultan, in Balban's view, was as much a responsibility as a privilege, and he maintained that one gains the effulgence of the sultan not by just sitting on the throne, but by the manner in which he rules, serving the interests of the people and ensuring their welfare. In his view only those rulers in whose kingdom there was not a single naked or hungry man deserved to be called a sultan.

Ala-ud-din Khalji also claimed absolute royal power, but he based that claim on realpolitik, not on any theological principle. As he once candidly told a qazi, he did not know, and did not care for, theological prescriptions, but did what was essential 'for the good of the state and the benefit of the people.' Ala-ud-din in fact, despite his dictatorial nature, was one of the few Delhi sultans who showed a genuine concern for the welfare of his subjects, and did what he could for the betterment of the conditions of their life.

Ala-ud-din was a political realist. He held that whatever be the Islamic theory of monarchy, and whatever be the pretence of sultans, in reality the basis of royal authority was the sultan's military might, his ability to coerce others to submit to his will. Though there were in Islam various socio-religious prescriptions about the scope of the sultan's power, and about what he should and should not do, most sultans in practice treated their kingdom as their private possession, which they could rule without any constraints whatever. The powers that an individual sultan exercised were limited only by what he was capable of exercising. In theory, the primary duty of the sultan was to protect his subjects and to provide for their welfare, but in practice his primary concern—often his sole concern—was to preserve and expand his power. According to Barani, haughtiness and egomania characterised the conduct of most sultans.

IN THEORY, SULTANS everywhere in the Muslim world were the proconsuls of the Caliph, who was the head of all Muslims throughout the world, in temporal as well as in spiritual matters. The practice in the Muslim world indeed matched this principle in the early period of Muslim history, when Muslim political power was largely confined to Arabia and its adjacent lands, and there was only one Caliph. Later however, as the Muslim empire expanded into the lands of several other races and cultures, and the religion itself split into different sects and factions, there also came to be several Caliphs, and their status declined to that of mere figureheads. Still, Muslim kings everywhere generally continued to acknowledge, at least nominally, the Caliph as their overlord, and they continued to receive honours from him with a show of deep respect. It was useful to do so, for it legitimised their rule and validated their policies and actions, particularly in the eyes of orthodox Muslims. The sultans therefore usually included the Caliph's name in the khutba recited in their kingdoms, and had his name inscribed on the coins they issued. Several Delhi sultans in fact expressly sought investiture by the Caliph, and some, notably Muhammad Tughluq, were ostentatiously demonstrative in displaying their subservience to him, though in reality they ruled as totally independent autocrats.

Rajas had no such pretence of grand, transnational affiliations. But in other respects Hindu kingdoms were also marked by the dichotomy between the professions and the practices of their rulers. The political ambiance of Hindu kingdoms therefore was not very different from that of Muslim kingdoms, in broad terms though not in detail. The primary concern of rajas, as of sultans, was for the preservation and expansion of their power, rather than for the welfare of their subjects, as they generally professed. As a medieval Indian saying had it,

> What matters it to us
> whether Rama reigns
> or Ravana reigns?

That was the reality. But kings, particularly rajas, generally professed commendably high ideals, which are fascinating in themselves, though they had little connection with political reality. Thus in a story told by Muhammad Ulfi, a fourteenth century chronicler, a Hindu raja asserts: 'It is the paramount duty of all those in whose hands authority and power are placed, to walk in the path of justice and benevolence, in order that those who are weak should be strengthened and protected by the law, and that those who are wealthy should enjoy their riches in peace and security.'

Similar professions were made by king Krishnadeva of Vijayanagar in his poetic opus *Amukta-malyada*. Pay particular attention to the welfare of your subjects, he counsels rajas; keep the company of sages and scholars; cultivate piety; avoid vices like womanising and gambling; ensure administrative efficiency and strictly supervise the work of officers; and maintain a strong army as well as an efficient spy network. Krishnadeva further directs kings to promote the prosperity of their kingdom by constructing irrigation networks to facilitate the expansion of agriculture, and by encouraging trade, particularly foreign trade. They are also advised to try to reform criminals, rather than punish them summarily, and that in any case their punishments should not be too harsh. Above all, kings should tend their kingdoms with devoted care, like a farmer tending his field with care, the raja advises.

ONE OF THE major reasons for the upheavals and instabilities in medieval Indian kingdoms, of Hindus as well as of Muslims, was that there were no well-defined and generally accepted rules of royal succession. The throne belonged to whoever could seize it. Contested royal succession was therefore the norm in India. And these contests were invariably marked by much brutality and bloodshed, even though the rivals were often brothers or other close relatives. Killing a father, brother, cousin or uncle for the throne was not considered a crime or a sin, but as a normal and legitimate action in royal politics. Kings were often murderers.

The career path of men in royal families was often from prison to throne or death, or from throne to prison or death. Those who ascended the throne by murdering its occupant, or their succession rivals, were themselves in turn often murdered by other aspirants for the throne. And nobles played an equally ignominious role in this vicious game; they usually had no enduring loyalty to anyone, and the usurper invariably won their support by scattering gold among them. Those who were obsequious towards a sultan one day, were equally obsequious towards his assassin-successor the next day. In India, as Mughal emperor Babur would later remark in his memoirs, 'there is . . . this peculiarity . . . that any person who kills the ruler and occupies the throne becomes the ruler himself. The amirs, viziers, soldiers and peasants submit to him at once and obey him.'

One reads with dismay about the pervasive political violence and criminality of the age. But these were not considered as deviant and condemnable conduct in that age; rather, they were widely accepted as the norm, and it is seldom that we hear any voice raised against such acts in the chronicles of the age.

In ancient Indian kingdoms there was a custom of kings in their old age handing over their power to a successor and leading a retired life, and this sometimes happened even in medieval times also. And in some dynasties—among the Pandyas, for instance—the king shared his power with his brothers. But there were hardly any instances of such practices in Muslim kingdoms. In the entire history of the Delhi Sultanate there is only one case of a sultan voluntarily, by his own will, giving up his throne—that was Alam Shah of the Sayyid dynasty, who relinquished his throne and moved to a small town well away from Delhi, where he lived for three full decades in contentment and tranquillity.

THE THRONE WAS no bed of roses. The sultan, for all his great power, led an ever-harried, perilous life. The sword of an enemy, or of a rebel or usurper, ever hung over his head. There were of course compensating rewards for taking these risks: the enjoyment of power itself—the highest of the highs that any political animal could aspire for—as well as the enjoyment of matchless luxuries, the very best that the contemporary world could provide. The sultans also found some diversion from the pressures of their life in various pastimes, particularly in hunting, which was the favourite means of relaxation for most sultans, as it had the excitement of a battle without its peril. The other common pastimes of the sultans were playing polo and horse-racing. Some sultans also enjoyed the pastimes of the common people. The favourite summer pastime of Sikandar Lodi, for instance, was fishing. According to Ni'matullah, an early seventeenth century chronicler, in summer the sultan often pitched his tents on the banks of the Yamuna, 'whither he retired in order to avoid the heat, and amuse himself with fishing . . . He [also] enjoyed himself in field sports.' And once when he was in Mathura, he travelled by boat on the Yamuna, 'amusing himself on the way with various kinds of sport.'

Several of the sultans were vain enough to build new cities and palaces of their own, named after themselves. Even Firuz Tughluq, a relatively modest sultan, built, according to Afif, a fourteenth-century chronicler, as many as 'thirty-six royal establishments, for which enormous supplies of articles were collected . . . [Some of these palaces were very large, with] elephant, horse, and camel stables, the kitchen, the butlery, the candle department, the dog-kennels, the water cooling department, and other similar establishments.'

The Delhi sultans normally, with rare exceptions, lived in a grand style in huge fortified palaces, and had vast domestic establishments to take care of their every need. In addition, the royal palaces were served by various ancillary establishments that met the diverse requirements of the sultan and his court. Muhammad Tughluq, for instance, employed 4000 silk weavers, who supplied the materials for making the great number of the robes of honour that the sultan needed for distributing to his favourites. In a related activity, he had 500 craftsmen working on gold embroidery. 'In the winter season six lakh tankas were expended on the [royal] wardrobe, besides the outlay for spring and summer,' notes Afif about Firuz Tughluq. There were similar expenditures in other departments also. The royal workshops also served the needs of the army.

The royal kitchen, like everything else associated with royalty, was a large and tightly organised establishment. 'The king has ten cooks for his personal service, and has others kept for times when he gives banquets; and these ten prepare the food for no one save for the king,' reports Fernao Nuniz, a sixteenth century Portuguese traveller, about the practice in Vijayanagar. 'He has a eunuch for guard at the gate of the kitchen, who never allows anyone to enter for fear of poison. When the king wishes to eat every person withdraws, and then come some of the women whose duty it is, and they prepare the table for him. They place for him a three-footed stool, round, made of gold, and on it put the messes. These are brought in large vessels of gold, and the smaller messes in basins of gold, some of which are adorned with precious stones.'

And all these palace-related services were supervised by a high-ranking official, Wakil-i-dar, through whom 'all orders were issued to the respective establishments', and salaries and allowances paid to the personal staff of the sultan.

A PRODIGAL AND EXTRAVAGANT lifestyle was considered indispensable for kings, to demonstrate their unique status in society. As Barani would comment, overweening pride, haughtiness and self-glorification were normal and essential qualities in monarchs. In the view of the eleventh-century Ghaznavid chronicler Baihaqi, it was essential for the sultan to have 'pomp, servants, officers of the state, lords of the sword and pen, countless armies, elephants and camels in abundance, [and] an overflowing treasury.' Similarly, according to Barani, nobles in Delhi held that 'two things were required in kings: firstly, princely expenditure and boundless liberality . . . and, secondly, dignity, awe and severity, by which enemies are repulsed and rebels put down . . .' The lifestyle of most of the Delhi sultans matched these prescriptions, and was indeed often extravagantly flamboyant.

One could not be a sultan and be self-effacing. This was the general view. But there were a few sultans in medieval India who were quite modest in their lifestyle. For instance, Jalal-ud-din, the late-thirteenth-century founder of the Khalji dynasty, was so unostentatious that his nobles scorned his conduct as unbecoming for a sultan. Even more modest was the lifestyle of the early fifteenth century Bahmani sultan Firuz Shah, even though he was one of the most adventurous and successful of the Bahmani sultans—he met his personal expenses by copying the Koran, and required the ladies of his harem to support themselves 'by embroidering garments and selling them.' There were a couple of other kings like them in medieval India. But these were truly exceptional cases.

In contrast to the generally ostentatious lifestyle of sultans, the traditional lifestyle of rajas was relatively simple. But in time many of the rajas adopted some of the Turko-Afghan royal practices. While most Hindu kings customarily held court sitting on a mat or carpet, or on a low stool or chair, during the medieval period many of them gradually took to sitting on opulent and elaborately bejewelled thrones in the style of the sultans. According to Abdur Razzak—who visited India in mid-fifteenth century as an envoy of Timur's son Shah Rukh—the throne of king Devaraya II of Vijayanagar 'was of an extraordinary size; it was made of gold, and was enriched with precious stones of extreme value . . . The king was seated in great state in the forty-pillared hall, and a great crowd of Brahmins and others stood on the right and left of him. He was clothed in a robe of green satin, and he had around his neck a collar composed of pure pearls of regal excellence, the value of which a jeweller would find difficult to calculate.' And when the raja travels 'not less than a hundred thousand warriors go with him,' states Barbosa, an early sixteenth century Portuguese traveller, rather exaggeratedly.

Unlike the opulence of the North Indian and Deccani kings, the lifestyle of the Dravidian kings of South India, particularly of the Chera kings of Kerala, was quite simple. Battuta, a fourteenth century Moorish traveller in India, saw the king of Kozhikode on the beach 'wearing a large white cloth round his waist and a small turban, barefooted, with a parasol carried by a slave over his head and a fire lit in front of him.' According to Barbosa, when the king of Kerala travels, he 'comes forth in his litter borne by two men, which is lined with silken cushions . . . [The litter] is hung on a bamboo pole covered with precious stones.' The bearers of the litter run at a jog-trot pace, all the while humming and grunting 'in a curious antiphonic manner.' Barbosa also notes the curious Kerala custom in which, when a raja dies and has been cremated, all the members of the royal family 'shave themselves from the crown of the head to the soles of the feet, saving only their eyelashes and eyebrows. This they do from the prince to the least heir of the kingdom.'

A commendable attribute of the early medieval Indian rulers, of sultans as well as rajas, in Delhi as well as elsewhere, is that many of them were keen and knowledgeable patrons of art, literature and learning, and some of them were distinguished scholars and writers themselves. But erudition in itself made little difference in the performance of a ruler; it was only his pragmatism, as well as his administrative and military capabilities, that really mattered. Muhammad Tughluq was probably the most erudite of the Delhi sultans, but he was a pathetic failure as a ruler; on the other hand, Ala-ud-din Khalji was illiterate, but was the most successful of the Delhi sultans.

MOST OF THE medieval Indian sultans and rajas were polygamous; they had several wives, and in addition maintained huge harems, as befitting their Olympian stature and lifestyle. This was mainly for pomp, but partly also for pleasure. Yet another reason for a king to have a large number of wives was for him to beget many children, to ensure that he would have enough sons to survive him in the perilous political environment of the age, so that his dynasty may endure.

Islamic convention allowed only four lawful wives to a man, whatever be his status, but among Hindus there was no such restriction. Achyutadeva-raya, the king of Vijayanagar, according to a probably exaggerated account of Nuniz, had as many as 500 wives. 'And when he journeys to any place he takes with him twenty-five or thirty of his most favourite wives . . . each one in her palanquin with poles. The palanquin of the principal wife is all covered with scarlet cloth tasselled with large and heavy work in seed-pearls and pearls, and the pole itself is ornamented with gold.' More credible is what Domingos Paes, an early sixteenth-century Portuguese traveller, says about Krishnadeva. 'This king,' he reports, 'has twelve lawful wives, of whom there are three principal ones . . . [The three] are in all respects treated and provided for equally,] so that there may never be any discord or ill feeling between them. All of them are great friends, and each one lives by herself . . . The king [too] lives by himself inside the palace, and when he wishes to have with him one of his wives, he orders a eunuch to go and call her.'

The queens of Vijayanagar, particularly the three chief queens, were sumptuously provided with all luxuries. 'Each one of these wives has her house to herself, with her maidens and women of the chamber, and women guards, and all other women servants necessary; all these are women, and no man enters where they are, save only the eunuchs, who guard them,' continues Paes. 'These women are never seen by any man except perhaps by some old man of high rank by favour of the king. When they wish to go out they are carried in litters shut up and closed, so that they cannot be seen.'

This evidently was a practice that spread to the Hindu royal families under Turko-Afghan influence, for previously there was no such seclusion of the royal women in Hindu kingdoms. 'Most of the princes of India, when they hold court allow their women to be seen by the men who attend it, whether they be natives or foreigners,' writes Abu Zaid, an early medieval Arab historian. 'No veil conceals them from the eyes of the visitors.' However, whether the royal women remained in the zenana and behind the veil, or appeared openly in public, they usually played an important role in public affairs, through their influence on kings.

Apart from the queens, a large number of women, including several foreigners, lived in the royal harem. Some of them served as royal concubines— there was no restriction on the number of concubines a raja or a sultan could have—while the others provided various routine services in the palace. All the king's female relatives, such as his mother, unmarried aunts, sisters and daughters, as well as his young sons, lived in the harem. His adult sons lived apart. There were also several female entertainers in the harem. According to Nuniz, the raja of Vijayanagar had 'within his gates more than 4000 women, all of whom live in the palace; some are dancing girls, and others are bearers . . . He has also women who wrestle, and others who are astrologers and soothsayers; and he has women who write all the accounts of expenses that are incurred inside the gates, and others whose duty it is to write all the affairs of the kingdom . . . He has women also for music, who play instruments and sing. Even the wives of the king are well versed in music.' Paes reports that Krishnadeva had 12,000 women in his harem, some of whom 'handle sword and shield, others wrestle, and yet others blow trumpets and others pipes, and [various] other instruments . . . [There were also there] women bearers and washing-folk . . .' The sultans too maintained huge harems. Portuguese sources report that sultan Ghiyas-ud-din Mahmud Shah of the mid-sixteenth century Bengal, had 10,000 women in his harem.

THE APPEARANCE AND lifestyle of some of the medieval Indian kings were odd beyond belief. Such was the case of Sultan Mahmud Shah Begarha of Gujarat. 'The said sultan has mustachios under his nose so long that he ties them over his head as a woman would tie her tresses, and he has a white beard which reaches to his girdle,' writes the early sixteenth-century Italian traveller Varthema, who was in Gujarat during Begarha's reign. 'Every day he eats poison. Do not, however, imagine that he fills his stomach with it; but he eats a certain quantity, so that when he wishes to destroy any great personage he makes him come before him stripped and naked, [and he spits on him the juice of the various fruits and leaves he has masticated, so that, because of the highly poisonous quality of spittle,] the man falls dead to the ground in the space of half an hour.

'This sultan has also three or four thousand women [in his harem], and every night he sleeps with one, and she is found dead in the morning. Every time that he takes off his shirt, that shirt is never again touched by any one; and so also his other garments; and every day he chooses new garments . . . [The sultan could consume poison daily, because] his father had fed him upon poison from his childhood.' This portrait, bizarre though it might seem, is at least partly confirmed by Barbosa, who visited Gujarat around this time. 'I have heard that he was brought up from childhood to take poison, for his father, fearing that, in accordance with the usage of the country, he might be killed by that means, took this precaution against such a catastrophe,' writes Barbosa. 'He began to make him eat of it in small doses, gradually increasing them, until he could take a large quantity, whereby he became so poisonous, that if a fly lighted on his hand, it swelled and died at once, and many of the women with whom he slept died from the same cause.'

Begarha had other strange practices too. 'In the morning, when he rises, there come to his palace fifty elephants, on each of which a man sits astride; and the said elephants do reverence to the sultan, and they have nothing else to do,' reports Varthema. 'And when he eats, fifty or sixty kinds of [musical] instruments play, namely, trumpets, drums of several sorts, and flageolets, and fifes, with many others, which for the sake of brevity I forbear mentioning. When the sultan eats, the said elephants again do reverence to him.' Curiously, the raja of Vijayanagar also had a custom of being greeted by an elephant in the morning. 'The king has a white elephant, exceedingly large,' reports Razzak, 'Every morning this animal is brought into the presence of the monarch, for to cast eye upon him is thought a favourable omen.'

IN CONTRAST TO the rigid and grandiose formality of the court customs of most kings of the middle and late Sultanate period, court customs in the early Sultanate period were quite simple. But they became rigidly formal during the reign of Balban, who had a very lofty concept of kingship and considered it an imperative practical necessity, for good governance, to elevate the sultan to a status far above the nobles, and thus create an unbridgeable psychological distance between him and the nobles, so that royal diktats would be unquestioningly obeyed by all. Balban therefore enforced in Delhi a court etiquette somewhat similar to that of the pre-Islamic Sassanian monarchy of Persia, such as requiring courtiers to prostrate before the sultan, and kiss his throne or his feet.

To match his exalted concept of kingship, Balban always maintained a sternly regal demeanour in public, and took every care to be impeccably ceremonious in all he did. And he demanded that his courtiers also should behave becomingly in his presence. He permitted absolutely no frivolity, even loud laughter, in the court. The later sultans were not quite as stern as Balban, but most of them did maintain a fair amount of formality in the court. The only sultan who notably relaxed the court practices was Khizr Khan, the founder of the Sayyid dynasty, who reverted to the simplicity and camaraderie in the relationship between the courtiers and the sultan that had existed in the early Sultanate period.

There was usually a master of the ceremonies at the court, to regulate the people who entered the court and to ensure that proper order was maintained there, and that all observed the formalities required of them. All strangers presenting themselves to the sultan were required to make an offering to him as a homage. 'No stranger admitted to court can avoid offering a present [to the sultan] as a kind of introduction, which the sultan repays by one of much greater value,' states Battuta. And the sultan when he wanted to honour a courtier or a visitor invested him with a *khilat*, a ceremonial robe.

Court etiquette was fairly elaborate in Vijayanagar also. There, as Paes notes, those attending the court, 'as soon as they enter make their salaam to him (the raja), and place themselves along the wall far off from him. They do not speak to one another, nor do they chew betel before him, but they place their hands in the sleeves of their tunics and cast their eyes on the ground. And if the king desires to speak to anyone, it is done through a second person ... The salaam, which is the greatest courtesy that exists among them, is that they put their hands joined above their head as high as they can.' And all men respectfully removed their footwear before entering the royal court.

Most courtiers were servile sycophants, and were obsequious towards the king, and they passively conformed to the abject subservience required of them in the royal court, for their career depended on the whim and pleasure of the sultan. It was very rarely that anyone spoke out in the court; usually when the king asked his nobles for some advice, they in turn asked him what was in his mind, and they generally agreed with whatever he suggested.

THE CUSTOMS AND practices observed in the Delhi court are described in detail by Battuta. 'The sultan's palace in Delhi is called Dar Sara, and has many doors. At the first door there are a number of guards ... trumpeters and flute-players,' states Battuta. 'When any amir or person of note arrives, they sound their instruments and announce, "So-and-so has come! So-and-so has come!" The same takes place also at the second and third doors.

'Outside the first door are platforms on which executioners sit, for the custom amongst them is that when the sultan orders a man to be executed, the sentence is carried out at the door of the audience hall, and the body lies there for three nights.

'Between the first and second doors there is a large vestibule with platforms along both sides, on which sit those whose turn of duty it is to guard the doors. Between the second and third doors there is a large platform on which the principal *naqib* (chief usher) sits . . . [He holds a gold mace in his hand] and on his head he wears a jewelled tiara of gold, surmounted by peacock feathers. The second door leads to an extensive audience hall in which the people sit.

'At the third door there are platforms occupied by scribes . . . One of their customs is that none may pass through this door except those whom the sultan has authorized, and for each such person he assigns a number of his staff to enter [the court] along with him. Whenever any person comes to this door the scribes write down "So-and-so came at the first hour", or the second [hour], and so on, and the sultan receives a report of this after the evening prayer. Another of their customs is that anyone who absents himself from the palace for three days or more, with or without excuse, may not enter this door thereafter except by the sultan's permission. If he has an excuse of illness or otherwise, he presents the sultan with a gift suitable to his rank. The third door opens into an immense audience hall called Hazar Uslun, which means "a thousand pillars". The pillars are of wood and support a wooden roof, admirably carved. The people sit under this, and it is in this hall that the sultan holds public audiences.' According to Nikitin, a Russian traveller in India in the fifteenth century, 'the sultan's palace has seven gates, and at each gate are seated 100 guards and 100 Muhammadan scribes, who enter the names of all persons going in and out.'

IT WAS AN indispensable duty of the sultan to hold a durbar every day, sometimes even twice a day, morning and afternoon. 'As a rule his audiences are held in the afternoon, though he often holds them early in the day [also],' reports Battuta about the practice of Muhammad Tughluq. 'He sits cross-legged on a throne placed on a dais carpeted in white, with a large cushion behind him and two other as armrests, on his right and left. When he takes his seat, the vizier stands in front of him, the secretaries behind the vizier, then the chamberlains, and so on in the order of precedence. As the sultan sits down the chamberlains and *naqibs* say in their loudest voice: *Bismillah!*

'[Behind the sultan stands a man] with a fly-whisk in his hand to drive off flies. A hundred armour-bearers stand on his right, and a like number on his left, carrying shields, swords, and bows. The other functionaries and notables stand along the hall to the right and the left. Then they bring in sixty horses with royal harness, half of which are arranged on the right and half on the left, where the sultan can see them. Next fifty elephants are brought in, which are adorned with silken cloths, and have their tusks shod with iron for greater efficacy in killing criminals. On the neck of each elephant sits its mahout, who carries a sort of iron axe with which he punishes it and directs it to do what is required of it. Each elephant has on its back a sort of large chest capable of holding twenty warriors or more or less, according to the size of the beast.

'These elephants are trained to make obeisance to the sultan and incline their heads, and when they do so the chamberlains cry in a loud voice: *Bismillah!* The elephants are also arranged half on the right and half on the left, behind the persons standing. As each person enters . . . he makes an obeisance on reaching the station of the chamberlains, and the chamberlains say *Bismillah*, regulating the loudness of their utterance to the rank of the person concerned; he then goes to his appointed place, beyond which he never passes. If it is one of the infidel Hindus who makes obeisance, the chamberlains say to him, "May god guide thee".

'If there should be anyone at the door who has come to offer the sultan a gift, the chamberlains enter the sultan's presence in their order of precedence, make obeisance in three places, and inform the sultan of the person at the door. If he commands them to bring him in, they place the gift in the hands of the men who stand . . . in front of the sultan, so he can see it. He then calls in the donor, who makes obeisance three times before reaching the sultan and makes another obeisance at the station of the chamberlains. The sultan then addresses him in person with the greatest courtesy and bids him welcome. If he is a person who is worthy of honour, the sultan takes him by the hand or embraces him, and asks for some part of his present. It is then placed before him, and if it consists of a weapon or fabric he turns it this way and that with his hand and expresses his approval, to set the donor at ease and encourage him. He then gives him a robe of honour and assigns him a sum of money . . . proportionate to his merit.'

Similar formalities were observed when the sultan went on tour, and great precautions were taken for his safety—he was, in the case of Balban, always accompanied by a commando force of 1000 soldiers. And the return of the sultan to the capital was invariably a grand celebratory occasion. 'When the sultan returns from a journey, the elephants are decorated, and on sixteen of them are placed sixteen parasols, some brocaded and some set with jewels,' continues Battuta. 'Wooden pavilions are built several storeys high and covered with silk cloths, and in each story there are singing girls wearing magnificent dresses and ornaments, with dancing girls amongst them. At the centre of each pavilion is a large tank made of skins and filled with syrup-water, from which all the people, natives or strangers, may drink, receiving at the same time betel leaves and areca nuts. The space between the pavilions is carpeted with silk cloths, on which the sultan's horse treads. The walls of the street along which he passes from the gate of the city to the gate of the palace are hung with silk cloths. In front of him march footmen from his own slaves, several thousands in number, and behind him come the mob and soldiers. On one of his entries into the capital I saw three or four small catapults placed on elephants throwing gold and silver coins amongst the people from the moment he entered the city till he reached the palace.'

The Bahmani sultans also maintained a grand style when they appeared in public. 'The Sultan, riding on a golden saddle, wears a habit embroidered with sapphires, and on his pointed headdress a large diamond,' notes Nikitin. 'He also carries a suit of gold armour inlaid with sapphires, and three swords mounted in gold.' The sultan's way through the crowd was cleared for him by a huge armoured elephant. And the sultan was accompanied by a large troupe of armoured soldiers, as well as by several hundred women singers and dancers. The rear of the procession was made up of 300 armoured elephants, each of which held heavy chains in its trunk, and carried several soldiers on a platform fitted to its back. Similar pomp was displayed by the rajas of Vijayanagar also when they appeared in public. The horse on which the raja rode, according to Varthema, was 'worth more than some of our cities on account of the ornaments which it wears.'

2

By the King, For the King

The Delhi Sultanate, at the peak of its territorial expansion during the reign of Muhammad Tughluq, was the largest empire in the history of India in the two-millennium-long period between the Mauryan empire at its zenith under Asoka in the mid-third century BCE and the Mughal empire at its zenith under Aurangzeb in the late seventeenth century CE, and it covered virtually the entire Indian subcontinent, except Kerala in the far south, Kashmir in the far north, and a few pockets here and there in between.

But bulk did not mean stability. Or even strength. The Delhi Sultanate was in fact the least stable of all the great empires in Indian history, and was ever roiling with rebellions and usurpations. Nor did it have the administrative capacity needed to effectively govern its vast and diverse realm. The only notable exception to this dismal state of affairs was the reign of Ala-ud-din Khalji, whose empire was extensive, and his government administratively and militarily strong.

Waging wars was the primary occupation of medieval Indian sultans and rajas, to suppress rebellions, to defend or expand their kingdom, and to seize plunder. Civil administration, except revenue collection, had only a low priority for most of them. With very rare exceptions, providing good government and caring for the welfare of the people hardly concerned the sultans or the rajas.

Most kings in medieval India were just warlords. In the entire history of the Delhi Sultanate, there were no notable periods of stability and peace, except for a time during the reigns of Ala-ud-din Khalji and Firuz Tughluq. Normal life in the Delhi Sultanate was hardly normal. Everything there was ever in a turbulent state, ever seething with violence. This was true of all political relationships in the Sultanate, such as the relationship between the sultan and his nobles and provincial governors, between the sultan and the Hindu chieftains, even between the sultan and his family members. Anyone at any time could be anyone's adversary. No loyalty could be ever taken for granted.

The government of the Delhi Sultanate was a minimum government. The sultans occupied the realm, but hardly governed it. Brigands and wild hill tribes often rampaged through the land, swooping down from their inaccessible forest habitats. At times they even menaced major towns. Protection against them was mainly the concern of the local people, seldom that of the sultan. And when the sultan acted against brigands, it was mainly to safeguard his revenue, hardly ever to protect the people. Indeed, the sultans themselves at times acted like brigands, pillaging their own subjects, to collect the overdue taxes from them. And at times even common villagers turned into rampaging brigands.

The usual means of the Delhi sultans to pacify their refractory subjects was to devastate their lands and slaughter the people there en-masse. In the case of Vijayanagar, even its most successful king, Krishnadeva, found it difficult to control the depredations of marauding hill tribes. So he sought to placate them, or to divert their raids into other kingdoms, holding that, as he wrote in *Amukta-malyada*, 'if the king grows angry with them, he cannot wholly destroy them, but if he wins their affection by kindness and charity, they serve him by invading the enemy's territory and plundering it.'

MEDIEVAL INDIAN STATES had no fixed frontiers—their frontiers were what their army controlled at any given time. So the territory of the state varied from reign to reign, and even from time to time during the reign of each sultan or raja. And the control of the central government over the provinces of the kingdom also varied from reign to reign. The sultans and the rajas usually kept a certain portion of their kingdom, its richest districts, under their direct administration. The rest of the kingdom was divided into provinces, and given to royal favourites to govern and collect revenue.

During the reign of Ala-ud-din Khalji the Delhi Sultanate was divided into twelve provinces (subas), each under a governor. Each province in turn was divided into a number of districts (sarkars), and the districts again into taluks (parganas). Each taluk was made up of a number of villages, which were the basic administrative units of the state all through pre-modern history of India. Villages were virtually autonomous, and royal officers did not normally intrude into their affairs as long they paid their revenue dues to the king, and did not create any major law and order problem, like breaking out into rebellion or taking to brigandage.

The other divisions of the state—provinces, districts and taluks—also, like villages, enjoyed considerable autonomy in medieval India, in Muslim as well as Hindu kingdoms. Provinces were in fact semi-independent states, and provincial governors functioned like semi-independent rulers, except that the king exercised hegemonic control over them. In Vijayanagar, as Sewell notes, each provincial chief 'was allowed entire independence in the territory allotted to him so long as he maintained the quota of horse, foot, and elephants . . . [assigned to him, and kept them] in perfect readiness for immediate action, and paid his annual tribute to his sovereign. Failing these he was liable to instant ejection, as the king was lord of all and nobles held [their office] only by his goodwill.'

The ultimate authority in the Sultanate in all matters was the sultan. In theory he was expected to rule according orthodox Islamic laws and conventions, but in practice he was usually an autocrat, who did whatever he pleased and could get away with. Autocracy did not however necessarily mean tyranny. Though several of the sultans were indeed dreadful tyrants, there were also several sultans who were benevolent rulers. And some of the tyrannical sultans—Ala-ud-din, for instance—were exceptionally caring about the welfare of the common people.

Next to the sultan in authority was the wazir, chief minister. The entire civil administration of the empire was under his purview, and it was he who appointed all the top civil servants and oversaw their work. The management of the finances of the empire—the collection of revenue and the allocation of funds to various government departments—was his particular responsibility. He also had the responsibility of getting the accounts submitted by various government departments and provinces audited, and of taking measures to recover from officers the funds they had misappropriated or squandered. And it was he who disbursed funds to deserving scholars and writers, and sanctioned charitable payments to the indigent. The responsibilities and powers of the wazir were so wide and important that his role in the state was held to be as crucial for its survival as the role of the soul for the survival of a man.

Alongside the wazir there were three other senior ministers in the Delhi Sultanate, each in charge of a crucial government department: Diwan-i-risalat, which administered religious institutions and allotted financial support to the pious and the scholarly; Diwan-i-arz, which controlled the military establishment; and Diwan-i-insha, which handled the state correspondence, collected intelligence reports from the various provinces of the empire, and supervised the transactions between the central government and the provincial officials. These three officers, along with the wazir, were considered the four pillars of the government.

These officers, like all the other top officers of the state, held their posts at the pleasure of the sultan. So what mattered most to them, in terms of their career prospects, was their ability to please the sultan, rather than their ability to discharge their official duties efficiently. And no one was ever secure in his office, his position being subject to the whims of the sultan as well as the conspiratorial intrigues of rival officers. Inevitably, it was the most earnest and efficient officers who were in the greatest peril, as they most roused the envy of their fellow officers.

IN THE EARLY period of the Delhi Sultanate, till the reign of Balban, the relationship of the nobles with the sultan was of camaraderie than of subservience. Balban changed that, and raised the status of the sultan far above that of the nobles. Consequently most of the nobles became abjectly servile towards the sultan, though there were still a few rare instances of royal officers boldly asserting themselves before the sultan. Such was the case of Ainu-l Mulk, 'a wise, accomplished . . . [and] clever man,' as Afif describes him. He held a senior position in the government under Firuz Tughluq, but had a personality clash with the wazir and was therefore dismissed from service. However, a few days later, the sultan, unwilling to lose the services of this able officer, assigned to him the charge of three fiefs along the critically important north-west frontier of the empire. But Ainu-l Mulk submitted that he would accept the appointment only if he was allowed to submit his reports directly to the sultan, and not through the wazir, and he took charge of the assignment only when the sultan acceded to that condition.

That was an exceptional case. The normal attitude of the nobles towards the sultan was of obsequiousness, and this was evident even in the manner in which provincial governors formally received royal orders. 'It was the custom for every chief when he heard of the coming of a royal order to go out two or three kos to meet its bearer,' records Abdullah, a late medieval chronicler, about the practice in the Sultanate during the reign of Sikandar Lodi. 'A terrace was then erected, on which the messenger placed himself, whilst the nobleman standing beneath received the firman in the most respectful manner with both hands, and placed it on his head . . . If it was to be read privately he did so, and if it was to be made known to the people, it was read from the pulpit of the mosque.'

Such shows of servility by the nobles were however just pretences in most cases—if the sultan grew weak, or the noble grew powerful, the noble's attitude towards the sultan changed from servility to defiance. Provincial insubordination and rebellion were in fact perennial problems in the Delhi Sultanate.

The provincial governments of the Delhi Sultanate were virtual replicas of its central government, with the governor in the provincial capital occupying a position similar to that of the sultan in Delhi. The main duties of the governor were to collect revenue from his province, and to maintain law and order there. From the revenue of his province the governor had to remit a specified portion to the royal treasury, and with the rest of the revenue meet his administrative expenses, maintain a military contingent for the sultan, and also meet his personal expenses. The provincial governor in turn farmed out his territory to his subordinates, to administer and to collect revenue.

A BAFFLING FEATURE of the Delhi Sultanate was the open and rampant corruption in its government at all levels, from the highest to the lowest. 'It was well known in the world that government clerks and servants were given to peculation,' states Afif. And they often indulged in venality right under the sultan's nose. 'It usually happens that there is a long delay in the payment of the money gifts of the sultan,' grouses Battuta, who once had to wait for six months before receiving the twelve thousand dinars awarded to him by Muhammad Tughluq. 'They have a custom also of deducting a tenth from all the sums given by the sultan.' Once when the sultan sanctioned a payment to Battuta and ordered the treasurer to pay it, 'the treasurer greedily demanded a bribe for doing so and would not write the order,' states Battuta. 'So I sent him two hundred tankas (silver coins), but he returned them. One of his servants told me from him that he wanted five hundred tankas, but I refused to pay it.' Eventually the sultan had to intervene before the money was paid to Battuta.

Provincial governors and other high government officials, even the sultan himself, were not above seeking recompense for doing favours, the only difference being that in their case the offerings were treated as presents, not as bribes. Also, with them it was the rarity of the items offered, and the sentiment behind the offering, that were esteemed more than the cash value of what was offered. Thus when Battuta first arrived in India he presented to the governor of Sind 'a white slave, a horse, and some raisins and almonds.' Of these, what the governor appreciated most were the raisins and almonds. 'These,' comments Battuta, 'are among the greatest gifts that can be made to them, since these do not grow in their land and are imported from Khurasan.'

Another aspect of the medieval Indian custom of giving presents was that just as subordinates gave presents to their superiors to win favours from them, superiors often gave presents to their subordinates to secure their loyalty. This was done even by the sultans. Loyalty was invariably on sale in medieval India. All were equally perfidious, at all levels of government and society. Probity was a luxury that virtually no one in medieval India could afford, neither kings nor nobles, nor the common people. Thus Ala-ud-din Khalji, who usurped the throne by murdering his uncle, had no difficulty in winning over to his side the top officers of the empire by liberally presenting to them large sums of money. And 'those unworthy men, greedy for gold . . . and caring nothing for loyalty . . . joined Ala-ud-din,' observes Barani. Similarly, Ala-ud-din won over the common people of Delhi by showering gold stars on them with a portable catapult. 'He scattered so much gold that the faithless people easily forgot the murder of the late sultan, and rejoiced over his succession,' concludes Barani. And, according to Mughal chronicler Yadgar, Sultan Ibrahim Lodi, who faced opposition from a brother on his accession, one day 'summoned all the nobles into his private apartment and gained them to his side by making them presents in gold, and giving them titles and dignities.'

THE ATTITUDE OF the sultans towards their nobles during most of the Delhi Sultanate history was a bizarre mixture of two contrary modes, tyrannical as well as complaisant. The scene was however quite different in the first phase of the history of the Sultanate, for at that time there was no great difference in the status of the sultan and of the nobles, and the relationship between them was like that of comrades, rather than that of a king and his subjects, as it became later. This amity was in part because of the egalitarian ethos of early Islam, and also because the early sultans of Delhi were, like several of their top officers, manumitted slaves or their descendants.

In early Islamic society it was no disgrace or handicap for one to be a slave, for slaves could rise to any position—including that of the sultan—that they merited by their abilities. Though hardly anyone initially became a slave by choice, and most of them had been sold into slavery as children, or were captured and enslaved by marauders or conquerors, many slaves rose to high positions by their ability, dedication and hard work.

Many slaves no doubt led degrading lives, but being a slave was not in itself a disability or disgrace in early medieval Muslim society. There was no social or political prejudice against slaves as a class. Indeed, to be the favourite slave of a monarch or a high noble was a great advantage for a careerist, for that opened up major avenues for professional advancement for him, and several such slaves rose to be top officers in the Delhi Sultanate. Some nobles, even some sultans, honoured their favourite slaves by giving their daughters in marriage to them. Indeed, being a royal slave was a high honour and distinction, and three of them—Aibak, Iltutmish and Balban—succeeded their masters to the throne.

Another curious feature of the Delhi Sultanate was that the sultans generally preferred to appoint foreign migrants—Arabs, Turks and Persians—to top administrative and military posts in their government, reflecting their disdain for native Indians. And they usually treated foreign visitors with high regard. 'It is a custom of the sultan of India . . . to honour strangers, to favour them, and to distinguish them in a manner quite peculiar, by appointing them to . . . [high government posts],' records Battuta about what he observed in Delhi in the fourteenth century. 'Most of his (sultan's) courtiers, chamberlains, wazirs, magistrates, and brothers-in-law are foreigners.' Battuta himself, a Moorish adventurer, was appointed by Muhammad Tughluq as a judge in Delhi on a high salary of 12,000 dinars a year. And when he left to continue his travels, he was designated as the royal ambassador to China.

This partiality of the sultans for foreigners sometimes led to tension between foreign and native officials, and, in the case of Bahmani Sultanate, it even led to a few gory riots. However, despite the bias of the sultans in favour foreign migrants, paths for the advancement of talented natives remained open in Muslim kingdoms, and several Hindu converts to Islam rose to high positions in those states over time. The prominence gained by Raihan, a mid-thirteenth century Hindu convert to Islam, who became powerful enough in royal service even to overshadow Balban, the then topmost royal officer in the Delhi Sultanate, was indicative of the growing prominence of Indian Muslims in government. From the reign of Khaljis on the number and importance Indian Muslims in government increased considerably. This was partly because of the proven ability of the Indian Muslim officers, like Malik Kafur under Ala-ud-din Khalji, and partly because their appointment to high offices had become a practical necessity for the sultans from the thirteenth century on, because the interposition of Mongols between India and the Turko-Persian homelands drastically reduced the migration of foreign Muslims into India.

One of the most remarkable of the Indian Muslim officers of the Delhi Sultanate was Khan-i Jahan Maqbul, a Hindu convert from Telingana, who, though illiterate, rose to the highest position in the Sultanate by his sheer ability. He joined the service of the Sultanate during the reign of Muhammad Tughluq who, recognising his merit, raised him rapidly in official positions, and finally appointed him as the deputy wazir. 'Although he had no knowledge of reading and writing, he was a man of great common sense, acumen and intelligence, and was an ornament of the court,' reports Afif. Firuz Tughluq appointed Maqbul as his wazir, and left him as his deputy in Delhi whenever he set out on military campaigns.

Maqbul was in every respect a most extraordinary person—his physical prowess matched his mental prowess, and so did his sexual prowess. 'He was,' according to Afif, 'much devoted to the pleasures of the harem, and sought eagerly for pretty handmaids. It is reported that he had 2000 women of Europe and China in his harem, where he spent much of his time notwithstanding his onerous official duties,' and he fathered a great many children. And to cap it all, Maqbul lived in so grand a style that Firuz Tughluq was often heard jocularly remarking that Maqbul was indeed 'the grand and magnificent king of Delhi.'

APART FROM THE Hindu converts to Islam, Hindus themselves also played vital roles in the affairs of the Delhi Sultanate. Right from the beginning of the Sultanate, in fact even from the time of Mahmud Ghazni, several Hindu chieftains served as captains in the armies of Muslim kings, and they sometimes played crucial roles in the campaigns of sultans, leading their own contingents into battle. And a good number of the common soldiers in the armies of the sultans in India were Hindus.

In civil administration, the preponderant majority of the staff of the Delhi Sultanate, at all but the top one or two levels, were Hindus, particularly in the provinces. The sultans did not have the manpower from their own people to man the entire administration, or even to man all the crucial offices of their extensive Indian empire with its vast and diverse population. Nor did they have the local knowledge needed to run the local administration. They therefore necessarily had to depend heavily on Hindus to run the government.

At the district and village levels the administration in Muslim states was almost entirely manned by Hindus, and there the traditional indigenous administrative institutions and hereditary officers generally—except during the reign of Ala-ud-din Khalji—continued to function as they had done for centuries before the Muslim invasion. This was particularly true of village administration. Villages were virtually autonomous during the medieval period, as they had been for very many centuries. The government of the sultans did not normally intrude into village administration at all, except for revenue collection and for the maintenance of law and order. But even in these functions, Muslim officers and fief-holders generally played only a supervisory role, for villages policed themselves in normal times, and revenue collection was mostly managed by the traditional local functionaries.

In a very real sense, it was Hindus who ran the government in Muslim kingdoms. What Dubois said of India in the early nineteenth century—that 'the rule of all the Hindu princes, and often that of the Mahomedans, was properly speaking, Brahminical rule, since all posts of confidence were held by Brahmins'—was substantially true of the early medieval period as well. The rule of the sultans was sustained—indeed, was made possible—by the service of Hindu officers and staff.

The majority of Hindu officers in the service of Muslim kings were in subordinate positions. There were however a few notable exceptions to this, of Hindu officers rising to the top echelons of government in Muslim states. For instance, in the early sixteenth century Hindus held several top positions in the Muslim kingdom of Malwa, and one of them, Basanta Rai, even rose to be the wazir. This dominance of the Hindus in the government led to a conflict between the Hindu and Muslim officers of the state, resulting in the murder of Basanta Rai. But presently another Hindu officer, Medini Rai, rose to dominance in the state, and he grew so powerful and overweening that the sultan himself was forced to flee from the state and take refuge in Gujarat. Similarly, the *de facto* ruler of Bengal in the early fifteenth century was a

Hindu officer named Ganesa; his son, who became a Muslim, even ascended the throne of Bengal.

The appointment of Hindus to high official positions was fairly common in the Deccan sultanates at this time—Bahmani sultan Firuz Shah, for instance, appointed several Brahmins and other Hindus to crucial offices in his government. Generally speaking, the establishment of the Turko-Afghan rule made no significant difference in the lives and functions of most Hindu officials from what they had been before the Muslim invasion.

NOR DID THE life of the common folk in India change in any notable way consequent of the displacement of rajas by sultans. This was partly because the Sultanate did not have the administrative capacity or the manpower needed to intrude in any significant manner into rural India, where most Indians lived, and partly also because the rajas were nearly as exploitative of the common people as the sultans were. It was mainly the Hindu political elite who suffered loss—the loss of power and prestige and wealth—because of the Turko-Afghan invasion.

And what the Hindu political elite lost was gained by the Muslim political elite—the gain of power and prestige and wealth. The top Turko-Afghan officers of the Sultanate were paid fabulous salaries; in fact, what they received were not just salaries, but what amounted to be shares in the revenues of the empire. The wazir under Firuz Tughluq, for instance, received, 'exclusive of the allowance for his retainers, friends and sons . . . a sum of thirteen lakh tankas—or, instead of it, sundry fiefs and districts,' states Afif. Not surprisingly, when Malik Shahin Shahna, a senior officer of the Sultanate, died and his effects were examined by royal auditors, it was found that he had accumulated 'a sum of fifty lakh of tankas in cash . . . besides horses, valuables, and jewels in abundance.'

The normal practice of most Delhi sultans was to assign to their officers, and sometimes even to the soldiers of their central army, lands in lieu of cash salaries, lands from which they could collect taxes. This reinforces the impression that the sultan was not merely paying salaries to his officers, but sharing the revenues of the empire with them. This practice also had a major advantage for kings, in that it considerably reduced the tax collection burden of their rudimentary administrative organisation.

Under this system, soldiers were usually assigned villages, while officers received districts, or even provinces, depending on their rank. The principal assignees in turn often sub-assigned parts of their territory to their subordinates, on terms similar to those on which they received their assignments from the sultan. In all these cases what was given to the assignees was only the revenue from the allotted land, not the land itself. The assignee had no hereditary ownership right over the land. Besides, the land assignments were transferable, and were usually reassigned every four years or so, so that the assignees did not get rooted in their jagirs and turn themselves into zamindars. The land revenue assignment system, termed *iqta*, therefore did not lead to feudalism.

The *iqta* system was a highly inefficient system of revenue administration, and it led to a great deal of corruption, as well as to the exploitation of peasants by the assignees. But it was the only workable system in most medieval Indian kingdoms, because of their poor administrative capability. Even Ala-ud-din, who sought strict administrative control over his empire, had to retain the *iqta* system in the provinces, even though he abolished it in his central army, whose soldiers and officers were paid in cash directly from the royal treasury. Muhammad Tughluq also sought to tightly control *iqta* assignments, but his successor Firuz reverted to the old practice of general *iqta* assignments. In Vijayanagar land assignments to Nayaks (chieftains) was the common practice; there were, according to Nuniz, over 200 such assignments in the kingdom.

THE REVENUE AND military departments were the most important departments of the Delhi Sultanate, as in any medieval state. These were interdependent departments—there could be no army without revenue, and quite often the army was needed to enforce revenue collection. And just as the sultans maintained a large army, so also they maintained a large finance department with numerous accountants, to keep track of the state's income and expenditure. The accounts submitted by the officers of the fiefs were regularly audited by this department; similarly the accounts of the various royal establishments were also regularly audited.

There were four legitimate sources of revenue for the sultan, sanctioned by Sharia: tax on agricultural produce, poll tax on non-Muslims, income tax on Muslims, and war booty. Of these, the primary source of revenue of the Delhi Sultanate, as of all medieval Indian states, was agricultural tax. The sultans also received a good amount of income from the produce of the crown lands, the *khalisa*, which was remitted directly into the royal treasury. All the lands of the empire other than the crown lands were assigned to royal officers as *iqta* lands, from the revenue of which they were to take their salary, meet their administrative expenses, and maintain the military contingents assigned to them.

In addition to the four revenue sources sanctioned by Islam, most Muslim kingdoms also collected a variety of minor taxes, which varied from kingdom to kingdom, even from ruler to ruler. Many of these additional taxes were in violation of Islamic regulations, and were therefore abolished by Firuz Tughluq.

Hindu kingdoms also collected a wide variety of taxes in addition to agricultural tax; they indeed generally collected a far wider variety of taxes than Muslim kingdoms, such as tax on forest produce, customs duties, octroi, police or military protection taxes, profession taxes (such as on barbers, goldsmiths, leather-workers, dhobis, etcetera), tax on workshops, social taxes (such as marriage tax), taxes on herdsmen, commercial taxes on merchants and artisans, and so on. In fact, virtually all productive activities in the kingdom, however trivial, were taxed—the government took a share of whatever money anyone made in any activity. Besides all these, rajas often charged special taxes to meet temple expenses.

The orthodox Muslim view of state revenue was that it belonged to the state, and was not the sultan's personal income, and that it should to be used only to meet state expenses. Sultans were however permitted to spend a good part of the state revenue on themselves and their families, to maintain their exalted status, which was considered an essential requirement for maintaining the authority of the state. 'Whatever is expended on your family could be increased a thousand fold, in order that the royal dignity might be thereby enhanced in the eyes of the people,' a qazi once advised Ala-ud-din Khalji. 'This enhancement of the royal dignity is politically essential and expedient.' This in effect meant that the sultan could treat the kingdom as his private property, use the state revenue as his personal income, and spend it as he pleased.

THE MOST IMPORTANT source of revenue for the medieval state was agricultural tax. This was collected soon after each of the two harvests normally gathered in India: *rabi*, the winter harvest, and *kharif*, the rainy season harvest. The state usually sought to enhance its agricultural tax revenue by encouraging farmers to expand the land under their cultivation, and to plant more valuable crops.

The agricultural tax rates charged by kings varied considerably from kingdom to kingdom, and from king to king. The normal tax rate in Muslim states was probably around one-fifth of the gross farm produce, but some sultans, Ala-ud-din Khalji for instance, collected much higher taxes. Sometimes, where special facilities had to be built by the farmer for irrigation, like the bucket or wheel system, there, unlike in the rain-fed fields, taxes were sometimes reduced by kings to as much as one-twentieth of the produce, to compensate the farmer for the extra labour he had to put in to cultivate his field.

In Hindu kingdoms, the tax rate demanded by the rajas varied considerably with the exigencies of their situation, from the traditional one-sixth to as much as one-half of the gross produce. The Agricultural tax rate in Vijayanagar was between one-sixth and one-third of the gross produce. A complicating factor in the tax system of Vijayanagar and of several other Hindu kingdoms— often of Muslim kingdoms as well—was the practice of the state farming out tax collection to the highest bidders. This was a pernicious practice, for the speculators who bid for tax collection were usually exploitative towards cultivators, so the tax burden on them in kingdoms like Vijayanagar was usually very high and oppressive.

A curious practice of the Delhi sultans was that they sometimes raised agricultural tax exorbitantly to punish unruly villagers. Thus Muhammad Tughluq once raised 'the taxes on the inhabitants of the Doab by ten or twenty per cent, as they had shown themselves refractory,' notes Mughal chronicler Badauni. 'He instituted also a cattle-tax, a house tax, and several other imposts of an oppressive nature, which entirely ruined and desolated the country, and brought its wretched inhabitants to destruction.' And this led to a vicious cycle of rebellion by peasants and brutal repression by the sultan—driven to extremities, peasants sometimes rose in rebellion, burned their grain stacks and drove away their cattle; and the sultan responded to that by desolating the villages, and slaughtering or blinding the villagers.

This was typical of the eccentric policies and actions of Muhammad Tughluq. On the other hand some of the Delhi sultans did indeed take elaborate measures to systematise land revenue assessment and collection. Thus Ala-ud-din Khalji had all the cultivated land in his empire measured and categorised, and fixed the tax on them on the basis of their standard yields. His tax demands were high—he demanded half the agricultural produce as tax, based on the average yield of a particular area; in addition he also collected tax on pastures. But despite these high tax demands, peasants were on the whole better off under Ala-ud-din than under most other sultans, for his high tax demands were balanced by measures providing security to villagers from marauders, protecting them from exploitation by village headmen, and encouraging them to expand cultivation.

Unlike most other sultans, Ala-ud-din collected agricultural taxes directly from peasants though his officers, and did not depend on village chieftains for tax collection, because the vested interests of the chieftains clashed with the interests of the state as well as of the cultivators. He also rescinded the tax exemptions and privileges that village chieftains traditionally enjoyed, and treated all farmers on par. Further, he abolished the system of collective tax on villages, but taxed each farmer individually, so that the village chieftains did not transfer their tax burden on to the common villagers, as they used to do.

All this considerably increased the administrative burden of the state, but Ala-ud-din met that challenge by appointing an army of officers to deal with land revenue assessment, collection, and audit. Later Firuz Tughluq also sought to systematise land revenue assessment and collection. One of the radical measures he took in this matter was to organise a six-year survey of agricultural production in the empire, which enabled him to make an informed estimate of the revenue potential of the empire, and tailor his tax demand accordingly.

JIZYA WAS ANOTHER source of revenue for the Muslim state. This was a tax imposed by Muslim states on zimmis, protected non-Muslims, and its collection was mandatory for Muslim rulers. It was a discriminatory communal tax, but its collection imposed certain reciprocal obligations on Muslim rulers, to protect the life and property of non-Muslims, to grant them the freedom to live according to their traditional way of life, and to perform their customary religious rites without any hindrance. In the early history of Islam the zimmi privilege was granted only to Jews and Christians, but it was extended to the followers of other religions when the political power of Muslims extended beyond Arabia.

Did Hindus merit to be treated as zimmis? Some Muslim theologians held that they did not, and that they should be forced to become Muslims or be killed. But this was not a sensible or practical idea. Hindus were far too many to be exterminated. Besides, they had a crucial and indispensable role in Indian economy, particularly in agriculture, which was entirely dependent on their labour. It was in fact the labour of Hindus that that provided the Muslim state its sustenance. Hindus also provided many essential services in the Muslim army and administration. Their contributions were an absolute requirement for the very survival of the Sultanate.

But there was a curious anomaly in the collection of jizya in India, for Brahmins, who headed the Hindu society, were exempted from this tax. This was presumably because Brahmins played an important and essential role in running the administration of Muslim states, as officers and clerks. Further, Brahmins were not considered an economically productive people, so they could be exempted from jizya, just like the other people considered to be non-productive, such as women, were exempted from it. It was also probably feared that antagonising Brahmins, the most revered people in Hindu society, would antagonise a large section of the Indian population, and make the administration of the country difficult. Most sultans therefore exempted Brahmins from jizya. But these considerations did not influence hyper-orthodox Firuz Tughluq, and he imposed jizya on Brahmins, as on other Hindus, though at a reduced rate.

Jizya was a poll tax, not an income tax. However, for the fair distribution of the burden of jizya, non-Muslims were divided into three economic groups—the affluent, the middle class, and the commoners—paying different amounts of the tax. The actual amount charged on the people of each of these categories is given variously in different medieval texts, but their ratio seems to have been the same as what Arabs charged on non-Muslims during their rule in Sind, requiring the affluent to pay 48 dirhams a year, the middle class 24 dirhams, and the others 12 dirhams. Women, children, and the disabled, as well as government servants, were exempted from this tax. In towns jizya was collected separately from each individual, but in villages it was usually assessed as a collective tax. The collection of jizya does not seem to have been rigorously enforced in the Delhi Sultanate, and it does not seem to have been a major source of revenue for the state.

Similar to jizya paid by Hindus, Muslims paid an alms tax called zakat. The revenue from zakat was not allowed to be used for state expenses, but was for distribution in charity among needy Muslims and Muslim institutions. In fact, under Firuz Tughluq the revenue from zakat was remitted into a separate treasury. Zakat was not a poll tax, but a wealth tax, and was collected as a percentage of the wealth of individual Muslims. But it was charged only on the wealth that was in the possession of an individual for at least one full year. This provision was often misused by people to evade the tax, by transferring their property to a wife at the end of a year and then repossessing it at the beginning of the following year.

Yet another source of income for the Muslim state was booty, collected during wars. The Sharia prescription on this was that one-fifth of the booty collected may be kept by the sultan for charitable and religious purposes, and that the rest should be distributed among soldiers. But the Delhi sultans (except Firuz Tughluq) usually reversed this ratio, and took four-fifth of the booty for themselves, and gave only one-fifth to soldiers. This reversal was justified by the sultans on the ground that while Muslim soldiers had originally received no salary but only a share of the booty—as they were not employees, but partners in a common endeavour—later, as soldiers were recruited as employees of the state, they merited only one-fifth share of the booty, for they were then paid regular salaries by the state all through the year, whether they were deployed in war or not.

Plunder, similar to war booty, was another major source of revenue for the state. Plundering raids were a legitimate state activity in medieval India, and the sultans as well as the rajas periodically launched these raids into neighbouring kingdoms, to replenish their treasury. The other normal revenue sources for the state were judicial fines, and the presents that the king received from favour seekers.

Tax collection was a difficult task for the state in early medieval India, because of the general laxity of administration in those days, in Hindu as well as Muslim kingdoms. Besides, people everywhere and at all times were reluctant to pay taxes, especially so in medieval India, as very few people there had any disposable income, and in any case they received hardly any benefits from their rulers. Kings therefore often had to use force to collect taxes; sometimes they even had to send their soldiers into the refractory villages to plunder the people there, as that was the only way to collect the tax dues from them.

The state was usually assisted in tax collection by the village headmen, who normally received 2.5 per cent of the collection as their reward. The headmen themselves did not normally (except under the rigorous rule of Ala-ud-din) pay any taxes, or even pay jizya (presumably because they considered themselves to be government officers) but enjoyed various perquisites. In the Delhi Sultanate tax collection was sometimes farmed out to officers, who were required to remit a fixed annual amount into the state treasury, irrespective of their actual revenue collection, whether high or low.

Despite all the irregularities and inefficiencies in revenue administration, sultans and rajas usually had overflowing coffers. 'In the king's treasury there are chambers, with excavations in them, filled with molten gold, forming one mass,' writes Razzak about Vijayanagar. The raja there maintained two treasuries, one to meet the current expenditure of the kingdom, and the other to store savings to meet emergencies. Under Krishnadeva, the ideal was to divide the state revenue into four equal parts: one part for palace expenditure and charity, two parts for the army, and the remaining part for depositing in the reserve treasury.

THE LAWS THAT applied to Hindus and Muslims in a Muslim state were entirely different—while Muslims were subject to Sharia (the prescriptions of the Koran and the traditions of Prophet Muhammad) it was caste rules and local conventions that applied to Hindus. Though Hindus were normally subject only to their own laws, if one of the litigants in a case was a Muslim, the matter had to be taken to a Muslim court, and judged according to Sharia.

The Hindu legal system was incredibly complex, as its laws and legal conventions, as well as its legal institutions and practices, varied from place to place and caste to caste. An act considered as an abominable crime in one caste could be considered as a perfectly legitimate act in another caste, and what was considered as the lawful punishment for a crime in one caste could be considered as entirely unlawful for the same crime in another caste. And, as these rules were enforced by caste courts, political authority had only a marginal role in the process.

Even in the case of the Muslim legal system there was a good amount of variability in the law that was applicable in any given situation. Though Muslim law everywhere in the world was based on Sharia, these were only guidelines, and what law applied in any specific case depended on the interpretations of Sharia by the ulama (religious scholars), and these interpretations varied from country to country, sect to sect, and from scholar to scholar.

The sultan, advised by his chief qazi (judge), was the highest judicial authority in a Muslim state. In the case of capital punishments, the judgements of the lower courts had to be brought before the sultan, and his confirmation was required before the sentence could be executed. Further, the sultan could intervene in the administration of justice at any point, and when he did that, his decision, whether it was in conformity with conventions or not, invariably prevailed.

In Delhi the sultans usually set aside certain days in the week to deal with people's complaints—Muhammad Tughluq, for instance, heard complaints on Mondays and Thursdays—but they were normally accessible to suppliants on other days too. Iltutmish even set up at the entrance of his palace a great bell that people could ring to draw his attention and seek justice. People could even sue the sultan in a court of law—there are recorded instances of Muhammad Tughluq appearing humbly in a qazi's court and submitting to its judgement against him. On the other hand, if anyone, however great he might be, incurred the wrath of the sultan, he was often summarily executed without any trial.

As in Muslim kingdoms so also in Hindu kingdoms the highest judicial authority was the king. And in both systems there was a hierarchy of courts beneath the king. In the Hindu system, the lowest courts were the village panchayat courts and the caste courts. Appeals could be made against the judgement of a lower court to a higher court, and ultimately to the king. The rajas, like the sultans, were usually accessible to anyone seeking justice. In Vijayanagar, according to Nuniz, 'when anyone suffers wrong and wishes to represent his case to the king he shows how great is his suffering by lying flat on his face on the ground till they ask him what it s he wants.' In the Muslim judicial system there were normally four types of courts: the Diwan-i-mazalim, the court of complaints, presided over by the sultan or his representative; the qazi's court, which administered the law of Islam; the court of the muhtasib, which dealt with issues of public morals and offenses against religious ordinances; and the shurta, police courts.

Despite all these elaborate legal systems and hierarchy of courts, the treatment of criminals in early medieval India, in Hindu as well as in Muslim states, was usually arbitrary and often horribly barbarous. Suspects were invariably tortured to extract confession from them—and tortured so savagely that they often confessed even to the crimes they had not committed, preferring execution to torture. 'People consider death a lighter affliction than torture,' notes Battuta.

The punishment of rebels by the state in medieval India was particularly savage, and involved mutilation, impalement, flaying alive, hacking off limbs, trampling by elephants, being shot through a cannon, and so on. Sometimes an entire group of people was summarily executed, on suspicion of being rebels or thieving tribes. Thus Balban, when he was serving Sultan Nasir-ud-din Mahmud as the Lord Chamberlain, slaughtered the entire lot of hill tribes living in the environs of Delhi, because they were all, according to Siraj, a thirteenth-century chronicler, 'thieves, robbers, and highwaymen.' This carnage went on for twenty days, butchering all who were caught. Balban, according to Siraj, offered his soldiers 'a silver tanka for every [severed] head, and two tankas for every man brought in alive.' Many of those captured were cast under the feet of elephants. 'About a hundred met their death at the hands of flayers, being skinned from head to foot; their skins were all then stuffed with straw, and some of them were hung over every gate of the city.'

Battuta, who was in Delhi during the reign of Muhammad Tughluq, has left a vivid description of how elephants were used to execute rebels and criminals. 'The elephants which execute men have their tusks covered with sharp irons, resembling the coulter of the plough . . . and with edges like those of knives . . . When a person is thrown in front [of the elephant], the animal winds its trunk round him, hurls him up into the air, and catching him on one of its tusks, dashes him to the ground . . . [And then it] places one of its feet on the breast of the victim' and crushes him to death.

The punishments meted out to traitorous royal relatives and high nobles were particularly fiendish in the Delhi Sultanate, because they posed the greatest threat to the sultan. According to Battuta, Muhammad Tughluq once had a rebellious prince 'skinned alive . . . His flesh was then cooked with rice, and some of it was sent to his children and his wife, and the remainder was put in a great dish and given to elephants to eat, but they would not touch it. The sultan ordered his skin to be stuffed with straw, and . . . exhibited throughout the country.'

THE DREAD OF such savage punishments by kings was the primary means for preserving law and order in early medieval India, as it was in ancient India, for, as the Hindu lawgiver Manu held, 'the whole world is controlled by punishment, for a guiltless man is hard to find.' This was acknowledged even by Firuz Tughluq, one of the most humane of the Delhi sultans. 'In the reigns of former sultans the blood of many Mussulmans had been shed, and many varieties of torture employed,' writes the sultan in his memoirs. 'Amputation of hands and feet, ears and noses, tearing out the eyes, pouring molten led into the throat, crushing the bone of the hand and feet with mallets, burning the body with fire, driving iron nails into the hands, feet, and bosom, cutting the sinews, sawing men asunder; these and many similar tortures were practised . . . All these things were practised so that fear and dread might fall upon the hearts of man, and that the regulations of government might be duly maintained.'

Not only were the punishments savage, but its savagery was ostentatiously put on display to horrify people, and thus to deter them from committing offences. Thus when a top official in Ghazni, who had incurred the displeasure of Sultan Masud, was executed, his body was kept on the gibbet for seven years, so 'his feet dropped off and his corpse entirely dried up, so that not a remnant of him was left to be taken down and buried,' records Baihaqi. And in Delhi, according to Battuta, 'it is the custom with this people that whenever the sultan orders the execution of a person, he is despatched at the door of the hall of audience, and his body left there for three days . . . It was only rarely that the corpse of someone who had been executed was not seen at the gate of the palace.' This was done even to the princes who were suspected of disaffection. Nor were royal ladies spared—thus during the reign of Muhammad Tughluq a princess, who was suspected of debauchery, was stoned in public at the entrance of the durbar hall. The only sultan of Delhi who abolished these barbaric practices was Firuz Tughluq. 'Through the mercy which god has shown to me these severities and terrors have been exchanged for tenderness, kindness and mercy,' he writes.

Vijayanagar and Bahmani kings also inflicted barbarous punishments similar to those inflicted by the Delhi sultans. 'The punishments that they inflict in this kingdom are these: for a thief, whatever theft he commits, however little it be, they forthwith cut off a foot and a hand, and if his theft be a great one he is hanged with a hook under his chin,' notes Nuniz about the practices in Vijayanagar. 'If a man outrages a respectable woman or a virgin, he has the same punishment . . . Nobles who become traitors are sent to be impaled alive on wooden stakes thrust through the belly. And people of the lower orders, for whatever crime they commit, . . . [the raja] forthwith commands to cut off their heads in the market-place. And the same [is done] for a murder, unless the death was the result of a duel.' In the Bahmani Sultanate during the reign of Nizam Shah, when a rebel noble was executed, 'his body was hewn in pieces, which were affixed on different buildings,' records Ferishta.

THE ROUTINE POLICING of their kingdoms was not an onerous burden for Indian kings, for Indian villages were self-administering, and they generally policed themselves. The main policing task of Indian states was therefore confined to the cities. In this, the scene varied considerably from city to city. According to a rather incredible report of Abdur Razzak, Kozhikode in north Kerala was a haven of peace and security in the mid-fifteenth century. 'Security and justice are so firmly established in this city,' he writes, 'that the most wealthy merchants bring thither from maritime countries considerable cargoes, which they unload, and unhesitatingly send them into the market and bazaars, without thinking in the meantime of any necessity of checking the account, or of keeping watch over the goods.'

The scene in most other Indian cities was entirely different, and they required elaborate law enforcement setups to preserve order in them. The head of the town police in Muslim states was the kotwal, who worked in tandem with the military officers in the town. His main responsibility was to maintain law and order in the city, but he was also responsible for the upkeep of public utilities and for the regulation of markets. He also had diverse social responsibilities, such as the prevention of the circumcision of boys under twelve years age, the prevention of forced sati, the expulsion of religious impostors and charlatans, and so on. At night the towns were patrolled by the police. 'Throughout the night the town of Bidar is guarded by 1000 men . . . mounted on horses in full armour, each carrying a light,' reports Nikitin. The town gates were usually closed at sunset for security reasons, and would not be opened again till morning; those who arrived at the town after its gates were closed had to spend the night outside the town walls, but there were inns there for their accommodation.

Protecting the frontiers of their kingdom was a major concern of Indian rulers, and the Delhi sultans paid special attention to this, particularly in guarding their ever-vulnerable north-west frontier. 'When we reached this river called Panj-ab, which is the frontier of the territories of the sultan of India and Sind, the officials of the intelligence service came to us and sent a report about us to the governor of the city of Multan,' reports Battuta about his experiences at the frontier. 'When the intelligence officials write to the sultan informing him of those who arrive in his country, he studies the report very minutely. The reporters therefore take utmost care in this matter, telling the sultan that a certain man has arrived of such-and-such appearance and dress, and noting the number of his party, salves and servants and beasts, his behaviour both in action and at rest, and all his doings, omitting no detail. When the new arrival reaches the town of Multan, which is the capital of Sind, he stays there until an order is received from the sultan regarding his entry and the degree of hospitality to be extended to him. A man is honoured in that country according to what may be seen of his actions, conduct, and zeal, since no one knows anything about his family or lineage . . . On the road to Multan . . . [at a river crossing] the goods and baggage of all who pass are subjected to a rigorous examination. Their custom at the time of our arrival was to take a quarter of everything brought in by merchants, and exact a duty of seven dinars for every horse.'

GATHERING INTELLIGENCE AND maintaining an efficient communication network were matters of high priority for most Indian rulers. Battuta was greatly impressed by the intelligence network of the Delhi Sultanate, by which the sultan was kept regularly and speedily informed about all that was happening in the various parts of his empire. This system was initially set up by Ala-ud-din Khalji, but it fell into disuse after him, till it was restored by Ghiyas-ud-din Tughluq. According to Battuta, the postmaster (chief intelligence officer) of a region 'is the person who keeps the sultan informed of the affairs in his town and district and all that happens in it and all who come to it.'

'In India the postal service is of two kinds,' continues Battuta. 'The mounted couriers travel on horses belonging to the sultan, with relays at every four miles. The service of couriers on foot is organised in the following manner. At every third of a mile there is an inhabited village, outside which there are three pavilions. In these sit men girded up and ready to move off, each of whom has a rod a yard and a half long with brass bells at the top. When a courier leaves the town he takes the letter in . . . one hand, and the rod with bells in the other, and runs with all his might. The men in the pavilions, on hearing the sound of bells, prepare to meet him, and when he reaches them one of them takes the letter in his hand and passes on, running with all his might and shaking his rod until he reaches the next station, and so the letter is passed on till it reaches its destination. This post is quicker than the mounted post. It is sometimes used to transport fruits from Khurasan which are highly valued in India; they are put in covered baskets and carried with great speed to the sultan. In the same way they transport notorious criminals; they are each placed on a wooden frame and the couriers run carrying it on their heads. The sultan's drinking water is brought to him by the same means when he resides at Daulatabad, from the river Kank (Ganga) . . . which is at a distance of forty days' journey from there.'

Apart from this government postal system, there seems to have been also a private postal system in medieval India, presumably maintained by prominent trade guilds. The carriers of this system stationed themselves at markets and announced the names of those for whom he was carrying mail, so they could go to him and collect their letters.

3

Wars Forever

The Delhi sultans were warlords. And so were most Hindu rajas. For instance, Vijayanagar, as Sastri comments, was 'a war state . . . and its political organization was dominated by its military needs.' Waging wars was the normal mode of life of most early medieval kings, as hunting is for predatory animals. And their hunger for land was generally insatiable. As the medieval Persian poet Saadi puts it:

> If a holy man eats half his loaf,
> he will give the other half to a beggar.
> But if a king conquers all the world,
> he will still seek another world to conquer.

Even if a king did not have any belligerent intentions, he had to be ever prepared for war, for his very survival depended on it, as medieval Indian kingdoms were all invariably bordered by potential aggressors. In that environment, it was inevitably the martial capabilities of a king that primarily defined his worth. This attitude is reflected in the Rajput custom of a newly enthroned king engaging in a battle, or at least in a mock battle, right after his accession, for him to prove his worthiness for the throne.

The incessant sweep of armies all across the subcontinent—invariably accompanied by ravaging, pillaging wild tribes—was fatally disruptive of normal life in India and was ruinous to its economy. Medieval Indian armies were all predatory by nature. Pillaging the enemy or rebel lands was part of their normal operations, and even their advance through their own kingdom was often devastating. Men in fact joined the army not so much for the salary they were

295

given, as for the opportunity it offered for plunder during campaigns. For kings too, plundering the enemy or rebel lands was a normal and legitimate means for filling their treasuries. According to Ni'matullah, during Sikandar Lodi's campaign against a rebel in Bayana, 'the whole army was employed in plundering, and all the groves which spread their shade for seven kos around Bayana were torn up from their roots . . . He butchered most of the people who had fled for refuge to the hills and forests, and the rest he pillaged and put in fetters.'

Waging war on non-Muslims was considered as holy war in Islam, and it had the sanction of religion. But in most cases the claims made by sultans of waging holy wars were mere pretexts to mask their essentially predatory purpose. Their wars, even their wars against Hindu kings, usually had little or nothing to do with religion. In fact, sultans often waged pillaging wars against fellow Muslim kingdoms, just as they waged such wars against Hindu kingdoms. And rajas too often waged pillaging wars against fellow Hindu kingdoms, just as they waged such wars against Muslim kingdoms. In both cases, the invocation of religious spirit by kings at best served to rouse the combative fervour of their soldiers.

Medieval Indian wars were often unspeakably savage orgies of violence. In the case of Turco-Afghans, a relatively small troop of men in military occupation of a vast country teeming with alien people, ferocity was an essential survival requirement, to instil terror in their adversaries and thus gain a critical psychological advantage over them.

This, however, was only a contributing factor in the savagery of medieval wars. Wars, at all times and among all people everywhere in the world were savage. And Hindu kings were not far behind Turks in bestial ferocity in wars. Thus Bukka, the mid-fourteenth century king of Vijayanagar, during his campaign in the Raichur Doab, ordered all the inhabitants of a town there—men and women and even children—to be slaughtered. And when Bahmani sultan Muhammad Shah heard of this outrage, he, according to Ferishta, took a solemn oath 'that till he had put to death one hundred thousand infidels, as an expiation for the massacre of the faithful, he would never sheathe the sword of holy war nor refrain from slaughter.'

In the ensuing battle the sultan routed the Vijayanagar army, and then set about slaughtering Hindus en-masse, 'putting all to death without any distinction,' reports Ferishta. 'It is said that the slaughter amounted to 70,000 men, women and children . . . Not even pregnant women, or even children at the breast, escaped the sword . . . The slaughter was terrible . . . The inhabitants of every place around Vijayanagar . . . [were] massacred without mercy.' Similarly, sultan Jalal-ud-din Khalji of Delhi during one of his campaigns 'made the blood of the infidels flow in streams, and formed bridges with their heads,' writes medieval poet Amir Khusrav.

SO IT WENT on and on. Thus when Devaraya of Vijayanagar fought against the Bahmani sultan Firuz Shah, 'Hindus made a general massacre of Muslims, and erected a platform with their heads on the field of battle,' recounts Ferishta. 'And they wasted [the land] with fire and sword . . . demolished many mosques and holy places, slaughtered people without mercy . . . seeming to discharge their treasured malice and resentment of ages.' Even Krishnadeva, one of the most cultured rulers of the age, burnt down villages and pillaged the countryside during his campaigns in Orissa and Bijapur.

European armies in India also indulged in the barbaric slaughter of innocent civilians at this time. Thus Vasco da Gama, the Portuguese explorer, during his 1504 second Indian campaign, wantonly butchered several hundred people in a vessel he captured along the Kerala coast, and soon after, on reaching Kozhikode, immediately bombarded the city, and set about slaying in cold blood some 800 harmless fishermen at the port. Similarly, Albuquerque, the early sixteenth-century Portuguese governor of Goa, on being attacked by the Bahmani army once, decapitated 150 principal Muslims in the town, and also slaughtered their wives and children, before evacuating the port. And a few months later, when he recaptured the port, he had some 6000 Muslim men, women and children there mercilessly slain. On the whole the behaviour of Christian soldiers was no different from the behaviour of Hindu and Muslim soldiers. All were equally savage. As Sewell comments, 'Europeans seemed to think that they had a divine right to pillage, rob, and massacre the natives of India . . . Their whole record is one of a series of atrocities.'

In Kerala the chieftains there had the odd custom of turning battles into duels, which, though a savage sport, had the advantage of minimising bloodshed. 'When they are in battle, and one army is distant from the other two ranges of a crossbow, the king says to the Brahmins, "Go to the camp of the enemy, and tell the king to let one hundred of his Naeri come, and I will go with a hundred of mine." And thus they both go to the middle of the space, and begin to fight in this manner,' reports Varthema. 'And when four or six on either side are killed, the Brahmins enter into the midst of them, and make both parties return to their camp. And the said Brahmins immediately go to the armies on both sides, and say, "*Nur manezar hanno?*" The king answers, "*Matile?*" That is, the Brahmins ask, "Do you wish for any more fight?" And the king answers, "Enough, no?" And the rival king does the same. In this manner they fight, one hundred against one hundred. This is their mode of fighting.'

THIS MODE OF battle was evidently feasible only in small kingdoms with small armies. Major Indian kingdoms, of Hindus as well as of Muslims, but particularly Hindu kingdoms, deployed immense armies in battle, sometimes as many as several hundred thousand soldiers.

These armies consisted of a number of permanent divisions, as well as a large number of temporary recruits. In the case of the permanent Delhi Sultanate army, its core was made up of a central elite corps, a major division of which was stationed in the royal capital and it always accompanied the sultan on his campaigns, and served as his bodyguards. The other divisions of this elite army were stationed in various provincial forts and along the frontiers of the empire. Apart from this central army, the Sultanate army had several other contingents, recruited and maintained in the provinces by the fief (*iqta*) holders of the empire, and these contingents made up the bulk of the Sultanate army. The overall command of the entire army of the Sultanate was with an officer titled Ariz-i-mumalik, who functioned directly under the sultan.

The soldiers of the central elite corps were recruited with great care, their strength and skill tested in various ways, and their salaries adjusted according to their merit. 'When anyone comes desiring to be enrolled in the army as an archer, he is given one of the bows to draw,' reports Battuta. 'They differ in stiffness, and his pay is graduated according to the strength he shows in drawing them. Anyone desiring to be enrolled as a trooper sets off his horse at a canter or gallop, and tries to hit a target set up there with his lance. There is also a ring there, suspended from a low wall; the candidate sets off his horse at a canter until he comes level to the ring, and if he lifts it off with his lance he is considered a good horseman. For those wishing to be enrolled as mounted archers there is a ball placed on the ground, and their pay is proportioned to their accuracy in hitting it with an arrow while going at a canter or gallop.' There were presumably similar procedures for the recruitment of soldiers in the provincial armies of the Sultanate as well.

All soldiers were required to keep themselves fighting fit always, but the rigour of the royal control of the army varied from sultan to sultan, Balban and Ala-ud-din being particularly strict about it. On the whole, the Indian armies of the age were usually in fine fettle, as they were almost continuously engaged in wars.

THE MAIN WEAKNESS of the Indian armies was that none of them were cohesive forces, but were made up of different groups of soldiers based on their race, language and religion. In addition to these, Hindu soldiers were further divided by inviolable sect and caste taboos. These Hindu social divisions affected the armies of Muslim kings also, for they all had a large number of Hindus in them, particularly in the infantry.

The custom of recruiting Hindus into Muslim armies began right from the very first Muslim military penetration into India, the Arab conquest of Sind in the early eighth century. The practice continued under the Ghazni and Ghuri sultans, and it became quite pronounced under the Delhi sultans. The provincial armies of the Delhi Sultanate in particular had a large proportion of Hindus. The dependence of the sultans on Hindu recruits became even more pronounced when the migration of Turks into India dwindled soon after the founding of the Delhi Sultanate, because of the interposition of Mongols between India and Central Asia. Later a small number of Europeans, mainly the Portuguese, joined the Indian armies, particularly in the Bahmani and Vijayanagar kingdoms.

And just as a large number of Hindu soldiers served under sultans, so also a fair number of Muslim soldiers served under rajas. Both these practices began from the very beginning of the history of the Hindu-Muslim military engagements—while Muhammad Qasim, the commander of the very first Muslim army invading India, had a number of Hindus in his army, his adversary, Dahar, the raja of Sind, had some 500 Arabs in his army. Similarly, in the mid-twelfth century, half a century before the establishment of the Delhi Sultanate, a number of Muslim soldiers are known to have served in the army of the Hoysalas in peninsular India. Later, the rajas of Vijayanagar also recruited a good number of Muslims for their armies.

There was a general preference in India at this time, in Muslim as well as Hindu kingdoms, to recruit foreigners for the army, particularly as cavalrymen, cannoneers and musketeers. According to Ferishta, the sultan of Bijapur employed in his army a large number of foreign soldiers, such as Afghans, Abyssinians, Arabs, Persians, Turks, Uzbeks, and so on. And both Bahmani and Vijayanagar kingdoms had several European soldiers in their armies, serving as cannoneers and musketeers. A number of Portuguese marksmen are recorded to have served in the army of Krishnadeva of Vijayanagar during his campaign against Adil Shah of Bijapur, and were particularly effective in shooting down the defenders on the fort walls of Raichur.

THE OFFICERS OF the Delhi Sultanate were paid their salaries either in cash or by assigning to them the revenues of particular tracts of land. Of these two modes of payment, the land revenue assignment, *iqta*, was generally preferred by the Delhi sultans—as well as by most Hindu kings—as it substantially reduced the administrative burden of the state. The officers who were thus allotted lands were required to meet, from the revenue of the lands given to them, the administrative expenses of their fiefs, maintain the military contingent assigned to them, and take their own salary.

The revenue from *iqta* lands was however only a part of the income of army officers. A major part of their income, as well as of the income of common soldiers, came from their share of war booty. Even though they were in medieval Indian sultanates generally allowed to keep only one-fifth of the booty they collected—instead of the four-fifth they were originally allowed to keep under the Sharia prescription—this restriction was probably more than compensated by the abundance of booty they could collect during the innumerable wars waged by their kings. Cavalrymen, who played the most decisive role in medieval wars, were usually paid double the salary of infantrymen, and those who showed high valour in battle received special bonuses from the king.

Most Indian kingdoms maintained incredibly large armies, but it is hard to believe some of the figures given in medieval chronicles. Muhammad Tughluq's army, according to Barani, was 'as numerous as a swarm of ants or locusts.' Arabic sources claim that the sultan's army, central and provincial forces together, had a total strength of 900,000 soldiers! And Afif states that when Firuz Tughluq campaigned in Bengal he led an army that 'consisted of 70,000 cavalry, innumerable infantry, 470 warlike elephants, and many barrier-breaking boats,' and that the army that he led into Sind 'consisted of 90,000 cavalry and 480 elephants.'

According to Barbosa, the king of Vijayanagar had 'more than a hundred thousand men of war continually in his pay.' And Krishnadeva in his battle against Adil Shah of Bijapur is said to have led an army 'of about a million men, if camp-followers are included,' according to the report of Nuniz. And Ramaraya in the battle of Talikota is said to have deployed, according to one estimate given by Ferishta, 900,000 infantry, 45,000 cavalry, and 2000 elephants, besides a large number of auxiliaries.

Most of these figures are quite probably hyperbolic. But whatever be the factuality of these figures, Indian armies were usually of mammoth size. Large size however did not necessarily mean great strength. In fact, the huge size of Indian armies often turned them into unwieldy, uncontrollable rabbles, which could be easily routed by a small, tightly organised army, as Mahmud Ghazni proved again and again during his Indian campaigns, and as Babur would later prove in his battle against Ibrahim Lodi. Similarly, in the peninsula, the Bahmani sultans usually won their battles against the much larger forces deployed by the rajas of Vijayanagar.

Adding to the unwieldiness and bedlam of Indian armies were the hordes of non-combatants that accompanied the army, such as various vendors and service providers, as well a large number of prostitutes. In the train of the Vijayanagar army there were, according to Barbosa, five or six thousand women, paid for by the raja, evidently to provide the soldiers with essential sexual services. The army on the march was also invariably followed by hordes of irregulars, adding to the chaos in the army and the devastation it caused all along the route of its march.

INDIAN ARMIES IN the early medieval period consisted of four main divisions: elephants, cavalry, archers, and infantry. The army usually also had a few non-combatant wings in it, such as engineers—to serve as sappers and miners, and to man siege engines—surgeons, physicians, and scouts.

In time two new corps—cannoneers and musketeers—were added to the Indian army, and they would play an increasingly prominent role in battles. But chariots, which had a crucial role in battles in ancient India, had virtually disappeared from the scene by the late classical period; they are not even mentioned in Harsha's army. As for the navy, some South Indian kingdoms, the Cholas for instance, had a strong naval presence in the Indian Ocean in the classical period, but their role sharply declined by the early medieval period, and the control of the seas around India passed on to Arabs and Chinese, and eventually to Europeans. Some Indian kingdoms probably still maintained small naval fleets at this time, but there is hardly any information on this. There was however a strong presence of pirates on the western peninsular coast of India, with some of the pirate chieftains commanding as many as thirty warships.

The major reliance of Indian armies in the early medieval period was on their war elephants, and kings and generals usually rode into battle on elephants, for safety as well as to have a commanding view of the battle. War elephants have been in use in India from ancient times. King Porus of north-western India is recorded to have deployed 200 elephants in his battle against the invading army of Macedonian king Alexander in the fourth century BCE. Alexander however did not think much of the value of elephants in battle, and he devised a tactic to turn them against their own side, and thus rout the raja. Similarly, Timur in his battle against sultan Mahmud of Delhi in the late fourteenth century[1] also devised a tactic to counter the threat of elephants, and win the battle.

But these were rare incidents. Elephants normally played a decisive role in Indian battles. And the size of the elephant corps in Indian armies grew greatly over the centuries, and in time their use in war spread from India to Central Asia, and even to Europe. Ghaznavids were the first Muslim kings to use elephants in large numbers in battle—Mahmud Ghazni is said to have maintained a stable of 1000 elephants, tended by Hindu mahouts. Balban valued elephants very highly, and held that 'one elephant was worth 500 horsemen.' The 'elephant possesses more intelligence than any other animal in the world,' states Varthema. 'I have seen some elephants which have more understanding, and more discretion and intelligence, than many kind of people I have met with.'

Confronting elephants in the battlefield was a horrifying experience for most invading armies. Elephants, notes Razzak, 'in their size resemble

[1]See Part 5, Chapter 5

mountains and in their form resemble devils.' In battle they were usually made even more terrifying by being armoured and armed. 'Large scythes are attached to the trunks and tusks of the elephants, and the animals are clad in ornamental plates of steel. They carry a howdah, and in it are twelve men in armour with guns and arrows,' reports Nikitin. These soldiers, according to Timur, also threw grenades and fireworks, and shot rockets at the enemy.

The very sight and smell of elephants, as well as their trumpeting, threw the horses of invaders into panic. And the terrifying charge of elephants, which could reach speeds of up to thirty kilometres an hour, usually disarrayed the enemy infantry and cavalry, and made them flee pell-mell. All this made elephants an object of absolute terror for invading armies, more so as the all too real terrors of these beasts were magnified fantastically in the legends about them. Even as late as the close of the fourteenth century, when Timur invaded India, these legends persisted, and they dispirited the Mongol soldiers.

A major problem with elephants in battle was that they often ran amuck, throwing their own army into disarray. Still, elephants continued to play a crucial role in Indian battles till the late medieval period. But their role gradually declined thereafter, for the use of firearms made them obsolete. Moreover they were easy targets for cannons. The role of elephants in the army then became limited to hauling heavy military equipments.

NEXT IN IMPORTANCE to elephants in the early medieval Indian armies were mounted archers, who usually carried spears, swords and battle-axes, apart from bows. Their arrow heads were sometimes poisoned. Several thousands of these cavalrymen simultaneously charging at full tilt and shooting arrows was an onslaught which few infantry formations could withstand. Balban, according to Barani, held that a cavalry force of six or seven thousand could easily rout a hundred thousand strong infantry force.

India did not breed good quality horses at this time, so they had to be imported in large numbers from the Middle East and Central Asia. This was done by rajas as well as sultans. 'The king,' says Nuniz about the raja of Vijayanagar, 'every year buys thirteen thousand horses of Ormuz, and country-breds, of which he chooses the best for his stable, and gives the rest to his captains.' This had to be done every year, for, as Barbosa states, 'horses do not thrive well in their country and live therein but a short time,' because of the hot and humid climate of India.

Indian kings also regularly recruited a good number of foreign cavalrymen—Turks and other steppe people—as they were far superior to local cavalrymen. But they too, like imported horses, had to be recruited afresh periodically, as the spirit and energy of foreign soldiers tended to decline in the enervating climate of India.

Elephant and cavalry divisions were the most powerful units of the early medieval Indian armies, to which artillery and musketry divisions were later added. But the largest numerical constituent of Indian armies has always been the infantry. This however was also its weakest wing, being an ill-disciplined horde with hardly any military training, many of them just temporary recruits from among peasants.

A curious constituent of the medieval Indian armies was its contingent of martial 'ascetics', about whom there are several vivid accounts in the chronicles of the Mughal period, and they were no doubt a notable presence in the Indian armies of the early medieval period as well. These 'ascetics' entered into battle stark naked, but with their bodies daubed all over with paint and ash. Elsewhere in Asia too, as well as in Europe, there were bands of warrior monks in medieval times, but the Indian warrior monks were entirely different from them, and were rather like bands of primitive predators. 'Never have I seen yogis like this,' comments Kabir, a fifteenth-century mystic poet of North India. 'Shall I call such men ascetics or bandits?'

MOST MEDIEVAL INDIAN armies were not integrated units, but amalgams of disparate and incongruent elements. The clothes and weapons of their soldiers varied from group to group, even from person to person. There were no uniforms for soldiers, so each dressed as he liked. Often the dress of soldiers, particularly of the infantry, was minimal, as of the common people. South Indian soldiers at this time were 'all naked and bare-footed,' reports Nikitin, apparently ignoring the loincloth that they no doubt wore.

In contrast to this, soldiers in Afghanistan were well-dressed and well-armoured. 'It is the practice in the armies of Ghur for the infantry to protect themselves in battle with a covering made of a raw hide covered thickly on both sides with wool or cotton,' writes Siraj. 'This defensive covering is like a board, and is called *karoh*. When men put it on they are covered from head to foot, and their ranks look like walls. The wool is so thick that no weapon can pierce it.' Similarly, Yadgar found that some soldiers in North India, presumably migrants from Central Asia, were 'clothed in chain armour, which was concealed by white clothing.'

Most Indian kings and chieftains, as well as their senior officers, unlike the common soldiers, dressed in their best for battle, and wore their finest jewellery, presumably to impress and inspire their soldiers, and to awe the enemy. Thus when King Jayapala of Punjab was captured by Mahmud Ghazni in a battle, he, according to Al-Utbi, was found to be wearing several opulent jewels, such as a necklace 'composed of large pearls and shining gems and rubies set in gold.' Similarly, Ibrahim Lodi was heavily bejewelled when he fought against Babur in the battle of Panipat.

As in dress and ornaments, so also there were wide variations in the weapons carried by Indian soldiers, for these were not supplied by the state, but procured by each soldier, according to what he preferred or could afford. According to *Chach-nama*, an eighth century Arabic chronicle, the common weapons of the Indian soldiers in early medieval India were 'swords, shields, javelins, spears, and daggers.' Other sources indicate that they also carried lances, maces and lassos. Battuta found that in North India mounted soldiers usually carried two swords: one, called the stirrup-sword, was attached to the saddle, while the other was kept in his quiver. In South India, according to Nikitin, foot-soldiers carried 'a shield in one hand and a sword in the other.' And Nuniz reports that the soldiers of Vijayanagar 'were all well armed, each after his own fashion, the archers and musketeers with their quilted tunics, and shield-men with swords and poignards in their girdles. Their shields are so large that there is no need for armour to protect the body, which is completely covered. Their horses were in full clothing. The men wore doublets, and had weapons in their hands. And on their heads were headpieces after the manner of their doublets, quilted with cotton.' Says Razzak about Kerala soldiers: 'In one hand they bear a . . . dagger . . . and in the other a shield made of cowhide.'

Mangonels and other naphtha and missile-throwing devices were in general use in the army of the Delhi Sultanate right from the beginning, and it was common for Indian armies to hurl incendiary arrows and javelins, as well as pots filled with combustible materials, into enemy forts and against enemy soldiers. But it was only in the mid-fourteenth century that gunpowder, invented in China in the ninth century, was introduced into India, presumably by Mongols or Turks. This was then used in various explosive devices by the army. But it took another century before Indian armies began to use firearms regularly in battle. And it was still later that cannons came to be used in India—the first recorded instance of the use of cannons in India was by Babur in the battle of Panipat in 1526. But thereafter the use of cannons became fairly widespread in field battles in India, and they played a decisive role in the battle of Talikota in 1565.

Indian kings generally preferred to recruit foreign soldiers to serve as musketeers and to man their artillery, because of their greater experience and superior skills in the use of these weapons. The artillery of the Deccan sultans in the battle of Talikota was, for instance, commanded by a Turk. There were also a number of Portuguese gunners in the armies of South Indian kingdoms.

THE PACE OF advance of an Indian army into battle was slow, because of the slow pace of its infantry, which was normally its largest division. 'In ordinary cases eight kos (about 26 kilometres) would be one day's march,' states Siraj.

But in an emergency the army could cover double that distance or even more. Timur in his autobiography states that he once covered twenty kos in one day, though usually he covered only six kos in a day. Laden with plunder his army marched even more slowly, covering only four or five kos a day on the average.

The armies on the march were often ruthlessly predatory. They advanced trampling down everything on their way, and devastating the country— pillaging, slaughtering people, and spreading terror—even in their own kingdom. According to Amir Khusrav, wherever the army marched, every inhabited spot was desolated. And since the army was constantly on the march, the devastation it caused was also ceaseless. The only way people could save themselves was by fleeing from the path of the army. And this they invariably did.

If this was the manner in which the army advanced into battle, its retreat from the battlefield was often even more chaotic, especially after a defeat or some other calamity. Thus when the Delhi Sultanate army retreated from Sind following the death of Muhammad Tughluq, 'every division of the army marched without leader, rule, or route, in the greatest disorder,' states Barani. 'No one heeded or listened to . . . anyone.'

In sharp contrast to the chaos in the army on the march, military camps were usually well laid out and well organised in medieval India. Though there is hardly any information on the military camps of the Delhi Sultans, there is a fair amount of information on the practices in peninsular India, in Hindu as well as Muslim camps. Presumably the camp scene in North India was not much different from this. In all cases particular care was taken to protect the army camp against surprise attacks. According to Ferishta, the Bahmani sultan while on a campaign 'surrounded his camp with carriages after the usage of Turkey, to prevent the enemy's foot from making night-attacks.'

The most detailed account we have of a medieval military camp is about the camp of the Vijayanagar army. 'The camp was divided into regular streets,' reports Nuniz. 'Each captain's division had its own market,' which was well-stocked with all kinds of provisions and other supplies, as in a city market; and there were there a number of craftsmen of all sorts, even jewellers. Such was the appearance of the Vijayanagar army camp that in it one 'would think that he was in a prosperous city,' and it was hard to believe that a war was going on.

Apart from stocking all that was required for the soldiers, the army camp also stocked immense quantities of grass and straw, needed to feed the vast number of animals in the army. 'Anyone can imagine what amount of grass and straw would be required each day for the consumption of 32,400 horses and 551 elephants, to say nothing of the sumpter-mules and asses, and the great number of oxen which carry all the supplies and many other burdens, such as tents and other things,' writes Nuniz.

AS IN THE case of military encampment, so also there were detailed and well-established conventions about the array of the army for battle, in the Hindu as well as the Sultanate armies. In the Delhi Sultanate, the battle array consisted of the centre, two wings, two flanking contingents, a vanguard and a rearguard. Armour-clad elephants carrying soldiers in the howdah mounted on them were usually deployed in front of this array, with a protective contingent of infantry and archers in front of them. Wide gaps were left in this frontal formation, for the cavalry, stationed at the back, to charge through the gaps and attack the enemy.

Military campaigns were normally launched, by rajas as well as by sultans, on days chosen by astrologers as lucky. This was a major factor in infusing confidence in soldiers. The king also usually went around the camp on the eve of the battle, to rouse the spirit of his soldiers. And the army stormed into battle to the sound of martial music, with the soldiers themselves yelling war cries and flinging challenges at the enemy, to psyche themselves up and to scare the enemy. Rajputs customarily entered the battle blowing conch-shells, as in a religious ritual, while Muslims struck kettledrums and blew trumpets.

At daybreak on the day of the battle 'they strike up their music as sign that they are about to give battle,' writes Nuniz about the practice in the Vijayanagar army, which he had probably observed personally, as he had spent about three years in the kingdom, during the reign of Achyutadeva. 'The drums and trumpets and other music in the king's camp then began to sound and the men to shout, so that it seemed as if the sky would fall to the earth; then [there was] the neighing and excitement of the horses, and the trumpeting of the elephants . . . [So fearsome was the din of all this] that even the very men that caused the noise were frightened by it. And the enemy on its part made no less noise, so that if you asked anything you could not hear yourself speak, and you had to ask by signs, since in no other manner could you make yourself understood.' Timur in his autobiography records that the soldiers of the raja of Jammu 'howled like so many jackals' while confronting Mongols

Nearly everywhere in medieval India, the battle began with the rival armies shooting arrows at each other. Then, 'when the time for shooting arrows was past, they used their spears and swords,' writes Afif. 'And when the conflict became even yet closer, the brave warriors seized each other by the waistbands, and grappled in deadly strife.' It was a savage scene, an animal fight, except that the combatants used sword and spear and axe, instead of tooth and claw. The battlefield after a clash was usually slush with blood, and strewn with the bodies and limbs of the fallen soldiers.

Fortunately, medieval Indian battles were usually, again like animal fights, very short affairs, lasting just a few hours, seldom more than a day. Sometimes however, though rarely, a battle lasted several days. Thus Mahmud Ghazni in one of his campaigns in Punjab fought a battle 'for three days and nights,' according to medieval Arabic chronicler Al-Utbi. 'On the fourth morning [Mahmud] made a most furious onslaught with swords and arrows, which lasted till noon,' and that carried the day for him.

Desertions were fairly common in Indian armies, and were generally not taken as a serious matter by kings, though we do sometimes hear of severe action being taken against runaways. Thus, according to Nuniz, Krishnadeva during one of his campaigns commanded his loyal soldiers 'to slay without mercy every one of those who had fled.' But if deserters were common in Indian armies, so were warrior heroes, who preferred to fight to death rather than to flee and save their lives, thinking that it was 'worse to be conquered than to die,' as Nuniz puts it.

One of the most difficult tasks in medieval wars was to capture forts, because armies those days did not have the heavy weapons needed to breach fort walls, which were usually several feet thick. Even after field artillery came into use in India, these crude weapons were of little use in breaking through fort walls. To get around this difficulty, the attackers tried to mine the fort walls, or to ram down the fort gates. They also cannonaded the fort by hurling stones and fireballs into it with catapults, and they shot at targets inside the fort by raising earthen mounds as tall as the fort wall and mounting cannons on them. Mahmud Ghazni is said to have hurled sacks of live serpents into an enemy fort by using catapults. The besiegers also used zigzag trenches or covered trenches to approach the fort walls without exposing themselves to enemy missiles.

Typical of the attack on a fort was Ibrahim Lodi's siege of Gwalior. According to Yadgar, the sultan had 'trenches dug [alongside the fort] in which he sheltered his men whilst he made his approaches, and distributed several batteries amongst his officers. He then projected fiery missiles, or shells, into the fort.' But none of these measures was particularly effective, as the defenders on the fort walls countered them by throwing down heavy stones or ignited bundles of cloth on the attackers. 'Hindus filled bags with cotton steeped in oil, which they ignited and threw down upon the enemy,' states Yadgar. Similarly, during the eighth century Arab conquest of Sind, according to *Chach-nama*, 'the garrison [in the local raja's fort] began to beat drums and sound clarions, and they threw down from the ramparts and bastions stones from mangonels and ballistas, [shot] arrows, and [hurled] javelins' at the assailants.

Quite often the only means of reducing a fort was to starve its defenders to submission, but that took a long time, for forts were usually well-stocked with provisions. So it often took several weeks or even several months, to capture a fort. Sometimes the only means of capturing a fort was by bribing some of its defenders.

ONE OF THE puzzles of the history of early medieval India is why the Hindu kings of the age were invariably routed in battle by Muslim armies, first by the Arabs, then by the Turko-Afghans in North India, and in the peninsula by the Deccan sultans, even though the rajas usually had more extensive territories, greater population and resources and much larger armies than the sultans. Devaraya II, the mid-fifteenth century king of Vijayanagar, once posed this puzzle to his courtiers. The courtiers then discussed the issue in detail among themselves, and came to the conclusion that the sultans invariably won their battles because of the superiority of their cavalry and archers.

This was not quite true. There was no difference at all in the quality of the horses used by Bahmani sultans and Vijayanagar rajas, for in both cases the horses were imported from the Middle East and Central Asia. As for cavalrymen and archers, their quality difference in the two armies could not have been the crucial factor in their military fortunes, as is evident from the fact that the induction of a large number of Muslim cavalrymen and archers into the Vijayanagar army did not make any significant difference in the outcome of its battles with Bahmani. Except Krishnadeva and Ramaraya, hardly any of the other Vijayanagar kings was ever victorious in his battles against the sultans. Equally puzzling is why the Delhi sultans in turn were defeated by the smaller invading forces of Timur and of Babur.

Apparently the size of the army and the quality of its mounts and equipments were not the decisive factors in the outcome of battles. What was decisive was the army's spirit. And discipline. 'The princes of the house of Bahmani maintained themselves by superior valour only, for in power, wealth and extent of country the rajas of Vijayanagar were greatly their superiors,' observes Ferishta. Hindu armies—particularly their vast infantry contingents— were just mobs, with hardly any military training. The immense size of the Hindu armies was often more a disadvantage than an advantage.

Occasionally there were some efforts to tighten the discipline of the Hindu soldiers, and to rouse their martial spirit by instilling in them religious fervour, as in the Muslim armies. But these do not seem to have yielded any significant change in the fortunes of Hindu armies. Thus, according to Ferishta, Bukka I in his battle against Bahmani sultan Muhammad Shah 'commanded the Brahmins to deliver every day to the troops discourses on the meritoriousness of slaughtering the Mohammedans, in order to excite [their zeal] . . . He ordered them to describe the butchery of cows, the insults to sacred images, and the destruction of temples [committed by Muslims].' Despite this harangue by Brahmins, Bukka lost the battle.

This was the usual outcome of the battles between rajas and sultans. And the frequent defeats that rajas suffered at the hands of sultans dispirited and demoralised Hindu armies. They often engaged in battle expecting defeat, and they were therefore often more ready to flee than to fight. In contrast, the confidence of victory and the prospect of plunder galvanised the Muslim armies.

Yet another reason for the defeat of the Hindu armies was that they were not cohesive or well-disciplined forces. Even though the armies of the sultans were also not cohesive forces—their soldiers were racially diverse, and they had a good number of Hindus of different castes and sects in them—they were far more tightly organised and disciplined than the armies of the rajas. There was no integrating spirit at all in the Hindu armies, no unifying emotional bond between the soldiers and their raja. Besides the caste divisions of the Hindu society also divided the Hindu army. Soldiers of different castes would not even sit together for a meal. In personal valour Hindu soldiers were quite probably in no way inferior to Muslim soldiers, but Hindu soldiers were not trained to fight as integrated units, so they lacked group discipline, and were consequently weak as an army. Even in the case of the renowned martial valour of the Rajput soldier, what mattered to him was not so much the victory of the army as the demonstration of his personal heroism. His view, as al-Biruni puts it, was that 'if he conquers, he obtains power and good fortune. If he perishes, he obtains paradise and bliss.' The outcome of the battle therefore did not matter much to him.

THERE WAS NO spirit of unity at all among the people of any state in early medieval India, to bind together the king and the people and the army. This was how it was in Hindu as well as Muslim kingdoms. But the armies of the sultanates—their dominant Muslim soldiers anyway—were united in their religious fervour and in their aggressive spirit as conquerors ruling over an alien subject people. There was no such galvanising spirit in the armies of most Hindu kingdoms. Their soldiers were fighting for pay and plunder, not for their king or for any large cause. The soldiers belonged to their caste, not to their kingdom, especially as the kingdoms, unlike the castes, were ephemeral entities. What happened to their king—whether he won or lost the battle—made hardly any difference in the lives of the common people, for the state played only a peripheral role in their lives.

This absence of any emotional bond between Hindu soldiers and their raja was evident even in the battles that rajas waged against sultans. Turks were of course an alien people, and belonged to an alien religion, but even that made very little difference in the lives of the common people, to rouse their spirit against them. The common people, even the rajas, viewed Turks as just one of the many diverse people in the subcontinent, each belonging to a different race, tribe, religion, sect, or caste, and each speaking a different language. The absence of antagonism among Indians towards Turks was also because there was hardly any interaction between these two people, for Turks were almost entirely confined to urban centres, while the preponderant majority of Indians lived in villages into which the Turkish rule barely intruded. The Turkish invasion of India therefore did not make any notable difference in the lives of the common people of India, and it roused no strong feeling of antagonism among them against Turks. They were of course exploited by the Turkish rulers, but then they were exploited by the Hindu rulers as well.

There was no awareness among Indians, among people or kings, of the radically different and historic nature of the Turkish invasion—that the Turkish invasion, unlike all the previous invasions of India by foreigners, entailed the displacement of virtually the entire traditional political class of India, and, even more importantly, the superimposition of a foreign civilisation and religion over Indian civilisation and religion. This lack of awareness meant that there was no general, united opposition among rajas against sultans. Even when Turks were rolling up Hindu kingdoms one after the other, rajas and chieftains went on with their usual endless petty squabbles and fights among themselves, as if nothing whatever in their world had changed, while everything had in fact changed radically. Not surprisingly, there were many instances of senior Hindu officers betraying their rajas to sultans, as if they were merely shifting their allegiance from one local ruler to another local ruler. And it was common for Indians to serve Turks as informers and guides. And once the Delhi Sultanate was established, multitudes of Hindus would serve the sultans in various administrative and military capacities without any antipathy whatever.

The pervasive attitude of fatalism among Indians of all classes was yet another factor affecting the spirit of Indian armies—victory and defeat were not in their hands, they believed; whatever was destined to happen would happen. This inculcated a negativist, defeatist attitude in Indian soldiers. They lacked the confident aggressiveness essential for success in battle. The enervating climate of India also played a role in desiccating the martial spirit of Indians. In the case of the Delhi Sultanate, regular fresh arrivals of men from Central Asia reinvigorated its army periodically, even as earlier migrants slowly lost their vigour and spirit. Not surprisingly, the dwindling of fresh arrivals of foreigners in the later part of the Sultanate history greatly weakened the kingdom.

VICTORY IN A BATTLE in medieval India was immediately followed by the victorious soldiers frenziedly rampaging through the enemy camp and the enemy country, indiscriminately slaughtering enemy soldiers as well as the common people, even women and children, and pillaging whatever valuables they could find, to glut their bloodlust and their lust for plunder. And this was, for the common soldiers, among Hindus as well as Muslims, the real reward for risking their lives in battle. Says al-Biruni about Mahmud Ghazni's Indian campaigns: 'Mahmud utterly ruined the prosperity of the country, and performed there wonderful exploits, by which Hindus became like atoms and dust, and scattered in all directions.' Similarly, when Vijayanagar once invaded Ahmadnagar, its soldiers, according to Ferishta, 'committed the most outrageous devastations, burning and razing buildings, putting up their horses in mosques, and performing their idolatrous worship in holy places.' In the frenzy of war, soldiers often did not even spare their coreligionists. Thus when Muhammad Tughluq once stormed into Devagiri to suppress a rebellion there, his soldiers plundered 'the inhabitants of Devagiri, Hindus and Muslims, traders and soldiers' without any discrimination, reports Barani.

This mode of military operation persisted in India till late medieval times. Thus we repeatedly come across phrases like 'attack and lay waste the country', 'ravage the country from end to end', 'kill and ravage as much as possible', 'plunder and lay waste all the country,' 'plunder and destroy every inhabited place', in the orders given to the Mughal army during the reign of Shah Jahan, as recorded by the contemporary chronicler Abdul-Hamid Lahauri. The conditions in the countryside around the battlefield, as well as in conquered cities, usually remained anarchic for several months after a battle. Thus Caesar Frederic, a sixteenth-century Venetian traveller in India, was held up for seven months in Vijayanagar after the battle of Talikota, as brigands were then rampaging through the land.

Fair treatment of the defeated enemy was uncommon in medieval India, the attitude of the victor being that he who is an enemy today could be an enemy again tomorrow, so it was best to exterminate him. Theirs was a feral relationship. Sometimes the defeated king and his chief officers were gibbeted, as a warning to other potential enemies. Often the enemy soldiers were herded into prison camps and sold as slaves. Muhammad Ghuri during one of his Indian campaigns is said to have captured so many of the enemy soldiers that they glutted the slave market, and their price fell so sharply that they had to be sold for just a dinar each. It was only very rarely that the victor treated the people of a conquered region with fairness and compassion, as Krishnadeva, according to Nuniz, is said to done when he captured Raichur.

Sometimes a raja, defeated by a sultan, became a Muslim, even ate beef, to save his life and throne, as a king of Jammu is said to have done once. 'Among these infidels there is no greater crime and abomination than eating the flesh of a cow or killing a cow, but he ate the flesh in the company of Muslims,' writes Timur in his autobiography. Often the defeated raja gave one of his daughters in marriage to the victor as a peace offering.

There were however several exceptions to such servile conduct, instances of Hindu kings preferring death to the humiliation of defeat and servitude.

According to Al-Utbi, 'there is a custom among . . . [some Hindu kings] that if any of them is taken prisoner by an enemy . . . it is not lawful for him to continue to reign . . . [So king Jayapala of Punjab, on being captured in war and later released by Mahmud Ghazni, decided that] death by cremation was preferable to shame and dishonour. So he commenced with shaving off his hair, and then threw himself upon the fire till he was burnt.'

A variation of this practice was jauhar, mass ritual suicide by the residents of a fort in imminent danger of being captured by the enemy. This involved the women and children of the raja, as well as the women and children of his nobles, immolating themselves, voluntarily or by force, in a funeral pyre built in the fort, and then the men storming out to fight the enemy, to kill and be killed.

The first known account of this practice is in *Chach-nama*. The custom was probably introduced into India by Central Asian migrants in the late classical period, and seems to have been initially confined to Rajputs, who were mostly migrants. In time the custom spread to the ruling class of some other people also. Thus, according to Battuta, the raja of Kampili in Karnataka, on the verge of his castle being stormed by the army of Muhammad Tughluq, 'commanded a great fire to be prepared and lighted. Then . . . he said to his wives and daughters, "I am going to die, and such of you as prefer it, do the same." Then it was seen that each one of these women washed herself, rubbed her body with sandalwood paste, kissed the ground before the raja . . . and threw herself upon the pyre. All perished. The wives of his nobles, ministers, and chief men imitated them, and other women also did the same. The raja, in his turn, washed, rubbed himself with sandalwood paste, and took his arms, but did not put on his breastplate. Those of his men who resolved to die with him followed his example. Then they sallied forth to meet the troops of the sultan, and fought till every one of them fell dead.'

PART VIII

SOCIO-ECONOMIC SCENE

I do repent of wine and talk of wine
Of idols fair with chins like silver fine
A lip-repentance and a lustful heart,
O god, forgive this penitence of mine.

—ASJADI

1

Paradise on Earth?

'India . . . is the most agreeable abode on the earth, the most pleasant quarter of the world,' states Abdullah Wassaf, an early fourteenth-century Persian writer, in his long and fanciful paean on India. 'Its dust is purer than air, and its air purer than purity itself; its delightful plains resemble the garden of paradise, and the particles of its earth are like rubies and corals . . . [It] is distinguished from all parts of the globe by its extreme temperateness, and by the purity of its water and air . . . Indeed, the charms of the country and the softness of the air, together with the variety of its wealth, precious metals, stones, and other abundant products, are beyond description . . . Its treasuries and depositories are like the oceans full of polished gems; its trees are in continual freshness and verdure; and the zephyrs of its air are pure and odoriferous; the various birds on its boughs are sweet-singing parrots; and the pheasants in its gardens are all graceful peacocks.

> It is asserted that Paradise is in India,
> Be not surprised because Paradise itself
>   is not comparable to it.'

All this was mere poetic fancy by a writer who had never been to India. But even Indian writers were susceptible to such mythifications, as in the case of poet Amir Khusrav extolling India as a heavenly country—'Hindustan is like heaven,' he writes—even though he could plainly see before his very eyes an entirely different reality. Similarly over-effulgent is the description of India by the fourteenth-century Syrian writer Shahab-ud-din. 'India,' he writes, 'is a most important country, with which no other country in the world can be compared in respect of extent, riches, the numbers of its armies, the pomp and splendour displayed by the sovereign in his progresses and habitations, and the power of his empire . . . Its inhabitants are remarkable for their wisdom and intelligence; no people are better able to restrain their passion, nor more willing to sacrifice their lives, for what they consider agreeable in the sight of god.'

Closer to reality, but still rather exaggerated, is the praise of medieval India given in *Mukhtasiru-t Tawarikh*, a chronicle by an anonymous writer who lived in India during the reign of Mughal emperor Shah Jahan. 'India is a very large country, and it is so extensive that the other countries are not equal to a hundredth part of it. Notwithstanding its extensive area, it is populated in all places. It abounds in all quarters and every district with cities, towns, villages, caravanserais, forts, citadels, mosques, temples, monasteries, cells, magnificent buildings, delightful gardens, fine trees, pleasant green fields, running streams, and impetuous rivers . . . In this country there are mines of diamonds, ruby, gold, silver, copper, lead, and iron.'

SUCH FANCIFUL IMAGES of India were common in the premodern world, and they played a key role in enticing numerous migrants and invaders into India all through history. And Indians themselves, like most other people, were addicted to self-mythification. But gradually a more realistic view of India began to emerge in the reports of medieval Turkish writers and European travellers, though there was still a good amount of fancy even in these accounts, and they were inevitably marred by the racial prejudice and socio-religious bias of the chroniclers. Typical of the dichotomous view of medieval foreigners about India was what a noble told Timur when he was planning to invade India. India, he said, was an excellent country to raid and plunder, for it was fabulously wealthy, but it would be self-destructive to occupy and rule it. 'If we establish ourselves permanently therein, our race will degenerate and our children will become like the natives of those regions, and in a few generations their strength and valour will diminish,' he cautioned.

There is a good amount of information about medieval India in the chronicles of the age by Muslim writers, far more than on any of the previous ages in Indian history, but these almost solely deal with political history, and there is hardly any information in them about the towns and villages of India, or about the way of life of the common people. Though there is some information on these matters in the accounts of contemporary European travellers in India, these are quite meagre, just some casual sketches of a few random places, communities and incidents.

The Indian city on which we have the most information in medieval chronicles is, predictably, Delhi. According to a widely held but unverifiable tradition, Delhi was originally Indraprastha, City of Indra, mentioned in *Mahabharata* as the capital of Pandavas. In historical times the city, termed Dilli or Dillika, is believed to have been founded in the mid-eighth century by Tomaras (a Rajput clan ruling Haryana) as their capital. The name first occurs in an inscription in the late twelfth century.

But Delhi was at this time just an obscure provincial city. It was only in the early thirteenth century, after it became the capital of the Delhi Sultanate, that it gained subcontinental prominence. It would thereafter, except for a few short interludes, remain the political hub of India, first as the capital of the Delhi Sultanate, then of the Mughal empire, then of the British-Indian empire, and finally of the Republic of India.

The city became the capital of the Delhi Sultanate when Aibak, the Turkish general in India, assumed sovereign power in Delhi in 1206, on the death of his overlord, Muhammad Ghuri. The location of the city was ideal for the Delhi sultans, for it was near the centre of their extensive kingdom, which stretched from Punjab to Bengal across the Indo-Gangetic Plain. Further, Delhi had the advantage of being quite distant from the vulnerable western frontier of the Sultanate menaced by the Mongols, and yet close enough to the frontier to defend it.

Delhi grew immensely in size and prominence under the sultans, and in time it became a much admired city in the medieval Muslim world. It was 'the envy of the cities of the inhabited world,' claims Barani, an early medieval chronicler. Battuta, a Moroccan traveller who was in Delhi during the reign of Muhammad Tughluq, is equally lavish in his praise of the city. 'Delhi, the metropolis of India, is a vast and magnificent city, uniting beauty with strength,' Battuta testifies. 'It is surrounded by a wall that has no equal in the world, and is the largest city in India, nay, rather largest city in the entire Muslim Orient. The city of Delhi is now made up of four neighbouring and contiguous towns. One of them is Delhi proper, the old city built by the infidels . . . The second is called Siri . . . The third is called Tughluqabad . . . The fourth is called Jahan Panah (Refuge of the World), and is set apart for the residence of the reigning sultan, Muhammad.' Like all the cities and major towns of the age in India, Delhi was a fort city, and it had, according to Battuta, twenty-eight gates.

Towards the close of the history of the Delhi Sultanate its capital was shifted from Delhi to Agra by Sikandar Lodi. But Agra was not a lucky city for Sikandar, for on 6 July 1505, soon after he shifted his residence there, a violent earthquake shattered the town, reducing most of it to rubble. 'Even the very hills quaked, and lofty buildings crashed to the ground,' writes Ni'matullah, an early seventeenth-century chronicler. 'The living thought that the Day of Judgment had arrived; the dead, the day of resurrection.' The quake was so intense that it was felt nearly all over India, and even in far away Persia.

Very little is known about the early history of Agra. According to Abdullah, a seventeenth century chronicler, Agra before the time of Sikandar Lodi was 'a mere village, but one of old standing.' There was an old fort there, which was used by the raja of Mathura as a state prison before the advent of the Turks. Agra was ravaged by Mahmud Ghazni during one of his raids into India, and he so utterly devastated it that 'it became one of the most insignificant villages in the land,' states Abdullah. 'After this, it improved from the time of Sultan Sikandar [Lodi], and at length, in Akbar's time, became the seat of government . . . and one of the chief cities of Hindustan.'

ANOTHER MUCH ADMIRED early medieval Indian city was Vijayanagar, founded in 1336 by Harihara. In the beginning it was just a small fortified settlement in the hill country along the southern bank of the Tungabhadra, but in time it grew into a very large city, which probably had a population of half a million or more. The ruins of the city today cover nearly thirty square kilometres. 'The city of Vijayanagar is such that eye has not seen nor ear heard of any place resembling it upon the whole earth,' writes Abdur Razzak, the mid-fifteenth century Persian envoy in Vijayanagar. 'It is so built that it has seven fortified walls, one within the other. Beyond the circuit of the outer wall there is an esplanade extending for about fifty yards, in which stone slabs are fixed near one another to the height of a man . . . so that neither foot nor horse . . . can advance with facility near the outer wall . . . The fortress [which is within the seventh enclosure of the city] is in the form of a circle, situated on the summit of a hill . . . In that is the palace of the king . . . Between the first, second, and third walls, there are cultivated fields, gardens and houses. From the third to the seventh enclosure, shops and bazaars are closely crowded together . . . There are many rivulets and streams flowing through channels of cut stone, polished and even.'

Some eight decades after Razzak, in the first quarter of the sixteenth century, Portuguese traveller Domingos Paes visited the city and described it 'as large as Rome, and very beautiful to the sight,' having gardens and lakes in it. The city had, according to Paes, some 100,000 houses. Another Portuguese traveller, Duarte Barbosa, also visited Vijayanagar around this time. The king of Vijayanagar, he writes, has 'very large and handsome palaces, with numerous courts . . . There are also in this city many other palaces of great lords . . . All the other houses of the place are covered with thatch. The streets and squares are very wide. They are constantly filled with innumerable crowd of all nations and creeds . . . There is an infinite trade in this city.'

About 600 kilometres to the north of Vijayanagar, in Maharashtra, is Daulatabad, a fort unlike any other in the world. Originally built by Yadavas around the turn of the twelfth century, the fort was captured by Ala-ud-din

Khalji towards the close of the thirteenth century. In 1327 Muhammad Tughluq shifted his capital from Delhi to it for a while, partly because of his resentment towards the truculent people of Delhi, but mainly because of the surpassing strength of the Daulatabad fort, which stands on a conical hill some 200 metres high. Daulatabad, writes Battuta, is an 'enormous city which rivals Delhi . . . in importance and in the spaciousness of its planning . . . [Its fortress] is on a rock situated in a plain; the rock has been excavated and a castle built on its summit.'

The most detailed medieval description of the fort is given by Abdul-Hamid Lahauri, the official chronicler of Mughal emperor Shah Jahan. 'This fortress . . . is on a mass of rock which raises its head towards heaven,' he writes. The sides of the hill at the bottom were chiselled away all around to form a sheer vertical barrier of about fifty metres high from the ground. And the barrier in turn was scraped smooth and even so that, according to Lahauri, 'not even an ant or a snake could crawl up the slippery surface.' For additional defence, the barrier was girded at its base by a broad and deep moat—'40 cubits broad and 30 cubits deep'—hewn into solid rock. Further, the citadel, which was at the top of the hill, was itself girded by three concentric defensive walls, with bastions on them.

The only access to the citadel was through an iron gate at the base of the hill, which opened into a tortuous, zigzag cave passage hewn into the interior of the rock. 'This passage,' notes Lahauri, 'is so dark that even on the brightest day you could not grope your way through it without lamps and torches . . . In order to obstruct this passage in case of emergency they have constructed some iron plates to close it up, which they can heat up with fire and thus render it utterly impossible for any living creature to pass through. From the middle to the crest of the hill, by way of additional security, strong forts have been erected of stone and quicklime.'

All this made Daulatabad entirely impregnable. 'Thus the usual means for the reduction of forts—such as mines, covered galleries, and batteries—are all utterly useless in besieging such an impregnable fortress as this,' concludes Lahauri. 'In fact, its capture is impossible except through the agency of accidental or miraculous means; hence drought, famine and pestilence became the instruments of its final overthrow.'

THERE ARE A FEW brief descriptions of several other Indian cities in medieval chronicles. One such city is Gwalior, which Hasan Nizami, a contemporary of Qutb-ud-din Aibak, describes as 'the pearl on the necklace of the castles of Hind.' Adds Battuta: 'The fort of Gwalior . . . is situated on the top of a high mountain, and appears . . . to be cut out of the rock itself . . . There are subterranean cisterns in it, and it contains also about twenty bricked wells . . . Near the gate of the fort there is the figure of an elephant with its mahout, carved in stone, which when seen from a distance seems to be a real elephant. At the base of the fortress there is a fine town, built entirely of white hewn stone, mosques and houses alike. No wood is used except for the doors. '

Urban centres had generally become derelict in India in the late classical period, because of economic decline and the slide of India into the Dark Ages. Though there was some revival of urbanisation during the sultanate period, most of the towns in India were still in a dilapidated state at this time. This was the condition of many villages also, as Battuta in the fourteenth century found. Most medieval Indian villages were secluded settlements, surrounded by thickets or forests, which covered most regions of the subcontinent at this time. Battuta, for instance, found that the Tamil country 'was an uninterrupted and impassable jungle of trees and reeds.'

Villages in early medieval India were just clusters of huts, with fields and pastures alongside them. They were often temporary habitations, as the population kept shifting periodically, abandoning old villages and setting up new ones, seeking fresh lands for cultivation. 'In Hindustan hamlets and villages, even towns, are depopulated and set up in a moment,' noted Mughal emperor Babur in the early sixteenth century. 'If the people of a large town, one inhabited for years even, flee from it, they do it in such a way that not a sign or trace of them remains in a day, or a day and a half.'

The village scene in medieval India varied considerably from region to region, India being a vast and diverse country. In most parts of India villagers led an isolated, self-sufficient life in medieval times, needing hardly anything from outside the village to meet their meagre requirements. It was only the temple fairs in the neighbouring towns once a year or so that brought villagers out of their seclusion. But there were also regions in India where villages were contiguous, and villagers had a broad social life. 'The country is but small, yet it is so full of people, that it may well be called one town,' says Barbosa about Kerala.

TRAVEL FACILITIES, LIKE everything else in medieval India, varied considerably from region to region. The best roads in India at this time were in the Indo-Gangetic Plain, the east-west and the north-south arterial roads passing thorough Delhi. It was a laudable traditional practice of kings and chieftains in premedieval India to plant shade trees and fruit trees along roads, and this practice was continued by medieval rulers. Thus Battuta found that the nearly 1000 kilometre long road between Delhi and Daulatabad was all along the way 'bordered with trees, such as the willow and others, so the traveller might think himself in a garden.' Similar was the observation of the anonymous author of *Mukhtasiru-t Tawarikh* some three centuries later: 'On all roads shady and fruit trees are planted on both sides. Wells and tanks are dug which contain fresh and sweet water in abundance. The passengers go along the roads under the shadow of the trees, amusing themselves, eating the fruits and drinking cold water, as if they are taking a walk along the beds of a garden.' And in faraway Kerala, Battuta found that the roads there 'run through orchards.'

Mukhtasiru-t Tawarikh further states that 'on all public roads and streets strong bridges are made over every river and rill, and embankments are also are raised.' This clearly is an exaggeration. Bridges across rivers were rare in medieval India—rivers were usually crossed by boats, or waded across during the dry season. Paes found that in Vijayanagar people crossed rivers 'by boats which are round like baskets; inside they are made of cane, and outside are covered with leather. They are able to carry fifteen or twenty persons. Even horses and oxen cross in them if necessary, but for the most part these animals swim across. Men row the boats with a sort of paddle, and the boats are always turning round, as they cannot go straight like others. In all the kingdom . . . there are no other boats but these.'

There was a fair amount of long-distance river traffic in medieval India, particularly down the Ganga-Yamuna river system. But road travel was easier and faster, and had greater facilities. Pillars with travel directions were erected on all important roads. 'All along the road [from Delhi to central India] . . . there are pillars, on which is engraved the number of miles from each pillar to the next,' reports Battuta. 'Lofty minarets are made at the distance of each kos to indicate the road,' states *Mukhtasiru-t Tawarikh*. There were even public transport facilities in some places. According to Afif, a courtier chronicler of Firuz Tughluq, there was in his time very heavy traffic between Delhi and Firuzabad, and 'to accommodate this great traffic, there were public carriers who kept carriages, mules and horses, which were ready for hire at a settled rate every morning . . . Palanquin-bearers were also ready to convey passengers. The fare of a carriage was four silver jitals for each person; for a mule, six; for a horse, twelve; and for a palanquin, half a tanka. There were also plenty of porters ready for employment by anyone, and they earned a good livelihood.'

There were also rest houses along the main roads. 'At every two *parasangs* inns are built of strong masonry for travellers to dwell in and take rest,' states *Mukhtasiru-t Tawarikh*. 'Every kind of food and drink, all sorts of medicines, and all kinds of necessary instruments and utensils can be obtained at each inn.' This is also reported by Battuta: 'At each of these stations the traveller finds all that he needs, as if his . . . journey lay through a market.' According to the mid-fifteenth century Russian traveller Nikitin, 'In the land of India it is the custom of foreign traders to stop at inns; there the food is cooked for the guests by the landlady, who also makes the bed and sleeps with the stranger. Women that know you willingly concede their favours, for they like white men.'

Similar facilities were available even in the peripheral regions of India. 'The road over the whole distance runs beneath the shade of trees, and at every half-mile there is a wooden shed with benches on which all travellers, whether Muslims or infidels, may sit,' reports Battuta about his experience in Kerala. 'At each shed there is a well for drinking water and an infidel in charge of it. If the traveller is an infidel he gives him water in vessels; if he is a Muslim he pours the water into his hands, continuing to do so until he signs to him to stop . . . At all the halting places on this road there are houses belonging to Muslims, at which Muslim travellers alight, and where they buy all that they need.'

In North India there were, in medieval times, several deep and elaborately constructed step-wells along the main roads, which had pavilions attached to them, providing resting places for travellers. 'Kings and nobles of the country vie with one another in constructing them along the highroads where there is no water,' notes Battuta.

THESE FACILITIES WERE however available only on just a few major roads. Travel in medieval India was usually quite hazardous, especially in the sparsely populated regions, because of the menace of highwaymen and the lack of proper roads there. Even the environs of major cities, including Delhi, were not always secure, as brigands openly rampaged through the land at the slightest sign of weakness in government. And trans-regional travellers often had to pass through dense forests, which were particularly dangerous places, as they were infested with bandits and wild tribes, apart from wild animals.

Travel security varied greatly from region to region in India. *Mukhtasiru-t Tawarikh* is clearly utopianising medieval India when it states that 'merchants and tradesmen and all travellers, without any fear of thieves and robbers, take their goods and loads safe to distant destinations.' Battuta also at times indulged in similar fantasies. 'I have never seen a safer road than this,' he writes about his experience in Kerala, 'for they put to death anyone who steals a single nut, and if any fruit falls no one picks it up but the owner.'

Several regions of India in medieval times were entirely trackless, and sometimes even sultans lost their way there, as it once happened to Firuz Tughluq while returning to Delhi from Orissa. And nearly everywhere in India monkeys were a major nuisance to travellers, even to armies. 'Several times when I encamped in these mountains great numbers of monkeys came into the camp from the jungles and woods, both night and day, and laid their claws upon whatever they could find to eat, and carried it off . . . At night they stole little articles and curiosities,' writes Timur about his experience in India.

Because of all these diverse perils people usually travelled in large groups, and whenever possible they accompanied trade caravans, which had armed guards.

Indian summer was yet another hazard that travellers had to cope with. 'The heat was so intense that my companions used to sit naked except for a cloth around the waist and another cloth soaked with water on their shoulders; this dried up in a very short time, so they had to keep wetting it constantly,' writes Battuta about his experience in Sind. Summer was particularly brutal in 1505, the year in which a devastating earthquake struck Agra. That year, recounts Ni'matullah, 'the heat of the air became so intense that almost all people fell grievously sick of fevers.'

As in everything else in medieval India, the mode of travel also varied from region to region. In peninsular India, according to Nikitin, people did not travel on horses, but used 'oxen and buffaloes . . . for riding, conveying goods, and every other purpose.' And in Kerala 'no one travels on an animal . . . and only the sultan possesses horses,' states Battuta. 'The principal vehicle of the inhabitants is a palanquin carried on the shoulders of slaves or hired porters; those who do not travel on palanquins go on foot, be they who they may. Baggage and merchandise is transported by hired carriers, and a single merchant may have a hundred such or thereabouts carrying his goods.'

Because of these diverse modes of travel and transport, and the general difficulties of the roads, the pace of travel was very slow in medieval India. Thus, according to Battuta, it took forty days to cover the 1000 kilometres between Delhi and Daulatabad, even though the highway between these two cities was one of the best in India. Travel was considerably slower in the peninsula, because there were hardly any roads there. 'The country of Ma'bar (the Tamil country), which is so distant from the city of Delhi that a man travelling with all expedition could reach it only after a journey of twelve months,' states Amir Khusrav, medieval Indian poet-chronicler.

2

Polymorphic Society

Over the millennia, from the Old Stone Age, or perhaps from an even earlier period, to well into late medieval times, many diverse races had debouched into India, as migrants or invaders, through the defiles in the Hindu Kush mountains on the north-west border of the subcontinent. These mountain passes were among the most active trans-continental migration routes of races in the premodern world. And nearly all the diverse people who entered India through these passes made India their homeland. The many different races in the subcontinent today are all migrants. None are natives.

The invasions of Turko-Afghans and Mughals into India in medieval times were the last of the major people movements into India, and they radically altered the socio-cultural profile of the country. Though India would later, in early modern times, come under the dominance of yet another foreign power, the British, that involved no notable alteration in the population profile of India, as there was hardly any migration of Englishmen into India. In contrast to this, both the Turko-Afghan and the Mughal invasions of India resulted in radical changes in the racial makeup of India, as those invasions led to large-scale migrations into India by Central Asian and the Middle Eastern Muslims, who saw India as a land of opportunity, and were drawn to it by the prospect of gaining wealth and power. Further, India was for many of them a safe haven into which to escape from the racial and political turmoil in their homeland.

The consequences of the invasion of India by Turko-Afghans were fundamentally different from those of all previous invaders—while all the people who previously entered India had eventually blended smoothly and indistinguishably into Indian society by adopting Indian religion, social customs, cultural values, and even local languages, this did not happen in the

324

case of Turko-Afghans, because in all these matters the culture of Indians was totally antithetical to that of Turks.

Unlike polytheistic Hinduism, which could absorb into it any number of new deities, beliefs and practices, and had a society divided into numerous hereditary, hierarchal and exclusive castes, each of which had its specific profession, Islam was a monotheistic religion which, though it had some sectarian divisions in it, was essentially a cohesive religion with only one god and one basic set of beliefs and practices. And its society was egalitarian, without any birth determined, caste-like social divisions in it, so anyone from any racial, social or family background could take up any vocation in it, aspire to occupy any office, and gain any social status.

These socio-religious differences led to a sharp divergence in the attitudes of Muslims and Hindus towards each other. The Hindu attitude towards Muslims was similar to the tolerant-intolerant attitude of Hindu castes towards each other. Hindus had no objection to Muslims keeping to their beliefs and practices, just as they had no objection to the different castes and sects of Hindus keeping to their particular beliefs and practices. But they would not tolerate the intermixing of the two communities, just as they would not tolerate the intermixing of different castes. Similarly, though Hindus normally had no objection to serve under a Muslim employer, they would avoid all social interaction with him. Typical of this was the experience of Battuta in Kerala, about which he writes: 'It is the custom of the infidels in the Mulaybar lands that no Muslim may enter their houses or eat from their vessels.' For Hindus, particularly for high caste Hindus, Muslims were untouchables. Muslims had no such apartheidal prejudices. They did treat Hindus as second class citizens, but this was not an irreversible birth-determined status division, as in Hindu society, for even Hindus of the lowest of the low outcastes were, on being converted into Islam, treated as equals to everyone else in that society, and the personal status of an individual depended solely on his abilities and achievements, not on his birth. So a person who was on the bottom rung of Hindu society could rise to the highest rung of Muslim society.

BECAUSE OF THIS antithetical character of Hinduism and Islam, there was very little socio-cultural interaction or mutual influence between the two communities, despite their several centuries long coexistence in India. In fact Muslims and Hindus mostly lived physically separated from each other—while most Muslims lived in towns (serving the government as soldiers and civil servants, or engaged in various occupations, as artisans, merchants, and so on) the vast majority of Hindus lived in villages (mostly as farmers and farm-labourers). And even in towns, where the two communities coexisted, they lived in different wards of towns, as an extension of the traditional Hindu practice of different castes living in different parts of towns and villages.

However, despite the sharp socio-religious segregation between Hindus and Muslims, there was some amount of interaction between the two communities in towns, and they did have some influence on each other. But these influences were mostly superficial, and were confined to a few small groups. The most obvious instance of this was that the Hindu political elite in North India gradually took to the Turkish mode of dress and adopted some Turkish social practices, and the Turks in turn adopted certain practices of the Hindu aristocracy. And in religion, the mystic movements in both religions did exert some influence on each other.

On the whole, Muslim rule did not make any notable difference in the lives of the vast majority of Indians, and hardly anything changed in Hindu society because of Muslim influence. Nor did anything change in Muslim society consequent of its interaction with Hindu society, except that the Hindu converts to Islam carried some of their traditional practices with them into Islamic society. For the most part, the two communities remained sharply divided and incompatible. They coexisted, but did not interact.

There were some curious internal paradoxes in both Hindu and Muslim socio-religious systems. Islam as a religion was adamantine in character and was generally impervious to external influences, but Islamic society was open and fluid, into which people of any race or clan or social background could enter on becoming Muslims, and play any role according to their interest and ability, without being restricted to any birth-determined roles. The values and practices of Hindu religion and society were the exact reverse of this. Hinduism was a fluid, diversified and ever-changing religion, open to various external influences, but Hindu society was adamantine in character, which had place only for those who were born as Hindus, and in which a person born into a particular caste could not ever change his caste and social status, and was bound to the occupation of that caste, whatever be his interest and ability.

There were however some exceptions in these matters, in Hindu as well as Muslim society. Thus, even though Muslim society in theory was an open and egalitarian society, which had no social divisions based on race or clan or birth, in practice it had divisions based on these factors. On the other hand, Hindu society, despite its seeming rigidity and imperviousness, was in fact a porous society, and it had over the centuries absorbed numerous foreign people and non-Aryan local tribes and their cults into it. This however was not done by performing any rite, as in the case of the conversions of outsiders into Islam or Christianity, but through a process of osmosis, by which outsiders and their cults inconspicuously, and without any formal process, seeped into Hindu society over several centuries.

But this was a process of community transition, not of individuals. Normally it was impossible for any outsider individual to enter Hindu society, for Hinduism has no conversion rites to admit non-Hindus into its fold. To be a Hindu one has to be born a Hindu. But in this too, as in nearly everything else in the ever-rigid-ever-flexible Hindu society, there were exceptions, though rare, by which elaborate rites were performed to induct non-Hindu rajas, chieftains and other important persons into Hindu society at appropriate social levels. This process involved the fabrication, through the connivance of colluding priests, of a myth that the conversion seeker belonged to a family that had originally been a Hindu, but had lost its religion and caste because of its deviant practices, and that he could be therefore restored to his family's original religion and caste through certain purification ceremonies.

ISLAM AND HINDUISM were totally antipodal in religion and society. Nevertheless the attitude of the Muslim rulers in India towards their Hindu subjects was in most cases accommodative rather than suppressive. It necessarily had to be so, for pragmatic reasons. From the purely religious point of view, the sultans had to do what they could to fetter or eradicate Hinduism, and thus promote Islam, but from the practical point of view they needed to patronise Hindus, for they could not possibly govern their Indian kingdoms without the services of Hindus, as they did not have the requisite administrative organisation or personnel, or the local knowledge, to do that. The sultans therefore treated Hindus as zimmis, protected non-Muslims, by which Hindus were allowed, though with some restrictions, to maintain their social customs and observe their religious practices; they were even allowed to perform rites which were abominable to orthodox Muslims, such as sati, and animal and human sacrifices.

In the early history of Islam, the zimmi privilege was accorded only to Jews and Christians, while the followers of other religions were required to become Muslims or be exterminated. But when Islam expanded beyond Arabia, its homeland, the zimmi privilege was, for various practical reasons, extended to the people of other religions as well, including Hindus. In India, the sheer vastness of the non-Muslim population made it in any case physically impossible to extirpate them. Furthermore, Hindus were the primary economically productive people of the land, particularly in agriculture, so to massacre them, or even to oppress them beyond endurance, would have been counterproductive for the sultans, for that would have been to uproot the very plants that nourished them.

Hindus were treated as second class citizens in Muslim states, but as citizens nevertheless. They had their own rights. The discriminatory treatment that Hindus received at the hands of Muslim rulers would not have troubled them much, for most Indian communities were subject to worse discrimination in their own rigidly hierarchal caste society. For most Hindus, Muslims would have seemed like just another segment in their own labyrinthine society. Hindus and Muslims did live separately; but then so did the different Hindu castes. Even in the matter of jizya, not many Hindus would have felt it as a particularly discriminative tax, for Muslims also had to pay a community tax, zakat. Besides, jizya was usually imposed on individuals only in towns, while in villages it was imposed as a collective tax.

ON THE WHOLE the life of the vast majority of the common people under Muslim rule in India remained the same as what it was before the Muslim invasion. This was mainly because the impact of Muslim rule was largely confined to towns, while most Indians lived in villages where there were hardly any Muslims. Even in towns, where there was a fair amount of interaction between Hindus and Muslims, the treatment of Hindus by the sultans, even by the most bigoted of them, would not have been anywhere near as ruthless as described by Muslim chroniclers seeking to eulogise their kings. To most Indians, the sultans would not have seemed any more oppressive than their own rajas. Whether it was a raja or a sultan who ruled over them made little difference in the generally wretched life of the common people in India.

Muslim courtier chroniclers, most of whom were hyper-orthodox, generally tended to gloatingly exaggerate the severity of the persecution of Hindus by sultans, which they considered as a most praiseworthy act. Thus Barani, while lauding the slaughter of Hindus by Mahmud Ghazni, wished that the sultan had campaigned in India once more, and had 'brought under his sword all the Brahmins of Hind who . . . are the cause of the continuance of the laws of infidelity and the strength of idolaters . . . [and had] cut off the heads of two hundred or three hundred thousand Hindu chiefs.' Similarly, Barani exaggeratedly lauded Ala-ud-din for his oppression of Hindus, stating 'that by the last decade of his reign the submission and obedience of the Hindus had become an established fact. Such a submission on the part of the Hindus has neither been seen before nor will be witnessed hereafter.' Reality, though harsh, was not quite so harsh.

Curiously, while the Muslim intelligentsia was generally aggressive in its attitude towards Hinduism, the Hindu intelligentsia was entirely passive in its response to the establishment of the Muslim rule in India. There is hardly any mention of the Turkish conquest of India in the Sanskrit works of the early middle ages. This was perhaps because the preoccupation of the Hindu intelligentsia was with transcendental matters. The general attitude of fatalism among Indians—that whatever happens is fated to happen—also no doubt contributed to the apathetic attitude of Indians to the circumstances of their life. And this was one of the major factors that enabled a small group of Turko-Afghans to rule over an infinitely larger number of Indians for several centuries without any major resistance.

The general attitude of Muslims, the masters, towards Hindus, the subjects, was of scorn. And there was, inevitably, a good amount of persecution of Hindus by the sultans, though it was nothing comparable to what it could have been, given the totally antithetical nature of the two socio-religious systems. Very many Hindu temples were demolished by the sultans, and their idols smashed or defiled. Ostentatious Hindu religious celebrations were forbidden in Muslim states. And there were several instances of the general massacre of Hindus by the sultans. Some of these acts were revoltingly savage, such as the mass slaughter of Hindu men, women and children by a mid-fourteenth century sultan of Madurai, which was excoriated even by Ibn Battuta, a fellow Muslim. 'This,' commented Battuta, 'was a hideous thing such as I have never seen being indulged in by any king.' But such acts of savagery were random, not systematic, and they seem to have been motivated more by the need to terrorise a conquered people into servility, than by religious fervour, though religious fervour was also undeniably present.

FORTUNATELY, THE ANTI-HINDU venom was more on the tongues of Muslim clerics and chroniclers than on the swords of the sultans. Except in a few rare instances, Hindus were not oppressed beyond endurance in Muslim kingdoms. This is evident from the fact that a very large number of Hindus served in the government and the army of Muslim states. Most of the service providers in Muslim states—merchants, craftsmen, moneylenders, and so on— were also no doubt Hindus. And nearly all the farmers in India were Hindus.

Hindus generally had no compunction about serving under sultans in any capacity, even as soldiers and captains in the battles of the sultans against rajas. Many of the top officers of even the hyper-orthodox Mughal emperor Aurangzeb were Hindus. Equally, many Muslims served in the army and administration of Hindu kingdoms. In that freewheeling political environment rajas often allied with sultans, even in the battles of sultans against fellow rajas, and sultans often allied with rajas, even the battles of rajas against fellow sultans.

In the personal life of the sultans also there were some curious intercultural and interreligious influences and practices. The sultans, despite their professed orthodoxy, sometimes even sought the counsels of Hindu and Jain sages. According to Jain sources, Ala-ud-din Khalji used to hold discussions with Jain sages, and he is said to have once specially summoned Jain sage Acharya Mahasena from Karnataka to Delhi for consultations. Muhammad Tughluq is also known to have had Jain counsellors; and he, according to Battuta, used to consort with Hindu yogis. Some of the sultans were exceptionally liberal in their treatment of Hindus—Ala-ud-din Husain Shah, the early sixteenth century sultan of Bengal, for instance, is said to have been so benevolent in his treatment of all his subjects, irrespective of their religion, that local Hindu poets eulogised him as Arjuna or Krishna, Hindu mythical heroes.

SUCH LIBERAL TREATMENT of Hindus by sultans was odious to orthodox Muslims, for Islam was traditionally an aggressively proselytising religion, which had little tolerance for the people of other religions, and had in its early history forcefully converted a large number of people into the religion. But such conversions were rare in India. The practice however varied from sultan to sultan. The Tughluqs, Muhammad and Firuz, are known to have coerced the families of some defeated rajas to become Muslims. But the primary concern of most sultans was to preserve and expand their power, and they had hardly any inclination to work as missionaries.

There were however a good number of voluntary converts to Islam from low caste and outcaste Hindu communities, and this went on all through the medieval period. It was a great advantage for this class of Hindus to become Muslims, for conversion opened up unprecedented career and social advancement opportunities for them, which they would never have had in Hindu society. As Muslims they could occupy any position that they merited by their abilities, and thus move up in society, free from the caste bond that confined them to a particular social niche and profession. Not surprisingly, many of the underclass conversions to Islam were mass conversions, following community or clan decisions.

Apart from low caste and outcaste Hindus, many traders, craftsmen and other service providers also found it to be a temporal advantage for them to become Muslims, as that widened their business opportunities, as most of their affluent customers were now Muslims. A few upper class Hindus also voluntarily became Muslims, thereby to gain various socio-political and material advantages. There are said to have been even a few instances of men becoming Muslims because of their conviction of the superiority of Islam over Hinduism as a religion

Despite all this, even at the close of the eighteenth century, after six centuries of dominant Muslim rule in India, the region around Delhi, the core area of Muslim power in India, had only around 14 per cent Muslims in its population. However, in some other regions of the subcontinent, particularly in the western and eastern flanks of the Indo-Gangetic Plain—the regions that in the twentieth century became Pakistan and Bangladesh—Muslims constituted a much larger part of the local population, presumably because of the mass conversion to Islam of tribal people in those mountainous regions.

The proportion of Muslim population in the subcontinent increased over the next century and half, because of the higher birth-rate in the community, so that by the end of the British rule in 1947 they formed about a quarter of the subcontinent's population.

INDIA IN MEDIEVAL times was already a densely populated land, compared to the other regions of the world. 'This country is so well-populated that it is impossible in a reasonable space to convey an idea of it,' notes Razzak. Moreover, the population profile of India was highly complex, because of the racial, linguistic, social, cultural, religious and sectarian diversity of Indians, resulting from the socio-cultural-religious developments within the country, as well as from the migration of very many different races into India over the millennia.

Migrants continued to pour into India during the medieval period; indeed, the Delhi sultans eagerly sought fresh migrants from Central Asia, to swell the Muslim population in India, so that Muslims in India would not get totally submersed in the vast sea of native Indians. The sultans also needed migrants to strengthen their army and administration with fresh recruits. And Central Asians on their part were eager to migrate to India, because of the legends about its fabulous wealth, and the grand career opportunities offered to them by Indian rulers. They also saw India as a safe haven for them to escape to, from the Mongol flood that was at this time raging through their homeland.

Hindu society, because of its polymorphic nature, was generally quite tolerant of the beliefs and practices of other religions, just as it was tolerant of the beliefs and practices of the diverse sects and castes within its own society. But the tolerance of Hindu society was tolerance by segregation; it was in fact a form of intolerance. Any community was free to live in any way it liked, but none was allowed to intrude into the life of other communities. This meant that Hindu society, despite its broad attitude of tolerance, was a highly discriminatory, inequitable and intolerant society, which sharply and unalterably segregated people by religion, sect and caste, and treated each group differently.

However, the Hindu caste segregation involved no overt oppression, as it was birth determined, and was not the result of any deliberate social action by any group. Though segregation itself was an oppressive practice, the underclasses did not generally feel oppressed, but passively accepted the circumstances of their life, as the natural and inevitable outcome of the transmigratory process, the conditions of their life being foreordained by their acts in their previous lives. Besides, the pervasive fatalistic attitude of the Indians of that age made them limply accept the conditions of their life, whatever those conditions were, and not struggle against them, as they believed that those conditions were inexorably fated. The social ethos of medieval India was thus a peculiar mixture of tolerance and intolerance. This was evident as much in the relationship of Hinduism with other religions, as in the relationship between the various sects and castes within Hindu society.

Because of these factors, the traditional Indian society had been, for very many centuries before the Turkish invasion, an exceptionally peaceful and harmonious society, despite its numerous caste divisions and harshly exploitative character. Though there were occasionally some social conflicts here and there in the subcontinent, they were usually minor and transient. There are no records of any serious and enduring inter-caste rivalries or clashes in pre-modern India. Nor were there any major inter-sectarian, inter-religious or inter-racial conflicts in India during this entire period. In all this, India was like no other country in the world.

And, paradoxical though it might seem, Hindu India's social diversity was the basis of its social cohesion and efficiency, for the divergent groups and castes in India, though they were rigidly segregated from each other socially, were tightly integrated with each other in their functions, with each caste, from the highest to the lowest, including the outcastes, providing a distinct and indispensable service in society. All the castes belonged together as the integral organs of one social entity, each caste occupying a specific social niche and performing a specific socio-economic function, like the different organs and limbs of a living being. And this enabled the caste society, despite its diversity and appalling inequity, to function efficiently and peacefully for very many centuries. The caste society was a cooperative society, not a competitive society. The diverse castes in it were not adversaries, but co-operators. And together they all constituted one cohesive society.

UNFORTUNATELY, THE CASTE system had a serious negative aspect to it, which nullified most of its benefits—it was a singularly unjust system, and was dreadfully wasteful of human resources, for its division of labour was not based on the merit of individuals, but on their birth, so that men of low ability often had to perform high functions, while men of high ability often had to perform low functions. Moreover, the caste system kept society sedated, in a state of coma, precluding mutation and progress in Indian civilisation. Though all human societies all over the world, and all through history, had functional and hierarchic divisions, Indian society was unique in that its divisions were unalterably hereditary. An individual's social function and status were solely dependent on his birth—not on his aptitude or ability—and they remained the same for his family from generation to generation over the centuries. Though there were a few minor deviations from this rule in history, the caste system on the whole remained virtually the same for very many centuries, well into the twentieth century.

One would have thought that this iniquitous system would weaken over time and disintegrate, and that there would be revolts against the system by the underclasses. But it was the opposite of this that happened. Instead of weakening, the caste system became more rigid over time, and the social distance between the castes widened. This was largely because India had slid into the Dark Ages in the late classical period, consequent of the decline of its urban prosperity and the general ruralisation of Indian culture. The caste system was the ideal social system for the Dark Ages.

In that setting, the social dominance of Brahmins became absolutely unassailable. But their status was not based on wealth or power, but on their birth determined ritual ranking. But ritual ranking in Hindu society meant social ranking, so very many social privileges and material benefits went with the Brahmin rank.

Some of the privileges enjoyed by Brahmins were conceded to them even by Muslim rulers. Brahmins, for instance, usually paid little or no tax, even in Muslim kingdoms. And if any king or chieftain sought to impose dues on a Brahmin, he, according to Kosambi, 'would threaten to spill his own blood, kill a child, burn alive some old woman of his family, or fast to death, the sin of which would fall on the head of the feudal lord.' Brahmins were exempted even from jizya by most Delhi sultans, and when Firuz Tughluq imposed it on them, the Brahmins of Delhi and its environs took to mass fasting in protest and threatened to burn themselves to death at the walls of the royal palace. They withdrew their protest only when the amount of jizya demanded from them was reduced by the sultan, and the other Hindu castes offered to pay the tax on their behalf—Brahmins evidently had no objection to jizya being imposed on them, as long as Hindus of other castes would pay the tax on their behalf!

The social status of Brahmins was based on their ritual status and function. But with the passage of time, and the growth in Brahmin population, many Brahmins spread out into other fields of activity. Many of them took to providing financial services, as bankers and tax-farmers, or served as scribes or accountants, under Hindu as well Muslim rulers. Some even served as military commanders, mostly in the Vijayanagar army.

There were similar changes in the profession of some other Hindu communities also. And, even though these changes did not lead to any significant alteration in the status hierarchy of the caste society, they did alter the material conditions of the life of some castes, with some castes gaining and some losing advantages. The main losers were Kshatriyas, the elite Hindu politico-military caste, many of whom lost their power and privileges to

Turks. Though some Kshatriyas salvaged their material privileges by serving as the subordinates of sultans or their provincial governors, such service itself was considered an appalling degradation by orthodox Hindus. But what the Kshatriyas lost was power and wealth, not their social status within the caste society, which remained the same as before.

In material gains, artisans and traders were the main beneficiaries of the establishment of the Delhi Sultanate, for there was a sharp revival of urban prosperity during this period, and that led to the resuscitation of the commercial economy which had been comatose in India for several centuries. Some of the low castes in Indian society, particularly the outcastes, also benefited from the establishment of the Turko-Afghan rule, for Muslims generally ignored caste distinctions, and treated the outcastes in the same manner as they treated the other members of Indian society. Indeed, some of the outcaste communities became Muslims en-masse, thereby instantly transforming their social status from that of the underclass to that of the upper-class.

THE ETHOS AND structure of Muslim society was entirely different from that of Hindu society. Muslim society was a brotherhood, and had no caste-like hereditary social divisions in it. There were functional and status divisions in it, but these were based on an individual's ability and accomplishments, not on his birth. Anyone could rise to any position that he merited by his abilities.

This was the Islamic ideal. The reality of Muslim society did not quite match this egalitarian, merit-oriented ideal. There were social divisions in Muslim society based on race and clan and sect, and these played a key role in determining a person's social status. For instance, Sayyids, persons of Prophet Muhammad's lineage, enjoyed a birth-determined, caste-like high social status everywhere in the Muslim world, irrespective of their personal merit. Further, people of foreign origin (Persians, Arabs, Turks and Afghans) generally formed the upper class of the Muslim society in India, followed by converts from the Hindu upper castes. Persians in particular enjoyed a high social status in India, and they looked down on Turks; and Turks in turn looked down on Afghans and Mongols; and all looked down on low caste Hindu converts.

Foreign Muslims 'alone are capable of virtue, kindness, generosity, valour, good deeds, good works, truthfulness, keeping of promises . . . loyalty, clarity of vision, justice, equity, recognition of rights, gratitude for favours, and fear of god,' states Barani, reflecting the stark social prejudice of upper class Muslims in medieval India. 'They are, consequently, said to be noble, free born, virtuous, religious, of high pedigree and pure birth. These groups alone are worthy of offices and posts in the government . . .'

Even among the Muslims of foreign origin, the early migrants and their children were held in lower esteem than the later migrants. According to

Francois Bernier, a late-seventeenth-century French physician in India, the 'children of the third and fourth generation, who have brown complexion . . . are held in much less respect than newcomers, and are seldom invested with official positions: they consider themselves happy, if permitted to serve as private soldiers in the infantry or cavalry.'

Converts from Hindu low castes and outcastes formed the bottom rung of Muslim society in India. The vast majority of Indian Muslims were in fact converts from low castes, and they mostly served as common soldiers, artisans and menials. These class distinctions were particularly important in arranging marriages. But inter-dining was not a taboo among Muslims, as it was among Hindus, though low-class menials were usually segregated.

These social divisions in the Muslim society in India were, however, porous, and over time there came about some amount of social coalescing among the various Muslim communities in India. The status of Indian converts to Islam began to improve from the late thirteenth century on, and in time a number of them rose to high positions in government. The classic case of this was the career of Malik Kafur—a Gujarati eunuch-slave, he rose to be the top general under Ala-ud-din Khalji, and even became, for a few months during the last phase of the life of the ailing sultan, the virtual ruler of the empire.

In time, a number of inter-community marriages took place at all levels of the Muslim society in India, and this led to a good amount of social levelling among Muslims in India. In a parallel development, Indian Muslims in high positions now took to fabricating elaborate genealogies to claim patrician foreign family backgrounds.

In addition to the social status divisions among Muslims in India, there were also some functional divisions in Muslim society, such as between those of military profession and those of civilian profession. The civilian professionals in turn were divided into those of administrative vocation and those of religious vocation. Religious leaders played a major role in Muslim polity, especially in the formulation of policies and laws, to ensure that these conformed to religious prescriptions. Unlike in Christianity, there were no ordained priests in Islam, no bishops, no pope. But there were religious leaders (imams) in Islam, who led the congregational prayers in mosques and at other gatherings of Muslims. Some of these religious leaders were highly influential, and the sultans could ignore their advice or ill-treat them only at their own peril.

THE MUSLIM ARISTOCRACY in medieval India mainly consisted of men in government service, whose status depended on the post they held. And the post they held depended on the will and pleasure of the sultan. Inevitably most of the royal officers lived in a state of perpetual anxiety about their future, and this was one of the determinants of their lifestyle, which was characterised by incredible extravagance, without any thought for the future—because they could not be certain that they, or their families, had a future.

Muslim nobles lived in palatial mansions, opulently furnished with tapestries and carpets imported from Central Asia, and provided with gold and silver tableware, as well as fine chinaware. They were usually deep in debt, living far beyond even their fabulous means—it was indeed considered prestigious for one to be heavily in debt, as proof of his profligacy. There was in any case no point in they saving anything for the future, for they could not bequeath their saved wealth to their progeny. This was because their wealth was derived from the estate assigned to them by the state to meet their official and personal expenses, so whatever wealth they saved from their estate after meeting these expenses belonged to the state.

Not only did the nobles pamper themselves opulently, but they were also equally extravagant in their charity, and in the gifts they gave to those who pleased them in any way. Says Abdullah, a late medieval chronicler, about Asad Khan, a high officer of Sikandar Lodi: 'Whenever the cloth was spread before him at meal-times, he first filled large china plates with food, on which he placed great quantities of bread and pickles of every description, and on them a betel leaf, and on that a gold mohur, all of which he gave to beggars, and [only] then he began to eat.' Once he gave to a needy relative a heap of gold pieces amounting to 70,000 tankas. Likewise, on several occasions he filled cups and bowls with gold and gave them away to whoever pleased him at the moment.

These were laudable benevolent acts. But what characterised the lifestyle of most nobles was their extravagant self-indulgence. Thus Dilawar Khan, another noble of Sikandar Lodi, everyday purchased 500 tankas worth of roses for his harem. According to Varthema, an early sixteenth century Italian traveller in India, many of the officers of the sultan of Bijapur 'wear on the insteps of their shoes rubies and diamonds and other jewels; so you may imagine how many are worn on the fingers of the hand and on the ears.'

MEDIEVAL INDIAN SOCIETY, like medieval societies everywhere in the world, was characterised by shocking social and economic disparities, with the nobles living in incredible luxury and the common people living in abject poverty. This was true of Hindu as well as Muslim society. 'The land is overstocked with people, but those in the country are very miserable, whilst the nobles are extremely opulent and delight in luxury,' observes Nikitin. 'They are wont to be carried on their silver beds, preceded by some twenty chargers caparisoned in gold, and followed by 300 men on horseback and 500 on foot, and by horn-men, ten torchbearers and ten musicians.'

There is a good amount of information about the lifestyle of the upper classes in medieval India in the chronicles of the age, but there is hardly any information about the life of the common people. Circumstantial evidence shows that even when the common people had the means to live in comfort, they usually dared not to do so, for fear of attracting the attention of vulturous government officers and other predators. Besides, they were anxious to save for the contingency of any future adversity, which they feared was always around the corner. So they generally lived frugally, often well below their means. And what wealth they could save, they buried, usually in pits dug inside their houses. The buried treasure might not grow, but it would be at least safe, they felt, and it gave their owners a sense of security. According to Shahab-ud-din, 'the inhabitants of India like to make money, and hoard it.' This was their insurance against the uncertainties of life.

Nearly all the rulers of the early medieval India, rajas as well as sultans, were predators, concerned primarily with the preservation and expansion of their wealth and power, scarcely ever with the welfare of the people. They were all warlords. And if kings had no vital interest in the welfare of their people, the people had no vital interest in the welfare of their kings either. Whether their king was a Hindu or a Muslim, the common people had no sense of identity with him, and were indifferent to what happened to him, whether he rose or fell, or was killed.

This attitude of fatalism, which was pervasive in medieval India, was the reason why people's rebellions were very rare in India, despite their inhuman oppression by the rulers. By and large people acquiesced with the conditions of their life, however harsh they might be. As Dubois, an early nineteenth century French missionary in India, would comment in another context, 'The people of India have always been accustomed to bow their heads beneath the yoke of a cruel and oppressive despotism, and moreover, strange to say, have always displayed mere indifference towards those who have forced them to it. Little cared they whether the princes under whom they groaned were of their own country or from foreign lands. The frequent vicissitudes that befell those in power were hardly noticed by their subjects. Never did the fall of one of these despots cause the least regret; never did the elevation of another cause the least joy. Hard experience had taught Hindus to disregard not only the hope of better times but the fear of worse.'

A COMMON FEATURE OF premodern societies nearly everywhere in the world was slavery, and it was widespread in India too in medieval times. Slaves were an indispensable part of the household of affluent Indians in most parts of the subcontinent. Even some mystics kept slaves. As for nobles, most of them kept a large number of slaves, including many concubines. That was an essential part of their ostentatious lifestyle. Khan Jahan Maqbul, Firuz Tughluq's vizier, for instance, is said to have maintained, according to Afif, as many as 2000 concubines! The largest number of slaves in medieval India was, predictably, in the service of the Delhi sultans, who employed them in various government departments and in the royal army, as well as in their personal service. The sultan's personal attendants were all invariably slaves.

The number of slaves maintained by the Delhi sultans varied considerably from reign to reign, depending on the requirements of each sultan. The sultan who had the largest number of slaves was Firuz Tughluq, who is reported to have had as many as 180,000 slaves, and is said to have issued an order to his officers that the best of the captives they enslaved during military campaigns should be reserved for him. It was not however to pander to his personal vanity that Firuz kept so many slaves, but to give them training in crafts and to employ them in productive work, so that they became economic assets and contributed to the revenue of the state and the prosperity of the land.

Capturing people to enslave them was part of the spoils that sultans, officers and soldiers sought during military campaigns. For instance, Qutb-ud-din Aibak during his Gujarat campaign captured 20,000 people to be enslaved, and in his Kalinjar campaign he herded as many as 50,000 people into slavery. This was the usual practice of the sultans during their campaigns of conquest. They also enslaved captives during their punitive campaigns within the empire. Captured professionals too were enslaved, as Timur did during his Indian campaign, when he, according to the early fifteenth century Persian chronicler Yazdi, captured as slaves 'several thousand artisans and professional people.' Like invaders, marauders too often seized men, women and children, to sell them as slaves. Sometimes children were sold into slavery by their needy parents or by hostile relatives.

Slavery was prevalent in most ancient, medieval and early modern societies all over the world. It was common in India too from ancient times, but it had never been as widespread as it was during the early medieval period, when slave trade became an important part of the Indian economy. There was even a regular export of slaves from India during this period, but Firuz Tughluq forbade it, presumably because he himself wanted to accumulate a large number of slaves. All major cities in medieval India had slave markets, where slaves were sold like cattle; in Delhi, adequate availability of slaves in the market was maintained by regular fresh supplies, as Barani indicates.

The price of slaves, as of any other commodity, depended on the prevailing demand and supply equation in the market, as well on the quality of individual slaves. According to Battuta, rustic women captured during raids fetched only very low prices, because of their large numbers and crude ways. During the reign of Ala-ud-din Khalji the prices of various categories of slaves were fixed by the sultan himself, as part of his market regulations. On the whole slaves were quite cheap in Delhi; they were even cheaper in other Indian cities. According to Shahab-ud-din, 'the value . . . of a young slave girl for domestic service does not exceed eight tankas' in Delhi. More charming girls, those fit for concubinage, fetched fifteen tankas. However, some Indian slave-girls cost as much as '20,000 tankas, and even more . . . [for they] are remarkable for their beauty, and the grace of their manners.'

THE POSITION OF slaves in Islamic society was quite different from what it was in most other societies. Muslims generally treated their slaves in the same manner as they treated their other servitors, and the position that a slave occupied, as well as the privileges he enjoyed, depended, as in the case of other servitors, on his aptitude and merit. On the whole, the life and career of a slave in Islamic society was not much different from what he could have had as a free man.

Slaves were of course bonded to their owners, so they had very little personal freedom. But talented and loyal slaves were usually rewarded by their masters by manumitting them. In some cases it was an advantage to be a slave, particularly to be the favourite slave of a sultan or a high official, for that opened up for the slave an avenue for rapid career advancement. A royal slave could even succeed his master on the throne, as indeed three slaves did in the Delhi Sultanate. The first dynasty of the Delhi Sultanate—which ruled the empire for 84 years, from 1206 to 1290—is usually described as the Slave Dynasty, for all the ten rulers of the dynasty were either manumitted slaves or descendants of slaves.

Slaves served in a wide variety of occupations in early medieval India, in administration, army and economy, as well as in households. Royal bodyguards were invariably slaves, Ethiopians slaves being particularly favoured for that service. But very few of the royal slaves were for personal attendance on the sultan; rather, they were mostly treated like any other government staff and assigned to various official duties. This was particularly so in the case of the slaves of Firuz Tughluq, who took special care to treat them well and to employ them in various productive occupations, and thus turn them into economic assets of the state. 'In all cases, provision was made for their support in a liberal manner,' states Afif about Firuz's treatment of his slaves. Sultans generally assigned responsible work to most of their slaves, though some slaves were also employed as entertainers or as menial workers in the royal household. During the reign of Kaiqubad, the last slave sultan, who was a heedless voluptuary, slave boys and girls were, according to Barani, given special training in music, dance, coquetry, and the erotic arts, for those were the primary interests of the sultan.

Slavery declined in the late Sultanate period, and became quite insignificant during the Mughal rule. Babur does not mention slaves at all in his autobiography. However, slavery did exist in India during the Mughal period, as European travellers noted, but their numbers were insignificant, and nearly all of them were domestic slaves. There were no state slaves under the Mughals.

WOMEN GENERALLY SUFFERED far more discrimination than slaves in medieval India, in all sections of society, but more so in upper caste Hindu society, though there were some commendable exceptions to this. Their life was confined to their family. They had no social role whatever. In fact, in medieval Hindu society their position was much worse than what it was in ancient India, where there were hardly any lifestyle restrictions on women, and they ate and drank whatever their men ate and drank. *Ramayana*, for instance, relates that Sita, the ultimate Hindu ideal of wifely propriety, drank wine in the company of Rama, her husband. But later the scene changed altogether, and Smriti rules of medieval India severely circumscribed the life of Hindu women, and ordained that a wife who drank liquor should be superseded, or even abandoned.

On the whole, women had very low social standing in medieval India. The only notable exception to this was in the matrilineal Nair society of Kerala, where women enjoyed a status equal to that of men. Also, among the poor all over India, women enjoyed a good amount of freedom, for their lives were too basic to be segregated into male and female domains. It was mainly the middleclass women who suffered most from social constraints.

Illiteracy was very common among medieval Indian women, and in some Hindu castes it was even considered shameful for respectable women to be literate. In upper class Muslim society, women had to observe purdah, and were secluded in the zenana, the female quarters of their home. They were not allowed to have any contact with any men other than the members of their immediate family. And when they appeared in public, they had to wear the burqa, a shapeless, sack-like outer garment that covered their entire body from head to foot, leaving only a narrow veiled opening over the eyes. Among the affluent, women travelled in closed litters. Even in mosques women were segregated from men. In some Islamic societies women were not even allowed into mosques, as Prophet Muhammad is said to have preferred women to pray at home. Affluent Hindus, particularly the political aristocracy in North India, in time adopted some of the Muslim social practices, such as sequestering their women, to gain social recognition by the Muslim ruling class.

Despite these various restrictions on the life of women in medieval India, women in royal and aristocratic families, in Hindu as well as Muslim society, generally led a good life, and enjoyed all the creature comforts available in that age. They also exercised a fair amount of influence on government and society from behind the curtain of the zenana, by acting through intermediaries. Sometimes they even took part in battles. Thus when Delhi was attacked by a rebel force when sultan Buhlul Lodi was away on a campaign, and there were only very few soldiers in the fort then, a number of women under the leadership of a woman, Bibi Matu, put on male attire and took up combat positions on the battlements of the fort, to scare away the attackers. Similarly, the concubine of a rebel noble in Sind—'a strumpet who was indeed surpassingly beautiful'—took over the captaincy of the noble's army when he fell in battle. She, according to Yadgar, 'put on a suit of armour, bound round her waist a gilt quiver and, placing a helmet on her head, joined the army.' The ultimate political status that any woman gained during the Sultanate period was by Raziya, who ascended the throne in Delhi on the death of her father, Sultan Iltutmish, and proved herself to be better than many sultans, in administration as well as in battle.

On the whole Muslim women, despite purdah, enjoyed higher status and greater freedom in society than most Hindu women. They could inherit property and obtain divorce, privileges that Hindu women did not have. In several Hindu communities, such as among the Rajputs, the birth of a girl child was considered a misfortune, and female infanticide was widespread, but Muslims did not have that practice.

3

Ideal and Reality

The traditional Indian prescription for sensible living was to divide man's life into four successive stages—*brahmachari* (student), *grihastha* (householder), *vanaprastha* (anchorite), and *sanyasi* (religious mendicant). Each of these stages, except the last stage, had its own specific pursuits: acquisition of knowledge as *brahmachari*, fulfilment of social and family responsibilities as *grihastha*, and spiritual quest as *vanaprastha*. And finally, after fulfilling all these duties, in the last stage of his life, as *sanyasi*, man renounces all human pursuits, both temporal and spiritual, and frees himself from life even while living.

This was the ideal. The reality was quite different. Hardly anyone, except a few exceptional individuals, went through all the prescribed four stages of life. The sole concern of nearly everyone was to earn a good livelihood and lead a pleasant life as a householder. In this mundane scheme of life, the most important events in the life of an individual were getting married and begetting children. These were the essential first steps for man to fulfil his responsibilities to his family, his society, and his species.

Marriage was considered particularly essential for women, and it was a matter of disgrace for a family to have unmarried adult women at home. But getting daughters married off entailed huge expenses—in Hindu as well as Muslim society, but more so in Hindu society—which were beyond the means of many families. In Delhi the sultans sometimes provided financial assistance to needy Muslim parents, to help them out of their embarrassing predicament of not having funds to marry off their daughters suitably. Thus Firuz Tughluq, according to Afif, 'founded an establishment for the promotion of marriages', which granted funds to poor Muslims to dower their daughters. Hearing about this, 'people . . . flocked to the city from all parts of the country, and received grants for purchasing housekeeping requisites for their daughters.'

Among the affluent, it was considered essential to celebrate marriages lavishly, as demonstrations of their family status. Marriage celebrations in royal families were naturally the grandest, and were festive occasions for all in the royal capital. Thus, according to Amir Khusrav, on the occasion of the marriage of prince Khizr Khan, Ala-ud-din Khalji's son, the whole city of Delhi was magnificently decorated with triumphal arches, and the public were entertained with music and dance, illuminations, jugglery, acrobatics, and so on.

MOST MIDDLE AND upper class families in medieval India were polygamous, in Hindu as well as Muslim society. Muslims were permitted by their religion to have four legal wives. Besides, they could have any number of concubines they fancied, and some Muslim kings and nobles maintained incredibly large harems. Thus Begarha, the sultan of Gujarat, had in his harem 'three or four thousand women,' reports Varthema. And Khan-i Jahan, an Andhra Hindu convert to Islam who became the vizier of Firuz Tughluq, was, according to Afif, 'much devoted to the pleasures of the harem, and sought eagerly for pretty handmaids. It is reported that he had 2000 women of Rum and Chin in his harem, where he spent much of his time notwithstanding his onerous official duties.' Such sexual profligacy involved no social disapprobation in medieval Indian society; rather, it was prestigious for a man to have a large number of wives and concubines. Says Battuta about himself: 'It is my habit never to travel without [my slave girls].'

As for the rule that Muslims could have only four legal wives at a time, it could be easily circumvented, for divorce and remarriage were easy in Islam. The process for divorce was for the husband to merely say *talaq*—I divorce you—three times before his wife, after which he could right away marry another woman. This meant that men could divorce and marry any number of wives in succession, without going through any elaborate legal process. Similarly, a woman too could divorce her husband and marry another man, though the process involved in this was more complicated than in the case of divorce by men. And she could have, at least in theory, any number of husbands in succession, though at any given time she could have only one husband.

The facility for easy divorce in Islam led to the practice of some people entering into temporary marriages, sometimes for just a few hours. This form of marriage, termed *muta* marriage among Shias, was common in Maldives, the island chain off the southern tip of India. 'When ships arrive, the crew marry wives, and when they are about to sail they divorce them,' reports Battuta from his personal experience. 'The women never leave their country.'

Unlike in Islam, there was no restriction at all in Hindu society about the number of wives a man could have. 'The inhabitants of this region marry as many wives as they please,' comments Venetian traveller Nicolo Conti about what he observed in Vijayanagar in the early fifteenth century. Indeed, having a large number of wives was, for upper class Hindus, a means to flaunt their socio-economic status—as well as their sexual prowess! Some Hindu rajas are known to have had a prodigious number of wives. Achyutadeva, the mid-sixteenth century king of Vijayanagar, had as many as 500 wives, according to Fernao Nuniz, a contemporary Portuguese trader-traveller. This is most likely an exaggeration, but probably not a gross exaggeration. Even Krishnadeva, whose preoccupation with wars and administration would have left him with little time for dalliance, had twelve wives, according to Paes.

Unlike polygamy, polyandry was rare in India, and the only people who practiced it routinely were Nairs of Kerala. 'Among them there is a tribe in which one woman has several husbands,' notes Abdur Razzak, the mid-fifteenth century Persian royal envoy in India, about what he observed in Kerala. 'They (the husbands) divide the hours of the night and day amongst themselves, and as long as any one of them remains in the house during his appointed time, no other can enter. The Samuri (Zamorin) is of that tribe.'

'Each [Nair] woman has from two to ten known [lovers],' states Tome Pires, an early sixteenth century Portuguese pharmacist-traveller in India. 'The more lovers a Nair woman has, the more important she is.' Adds Portuguese traveller Duarte Barbosa, who was also in India in the sixteenth century: 'Nayre women of good birth are very independent, and dispose of themselves as they please with Bramenes and Nayres, but they do not sleep with men of castes lower than their own under pain of death . . . The more lovers she has the greater her honour. Each one of them (her lovers) passes a day with her from midday on one day till midday on the next day, and so they continue living quietly without any disturbance or quarrels among them. If any of them wishes to leave her, he leaves her, and takes another woman, and she also, if she is weary of a man, tells him to go, and he does so, or makes terms with her.' No ceremony at all was involved in accepting or discarding a lover.

This freewheeling amatory practice continued among Nairs well into modern times, as Francis Buchanan-Hamilton, a Scottish physician who was in India in the first decade of the nineteenth century, noted. Nair women, he writes, 'marry before they are ten years of age . . . but the husband never cohabits with his wife . . . She lives in her mother's house, or, after her parent's death, with her brother, and cohabits with any person she chooses of an equal or higher rank than her own . . . It is no kind of reflection on a woman's character to say that she has formed the closest intimacy with many persons; on the contrary, the Nair women are proud of reckoning among their favoured lovers many Brahmins, Rajas, or other persons of high birth . . . In consequence of this strange manner of propagating the species, no Nair knows his father, and every man looks on his sisters' children as his heirs.'

Marriage customs in medieval India, like everything else, varied greatly from region to region and community to community. But generally speaking, women were not allowed to marry below their caste, though men could do that. In most communities marriage between close relatives was also forbidden. For instance, among high caste Maharashtrians, they 'do not marry their relatives, except those who are cousins six times removed,' notes Battuta. But first cousin marriages and uncle-niece marriages were common in South India.

SEXUAL PROMISCUITY WAS pervasive in medieval Hindu society. 'Great licentiousness prevails in this country among women as well as men,' writes Abu Said, an early tenth century Arab historian. Ibn Khurdadba, another Arab writer of about the same period, confirms: 'The king and people Hind regard fornication as lawful.' In that social milieu, illegitimate children were common, and they usually had no stigma attached to them. Indeed, even a child born out of the extramarital liaison of a woman was considered legitimate. 'If a stranger has a child by a married woman, the child belongs to her husband, since the wife, . . . the soil in which the child is born, is the property of the husband,' observes al-Biruni, an eleventh century Ghaznavid chronicler.

Because of this general laxity in sexual matters in Hindu society, abnormal sexual practices like homosexuality and pederasty were rare in it. According to al-Biruni, Hindus considered sodomy as revolting, as revolting as eating beef, which was the ultimate revolting act a Hindu could commit. But these deviant sexual practices were common in Muslim society. Even some of the sultans were bisexual or homosexual. In medieval Muslim society, as in ancient Greece, none of that entailed any strong disapprobation. Thus sultan Mubarak, a successor of Ala-ud-din Khalji, spent his whole time 'in extreme dissipation,' reports Barani. 'He cast aside all regard for decency, and presented himself decked out in the trinkets and apparel of a woman before his assembled company.' Similar was the conduct of Kurbat Hasan Kangu, a fourteenth century sultan of Ma'bar (Tamil Nadu), who, when he held court, 'appeared decked out hand and foot with female ornaments, and made himself notorious for his puerile actions,' notes Afif.

Muslim women too sometimes strayed, though they were usually very carefully guarded. But when caught, they, even royal women, were savagely punished. Thus, according to Battuta, Sultan Muhammad Tughluq once had a princess stoned to death 'on a charge of debauchery or adultery.' Muhammad's successor, Firuz, was also quite severe in dealing with such matters, and he, as he notes in his autobiography, even prohibited women from going to the tombs on holy days, for that offered an opportunity for 'wild fellows of unbridled passion and loose habits . . . [to indulge in] improper, riotous actions. I commanded that no woman should go out to the [sacred] tombs under pain of exemplary punishment.'

Another matter in which Muslims and Hindus differed radically was in their attitude towards prostitution. Islam considered prostitution a major sin, but Hindus viewed it as a normal and legitimate aspect of social life. In ancient India, in Mauryan Empire for instance, there were even state run brothels. Similarly, in medieval times brothels were run as a government sanctioned service in Vijayanagar, and they were a source of revenue for the state. According to Razzak, the state derived 12,000 fanams (small silver coins) a day from 'the proceeds of the brothels,' and used that revenue to meet the salary of a large number of policemen.

The brothels in Vijayanagar city were located on both sides of a long and broad avenue behind the state mint. 'The splendour of those houses, the beauty of the heart-ravishers, their blandishments and ogles, are beyond description . . .,' reports Razzak. '[In the afternoon] they place at the doors of these houses, which are beautifully decorated, chairs and settees on which the courtesans seat themselves. Everyone is covered with pearls, precious stones, and costly garments. They are all exceedingly young and beautiful. Each has one or two slave girls standing before her, to invite and allure [passers-by] to indulgence and pleasure. Any man who passes through this place makes choice of whom he will.'

THE FOOD HABITS of Hindus in medieval India were quite different from what they were in earlier times. Indian society in ancient and early classical period was quite permissive in the matter of food, and allowed all people, irrespective of their class and sex, including the priestly class, the freedom to eat whatever they liked, even beef, drink alcohol and take psychotropic drugs. The scene changed altogether by the middle of the first millennium CE, when the caste system tightened its iron grip on Hindu society. Caste regulations then defined and enforced the food and drink rules applicable to each caste, and these rules played a crucial role in segregating castes.

The old adage that you are what you eat thus acquired a new meaning in India. Predictably, the highest dietary restrictions were on those of the highest caste, Brahmins, who, because of their primary priestly function, were generally forbidden to eat any meat or fish, and had to avoid even certain vegetables—garlic, onions, leeks, and so on—which were thought to stimulate carnal desires. On the other hand, those on the bottom rung of the caste society, the outcastes, had virtually no food restrictions at all.

Caste rules specified not only the dietary taboos to be observed by different castes, but also the dining practices they had to observe. 'No man of one creed will drink, eat, or marry with those of another,' observes Nikitin. 'Some of them feed on mutton, fowls, fish, and eggs, but none on beef . . . The [high caste] Hindus eat no meat, no cow flesh, no mutton, no chicken. They take their meals twice a day, but not at night, and drink no wine or mead. They neither eat nor drink with Mohammedans. Their fare is poor . . . They live on Indian corn, carrots . . . and different herbs. Always eating with their right hand, they will never set the left hand to anything. Nor do they use a knife; the spoon is unknown. While travelling every one carries a stone pot to cook his broth. They take care that Mohammedans do not look into their pot, nor see their food, and should this happen, they will not eat it; some therefore hide themselves under a linen cloth lest they should be seen when eating . . . They sit down to eat, and wash their hands and feet, and rinse their mouths before they do.' Adds Battuta: 'The nobles of the Marathas are Brahmins and Katris (Kshatriyas). Their food consists of rice, vegetables, and oil of sesame . . . They wash themselves thoroughly before eating . . .'

'In eating, they use the right hand only,' confirms Marco Polo, a late thirteenth century Venetian traveller. 'So also they drink only from their own drinking vessels, and every man has his own; nor will anyone drink from another's vessel. And when they drink they do not put the vessel to their lips but hold it aloft and let the drink spout into the mouth . . . They are very strict . . . in abstaining from wine. Indeed, they have made a rule that wine-drinkers and seafaring men are never to be accepted as sureties.'

Not only was interdining between castes prohibited in the Hindu society, but even within a family each individual usually took his or her meal separately. The family did not ever sit together for meals. 'They eat not with one another, nor with their wives,' states Nikitin. 'It is an established usage of infidels never to eat in the presence of each other,' adds Ferishta. Hindus considered eating to be a private act, and that it was preferable to do it in private, like other private acts.

There were of course occasions when several Hindus (all of the same gender, and usually all of the same caste) feasted together, as at a wedding reception. But even on such occasions, though they sat down together for the feast, they were only physically together, not socially together, for they ate in silence, and did not engage each other in conversation. And it was unthinkable for anyone to touch the food served to anyone else. 'When someone takes something from your food, what remains is a leftover, and cannot be eaten,' notes al-Biruni.[1]

---

[1]For Indian dietary practices, see *The First Spring*, Part VII, Chapter 3

THE ESTABLISHMENT OF the Delhi Sultanate and the large scale migration of Turks into India added several new elements to the dietary diversity of Indians. Muslims feasted on beef, but considered it abominable to eat pork; Hindus on the other hand considered it abominable to eat beef, but many Hindus, including high caste Rajputs, feasted on pork. While Hindus preferred to sit alone to eat, Muslims preferred to dine together in groups. And while the cuisine of Hindus, even of nobles and rajas, was quite simple, Muslim aristocracy favoured gourmet food. A medieval chronicle describes, no doubt with some exaggeration, a sultan being served a dish prepared with '300 and more ingredients in it.' Several of these ingredients were no doubt Indian spices, to the use of which Turks took to in India. At the same time, Indians on their part added pilau and kuruma to their cuisine under the influence of Turks.

Turks loved to feast on rich food. According to Shahab-ud-din, 2500 oxen, 2000 sheep, as well as a large number of other animals, and many different kinds of birds, were daily slaughtered in the kitchen of the sultan of Delhi. This claim might be rather hyperbolic, but it is not entirely incredible, when we consider that the raja of Vijayanagar every day supplied for the kitchen of Abdur Razzak, the visiting Persian envoy, 'two sheep, four couple of fowls, five *mans* of rice, one *man* of butter, and one *man* of sugar, and two varaha gold coins,' as the ambassador himself states.

Some of the stories told about the gluttons of the age are quite astounding. Battuta, for instance, speaks of an Ethiopian who was renowned as much for his appetite as for his valour: 'He was tall and corpulent, and used to eat a whole sheep at a meal, and I was told that after eating he would drink about a pound and a half of ghee.' Even more fantastic are the dietary practices attributed to Begarha, the sultan of Gujarat. A man of gigantic size and gargantuan appetite, he, according to legend, ate about fourteen kilos of food every day, and his breakfast consisted of a cup of honey, a cup of butter, and over a hundred plantains. And, most curious of all, his daily diet included of a swig of poison!

As for the food served at Muslim feasts, Isami, a mid-fourteenth century chronicler, gives an account of a banquet held in the Deccan in honour of the local sultan. 'It was the eighth part of the day when trumpets announced that the banquet was ready. Silk tapestries were spread and table cloths laid. Leavened and unleavened bread were kept ready, various items of salad were there, green and crisp. Then came roast quail and partridge and roast chicken and roast lamb. Curry puffs and cooked vegetables were there as accompaniments. Juicy almond puddings and halvahs were served as dessert and these were scented with camphor and musk. The meal ended with the distribution of betel and the tambula . . .' The tableware used at this feast were imported from China.

THERE WAS NO bar on anyone drinking alcoholic beverages in ancient India, but their consumption fell sharply in the late classical period due to the decline of economic prosperity, the collapse of towns and the virtual disappearance of urban lifestyle, as well as due to the enforcement of caste taboos. Brahmins were now required to totally abjure alcoholic drinks. They, notes Battuta, do not 'drink wine, for this in their eyes is the greatest of vices.' Al Masudi, a tenth century Iraqi historian, offers a curious (but sensible) explanation for this. 'Hindus,' he writes, 'abstain from drinking wine, and censure those who consume it; not because their religion forbids it, but in the dread of it clouding their reason and depriving them of their powers.'

In Islam too wine drinking was considered a major sin. Nevertheless, drinking was fairly common among the Muslim aristocracy in India and Afghanistan. And some of them were very heavy drinkers. According to Baihaqi, an eleventh century historian of the Ghaznavids, nobles at garden parties often 'drank to excess. They passed the night there and the next morning they again drank . . . [One noble] when he once sat down to drink, would continue boozing for three or four entire days.'

Baihaqi once witnessed a garden cocktail party hosted by Sultan Masud of Ghazni, and offers an amusing account of it. As the feast progressed, the courtiers, reports Baihaqi, 'began to get jolly, and the minstrels sang . . . [One noble] drank five goblets, his head was affected at the sixth, he lost his senses at the seventh, and began to vomit at the eighth, when the servants carried him off.' Some drank as many as twelve cups, and fell into torpor. One noble drank eighteen cups, then politely requested the sultan's permission to leave. Presently 'the singers and buffoons all rolled off tipsy.' But the sultan continued to drink. 'He drank twenty-seven full goblets . . . He then rose, called for a basin of water and his praying carpet, washed his face, and read the mid-day prayers as well as the afternoon ones, and so acquitted himself that you would have said he had not drunk a single cup. He then got on an elephant and returned to the palace.'

In Delhi the attitude of rulers towards drinking varied from sultan to sultan. Several of them were heavy imbibers, who regularly held convivial parties with their courtiers. But some others, even when they were secret drinkers themselves, prohibited that indulgence to their courtiers, or at least prohibited them from holding cocktail parties, for drunkenness often led to indiscipline and rebellions. In Delhi the strictest measures against drinking were those taken by Ala-ud-din Khalji, who sought to enforce prohibition by seizing the vast quantities of liquor stored in the homes of nobles and pouring them out on streets, and by imprisoning prohibition violators. He had so many of them arrested that in a short while there was no more any room for them in the prisons, so the guilty were interned in pits dug along the road near the royal palace. But despite such harsh and humiliating punishments, people persisted in wine drinking, so the sultan had to eventually modify his regulations, and permit people to drink privately at home. Muhammad Tughluq also tried to enforce prohibition—'Any Muslim who drinks is punished with eighty stripes, and shut up . . . for three months,' notes Battuta—but he had no more success in it than Ala-ud-din. The common attitude of the Muslim aristocracy of the age, as the early medieval Ghaznavid poet Asjadi puts it, was:

I do repent of wine and talk of wine
Of idols fair with chins like silver fine
A lip-repentance and a lustful heart,
O god, forgive this penitence of mine.

The most widespread indulgence of medieval Indians—indeed, the universal indulgence of medieval Indians, irrespective of class and caste and religion and sex—was chewing betel leaves, a mild stimulant with antiseptic and breath-refreshing qualities. Commonly termed paan, this was a treat that even the poorest of the poor could afford, and was considered a healthy habit. 'The inhabitants of India have little taste for wine and intoxicating drinks, but content themselves with betel, an agreeable drug, the use of which is permitted without the slightest objection,' comments Shahab-ud-din. For chewing, the betel leaf was lightly daubed with slaked lime, and then put in the mouth along with a few shavings of areca-nut. Those who could afford it added pinches of various spices and flavouring ingredients to the chew, but that was not essential, for though it improved the taste of the chew, added little or nothing to its effect.

'The betel is a leaf which resembles that of orange,' writes Razzak. 'It is held in great esteem in Hindustan, in the many parts of Arabia, and the kingdom of Hormuz, and indeed it deserves its reputation. It is eaten this way: they bruise a piece of areca nut . . . and place it in the mouth; then moistening a leaf of betel . . . together with a grain of quicklime, they rub one on the other, roll them up together, and place them in the mouth. Thus they place as many as four leaves together in their mouths, and chew them. Sometimes they mix camphor with it, and from time to time discharge their spittle, which becomes red from the use of the betel. This masticatory lightens up the countenance and excites an intoxication like that caused by wine. It relieves hunger, stimulates the organs of digestion, purifies the breath, and strengthens the teeth . . . [And it has] strong invigorating and aphrodisiac virtues . . . It is probably owing to the stimulating properties of this leaf . . . that the king of that country (Vijayanagar) is enabled to entertain so large a seraglio.'

NOTHING MUCH IS known about the sport and pastime of medieval Indians, except that the Muslim aristocracy were avid about polo; Sultan Qutb-ud-din Aibak in fact died in an accident while playing polo. The game is believed to have originated in Persia several centuries before the Common Era, and was introduced into India by Turkish invaders. In time the Hindu aristocracy also passionately took to it, and later so did the British officers in India.

Polo was a game of the elite. Virtually nothing is known about the games played by the common people in medieval India. Villagers no doubt played various rustic games, but the entertainment high points of their lives would have been attending the fairs, carnivals and temple festivals held in nearby towns, to which people from all the nearby villages flocked. The major attractions at these carnivals were performances by touring magicians, jugglers and acrobats. The feats performed by some of them were indeed astounding, if we are to believe medieval chroniclers. 'The juggler swallowed a sword like water, drinking it as a thirsty man would drink sherbet,' reports Amir Khusrav about a performance. 'He also thrust a knife up his nostril. He mounted a little wooden horse and rode in the air. Large bodies were made to issue out of small ones; an elephant was drawn through a window, and a camel through the eye of a needle . . . Sometimes they (the jugglers) transformed themselves into angels, sometimes into demons. . . They sang enchantingly . . .' There is no doubt a good amount of poetic fancy in this report of Khusrav, but Indian magicians of the age were indeed reputed for the awesome illusions they created.

Similar are the feats attributed to Indian sorcerers and yogis, many of which are truly incredible. 'First of all, they can bring a dead man to life,' writes Khusrav credulously. 'If a man has been bitten by a snake and is rendered speechless, they can resuscitate him after even seven months . . . They can procure longevity by diminishing the daily number of the expirations of breath. A yogi who could restrain his breath in this way lived . . . to an age of more than 350 years . . . They know how to convert themselves into wolves, dogs and cats . . . They can also fly like fowls in the air, however improbable it may seem. They can also, by putting antimony on their eyes, make themselves invisible at pleasure . . .'

These acrobatic and magical shows were usually held in towns during their annual temple festivals, to which people from all the nearby villages flocked. Apart from attending these annual events the everyday life of medieval Indian villagers would have been quite drab and routine. Most people of medieval India, villagers as well as townsmen, were addicted to taking siesta daily, which was an essential restorative for them in the generally sweltering climate of India. In summer 'the weather was very hot that at midday people kept indoors taking their siesta, so there were few people in the streets,' Barani observed. And everyone, including the sultan, slept in the open at night in summer—'the

sultan slept on the roof of the palace, having only a few eunuchs around him,'
reports Battuta.

THERE IS VERY little information about the lifestyle of the common people
in medieval chronicles, but there is in them a good amount of data on the
lifestyle of the affluent. The urban rich in peninsular India in the mid-fifteenth
century lived in palatial, multi-storeyed mansions, according Razzak. This
was confirmed a few decades later by the Portuguese traveller Paes, who noted
that the cities in the peninsula had large populations and had several rows of
handsome buildings. The city of Vijayanagar, according to him, was as large
as Rome and very beautiful, and had lakes and shady parks in it. But while the
nobles lived in grand mansions, the common people lived in modest houses of
just three or four small rooms, including kitchen. And the poor everywhere
in India lived in mud-and-thatch single room hovels. In Kerala, kings even
forbade the common people from roofing their houses with tiles instead of
with thatch; they had to get royal permission to use tiles.

The walls and floors of the houses of commoners, and the mats on which
their residents sat and slept, were invariably plastered with cow-dung, which
Indians 'looked upon as a clean substance,' according to Chau Ju-Kua, an early
thirteenth century Chinese chronicler. Confirms Marco Polo: 'The people of
this country have a custom of rubbing their houses all over with cow-dung.'
Another common feature of the Hindu homes was that people generally, even
the poor, adorned their front-yard with rangoli, auspicious decorative designs,
plain or colourful.

As for chairs and tables, there would have been hardly any of that in the
homes of most medieval Indians, for, as Marco Polo notes, all the people of
India, 'great and small, kings and barons included, do sit upon the floor only.'
But beds seem to have been fairly common in the homes of the affluent, and are
described in detail by Battuta. 'The beds in India are light, and can be carried
by a single man,' he writes. 'Every person when travelling has to transport his
own bed, which his slave boy carries on his head. It consists of four conical
legs with four crosspieces of wood on which braids of silk or cotton are woven.
When one lies down on it, there is no need for anything to make it pliable, for
it itself is pliable. Along with the bed they carry two mattresses and pillows
and a coverlet, all made of silk. Their custom is to put linen or cotton slips
on the mattresses and coverlets, so that when they become dirty they wash
the slips, while the bedding inside remains clean.' According to Marco Polo,
'nobles and great folks slept on beds made of very light cane work, hanging
from the ceiling by cords for fear of tarantulas and other vermin, while the
common folk slept on the streets.'

THE DRESS AND ornaments of the people, as well as their lifestyle, varied considerably from region to region in medieval India, and even within each region these varied according to the religion, class and caste of the people. But the common people everywhere in India, particularly in the peninsula, were scantily dressed, because of the warm and humid climate of India, and also because they could afford nothing better. 'The common people go quite naked, with the exception of a piece of cloth about their middle,' states Varthema, about what he saw in peninsular India. 'The blacks of this country go about with nearly naked bodies, wearing only a piece of cloth called langoti, extending from the navel to above their knees,' writes Razzak about Kerala. 'The king and the beggar both go about in this way . . .'

In coastal Maharashtra, according to Nikitin, 'people are all naked and barefooted. Women walk about with their heads uncovered and their breasts bare. Boys and girls all go naked till seven years, and do not hide their shame.' Adds Battuta: 'The women of . . . all the coastal districts wear nothing but loose unsewn garments, one end of which they gird round their waists, and drape the rest over their head and shoulders. They are beautiful and virtuous, and each wears a gold ring in her nose.'

Men and women of the upper classes, unlike the near naked common people, dressed luxuriously in most regions of India. Notes Varthema about the nobles of Vijayanagar: 'Their dress is this: the men of condition wear a short shirt, and on their head a cloth of gold and silk in the Moorish fashion . . . The king wears a cap of gold brocade two spans long, and when he goes to war he wears a quilted dress of cotton, and over it he puts another garment full of gold piastres, and having all around it jewels of various kinds. His horse is worth more than some of our cities, on account of the ornaments which it wears.' Barbosa also offers a similar description; according to him the affluent men in Vijayanagar wore a girdle and a short silk or cotton shirt, often brocaded; they also wore a small turban or a brocaded cap.

As for upper class women, they, according to Barbosa, 'wear white garments of very thin cotton, or silk of bright colours, five yards long, one part of which is girt round them below, and the other part is thrown over one shoulder and drawn across their breasts in such a way that one arm and shoulder remains uncovered . . . Their heads are uncovered and the hair is tightly gathered into a becoming knot on the top of the head, and in their hair they put many scented flowers . . . These women are very beautiful and very bold.'

The reports of various foreign visitors in medieval India on the dress and ornaments of the people are, in general terms, consistent, but there are several inconsistencies in the details they provide. Thus, while Varthema states that the people of Vijayanagar, even the nobles, wore 'nothing on their feet,'

Paes notes that though 'the majority of the people there, or almost all, go about the country barefooted,' the affluent men in Vijayanagar wore shoes with pointed ends, or sandals fitted with straps, 'like those which of old the Romans were wont to wear . . .' According to Barbosa, even women of the affluent families in Vijayanagar wore shoes, embroidered leather shoes. And they dressed luxuriously.

One of the most commendable practices of the people of medieval India was that most of them, whatever their class and caste, generally maintained good personal hygiene. 'It is their practice that everyone, male and female, washes their body twice every day,' observes Marco Polo. According Barbosa, nobles in Vijayanagar after bath daubed their bodies with 'white sandalwood, aloes, camphor, musk and saffron all ground fine and kneaded with rose water.' And Chau Ju-Kua notes: 'The inhabitants [of India] morning and evening besmear their bodies with turmeric so as to look like gold covered images.'

MEDIEVAL INDIANS, THE elite as well as the commoners, men as well as women, generally paid more attention to ornaments than to garments. 'All the inhabitants of the country, whether high or low, even down to the artificers of the bazaar, wear jewels and gilt ornaments on their ears and around their necks, arms, wrists, and fingers,' notes Razzak. 'In the side of one of their nostrils they make a small hole, through which they put a fine gold wire with a pearl, sapphire or ruby pendant,' reports Barbosa about the ornaments worn by affluent women in Vijayanagar. 'They have their ears bored as well, and in them they wear earrings set with many jewels; on their necks they wear necklaces of gold and jewels and very fine coral beads; bracelets of gold and precious stones and many good coral beads are fitted to their arms.' A common luxury which nearly everyone in India could afford was to adorn themselves, and their homes, with flowers. Notes Razzak about Vijayanagar: 'Sweet-scented flowers are always procurable fresh in that city, and they are considered as even necessary sustenance, seeing that without them people could not exist.'

In medieval times there was some mutual influence in the sartorial styles of the Hindu and Muslim upper classes, especially in North India. Rajput chieftains, for instance, took to wearing a tight-fitting cloak under the influence of Muslim nobility, and their women adopted Muslim style tight-fitting trousers and a cloak over it. Muslims in turn adopted the Rajput headgear, took to wearing luxurious garments, and began to adorn themselves with elaborate jewellery. 'Muslims clothe themselves in costly garments . . . and display various kinds of luxuries,' notes Razzak.

These ostentations in dress and ornaments by Muslims were disapproved by Firuz Tughluq; he considered them uncanonical, and sought to enforce

orthodox Muslim dress regulations. 'Under divine guidance I ordered that
. . . [only] such garments should be worn as are approved by the Law of the
Prophet,' states Firuz in his autobiography.

THE MEDIEVAL INDIAN society was characterised by several bizarre
practices. The most conspicuous of these was the practice of ritual suicide, of
which there were different forms. Though suicide in any form was considered
a great sin by Muslims, the sultans generally tolerated its practice by Hindus,
for they, as zimmis, were, according Muslim political tradition, free to follow
their social and religious customs without any hindrance.

One form of Hindu ritual suicide was for people in woe or debility,
because of illness or old age, to end their life in fire or water, to escape from
the miseries of life and to attain salvation. This was noted by Abu Zaid, a
tenth century Iraqi chronicler, in his account of early medieval India: 'When
a person . . . becomes old, and his senses are enfeebled, he begs someone of
his family to throw him into a fire, or to drown him in water; so firmly are
the Indians persuaded that they shall return to [life on] the earth.'

Jauhar,[2] mass ritual suicide, was another practice of Hindus, but this was
confined to the ruling class and the military aristocracy. Yet another form of
ritual suicide, again practiced mainly, though not exclusively, by the Hindu
aristocracy, was sati, the self-immolation by the widow or widows of a dead
king or chieftain on his funeral pyre. 'When the king dies four or five hundred
women burn themselves with him,' claims Barbosa. The number of royal
women committing sati given by Barbosa is evidently a gross exaggeration,
but it was not uncommon in medieval India for several queens to commit sati
on the death of their lord.

There is a detailed description of a sati rite in Vijayanagar in the report
of Nuniz. 'They place the dead man on a bed with a canopy of branches and
covered with flowers,' he writes. 'Then they put the woman on the back of a
worthless horse, and she [follows the funeral procession] . . . with many jewels
on her, and covered with roses. She carries a mirror in one hand and in the other
a bunch of flowers, and [is accompanied by] many kinds of music . . . A man
goes with her playing on a small drum, and he sings songs to her telling her
that she is going to join her husband, and she answers, also in singing, that so
she will do. As soon as she arrives at the place where they are always burned,
she waits with the musicians till her husband is burned . . . in a very large pit
that has been made ready for it, covered with firewood. Before they light the
pyre his mother, or one of his nearest relatives, takes a vessel of water on the
head and a firebrand in the hand, and goes three times round the pit, and at

[2]See Part VII, Chapter 3

each round makes a hole in the pot; and when these three rounds are done breaks the pot; which is small, and throws the torch into the pit.

'Then they apply the fire. And when the body is burned, the wife comes with all the feasters and washes her feet. Then a Brahmin performs over her certain ceremonies according to their law; and when he has finished doing this, she draws off with her own hand all the jewels that she wears, and divides them among her female relatives, and if she has sons she commends them to her most honoured relatives. When they have taken off all she has on, even her good clothes, they put on her some common yellow cloths, and her relatives take her by hand, and she takes a branch in the other hand, and goes singing and running to the pit where the fire is, and then mounts some steps which are made high up by the pit. Before they do this, they go three times round the fire, and then she mounts the steps and holds in front of her a mat that prevents her from seeing the fire. They throw into the fire a cloth containing rice, and another in which they carry betel leaves, and her comb and mirror with which she had adorned herself, saying that all these were needed to adorn herself by her husband's side.

'Finally she takes leave of all, and puts a pot of oil on her head, and casts herself into the fire with such courage that it is a thing of wonder. As soon as she throws herself in, her relatives, who are ready with firewood, . . . quickly cover her with it, and after this is done they all raise loud lamentations.' Adds Barbosa: At the pyre the woman removes all her clothes 'except a small piece of cloth with which she is clothed from the waist down. All this she does . . . with such a cheerful countenance that she seems not about to die . . . Then they place in her hands a pitcher full of oil, and she puts it on her head, and with it she . . . turns around thrice on the scaffold and . . . worships the rising sun. Then she casts the pitcher of oil into the fire and throws herself after it with as much goodwill as if she were throwing herself on a . . . [bed of] cotton . . . Then the kinsfolk all . . . cast into the fire many pitchers of oil and butter which they hold ready for this purpose, and much wood . . . [so that the pyre] therewith bursts into such a flame that no more can she be seen.[3]

[3]See *The First Spring* Part VI, Chapter 3 for Battuta's description of sati.

4

Rich Land, Poor People

The high period of Indian civilisation, in material prosperity as well as cultural efflorescence, was the thousand year period from the middle of the first millennium BCE to the middle of the first millennium CE. During that age India was one of the most urbanised, prosperous and civilised countries of the world. The scene changed altogether thereafter, as India slid into the Dark Ages, around the same time as Europe did. India's commercial economy and urban culture then collapsed. Towns turned derelict. And India slid into a state of dreary rusticity. India then, like Europe, curled up in a several centuries long slumber. But while Europe woke up from the slumber in the fourteenth century, during Renaissance, and made rapid economic, social and cultural progress, India remained in a comatose state well into the twentieth century.

Though there was some urban revival during the Sultanate period, India's socio-economic and cultural progress remained sluggish. The preponderant majority of Indians during the Sultanate period lived in villages, as they had done in the preceding several centuries, and would continue to do in the succeeding several centuries. And the life of the villager remained very much the same all through these centuries. The urban affluence that had characterised classical India was mostly missing in medieval India.

But despite its civilizational collapse, India remained a singularly enticing land in the eyes of foreigners virtually all through its history, well into modern times. This was largely because of India's fabulous natural resources. 'The whole of this country is very fertile, and the resources of Iran, Turan, and other lands are not equal to those of even one province of Hindustan,' states *Mukhtasiru-t Tawarikh*. 'In this country there are also mines of diamonds,

357

ruby, gold, silver, copper, lead and iron. The soil is generally good, and is so productive that in a year it yields two crops, and in some places more. All kinds of grain, the sustenance of human life, are brought forth in such quantities that it is beyond the power of pen to enumerate . . . Men of refined and delicate taste find great relish in eating the fruits of Hindustan. A separate book would have to be written if a full detail were to be given of all the different kinds of fruits which are produced in spring and autumn, describing all their sweetness, fragrance and flavour.'

There is a fair amount of exaggeration in this radiant medieval portrait of India, but in broad terms it is factual. India was indeed blessed with rich natural resources. And the basic survival requirements of the common people—food and shelter—were easily available there for all in normal times. But it is equally true that the common people of medieval India lived at a bare subsistence level. The land was rich, but the people were poor.

And the richness of the land continued to fascinate foreigners, and it attracted many adventurers, migrants and invaders into India all through history, well into modern times. And foreign visitors continued to write glowingly about the riches of India.

But there was a dark side to this luminous medieval image of India. India, like most other regions of the medieval world, was periodically ravaged by famine, for its agricultural production at this time was mostly dependent on the vagaries of weather. When weather failed, famine felled thousands and thousands of people in one sweep.

And those who survived did so by eating whatever they could find, however filthy or rotten, even putrefied carrion, and by taking to cannibalism. 'One day I went out of the city, and I saw three women . . . cutting in pieces and eating the skin of a horse which had been dead for some months,' writes Battuta about the horrors of famine he witnessed in India. 'Skins were cooked and sold in the markets. When bullocks were slaughtered, crowds rushed forward to catch the blood, and consumed it for their sustenance.' Adds Barani: 'Distress and anarchy reigned in all the country and towns . . . [In Delhi] famine was very severe, and man was devouring man.'

On such occasions the sultans, despite their general indifference to the plight of the people, often did what they could to alleviate their sufferings. Even Muhammad Tughluq, a sultan not particularly known for his compassion, once, during a time acute scarcity, 'ordered provisions for six months to be distributed to all the people of Delhi,' reports Battuta. In normal times too Delhi sultans usually took care to open almshouses in towns to succour the poor, as a pious act. This was mainly for the benefit of poor Muslims, but low caste Hindus, who could eat the food cooked by Muslims, also benefited from it.

THE EFFULGENT VIEW of India propagated by ancient and early medieval foreign visitors to India began to change gradually in the late medieval period, as the contrast between regressive India and progressive Europe sharpened, and as more and more European travellers visited India, and India became a familiar land to them. The fabled luminous images of India were then gradually replaced in their accounts with the images of the stark reality of India. Many visitors were now appalled by what they saw as the abysmal conditions of the life of the common people in India. Typically, Pelsaert, a Dutch traveller in India during the Mughal period, writes: The common people of India live in a 'poverty so great and miserable that the life of the people can be depicted or accurately described only as the home of stark want and the dwelling place of bitter woe. Their houses are built of mud, with thatch roofs. Furniture there is little or none, except some earthenware pots to hold water and for cooking.'

These and similar reports about the abject conditions of life of the common people in medieval India are in many cases rather exaggerated, just as the earlier glowing reports about India were exaggerated. There was still great wealth in medieval India, and though most of it was in the hands of the small ruling class, there was enough of it left over for the subsistence of the common people. Daily provisions were usually quite cheap and abundantly available everywhere. The disparity between the incredibly luxurious lifestyle of the ruling class and the dreary life of the common people was of course shocking, but this was a common feature of human societies nearly everywhere in the premodern world, though in European countries the conditions of life of the underclasses were not as dismal as it was in India.

Curiously, despite the growing awareness among Europeans of the abject poverty of the common people of India, many European powers were drawn to India in medieval times. This was because there were vast untapped natural resources in India to be exploited. And the very poverty and backwardness of Indians made the invasion of India seem easy. India thus remained, till modern times, a most enticing land in the eyes of foreigners, and migrants and invaders continued to stream into India.

THE ECONOMIC CONDITIONS in medieval India varied considerably from region to region, but most of the land was quite fertile and was extensively cultivated. 'This is a vast country, abounding in rice, and nowhere in the world have I seen any land where prices are lower than there,' notes Battuta about what he observed in fourteenth-century Bengal. And he goes on to report that an old inhabitant there once told him that he could maintain his family for a whole year with just eight dirhams, small silver coins. And Battuta found that in Kerala 'there is not a foot of ground but is cultivated. Every man has his own orchard, with his house in the middle and wooden palisade all around it.'

Orissa too was luxuriantly verdant. Afif, who visited the region during the reign of Firuz Tughluq, found it 'in a very flourishing state . . . [with] abundance of corn and fruit . . . The numbers of animals of every kind were so great that no one cared to take them. Sheep were found in countless numbers.' The scene in Jammu too was similar. 'The five or six kos which I traversed in this day's march was entirely through a cultivated country; nowhere did I see any dry or waste land,' writes Timur about Jammu in his autobiography. In addition to cultivating fields, most villagers in medieval India also maintained cattle-pens, for that involved virtually no expenditure, as there was plenty of open land in India for cattle-grazing.

Most farmlands in early medieval India were rain fed. Though Indian villages generally had water tanks in them, these were usually small and were used only to provide drinking water to villagers. 'They have a custom in those villages of making tanks in which the rain-water collects, and this supplies them with drinking water all the year round,' notes Battuta about what he observed in North India. As for irrigation facilities, pre-medieval India had a system known as *araghatt*—the precursor of the Persian wheel—for lifting water from wells and channelling it into fields, and these were modified and made more efficient in medieval times under Turkish influence. The spread of tank irrigation, and the cultivation of cash crops like cotton and indigo, notably boosted the income of farmers, and improved the living conditions in rural India at this time, even in dry regions.

The building of tanks to irrigate fields and to provide drinking water for people was a major community activity in ancient and medieval Indian villages. Kings also built them, huge reservoirs, to serve several villages. One of the oldest and largest of these reservoirs was the Sudarsana Lake in Gujarat built by Mauryan emperor Chandragupta in the fourth century BCE. Similar major irrigation works were constructed by kings in several other regions of India over the centuries. Paes saw a great reservoir being built in Vijayanagar by Krishnadeva, the embankment of which was a 'falcon-shot wide.' This reservoir, notes Paes, was built 'at the mouth of two hills, so that the water which comes from either one side or the other collects there.' In addition to rain water, the reservoir was also fed with water brought through pipes from a nearby lake. This was a gigantic enterprise, and it took several thousand men very many months to build it. 'In the tank I saw so many people at work that there must have been fifteen or twenty thousand men there, looking like ants, so that you could not see the ground on which they walked, so many were there,' states Paes. And while the dam was being constructed the raja had sixty men, presumably prisoners, and a number of horses and buffaloes sacrificed at the gate of the local temple, to appease gods and thus ensure the safety of the dam. Apart from this huge reservoir, the Vijayanagar rajas also built a number of other irrigation facilities, and this substantially increased the agricultural prosperity of the kingdom.

Some of the Delhi sultans also took care to build irrigation facilities to promote agriculture. Firuz Tughluq in particular was active in this; he built a vast network of canals in the Indo-Gangetic Plain, which drew water from several rivers—Yamuna, Sutlej, Ghaggar and so on—and distributed it for irrigation. This canal system is considered to be the largest such network ever built in India in pre-modern times. Provincial governors also played a notable role in expanding irrigation facilities in their territory. Besides these massive canal networks built by the state, several villages also built local canals to feed their fields.

A great variety of cereals, fruits, nuts, kitchen vegetables and spices were cultivated in medieval India. In addition to these native agricultural products, India in medieval times also took to the cultivation of tobacco, maize and potatoes, produce of the Americas brought into India by the Portuguese, and these in time became major crops.

Cereals were usually harvested twice a year in India: an autumn harvest (kharif) and a spring harvest (rabi). 'When they have reaped the autumn harvest, they sow spring grains in the same soil in which autumn grains had been sown, for their country is excellent and the soil is fertile,' reports Battuta. 'As for rice, they sow it three times a year.' Most of the agricultural produce in medieval India were consumed locally, in the villages that produced them, but there was also some trade across the subcontinent in them, particularly in cereals, carried by Banjaras, wandering grain traders.

In early medieval India farming was almost entirely in the hands of Hindus. Most of the farm holdings at this time were small, and were cultivated by their owners themselves. There were however also a few large estates owned by landlords, who cultivated them by hiring farm labourers. Hindu temples also played a major role in agriculture—they owned extensive tracts of land, which they usually rented out to tenants, but sometimes they themselves cultivated them by employing labourers. Temples also financed agriculture by advancing loans to farmers on the security of their lands. The state too played a notable role in promoting agriculture, inducing farmers to expand cultivation by granting them tax remissions or concessions, and by encouraging them to plant more valuable crops—sugarcane, oil-seeds, spices and poppies—instead of cereals.

Another development of economic importance in medieval India was the mass migration of people from one region to another. A major instance of this was the migration of a large number of farmers from the dry areas of Karnataka to the fertile lower Kavery valley. There was also a notable movement of Telugus into the Tamil country at this time, so that Telugu farmers and merchants came to constitute significant elements in the population of several districts in Tamil Nadu.

THE MOST SIGNIFICANT economic development of the early medieval period in India was the gradual revival of urban prosperity, and the related expansion of industrial production and trade. Some of the traditional industrial products of India, such as high quality textiles, underwent notable changes at this time, to reflect the Turkish taste, as Turks had become the major consumers of these products. Even the very mode of textile production changed at this time, as Indians now, in the thirteenth century, took to the use of the spinning wheel under Turkish influence, replacing the traditional the hand spindle. This technology became widespread in India over the next century, and it greatly speeded up textile production. Indians also took to the use of cotton-carder's bow around this time. Possibly the weaver's loom also underwent a modification in the medieval period, but information about this is scanty. Bengal was the main textile manufacturing region of India at this time, with Gujarat close behind it.

Cloth-weaving was the most widespread industrial activity in medieval India, but there were also several other crafts flourishing in India at this time. Metal crafts, for instance, boomed during this period, manufacturing war materials like swords and guns, as well as several household items. Indians also took to the manufacture of paper now, around the thirteenth century.

A notable economic development in India in the middle ages was the growing prominence of state run manufacturing units, producing a variety of luxury goods. This happened in nearly all the kingdoms of the period, but most prominently in Delhi. What the royal factories produced were not, however, for sale in the market, but for the consumption of the vast royal establishments, and for the king and his family members to give away as presents.

'The sultan has a factory, in which 400 silk weavers are employed,' notes Shahab-ud-din. 'And there they make stuffs of all kinds, for the dresses of persons attached to the court, for robes of honour and presents, in addition to the stuffs which are brought every year from China, Iraq and Alexandria. Every year the sultan distributes 200,000 complete dresses; 100,000 in spring and 100,000 in autumn. The spring dresses consist principally of the goods manufactured in Alexandria. Those of the autumn are almost exclusively of silk manufactured in Delhi or imported from China or Iraq . . . The sultan keeps in his service 500 manufacturers of golden tissues, who weave the gold brocades worn by the wives of the sultan, and those given away as presents to the amirs and their wives.'

Indian craftsmen enjoyed a high reputation in the medieval world for their skills. 'I tell you that they are the greatest and the most expert workmen ... in all the world,' states Varthema. But the crafts environment in India also had a negative aspect to it, in that the top Indian craftsmen were usually very secretive about their skills, passing them on to their sons or favourite disciples late in their lives, often near the time of their death. Sometimes they failed to do this, so that their unique skills died with them.

DOMESTIC TRADE IN India had declined sharply in the post-Gupta period, due to the ruralisation of Indian society and economy. Around that time India's foreign trade too petered out, because of the collapse of the Roman Empire and the slide of Europe into the Dark Ages. But now, with the establishment of the Delhi Sultanate, internal trade gradually revived, stimulated by the insatiable demand for luxury goods by the sultans and nobles. India's foreign trade also revived at this time, as the demand for Indian goods rose in Europe as it emerged out of the Dark Ages. These economic developments in India were noted by several contemporary foreign visitors—Battuta, for instance, found cities flourishing in the upper Gangetic valley, Gujarat, Bengal, the Deccan, Vijayanagar and Kerala. Barbosa and Paes also speak of the lively commercial scene in India at this time. Gold coins, which were rarely issued in India after the collapse of the Gupta Empire, now once again began to appear, indicating the revival of Indian economy.

Towns now rose to prominence again, with flourishing markets, where trade fairs were held periodically. Also, the political integration of a large part of the subcontinent under the Delhi sultans led to the economic integration of the subcontinent, as well as to the expansion of trade and to the close commercial interlinking of villages and towns. New towns now began to sprout all over the land. And alongside the existing major towns there appeared flourishing suburbs, indicating the spread of prosperity and the increased feeling of security among the people. The travel of people and the transport of goods across the land were now safer than in the previous period, though they were still quite hazardous. Caravanserais now appeared along major trade routes, and this also greatly facilitated regional and inter-regional trade.

There was however no notable change in the pattern of India's trade, or in its merchandise, from what they had been for many centuries previously. Nor was India's economic growth vigorous enough to bring about any civilizational change in India, or to markedly improve the standard of life of the common people. It is significant that there is no evidence at this time of the existence of trade guilds, which had played a crucial role in Indian economy in the classical age.

THE PROMINENT TRADING communities of medieval India were Banias of Gujarat, Multanis of Punjab, Marwaris of Rajasthan, and Chettis of peninsular India. Apart from these major trading communities, there were also several other Hindu communities engaged in trade in medieval times. Muslims too played an important role in trade at this time, in local as well as foreign trade. Banjaras—a nomadic people divided into several tribes and based in different parts of the subcontinent, but probably originally from Rajasthan—also played a prominent role in Indian economy at this time, as itinerant grain traders.

Brahmins too, according to Marco Polo, played a key role in trade at this time, as agents of foreign traders, and were highly respected for their integrity. Nuniz also speaks highly of Brahmin traders, and notes that they 'are honest men, given to trade, very acute and of much talent, very good at accounts, lean men and well-formed, but little fit for hard work.'

Did Brahmins at this time really play the prominent role in trade that is attributed to them by Polo and Nuniz? That is doubtful. It is quite probable that these chroniclers were mistaking Jains for Brahmins, for Brahmins were not known to have been active in trade in medieval India, except along the northern Karnataka coast, where the Konkani-speaking Saraswat Brahmins were prominent regional traders. Elsewhere in India too Brahmins played a major role in trade, but as financiers of traders, not as traders themselves.

In medieval India, as in classical India, trade in particular commodities was handled by particular communities, as an extension of the occupation specialisation of castes. Similarly, financing business was also usually a community specialisation. Two of the most prominent financier communities of medieval India were Shahs and Multanis, of whom the latter also directly participated in trade. Hindu temples, like Buddhist monasteries in earlier times, also played a major role in the economy and social life of medieval India. 'The temple,' as Thapar notes, 'was the bank, the landowner, the employer of innumerable artisans and servants, the school, the discussion centre, the administrative centre for the village, and the place for major entertainments in the form of festivals.' Muslims had virtually no role in financial services, as Islamic law condemned lending money on interest as a sin.

As for business ethics, it varied from community to community, and region to region. In Gujarat traders were invariably straightforward in their dealings, and charged only the right price for what they sold. On the other hand, traders in Lahore, whose customers were mostly itinerant foreigners, usually quoted inflated prices, and entered into a battle of wits in bargaining with their customers before agreeing on the price.

Traders in major towns in India at this time were generally very wealthy and lived in luxurious mansions. Battuta, for instance, mentions the case of one Mithqal—quite probably an Arab trader—in Kozhikode in north Kerala, who possessed 'great riches and many ships for trading with India, China, Yemen and Fars (Iran).'

ISLAM DISAPPROVED ITS votaries from taking to money lending business, but it had no serious objection to Muslims borrowing money on interest. In fact, the Muslim aristocracy in India were heavy, reckless borrowers of money, often at exorbitant interest rates. Notes Barani: 'The Multanis and Shahs of Delhi, who have acquired abundant wealth, have derived it from the resources of the old nobles of Delhi.' The nobles took huge loans from these moneylenders, and repaid them by assigning to them shares in the revenue of their fiefs. Being deep in debt was for these nobles even something to be proud of, as a demonstration of their extravagant and carefree lifestyle.

Muslim travellers, traders and migrants were also heavy borrowers, and they were served by Hindu moneylenders, particularly in the north-western frontier towns of India. 'The merchants of Sind and India began to furnish each newcomer with thousands of dinars as a loan, and to supply him with whatever he might desire, to offer as gift or for his own use, such as riding animals, camels, and goods,' reports Battuta. 'They place both their money and their persons at his service, and stand before him like attendants. When he reaches the sultan, he receives a magnificent gift from him and pays off his debt to them.'

The common people were also heavy borrowers in medieval times, but they often defaulted in their repayments, so the relationship between the lender and the borrower was seldom cordial in India, and sometimes the lender had to take coercive measures to recover his money. Marco Polo describes a curious South Indian practice of a creditor drawing a circle around his defaulting debtor, for the custom of the region required that 'the latter should not pass out of this circle until he had satisfied the claim, or given security for its discharge.'

Apart from financiers, brokers (dallals) also played a key role in trade deals, particularly as intermediaries in the transactions between Indians of different regions, or between Indians and foreigners, because the cultural and language differences between such persons made direct negotiations between them virtually impossible. This, the prominent role played by brokers in trade, was a relatively new development in India in medieval times, and was indicative of the expansion of inter-regional and foreign trade in India at this time. Brokers also served as clearing agents, transporters, and stockers of trade goods.

Trade negotiations in the market at this time were carried out in a peculiarly secretive manner in some Indian towns. 'They always sell by the hands of the . . . broker,' notes Varthema. 'And when the purchaser and the seller wish to make an agreement, they all stand in a circle, and the broker takes a cloth and holds it there openly with one hand, and with the other hand he takes the right hand of the seller, that is, the two fingers next to the thumb, and then he covers with the said cloth his hand and that of the seller, and touching each other with these two fingers, they count from one ducat up to one hundred thousand secretly, without saying "I will have 60" or "so much." But by merely touching the joints of the fingers they understand the price and say "Yes" or "No". And broker answers "No" or "Yes". And when the broker has understood the will of the seller, he goes to the buyer with the said cloth, and takes his hand in the manner above mentioned, and by the said touching he tells him he wants so much. The buyer takes the finger of the broker, and by the said touches says to him: "I will give him so much." And in this manner they fix the price.'

POLITICAL CONSOLIDATION IN India in early medieval times—in North India under the Delhi Sultanate, and in the peninsula under the Bahmani Sultanate and Vijayanagar—facilitated the economic recovery of India from the morass into which it had sunk in the late classical period. Though Mahmud Ghazni's pillaging raids in the early eleventh century had devastated the already moribund Indian economy, now, two centuries later, with the establishment of the Delhi Sultanate, the economy stabilised and began to expand. There were still incessant wars in many regions of the subcontinent at this time, but conditions were on the whole better than what they had been in the previous several centuries. There was now relative political stability in the subcontinent, and that facilitated the expansion of trade. Moreover, trade at this time was greatly stimulated by the patronage it received from the fabulously affluent and extravagant Muslim ruling class. And kings generally sought to promote trade by granting tax concessions to traders and by conferring on them various privileges, for the prosperity that traders brought to kingdoms strengthened the economic base of royal power.

The primary concern of the medieval Indian kings in their tax policies, as in everything else, was to consolidate and enhance their own power and resources; ruling for the benefit of the people was more a pretence than a practice with nearly all of them. But even from the narrow point of view of self-interest, it was very much in the interest of kings to nourish trade and be facilitative towards traders, especially towards foreign traders, for kings were dependent on those traders to provide them with the luxuries essential for their lifestyle, and also, more importantly, to supply them with the horses their armies needed. Besides, traders often operated across kingdoms, and if a king overtaxed or oppressed them, they could easily move their business elsewhere.

In every respect it was very much in the interest of kings to maintain good relationship with traders. And traders on their part usually avoided getting embroiled in political tussles, for that could jeopardise their business interests. But major traders, because of their great wealth, and the armed escorts they maintained, were sometimes tempted to enter into the perilous arena of politics. Thus the Tibi family, trade tycoons in peninsular India in the late thirteenth century, once played the role of kingmakers in the Pandya kingdom, in a tussle between two brothers for the throne. Similarly, according to Battuta, there was once, on the west coast south of Goa, a very rich trader named Jamal-ud-din, who maintained an army of 6,000 and a fleet of over fifty ships, styled himself 'sultan', and exercised considerable political power for a while in the late fifteenth century.

COMMERCIAL TAX PRACTICES and rates in India varied considerably from kingdom to kingdom, even from ruler to ruler in a kingdom. This was inevitable, given the political, economic and social diversity of India. The most rigorous of the trade control measures enforced by any medieval Indian king were those of Ala-ud-din Khalji, who sought to firmly control all economic activities in his empire, particularly in Delhi, by regulating both the movement of goods as well as their prices. The major trade objective of the sultan was to stabilise the price of grains, the essential food of Indians of all classes, and in this he was entirely successful. He achieved this by fixing and enforcing the price of grains, and by carefully balancing supply and demand, releasing into the market grains from the royal stores during times of scarcity. 'The unvarying price of grain in the markets was looked upon as one of the wonders of the age,' comments Barani.

Ala-ud-din's economic policies were comprehensive. In addition to the price of grains, he also sought to control the prices of all essential commodities, such as 'piece goods, garments, sugar, vegetables, fruits, animal oil, and lamp oil,' states Barani. The prices of slaves and concubines (essential commodities in that age!) were also fixed by the sultan. Even in the case of 'articles . . . of the most trifling value . . . the sultan took the greatest trouble to fix their prices and to settle the profit of vendors.' These were not mere paper regulations, but were rigorously enforced. And the sultan kept himself regularly informed about the market conditions through the reports of three independent sources—the superintendent of the market, reporters, and spies—and he took prompt remedial measures whenever required to restore market stability. Merchants who used short-weights were punished with 'blows and by cutting off flesh [of an equal weight] from the haunches of those who gave short weight.'

To enforce his market regulations, Ala-ud-din held the families of the major suppliers of goods in the market as hostages, and held out the threat of severe punishment to those who violated government regulations. But this was only one side of the sultan's policy. His was a carrot-and-stick policy, by which, on the one side, he coerced traders to abide by his market regulations, and, on the other side, encouraged and supported fair traders by honouring them with robes of honour, and by granting them loans from the royal treasury for financing their business. An equally creditable aspect of Ala-ud-din's trade regulations was that they were as much beneficial to the common people as to the state, as they created stable market conditions and kept the prices of essential commodities low. Ala-ud-din was an autocrat, but a benevolent autocrat. Unfortunately, his market regulations 'came to an end on his death, for his son . . . was not able to maintain even a thousandth part of them,' comments Barani.

THE ECONOMIC POLICIES of Krishnadeva of Vijayanagar was the exact opposite of the policies of Ala-ud-din—the raja's objective was to stimulate economic activity, while the sultan's objective was to control it—but in both cases their policies were beneficial to the king as well as to the people.

Of all the Indian kings of the early middle ages, Krishnadeva's economic policies were the most liberal. 'A king should improve the harbours of his country and encourage its commerce, so that horses, elephants, precious gems, sandalwood, pearls, and other articles are freely imported into the country,' he advises in *Amukta-malyada*, his poetic work. 'He should arrange that foreign sailors who land in his country on account of storm, illness, and exhaustion are looked after in a manner suitable to their nationality . . . [He should] make the merchants of distant foreign countries who import elephants and good horses be attached to him by providing them with daily audience and presents, and by allowing decent profits. Then those articles will never go to his enemies. . . .'

This liberal import policy however applied only to the items that the state itself did not produce. In other items the protection of local producers and traders was a high priority for Vijayanagar kings, and they usually imposed high taxes on the goods brought from outside the state. This was the common practice of most Indian kingdoms.

Import taxes were usually collected at the frontiers of kingdoms. For instance, at a river crossing near Multan, 'the goods and baggage of all who pass are subjected to a rigorous examination,' reports Battuta. 'Their custom at the time of our arrival was [for government officers] to take a quarter of everything brought in by merchants, and exact a duty of seven dinars for every horse.' These were quite high rates. Further, in addition to import duties, medieval Indian states also collected octroi at the gates of towns.

The range of commercial taxes in medieval Indian kingdoms was indeed very broad. Indian kings usually imposed tax on all trade and economically productive activities in the state, however trivial, because, from the point of view of kings, the very existence of those activities depended on the protection that the state provided to them through the maintenance of law and order.

However, despite the wide range of commercial taxes collected by Indian states, these taxes were relatively fewer than the other taxes collected by medieval Indian states. And the rates of commercial taxes were usually lower than the rates of agricultural taxes. In Vijayanagar, for instance, agricultural tax was between one-third and one-sixth of the produce, but customs duty was only between 2.5 and 5 per cent of the sale price. But even at such low rates, commercial taxes yielded high revenue for the state, next only to the revenue from agricultural taxes.

Kings were generally protective towards traders, because it was very much in their interests to do so. But practices in this varied considerably from kingdom to kingdom. And sometimes kings acted like brigands or pirates. For instance, in Kerala, according to Battuta, it was 'a custom of theirs that every ship that passes by a [port] town must drop anchor there and give a present to the [local] ruler . . . If anyone omits to do this, they sail out in pursuit of him, bring him into the port by force, double the tax on him, and prevent him from proceeding on his journey for as long as they wish.' Kerala kings apparently considered the coastal seas as their territorial waters.

SUCH PIRATICAL CONDUCT by kings was however rare. Usually the relationship between kings and traders was mutually supportive, and mutually beneficial. This was reflected in the fact that the most flourishing markets in kingdoms were generally in royal capitals. 'By the palace of the king there are four bazaars, situated opposite one another . . .,' reports Razzak about Vijayanagar. 'At the head of each bazaar there is a lofty arcade and magnificent gallery . . . The bazaars are very broad and long . . . The tradesmen of each separate guild or craft have their shops close to one another. Jewellers sell their rubies and pearls and diamonds and emeralds openly in the bazaar.' The largest market in medieval India was, as was to be expected, in Delhi, which Battuta considered the largest market in the world. Apart from these permanent markets, large temporary trade fairs were usually organised in towns and major villages during temple festivals.

A major item of trans-regional trade in medieval India was salt, the main source of which was the Sambhar Salt Lake in Rajasthan. Several metals of commercial value were also mined in India. Of these, the most important item was iron, which was quarried in several places in the extensive region stretching from the southern Gangetic Valley to almost the very tip of India. Indian iron had a good overseas market in medieval times, as it was considered ideal for making swords. Copper was another notable metal mined in India, mainly in Rajasthan. But gold and silver were scarce in India, and only very small quantities of them were mined there. Diamonds were mined in the Deccan. And pearl fishery was a major industry on the southern Tamil Nadu coast.

In medieval times there was also some inter-regional and international trade in a few items manufactured in India, particularly in cloth. A variety of fabrics were woven in India at this time—in cotton, silk, and wool—and some of the special regional textile products were of very high quality and were marketed across India, and also exported. Gold and silver embroidery was a speciality of Gujarat; shawls and carpets of Kashmir.

MEDIEVAL INDIA HAD, for that age, fairly good transportation and communication facilities, with its main roads running east-west across the breadth of the Indo-Gangetic Plain, and north-south from the Gangetic Valley to deep into peninsular India. These roads had halting stations at regular intervals, where there were caravanserais and shops, as well as porters, horses, horse-carriages, bullock-carts and palanquins for hire. There was also an efficient long distance postal system in India at this time, with runners and horsemen posted at regular intervals along the main roads to carry mail. This facility was primarily for government use, but presumably it, or a similar service, was also available to traders.

These services however linked only the major political and commercial centres of India, and did not cover the interior regions of the subcontinent, where roads were rare, and communication facilities poor or nonexistent. Because of this, carts were seldom used to transport goods in India, except for short haul. The common mode of transport of goods in medieval India was to carry them on bullocks, which travelled in huge caravans, often consisting of thousands of bulls—Battuta mentions a caravan of 3000 bulls carrying 30,000 maunds of grain; other reporters mention caravans of 10,000 and even 20,000 bulls.

In Kerala most of the bulk goods were transported in boats on the backwaters or rivers; alternately men carried the goods on their heads. Animals were seldom used for transporting goods in Kerala—'There are no beasts of burden in this land,' states Barbosa. In North India, the Ganga-Yamuna river system was extensively used for transporting goods by boat, which was relatively cheaper and safer than road transport, and boats and guards were available for hire by traders at jetties along these rivers. There was also some amount of coastal shipping in India at this time.

Apart from the poor network of roads in the interior regions of India, there were several other hazards for the transport of goods in India in medieval times. Travel routes in several regions of India passed through dense forests inhabited by brigands, so traders usually travelled in groups and under the protection of hired guards. Wars and rebellions, which were perennial in medieval India, also disrupted trade. Venetian trader Caesar Frederic, for instance, was once held up in Vijayanagar for seven whole months, for the roads in the region were at this time, following the defeat of Vijayanagar in the battle of Talikota, infested by bandits.

Another major impediment to the free flow of trade in medieval India was the confusing diversity of currencies, weights and measures in use in different parts of the country. These often varied from region to region, and from kingdom to kingdom, sometimes even in the different parts of the same kingdom, or from king to king. Coins of the same name, as well as weights and measures of the same name, often had different values in different places and in different times. Vijayanagar had several mints, one at each provincial capital, which would have made it very difficult to maintain uniform standard in its coins. Adding to the confusion of all this was the free circulation of foreign coins in India, particularly the coins of Portugal, Italy, and the Middle Eastern kingdoms. Comments Caesar Frederick, a mid-sixteenth century Italian trade prospector in India: 'The money we take this day would not serve the next.'

All this impeded the smooth transaction of business in the subcontinent. What prevented Indian trade from collapsing altogether in this monetary chaos was the presence of money changers in all major markets, who would, for a commission, give local coins in exchange for the coins of different Indian kingdoms and of foreign lands. Besides, the barter system was still extensively used in India for small transactions, with grain as the medium of exchange. According to Battuta, the common people in Bengal and Maldives used cowrie as money.

AN IMPORTANT ELEMENT in the Indian economy of the early medieval period was the participation of Indians in the brisk maritime trade in the Indian Ocean, particularly in the trade with South-east Asia and China. 'The curiosities of Chin (China) and Machin (Canton) and the beautiful products of Hind and Sind, laden on large ships . . . sailing like mountains . . . are always arriving there (at Mabar: Coromandel Coast) . . . which is so situated as to be the key of Hind,' writes Wassaf.

The major players in the Indian Ocean trade at this time were Indians, Arabs, Chinese and South-East Asians. Of these, Arabs were the most active and successful traders, and their dominant presence in the Arabian Sea eventually obliged Indian traders to gradually retreat from there, though they still maintained a residual presence in a few Middle Eastern trade centres, like Aden. Indians thereafter largely confined themselves to trade with South-east Asia and China; Indian traders, particularly Chettis of the Tamil country, had at this time a notable presence in places like Malacca.

Arab traders had been active in the Indian Ocean long before the founding of Islam, but now, energised by their new faith, they surged ahead, and went on to dominate the sea trade in the entire region. This was the result of peaceful though fierce competition; virtually no military action was involved in it. And, as Arab trade in the region expanded, Arab settlements in India's coastal towns increased in number and size, and they generally enjoyed great prosperity. Arab traders in Cambay in Gujarat were very affluent, and lived in grand mansions, Battuta noted. And he found numerous mosques along the coast of Kerala, which indicated the presence of a large number of Arabs and local Muslims there, and their general prosperity.

Peninsular Indian kings, sultans as well as rajas, generally patronised Arab traders, as these traders contributed to the prosperity of their kingdoms, and because the kings were dependant on Arabs for the regular supply of horses, a perennial military requirement of most Indian kings. Arab traders enjoyed virtual autonomy in Kerala, as the local rulers there allowed them to live there under their own laws, and to have their own governors to regulate their lives and to punish their criminals, without any reference to the raja. According to Barbosa, fresh batches of Arab merchants arrived in Kerala periodically, and they were favoured by the local raja by assigning to each of them attendants like bodyguards, accountants and brokers, to help them in their local transactions. Many of these merchants settled in Kerala, married local women, and they and their descendants, called Mapilas, in time became a notable element in the local population.

Arabs dominated the Arabian Sea trade for several centuries, till the early sixteenth century, when the Portuguese wrested control from them. The Portuguese had arrived on the scene at the close of the fifteenth century, and soon they became absolute masters of the seas around India, because of their superior naval capabilities. Presently they built their fortified settlements on the eastern and western coasts of peninsular India, with Goa as their chief centre, and thus entrenched themselves on land in India, to backup their dominant naval presence in the Indian seas.

The Portuguese then considered the Indian Ocean as their sovereign territory, and controlled all the traffic there by laying down the rule that the ships of all other nations sailing there, particularly in the Arabian Sea, should do so only by calling at a Portuguese port in the region, to pay duty on their cargo and to obtain a pass for their safe journey. And they decreed that no ship plying in the Arabian Sea should carry certain items, especially spices and ammunitions, which they considered as their monopoly. They also required that merchantmen should sail in small convoys, and under the escort of Portuguese warships. This hegemony of the Portuguese in the Indian seas lasted for about a century, but they were eventually, in the early decades of the seventeenth century, displaced by other European powers, particularly the British.

BY THE SIXTEENTH century the port cities of peninsular India emerged as the most prominent foreign trade centres in the subcontinent, displacing the cities in north-western India which had dominated this trade for many centuries. This change was because foreign trade, which had been mostly by land route previously, was now mostly by sea route, and the peninsular ports were ideally situated to serve both eastern and western sea traders.

There is a good amount of information about the trade activities in peninsular India at this time, because the region was then visited by very many foreign traders and travellers, and several of them maintained records of what they observed. In particular, the Kerala coast, which was studded with several natural harbours, was abuzz with commercial activity at this time. Kozhikode (Calicut, in north Kerala) and Kollam (Quilon, in south Kerala), according to Battuta, were among the best ports he had seen anywhere in the world, and were equal to Alexandria. 'It has fine bazaars, and its merchants . . . are immensely wealthy,' writes Battuta about Kollam. 'A single merchant will buy a vessel with all that is in it and load it with goods from his own house. There is a colony of Muslim merchants there; the cathedral mosque there is a magnificent building. This city is the nearest of the Mulaybar (Malabar: Kerala) towns to China, and it is to it that most of the merchants [from China] come.' Kollam was the main centre for the transhipment of East Asian goods to the West, and of European goods to the East.

This trade prominence of Kollam was rivalled by Kozhikode, but the town seems to have gained importance only around the fourteenth century, for Marco Polo, who visited Kerala in the thirteenth century, does not mention it at all. But by the next century the town emerged into great prominence, and became renowned as the City of Spices. Battuta, who was in Kerala in the mid-fourteenth century, found the town flourishing. 'Qaliqut,' he writes, 'is one of the chief ports in Mulaybar and one of the largest harbours in the world. It is visited by men from China, Sumatra, Ceylon, the Maldives, Yemen and Fars (Persia), and in it gather merchants from all quarters.'

Razzak also is all praise for the prosperity of Kozhikode, and its good government. The city, he reports, 'brings together merchants of every city and every country . . . It is the practice at other ports, that if any vessel be consigned to any particular port, and unfortunately by the decree of the Almighty it is driven to any other [port] than that to which it is destined, the people plunder it, on the plea that it is sent [to them] by the winds. But at Kozhikode every vessel, wherever it comes from, and whichever way it arrives, is treated like any other, and no sort of trouble is experienced by it.'

Several other Indian towns engaged in foreign trade are also mentioned in medieval texts. Khambhat (Cambay) in Gujarat is one such town, where, according to Varthema, 'about three hundred ships of different countries come and go.' The town was also renowned for the excellent jewellery made there. Daulatabad in Maharashtra was another famed centre for jewellery—'the infidels of this town are merchants, dealing principally in jewels, and their wealth is enormous,' states Battuta. The entire stretch of the Coromandel Coast was also involved in overseas trade in medieval times.

SPICES WERE WHAT medieval foreign traders mainly sought for export from India, and that gave Kerala exceptional prominence in the world trade of that age, for it was, as Battuta describes it, 'the pepper country'. The main items exported from India in medieval times were pepper, cloves, ginger, cardamom and cinnamon; India also exported saffron, indigo, sugar, rice, tamarind, coconut and rhubarb, as well as sandalwood, brazilwood, musk, ambergris and myrobalan. Incense, precious stones, beads, and seed pearls were the other common items exported from India. Another product of India that was keenly sought by foreigners was fine cotton fabrics, manufactured in many parts of India, but which was a speciality of Bengal. Elegant leather shoes made in Sind were yet another prized item of export from India.

Because of this flourishing overseas trade a great amount of gold flowed into India in medieval times, and it remained there. 'I have calculated that for the last 3000 years that country has not exported gold to other countries, and whatever has entered it has never come out again,' Syrian chronicler Shahab-ud-din was once told by one of his informers. China also had an adverse trade balance with India. Consequently there was a drain of gold from China into India, and this so bothered the Chinese government that it at one time banned imports from India.

But it was not all a one-way trade for India. Just as India exported a wide variety of goods, it also imported a wide variety of goods. But the total value of its imports seems to have been far less than that of its exports. The most notable item imported into India in early medieval times was horses, several thousands of which were brought into the country every year. It was also the most expensive item that India imported, a single horse costing as much as 220 dinars! Horses were brought into North India by land through the north-western mountain passes, and by sea into the peninsula. India also imported perfumes, coral, quicksilver, vermilion, lead, gold, silver, alum, madder, and saffron from the Middle East; and from China it imported silks, taffetas and satins, blue and white porcelain, gold, silver, copper, vermilion, quicksilver, and so on. Various spices were also imported into India from South-east Asia. The opulent lifestyle of Muslim kings and nobles in medieval India led to an exponential growth in India's demand for imported luxury products like silks, velvets, damasks, camlets and satins. India also imported dates. In time India's export of manufactured goods declined, while its import of such goods increased.

A wide variety of ships from different nations were engaged in trade with India in medieval times. The largest of these were the Chinese junks, but the Chinese also plied medium and small ships in the Indian seas. Indian ships were smaller than the junks, but larger than the European ships, according to Nicolo Conti. But European ships, despite their relatively small size, had a decisive advantage over Asian ships, as they were more robustly built. While the Indian, Arab and Chinese ships were not strong enough to sail in the open seas in rough weather, European ships could do that. European ships also carried superior artillery. These were the key factors that enabled Europeans to eventually dominate the Asian seas.

Medieval sea transport was slow, averaging only around sixty kilometres a day, and was often further delayed on the way for various reasons—a delegation sent by a Chola king to China in the early eleventh century, for instance, took as many as three years to reach the Chinese capital. Not surprisingly, it took ships around fifteen days to reach Colombo from Kozhikode.

Sea travel was also hazardous, because of violent storms in the Indian Ocean, and also because the sea was infested with pirates at this time. These pirates belonged to different nations, but many of them operated from the west peninsular coast of India, no doubt with the connivance of the local rulers, who received a share of the booty. According to Marco Polo, these pirates were 'the most arrant corsairs of the world.' Because of the ever present menace of pirates in the Indian seas, merchantmen usually sailed in fleets, just as trade caravans in India travelled in large groups for protection against brigands. For the same reason, Chinese junks in the Indian seas usually carried a good number of soldiers in them. According to Battuta, a large Chinese ship carried a crew of 1,000, of whom 600 were sailors and 400 warriors: 'archers, shield-bearers and crossbow archers . . . who shoot naphtha missiles.'

PART IX

CULTURE

Make thy mind the Kaaba,

thy body the temple

thy conscience the primary teacher . . .

Hindus and Muslims have the same lord.

—KABIR

1

Pearls and Dung

'Seldom in the history of mankind has the spectacle been witnessed of two civilisations, so vast and so strongly developed, yet so radically dissimilar as the Muhammadan and Hindu, meeting and mingling together,' observes John Marshall, distinguished early twentieth century British archaeologist-historian. 'The very contrasts which existed between them, the wide divergences in their culture and their religions, make the history of their impact peculiarly instructive . . .'

Such civilisational confrontations have indeed been very rare in world history. But what is even more curious is that though Hindu and Muslim civilisations coexisted in India for very many centuries, there was hardly any creative interaction between them, no significant change in either, in response to the challenge by the other. The two coexisted, but did not interact. They were like water and oil in the same pot.

The entire early medieval period in India was culturally quite barren, in sharp contrast to the lush cultural efflorescence of the preceding classical period or the succeeding Mughal period. Except for the patronage of Indian culture by a few provincial sultans, the explorations into Indian heritage by a couple of Persian scholars and writers like al-Biruni and Amir Khusrav, the conservation of some ancient Indian monuments by a few sultans like Firuz Tughluq, and the construction of a few grand monuments like Qutb Minar, there was nothing notably positive in the cultural history of the Delhi Sultanate and its provincial offshoots.

Nor was there any notable creative response by Hindu civilisation to the challenge of Islam, except the superficial adoption of a few Persian cultural modes and lifestyle by some rajas. For many centuries, roughly from the sixth to the eleventh century, Indians had lived hermetically sealed within the subcontinent, with virtually no contact with the outside world. There were no major invasions or racial migrations into India during this period, unlike in the previous periods. The only exception to this was the Arab conquest of Sind in the early eighth century, but that was a peripheral event, more important in what it portended than in what it achieved. As for Indian kings, they had never-ever, in the entire long history of India, ventured outside the subcontinent for conquest.

Because of all this, Indians of the late classical period had hardly any knowledge of the outside world. And they in their ignorance viewed all foreign civilisations as contemptibly inferior to their own civilisation, and held that any contact with foreign people would be degrading.

THE CULTURAL INSULARITY and torpor of medieval India was appalling. 'I can only compare their mathematical and astronomical literature, as far as I know it, to a mixture . . . of pearls and dung, or of costly crystals and common pebbles,' comments al-Biruni, an exceptionally liberal-minded and perceptive early medieval Iranian intellectual, who was a keen student of Indian civilisation. 'Both kinds of things are equal in their eyes, since they cannot raise themselves to the methods of a strictly scientific deduction.' This lack of discrimination, the blind acceptance of whatever ancient knowledge had come down to them, often in a corrupt form, and disdaining even to look at the achievements of other civilisations, characterised the Indian cultural elite of the early medieval period. Equally, Indians were averse to share their knowledge with the people of other lands, scorning them as unworthy of such knowledge. And even among Indians themselves caste rules restricted the dissemination of particular fields of knowledge to particular castes.

'Hindus believe that there is no country like theirs, no nation like theirs, no kings like theirs, no religion like theirs, no science like theirs,' continues al-Biruni. 'They are haughty, foolishly vain, self-conceited, and stolid. They are by nature niggardly in communicating that which they know, and they take the greatest possible care to withhold it from men of another caste among their own people, still much more, of course, from any foreigner. According to their belief . . . [no people] besides them have any knowledge or science whatsoever . . . [And if you tell them of the achievements of other civilisations] they will consider you to be both an ignoramus and a liar.' All these were fatal flaws in the Indian civilisation of the early medieval period. With no challenge to stimulate creativity, Indian civilisation had over many centuries become comatose, while most of the rest of the world woke up from their medieval slumber and surged ahead.

According to al-Masudi, a tenth-century Arab scholar, 'India was the portion of the earth in which order and wisdom prevailed in distant ages.' True indeed. But the scene in medieval India was entirely different from that. India at this time had hardly any creative vitality in any field of culture. Not surprisingly, India's primary response to the Turkish invasion and the challenge of Islam was to defensively curl up tighter into itself. In the Sanskrit literature of the age there is virtually no mention of the establishment of the Turkish rule in India, and no indication of any socio-cultural response by Indians to the challenge of Islam.

TURKS WERE ORIGINALLY a wild nomadic people of mixed racial and tribal origin, spread over a vast area in Central Asia. But gradually, from around the eighth century, they became Islamised in religion and Persianised in culture. And by the time they invaded India, they had become an urbane, sophisticated people, though some of their old feral nature still persisted in them. Several of their sultans, in Delhi as well as elsewhere in India, were ardent patrons of culture, and some—Firuz Tughluq, for instance—were themselves respected writers. According to Afif, a fourteenth-century chronicler, Firuz Tughluq spent a vast sum of money on allowances to scholars; further, according to Mughal chronicler Ferishta, the sultan encouraged scholars to fan out in his empire and spread learning. There were said to have been as many as a thousand educational institutions flourishing in Delhi during the Tughluq period.

Intellectuals and creative people from many regions of the Muslim world migrated to India at this time, for the Delhi Sultanate was one of the most powerful Muslim kingdoms of the age, and most of the sultans were generous patrons of scholars and writers. A notable exception to this was Ala-ud-din Khalji, who considered cultural pursuits a waste of time and resources. But even during his reign, Delhi continued to attract cultural leaders from around the Muslim world, drawn by the great prosperity of the sultanate at this time. 'During the time of Sultan Ala-ud-din, Delhi was the great rendezvous for all the most learned and erudite personages,' writes Abdul Hakk Dehlawi, a chronicler of the Mughal age. 'For, notwithstanding the pride and hauteur, the neglect and superciliousness, and the want of kindness and cordiality, with which that monarch treated this class of people, the spirit of the age remained the same.'

The benefaction of Delhi sultans, as had to be expected, was primarily for Muslim scholars and writers, but some of the sultans also extended their favour to Hindu scholars and to the promotion of the traditional knowledge of India, particularly to the study of secular subjects. And they took the initiative to get several ancient Indian texts on scientific subjects, such as medicine, translated into Persian. Thus when Firuz Tughluq found a vast collection of manuscripts in the temple of Jvalamukhi at Nagarkot (Kangra) in Himachal Pradesh, he took care to have several of them translated into Persian. 'In this temple was a fine library of Hindu books, consisting of 13,000 volumes,' records Ferishta. 'Firuz sent for some of the wise men of that religion and ordered some of the books to be translated, and especially directed one of those books, which dealt with philosophy, astrology and divination, to be translated [into Persian] . . . It is in truth a book replete with various kinds of knowledge, both practical and theoretical.' According to Mughal historian Badauni, some 'unprofitable and trivial works on prosody, music and dancing' were also translated under the sultan's patronage.

The patronage of culture by kings was an ancient tradition in India, and even in medieval times, despite the general decline of Hindu political power, there were several rajas who had serious cultural interests and accomplishments. Particularly noteworthy among them was Rana Kumbha of Mewar, who, notwithstanding his many military engagements, found time and interest not only to earnestly promote culture, but also to turn himself into a distinguished scholar in several fields, from ancient Hindu scriptures to political theory, grammar, literature, and music. He also wrote four plays, three texts on music, and had to his credit the writing a highly regarded commentary on Jayadeva's *Gita-Govinda*. Unfortunately he went insane towards the end of his life, and was murdered by his son.

SUCH EARNEST SCHOLARSHIP and creativity as that of Rana Kumbha were relatively rare in Hindu society in medieval times, compared to its marvellous cultural luxuriance in the earlier age. Even the study of the ancient Indian systems of knowledge was in a dismal state of decay at this time, particularly in North India, though there were some lingering sparks of vitality in them in South India. Generally speaking, the purpose of scholarly pursuits by Indians in this age was not for advancing knowledge, but almost entirely for learning old texts by rote. And since many of the old texts had become hopelessly corrupt over the centuries, this mode of learning meant the perpetuation of flawed, decayed knowledge.

There were however still a few major centres of traditional learning in India at this time. Varanasi (Benares) was one such centre. The city specialised in the *gurukula* system of education, of eminent scholars taking under their care a few chosen students. 'The town of Benares situated on the Ganges . . . in the midst of an extremely rich and fertile country may be considered the general school of gentiles,' writes Bernier, a late seventeenth century French physician in India. 'It is the Athens of India, whither resort Brahmins and other devotees . . . The town contains no colleges or regular classes as in our universities, but resembles rather the schools of the ancients, the masters being dispersed over different parts of the town in private houses, principally in the gardens of the suburbs, which the rich merchants permit them to occupy. Some of these masters have four disciples, others six or seven and the most eminent may have twelve, but this is the greatest number.'

Varanasi was a Hindu centre of learning, but there were also a few major Buddhist and Jain centres of learning in early medieval India. These, unlike the guru-centred Hindu educational system, provided institutionalised education, in large university-like campuses, which had a good number of teachers in diverse subjects. The most renowned of the Buddhist educational centres of the age was the University of Nalanda in Bihar, which, because it was a walled campus, was mistaken for a fort and was destroyed by Turkish commander Bakhtiyar Khalji in the early thirteenth century, during the reign of Qutb-ud-din Aibak. 'Most of the inhabitants of the place were Brahmins with shaven heads,' writes Siraj, an early medieval chronicler, mistaking Buddhist monks for Brahmins. 'They were all put to death. A large numbers of books were found there, and when the Mohammedans saw them, they called for some persons to explain their contents, but all the men had been killed. It was then discovered that the whole fort and city was a place of study.' There were several other such instances of wanton destruction of Indian cultural and religious centres by Turks.

ON THE POSITIVE side, one of the major cultural developments of the early medieval period was the spread of Persian language and literature in India. Persian was the favoured language of the sultans and the Muslim elite in India, for official business as well as for cultural pursuits. The language was also increasingly cultivated by upper class Hindus—especially by those who were in any way connected with the administration of Muslim kingdoms—somewhat in the same manner in which many Indians would later take to the study of English during the British rule. And, along with the use of Persian language, the adoption of Persian dress and lifestyle became the mark of high culture among the political elite—among Muslims as well as Hindus—in most regions of India, except in the deep south, which was outside the pale of Muslim rule and direct Muslim cultural influence.

A number of books on India were written by Muslim scholars in the early medieval period, and they provide invaluable information on many aspects of life in India in that age. One of the earliest and finest of these works is al-Biruni's *Ta'rikh al-Hind*: Chronicles of India. Hardly anything is known about al-Biruni's family background or about his early life, except that he was a Persian by birth, and spent his early life in Khwarazm. He was a contemporary and one-time colleague of Avicenna, the renowned intellectual and physician of the age. When Mahmud Ghazni conquered Khwarazm, he induced or forced al-Biruni (along with several other scholars) to move to Ghazni, and there the young scholar immersed himself in his studies under the patronage of Mahmud and his successors.

Al-Biruni, according his medieval biographer Shams-ud-din Muhammad Shahrazuri, was so dedicated to his studies that 'he never had a pen out of his hand, nor his eye off a book, and his thoughts were always directed to his studies . . . [He had no interest in temporal acquisitions, and was content with] procuring the necessaries of life on such a moderate scale as to afford him bare sustenance and clothing.' Once when sultan Masud rewarded him with an elephant load of silver, he politely declined to accept the gift and returned it to the treasury. This indifference to temporal gains was a major factor that enabled al-Biruni to be totally unbiased in his works—he did not write to please anyone but himself. He had 'a most rigid regard for truth,' comments Baihaqi, who lived half a century after al-Biruni.

Al-Biruni does not seem to have had a family of his own—he probably never married—and his single-minded devotion to scholarship, and indifference to wealth, were probably in part because he did not have to provide for a family. The absence of family also enabled him to travel freely, wherever the pursuit of his studies took him. He spent several years in India, in Punjab, interacting with Brahmin pundits there and translating into Persian or Arabic some Indian books, such as on Samkhya and Yoga, the principal Indian philosophical schools of the age. A facile linguist, he knew several languages, including Sanskrit and Greek, but wrote mostly in Arabic.

One of the most brilliant polymaths of the medieval world, al-Biruni is said to have written over a hundred books—a camel load of books, it is said. Of them only twenty-two books are extant now, but even these cover a wide range of subjects, including various sciences, as well astrology, history, sociology, geography, philosophy and theology. There was hardly any field of contemporary knowledge that al-Biruni did not deal with. He was the first scholar anywhere in the world to study Indian culture methodically, and he may be rightly considered the patriarch of Indology. His treatment of Indian culture was fair and objective, almost entirely without racial or religious prejudice.

ANOTHER VERSATILE GENIUS of early medieval India was Amir Khusrav. He, like al-Biruni, was a prolific writer, and is credited with writing a large number of books—there is tradition that he wrote 99 books, on different subjects and in a variety of literary modes—and also some 400,000 verses. He is also said to have introduced several innovations in music. We do not know whether all the achievements attributed to him are true—it is not impossible that he did all that, but we have to also bear in mind that there was a tendency in India at this time to attribute innovative works to some renowned person, in order to gain general acceptability for the innovations.

Khusrav was born in 1253 in Patiali, a small town near Delhi, and he died in 1325, aged seventy-two. His father was a migrant Turk, but his mother, according to some accounts, was a Hindu convert to Islam, and it is probable that it was this genetic and cultural hybridity that enabled him to smoothly blend Hindu and Muslim cultural traditions in his works.

Khusrav was a child prodigy, and wrote his first collection of poems in his teens. He then went on to serve eight successive Delhi sultans, from Balban to Ghiyas-ud-din Tughluq, as their court poet, and he kept himself in royal favour by writing panegyrics on all those sultans. He was particularly favoured by Jalal-ud-din Khalji, who, according to Barani, a fourteenth century Delhi chronicler, 'was a great appreciator and patron of talent . . . [The sultan appointed Khusrav as] one of his chosen attendants . . . [and] invested him with such robes as are given to great nobles, and girded him with a white sash.' He was also given generous cash awards. Ala-ud-din Khalji also favoured Khusrav, and appointed him as his court poet. On the whole Khusrav had a remarkably smooth and successful career in those turbulent times. But in his old age he abandoned all temporal pursuits, became a follower of the Sufi saint Nizam-ud-din Auliya, and lived a cloistered life, though he still wrote poetry.

Khusrav wrote mainly in Persian, but he freely used Hindi words in his compositions, as in the mixed Hindi-Arabic-Persian-Turki language called Hindawi, the precursor of Urdu, that was taking form in the region around Delhi in his time. He often set his poems to music, and is thought to be the father of Qawwali, the Sufi devotional music.

Khusrav's works are characterised by luxuriant literary flourishes, and are marvellously mellifluous, qualities which were greatly admired in medieval times, but are mostly lost in English translation, as of these verses:

Bakhubi hamcho mah tabindah baashi;
Bamulk-e dilbari paayindah baashi.
Man-e darvish ra kushti baghamzah;
Karam kardi Ilahi zindah baashi.
Jafaa kam kun ki farda roz-e mehshar;
Baru-e aashiqan sharmindah baashi.
Ze qaid-e dojahan azad baasham;
Agar tu hum-nashin-e bandah baashi.
Barindi-o bashokhi hamcho Khusrau;
Hazaran khanuman barkandah baashi.

May your charming face ever shine like the full moon;
May you hold eternal sway over the realms of beauty.
By your amorous glance you have killed me, a vagrant;
How generous of you? May god give you a long life.
Pray do not be cruel lest you feel ashamed of yourself
Before your lovers on the day of judgment.
I shall be set free from the bonds of the two worlds
If you become my companion for a while.
By your wanton playfulness you must have destroyed
Thousands of hearts of lovers like that of Khusrav.

AN IMPORTANT CULTURAL development of the early medieval period
was the translation of several Sanskrit works into Arabic and Persian. The
first book thus translated was *Suka-saptati* (Parrot's Seventy), a circa twelfth
century compilation of amusing ancient Indian tales, told by a clever parrot
to a forlorn woman (whose husband was away), to distract her from straying.
This was translated into Persian by Zia Nakhshabi in the early fourteenth
century. The Persian book, titled *Tuti-nama* (Book of the Parrot), gained
wide popularity in India and the Middle East, and was in time translated
from Persian into Turkish and several European languages. Zia Nakhshabi
also translated *Koka-shastra* (also known as *Rati-rahasyam*: Secrets of Love),
a popular early medieval Sanskrit work on erotica written by Kukkoka. During
the reign of Firuz Tughluq, a number of other Sanskrit works on a variety
of subjects were translated from Sanskrit into Persian under royal patronage.
Similarly *Mahabharata* and Kalhana's *Rajatarangini* were translated into
Persian under the patronage of Zain-ul-Abidin, a mid-fifteenth century sultan
of Kashmir. Such liberal royal patronage of the ancient Indian cultural heritage
would continue till almost the very end of the Delhi Sultanate, with Sikandar
Lodi commissioning the translation of several Sanskrit works into Persian.

In contrast to this vigorous Sanskrit-to-Persian translation activity,
there was hardly any attempt at this time to translate Persian literature
into Sanskrit or any other Indian language. The Indian intelligentsia, in
their characteristic cultural insularity, almost totally ignored the dominant
Muslim cultural presence in India. The Turkish invasion of India, as
Kosambi comments, did not make 'the slightest impression upon the
mannerisms or complacency of the local intelligentsia. The last great
Sanskrit literature, written about this time . . . contains not the slightest
mention of contemporary events.' Thus even when the Turkish advance was
threatening to overwhelm Jayachandra Gahadavala, king of Kanauj, the last
great Hindu ruler of North India, his court poet Sriharsha was turning out
self-indulgent romances and lyrics in Sanskrit.

The cultural scene was not much different elsewhere in India either, with the court poets of the rajas continuing to indulge in their 'mannered stupidities,' as Kosambi describes it. Typical of this was 'the *Rama-charita* of Sandhyakara-nandin, [which] reduced Sanskrit poetry to the level of an acrostic . . . In effect, it cannot be understood at all,' comments Kosambi. Hardly any of the Sanskrit works of the medieval period had any merit, they being mostly mediocre reworkings of old classics. The preoccupation of the Sanskrit writers of medieval India was with form, not substance.

The dreary state of Sanskrit literature at this time was not surprising, for it was then the dead language of a comatose civilisation. What mainly sustained literary activity in it in medieval times was the pretentious patronage of Sanskrit writers by the rajas, for whom it was prestigious to patronise literature in India's classical language. But as most rajas lost their power consequent to the Turkish invasion of India, Sanskrit scholars and writers lost their main source of patronage, and that led to a sharp decline in the quality and quantity of Sanskrit literary output in medieval India.

Still, some amount of Sanskrit literary activity continued at this time, mainly in regions outside the Muslim rule, particularly in Vijayanagar, under the vigorous patronage of its rajas, some of whom, like Krishnadeva, were themselves literary figures of merit. The old Indian tradition of poets writing panegyrics in Sanskrit on kings also continued during this period, and such poems were written even on sultans, like the one on Mahmud Begarha of Gujarat. In fact, similar eulogies continued to be written in modern times too, such as *Victoria-charita*—on Victoria, queen of England and empress of India—published in Dacca in the late nineteenth century. But none of these works had any literary merit compared to the Sanskrit classics of the ancient period.

A positive consequence of the decline of Sanskrit in medieval times was that it opened up literary space for regional Indian languages to grow and flourish. Sanskrit, or rather Prakrit, had spawned a number of regional offshoots in North India in the late classical times, and from around the eighth century on some of these regional languages began to produce their own literatures, and this gathered considerable momentum over the years. Many of the early writers in these languages were Buddhists and Jains, as they sought to reach out to the common people by writing in their languages, rather than in Sanskrit, which was understood only by the erudite. Buddhists in particular made major contributions in promoting regional languages—the earliest writers in Bengali, for instance, were Buddhists.

The spread of the Bhakti movement in Hinduism at this time was another factor that stimulated literary activity in regional languages—as Bhakti was a movement of the common people, it used the language of the common people for its devotional literature. At this time there were also several translations of popular Sanskrit works, like the *Puranas* and the epics, into regional languages, and that greatly enriched the literature in these languages.

IN CONTRAST TO the moribund state of Sanskrit literature in medieval times, Tamil, the only other ancient Indian language which had a literature of its own, remained vibrantly alive during this period. But the ethos of Tamil literature in the medieval times had changed altogether from what it had been in the classical period. While Tamil in the classical period produced sensitive secular literature, depicting the chiaroscuro of everyday life, its miseries and pleasures, mainly under Buddhist and Jain influence, its emphasis now shifted to religious literature, both devotional and expository, under the influence of resurgent Hinduism and its devotional cults. Religious fervour now replaced the calm reflectiveness that had earlier characterised Tamil literature.

The golden age of this new Tamil literature was the imperial Chola period, from the mid-ninth to the late twelfth century, when a great amount of Shaiva and Vaishnava texts, and even a few Buddhist and Jain texts, were written. The age also produced a few quasi-historical works in the style of the Puranas, mainly describing the legends about prominent South Indian temples. A few secular works on the exploits of local heroes, and some anthologies of old Tamil works, with commentaries appended to them, were also compiled at this time. A major lexicographic work on Tamil, *Nigandu-cudamani* by Mandalapurusha, a Jain scholar, also belongs to this period. But the best known Tamil literary work of the age is the *Ramavatharam*, popularly known as *Kambaramayanam*, a retelling of the story of the *Ramayana* by Kamban in the twelfth century. Its story is drawn from the Sanskrit epic, but Kamban enriches it by introducing a good amount of local flavour into it.

This emphasis on local flavour is particularly evident in the literature of the regional offshoots of Tamil that appeared in the late classical period, around the same time when literature in the regional offshoots of Sanskrit appeared. Tamil spawned three offshoots—Kannada, Telugu and Malayalam—and these in time produced impressive literatures of their own in the medieval period, each distinguished by the distinctive flavour of its region. As these offshoots of Tamil evolved, their literature came to be heavily influenced by Sanskrit, while Tamil literature itself remained relatively unaffected by it. In fact, a major part of the early literature in these regional languages consisted of reworked old Sanskrit texts. But in time these languages developed distinctive literatures of their own. The individuation of these languages, and the growth of literature in them, were facilitated by the use of these languages by Bhakti sages, and by the patronage of the literature in them by local rulers.

The earliest of the offshoots of Tamil to develop a literature of its own was Kannada, in which literary works began to appear around the middle of the first millennium, and by around the tenth century it produced some major works. The oldest extant literary work in Kannada is considered to be *Kavirajamarga* (Royal Path of Poets) of around the ninth century, its very title indicating the existence of older literature in the language. Most of the early works in Kannada were by Jains, and this was followed by the contributions of Vira-Shaivas, a sect of Shiva devotees.

A fascinating development in Kannada literature at this time was the introduction in it of a folksy style known as *vacana*, using simple, clear prose without any literary flourishes. The pioneer of this style is thought to be Madara Chennaiah, an eleventh century cobbler-sage. In the following century, this form of literature flourished under the patronage of Basava, the chief minister of the local kingdom, and himself a distinguished poet.

Early Telugu had a very close affinity with Kannada, and the two shared virtually the same script. But by around the fifth or sixth century, Telugu acquired many distinctive characteristics of its own, and it gradually grew into a separate language. The first major literary work in Telugu is *Mahabharatam*, written by Nannaya in the early eleventh century. But Nannaya died before he could finish the work. Two centuries would pass before the gargantuan task of completing the work was taken up by another poet, Tikkana, the greatest Telugu poet of all time, who, because of his brilliant literary skills, came to be known as Kavi Brahma. But even he left out a portion of the epic, and it was Yerrapragada (Errana) of the fourteenth century who finally completed the translation.

Around this time Telugu developed its own distinctive script, in the place of the Kannada script it had been using all along. Further, literary Telugu then began to diverge from the language of the common people, because of its heavy Sanskritisation. The high period of Telugu literature was the early sixteenth century, during the reign of Krishnadeva of Vijayanagar, who was himself a noted writer.

The last of the Dravidian languages to break free from Tamil was Malayalam, the language of Kerala. This separation began around the sixth century, and in the following centuries the language in its literary form became heavily Sanskritised, and came to have a very large number of its words drawn from Sanskrit. Its script however remained a variant of the Tamil Grantha script. It is believed that Malayalam began to evolve a distinct literature of its own by around the eleventh century, but the oldest extant literary works in the language are only of the fourteenth century, the best known among them being *Unnuneeli-sandesam*, an anonymous work modelled on Kalidasa's *Megha-sandesam*, and uses a rich mixture of Sanskrit and Malayalam called Manipravalam: ruby-coral.

2

Duplex Culture

Music was an integral part of the social and religious life of Indians from very early times, but it is hard to trace its early history, as very little data is available on it. In early medieval times Indian classical music split into two distinct streams: Carnatic music of South India, and Hindustani music of North India. This was because North Indian music had at this time come under the influence of Perso-Arabic musical tradition, while South Indian music remained virtually unaffected by it. Further, Hindustani music at this time became primarily court music (because its main patronage now, consequent of the collapse of the Hindu political power in North India, came from sultans and Muslim nobles) while Carnatic music (which flourished mainly in peninsular India, in regions outside Muslim rule) largely retained its old character as devotional music. Besides, Carnatic music remained essentially a vocal music, as most of its compositions were written to be sung, and even when this music was played on instruments, it usually mimicked singing. In contrast, musical instruments came to play a much larger role in Hindustani music, and it used far more instruments than Carnatic music. But despite all these differences, the two schools of music share the same basic compositional and improvisational elements: sruti (pitch), swara (note), raga (melody) and tala (rhythmic pattern).[1]

Carnatic music took its final form in the early sixteenth century. Its systematisation at this time was largely due to the efforts of Purandara-dasa, a musicologist-composer-performer of Karnataka, who laid down definitive guidelines for the composition and performance of Carnatic music, and is therefore generally regarded as the *pitamaha* (grandfather) of Carnatic music.

---

[1] For more on Indian music, see *The First Spring*, Part XI, Chapter 1

Around this time Hindustani music too was greatly enriched by the contributions of two seminal, marvellously creative musicians: Amir Khusrav of the thirteenth-fourteenth century, and Tansen of the sixteenth century. Khusrav is also generally credited with the invention of tabla (the popular Indian percussion instrument consisting of a pair of hand drums of different sizes and timbres) and the long-necked lute. Further, he is said to have written several treatises on music, and to have devised several melodic forms, such as khyal (a meditative form of music which allows considerable improvisation), qawl (the precursor of qawwali, the Sufi devotional music), tarana (which uses meaningless syllables to turn voice into a musical instrument), and so on. Khusrav is in fact credited with the invention of as many as nineteen melodic forms.

There is no way of verifying these claims. But it is quite probable that Khusrav played a major role in the evolution of Hindustani music by blending Hindu and Muslim musical modes. Khusrav was an admirer of Hindu music, which he considered to be more soul-stirring than any other music. He is said to have studied Carnatic music and to have fused some of its elements into his own music. The blending of Hindu and Muslim musical systems was further facilitated by the conversion of a number of Hindu musicians to Islam at this time, as they sought to secure the patronage of the new rulers. The affinity of Sufis for Indian music also played an important role in the fusion of the two musical traditions.

Many of the Delhi sultans were keen patrons of music, even though hyper-orthodox Muslims frowned on music as a frivolous diversion, and strictly forbade the playing of music in mosques. Even Firuz Tughluq, despite his general compliance with orthodox religious prescriptions, was avid about music. Holding musical soirees at the court was a common practice of several Delhi sultans. Though some sultans—Iltutmish and Ghiyas-ud-din Tughluq, for instance—banned this practice, it was restored by their successors. Several rulers of the other Muslim kingdoms in India were also keen patrons of music. Notable among them was Ibrahim Adil Shah II, the late sixteenth-early seventeenth century sultan of Bijapur, who was an ardent patron of art and music, and was himself a poet and musician, as well as the author of a book on music.

There were troupes of professional musicians in most of the major cities of medieval India, and in some cities there were regular public performances by them. 'In Daulatabad there is a very fine and spacious bazaar for singers and singing girls, containing numerous shops, each of which has a door leading to the house of its proprietor,' reports Battuta. 'The shop is beautified with carpets and in the centre of it there is a sort of large cradle on which the singing girl sits or reclines. She is adorned with all kinds of ornaments, and her attendants swing her cradle. In the centre of the bazaar there is a large carpeted and decorated pavilion in which the chief musician sits every Thursday after the afternoon prayer, with his servants and slaves in front of him. The singing girls come in relays and sing and dance before him till the sunset prayers, when they withdraw . . . One of the infidel rulers in India, on passing through this bazaar, used to alight at the pavilion, and the singing girls used to sing before him. Once the Muhammadan sultans too used to do the same.'

Hindu rajas were traditionally ardent patrons of music, but their role in this declined sharply in medieval times, particularly in North India, because of their loss of power and the consequent loss of the material means to patronise cultural activities. The most prominent of the Hindu royal patrons of music during the Sultanate period was Raja Man Singh of Gwalior, who was himself a gifted musician, under whose patronage his court musicians compiled a book titled *Man Kautuhal* (Curiosities of Man), describing the rules governing various ragas, including those of the new musical modes introduced under Perso-Arabic influence. Perso-Arabic influence in music was present even in the Carnatic music patronised by the rajas of Vijayanagar, and this is acknowledged in such texts as Kallina's *Sangita-ratnakara* of the mind-fifteenth century, and *Svaramela-kalanidhi* of Vijayanagar king Ramaraya of the mid-sixteenth century.

AS IN MUSIC, so also in art and architecture, there was some amount of mutual influence between Hindu and Muslim traditions. But a harmonious blending of the two architectural styles was difficult, for they were entirely unlike each other in nearly every respect. While the structure of the Hindu temple was complex, dark and mysterious, the structure of the mosque was bright and open, its lines smooth and simple and elegant. Their very construction methods were different. As Marshall describes it, 'The Hindu system of construction was trabeate, based on column and architrave; the Muslim [system] was arcuate, based on arch and vault.' And while temples were richly adorned with the paintings and sculptures of life-forms, mosques used only floral, calligraphic, arabesque and geometric designs for decoration, as Islam considered figurative art as sinful imitations of god's work. Because of these differences, when Hindu and Muslim architectural styles were combined, the two did not usually blend smoothly. This was evident particularly in the mosque that Aibak built in Delhi, which, as Percy Brown describes it, is 'mainly a patchwork of older materials, beautiful in detail . . . but as a whole a confused and somewhat incongruous improvisation.'

The incorporation of Muslim architectural forms into Hindu structures was more harmonious than the incorporation of Hindu architectural forms into Muslim structures, just as the adoption of Muslim cultural modes into Hindu culture was smoother than their reverse adoption. This was because Hindu culture had a great amount of diversity within itself, so that new elements introduced into it seldom seemed incongruous.

The structure of the early mosques everywhere in the Muslim world was very simple, just a square or rectangular courtyard bordered with cloisters on three sides, and an alcove on the fourth side, from which the imam led prayers. In India the alcove was on the west side of the courtyard, in the direction of Mecca, facing which the devotees knelt in prayer. On the side of the alcove there was usually a pulpit for delivering sermons. Initially, the alcove had only a flat roof, but later a dome was commonly built over it. An essential feature of the mosque architecture is the tall minaret built at a corner of its courtyard, from which the muezzin announced the time for the five daily prayers, and summoned the faithful for the Friday congregational prayers. In many mosques additional minarets were built at the other three corners of mosque, for visual harmony.

Arch and dome are the defining characteristics of Muslim architecture. India had no tradition of dome building, and arches were built in India by the method of corbelled horizontal courses, unlike the superior Muslim practice of building them with voussoirs. It was only in the late thirteenth century, on the tomb of Balban, that the true arch appeared in India for the first time.

THE ARCHITECTURAL SCENE in India, particularly in North India, changed radically during the Sultanate period, when a large number of forts, palaces, mosques and tombs built by Muslims dotted the land. Even though a number of mosques had been built in India even before the establishment of the Muslim rule there, these were mostly in port cities, built by Arab traders and their local converts. Later, in the eighth century, the Arab rulers of Sind built mosques in their kingdom, and still later the sultans of Ghazni and Ghuri built mosques in Sind and Punjab. But there were as yet no mosques in the Indo-Gangetic Plain, the heartland of India. The first mosque there, the Quwwat-ul-Islam mosque in Delhi, was built by Qutb-ud-din Aibak in the early thirteenth century, on the site of a tenth century Hindu temple.

This mosque was built mainly with the construction materials collected from a number of demolished Hindu and Jain temples—twenty-seven of them, according to an inscription at the entrance of the mosque. But it was necessity rather than choice that made Aibak use those materials, because the mosque was urgently needed for the Friday congregational prayers of Muslims, and it was easier and quicker to build it with the pillars and stones collected from the demolished temples, than to quarry fresh building materials for it. The use of the demolished temple materials to build the mosque was also symbolically appropriate, as a display of the triumph of Islam over Hinduism.

This method of construction, and the fact that the masons and artisans who were employed in planning and building the mosque were predominantly Hindus, gave this mosque a distinctive Indian appearance. The practice of Muslim rulers building mosques with the materials of demolished temples continued in India for a while under the successors of Aibak, but in time the practice declined, partly because not so many temples were demolished in later times—as Hindus, being then treated as zimmis, received government protection for their institutions and way of life—and partly because Muslims preferred to retain the purity of their architectural style, and Indian craftsmen and builders had by then learned to build in the Muslim style. The migration of a number of Muslim architects and artisans from the Middle East and Central Asia into India at this time also facilitated this transformation. However, some elements of the local architectural style continued to be evident in the structures built by Muslim rulers in provincial towns for quite a while.

The mosque that Qutb-ud-din built in Delhi was enlarged to more than double its size by Iltutmish, and was further expanded by later sultans, as the Muslim population in the city grew, and they had to be provided space for their congregational prayers. 'The cathedral mosque occupies a large area; its walls, roof, and paving are all constructed of white stones, admirably squared and firmly cemented with lead,' writes Battuta in his vivid but factually imprecise account of what he saw in Delhi in the mid-fourteenth century. 'There is no wood in it at all. It has thirteen domes of stone; its pulpit is also made of stone, and it has four courts. In the centre of the mosque is an awe-inspiring column[2], and nobody knows of what metal it is made. One of their learned men told me that it is called Haft Jush, which means "seven metals", and that it is constructed from these seven. A part of this column, of a finger's breadth, has been polished, and gives out a brilliant gleam. Iron makes no impression on it. It is thirty cubits high; we rolled a turban round it, and the portion which encircled it measured eight cubits. At the eastern gate [of the mosque] there are two enormous idols of brass prostrate on the ground and held [in place there] by stones, and everyone entering or leaving the mosque treads on them.

---

[2]This is a Gupta age iron pillar, which the builders of the mosque had the good sense not to tamper with. Most remarkably, the pillar has not rusted even after the passage of some sixteen centuries of exposure to weather.

The height of the pillar is 7.21 metres, of which 1.12 metre is below ground; its diameter at the bottom is 420 millimetres, and it tapers to 306 millimetres at the top. Its weight is estimated to be over six tons.

There is a common belief that anyone who can encircle the pillar with his arms while standing with his back to it and makes a wish, will have that wish granted.

The site was formerly occupied by an idol temple, and was converted into a mosque on the conquest of the city.'

Aibak's mosque complex in Delhi is dominated by its towering minaret, known as Qutb Minar. Its construction was begun by Aibak, but he could build only its bottom storey. The structure was completed by Iltutmish, Aibak's successor, by adding three storeys to it, each of diminishing girth and height. In 1370, during the reign of Firuz Tughluq, the fourth storey of the minaret was struck by lightning and severely damaged. Firuz then dismantled the storey and in its place built two new storeys of plain circular design, raising the total height of the minaret to about 73 metres, nearly as tall as a twenty-four storey building. The minaret was repaired again by Sikandar Lodi, towards the end of the history of the Delhi Sultanate. Qutb Minar was not just a minaret for the muezzin to call the faithful to prayer, but was also a victory tower proclaiming the establishment of the Turkish empire in India. According to some authorities it is 'the most perfect example of a tower known to exist anywhere' in the world.

Battuta saw the Minar before it was damaged by lightning. 'In the northern court [of the mosque] is the minaret, which has no parallel in the lands of Islam . . .,' he reports. 'Its passage is so wide that elephants could go up by it. A person in whom I have confidence told me that when it was built he saw an elephant climbing with stones to the top . . .' Despite its immense size, Qutb Minar is an elegant structure, its soaring upward thrust emphasised by vertical flutings—alternately round and angular—which in turn are decorated with horizontal bands of inscriptions and foliated designs. The starkness of the building is also relieved by its richly decorated balconies at the base of each storey. The bottom three storeys of the tower are built of grey quartzite faced with red sandstone, but its top two storeys, built by Firuz Tughluq, are of red sandstone faced with marble.

After the reign of Iltutmish till the reign of Ala-u-din Khalji there was hardly any major construction activity in the Delhi Sultanate. The only notable building of this period was the tomb of Balban. Building activity picked up again under the Khaljis and the Tughluqs, particularly under Firuz Tughluq, who was a compulsive builder of all sorts of structures, such as forts, palaces, mosques, tombs and so on. He even built some new towns.

A major innovation in the architectural style introduced in the late Sultanate period, during the reign of Sikandar Lodi, was the practice of building the double-dome, one enclosing the other. This, according to John Marshall, had become necessary 'in order to preserve the symmetry and relative proportions of the interior as well of the exterior . . . [of the mosque, when the exterior dome was] elevated on a lofty drum . . .'

THE FINEST EXPRESSIONS of Muslim architecture in India were, naturally, in Delhi, but there was a good amount of engaging construction activity in the provinces also. Particularly notable among them was the modification of the fort and city of Daulatabad by Muhammad Tughluq. Daulatabad was originally a Hindu fort named Devagiri, but it was substantially modified by the sultan in the fourteenth century, who renamed it Daulatabad and shifted his capital from Delhi to it for a while.

One of the main reasons for the sultan to shift his capital to Daulatabad was that its fort, built atop a solitary, precipitous rocky hill rising starkly from the surrounding plain, was virtually impregnable. 'Its inner citadel stands on an isolated conical rock 600 feet in height, with sides scraped sheer for 150 feet and a moat hewn out of the living rock at their base,' writes Marshall about Daulatabad. 'The only entrance is through a devious tunnel which in times of siege was rendered impassable by an ingenious contrivance. At a bend in the tunnel . . . near to the outer edge of the rock was a small chamber provided with a flue pierced through the thickness of the wall and fitted, in addition, with a staging of iron plates . . . [If] on these plates a charcoal fire was lit, . . . [it], fanned by the wind blowing incessantly through the flue, would quickly fill the tunnel with its fumes and make any ingress impossible.'[3]

Elsewhere in the peninsula too there are several notable Muslim structures, such as Gol Gumbaz, the tomb of Muhammad Adil Shah, a seventeenth century sultan of Bijapur. This is one of the largest domed structures in the world, and consists of a massive square tomb chamber, covering an area of 1693 square metres, and is crowned by an immense dome of nearly 44 metres diameter.

In time the dominant presence of Muslim architectural forms in urban India came to have a growing influence on the buildings of Hindus. This was particularly evident in North India, but several examples of it can be seen in peninsular India too, as in the arches and domes of the 'elephant stables' in Vijayanagar. There was however no notable Muslim influence on Hindu temple architecture anywhere in India, for temples were built strictly according to canonical prescriptions. There was in fact hardly any major new temple construction in northern and central India at this time, as the entire region was under Muslim rule and the sultans, in conformity with Islamic law, forbade the construction of new temples in their territories.

But there was at this time a good amount of temple construction in South India, the region outside Muslim rule; in fact, temple architecture now attained its zenith in India, in the colossal temples teeming with sculptures built in South India by the rajas. The last great phase of temple construction in pre-

---

[3]See Part VIII, Chapter 1, for Mughal chronicler Lahauri's description of the fort.

modern India was in Vijayanagar and its successor kingdoms, and this activity reached its peak in the sixteenth century. One of the main features of these temple complexes was the *kalyana-mandapam*, the 'thousand-pillared'—figuratively so called—marriage hall, built for the annual celebration of the marriage of the chief deity of the temple and his consort. This hall was usually adorned luxuriantly with sculptures, particularly so its numerous pillars, each of which had several sculptures of rampant horses, hippogryphs and other mythical creatures, all carved out of a single block of stone. Some of these pillars are called 'musical pillars', for they produce pleasant musical tones which when tapped.

The Vijayanagar temples were the most lavish temples ever built in India, unmatched for their decorative luxuriance, particularly so the Vittala temple in Hampi. This tradition of temple building was continued in the post-Vijayanagar period by the Marathas, especially by the Nayaks of Madurai. In many of the South Indian temples the gopurams (gate towers) are much taller than the shrines themselves, because the temples they fronted were usually old and sacred, and it would have been sacrilegious to demolish them and build anew.

AS IN ARCHITECTURE, so also in art, Hindu and Muslim ideals and practices were fundamentally different. Muslims abhorred the representation of living beings in art, but Hindu art was primarily figurative, in painting as well as in sculpture. So while mosques were entirely free of figurative art, Hindu temples generally teemed with the sculptures and paintings of people, gods, animals and mythological creatures. Furthermore, Hindu temple art often depicted men and women in erotic play, which Muslims considered as totally abhorrent.

Also, there were often whimsical elements in Hindu temple art, which would have seemed to Muslims as totally inappropriate in a place of worship. Thus a sculpture in the Varadaraja Perumal temple in Kanchipuram depicts a man with a beard and moustache on one side of his face, while on the other side his face is clean-shaven; also, he wears Muslim-style slacks on one side, but on the other side wears a dhoti like Hindus. Another sculpture in this temple shows a man sexually penetrating a bent over naked woman from the back, and at the same time triumphantly blowing a trumpet. And in Mamallapuram, among the numerous figures on the massive bas-relief panel of rock sculpture there, there is an amusing carving of an ascetic cat standing on its hind legs doing penance, in the presence of worshipful mice. Mamallapuram also has some engaging portrait sculptures, such as that of Mahendra-varman and his two queens on the Varaha cave temple there. Apart from these stone sculptures Hindu art at this time also produced some exquisite cast-bronze statues, such as the life-size portraits of Krishnadeva and his two consorts at the portals of the Tirupati temple in Andhra Pradesh.

As in the case of figurative sculptures, orthodox Muslim rulers also disfavoured figurative paintings. There were however some sultans who patronised such paintings, and even adorned their palaces with them. But many of these paintings were later erased by their orthodox successors. The classic example of this was the action of Firuz Tughluq, who, despite being a keen lover of art, not only prohibited the painting of portraits, but erased many of these paintings and other decorative elements in royal palaces. It should be however noted that orthodox sultans like Firuz were not against art as such, but only against the forms of art that offended their religious beliefs. Nor did they have any objection to Hindus patronising figurative sculptures and paintings. Some of the sultans did indeed destroy a number of Hindu temples and vandalised their idols, but this was part of their military campaigns to demoralize and subjugate Hindus, and was not an expression of philistinism.

During the early medieval period there was a fair amount of activity in miniature painting in India, mostly by Jains in their palm leaf manuscripts. These paintings were however mostly formulaic, and can hardly be described as works of art. In them, the faces of persons—always drawn in profile, but two-eyed, with the second eye protruding right out of the face at a right-angle— were all of a type and had little individuality in them. Several Buddhist palm leaf manuscripts of the period also had similar drab miniature illustrations.

But book illustrations underwent a major change by around the fifteenth century, because of the use of paper for writing texts. Paper, because of its larger size and smoother surface than palm leaf, allowed freer scope for painting illustrations, and this led to a great improvement in the quality of text illustrations, as Mughal and Rajasthani miniatures show. And some of the manuscript books made at this time were in themselves, as books, major works of art, their pages illuminated with gold, and adorned with floral, calligraphic and abstract designs, apart from having miniature illustrations.

SOME OF THE Delhi sultans, particularly Firuz Tughluq, were ardent conservationists. Firuz had to his credit transporting, with scrupulous care, two Asoka pillars from their original sites in Uttar Pradesh and Punjab, and installing them in Delhi with equal care. 'Quantities of . . . silk cotton were placed around the column, and when the earth at its base was removed, it fell gently over the bed prepared for it,' reports Afif, a courtier-historian of Firuz. 'The cotton was then removed by degrees, and after some days the pillar lay safe upon the ground. When the foundations of the pillar were examined, a large square stone was found as its base, which was also taken out. The pillar was then encased from top to bottom in reeds and raw skins, so that no damage would occur to it. A carriage, with forty-two wheels, was constructed . . . and after great labour and difficulty the pillar was raised on to the carriage. A strong rope was fastened to each wheel [of the carriage], and 200 men pulled at each of these ropes. By the simultaneous exertions of so many thousand men the carriage was moved, and was brought to the banks of the Yamuna. Here the Sultan came to meet it. A number of large boats had been collected, some of which could carry 5,000 and 7,000 *mans* of grain, and the least of them 2,000 *mans*. The column was very ingeniously transferred to these boats, and then taken to Firuzabad, where it was landed and conveyed into the *kushk* with infinite labour and skill.'

The pillar was then gradually, over several days, raised to an erect position, and its base properly embedded. 'After it was raised, some ornamental friezes of black and white stone were placed round [it] . . . and over these . . . was raised a gilded copper cupola . . . The height of the obelisk was thirty-two gaz; eight gaz was sunk in the pedestal, and twenty-four gaz visible. On the base of the obelisk there were engraved several lines of writing in Hindi characters. Many Brahmins and Hindu devotees were invited to read them, but no one was able. It is said that certain infidel Hindus interpreted them as stating that no one should be able to remove the obelisk from its place till there should arise in the later day a Muslim king named Sultan Firuz . . . '[4]

---

[4]See also Part V, Chapter 4

The Breath of All Breath

The socio-cultural profile of India changed radically with the establishment of the Delhi Sultanate. Never before in its millenniums-long history had India faced a civilizational challenge as potent and irreconcilable as that of Turco-Afghans, and never before had it failed to absorb invaders and migrants smoothly into its society and culture. Although there had been several radical transformations in Indian civilization over the millenniums, all these arose out of India's internal evolutionary processes, not out of external imposition, as it happened during the Sultanate period.

One of the most fundamental of these internal changes in Indian civilization took place in the late classical age, the period immediately preceding the Turkish invasion of India. This involved the collapse of India's commercial economy, the consequent decay of its towns, and the virtual disappearance of its urban lifestyle and culture. In a parallel and related development, Hinduism, which had remained dormant in the background of India's cultural landscape for very many centuries—ever since Buddhism and Jainism rose to subcontinental dominance in the last quarter of the first millennium BCE—now surged up like a mountainous tidal wave, and swept across the subcontinent, overwhelming Buddhism and Jainism and reducing them to the status of minor religions in India.

Hinduism then became *the* religion of India. But Hinduism itself had over the centuries become totally transformed from its Vedic and Upanishadic formulations, and had turned into a virtually new religion, Puranic Hinduism, a polymorphic religion unlike any other religion in the world. In fact, it was hardly a religion in the common sense of the word, but a loose conglomeration of the diverse and often contradictory creeds of India's diverse people and their diverse socio-cultural makeup.

400

These socio-religious transformations in India rarely involved any conflict or violence. Hinduism, Buddhism and Jainism were fraternal religions, and though they had several irreconcilable differences between them, they generally coexisted in peace with each other, and did not have the kind of adversarial or violent relationship that usually characterised the relationship between the other major religions of the premodern world.

This amiability was evident even in the relationship of Indian religions with the religions of the several foreign races that entered India over the centuries. In fact, Hinduism itself was a foreign religion, brought into India from Central Asia by invading Aryans around the middle of the second millennium BCE, which then, over time, smoothly absorbed into itself the pre-existing Dravidian culture and religion of the subcontinent. Similarly, all the subsequent migrants and invaders who entered India in premedieval times also brought with them their own traditional socio-religious systems, but these too over the centuries blended smoothly and indistinguishably into the existing Indian socio-religious milieu.

There were however a few small groups of migrant foreigners, mostly traders from Central Asia and Middle East, who, unlike most other migrant people who entered India, retained their ancestral socio-religious identity, and even won some local converts into their religion. This was how Judaism (brought into India by Jewish traders in the first millennium BCE), Christianity (introduced into Kerala by an apostle of Christ in the mid-first century CE), Islam (brought into India by Arab traders soon after the founding of the religion in Arabia), and finally Zoroastrianism (brought by Persian migrants around the eleventh century CE) took root in India. The introduction of these foreign religions into India, and the settlement of their devotees there, created no notable tension or conflict in India. These diverse people and their diverse religions mostly coexisted in harmony with the local people and their religions.

THIS AMICABLE SOCIO-RELIGIOUS scene in India changed altogether in the early medieval period, with establishment of the Delhi Sultanate. Unlike all the previous migrants and invaders, who had over the centuries merged smoothly into Indian society, Turks retained their distinct identity all through, and remained virtually as aliens in India throughout the over three-century long history of the Delhi Sultanate.

The establishment of the Delhi Sultanate altogether changed the religious scene in India as never before, for Islam, as the religion of the conquerors, assumed an aggressive posture against Indian religions, the religions of the subjects. The most evident and immediate adverse effect of this antagonism was on Buddhism. Buddhism, even in its atrophied state at this time, had a prominent presence in early medieval India, because of its large monasteries, stupas and educational institutions, and these drew Turks to them, who vandalised or destroyed several of them, sometimes, as in the case of Nalanda, mistaking the walled Buddhist universities to be enemy forts. They also butchered very many Buddhist monks, who were easily identifiable because of their distinctive saffron dress and shaven heads. In consequence of all this Buddhism virtually disappeared from India in early medieval times.

Turks were equally virulent towards Hinduism, but it survived without any critical damage because of its pervasiveness all over the subcontinent, as well as because of its polymorphic nature, without any nucleus, the destruction of which would have fatally damaged the religion. But there would never be any real harmony, or even any notable mutual influence between Hinduism and Islam, because they were diametrically opposite to each other in every respect. While Islam was monotheistic, Hinduism was polytheistic; while Islamic society was egalitarian and had no hereditary social divisions, Hindu society was hierarchic and divided into many hereditary castes which occupied different rungs in society and performed diverse and exclusive functions in society; while Muslims feasted on beef, Hindus venerated the cow and regarded cow slaughter and eating beef as most heinous sins.

Further, while Islam was a mono-layered and relatively immutable religion, Hinduism was a multi-layered religion which was forever in flux; and while Islam was an aggressive, proselytising religion, which was intolerant of other religions, Hinduism was a passive, non-proselytising religion, which could tolerantly coexist with any other religion, or any number of other religions. But while Hindu religion was inclusive, Hindu society was exclusive, into which one could enter only by being born into it. In contrast to this, Islam was exclusive in religion, but inclusive in its society, into which anyone could enter at any stratum by becoming a Muslim. It is significant that Hinduism, unlike Islam, had no provision at all for religious conversions; one could be a Hindu only by being born a Hindu. Further, the lifestyle and social customs and practices of the followers of the two religions—such as their succession laws, disposal of the dead, mode of dining, even their style of greeting—were all entirely different from each other. There was nothing at all common between Islam and Hinduism in any notable matter.

'They (Hindus) totally differ from us in religion, as we believe in nothing in which they believe, and vice versa . . .,' comments al-Biruni. 'All their fanaticism is directed against those who do not belong to them—against all foreigners. They call them *mleccha*, i.e. impure, and forbid having any connection with them, be it by intermarriage or any other kind of relationship, or by sitting, eating, and drinking with them, because thereby, they think, they would be polluted . . . In all manners and usages they differ from us as to such a degree as to frighten their children with us . . . [They] declare us to be of the devil's breed, and our doings as the very opposite of all that is good and proper.'

This view of al-Biruni, though factual, is one-sided. The irreconcilability between Hindu and Muslim civilisations was due as much to the attitudes and values of Muslims as of Hindus. In fact, the adamantine nature of Islam was in a way more responsible for this. Islam, even though it had a few rival sects in it, was essentially a rock-hard, monolithic religion, which did not have the malleability to modify itself under the influence of other religions and cultures. Indeed, according to one interpretation of Islamic cannon, if a Muslim became an apostate or adopted deviant religious practices, he could be executed by any Muslim without any legal formality.

In sharp contrast to Islam, Hinduism was an infinitely malleable, variegated, ever-changing religion. It had no inviolable core beliefs and practices, so it could companionably accommodate within it any number of contradictory beliefs and practices. It could be anything to anybody. Even though people of different sects and castes remained strictly segregated from each other in Hindu society, they all belonged to one religion. The rigidity of Hinduism was more of society than of religion. Indeed, Hinduism, left to itself, could have possibly accommodated Islamic beliefs and practices within itself, as it had done with innumerable Indian tribal cults, as well as with the cults of numerous migrants and invaders, all through its long history. Hinduism could do that without ceasing to be Hinduism. But Islam could not in any way accommodate Hinduism within its fold without altogether ceasing to be Islam.

The rigidity of Islamic civilisation was however only in religious beliefs and practices. In social and cultural matters Muslims were fairly open—Arabs, for instance, were greatly influenced by Greek civilisation; similarly Turks were greatly influenced by Persian civilisation. But Muslims were not quite so receptive to Hindu influence, partly because of the total contrariety of Hindu and Muslim civilisations, and also because the main preoccupation of the Turkish rulers in India was with their political survival, they being a tiny community precariously afloat in a vast and turbulent sea of aliens. Besides, Turks, as rulers, tended to scorn the culture of Hindus, their subjects.

Because of these fundamental differences, not only was there no synthesis of Hinduism and Islam, the two did not even have any major influence on each other, despite their several centuries long coexistence in India. They accommodated each other, but neither changed under the influence of the other.

Arabs had, in the early history of Islam, wiped out several local creeds as they swept from their homeland across the Eurasian continent and North Africa, and they had converted to Islam a large number of people in those lands, often by force. But they could not do that in India, because of the complexity and diversity of Indian society and religion, and the vastness of the Indian population. Islam could neither absorb nor exterminate Hinduism. Nor could Hinduism absorb or exterminate Islam. They had to coexist.

There were however a few kings and nobles in both these communities who were open to the cultural and religious influence of the other community. And there were a few Muslim scholars, such as al-Biruni and Amir Khusrav, who applied themselves earnestly and sympathetically to the study of the religion and culture of Hindus. Equally, there were a few Hindu scholars who studied the religion and culture of Muslims. At another level, many upper class Indians, particularly in North India, learned Persian and adopted the Persian dress and lifestyle, as the means for advancing their careers in the service of Muslim rulers. But these were all peripheral developments, and they did not lead to any notable change in either community.

STRANGELY, DESPITE THE total contrariness of Hinduism and Islam, there does not seem to have been any major communal clashes between the followers of the two religions in the medieval period. Presumably this was mainly because of the passive and accommodative nature of Hindu society and the general attitude of fatalism among Hindus; but partly it was also because Muslims mostly lived in towns, while Hindus mostly lived in villages. Though many temples were destroyed by the sultans during this period, and a large number of Hindus were slaughtered by them or were forcefully converted to Islam, these were mostly incidental to military campaigns, and were not very much different from what happened in the battles between Hindu kingdoms. For instance, during the wars between Cholas and Chalukyas in the eleventh century, Cholas, according to a Chalukya inscription, 'plundered the entire country, slaughtered women, children and Brahmins,' and carried away Brahmin girls and gave them in marriage to men of other castes.

Though the actions of Muslim armies were usually far more violent than that of Hindu armies—necessarily so, as they were in an alien country—they were not entirely dissimilar, and they do not seem to have had any serious adverse effect on the general Hindu-Muslim communal relationship. In normal times there was a fair amount of accommodativeness in the relationship between the two communities, and in the treatment that the rulers belonging to one religion meted out to their subjects of the other religion. 'The king allows such freedom that every man may come and go and live according to his own creed, without suffering any annoyance . . . whether he is a Christian, Jew, Moor or Heathen,' states Portuguese traveller Barbosa about what he observed in Vijayanagar in the sixteenth century. Hindus and Muslims mostly lived in peace with each other in medieval times. And they continued to do so with rare exceptions till the mid-twentieth century, when the partition of the subcontinent into India and Pakistan on the eve of the departure of the British rulers from the region led to unprecedented communal bloodbath.

There is no indication that Indians at any level were unduly perturbed by the establishment of the Turkish rule in India. In the view of the Hindu ruling class, Turks were just another contender for political power in India, like the many other contenders for power in the subcontinent. They were not viewed as aliens. As for the Hindu common people, it did not at all trouble them to live under Muslim kings—for them, the change of their rulers was a far away event that had virtually no bearing on their lives. Nor was there much social interaction between the common people of the two communities, as they generally lived physically separated from each other, Muslims being mostly urbanites and Hindus mostly villagers.

The general attitude of Hindus towards Muslims was to treat them as just another element in the highly variegated Indian society. This was quite in character with the history of Hinduism, which had made very many similar adjustments over the millennia, right from the beginning of its history, the Aryan migration into India. Over the centuries, as Aryans spread out in India, they absorbed into their religion many of the diverse sects and deities of the indigenous people; similarly, they also absorbed into it the cults of the many invaders and migrants who later entered India. Hinduism thus became an incredibly complex religion over the centuries, and its pantheon became fantastically multifarious.

It could not have been therefore any major problem for Hindus to be accommodative towards Islam. Indeed, it was not unusual for Hindus to revere Muslim sages or to offer devotions at Muslim shrines, just as they did at the shrines of the deities of different Hindu sects. For them Allah was just another deity, who had to be propitiated, or from whom favours could be sought. A classic example of the liberal attitude of Hinduism towards Islam was the decision of the administrators of the temple of Somnath in Gujarat to donate to a Muslim trader a plot of land close to the temple to build a mosque there—this, despite the fact that the temple had been desecrated and destroyed by Mahmud Ghazni just a few centuries earlier, the memory of which would have been still fresh in the minds of the local people.

Hindu kings seem to have viewed the Turkish invasion of India as a part of the normal churning political processes of medieval India. Communal considerations were seldom major factors in the calculations that determined the policies and actions of rajas or sultans, unless it was politically and militarily expedient for them to play the communal card. Hindu kings were especially liberal in their treatment of Muslims, partly because communal and religious diversity was the norm in India—had been so for very many centuries—and also because Muslims played a vital role in their kingdoms as traders and soldiers. Many Hindu kingdoms had fairly large colonies of Muslims in their towns, and the rajas usually did not discriminate against them in any way. Indeed, they often showed special favours to Muslims in their service, such as Devaraya of Vijayanagar placing a Koran on an ornate desk in front of his throne so that his Muslim officers would feel comfortable in bowing before him. And, even though the sultans generally forbade Hindus to build new temples in their kingdoms, the rajas had no objection to their Muslim subjects building mosques in their kingdoms.

In medieval India it was common for rajas to have a good number of Muslims in their armies, particularly in critical divisions like the cavalry, musketry and artillery, and to deploy them even in their wars against Muslim rulers. But then, so did sultans employ a large number of Hindus in their armies, and deploy them even in their wars against Hindu kings. They could do so without any unease, because the wars between sultans and rajas were not usually, with rare exceptions, fought in a crusading spirit by either side, and were not in any way different from their wars against their own coreligionists. These wars were all about power and wealth and territory, not about religion.

THE ACCOMMODATIVE SPIRIT of Hindus in matters of religion was an expression of their general tendency to bend with the wind, adjust to the prevailing conditions, whatever they might be. Equally, it was an expression of the widely held view of Hindus that the beliefs and practices of each group of people were legitimate for that group, and should not be interfered with, however repugnant those beliefs and practices might be to other groups.

Muslims did not share this liberal attitude. This is epitomized in an incident reported by Shaikh Nurul Haq, a sixteenth century chronicler. According to him, Sultan Sikandar Lodi was once told that a Brahmin religious leader held the view that Hinduism and Islam were both equally true religions. The Brahmin no doubt meant well, but unfortunately for him, the sultan found it odious that Hinduism and Islam should be thus equated. So he ordered the Brahmin to become a Muslim (since being a Muslim was as good as being a Hindu), and when he refused to do that (since being a Hindu was good as being a Muslim), he was put to death.

Many such incidents of the persecution of Hindus by sultans are reported by Muslim chroniclers. But the prominence given to these incidents by them seems to be rather excessive, considering the vast range of the interaction between Hindus and Muslims in medieval India, the immense number of people involved in it, and the many centuries long coexistence of the two communities. By and large Hindus and Muslims lived together peacefully in medieval India, without any serious communal clashes. But neither religion exerted any notable influence on the other religion. Hinduism, a couple of millenniums old and rather decrepit at this time, did not have the energy and spirit to respond creatively to the challenge of Islam; as for Islam, it was far too rigid a religion to accommodate any modifications under external influence. The most that happened was that both religions spawned a few minor and transient cults that synthesised some elements from both religions.

In any case, Hinduism and Islam were far too divergent from each other in every respect to have any major influence on each other. For instance, while Hinduism was flexible in its religious beliefs and practices, it was rigid in its social organisation—the caste compartmentalisation of its society—while Islam was flexible in its social organisation, but was rigid in its religious beliefs and practices. Conforming to caste rules was for Hindus far more important than conforming to religious beliefs and practices—anyone could adopt any religious belief and practice, worship any deity or any number of deities, but none could deviate from the prescriptions and practices of his caste without serious consequences, which involved even the risk of being ostracised by the entire Hindu society. Thus Hindus would be horrified at the mere thought of allowing Muslims to enter their homes or to share a meal with them, even though they generally had no qualms about serving under Muslim rulers or even about offering devotions at Muslim shrines.

ACCORDING TO THE strict interpretation of Koranic law, all non-Muslims in Muslim ruled lands, except Jews and Christians, had to become Muslims or be exterminated. But it was not practicable to apply this prescription against Hindus, as they were far too numerous to be put to death, even if very many years were spent on it. Further, in many fields the services of Hindus were essential for the very survival of Muslim rule in India. So Muhammad Qasim, the first Muslim invader of India, was permitted by his superiors to give the people of India the status of Zimmis, protected non-Muslims—like Jews and Christians—and thus spare their lives and allow them, on the payment of jizya, to lead their traditional way of life, and practise their religion without any interference.

That was the general rule. And it was generally observed. There was nevertheless a good amount of slaughter of Hindus and destruction of their temples throughout the history of the Delhi Sultanate, particularly during its early period. Gruesome savagery was an essential part of medieval warfare everywhere in the world, for soldiers to quench their bloodthirst and to demoralise the enemy. This was more so with Turks in India, because they, a miniscule minority in India, needed to terrorise Indians to keep them submissive. As for vandalising temples, that was, in their view, an essential demonstration of the powerlessness of Hindu gods. Moreover, looting temples

THE AGE OF WRATH

was a good means for collecting booty, for many of the temples were fabulously rich, with the accumulated offerings of their devotees over the centuries.

Ala-ud-din Khalji once asked his advisors about what he should do to keep Hindus submissive to his rule. And they, according to Barani, advised him that Hindus should be reduced to so abject a condition as to be unable to enjoy any luxuries and be hard-pressed even to have common comforts. Another day the sultan sought the opinion of a kazi on how to treat Hindus, and the kazi advised: 'When the revenue officer demands silver from them, they should, without question and with all humility and respect, tender gold. If the officer throws dirt into their mouths, they must without reluctance open their mouths wide to receive it . . . To keep Hindus in abasement is a religious duty.' Ala-ud-din smiled at this counsel, and said that he too considered Hindus to be a major source of turbulence in the state, and that it was therefore an imperative political necessity that they should be 'reduced to the most abject obedience,' and be deprived of 'wealth and property which fosters disaffection and rebellion.'

Ala-ud-din's anti-Hindu policy was primarily motivated by political and military considerations, not by religious considerations, and there is evidence that, despite his anti-Hindu professions, Hindus enjoyed greater security and prosperity under him than under many other sultans. In contrast, the primary motive of the anti-Hindu policy of Firuz Tughluq, which was quite oppressive, was to enforce orthodox Muslim religious prescriptions, than to gain political advantage. And, although he was on the whole a humane and cultured ruler, some of his actions against Hindus and Muslim heretics were horrendous. Thus when he was told that an old Brahmin in Delhi was 'publicly performing the worship of idols in his house, and that the people of the city, both Muslims and Hindus, were resorting to his house to worship the idol,' Firuz had the Brahmin brought to him and ordered him to become a Muslim, and when he refused, had him thrown alive into a burning pyre built in front of the durbar hall.

There were several other such incidents during the reign of Firuz, and he himself reports on some of them in his autobiography. 'There was a set of heretics . . . [who] met by night at an appointed time and place, both friends and strangers,' he writes about what was obviously the rite of a Hindu Tantric sect. 'Wine was served, and they said that this was their religious worship. They brought their wives, mothers, and daughters to these meetings. The men threw themselves on the ground as if in worship, and each man had intercourse with the woman whose garment he caught. I cut off the heads of the elders of this sect, and imprisoned and banished the rest, so that their abominable practices were put an end to.' Similarly, 'there was a sect which wore the garments of atheism, and having thrown off all restraint, led men astray. The name of their chief was Ahmad Bahari . . . His followers called him a god.' Firuz had the 'god' chained and imprisoned, and his followers banished from the city.

Firuz also sought, in conformity with orthodox Muslim prescriptions, to strictly enforce the collection of jizya from all non-Muslims, including Brahmins, who were till then exempt from it. When this policy was announced, the Brahmins of Delhi and its environs gathered in front of the royal palace and threatened to immolate themselves or starve themselves to death if the sultan did not revoke the order. But Firuz remained unrelenting, and eventually the Brahmins had to withdraw their agitation, after pleading with the sultan to at least reduce the quantum of the tax on them, to which he agreed.

OUR ONLY SOURCES of information on the persecution of Hindus by the sultans are the accounts given by Muslim chroniclers, who invariably embellished their reports with exaggerations in order to glorify their royal patrons, as the slaughter of Hindus and the destruction of their temples were, in their view, highly commendable acts. 'The blood of infidels flowed copiously and apostasy was often their only way of survival,' writes al-Utbi, a medieval Arab chronicler, about the plight of Hindus in the Delhi Sultanate. Adds Amir Khusrav: 'The land had been saturated with the water of the sword and the vapours of infidelity had been dispersed.'

These are hyperbolic statements. Though there is no doubt that severe persecution of Hindus were carried out by the Turko-Afghans, and that a large number of Hindus were slaughtered by them, the incidents were in all probability nowhere near of the scale described by Muslim chroniclers. Many of the sultans in fact treated Hindus quite fairly and employed a good number of them in crucial offices. Even Mahmud Ghazni, the reportedly ruthless iconoclast and exterminator of Hindus, had a large contingent of Hindu soldiers in his army. And so had his son and successor Masud, who even warned his Muslim officers to take care not to offend the religious sentiments of their Hindu colleagues. And there were several instances, even in the very early phase of the Delhi Sultanate history, of sultans employing Hindu captains and soldiers in their army, and of allying themselves with rajas, to wage war against rival Muslim rulers or chieftains. Zaynu'l-Abidin, a fifteenth century sultan of Kashmir, was particularly conciliatory towards Hindus; he employed several of them in high positions in government, even rebuilt some of their temples destroyed by his predecessors, and allowed Hindus who had been forced to become Muslims to revert to their ancestral faith, even though apostasy was a capital crime in Muslim society. And in Delhi, some of the Muslim nobles, even some members of the royal family, now came to be known by Hindu nicknames, a minor but culturally noteworthy development. It is significant that one of the reasons (or pretexts) for Timur's invasion of India was that he felt that the Delhi sultans were too lenient in their treatment of Hindus.

The accommodative policy of some sultans towards Hindus was in part an expression of their liberal and humane sentiments, but it was primarily dictated by political prudence, for the sultans could not have governed their Indian empire without the service of Hindus, who held very many crucial though subordinate positions in the civil and military wings of the government, and it was the productivity of the Hindu population that provided the material resources to the sultans to maintain their rule.

ONE OF THE most fascinating religious developments in India in the early medieval period was the rise of several mystical religious movements, in Islam as well as in Hinduism. These movements were inevitably confined to a small number of spiritually sensitive people, who scorned conventional religious practices as impediments—rather than as the means—to spiritual attainment. Typically, Bauls, a cult of Bengali mystic minstrels, asserted that 'the path to god is blocked by the temple and the mosque,' and that god dwelled within each man, so no one had to go to temple or mosque to worship god. 'The man of my heart dwells inside me,' declared a Baul poet. 'Everywhere I look, he is there . . . He is in the very sparkle of light.'

The Indian mystic sages of the middle ages were usually syncretic in their religious views, and had no hesitation to freely incorporate elements of different faiths in their teachings. 'There is only one god, though Hindus and Muslims call him by different names,' states sage Haridasa. 'This one god is the highest meaning of both the Puranas and the Koran.' This was the common credo of all mystic sects. There was in fact hardly any fundamental difference between the various mystic sects of medieval India. Their common view was that all gods (and goddesses) are manifestations of The One, though man, because of the limitations of his understanding, sees them as many. And, as the mystics did not discriminate between gods, they did not discriminate between men either, and they rejected or ignored caste and communal divisions. Another common characteristic of these mystic sects was that they generally were intensely emotion-charged movements.

One of the most prominent mystic saint-poets of medieval India was Kabir, who lived and preached in Varanasi in Uttar Pradesh. The details of his background and early life are uncertain. He probably lived around the late fifteenth or early sixteenth century, and was evidently born a Muslim, as his name indicates. There is a legend that he was the illegitimate son of a Brahmin widow, who abandoned him on birth, and that he was then brought up by a humble Muslim family of weavers. Kabir's family profession is reflected in the many similes drawn from weaving in his verses. We do not know what education he had, if any at all. His poems were all oral compositions, which were later written down by his disciples, so there is quite probably some amount of interpolations in them.

Kabir was probably inclined to mysticism from an early age, but the transformative event of his life was his adoption by Ramananda—the great Vaishnava saint-reformer of Varanasi—as his disciple. As Kabir set out on his spiritual journey he was quite confident of what he would achieve in life, and what his achievement would mean to others, as he states in one of his poems:

When I was born, the world smiled and I cried.
But I will do such deeds that when I die,
I will be smiling and the world will be crying.

The main thrust of Kabir's mission was to unite Hindus and Muslims in a common quest for god realisation. 'Hindus and Muslims have the same god,' he held. 'God is the breath of all breath . . . Look within your heart, for there you will find [god] . . . All men and women in the world are his living forms.' Although many of his sayings had a strong Hindu flavour in them—presumably because of Ramananda's influence—he made no distinction between Hinduism and Islam. Similarly, though he usually referred to god as Hari or Rama, he used those words as synonyms of god, and not as the names of particular deities. 'I am not Hindu nor Muslim; Allah-Ram is the breath of my body,' he stated, and went on to declare that

All that lives and dies,
    they are all one.
The this and that haggling,
    is done.

Kabir made no distinction between religions or castes. 'In the beginning there was no Turk, no Hindu, no race, no caste,' he maintained. Not surprisingly, he ridiculed many of the common Hindu beliefs and practices, such as the caste system, idol worship, belief in divine incarnations, the practice of going on pilgrimages, and so on. 'If by worshipping stones one can find god, I shall worship a mountain,' he mocked. He considered many of the conventional socio-religious customs and practices of all religions as utterly ludicrous. 'A Brahmin wears a sacred thread he himself has made. If you are a Brahmin, born of a Brahmin mother, why haven't you come into the world in some special way?' he taunted. 'If you are a Turk, born of a Turk, why weren't you circumcised in the womb of your mother? If you milk a black cow and a white cow, can you distinguish the milk that they give?'

Kabir's emphasis was on inward devotion, not on outward displays of faith. And he exhorted:

> Make thy mind the Kaaba,
> thy body the temple
> thy conscience the primary teacher . . .
> Hindus and Muslims have the same lord.

Kabir's disciples—Kabir-panthis—came from both Hindu and Muslim communities, but on his death they split into two sects, one of Hindus and the other of Muslims, each claiming that Kabir belonged to their religion. And they wrangled with each other about the funeral rites they should perform for him. But when, according to legend, they removed the sheet supposedly covering his body, all they found there was a heap of flowers. His Muslim and Hindu followers then divided the flowers between them, and performed over each lot their particular funeral rites. Subsequently even the Hindu followers of Kabir split into two groups, the Bap (father) sect, and the Mai (mother) sect. The Kabir-panthis are generally considered a Hindu sect.

Zillion Creeds

Hinduism in medieval times was a very different religion from what it was in Vedic times, having metamorphosed twice over a period of two thousand years, first into Upanishadic Hinduism around the middle of the first millennium BCE, a thousand years after Aryans brought the religion with them into India, and then into Puranic Hinduism yet another thousand years later, around the middle of the first millennium CE. These transformations of Hinduism however were not due to any external influence, but due to its own evolutionary process, as in the case of Upanishadic Hinduism, or due to its assimilation of numerous tribal cults over the centuries, as in the case of Puranic Hinduism.[1]

These evolutionary processes in Hinduism ended well before the Turkish invasion of India, and there were no radical, transformative new developments in the religion during the medieval period. The late classical period was the age of mystics in Hinduism, around whom several new cults had formed, many of which endured well into the medieval period. A few new mystic cults also appeared in Hinduism in medieval times. But far more fascinating than all this was the appearance of a few syncretic religious cults in India at this time, some of which had significant insights into the human predicament. But they all remained peripheral movements, and did not bring about any notable or enduring changes in Hindu religion or society.

An important development in Hinduism in the late classical period was the formation of monasteries, *mathas*, evidently in simulation of Buddhist

---

[1]For Upanishadic Hinduism, see *Gem in the Lotus*, Part III; for Puranic Hinduism, see *The First Spring*, Part XII.

monasteries. In time some of these monasteries grew enormously in wealth, power and influence, and their chiefs took to surrounding themselves with quasi-royal paraphernalia, holding court under ceremonial umbrellas, and touring around on elephants, accompanied by drummers and followed by large entourages.

But these were superficial changes, changes in appearance, not in substance, and they involved only a tiny fraction of the Hindu population, and had virtually no effect on the religious culture of the common people, which remained the same as it had been for several centuries. The approach of the common people to religion in Hindu society was rather casual, unlike the fervent earnestness of the devotees of monotheistic religions, like Christianity and Islam. Hindus, notes al-Biruni, are 'so little pious, that, when speaking of these things (religious matters), they do not even abstain from silly and unbecoming language.'

Hindus were devout in religion, but not fanatical. The main reason for this was the presence of countless gods in Hinduism, unlike in all the other major religions of the world. This multiplicity of gods in turn led to the existence of a great diversity of sects, rituals and beliefs in Hinduism. And this sectarian diversity in turn led to the practice of broad religious tolerance by Hindus. Though there were a few instances of clashes between rival Hindu sects, they by and large coexisted companionably. Nor was it uncommon for the devotees of one Hindu deity to also offer devotions to other Hindu deities, or even to the deities of other religions. Hindus, unlike Christians and Muslims, were not monomaniacal about their faith. Hinduism has no heresies, as any deviant belief and practice could be accommodated and legitimised in it.

Despite all this diversity there were a few universally held beliefs among Hindus. One such belief was in metempsychosis. This was noted by several medieval chroniclers. 'Metempsychosis is the shibboleth of the Hindu religion,' comments al-Biruni. This faith 'is rooted in their hearts, and about which they have not the slightest doubt,' adds Abu Zaid, a tenth century Iraqi chronicler. Life, Hindus held, does not begin with birth. Or end with death. Birth and death are only transformative phases of the eternal cycle of life that a being goes through, in which one could be reborn in any socio-cultural environment, or even as any creature, depending on one's karma.

FACTUAL, OBJECTIVE INFORMATION about medieval Hinduism is scanty, though there are some interesting sidelights on it in the reports of foreign travellers and scholars. The religious beliefs of medieval Hindus, according to al-Biruni, were similar to those of ancient Greeks: 'The heathen Greeks, before the rise of Christianity, held much the same opinions as Hindus; their educated classes thought much the same as those of Hindus; their common people held the same idolatrous views as those of Hindus.'

Belief in omens was universal in medieval India, and was often trivial and absurd in its expressions. In Kerala, according to Barbosa, 'if a cat crosses in front of any person who is about to do any business, he does it not; or if on going from the house for any purpose they see a crow carrying a stick, they turn back; or if while saying farewell to other persons with whom they have been, one of them sneezes, he who was going sits down and does not leave soon.'

For Hindus, as for the followers of all medieval religions, going on pilgrimages was a major goal of life, to secure a good afterlife. There were seven major holy sites in India for Hindus to visit, from Badrinath in the far north to Rameswaram in the far south. Major rivers, particularly Ganga, were considered sacred by Hindus, and bathing in them was a rite for them. 'The Hindu infidels worship Ganga, and once every year they come on pilgrimage to this place (Haridwar) which they consider the source of the river, to bathe and have their heads and beards shaved,' notes Timur in his autobiography. 'They believe these acts to be the means of obtaining salvation and securing future reward. They dispense large sums in charity among those who wear the Brahminical thread, and they throw money into the river. When infidels die in distant parts, their bodies are burned, and the ashes brought to this river and are thrown into it. This they look upon as a means of sanctification.'

According to Khondamir, an early sixteenth century chronicler, the reason why Hindus consider Ganga to be sacred is that they 'believe that the water of this river springs from the fountain of paradise.' Battuta also makes the same point. And so does al-Utbi. Hindus, he writes, regard Ganga 'as of exceeding sanctity, and consider that its source is in paradise ... Devotees come to it from a distance, and drown themselves in it, in the hope of obtaining eternal salvation.' Adds Yazdi, an early fifteenth century chronicler: up in the Himalayas, there is 'a stone in the form of a cow, and the water of the river [Ganga] flows out of the mouth of that cow. The infidels of India worship this cow, and come hither from all quarters, from distances even of a year's journey ... They throw gold and silver into the river, and they go down into the river, wash their feet, sprinkle water on their heads, and have their heads and beards shaved. This they consider to be an act of devotion, just as Muslims consider pilgrimage to Mecca a pious act.'

Medieval chroniclers also record the universal Hindu reverence for cows. 'Hindus call the bull father and the cow mother,' writes Nikitin, a mid-fifteenth century Russian traveller in India. 'With their excrements [as fuel] they bake bread and boil food, and with their ashes they mark the symbols of these animals on their own faces, foreheads and whole bodies.' Serpents were also venerated by Hindus. Notes Varthema, an early sixteenth-century

Italian traveller, 'Those who kill serpents receive capital punishment [in Hindu kingdoms]: the king would immediately put him to death. In like manner, if anyone kills a cow, he would also put that person to death. They say that these serpents are the spirits of god, and that if they were not his spirits, god would not have given them such power as to immediately kill a person with just a small bite.'

NICOLO CONTI, AN early fifteenth-century Venetian traveller in India, has left us some vivid descriptions of the Hindu festivals he witnessed. 'At a certain time of the year their idol is carried through the city, placed between two chariots, in which are young women, richly adorned, who sing hymns to the god. The chariots are accompanied by a great concourse of people. Many of them, carried away by the fervour of their faith, cast themselves on the ground before the wheels [of the chariot], in order that they may be crushed to death—a mode of death which they say is very acceptable to their god. Others, making an incision on their side, and inserting a rope thus through their body, hang themselves from the chariot by way of ornaments, and thus suspended and half dead accompany their idol . . .

'Thrice in the year they keep festivals of especial solemnity. On one of these occasions the males and females of all ages having bathed in the rivers or the sea, clothe themselves in new garments, and spend three entire days singing, dancing, and feasting. On another of these festivals they fix up within their temples, and on the outside on the roofs, an innumerable number of oil lamps . . ., which are kept burning day and night. On the third [festival], which lasts nine days, they set up on all the highways large beams, like the masts of small ships, to the upper part of which are attached pieces of very beautiful cloth of various kinds, interwoven with gold. On the summit of each of these beams is each day placed a man of pious aspect, dedicated to religion, capable of enduring all things with equanimity, who is to pray for the favour of god. These men are assailed by the people, who pelt them with oranges, lemons, and other odoriferous fruits, all of which they bear most patiently. There are also three other festival days, during which they sprinkle all passers-by, even the king and queen, with saffron water, placed for that purpose by the wayside. This is received by all with much laughter.'

Barbosa reports that during a temple festival in Kerala, when the idol is taken out in procession, 'in front of the idol walk many Nairs with bare swords, slashing themselves wheresoever they can, and foaming at the mouth, and shouting so that they seem possessed of devils.' Friar Odoric, an early fourteenth century Italian missionary-traveller, also reported on several Hindu festivals and temple rites. 'When any man offers to die in the service of his . . . god, his parents, and all his friends assemble themselves together with a consort of musicians, making him a great and solemn feast. Which feast being ended, they hang five sharp knives around his neck and carry him to the idol. As soon as he reaches there, he taketh one of his knives crying with a loud voice, "For the worship of my god do I cut [off] this my flesh", and then he casteth the morsel which is cut at the face of his idol. At the very last wound wherewith he murdereth himself, he uttereth these words: "Now do I yield myself to death in behalf of my god." And being dead, his body is burned, and [he] is esteemed by all men to be holy.'

Human sacrifices at temples were prevalent but rare in medieval India, but animal sacrifices were quite common. Barbosa reports about a peculiar rite at a Shiva temple in Vijayanagar, in which a virgin with 'a sharp-pointed stick' deflowers herself before the idol and sprinkles it with the oozing blood.

Temples played a prominent role in all facets of life of medieval Indians. Rajas were keen patrons of temples, and they gifted vast treasures to them, so as to root their power firmly in the local socio-cultural soil, and also, more importantly, to win divine favour, which was considered indispensible for success in any venture. Temples also played a notable role in the local economy, by providing finance for agriculture, trade and industry. Major temples were the nuclei around which towns formed, and were significant factors in the revival of urban economy and culture in medieval India.

'THERE ARE IN all eighty-four creeds,' states Nikitin about Hindu sects. Quite probably there were very many more Hindu sects than that. There were also several different ascetic orders in Hindu society, commonly called yogis. Battuta once witnessed the performance of feats by yogis at the court of Muhammad Tughluq, and reported on it.

'The men of this class do some marvellous things,' reports Battuta. 'One of them will spend months without eating or drinking, and many of them have pits dug for them in the earth, which are then covered up on top of them, leaving only a space for air to enter. They stay in these for months, and I heard them tell of one who remained thus for a year. People say that they make pills, one of which they take for a given number of days or months, and during that time they require no food or drink. They can tell what is happening at a distance. The sultan [Muhammad Tughluq] holds them in esteem and admits them to his company . . . The majority [of them] eat no meat. It is obvious that they have so disciplined themselves in ascetic practices that they have no need for any of the goods or vanities of this world.

'There are amongst them some who merely look at a man and he falls dead on the spot. The common people say that if the breast of a man killed in this way is cut open, it is found to contain no heart, and they assert his heart has been eaten. This is commonest in the case of women, and a woman who acts thus is called a *kaftar*. During the famine in Delhi they brought one of these women to me, saying that she had eaten the heart of a boy. I ordered them to take her to the sultan's lieutenant, who commanded that she should be put to test. They filled four jars with water, tied them to her hands and feet and threw her into the river Yamuna. As she did not sink she was known to be a *kaftar* . . . He ordered her then to be burned . . . Her ashes were collected by the men and women of the town, for they believe that anyone who fumigates himself with them is safe against a *kaftar's* enchantments during that year.'

Some of the Hindu ascetic sects in medieval India were like the warrior monks of medieval Europe, and there are some graphic accounts of their activities during the Mughal period. Following the collapse of the Mughal Empire, these ascetic gangs—known as Nagas, their generic name—came to play a notable role in the politics of the late medieval and early modern India, serving under various rajas and sultans—these Hindu warrior ascetics had no compunction to serve under Muslim rulers.

The Nagas were quite bizarre in their appearance as well as their mode of fighting. Colonel Malleson, a British officer in India in the mid-eighteenth century, describes a band of them he saw in the army of the nawab of Oudh as 'all perfectly naked and covered with paint and ashes.' Battle was a rite for them, and they, as modern historian W. G. Orr describes them, went into battle in 'a kind of whirling dance, during which they became wrought up to a pitch of uncontrollable excitement. Then, with ear-piercing yells, they rushed upon the enemy.'

The Nagas belonged to the extreme periphery of Hindu religion, and had virtually no role in the everyday life of Hindus. The most notable of the mainstream medieval Hindu religious movements were the Bhakti cults, which came to prominence in the centuries immediately preceding the Turkish invasion of India.[2] These supercharged devotional cults originated in South India around the sixth century, and gradually, over the next few centuries, spread all over the subcontinent. The Bhakti sages held that only total and unswerving *bhakti* (devotion to god) can save man from the pitfalls of life and earn him salvation. And for this one does not have to go to temples or perform rituals, for god is latent in every man, and this god within can be awakened through loving devotion.

The defining characteristic of the Bhakti sages was that they lived totally immersed in the sea of devotional ecstasy. Quite appropriately, the Tamil Vaishnavite Bhakti sages were known as *Alvars*, meaning the immersed. These

---

[2]For a detailed account of the Bhakti movement, see *The First Spring*, Part XII, Chapter 7.

sages ignored all class and caste distinctions, preached in vernacular languages, using simple maxims and parables, so their teachings were accessible to all right across the social spectrum, to the literate as well as to the illiterate. The movement had no intellectual pretensions, but had strong emotional fervour, which appealed to rustics and to urban underclasses. Orthodox Hindus, particularly Brahmins, initially disapproved the movement, as it was disruptive of the established social order and religious practices. But eventually the movement gained wide acceptance among all Hindu castes. In the process, however, it lost some of its radical features—it no longer opposed the caste system or idol worship—but fitted itself into a niche in the orthodox Hindu socio-religious structure.

ISLAM, UNLIKE HINDUISM, did not ever go through any transformative evolutionary processes. Its beliefs and practices were defined in detail by Prophet Muhammad, and these have remained unchanged since then. And, although several sects had appeared in Islam over the centuries, these differed only in organisational matters and social practices, not in religious faith. Similarly, authorities often differed in their interpretations of Koranic prescriptions, but the prescriptions themselves were never questioned.

The rigour of the enforcement of Koranic prescriptions however varied from sultanate to sultanate, and from sultan to sultan. The primary concern of sultans, even of the most orthodox of them, was with the preservation and expansion of their power, not with the enforcement of religious directives. Thus Balban, despite his strict personal observance of orthodox religious prescriptions, was, in matters of administration, guided primarily by the needs of the state, not by Islamic law. Ala-ud-din Khalji followed the same policy. 'When he became sultan he came to the conclusion that polity and government are one thing, and the rules and decrees of Islamic law are another,' observes Barani. 'Royal commands belong to the sultan, Islamic legal decrees rest upon the judgment of the qazis and muftis.'

Islam, like Judaism and Christianity, is a monotheistic religion. This is stated in the Kalimah, the Islamic confession of faith: *La Ilaha Illa-Allah; Muhammadur Rasul-ullah*: there is no god but Allah; Muhammad is the messenger of Allah. Sharia, the holy laws of Islam—based on the prescriptions of Koran, the sayings and conventions of prophet Muhammad (*hadith*), and the rulings of Islamic scholars (*fatwas*)—regulate every aspect of Islamic society, economy and government, as well as the totality of the life of individual Muslims. Islam makes no distinction between religious and secular laws. Every law has a religious base, and the violation of any law is a crime as well as a sin.

There are, however, a few purely religious duties for Muslims to perform. All Muslims, for instance, are required to pray five times a day at home or office, and to gather in a mosque for congregational prayers on Fridays. They are also required, if they can afford it, to go on Hajj, pilgrimage to Mecca, at least once in their lifetime.

Islam abhors idol worship, and maintains austerity and high decorum in its religious ceremonies. While temple worship in Hinduism is often accompanied by music and dance, Islam sternly prohibits them in mosques. Religious festivities in Islam are solemn acts of submission to god, unlike in Hinduism in which they are carnivals in celebration of deities. In fact, Islam, unlike most other religions, has no religious rituals at all, and therefore no ordained priests or bishops, no supreme religious authority like pope.

There are however religious leaders in Islam, termed Imams, men of piety and scholarship, who lead the prayer in mosques. The other prominent socio-religious functionaries in Islamic society are Mullahs (religious scholars), Pirs (spiritual guides), Sheikhs (tribal patriarchs), and above them all the Caliph (the supreme authority over all Muslims of his sect everywhere in the world, in temporal as well as spiritual matters). But all these functionaries, even the Caliph, hold their posts by their personal merit recognised by their community, not by ordination. The role of the Caliph was similar to the role of the sultan, except that the sultan's power was confined to his kingdom, while the Caliph had, in theory at least, authority over all Muslims of his sect everywhere in the world, though often he was just a figurehead.

ISLAM, LIKE ANY other religion, has a number of sects, the most prominent of which are Sunnis, Shias and Sufis. The difference between Sunnis and Shias is primarily in organisational matters. These two sects initially emerged out of their difference over the mode of succession to the Caliphate—while Shias preferred hereditary succession to the office through the descendants of Ali, prophet Muhammad's cousin and son-in-law, Sunnis wanted succession to be decided by the consensus of the Muslim community. Later other differences also arose between the two sects, and the gap between them widened. The Sunni is the predominant sect in the Muslim world, including the Indian subcontinent, while Shias are mostly in Iran.

Shia and Sunni, despite their differences, are both orthodox sects. Sufis are on another religious plane altogether; they are mystics and are regarded as heretics by many orthodox Muslims. Even al-Biruni, though he was generally quite broadminded, was censorious about Sufism, and condemned it for its flighty mysticism and lack of intellectual rigour and sophistication. Sultan Ghiyas-u-din Tughluq also disapproved of Sufis. A rigidly orthodox Muslim, he once summoned Nizamuddin Auliya, the great Sufi sage of medieval India, to the court to appear before a jury of orthodox theologians, and forced him to acknowledge, at least outwardly, the error of his ways.

Sufis hold that god realisation cannot be achieved through conventional religious practices, but only though obsessive, passionate devotion to god, and by awakening one's intuitive faculties through intense meditation. Such meditation, Sufis believe, would enable the devotee to gain insights into the true nature of god, and that this knowledge would liberate him from all worldly bonds, so that he becomes one with god. Typically, Khwaja Moinuddin, the founder of the Chishti sect in India, claimed: 'For years I used to go around the Kaaba, now the Kaaba goes around me.'

Many of the peculiar beliefs and practices of Sufis arose out of their conviction that doomsday, the end of the world—the day of final divine judgement and the arrival of Mahdi, the redeemer—was at hand, and that man should prepare himself earnestly for that day by ridding himself of all his temporal concerns, and thus transcend the human condition. Sufis therefore detached themselves from society, lived in seclusion, practised self-mortification, and indulged in dervish practices like rapturous singing and dancing, to induce in themselves spiritual ecstasy and to fall into a trance, and thus disengage themselves totally from the mundane world. Often they spoke in a cryptic language, not so much to say anything, as to create an otherworldly ambiance.

The beliefs and practices of Sufis were in many ways similar to those of the Bhakti cults of Hinduism, but while the Bhakti sages usually functioned within society, Sufis usually functioned outside society. In that they were rather like yogis. And yogis evidently did have some influence on some Sufi sects in India, whose members took to performing yogic exercises, particularly controlled breathing. Some Indian Sufi leaders even called themselves rishis, as the Hindu sages did. And some of them took Hindus as disciples.

Sufis in medieval India were divided into three major orders: Chishti (popular in Delhi and the Doab, and had poet Amir Khusrav as one of its distinguished followers), Suhrawardi (of Sind), and Firdausi (of Bihar). The best known Sufi sage of the early medieval period was Nizamuddin Auliya of the Chishti order, who had a large number of followers among the ruling class in Delhi. But the followers of Sufism, compared to the general Muslim population in India, were quite small even at the height of the movement's short-lived popularity, because the renunciatory and asocial character of the sect was not suited for the common people.

SOME OF THE Muslim mystic sects were quite weird in their practices, like some of the Hindu mystic sects. The oddest of them was the Qalandar sect, a loosely organized group of antinomian wandering dervishes. Their early history is obscure, but they probably originated in Iran or Central Asia, from where they entered India around the twelfth or thirteenth century. Qalandars were contemptuous of all social and religious conventions, habitually used psychedelic drugs, and considered themselves above all laws, including the Sharia laws. Unlike most Sufis, they shaved their head and face, even their eyebrows, wore iron rings on their ears and fingers, and went about clad in coarse, hip-length woollen blankets. Some members of this sect fitted a short iron rod transversely into their penis, to prevent any possibility of sexual intercourse by them.

Ibn Battuta once saw a performance by Qalandars at Amroha in Uttar Pradesh. 'Their chief,' he reports, 'asked me to supply him with firewood so that they might light it for their dance, so I charged the governor of that district . . . to furnish it. He sent about ten loads of it, and after the night prayer they kindled it, and at length, when it was a mass of glowing coals, they began their music recital and went into that fire, dancing and rolling about in it. Their chief asked me for a shirt and I gave him one of the finest texture; he put it on and began to roll about in the fire with it on and beat the fire with his sleeves until it was extinguished . . . He then brought me the shirt showing not a single trace of burning on it, at which I was greatly astonished.' In Maldives too Battuta once saw the dervishes perform this fire rite; they, he reports, went into a fire, 'treading it with their [bare] feet, and some of them ate it (the embers) as one eats sweetmeats.'

The early medieval period was the age of bizarre religious movements in India, in Hinduism as well as in Islam. Firuz Tughluq in his autobiography describes some of these sects, and the action he took to suppress them. One such heretic leader of the age was Rukn-ud-din, who claimed to be the Mahdi; Firuz set the rabble on him and had him killed—'the people rushing in tore him to pieces and broke his bones into fragments,' he writes with approbation. Firuz also mentions a heretic in Gujarat who 'used to say "Ana-l-Hakk" (I am god), and instructed his disciples that when he said these words they should say, "Thou art, thou art!" . . . He was put in chains and brought before me . . . I condemned him to punishment . . .'

ISLAM WAS AN aggressively proselytising religion, but there is no evidence of any extensive use of violence by Muslim rulers in India to force conversions. Though there were many instances of sultans converting Hindus into Islam by force, most of them were incidental to military campaigns. The sultans did not actively seek conversions, for their object in conquering India was to gain power and wealth, not to spread religion, though religion did subserve their other goals.

The greatest number of Hindu coverts to Islam came from the under-classes, who sought to gain socio-economic emancipation through conversion, by freeing themselves from the bondage of the Hindu caste system. As Muslims, their careers were no longer confined to their old degrading caste functions, so they could rise to whatever position they merited by their aptitudes and skills. And, more than anything else, conversion radically transformed their social status, from that of the underclass to that of the upper class.

'The heathens of these parts daily become Moors to gain the favour of their rulers,' writes Barbosa about what he observed in Bengal. Sometimes there were mass conversions, following clan or tribal decision. This was fairly common in north-east and north-west India, the predominantly tribal regions of the subcontinent. But most of the individual conversions were in urban areas—in rural areas there was very little for Hindus to gain by becoming Muslims, while in urban areas conversion opened up a whole new world for them, for economic as well as social advancement.

There were a few conversions to Islam from the Hindu upper castes also, of men who sought to advance their careers by becoming Muslims. Even some rajas and chieftains became Muslims, so as to retain their power. Conversion also freed Hindus from the obligation to pay jizya, though this does not seem to have been a major factor. Sufis too played a role, though only a small role, in attracting Hindus to Islam. In several cases, Hindu converts to Islam continued to observe their old sectarian socio-religious practices. Thus it was reported that Hindu converts to Islam in Punjab continued to worship their old village deities even after their conversion. Such practices were fairly common in other regions of India also.

Most Muslims in medieval India were in the regions under Muslim rule, but there were a good number of them even in Hindu kingdoms. These were mostly migrants from Central Asia, the Middle East and North Africa, though there were also some local converts there. Battuta in the fourteenth century found numerous mosques in Kerala, evidently built by Muslim traders from the Middle East who had peacefully settled there and prospered. According to Barbosa, even a Kerala king became a convert to Islam.

Incidental Data

Part II: Prelude

■ The Arabic word *islam* means 'submission', which, as applied to religion, means 'submission to god'. An adherent of Islam is called Muslim, meaning 'one who is submissive' to god.

    ■ Orthodox Indians, according to *Chach-nama*, scorned Arabs as 'outcaste cow-eaters'.

    ■ Buddhism was the dominant religion of Afghanistan before the region became Islamised.

    ■ Mahmud Ghazni was a ruthless military adventurer, but he had, according to medieval chronicler Khondamir, a weakness for fair-skinned young boys. At one time he became enamoured of the 'beauty of a boy of Turkistan . . . who was as white as silver . . . [and] looked as beautiful as a virgin of paradise.' Mahmud demanded the boy from the amir who owned him, and on the amir refusing, the sultan had him plundered and tortured to death.

    ■ Mahmud Ghazni, according to medieval chronicler Siraj, 'was the first Muhammadan king who received the title of sultan from the Caliph.'

    ■ Ibrahim, a grandson of Mahmud Ghazni and one of his successors, was physically rather frail, but had '36 sons and 40 daughters,' reports Siraj. He was 'a great king—wise, just, good, god-fearing and kind, a patron of letters, a supporter of religion, and a pious man.' He 'reigned happily for 42 years, and died in 1098, at the age of 60.'

Part III: Slave Sultans

■ Aibak's lavish generosity earned him the epithet Lakh-bakhsh: Giver of Lakhs. But he could not stand presumptuous fools. Thus when a court poet recited to him a poem full of obscenities, expecting to be rewarded with a gold coin for each line, all the sultan is said to have given him was a bowl of donkey's urine.

■ The term 'Forty', used to describe the clique of top nobles of the Delhi Sultanate at one time, was merely a conventional term. The actual number of the members of the group varied from time to time.

■ Part of the reason for the opposition of nobles to the reign of Raziya was that she seemed to be intimate with Yaqut, an Ethiopian slave. According to Isami, a fourteenth century chronicler, Yaqut 'used to stand by her side when she mounted her horse. With one hand he used to hold her arm and help her to mount her horse . . . When the grandees of the state noticed the liberties he took openly, they felt scandalised and said to one another privately, "From the way this demon has made himself more powerful in the State than all other servants, it would be no wonder if he found his way to seize the royal seal."'

■ The nobles opposing Raziya, according to Isami, grumbled: 'All women are in the snare of the devil; in privacy, all of them do Satan's work. No confidence should be placed in women . . . At no time can faithfulness be expected of women. Faithfulness is masculine; expect it only from men . . . When passions of a pious woman are inflamed, she concedes to intimacy even with a dog. If a man places confidence in a woman, she makes him a laughing stock. A woman is a source of danger wherever she be, since she is of devilish disposition . . . A woman cannot acquit herself well as a ruler, for she is essentially deficient in intellect . . . A woman who seeks pleasure and is at the same time ambitious, can be hardly free from the sway of passion.'

■ Barani: Balban was a man of 'fierce temper and implacable resolution.'

Part IV: Khaljis

■ According to Cambridge historian Wolseley Haig's calculation, Ala-ud-din in his Devagiri campaign seized '17,250 pounds of gold, 200 pounds of pearls, 58 pounds of other gems, 28,250 pounds of silver, and 1000 pieces of silk.'

■ The murderers of Jalal-ud-din Khalji soon met with divine retribution, states Barani. Many of the chief conspirators died in a short time. 'The hell-hound Salim, who struck the first blow, was a year or two afterwards eaten up by leprosy. Ikhtiyar-ud-din, who cut off the head, very soon went mad, and in his dying ravings cried out that Sultan Jalal-ud din stood over him with a naked sword, ready to cut off his head.'

■ Barani: When Ala-ud-din on his accession distributed vast sums as largess among the people, 'they gave themselves up to gaiety and pleasure, and indulged in wine and all kinds of revelry. Within the city they erected several wondrous pavilions, where wine, sherbet, and betel were distributed gratis, and in almost every house an entertainment was held. The maliks, amirs, and all the other men of note and respectability invited one another to feasts; wine, music and mirth became the order of the day.'

■ Barani: In the first year of Ala-ud-din's reign, because of this generous scattering of money, 'folks of all classes, both high and low, lived in such ease and affluence, that I cannot recollect seeing any age or period of such perfect happiness and contentment.'

■ From where did Ala-ud-din get his reform ideas? Some of his administrative measures 'were startlingly like that of *Arthasastra*,' comments modern historian Kosambi, and he goes on to speculate that it is possible 'that the sultan found someone to tell him of the Mauryan regulations.'

Part V: Tughluqs

■ Once, on the way back to Delhi from Deccan, Muhammad Tughluq suffered from severe toothache and had to have a tooth extracted. He then erected, over the spot where the extracted tooth was buried, a domed tomb which later came to be called the Dome of the Tooth.

■ The earliest use of paper money anywhere in the world was in China around the close of the eighth century CE. In the beginning it was more like a bank draft than a currency note. It enabled merchants to deposit gold and silver money in one town, receive a certificate of the deposit, and cash it in some other town. Shortly thereafter the Chinese government used this mode of transaction to transfer the tax collected in the provinces to the imperial capital.

Marco Polo, medieval Venetian world traveller, noted the use of paper currency in China, and wrote about it: 'All these pieces of paper are issued with as much solemnity and authority as if they were of pure gold or silver; and on every piece [of paper currency] a variety of officials . . . have to write their names, and to put their seals. And when all is duly prepared, the chief officer deputed by the Khan smears the Seal entrusted to him with vermilion, and impresses it on the paper . . . The money is then authentic. Anyone forging it would be punished with death.'

The use of paper money and its variants gradually spread westward from China, and eventually, after five centuries, it came into use in Persia. A few centuries later the practice finally spread to Europe, where paper currency was first issued in Sweden in the seventeenth century. Then, over the next century and half, the practice spread to the other parts of Europe as well as to America.

In India token currency—brass or copper coins marked as of the same value as silver coins—was first introduced by Muhammad Tughluq in the second quarter of the fourteenth century. But the reform failed utterly, like all his other innovations.

■ Muhammad Tughluq had two daughters in his early youth, but a surgery afterwards made him impotent. Consequently, according to Isami, a severely critical medieval chronicler, the sultan wished to see the whole world impotent like him. Perhaps the aberrations of his character had something to do with his sexual impotence.

■ Muhammad, according to Isami, was 'full of deceit and fraud,' and was 'a first-class hypocrite . . . who, while he made a display of justice, exercised oppression.'

■ Robert Sewell, an early modern historian, on Muhammad Tughluq: 'His whole life was spent on visionary schemes pursued by means equally irrational.'

Part VI: Three Kingdoms

■ The seventeenth-century English satirist Samuel Butler on Mahmud Begarha of Gujarat:

The King of Cambay's daily food
Is asp and basilisk and toad.

■ According to the fifteenth-century Italian adventurer Varthema, the title 'Zamorin' of the raja of Kozhikode means 'Lord of the Seas . . . The King of Calicut is a Pagan, and worships the devil.'

■ Ferishta on Parthal, the farmer's daughter, with whom Devaraya I of Vijayanagar got involved: 'There resided in the town of Mudgal a farmer, who was blessed with a daughter of such exquisite beauty, that the creator seemed to have united all his powers in making her perfect.' An old Brahmin told Devaraya about her, and the raja then sent opulent presents to her through the Brahmin and sought her for his harem. This overjoyed the girl's parents, but she refused the offer, as she did not want to be secluded in the royal harem, where even her parents would not be allowed to visit her. The Brahmin then returned to Vijayanagar, and told the raja about what had transpired. But the rejection by Parthal only inflamed the raja's passion, and he raided Mudgal to seize her. But by then Parthal and her parents had fled to Bahmani kingdom. The affair led to yet another war between Vijayanagar and the Sultanate.

■ Harihara and Bukka, according to Sewell, belonged to the Kuruba caste of Hindus, a warrior caste mostly living in Karnataka.

■ The Vijayanagar army in camp was found to have 120,000 infantry, 18,000 cavalry, and 150 elephants, reports Nuniz.

Part VII: Polity

■ Ambassadors in medieval times enjoyed virtually the same status as they do in modern times. According to Wassaf, a fourteenth-century Indian chronicler, 'To bring trouble on an ambassador is, under every system of religious faith, altogether opposed to the principles of law, social observance and commonsense.'

■ Battuta on he being confronted by brigands: 'I threw myself to the ground and surrendered, as they do not kill those who do that.'

■ A popular medieval Indian saying: All kings go to hell.

■ When Hasnak, a high official favoured by Mahmud Ghazni, was disfavoured and executed by Masud, Mahmud's successor, the victim's mother commented: 'What a fortune is my son's! Sultan Mahmud gave him this world, and Sultan Masud the next!'

■ Abu Zaid, an early medieval Arabic writer: When a king of Sri Lanka dies, his body is carried on a very low carriage so that his head, placed at the back, touches the ground and his hair drags in the dust. A woman follows the carriage with a broom and 'sweeps the dust [of the road] on to the face of the corpse, and cries out, "O men, behold! This man yesterday was your king . . . See now what he is reduced to."'

■ A medieval Indian saying: 'A common man with faults harms only himself with his faults, but through the faults of a king all his subjects too suffer destruction.'

■ Battuta: In Kerala 'there are twelve infidel sultans, some of them strong with armies numbering fifty thousand men, and others weak with armies of three thousand. Yet there is no discord whatever between them, and the strong does not desire to seize the possessions of the weak.'

■ The land revenue assignments, given to soldiers and officers by the Delhi sultans, instead of cash salaries, were in turn often reassigned by the assignees. 'It was the practice of certain persons in those days to buy up these assignments,' notes Afif. 'The purchasers of these assignments carried on a traffic in them, and gaining good profit, many of them got rich and made fortunes.'

■ Just as Muslim nobles kept Hindu mistresses, sometimes, though rarely, Hindu officers kept Muslim mistresses.

■ Mughal emperor Aurangzeb on jizya: 'By this means idolatry will be suppressed, the Muhammadan religion and the true faith will be honoured, our proper duty will be performed, the finances of the state will be increased, and infidels will be disgraced.'

■ Abdur Razzaq: 'The manner in which they catch elephants is this: they dig a pit in the way by which the animal usually goes to drink [water], which they cover over lightly. When an elephant falls into it, no man is allowed to go near the animal for two days; at the end of that period, a man comes up and strikes him several hard blows with a bludgeon, when suddenly another man appears who drives off the striker, and seizing the bludgeon, throws it away. He then retires, after placing some forage before the elephant. This practice is repeated for several days; the first lays on the blows, and the second drives him away, until the animal begins to have a liking for its protector, who by degrees approaches the animal, and places before it the fruits which elephants are partial to, and scratches and rubs the animal, until by this kind of treatment it becomes tame, and submits its neck to the chain.'

■ According to Barbosa, fighting duels was a sport in Vijayanagar. 'They are accustomed to challenge one another to duels, and when a challenge has been accepted, and the king gives his permission, the day for the duel is fixed . . .' The weapons to be used by both contestants were required to be of the same size. The king appointed seconds for the fight, which took place in a field allotted by the king. The contestants entered the field 'naked, covered only with some cloth wrapped round their middles, with very cheerful faces. Then after saying their prayers they begin to fight, and as they are bare it is over in a few strokes in the presence of the king and his court. No man may speak to them while they are fighting, except the seconds, each of whom stands by his own man. This is such a common practice among them, that some are slain daily.'

■ Private individuals in Indian kingdoms were not allowed to own elephants without royal permission; unauthorised ownership of elephants by individuals was considered an act of rebellion.

Part VIII: Socio-economic Scene

■ A legendary history of Delhi is given in *Khulasatu-t Tawarikh* by Munshi Subhan Rai Khattari, a late-seventeenth-century scholar living in Punjab. The text uses a lot of material copied from *Mukhtasiru-t Tawarikh*, an early seventeenth century anonymous work.

'In ancient times the city of Hastinapur was the capital of the rulers of Hindustan,' writes Subhan Rai. 'The city stood on the bank of the Ganga . . . When dissension broke out between Kauravas and Pandavas, the latter moved from Hastinapur to the city of Indarprast on the Yamuna, and made it their

capital. A long while afterwards, in the year 440 of Bikramajit, Raja Anang
Pal Tomar built the city of Delhi near Indarprast. Afterwards Rai Pithaura, in
the year twelve hundred and something of Bikramajit, built a fort and city to
which he gave his own name. Sultan Kutbu-d din Aibak and Sultan Shamsu-d
din Altmash occupied the fort of Rai Pithaura. In the year 666 Hijra (1267–8
AD) Sultan Ghiyasu-d din Balban built another fortress, which he called Shahr-
zaghan. In the year 686 Hijra (1287 AD) Sultan Muizzu-d din Kai-Kubad
built another city of handsome edifices on the Yamuna, to which he gave the
name of Kilu-gari . . . Sultan Jalalu-d din Khilji founded the city of Kushk-lal
(Red Palace) and Sultan Alau-d din the city of Kushk-Siri, and made them
their respective capitals. Sultan Ghiyasu-d din Tughlik Shah, in the year 725
Hijra (1325 AD) raised the city of Tughluqabad. His son, Sultan Muhammad
Fakhru-d din Jauna, founded another city, and erected in it a palace of 1000
pillars. He also built some other fine mansions of red stone. In the year 755
Hijra (1354 AD) Sultan Firoz Shah built the large city of Firoz-abad, and having
cut the river Jumna, he conducted the water to his city . . . Sultan Mubarak
Shah founded the city of Mubarak-abad. In the year 943 Hijra (1536 AD) . . .
Humayun Badshah, having restored and repaired the fort of Indarprast, gave
it the name of Din-panah, and made it his royal residence. Sher Shah Afghan,
having pulled down the city known as Kushk-Siri, built another one. Salim
Shah, his son, in the year 953 Hijra (1546 AD) built the fort of Salim-garh . . .
In the year 1048 Hijra (1638 AD), and in the twelfth year of his reign . . . [Shah
Jahan] built a city near Delhi, which he named Shah-jahan-abad.'

This text lists fourteen cities built on the site of Delhi, but tradition speaks
of only seven cities of Delhi, to which the British added the eighth. The oldest
of the seven cities of Delhi, according to archaeologist Johan Marshall, is
Qala-i-Rai Pithaura, within which is a fort called Lal Kot.

■ Battuta on Tughluqabad, the city that Ghiyas-ud-din Tughluq built to the
south of Old Delhi: 'Here were Tughluq's treasures and palaces, and the great
palace which he had built of gilded bricks, which, when the sun rose, shone
so dazzlingly that none could gaze steadily upon it. There he laid up great
treasures, and it was related that he constructed there a cistern and had molten
gold poured into it so that it became a solid mass, and his son Muhammad
Shah became possessed of all of it when the succeeded him.'

■ Battuta on Khambhat (Cambay): The city 'is situated on an arm of the sea
resembling a river; it is navigable for ships and its waters ebb and flow. . . This
city is one of the finest there is in regard to the excellence of its construction
and the architecture of its mosques. The reason for this is that the majority of
its inhabitants are foreign merchants, who are always building fine mansions
and magnificent mosques and vie with one another in doing so.'

■ Nizami: The Yamuna 'from its exceeding purity, resembled a mirror.'

■ Wassaf on Gujarat: It has '70,000 villages and towns, all populous, and the people abound in wealth and luxuries. In the course of the four seasons of the year seventy different species of beautiful flowers grow within that province . . . Its air is pure, its water clear, and the circumjacent country beautiful and charming both in scenery and buildings.'

■ Nikitin on the people of Bidar: 'They are all black and wicked, and the women are all harlots, or witches, or thieves and cheats, and they destroy their masters with poison.'

■ Abu Zaid: 'The Chinese are men of pleasure; but Indians condemn pleasure and abstain from it.'

■ Timur in his autobiography offers brief descriptions of some of the Indian communities he came across. The Jats, he writes, are 'a robust race . . . [They] had not their equals in theft and highway robbery . . . Jats were as numerous as ants or locusts, and . . . no traveller or merchant passed unscathed from their hands.' Timur decided to suppress them in order to secure the roads, and he claims that, marching into jungles, he 'slew 2,000 demon-like Jats, made their wives and children captives, and plundered their cattle and property.' Timur is more respectful in his description of Rajputs, the military aristocracy of North India, whom he describes as 'a class which supplies the most renowned soldiers of India.'

■ *Chach-nama* on Jats: 'They have the disposition of savages, and always rebelled against their sovereign. They plunder on the roads.'

■ Battuta, a keen admirer of female charms, is all praise for Maratha women: 'God has endowed Maratha women with special beauty, particularly in their noses and eyebrows.' And about Malwa he writes that 'their women . . . are exceedingly beautiful and famous for their charms of company.'

■ Idrisi, a twelfth-century Sicilian chronicler: 'Indians are naturally inclined to justice and never depart from it in their actions. Their good faith, honesty and fidelity to engagements are well-known, and they are so famous for these qualities that people flock to their country from every side; hence the country is flourishing.'

■ Siraj on the role of astrologers in India: In one instance, when a queen was about to deliver, astrologers cautioned that the child would be unlucky if born just then, 'but if the birth occurred two hours later the child would reign for eighty years. When his mother heard this opinion of the astrologers, she ordered her legs to be tied together, and caused herself to be hung with her head downwards. She also directed the astrologers to watch for the auspicious time. When they all agreed that the time for delivery had come, she ordered herself to be taken down, and Lakhmaniya was born directly, but he had no sooner come into the world than his mother died from the anguish she had endured.'

■ Battuta on a reservoir outside Delhi: It is 'a large reservoir . . . from which the inhabitants draw their drinking water. It is supplied by rain water, and is about two miles in length and half that in breadth. In the centre there is a great pavilion built of squared stones, two stories high. When the reservoir is filled with water it can be reached only in boats, but when the water is low the people go into it. Inside it is a mosque, and at most times it is occupied by mendicants . . . When the water dries up at the sides of the reservoir, they sow sugarcanes, cucumbers, green melons and pumpkins there. The melons and pumpkins are very sweet but of small size.'

■ Tome Piers on Kerala: 'In Malabar it is the custom for woman to have her eyes on the bed during coitus, and for man to have his eyes on the ceiling. This is the general practice among the great and small, and they consider anything else to be strange and foreign to their condition . . . The Nair women of Malabar have no virtue, nor do they sew and work, but only eat and amuse themselves.'

■ Barbosa: Among Nairs in Kerala, when a girl comes of age, her 'mother goes about searching and asking some young man to take her daughter's virginity . . . They regard it among themselves as a disgrace and a foul thing to take a woman's virginity . . . These Nayre women at their periods shut themselves up in a house apart for three days, touching no one, and prepare their food in separate pans and dishes . . . It is an article of faith with them (Nairs) that every woman who dies virgin is damned.'

■ Barbosa: 'The distinctive *kudumi* knot of the Malayali . . . does not hang down behind as with Tamils, but lies on the top of the head or is drawn around to the left of the forehead.'

■ Sati is not mentioned in *Manu-Smriti*, but it says that a widow 'may, if she so chooses, emasculate her body by subsisting on flowers, roots and fruits.' Kautilya prohibited sati as a punishable crime. In medieval times Sankaracharya condemned sati.

■ Mahatma Gandhi in *Young India*, 21 May 1931: 'If the wife has to prove her loyalty and undivided devotion to her husband, so had the husband to prove his allegiance and devotion to his wife. Yet, we have never heard of a husband mounting the funeral pyre of his deceased wife.'

■ Barbosa on coconut: Coconut is 'very sweet . . . when green . . . and each one when green has within it a pint of fresh and pleasant water, better than that from a spring. When they are dry this same water thickens within them into a white fruit as large as an apple which also is very sweet and dainty. The coconut itself after being dried is eaten, and from it they get much oil by pressing it . . . And from its shell . . . is made charcoal for the goldsmiths who work with no other kind. And from the outer husk . . . they make all the cord which they use . . . And from the sap of the tree itself they extract a *must*, from which they make wine . . . From this same *must* they make very good vinegar, and also a sugar of extreme sweetness which is much sought after in India. From the leaf of the tree they make many things, in accordance with the size of the branch. They thatch the houses with them . . . No house is roofed with tiles save temples or palaces . . . From the same tree they get timber for their houses and firewood as well . . .'

Part IX: Culture

■ In Islamic countries medical studies were part of the general curriculum in educational institutions, and some of the sultans—Muhammad and Firuz Tughluq, for instance—were hakims. The system of medicine they used was the Unani system, a Graeco-Arabic system formulated by Avicenna in the early eleventh century. Avicenna's system became increasingly popular in Delhi from the time of Sikandar Lodi.

   ■ Medieval writers were not given to modesty. Nizami, for instance, claimed that his work was 'superior to anything written by ancients or moderns.'

   ■ Poet Amir Khusrav was extolled as the Parrot of Hind. 'Amir Khusrav . . . is the prince of poets and the first among philosophers, for he was one of those steeped in spiritual wisdom, and such skill as he possessed in every kind and manner of literary composition, both in the use of ordinary or unusual phraseology, and of plain or obscure terms, has seldom been allotted to anyone,' comments medieval writer Abdu-l Hakk Dehlawi.

   ■ Khusrav on Indian literature: 'The language of Hind is like Arabic . . . If there is grammar and syntax in Arabic, there is not one letter less of them in Hindi. If you ask whether there are the sciences of exposition and rhetoric, I answer that Hindi is in no way deficient in these respects.'

   ■ Khusrav on Sanskrit: 'The common people know nothing of it. Brahmins know it, but Brahmin women do not understand a word of it. It bears a resemblance to Arabic in some respects, in its permutations of letters, its grammar, its conjugations, and polish.'

   ■ Khusrav: 'Brahmins here are as learned as Aristotle and there are among them many scholars in various fields . . .'

   ■ Abdur Razzak on musicians in Vijayanagar: 'The singers were for the most part young girls, with cheeks like the moon, and faces more blooming than the spring, adorned with beautiful garments, and displaying figures which ravished the heart like fresh roses. They were seated behind a beautiful curtain opposite the king. On a sudden the curtain was removed on both sides, and the girls began to move their feet with such grace that wisdom lost its senses, and the soul was intoxicated with delight.'

■ 'The contrast between the Hindu temples and the Muslim mosques could hardly have been more striking,' writes John Marshall, an early twentieth century British archaeologist in India. 'The shrine of the former was relatively small and constricted; the prayer chamber of the latter was broad and spacious. One was gloomy and mysterious, the other light and open to the winds of heaven. The Hindu system of construction was trabeate, based on column and architrave; the Muslim system was arcuate, based on arch and vault. The temple was crowned with slender spires or pyramidal towers; the mosque with expansive domes . . . [Hindu] monuments were enriched with countless idols of its deities; Islam rigidly forbade idolatry or the portrayal of any living thing. Decorative ornament in Hindu architecture delighted in plastic modelling; it was naturalistic . . . and . . . exuberant; Islamic ornament, on the other hand, inclined to colour and line or flat surface carving, and took the form of conventional arabesques or ingenious geometric patterning.'

■ Amir Khusrav on the new fort that Ala-ud-din Khalji built in Delhi: 'It is a condition that in a new building blood should be sprinkled; he therefore sacrificed some thousands of goat-bearded Mughals for the purpose.'

■ Kabir: 'Sanskrit is like water in a [deep] well; the language of the people is like a flowing stream.'

■ Tirupati, one of the most sacred Hindu shrines in modern India, acquired its prominence around the late fifteenth or early sixteenth century.

■ Odoric on Kerala: 'All the inhabitants of that country do worship a living ox, as their god, whom they put to labour for six years, and in the seventh year they cause him to rest from al his work, placing him in a solemn and public place, and calling him a holy beast. Moreover . . . every morning they take two basins, either of silver or of gold, and with one they receive the urine of the ox, and with the other its dung. With the urine they wash their face, their eyes, and all their five senses. The dung they put into both their eyes, then they anoint the . . . cheeks therewith, and thirdly their breast: and then they say that they are sanctified for the whole day. And as the people do, even so do their king and queen.'

■ Ramananda, a thirteenth century Vaishnava sage: 'I had an inclination to go with sandal and other perfumes to offer worship to Brahman. But the guru revealed to me that Brahman was in my own heart.'

■ The word *sufi* is derived from the word for wool: *suf*. Sufis wore wool instead of cotton or silk as an act of self-mortification. Sufis gained prominence in Persia around the tenth century.

■ The regions of India where Islam was most successful in winning converts were the regions where Buddhism still had a prominent presence in early medieval times. In time these regions came to have Muslim majorities, and they eventually, in the twentieth century, became independent Muslim states: Pakistan and Bangladesh. Muslims remained a minority in the Indo-Gangetic Plain, the heartland of Muslim power in India. In all, Muslims in the subcontinent at the time of India's independence constituted a quarter of its population.

■ The Portuguese brought the Inquisition to India. Those condemned by the inquisitor were burned.

Bibliography

Abdullah. *Tarikh-i-Daudi* (Elliot and Dowson:, henceforth referred to as E&D *The History of India as Told by Its Own Historians*, Vol. IV).

Achaya, K.T. *Indian Food* (Oxford University Press, 1998).

Afif, Shams-i-Siraj. *Tarikh-i-Firoz Shahi* (E&D, III).

Ahmad, Khwajah Nizam-ud-din. *Tabaqat-i-Akbari* (tr) B. De, 3 vols (Calcutta 1927–40).

Al-Biladuri. *Futuhu-l Buldan* (E&D, I).

Al-Biruni. *Alberuni's India* (tr) E.C. Sachau (London, 1888; Delhi, 1964).

Al-Masudi. *Muruju-l Zahab* (E&D, I).

Al-Utbi. *Tarikh-i-Yamini* (tr) James Reynolds (London, 1858; E&D, II).

Alam, M. *The Making of Indo-Persian Culture* (eds) F.N. Delvoye and M. Garborian (New Delhi, 2000).

Ali, D. *Courtly Culture and Political Life in Early Medieval India* (Cambridge, 2004).

Ali, Sharaf-ud-din. *Zafarnama* (Calcutta, 1887).

Anand, Mulk Raj. *Homage to Khajuraho* in *Marg* (Bombay, 1957).

Badauni. *Muntakhab-ut-Tawarikh* (trs) G.S.A. Ranking, W.H. Lowe, and W. Haig, (Calcutta, 1898–1925).

Baihaqi. *Tarikhu-s Subuktigin* (E&D, I).

Bakshi, Nizam-ud-din. *Tabaqat-i-Akbari* (Calcutta, 1913–40).

Banerjee, J.M. *History of Firuz Shah Tughluq* (Delhi, 1967).

Banga, Indu. (ed) *The City in Indian History: Urban Demography, Society, and Politics* (New Delhi, 1991).

Barani, Ziyauddin. *Tarikh-i-Firuz Shahi* (E&D, III).

Barbosa, Duarte. *An Account of the Countries Bordering the Indian Ocean and Their Inhabitants*, 2 vols, (tr) M.L. Dames (London, 1918–21; Delhi 1989).

Basham, A.L. (ed.) *A Cultural History of India* (Oxford, 1975).

Battuta, Ibn. *Travels in Asia and Africa* (London, 1889).

Bernier, François. *Travels in the Mughal Empire* (tr) Archibald Constable (1891).

Bihamad Khani, Muhammad. *Tarikh-i-Muhammadi* (tr) Muhammad Zaki (Aligarh, 1972).

Brijbhushan, J. *Sultan Raziya: Her Life and Times* (New Delhi, 1990).

Brown, Percy. *Indian Architecture* (Bombay, 1944).

The Cambridge History of Islam, (eds) P.M. Holt, Ann K.S. Lambton, and Bernard Lewis. 2 vols (Cambridge, 1970).

The Cambridge History of India, Vol. 3 (CUP, 1928; New Delhi, 1987).

Chandra, Satish. *History of Medieval India* (Orient Longman, 2007).

Chattopadhyaya, B.D. *Origins of the Rajputs: The Political, Economic, and Social Progress in Early Medieval Rajasthan* in *Indian Historical Review* (Delhi, March 1976).

Chettiar, S.M.L. Lakshmanan: *Folklore of Tamil Nadu* (New Delhi, 1973).

Comfort, Alex. (ed.) *The Koka Shastra and Other Medieval Indian Writings on Love* (London: Allen & Unwin, 1964).

Conti, Nicolo. *The Travels of Nicolo Conti* (tr) J.W. Jones (London, 1857).

Damodaran, K. *Keralacharitram* (Trichur: Current Book House, 1962).

Datta, V.N. *Sati: Widow Burning in India* (New Delhi, 1990).

Desai, Devangana. *Khajuraho* (OUP).

Devaraja, Maharaja. *Rati-ratna-pradipika*.

Dubois, Abbé J.A. *Hindu Manners, Customs and Ceremonies* (Reprint: Delhi, 1985).

Dughlat, Mirza Haidar. *Tarikh-i-Rashidi* (trs) E.D. Ros and N. Elias, (London, 1895).

Elliot H.M. and John Dowson. *The History of India as Told by Its Own Historians*, 8 vols (London, 1867–77).

Elphinstone, Mountstuart. *The History of India*, 2 vols (London, 1843).

Embree, Ainslie, T. *Sources of Indian Tradition* (Columbia, 1988).

Fakhr-i-Mudabbir. *Tarikh-i-Fakhruddin Mubarak Shah* (ed.) Sir Denison Ross, (London, 1927).

Ferishta, Mahomed Qasim. *Gulshan-i-Ibrahimi*, also known as *Tarikh-i-Ferishta* (tr) J. Briggs: *History of the Rise of Muhammadan Power.* (Lucknow, 1865; Calcutta, 1908–10).

Firuz Shah Tughluq. *Futuhat-i-Firoz Shahi* (E&D, III).

Fritz, John and George Mitchell. *City of Victory: Vijayanagara* (New York, 1991).

Frykenberg, R.E. *Delhi Through the Ages* (Oxford, 1988).

Gaynor, Barton and Laurraine Malone. *Old Delhi* (Calcutta, 1988).

Gommans, Jos and Dirk Kolff. *Warfare and Weaponry in South Asia: 1000–1800* (Oxford, 2001).

Grewal, J.S. *The State and Society in Medieval India* (Delhi, 2004)

Habib, Irfan. (ed.) *Medieval India* (New Delhi: Oxford, 1992).

Haq, Shaikh Nurul. *Zubdatu-t Tawarikh* (E&D, VI).

Hanafi, Muhammad Sharif. *Majalisu-s Salatin* (E&D, VII).

Harle, J.C. *The Art and Architecture of the Indian Subcontinent* (New York, 1986).

Heras, H. *Beginnings of Vijayanagara* (Bombay, 1934).

Hourani, G.F. *Arab Seafaring in the Indian Ocean in Ancient and Early Medieval Times* (Princeton, 1951)

Ibn-ul-Asir, Shaikh Abul Hasan. *Kamil-ut-Tawarikh* (E&D, II).

Ibn-ul-Asir. *Al-Tarikh-i Kamil* (E&D, II)

Isami. *Futuhu's-salatin* (tr) Mahdi Husain, 3 vols (Madras, 1948)

Jaffrey, Zia. *The Invisibles: A Tale of the Eunuchs of India* (Phoenix, 1998).

Jayadeva. *Rati-manjara.*

Jayakar, Pupul. *The Earth Mother* (New Delhi: Penguin, 1989).

Juwaini, Ala-ud-din. *Tarikh-i Jahan-kusha* (E&D, II).

Kalhana. *Rajatarangini* (tr) M.A. Stein, (Westminster, 1900; Delhi, 1961).

Karashima, N. *History and Society in South India* (New Delhi, 2001).

Kayanamalla. *Ananga Ranga* (16th c) (Internet).

Keay, John. *India: A History* (HarperCollins, 2000).

Khafi Khan. *Muntakhab-ul-Lubab* (Calcutta, 1869, 1925).

Khan, Mir Gholam Hussein. *Siyar-ul-Mutakherin* (tr) Haji Mustafa, (revised by) John
    Briggs (Allahabad, 1924; Internet).

Khondamir. *Khulasat-ul-Akhbar* (E&D, IV).

Khurdaba, Ibn. *Kitabu-l Masalik Wa-l Mamalik* (E&D, I)

Khusrau, Amir. *Miftah-ul-Futuh* (E&D, III).

———— *Tarikh-i-Alai* (E&D, III).

———— *Nuh Sipihr* (E&D, III).

Kidwai, Salim. *Sultans, Eunuchs and Domestics in Medieval India* (New Delhi, 1985).

Kosambi, D.D. *An Introduction to the Study of Indian History* (Bombay 1956, 1975).

———— *Myth and Reality: Studies in the Formation of Indian Culture* (Bombay, 1962).

Kufi, Ali Hamid. *Chach-nama* (tr) Mirza Kalichbeg Fredunbeg (Karachi 1900; Delhi
    1979).

Kukkoka. *Rati-rahasya* (Internet).

Kulke, Hermann. (ed) *The State in India, 1000–1700* (Delhi: OUP, 1995).

Kulke, Hermann and Dietmar Rothermund. *A History of India* (1986).

Kupl   Kuppuswami, A. *Sri Sankara* (Madras 1992).

Lal, K.S. *History of the Khaljis* (New Delhi, 1950, 1980).

———— *The Twilight of the Sultanate* (Bombay: Asia Publishing House, 1963).

Lane-Poole, Stanley. *The Muhammadan Dynasties* (London, 1894).

Lohari, Abdul Hamid. *Badshah Nama*, 2 vols (Calcutta, 1898).

Mahalingam, T.V. *Economic Life in the Vijayanagar Empire* (Madras, 1951).

———— *Administration and Social Life in the Vijayanagar Empire*, 2 vols (Madras,
    1969/1975).

Major, R.H. *India in the Fifteenth Century*, contains extracts from narratives of Nicolo
    Conti, Santo Stefano, etc. (London, 1857; Internet).

Majumdar, R.C. *The Classical Accounts of India* (Calcutta, 1960).

Majumdar, R.C. et al. *The History and Culture of the Indian People*, Vol. 5: *The
    Struggle for the Empire* (Bombay, 1957).

———— *The Delhi Sultanate* (Bombay, 1960).

Manrique. *Travels of Fray Sebāstien Manrique* (tr) Eckford Luard, 2 vols (London,
    1927).

Maulana Ahmad et al. *Tarikhi-Alfi* (E&D, V).

Menon, Sreedhara. *A Survey of Kerala History* (Kottayam, 1967).

Miller, Barbara Stoler. *The Powers of Art* (OUP, 1993).

Minahj, Siraj. *Tabaqat-i-Nasiri* (tr) H.G. Raverty, (E&D, II).

Michell, George. *The New Cambridge History of India, 1.VI: Architecture and Art of Southern India: Vijayanagara and the Successor States, 1350–1750* (Cambridge, 1995).

Moreland, W.H. *The Agrarian System of Moslem India* (London, 1929).

Muhammad Ufi. *Jami-ut-Hikayat* (E&D, II).

Mukhtasiru-t Tawarikh (E&D, VIII).

Mukund, Kanakalatha. *The Trading World of the Tamil Merchant* (London, 1999).

Mustaufi, Hamdullah. *Tarikh-i-Guzidah* (ed.) E.G. Browne (London, 1910; E&D, III).

Ni'matullah. *Makhzan-i Afghani and Tarikh-i Khan-jahan Lodi* (E&D, V).

Nikitin, Athanasius: *The Travels of Athanasius Nikitin*.

Nizami, Hasan. *Taju-l Ma-asir* (E&D, II).

Odoric, Friar. *The Travels of Father Odoric of Pordenone 1316–1330* (trs) H. Yule and H. Cordier.

Paes, Domingo. *Narrative of Domingo Paes* (in *A Forgotten Empire*).

Panikkar, K.M. *A Survey of Indian History* (1946).

Pires, Tomé. *The Suma Oriental of Tomé Pires (1512–15)* (tr) A. Cortesao, 2 vols (London, 1944).

Polo, Marco. *Travels* (trs) H. Yule and H. Cordier, (London, 1903, 1920).

Prasad, A.K. *Devadasi System in Ancient India* (Delhi, 1990).

Prasad, Ishwari. *History of Medieval India* (Allahabad, 1940).

Punja, Shobita. *Divine Ecstasy: The Story of Khajrāho* (Delhi: Viking, 1992).

Qazvini, Hamd-Ullah Mustaufi. *Tarikh-i-Guzida* (E&D, III) .

Ramanujan, A.K.. Velcheru Narayana Rao, and David Dean Shulman. *When God Is a Customer: Telugu Courtesan Songs* (Berkeley).

Ray, N., B.D. Chattopadhyaya, V.R. Mani, and R. Chakravarti. *A Sourcebook of Indian Civilization* (New Delhi, 2000).

Ray, T.N. (ed.) *Kokokam and Rati Rahasyam* (Calcutta: Medical Book Co., 1960).

Raychaudhuri, Tapan and Irfan Habib. *The Cambridge Economic History of India,* Vol. I (Longman, 1982).

Rizvi, S.A.A. *A History of Sufism in India,* 2 vols (New Delhi, 1983).

———— *The Wonder That Was India,* Vol. II (London, 1987).

Razzak, Abdur. *Matla'u-s Sadain* (E&D, IV).

Saletore, B.A. *Social and Political Life in the Vijayanagar Empire* (Madras, 1934).

Salman, Khwaja Masud bin Said bin Salman. *Diwan-i-Salman* (E&D, IV).

Sarkar, J. *Military History of India* (Orient Longman, 1960).

Sarwani, Abbas. *Tarikh-i-Sher Shahi* (E&D, IV).

Sastri, K.A.N. *Foreign Notices of South India from Megasthenes to Ma Huan* (Madras, 1939).

———— *The Cholas* (1955).

———— *A History of South India* (Oxford, 1955; Madras 1958).

Schoterman, J.A. *The Yonitantra* (New Delhi: Manohar Publications, 1980).

Sewell, Robert. *A Forgotten Empire* (London, Delhi, 1900/1962).

Shahab-ud-din. *Masaliku-l Absar Fi Mamaliku-l Amsar* (E&D, III).

Shami, Nizam-ud-din. *Zafar Nama* (E&D, III).

Sharma, R.S. *Early Medieval Indian Society: A Study in Feudalism* (Orient Longman).

Shirazi, Rafi-ud-din. *Tazkirat-ul-Muluk* (*History of the Bahmani Dynasty*) (tr) J.S. King (London, 1900).

Siraj. *Tabakat-i Nasiri* (E&D, II).

Sirhindi, Yahya bin Ahmad. *Tarikh-i-Mubarak Shahi* (tr) K.K. Basu (E&D, IV).

Spear, Percival. *India: A Modern History* (University of Michigan, 1961).

_____ *A History of India*, Vol. 2 (Penguin, 1965).

Stein, Burton. *Essays on South India* (Hawaii, 1975).

_____ (ed) *Peasant, State, and Society in Medieval South India* (New Delhi: OUP, 1980).

_____ *The New Cambridge History of India, I. 2: Vijayanagara* (Cambridge University Press, 1989).

Thapar, Romila. *A History of India,* Vol. I (Penguin, 1966).

_____ *Somanatha—The Many Voices of History* (New Delhi, 2004).

Thevenot, Jean De. *Indian Travels of Jean De Thevenot (1666–1667) & Gemelli Careri (1695–1696)* (ed) Surendra Nath Sen (New Delhi, 1949).

Thomas E. *The Chronicles of the Pathan Kings of Delhi* (London, 1871; Delhi, 1967).

Timur, Amir. *Malfuzat-i-Timuri* (E&D, III).

Tod, James. *Tod's Annals of Rajasthan* (New Delhi).

Ulfi, Muhammad. *Jami-ul-Hikayat* (E&D, II).

Vakpati. *The Gaudavaho: A Historical Poem in Prakrit* (eds) S.P. Pundit and N.B. Vatgikar (Poona, 1927).

Varthema: *The Itinerary of Ludovico di Varthema of Bologna* (ed) Sir Richard Temple (London, 1928; Google archives).

Veluthat, Kesavan. *The Political Structure of Early Medieval South India* (Orient Longman, 1993).

Visvanathan, Susan. *The Christians of Kerala* (Oxford, 1993).

Wagoner, P.B. *Sultan among Hindu Kings: Dress, Titles, and the Islamicization of Hindu Culture at Vijayanagara,* in *Journal of Asian Studies* 55 (1996).

Wassaf, Abdullah. *Tajziat-ul-Amsar wa Tajriyat-ul-Asar*, also called *Tarikh-i-Wassaf* (E&D, III).

Wayman, Alex. *Yoga of the Guhyasamaja Tantra: The Arcane Lore of Forty Verses* (Delhi, 1977).

Woodroffe, Sir John. *Tantra of the Great Liberation* (*Mahanirvana Tantra*) (New York: Dover, 1972).

Yadava, B.N.S. *Society and Culture in North India in the Twelfth Century* (Allahabad).

Yazdi, Sharafuddin. *Zafar Nama* (E&D, III).

Index